Table of Contents

Physicians' Fee Reference® 2007

PFR 2007 24th Edition

Yale Wasserman, D.M.D. ● Medical Publishers, Ltd.

P.O. Box 510949 ● Milwaukee ● Wisconsin 53203

www.medfees.com

PHOTOCOPYING IS ILLEGAL

Additional copies are available for $139. See last page for order form.

ISBN 1-59891-012-4

CPT® Notice

PFR GENERAL DISCLAIMER

PFR LIMITED WARRANTY AND LIABILITY DISCLAIMER:

INTRODUCTION

As stated in the DISCLAIMER, the **Physicians' Fee Reference**® **(PFR)** is designed as a marketing tool and is for reference only.

The **Physicians' Fee Reference**® is a nationwide fee compendium based on independent research. Fee information contained in the **PFR** is based primarily on the results of our annual independent direct mail confidential survey which was conducted in the fourth quarter of 2006. Survey participants include physicians, group practices, office managers, medical billing services, clinics, universities, hospitals, health care administrators and medical practice management consultants. Secondary sources include purchased data from claims clearinghouses. Included in our research is a review of public and private fee schedules.

The 2007 **PFR** uses current (2007) CPT and contains new CPT-4 codes. New codes are denoted with a ●. In previous editions we elected to exclude new CPT codes for lack of raw fee data. Through **PFR** feedback, we discovered that **PFR** users would prefer an estimate or approximation based on other methods rather than **IR** (Inconclusive Results) for new codes. For this reason, we are including new CPT codes as estimates derived from relative value techniques.

All CPT codes (5 digit numeric codes and descriptions) are taken directly from the American Medical Association (AMA), under licensed agreement for use in this publication. We strongly encourage our subscribers to purchase a current version of the official CPT code book for complete coding rules and instructions.

Relative Value Units (RVU)
(Total RBRVS Units)

Relative value studies have been available for many years and are used by third party payers and physicians as primary or secondary sources for fee setting. Medicare has fully phased in the **RBRVS** (**Resource Based Relative Value Scale**). Although this study was designed for Medicare, it is being incorporated into other government health plans and used by managed care and the private sector as an alternative to current UCR methodology. Whether you agree with **RBRVS** or not, it is important to have this information when evaluating your fees (especially new or rarely performed procedures).

The Medicare **RBRVS** system was developed by assigning weights to three factors that describe the value of each procedure code. Each code has three components: the physician work unit (the actual physician labor required to perform the procedure), the practice expense unit (the overhead of heat, lights, salaries, etc.) and the malpractice unit (the cost of insuring against malpractice claims). Each of these three components is multiplied by a geographic practice cost index that is specific to that component and geographic area. The sum of these calculations is multiplied by a monetary conversion factor, determined annually by the U.S. Congress. This result is the Medicare approved amount for that particular procedure code.

The Medicare **RVU** column used in the **PFR** is total **RBRVS** non facility relative value units. The **RVU** column value is the sum of the Physician Work RVUs, non-facility Practice Expense RVUs and Malpractice RVUs components (without any geographic adjustments or work adjuster applied). Total Medicare **RVUs** and National Medicare fees serve as a guide but cannot be used for calculating Medicare reimbursement without the work, practice and malpractice RVUs, regional geographic cost adjustment factors, work adjuster, and conversion factor. The 2007 conversion factor is $37.8975.

RBRVS for 2007

The publishers of the **PFR** offer a companion product for calculating RBRVS pricing for all U.S. Localities. **RBRVS EZ-Fees** is an easy-to-use Windows software application that calculates Medicare and other RBRVS-based fee schedules for all U.S. localities without any advanced computer skills or mathematical formulas. Visit **www.rbrvs.net** for a free demo download. See the back page of this book for order information.

2007 RBRVS fee schedule approved amounts are calculated using the following formulas:

2007 Non-Facility Pricing Amount = [(Work RVU * Work GPCI * Work Adjuster) + (Non-Facility Practice Expense RVU * PE GPCI) + (Mal Practice RVU * MP GPCI)] * Conversion Factor

2007 Facility Pricing Amount = [(Work RVU * Work GPCI * Work Adjuster) + (Facility Practice Expense RVU * PE GPCI) + (Mal Practice RVU * MP GPCI)] * Conversion Factor

Participating (PAR) providers automatically accept assignment on all claims. Non-participating (Non-PAR) providers may accept assignment on a claim-by-claim basis at any time. However, on assigned claims from non-participating providers, Medicare will only pay the provider 95% of the approved amount. For example, if the approved amount is $100, Medicare will pay the provider $76 (95% of $80) and the patient is still responsible for only the $20 (20%) co-insurance, in addition to an annual Part B deductible of $100.

For Medicare, Non-PAR status also means that the provider may not bill the patient more than the Medicare Limiting Charge (115% of the Medicare approved amount) on unassigned claims. For example, if the approved amount is $100, the provider may bill the patient up to $115 for the service. Medicare will pay the patient $80, and the patient is responsible for $35 out-of-pocket and the $80 Medicare payment to satisfy the $115 provider charge.

Using the PHYSICIANS' FEE REFERENCE® Percentiles

The **PFR** uses three fee percentile columns - the 50th, 75th, and 90th percentile. These numbers are nationwide references in U.S. Dollars which will vary for any given community. To "fine tune" the **PFR** fee information, use the Geographic Multipliers which are found in Appendix A.

A percentile is defined as the percentage of fees for that procedure that were equal to or less than that fee in our analysis. For example, if a physician is charging the 90th percentile for his/her community, 90% of the other physicians in that community are charging less than or equal to that fee. The 50th percentile is the middle value that separates an array of values in half. Many private third party payers use percentiles to set their maximum allowable charges. Unfortunately for physicians, different payers use different percentiles to set reimbursement limits. Not so long ago, the 90th percentile was considered the norm; however, many insurance companies today are only allowing up to the 50th or 60th percentile. If a physician submits a claim that is below the maximum, the claim is paid without comment. If the fee exceeds the maximum reimbursement, the physician and the patient are notified with an Explanation of Benefits (EOB). Tracking your EOBs is an excellent way to gain insight into your third party payer's maximum allowable charge limits.

Claims Monitoring (Tracking EOBs)

Explanation of Benefits (EOBs), along with their corresponding claims, should be monitored at the time the payment is posted to the patient's account. EOBs should be evaluated for three possible problems:

1) Full Payment - Full payment should not be seen as a success. If the insurance carrier approves or pays 100% of the fee charged, it is extremely likely that the fee is below the maximum that the insurance carrier is willing to pay. These cases should be evaluated to determine if the fee has been properly selected.

2) No Payment - No payment should be viewed as a coding error on the part of the physician or a coverage limitation on the part of the insurance carrier. Discuss these cases with the insurance carrier in the form of a coding discussion, rather than a payment (fee) discussion. Many carriers will help you code the claim so that it can be paid if coverage is available under the policy but will not discuss why they did not pay the claim nor will they tell you the UCR limit.

3) Reduced Payment - Reduced payment can be caused by improper coding or by fee schedule or UCR limitations. Fee schedule or UCR limitations are usually indicated on the EOB. If you suspect a coding problem, consider the possibility that this service should be coded using two or more codes rather than one. Some procedures require that supplies, drugs or related procedures be coded separately and will be paid according to the value of each code. However, be sure not to intentionally unbundle a procedure that should be coded as one code. Watch for the helpful "Unbundling Alerts" throughout the **PFR**.

Designing and Reviewing a Fee Schedule

The most commonly asked question regarding the **PFR** fee percentiles is "Which percentile column should I (the physician) use?" This is more a question of pricing philosophy than anything else. Some medical practice management consultants advise their physician clients to charge the maximum allowable charge (75th or 90th percentile depending on the patients policy), arguing that if it's allowable and you don't charge it, it's lost income.

Other consultants use a less aggressive reimbursement strategy. They try to place fees somewhere between the middle (50th percentile) and the maximum allowable charge, for example the midpoint between the 50th and 75th percentiles. With this approach, you can feel comfortable knowing that you are not in the bottom half (below the 50th percentile), yet below the maximum. This technique allows room for future increases and prevents unpleasant EOBs.

Independent of your pricing philosophy, review your fees often. Biannual consideration is recommended by reimbursement experts. Avoid sudden large fee increases. This will only create unhappy patients and hurt referrals. For some price-sensitive procedures, you may want to maintain lower than normal fees. This approach will help referrals and will pay off with increased volume. Be sure to carefully evaluate the fees for the procedures that are performed frequently or produce the largest amounts of revenue for your practice. This will provide maximum reimbursement and a minimum of unhappy patients.

To review a fee schedule, assemble copies of reference material, such as current CPT and HCPCS code books, current charge slips or superbills, your current fees, known fee schedules from any Managed Care contracts, Medicare's Relative Value Scale **RBRVS**, a fee guide such as this **PFR**, and sample EOBs for commonly used codes from major carriers.

Using the CPT and HCPCS books, your Superbills, and EOBs, determine which codes are used most frequently or produce large amounts of revenue. Construct a manual or computerized spreadsheet model, with the code and description at the left side of the spreadsheet. Add columns to collect data from each of the data sources (known fee schedules, relative value scales, **PFR**, and EOBs) and list the fees obtained from each source. Take into consideration any information obtained from the tracking of EOBs since the last fee review. Adjust your fees to meet your pricing strategy goals.

The determination of a physician's unique fee schedule, commensurate with his or her specialty, experience, office overhead (rent, salaries, utilities, insurance, malpractice insurance, equipment, and loan payments), is beyond the scope of this text. The reader is advised to stay abreast of changes in the medical marketplace by subscribing to medical/management magazines and journals that feature articles on medical pricing and health care issues. Two sources for medical economics information are *Medical Economics*, a semimonthly magazine published by Medical Economics Publishing, Inc. and *American Medical News*, a weekly newspaper published by the AMA.

Geographic Multipliers (Appendix A)

To help refine **PFR** fee information for your three digit zip code area, we have developed **PFR Geographic Multiplier**s or geographic adjustment factors (Appendix A). The **PFR** Multiplier is derived in part from Medicare's carrier locality areas, government wage indexes, and regional economic information. Do not use these multipliers for Medicare calculations.

Keep in mind that these multipliers describe overall relative differences of physicians' costs between three digit zip code prefixes and do not take into consideration economic disparities within these areas. You may need to modify these values. Geographic multipliers have their limitations but are found to be the best available measurement of the relative differences within geographic areas regarding medical practice costs.

PFR on CD ROM

We have developed an software version of the **PFR**. The **PFR Pricing Program**™ gives you the power of the **PFR** at your finger tips. For more information see the back page of this book. The **Physicians' Fee Reference Pricing Program**™ is a Windows® compatible version of the PFR book.

User Feedback

The editors of the **Physicians' Fee Reference**® would value any feedback including submission of your confidential price lists or suggestions on how the **PFR** can be more helpful. To participate in our independent research, we request survey participants to include the Zip Code and the date along with their fee schedules (names are optional). Other correspondence must be submitted on professional letterhead. Send to:

Research & Statistics
Physicians' Fee Reference®
P.O. Box 510949
Milwaukee, WI 53203

Additional copies of this publication are available on a limited basis for $139 each plus $11.95 shipping and handling. See the order form on the last page of this book for more information.

CODING OF PHYSICIAN SERVICES - AN OVERVIEW

What is the Current Procedural Terminology (CPT) coding system?

CPT is a coding system developed by the AMA and later adopted by the Centers for Medicare & Medicaid Services (CMS) formerly known as the Health Care Financing Administration (HCFA) for use in coding physician services. It continues to be maintained annually by the AMA and consists of 5 digit numeric codes covering the full spectrum of physician procedures and services. It is accepted by virtually all insurance carriers and is required when submitting claims to all government payers.

What is the Healthcare Common Procedural Coding System (HCPCS)?

Although often confused with CPT, HCPCS (pronounced "Hick-Picks") is not completely the same thing. CMS determined that while the CPT book described physician services, it did not contain descriptions of non-physician services and supplies that are performed or used in physician offices. Therefore, CMS developed its own coding system which incorporates CPT, in its entirety, and adds additional codes.

HCPCS includes 3 component levels:

Level I -　　The CPT book as published by the AMA. (See back pages for order information)

Level II -　　The CMS-developed 5 digit alphanumeric codes beginning with A0000 and ending with V9999. It is maintained at the CMS central office. (See back pages for order information)

Level III -　　Previously used 5 digit, alphanumeric codes , beginning with the letters W-Z. As of 1/1/04, these codes are no longer valid for processing claims due to the HIPAA Transactions and Code Sets requirements.

All HCPCS codes have a hierarchy for code assignment. A Level II code must be used before a Level I(CPT) code that may have the same description. In common usage, Level I codes are referred to as CPT codes and Level II codes are referred to as HCPCS codes.

To order the most current edition of the HCPCS Level II codes see the last page of this book. **HCPCS 2007 (list $59)**

Modifiers

Many CPT codes can be modified using a two digit modifier, which may affect payment. It should be noted that fee information throughout the **PFR** (except Radiology and a few Urology and Heart Catheterization procedures) is intended to represent the total charge unless otherwise indicated. These sections use the modifier -26 (professional component). For a complete list of CPT modifiers, see Appendix A of the CPT code book. For a discussion of coding using modifiers, see the Modifier section of this introduction. For a complete listing of CPT codes, guidelines, and modifiers, we encourage all of our subscribers to purchase and reference the latest version of the CPT code book, available from the AMA. Do not code directly from the **PFR**.

Inconclusive Results (IR)

The letters **IR** have been used to indicate an **I**nconclusive **R**esult due to insufficient/invalid source data or for unlisted procedures.

Global Surgical Package

Appendix B contains Global Fee Periods, expressed in days, to be included in certain pre- and postoperative care. The values presented in the **PFR** are taken directly from the Medicare Fee Schedule and can vary by carrier.

The global period starts the day prior to the procedure and extends throughout a time period defined by the third party payer. This global fee period is often referred to as follow up days (FUD). During this time period, no additional E/M codes can be coded unless the service was for an unrelated condition (see Modifiers list in this introduction), or was for a surgical complication. To code a visit for documentation purposes only, code 99024, "Postoperative follow-up visit, included in global service".

Multiple Surgical Procedure Reductions

When two or more procedures with the same global fee period are performed on the same day, these procedures share the pre- and postoperative care for the patient. They also share some intraoperative services such as, preparation, anesthesia and the surgical field. Therefore, Medicare and many private third party payers will reduce the second and subsequent procedures to account for the economy of these shared services. Second and subsequent procedures should be coded with a -51 modifier to indicate that they are multiple procedures.

There are a few procedures where the -51 modifier should not be used, mainly found in the integumentary section. Don't add a -51 modifier to any code where the description reads "each" or "each additional ... ". These codes have their allowable value already reduced and should not be reduced again.

It is appropriate to designate multiple procedures that are rendered on the same date by separate entries. This can be reported by using the multiple procedure modifier ('-51'). All add-on codes (see following definition) are exempt from the multiple procedures concept. For example: If individual medical psychotherapy (90841) is rendered in addition to subsequent hospital care (eg, 99231), the psychotherapy would be reported separately from the hospital visit. In this instance, both 99231 and 90841 would be reported.

Add-on Codes

Some of the listed procedures are commonly carried out in addition to the primary procedure performed. These additional or supplemental procedures are designated as "add-on" codes. All add-on codes found in CPT are exempt from the multiple procedure concept. They are exempt from the use of the Modifier -51, as these procedures are not reported as stand-alone codes. Add-on codes in CPT can be readily identified by specific descriptor nomenclature which includes phrases such as "each additional" or "(List separately in addition to primary procedure)".

Separate Procedure

Some of the procedures or services listed in CPT that are commonly carried out as an integral component of a total service or procedure have been identified by the inclusion of the term "separate procedure". The codes designated as "separate procedure" should not be reported in addition to the code for the total procedure or service of which it is considered an integral component.

However, when a procedure or service that is designated as a "separate procedure" is carried out independently or considered to be unrelated or distinct from other procedures/serviced provided at that time, it may be reported by itself, or in addition to other procedures/services by appending the modifier '-59' to the specific procedure code to indicate that the procedure is not considered to be a component of another procedure, but is a distinct, independent procedure. This may represent a different session or patient encounter, different procedure or surgery, different site or organ system, separate incision/excision, separate lesion, or separate injury (or area of injury in extensive injuries).

Modifiers

A modifier provides the means by which the reporting physician can indicate that a service or procedure that has been performed has been altered by some specific circumstance but not changed in its definition or code. The judicious application of modifiers obviates the necessity for separate procedure listings that may describe the modifying circumstance. Modifiers may be used to indicate that:

- A service or procedure has both a professional and technical component
- A service or procedure was performed by more than one physician and/or in more than one location
- A service or procedure has been increased or reduced

- Only part of a service was performed
- An adjunctive service was performed
- A bilateral procedure was performed
- A service or procedure was provided more than once
- Unusual events occurred

There are both CPT two digit numeric modifiers and HCPCS two digit alphabetic and alphanumeric modifiers, that should follow the code, separated by a hyphen.

This list includes all of the modifiers applicable to CPT 2007 codes.

- 21 Prolonged Evaluation and Management Services: When the face-to-face or floor/unit service(s) provided is prolonged or otherwise greater than that usually required for the highest level of evaluation and management service within a given category, it may be identified by adding modifier '-21' to the evaluation and management code number. A report may also be appropriate.

- 22 Unusual Procedural Services: When the service(s) provided is greater than that usually required for the listed procedure, it may be identified by adding modifier '-22' to the usual procedure number. A report may also be appropriate.

- 23 Unusual Anesthesia: Occasionally, a procedure, which usually requires either no anesthesia or local anesthesia, because of unusual circumstances must be done under general anesthesia. This circumstance may be reported by adding the modifier '-23' to the procedure code of the basic service.

-24 Unrelated Evaluation and Management Service by the Same Physician During a Postoperative Period: The physician may need to indicate that an evaluation and management service was performed during a postoperative period for a reason(s) unrelated to the original procedure. This circumstance may be reported by adding the modifier '-24' to the appropriate level of E/M service.

- 25 Significant, Separately Identifiable Evaluation and Management Service by the Same Physician on the Same Day of the Procedure or Other Service: The physician may need to indicate that on the day a procedure or service identified by a CPT code was performed, the patient's condition required a significant, separately identifiable E/M service above and beyond the other service provided or beyond the usual preoperative and postoperative care associated with the procedure that was performed. A significant, separately identifiable E/M service is defined or substantiated by documentation that satisfies the relevant criteria for the respective E/M service to be reported. The E/M service may be prompted by the symptom or condition for which the procedure and/or service was provided. As such, different diagnoses are not required for reporting of the E/M services on the same date. This circumstance may be reported by adding the modifier '-25' to the appropriate level of E/M service. Note: This modifier is not used to report an E/M service that resulted in a decision to perform surgery. See modifier '-57.'

- 26 Professional Component: Certain procedures are a combination of a physician component and a technical component. When the physician component is reported separately, the service may be identified by adding the modifier '-26' to the usual procedure number.

- 32 Mandated Services: Services related to mandated consultation and/or related services (eg, PRO, 3rd party payor, governmental, legislative or regulatory requirement) may be identified by adding the modifier '-32' to the basic procedure.

- 47 Anesthesia by Surgeon: Regional or general anesthesia provided by the surgeon may be reported by adding the modifier '-47' to the basic service. (This does not include local anesthesia.) Note: Modifier '-47' would not be used as a modifier for the anesthesia procedures.

- 50 Bilateral Procedure: Unless otherwise identified in the listings, bilateral procedures that are performed at the same operative session should be identified by adding the modifier '-50' to the appropriate five digit code.

- 51 Multiple Procedures: When multiple procedures, other than Evaluation and Management Services, are performed at the same session by the same provider, the primary procedure or service may be reported as listed. The additional procedure(s) or service(s) may be identified by appending the modifier '-51' to the additional procedure or service code(s). Note: This modifier should not be appended to designated "add-on" codes (see Appendix E of CPT Book).

- 52 Reduced Services: Under certain circumstances a service or procedure is partially reduced or eliminated at the physician's discretion. Under these circumstances the service provided can be identified by its usual procedure number and the addition of the modifier '-52', signifying that the service is reduced. This provides a means of reporting reduced services without disturbing the identification of the basic service.

- 53 Discontinued Procedure: Under certain circumstances, the physician may elect to terminate a surgical or diagnostic procedure. Due to extenuating circumstances or those that threaten the well being of the patient, it may be necessary to indicate that a surgical or diagnostic procedure was started but discontinued. This circumstance may be reported by adding the modifier '-53' to the code reported by the physician for the discontinued procedure.

- 54 Surgical Care Only: When one physician performs a surgical procedure and another provides preoperative and/or postoperative management, surgical services may be identified by adding the modifier '-54' to the usual procedure number.

- 55 Postoperative Management Only: When one physician performs the postoperative management and another physician has performed the surgical procedure, the postoperative component may be identified by adding the modifier '-55' to the usual procedure number.

- 56 Preoperative Management Only: When one physician performs the preoperative care and evaluation and another physician performs the surgical procedure, the preoperative component may be identified by adding the modifier '-56' to the usual procedure number.

- 57 Decision for Surgery: An evaluation and management service that resulted in the initial decision to perform the surgery may be identified by adding the modifier '-57' to the appropriate level of E/M service.

- 58 Staged or Related Procedure or Service by the Same Physician During the Postoperative Period: The physician may need to indicate that the performance of a procedure or service during the postoperative period was: a) planned prospectively at the time of the original procedure (staged); b) more extensive than the original procedure; or c) for therapy following a diagnostic surgical procedure. This circumstance may be reported by adding the modifier '-58' to the staged or related procedure. Note: This modifier is not used to report the treatment of a problem that requires a return to the operating room. See modifier '-78.'

- 59 Distinct Procedural Service: Under certain circumstances, the physician may need to indicate that a procedure or service was distinct or independent from other services performed on the same day. Modifier '-59' is used to identify procedures/services that are not normally reported together, but are appropriate under the circumstances. This may represent a different session or patient encounter, different procedure or surgery, different site or organ system, separate incision/excision, separate lesion, or separate injury (or area of injury in extensive injuries) not ordinarily encountered or performed on the same day by the same physician. However, when another already established modifier is appropriate it should be used rather than modifier '-59.' Only if no more descriptive modifier is available, and the use of modifier '-59' best explains the circumstances, should modifier '-59' be used.

- 62 Two Surgeons: When two surgeons work together as primary surgeons performing distinct part(s) of a single reportable procedure, each surgeon should report his/her distinct operative work by adding the modifier '-62' to the single definitive procedure code. Each surgeon should report the co-surgery once using the same procedure code. If additional procedure(s) (including add-on procedure(s)) are performed during the same surgical session, separate code(s) may be reported without the modifier '-62' added. Note: If a co-surgeon acts as an assistant in the performance of additional procedure(s) during the same surgical session, those services may be reported using separate procedure fee code(s) with the modifier '-80' or modifier '-81' added, as appropriate.

-63 Procedure Performed on Infants less than 4 kg: Procedures performed on neonates and infants up to a present body weight of 4 kg may involve significantly increased complexity and physician work commonly associated with these patients. This circumstance may be reported by adding the modifier '-63' to the procedure number. Note: Unless otherwise designated, this modifier may only be appended to procedures/services listed in the 20000-69999 code series. Modifier '-63' should not be appended to any CPT codes listed in the Evaluation and Management Services, Anesthesia, Radiology, Pathology/Laboratory, or Medicine sections

- 66 Surgical Team: Under some circumstances, highly complex procedures (requiring the concomitant services of several physicians, often of different specialties, plus other highly skilled, specially trained personnel, various types of complex equipment) are carried out under the "surgical team" concept. Such circumstances may be identified by each participating physician with the addition of the modifier '-66' to the basic procedure number used for reporting services.

- 76 Repeat Procedure by Same Physician: The physician may need to indicate that a procedure or service was repeated subsequent to the original procedure or service. This circumstance may be reported by adding the modifier '-76' to the repeated procedure/service.

- 77 Repeat Procedure by Another Physician: The physician may need to indicate that a basic procedure or service performed by another physician had to be repeated. This situation may be reported by adding modifier '-77' to the repeated procedure/service.

- 78 Return to the Operating Room for a Related Procedure During the Postoperative Period: The physician may need to indicate that another procedure was performed during the postoperative period of the initial procedure. When this subsequent procedure is related to the first, and requires the use of the operating room, it may be reported by adding the modifier '-78' to the related procedure. (For repeat procedures on the same day, see '-76'.)

- 79 Unrelated Procedure or Service by the Same Physician During the Postoperative Period: The physician may need to indicate that the performance of a procedure or service during the postoperative period was unrelated to the original procedure. This circumstance may be reported by using the modifier '-79'. (For repeat procedures on the same day, see '-76'.)

- 80 Assistant Surgeon: Surgical assistant services may be identified by adding the modifier '-80' to the usual procedure number(s).

- 81 Minimum Assistant Surgeon: Minimum surgical assistant services are identified by adding the modifier '-81' to the usual procedure number.

-82 Assistant Surgeon (when qualified resident surgeon not available): The unavailability of a qualified resident surgeon is a prerequisite for use of modifier '-82' appended to the usual procedure code number(s).

- 90 Reference (Outside) Laboratory: When laboratory procedures are performed by a party other than the treating or reporting physician, the procedure may be identified by adding the modifier '-90' to the usual procedure number.

-91 Repeat Clinical Diagnostic Laboratory Test: In the course of the treatment of the patient, it may be necessary to repeat the same laboratory test on the same day to obtain subsequent (multiple) test results. Under these circumstances, the laboratory test performed can be identified by its usual procedure number and the addition of the modifier '-91'. Note: This modifier may not be used when test are rerun to confirm initial results; due to testing problems with specimens or equipment; or for any other reason when a normal, one-time, reportable result is all that is required. This modifier may not be used when other code(s) describe a series of test results (e.g., glucose tolerance tests, evocative/suppression testing). This modifier may only be used for laboratory test(s) performed more than once on the same day on the same patient.

- 99 Multiple Modifiers: Under certain circumstances two or more modifiers may be necessary to completely delineate a service. In such situations modifier '-99' should be added to the basic procedure, and other applicable modifiers may be listed as part of the description of the service.

Modifiers Approved for Ambulatory Surgery Center (ASC)
Hospital Outpatient Use (Level I (CPT))

-25 significant, separately identifiable evaluation and management service by the same physician on the same day of the procedure or other service

-27 multiple outpatient hospital e/m encounters on the same date

-50 bilateral procedure

-52 reduced services

-58 staged or related procedure or service by the same physician during the postoperative period

-59 distinct procedural service

-73 discontinued out-patient procedure prior to anesthesia administration

-74 discontinued out-patient procedure after anesthesia administration

-76 repeat procedure by same physician

-77 repeat procedure by another physician

-78 return to the operating room for a related procedure during the postoperative period

-79 unrelated procedure or service by the same physician during the postoperative period

-91 repeat clinical diagnostic laboratory testy

Level II (HCPCS/National) Modifiers

A1	A1 Dressing for one wound
A2	Dressing for two wounds
A3	Dressing for three wounds
A4	Dressing for four wounds
A5	Dressing for five wounds
A6	Dressing for six wounds
A7	Dressing for seven wounds
A8	Dressing for eight wounds
A9	Dressing for nine or more wounds
AA	Anesthesia services performed personally by anesthesiologist
AD	Medical supervision by a physician: more than four concurrent anesthesia procedures
AE	Registered dietician
AF	Specialty physician
AG	Primary physician
AH	Clinical psychologist
AJ	Clinical social worker
AM	Physician, team member service
AP	Determination of refractive state was not performed in the course of diagnostic ophthalmological examination
AQ	Physician providing a service in an unlisted health professional shortage area (HPSA)
AS	Physician assistant, nurse practitioner, or clinical nurse specialist services for assistant at surgery
AT	Acute treatment (this modifier should be used when reporting service 98940, 98941, 98942
AU	Item furnished in conjunction with a urological, ostomy, or tracheostomy supply
AV	Item furnished in conjunction with a prosthetic device, prosthetic or orthotic
AW	Item furnished in conjunction with a surgical dressing
AX	Item furnished in conjunction with dialysis services
BA	Item furnished in conjunction with parenteral enteral nutrition (PEN) services
BL	Special acquisition of blood and blood products
BO	Orally administered nutrition, not by feeding tube
BP	The beneficiary has been informed of the purchase and rental options and has elected to purchase the item
BR	The beneficiary has been informed of the purchase and rental options and has elected to rent the item
BU	The beneficiary has been informed of the purchase and rental options and after 30 days has not informed the supplier of his/her decision
CA	Procedure payable only in the inpatient setting when performed emergently on an outpatient who expires prior to admission

CB	Service ordered by a renal dialysis facility (RDF) physician as part of the ESRD beneficiary's dialysis benefit, is not part of the composite rate, and is separately reimbursable
CC	Procedure code change (use 'CC' when the procedure code submitted was changed either for administrative reasons or because an incorrect code was filed)
CE	AMCC test has been ordered by an ESRD facility or MCP physician that is a composite rate test but is beyond the normal frequency covered under the rate and is separately reimbursable based on medical necessity
CF	AMCC test has been ordered by an ESRD facility or MCP physician that is not part of the composite rate and is separately billable
CR	Catastrophe/disaster related
E1	Upper left, eyelid
E2	Lower left, eyelid
E3	Upper right, eyelid
E4	Lower right, eyelid
EJ	Subsequent claims for a defined course of therapy, e.g., EPO, Sodium Hyaluronate, Infliximab
EM	Emergency reserve supply (for ESRD benefit only)
EP	Service provided as part of Medicaid early periodic screening diagnosis and treatment (EPSDT) program
ET	Emergency services
EY	No physician or other licensed health care provider order for this item or service
F1	Left hand, second digit
F2	Left hand, third digit
F3	Left hand, fourth digit
F4	Left hand, fifth digit
F5	Right hand, thumb
F6	Right hand, second digit
F7	Right hand, third digit
F8	Right hand, fourth digit
F9	Right hand, fifth digit
FA	Left hand, thumb
FB	Item provided without cost to provider, supplier or practitioner or credit received for replaced device (examples, but not limited to: covered under warranty, replaced due to defect, free samples)
FP	Service provided as part of Medicaid family planning program
G1	Most recent URR reading of less than 60
G2	Most recent URR reading of 60 to 64.9
G3	Most recent URR reading of 65 to 69.9
G4	Most recent URR reading of 70 to 74.9
G5	Most recent URR reading of 75 or greater
G6	ESRD patient for whom less than six dialysis sessions have been provided in a month
G7	Pregnancy resulted from rape or incest or pregnancy certified by physician as life threatening
G8	Monitored anesthesia care (MAC) for deep complex, complicated, or markedly invasive surgical procedure
G9	Monitored anesthesia care for patient who has history of severe cardio-pulmonary condition
GA	Waiver of liability statement on file
GB	Claim being re-submitted for payment because it is no longer covered under a global payment demonstration
GC	This service has been performed in part by a resident under the direction of a teaching physician
GE	This service has been performed by a resident without the presence of a teaching physician under the primary care exception
GF	
GG	Performance and payment of a screening mammogram and diagnostic mammogram on the same patient, same day
GH	Diagnostic mammogram converted from screening mammogram on same day
GJ	"Opt out" physician or practitioner emergency or urgent service
GK	Actual item/service ordered by physician, item associated with GA or GZ modifier
GL	Medically unnecessary upgrade provided instead of standard item, no charge, no advance beneficiary notice (ABN)
GM	Multiple patients on one ambulance trip
GN	Services delivered under an outpatient speech language pathology plan of care

GO	Services delivered under an outpatient occupational therapy plan of care
GP	Services delivered under an outpatient physical therapy plan of care
GQ	Via asynchronous telecommunications system
GR	This service was performed in whole or in part by a resident in a department of veterans affairs medical center or clinic, supervised in accordance with VA policy
GS	Dosage of EPO or darbepoietin alfa has been reduced and maintained in response to hematocrit or hemoglobulin level
GT	Via interactive audio and video telecommunication systems
GV	Attending physician not employed or paid under arrangement by the patient's hospice provider
GW	Service not related to the hospice patient's terminal condition
GY	Item or service statutorily excluded or does not meet the definition of any Medicare benefit
GZ	Item or service expected to be denied as not reasonable and necessary
H9	Court-ordered
HA	Child/adolescent program
HB	Adult program, non geriatric
HC	Adult program, geriatric
HD	Pregnant/parenting women's program
HE	Mental health program
HF	Substance abuse program
HG	Opioid addiction treatment program
HH	Integrated mental health/substance abuse program
HI	Integrated mental health and mental retardation/developmental disabilities program
HJ	Employee assistance program
HK	Specialized mental health programs for high-risk populations
HL	Intern
HM	Less than bachelor degree level
HN	Bachelors degree level
HO	Masters degree level
HP	Doctoral level
HQ	Group setting
HR	Family/couple with client present
HS	Family/couple without client present
HT	Multi-disciplinary team
HU	Funded by child welfare agency
HV	Funded state addictions agency
HW	Funded by state mental health agency
HX	Funded by county/local agency
HY	Funded by juvenile justice agency
HZ	Funded by criminal justice agency
J1	Competitive acquisition program no-pay submission for a prescription number
J2	Competitive acquisition program, restocking of emergency drugs after emergency administration
J3	Competitive acquisition program (CAP), drug not available through cap as written, reimbursed under average sales price methodology
JA	Administered intravenously
JB	Administered subcutaneousl
JW	Drug amount discarded/not administered to any patient
K0	Lower extremity prosthesis functional level 0
K1	Lower extremity prosthesis functional level 1
K2	Lower extremity prosthesis functional level 2
K3	Lower extremity prosthesis functional level 3
K4	Lower extremity prosthesis functional level 4
KA	Add on option/accessory for wheelchair
KB	Beneficiary requested upgrade for ABN, more than 4 modifiers identified on claim
KC	Replacement of special power wheelchair interface
KD	Drug or biological infused through DME
KF	Item designated by FDA as class III device
KH	DMEPOS item, initial claim, purchase or first month rental
KI	DMEPOS item, second or third month rental
KJ	DMEPOS item, parenteral enteral nutrition (pen) pump or capped rental, months 4 to 15

KM	Replacement of facial prosthesis including new impression/moulage
KN	Replacement of facial prosthesis using previous master model
KO	Single drug unit dose formulation
KP	First drug of a multiple drug unit dose formulation
KQ	Second or subsequent drug of a multiple drug unit dose formulation
KR	Rental item, billing for partial month
KS	Glucose monitor supply for diabetic beneficiary not treated with insulin
KX	Specific required documentation on file
KZ	New coverage not implemented by managed care
LC	Left circumflex coronary artery
LD	Left anterior descending coronary artery
LL	Lease/rental (use the 'LL' modifier when DME equipment rental is to be applied against the purchase price)
LR	Laboratory round trip
LS	FDA-monitored intraocular lens implant
LT	Left side (used to identify procedures performed on the left side of the body)
M2	Medicare secondary payer (MSP)
MS	Six month maintenance and servicing fee for reasonable and necessary parts and labor which are not covered under any manufacturer or supplier warranty
NR	New when rented (use the 'NR' modifier when DME which was new at the time of rental is subsequently purchased)
NU	New equipment
P1	A normal healthy patient
P2	A patient with mild systemic disease
P3	A patient with severe systemic disease
P4	A patient with severe systemic disease that is a constant threat to life
P5	A moribund patient who is not expected to survive without the operation
P6	A declared brain-dead patient whose organs are being removed for donor purposes
PL	Progressive addition lenses
Q2	HCFA/ORD demonstration project procedure/service
Q3	Live kidney donor surgery and related services
Q4	Service for ordering/referring physician qualifies as a service exemption
Q5	Service furnished by a substitute physician under a reciprocal billing arrangement
Q6	Service furnished by a locum tenens physician
Q7	One class A finding
Q8	Two class B findings
Q9	One class B and two class C findings
QA	FDA investigational device exemption
QC	Single channel monitoring
QD	Recording and storage in solid state memory by a digital recorder
QE	Prescribed amount of oxygen is less than 1 liter per minute (LPM)
QF	Prescribed amount of oxygen exceeds 4 liters per minute (LPM) and portable oxygen is prescribed
QG	Prescribed amount of oxygen is greater than 4 liters per minute(LPM)
QH	Oxygen conserving device is being used with an oxygen delivery system
QJ	Services/items provided to a prisoner or patient in state or local custody
QK	Medical direction of two, three, or four concurrent anesthesia procedures involving qualified individuals
QL	Patient pronounced dead after ambulance called
QM	Ambulance service provided under arrangement by a provider of services
QN	Ambulance service furnished directly by a provider of services
QP	Documentation is on file showing that the laboratory test(s) was ordered individually or ordered as a CPT-recognized panel other than automated profile
QR	Item or service provided in a Medicare specified study
QS	Monitored anesthesia care service
QT	Recording and storage on tape by an analog tape recorder
QV	Item or service provided as routine care in a Medicare qualifying clinical trial
QW	CLIA waived test
QX	CRNA service: with medical direction by a physician

QY	Medical direction of one certified registered nurse anesthetist (CRNA) by an anesthesiologist
QZ	CRNA service: without medical direction by a physician
RC	Right coronary artery
RD	Drug provided to beneficiary, but not administered "incident-to"
RP	Replacement and repair
RR	Rental (use the 'RR' modifier when DME is to be rented)
RT	Right side (used to identify procedures performed on the right side of the body)
SA	Nurse practitioner rendering service in collaboration with a physician
SB	Nurse midwife
SC	Medically necessary service or supply
SD	Services provided by registered nurse with specialized, highly technical home infusion training
SE	State and/or federally-funded programs/services
SF	Second opinion ordered by a professional review organization (PRO) per section 9401
SG	Ambulatory surgical center (ASC) facility service
SH	Second concurrently administered infusion therapy
SJ	Third or more concurrently administered infusion therapy
SK	Member of high risk population (use only with codes for immunization)
SL	State supplied vaccine
SM	Second surgical opinion
SN	Third surgical opinion
SQ	Item ordered by home health
SS	Home infusion services provided in the infusion suite of the IV therapy provider
ST	Related to trauma or injury
SU	Procedure performed in physician's office (to denote use of facility and equipment)
SV	Pharmaceuticals delivered to patient's home but not utilized
SW	Services provided by a certified diabetic educator
SY	Persons who are in close contact with member of high-risk population (use only with codes for immunization)
T1	Left foot, second digit
T2	Left foot, third digit
T3	Left foot, fourth digit
T4	Left foot, fifth digit
T5	Right foot, great toe
T6	Right foot, second digit
T7	Right foot, third digit
T8	Right foot, fourth digit
T9	Right foot, fifth digit
TA	Left foot, great toe
TC	Technical component
TD	RN
TE	LPN/LVN
TF	Intermediate level of care
TG	Complex/high tech level of care
TH	Obstetrical treatment/services, prenatal or postpartum
TJ	Program group, child and/or adolescent
TK	Extra patient or passenger, non-ambulance
TL	Early intervention/individualized family service plan (IFSP)
TM	Individualized education program (IEP)
TN	Rural/outside providers' customary service area
TP	Medical transport, unloaded vehicle
TQ	Basic life support transport by a volunteer ambulance provider
TR	School-based individualized education program (IEP) services provided outside the public school district responsible for the student follow-up service
TS	Follow-up service
TT	Individualized service provided to more than one patient in same setting
TU	Special payment rate, overtime
TV	Special payment rates, holidays/weekends
TW	Back-up equipment

U1	Medicaid level of care 1, as defined by each state
U2	Medicaid level of care 2, as defined by each state
U3	Medicaid level of care 3, as defined by each state
U4	Medicaid level of care 4, as defined by each state
U5	Medicaid level of care 5, as defined by each state
U6	Medicaid level of care 6, as defined by each state
U7	Medicaid level of care 7, as defined by each state
U8	Medicaid level of care 8, as defined by each state
U9	Medicaid level of care 9, as defined by each state
UA	Medicaid level of care 10, as defined by each state
UB	Medicaid level of care 11, as defined by each state
UC	Medicaid level of care 12, as defined by each state
UD	Medicaid level of care 13, as defined by each state
UE	Used durable medical equipment
UF	Services provided in the morning
UG	Services provided in the afternoon
UH	Services provided in the evening
UJ	Services provided at night
UK	Services provided on behalf of the client to someone other than the client (collateral relationship)
UN	Two patients served
UP	Three patients served
UQ	Four patients served
UR	Five patients served
US	Six or more patients served
VP	Aphakic patient

Unlisted Service or Procedure

It is recognized that there may be services or procedures performed by physicians that are not found in CPT. Therefore, a number of specific code numbers have been designated for reporting unlisted procedures. When an unlisted procedure number is used, the service or procedure should be described. Each of these unlisted procedural code numbers (with the appropriate accompanying topical entry) relates to a specific section of the book.

In addition, CPT has developed a new set of temporary codes to describe emerging technology, services, and procedures. These codes are called Category III codes and are part of the CPT book. They are 5-digit, alphanumeric codes, starting with 4 numbers and ending with a letter (eg, 1234T). They are accessed through the regular CPT index and are listed in their own section, directly following the Medicine Section of the CPT book. If a Category III code exists to describe a service, it must be used, rather than using an unlisted service code.

Special Reports

A services that is rarely provided, unusual, variable, or new may require a special report in determining medical appropriateness of the service. Pertinent information should include an adequate definition or description of the nature, extent, and need for the procedure; and the time extent, and need for the procedure; and the time, effort, and equipment necessary to provide the service. Additional items which may be included are:

- complexity of symptoms
- final diagnosis
- pertinent physical findings
- diagnostic and therapeutic procedures
- concurrent problems
- follow-up care

Fragmentation/Unbundling

Some procedures are considered to be part of another procedure and are not to be coded separately. In these cases, if two codes are used to describe a service that could be accurately coded using one code, it is considered unbundling or fragmented coding which can be considered fraud. In 1996 Medicare implemented its National Correct Coding Initiative in an attempt to eliminate this problem. Medicare and most third party payers have unbundling detection software and will not pay for unbundled codes. The PFR has hundreds of "Unbundling Alerts" associated with many of the commonly used CPT codes. Although these coding notes are helpful they are not a comprehensive listing of all CCI edits. The PFR recommends **CorrectCoder for Edits**™ **www.correctcoder.com**, a low cost easy-to-use Windows based software application that checks for CCI Edits. See back page of this book for an order form.

Over Utilization

Medicare carriers and other third party payers have the ability to track code utilization by individual providers over time. Some codes have individual frequency limitations (only a certain number of procedures allowed within a given time period). Other codes indicate that the physician performed extensive service, and therefore, warrant special tracking.

Be sure that the best possible code selection is made for each claim and that full documentation exists in order to protect yourself from delays, rejections, and audits.

Assigning a CPT Code

1. Analyze the documentation given by the physician and select the procedures, services, drugs, supplies and tests to be coded.

2. Identify the main term and the subterms and locate them in the Index under the procedure, anatomic site, condition, synonym, eponym, and abbreviation entries as necessary.

3. Note the code number(s) found with the selected main term or subterm.

    a. If a single code is listed - locate the code number in the body of the book. Verify that the description matches the item to be coded.
    b. If multiple codes are listed, separated by commas - locate each code in the body of the book. Do not automatically assign all codes. Choose from the list as options.
    c. If a range of codes is listed - locate the range in the body of the book and determine which description matches the item to be coded.

4. Never code directly from the index. Locate each code in the body of the book and read all section notes that apply to the codes.

5. Select appropriate modifiers, as necessary, to fully describe the item being coded.

Additional Information about CPT Coding

1. Use only codes that are valid at the time of the service.

2. Use new codes sparingly until the payment requirements have been tested.

3. Avoid using unlisted codes (XXX99) by fully researching all alternative codes. Consider using a detailed code and adding a -22 (additional service) or -52 (reduced service) modifier to accurately describe the service.

4. Send documentation with claims when there is a suspicion that more information will be required.

5. Diagnostic procedures are always included in the therapeutic procedures done by the same physician on the same day. When performed together, code only the therapeutic procedure. If coded separately, this is considered unbundling.

6. Remember that procedure descriptions can be compound, stopping at the semicolon (;) and replacing any indented descriptions for the portion following the semicolon.

What is the International Classification of Diseases - 9th Revision - Clinical Modification (ICD-9-CM) coding system?

ICD-9-CM is the recognized coding system for diagnoses in all health care settings, including physician services. Although the coding system does have codes for procedures in Volume 3, the ICD-9-CM procedures codes are not acceptable for physician services. As of 1988, the use of ICD-9-CM diagnosis codes is required when submitting claims to Medicare. Using ICD-9-CM for all insurance carriers greatly simplifies the claims submission process.

ICD-9-CM codes are updated annually on October 1st. Most carriers do not make the changes effective for physician billing until January 1st or after.

The ICD-9-CM codes have between 3 and 5 digits. When assigning a diagnosis code, be sure to use the code to the greatest specificity. That means that if the code has 5 digit subclassifications, you cannot use a 3 or 4 digit form of that code. If the code shows a maximum of 4 digits, then the 3 digit form cannot be used. The 3 digit form of the code can only be used if there are no 4 or 5 digit subclassifications.

Many payers use CPT-ICD crosswalks to audit and validate medical necessity. The PFR recommends CrossCoder for CPT/ICD www.crosscoder.com as a low cost solution for CPT/ICD crosswalks. (See last page)

ICD-9-CM Coding Basics

ICD-9-CM codes are three to five digits and can be either numeric or alphanumeric. The basic rule when coding with ICD-9-CM is that if the code is listed subdivided into four or five digits, the full amount of digits must be used. In other words, assign a three digit code only when no four digit codes are available. Assign a four digit code only when no five digit codes are available. Without the correct amount of digits as indicated in the code book, government payers will consider the code invalid, which is equivalent to being absent.

For physician services, only confirmed diagnoses should be coded. "Probable", "suspected" or "rule out" should not be considered as confirmed diagnostic statements. Rather, code the presenting symptoms until a confirmed diagnosis is made. In addition, ICD-9-CM codes must be correlated to the procedure code on the claim so that third party payers can determine why a service was performed. See **www.crosscoder.com** for more information.

Assigning an ICD-9-CM Code

1.   Look up the basic term in the alphabetic index and review any subterms listed. Investigate any cross references ("See", "See Also").

2.   YOU MUST VERIFY THE CODE IN THE TABULAR SECTION, reading all notes and exclusions and following any instructions.

3.   Add any necessary 4 or 5 digits indicated by the notes to assign the correct code.

Obtaining Information Under the Freedom of Information Act

The federal Freedom of Information Act requires that government agencies provide any information that they have in their possession when the information is requested. The difficult part is requesting the information specifically and using the correct terminology to obtain what you need. When successful, Freedom of Information requests can provide very helpful information about how items should be coded and whether Medicare considers a procedure covered under certain circumstances. Requests should be made in writing, be a specific as possible, and directed to the Freedom of Information unit at your local Medicare carrier.

Private Third Party Payers

Although many coding notes and tips in the **PFR** are based on Medicare rules, they are not to be avoided when coding for private payers. Rather than develop separate guidelines, many private payers are simply adopting Medicare's guidelines as their own. Because Medicare's guidelines are very stringent and attempt to save costs whenever possible, these guidelines are looking more and more attractive to private payers as well. Be watchful of Medicare rules as possible standards by other payers.

Workers' Compensation Carriers

Workers' Compensation carriers are also beginning to scrutinize claims as never before. In addition, some state agencies that govern Workers' Compensation policies have begun using fee schedules to help screen fee appropriateness. **RBRVS** has been chosen as the basis for some of these fee schedules, sometimes using multiples of the resulting Medicare payment (such as 1.2 times **RBRVS**) or by using a larger monetary conversion factor to calculate the payment. Many Workers' Compensation carriers are using conversion factors in the range of $35 to $70. (See last page of this book for information on **RBRVS EZ-Fees® Software**)

Managed Care and Commercial Carriers

Some Managed Care Organizations are using relative value studies to negotiate contracts. Over a dozen Blue Cross plans in the U.S. have adopted **RBRVS** for their physician payment plans and many more are planning or investigating a change to **RBRVS**. The conversion factor used by HMO's can also range from $35 to $70. (See last page for information on **RBRVS EZ-Fees® Software** or go to **www.rbrvs.net**)

CARRIER →

HEALTH INSURANCE CLAIM FORM

☐ PICA ☐ | PICA ☐ ☐

1. MEDICARE MEDICAID CHAMPUS CHAMPVA GROUP HEALTH PLAN FECA BLK LUNG OTHER	1a. INSURED'S I.D. NUMBER (FOR PROGRAM IN ITEM 1)
☐ (Medicare #) ☐ (Medicaid #) ☐ (Sponsor's SSN) ☐ (VA File #) ☐ (SSN or ID) ☐ (SSN) ☐ (ID)	

PATIENT AND INSURED INFORMATION

2. PATIENT'S NAME (Last Name, First Name, Middle Initial)

3. PATIENT'S BIRTH DATE MM | DD | YY   SEX   M ☐   F ☐

4. INSURED'S NAME (Last Name, First Name, Middle Initial)

5. PATIENT'S ADDRESS (No., Street)

6. PATIENT RELATIONSHIP TO INSURED Self ☐ Spouse ☐ Child ☐ Other ☐

7. INSURED'S ADDRESS (No., Street)

CITY | STATE

8. PATIENT STATUS Single ☐ Married ☐ Other ☐

CITY | STATE

ZIP CODE | TELEPHONE (Include Area Code) ( )

Employed ☐ Full-Time Student ☐ Part-Time Student ☐

ZIP CODE | TELEPHONE (INCLUDE AREA CODE) ( )

9. OTHER INSURED'S NAME (Last Name, First Name, Middle Initial)

10. IS PATIENT'S CONDITION RELATED TO:

11. INSURED'S POLICY GROUP OR FECA NUMBER

a. OTHER INSURED'S POLICY OR GROUP NUMBER

a. EMPLOYMENT? (CURRENT OR PREVIOUS) ☐ YES ☐ NO

a. INSURED'S DATE OF BIRTH MM | DD | YY   SEX M ☐ F ☐

b. OTHER INSURED'S DATE OF BIRTH MM | DD | YY   SEX M ☐ F ☐

b. AUTO ACCIDENT?   PLACE (State) ☐ YES ☐ NO

b. EMPLOYER'S NAME OR SCHOOL NAME

c. EMPLOYER'S NAME OR SCHOOL NAME

c. OTHER ACCIDENT? ☐ YES ☐ NO

c. INSURANCE PLAN NAME OR PROGRAM NAME

d. INSURANCE PLAN NAME OR PROGRAM NAME

10d. RESERVED FOR LOCAL USE

d. IS THERE ANOTHER HEALTH BENEFIT PLAN? ☐ YES ☐ NO **If yes**, return to and complete item 9 a-d.

READ BACK OF FORM BEFORE COMPLETING & SIGNING THIS FORM.

12. PATIENT'S OR AUTHORIZED PERSON'S SIGNATURE I authorize the release of any medical or other information necessary to process this claim. I also request payment of government benefits either to myself or to the party who accepts assignment below.

SIGNED _____ DATE _____

13. INSURED'S OR AUTHORIZED PERSON'S SIGNATURE I authorize payment of medical benefits to the undersigned physician or supplier for services described below.

SIGNED _____

PHYSICIAN OR SUPPLIER INFORMATION

14. DATE OF CURRENT: MM | DD | YY ◄ ILLNESS (First symptom) OR INJURY (Accident) OR PREGNANCY(LMP)

15. IF PATIENT HAS HAD SAME OR SIMILAR ILLNESS. GIVE FIRST DATE MM | DD | YY

16. DATES PATIENT UNABLE TO WORK IN CURRENT OCCUPATION MM | DD | YY FROM   TO   MM | DD | YY

17. NAME OF REFERRING PHYSICIAN OR OTHER SOURCE

17a. I.D. NUMBER OF REFERRING PHYSICIAN

18. HOSPITALIZATION DATES RELATED TO CURRENT SERVICES MM | DD | YY FROM   TO   MM | DD | YY

19. RESERVED FOR LOCAL USE

20. OUTSIDE LAB? ☐ YES ☐ NO $ CHARGES

21. DIAGNOSIS OR NATURE OF ILLNESS OR INJURY. (RELATE ITEMS 1,2,3 OR 4 TO ITEM 24E BY LINE) ⌐⌐

1. |___.___   3. |___.___

22. MEDICAID RESUBMISSION CODE   ORIGINAL REF. NO.

2. |___.___   4. |___.___

23. PRIOR AUTHORIZATION NUMBER

24. A DATE(S) OF SERVICE		B Place of Service	C Type of Service	D PROCEDURES, SERVICES, OR SUPPLIES (Explain Unusual Circumstances)	E DIAGNOSIS CODE	F $ CHARGES	G DAYS OR UNITS	H EPSDT Family Plan	I EMG	J COB	K RESERVED FOR LOCAL USE
From MM DD YY	To MM DD YY			CPT/HCPCS | MODIFIER							
1											
2											
3											
4											
5											
6											

25. FEDERAL TAX I.D. NUMBER SSN ☐ EIN ☐

26. PATIENT'S ACCOUNT NO.

27. ACCEPT ASSIGNMENT? (For govt. claims, see back) ☐ YES ☐ NO

28. TOTAL CHARGE $

29. AMOUNT PAID $

30. BALANCE DUE $

31. SIGNATURE OF PHYSICIAN OR SUPPLIER INCLUDING DEGREES OR CREDENTIALS (I certify that the statements on the reverse apply to this bill and are made a part thereof.)

SIGNED _____ DATE _____

32. NAME AND ADDRESS OF FACILITY WHERE SERVICES WERE RENDERED (If other than home or office)

33. PHYSICIAN'S, SUPPLIER'S BILLING NAME, ADDRESS, ZIP CODE & PHONE #

PIN# _____ GRP# _____

Health Insurance Claim Form CMS-1500

(Rev. 899, Issued: 03-31-06; Effective: 10-01-06; Implementation: 10-02-06)

The Form CMS-1500 (Health Insurance Claim Form) is sometimes referred to as the AMA (American Medical Association) form. The Form CMS-1500 is the prescribed form for claims prepared and submitted by physicians or suppliers (except for ambulance suppliers), whether or not the claims are assigned. It can be purchased in any version required i.e., single sheet, snap-out, continuous, etc. To purchase them from the U.S. Government Printing Office, call (202) 512-1800.

There are currently two versions of the Form CMS-1500. The current approved version of the form as of 2005 is the Form CMS-1500 (12/90). The current version is approved under the Office of Management and Budget (OMB) collection 0938-0008. The proposed version of the form will be the Form CMS-1500 (08/05) and is expected to receive OMB approval and receive a new collection number in April 2006. The current claim form is being revised to accommodate the implementation of the National Provider Identifier (NPI) which is scheduled for completion of the implementation in May 2007.

Because of the NPI dual usage period, there will be overlap between the use of the old and the new Form CMS-1500. Therefore, you will find information within this chapter that applies to both claim forms. The differences between the two forms will be noted within the body of the text that describes each of the items/boxes/fields of the Form CMS-1500. In addition to the text within the chapter, there are two exhibits at the end of this chapter that provide the print file specifications for each form. Exhibit 1 is the print file specification layout for the current Form CMS-1500 (12-90) and exhibit 2 is the print file specification layout for the Form CMS-1500 (08-05).

The Form CMS-1500 answers the needs of many health insurers. It is the basic form prescribed by CMS for the Medicare and Medicaid programs for claims from physicians and suppliers. It has also been adopted by the Office of Civilian Health and Medical Program of the Uniformed Services (OCHAMPUS) and has received the approval of the American Medical Association (AMA) Council on Medical Services.

There are a number of Part B services that have special limitations on payments or that require special methods of benefit computation. Carriers should monitor their processing systems to insure that they recognize the procedure codes that involve services with special payment limitations or calculation requirements. They should be able to identify separately billed procedure codes for physician services which are actually part of a global procedure code to prevent a greater payment than if the procedure were billed globally.

The following instructions must be completed or are required for a Medicare claim. Carriers should provide information on completing the Form CMS-1500 to all physicians and suppliers in their area at least once a year. Providers may use these instructions for completing this form. The Form CMS-1500 has space for physicians and suppliers to provide information on other health insurance. This information can be used by carriers to determine whether the Medicare patient has other
coverage that must be billed prior to Medicare payment, or whether there is a Medigap policy under which payments are made to a participating physician or supplier. (See Pub 100-05, Medicare Secondary Payer Manual, Chapter 3, and this manual, Chapter 28).

Providers and suppliers must report 8-digit dates in all date of birth fields (items 3, 9b, and 11a), and either 6-digit or 8-digit dates in all other date fields (items 11b, 12, 14, 16, 18, 19, 24a, and 31) are effective for providers and suppliers as of October 1, 1998. Providers and suppliers have the option of entering either a 6 or 8-digit date in items 11b, 14, 16, 18, 19, or 24a. However, if a provider of service or supplier chooses to enter 8- digit dates for items 11b, 14, 16, 18, 19, or 24a, he or she must enter 8-digit dates for all these fields. For instance, a provider of service or supplier will not be permitted to enter 8-digit dates for items 11b, 14, 16, 18, 19 and a 6-digit date for item 24a. The same applies to providers of service and suppliers who choose to submit 6-digit dates too. Items 12 and 31 are exempt from this requirement.

Item	Instructions
1	Show the type of health insurance coverage applicable to this claim by checking the appropriate box. Check "Medicare" to indicate this is a Medicare claim. Do not check any other box.
1a	Enter the patient's Medicare Health Insurance Claim Number (HICN) as it appears on the Health Insurance Identification Card (a.k.a, Medicare Card) - whether Medicare is the primary or secondary payer.
2	Enter the patient's last name, first name, and middle initial, if any, as shown on the patient's Medicare card. This is a required field.
3	Enter the patient's eight-digit birth date (MM | DD | CCYY) and gender.
4	If there is insurance primary to Medicare, either through the patient's or spouse's employment or any other source, list the name of the insured here. When the insured and the patient are the same, enter the word "SAME." If Medicare is primary, leave blank.
5	Enter the patient's mailing address and telephone number. On the first line, enter the street address; on the second line, the city and state; the third line, the ZIP code and phone number.
6	Check the appropriate box for the patient's relationship to the insured when item 4 is completed.

7	Enter the insured's address and telephone number. When the insured's address is the same as the patient's, enter the word "SAME." Complete this item only when items 4, 6, and 11 are completed. If Medicare is primary, leave blank.
8	Check the appropriate box for the patient's marital status and whether employed or a student.
9	Enter the last name, first name, and middle initial of the enrollee in a Medigap policy if it is different from that shown in item 2. Otherwise, enter the word "SAME." If no Medigap benefits are assigned, leave blank. **This field may be used in the future for supplemental insurance plans.** Medicaid plans are not Medigap insurance policies; refer to item 10D for instructions for claim crossovers to state Medicaid plans. NOTE: Only Participating Providers and Suppliers are to complete item 9 and its subdivisions, and only when the Beneficiary wishes to assign his/her benefits under a MEDIGAP policy to the Participating Physician or Supplier. Participating physicians and suppliers must enter information required in item 9 and its subdivisions if requested by the beneficiary. Participating physicians/suppliers sign an agreement with Medicare to accept assignment of Medicare benefits for **all** Medicare patients. A claim for which a beneficiary elects to assign his/her benefits under a Medigap policy to a participating physician/supplier is called a mandated Medigap transfer. Medigap - A Medigap policy meets the statutory definition of a "Medicare supplemental policy" contained in §1882(g)(1) of Title XVIII of the Social Security Act and the definition contained in the NAIC Model Regulation which is incorporated by reference to the statute. It is a health insurance policy or other health benefit plan offered by a private entity to those persons entitled to Medicare benefits and is specifically designed to supplement Medicare benefits. It fills in some of the "gaps" in Medicare coverage by providing payment for some of the charges for which Medicare does not have responsibility due to the applicability of deductibles, coinsurance amounts, or other limitations imposed by Medicare. It does not include limited benefit coverage available to Medicare beneficiaries such as "specified disease" or "hospital indemnity" coverage. Also, it explicitly excludes a policy or plan offered by an employer to employees or former employees, as well as that offered by a labor organization to members or former members. Do not list other supplemental coverage in item 9 and its subdivisions at the time a Medicare claim is filed. Other supplemental claims are forwarded automatically to the private insurer if the private insurer contracts with the carrier to send Medicare claim information electronically. If there is no such contract, the beneficiary must file his/her own supplemental claim.
9a	Enter the policy and/or group number of the Medigap insured *preceded* by **MEDIGAP**, **MG** or **MGAP**. (NOTE: Item 9d must be completed if you enter a policy and/or group number in item 9a.)
9b	Enter the Medigap insured's eight-digit birth date (MM | DD | CCYY) and gender.
9c	Leave blank if Medigap Payer ID is entered in item 9d. Otherwise, enter the claims processing address of the Medigap insurer. Use an abbreviated street address, two-letter postal code, and zip code copied from the Medigap insured's Medigap identification card. For example: 1257 Anywhere St Baltimore, MD 21204 is shown as "1257 Anywhere St. MD 21204"
9d	Enter the 9-digit PAYERID number of the Medigap insurer. If no PAYERID number exists, then enter the Medigap insurance program or plan name. If the beneficiary wants Medicare payment data forwarded to a Medigap insurer under a mandated Medigap transfer, all of the information in items 9, 9a, 9b, and 9d must be complete and accurate. Otherwise, the Medicare carrier cannot forward the claim information to the Medigap insurer.
10a-10c	Check "YES" or "NO" to indicate whether employment, auto liability, or other accident involvement applies to one or more of the services described in item 24. Enter the State postal code. Any item checked "YES" indicates that there may be other insurance primary to Medicare. Identify primary insurance information in item 11.
10d	Use this item exclusively for Medicaid (MCD) information. If the patient is entitled to Medicaid, enter the patient's Medicaid number preceded by MCD.

11	**THIS ITEM MUST BE COMPLETED, IT IS A REQUIRED FIELD.** By completing this item, the physician/supplier acknowledges having made a good faith effort to determine whether Medicare is the primary or secondary payer. If there is insurance primary to Medicare, enter the insured's policy or group number and proceed to items 11a-11c. Items 4, 6, and 7 must also be completed.
	NOTE: Enter the appropriate information in item 11c if insurance primary to Medicare is indicated in item 11. If there is no insurance primary to Medicare, enter the word "NONE" and proceed to item 12. If the insured reports a terminating event with regard to insurance which had been primary to Medicare (e.g., insured retired), enter the word "NONE" and proceed to item 11b.
	If a lab has collected previously and retained MSP information for a beneficiary, the lab may use that information for filling purposes of the non-face-to-face lab service. If the lab has no MSP information for the beneficiary, the lab will enter the word "NONE" in Block 11, when submitting a claim for payment of a reference lab service. Where there has been no face-to-face encounter with the beneficiary, the claim will then follow the normal claims process. When a lab has a face-to-face encounter with a beneficiary, the lab is expected to collect the MSP information and bill accordingly.
	Insurance Primary to Medicare - Circumstances under which Medicare payment may be secondary to other insurance include:
	• **Group Health Plan Coverage** Working Aged Disability (Large Group Health Plan) End-Stage Renal Disease • **No Fault and/or Other Liability** • **Work-Related Illness/Injury** Workers' Compensation Black Lung Veterans Benefits
	NOTE: For a paper claim to be considered for Medicare secondary payer benefits, a copy of the primary payer's explanation of benefits (EOB) must be forwarded along with the claim form.(See Pub. 100-05, Medicare Secondary payer Manual, chapter 3)
11a	Enter the insured's eight-digit birth date (MM | DD | CCYY) and gender, if different from item 3.
11b	Enter the employer's name, if applicable. If there is a change in the insured's insurance status, e.g., retired, enter either a six-digit (MM | DD | YY) or eight-digit (MM | DD | CCYY) retirement date preceded by the word "RETIRED."
11c	Enter the 9-digit PAYERID number of the primary insurer. If no PAYERID number exists, then enter the **complete** primary payer's program or plan name. If the primary payer's EOB does not contain the claims processing address, record the primary payer's claims-processing address directly on the EOB. This is required if there is insurance primary to Medicare that is indicated in item 11.
11d	Leave blank. Not required by Medicare.
12	The patient or authorized individual must sign and enter a six-digit date (MM | DD | YY) or eight-digit date (MM | DD | CCYY) unless the signature is on file. In lieu of signing the claim, the patient may sign a statement to be retained in the provider, physician, or supplier file in accordance with MDM §3047.1-3047.3. If the patient is physically or mentally unable to sign, a representative specified in MCM §3008 may sign on the patient's behalf. In this event, the statement's signature line must indicate the patient's name followed by "by," the representative's name, address, relationship to the patient, and the reason the patient cannot sign. The authorization is effective indefinitely unless patient or the patient's representative revokes this arrangement. *NOTE*: This can be "Signature on File: and/or a computer generated signature. The patient's signature authorizes release of medical information necessary to process the claim. It also authorizes payment of benefits to the provider of service or supplier, when the provider accepts assignment on the claim. Signature by Mark (X) - When an illiterate or physically handicapped enrollee signs by mark, a witness must enter his or her name and address next to the mark.
13	The signature in this item authorizes payment of mandated Medigap benefits to the participating physician or supplier if required Medigap information is included in item 9 and its subdivisions. The patient or his/her authorized representative signs this item, or the signature must be on file as a separate Medigap authorization. The Medigap assignment on file in the participating provider of service/supplier's office must be insurer specific. It may state that the authorization applies to all occasions of service until it is revoked. NOTE: This can be "Signature on File: and/or a computer generated signature.

14	Enter either a six-digit (MM | DD | YY) or eight-digit (MM | DD | CCYY) date of current illness, injury, or pregnancy. For chiropractic services, enter either a six-digit (MM | DD | YY) or eight-digit (MM | DD | CCYY) date of the initiation of the course of treatment and enter either a six-digit (MM | DD | YY) or eight-digit (MM | DD | CCYY) X-ray date in item 19. *Reminder: For date fields other than date of birth, all fields shall be one or the other format, 6-digit: (MM | DD | YY) or the eight-digit (MM | DD | CCYY). Intermixing the two formats on the claim is not allowed.*
15	Leave blank. Not required by Medicare.
16	If the patient is employed and is unable to work in current occupation, enter the six-digit (MM | DD | YY) or eight-digit (MM | DD | CCYY) date when patient unable to work. An entry in this field may indicate employment-related insurance coverage.
17	Enter the name of the referring or ordering physician if the service or item was ordered or referred by a physician. **Referring physician:** A physician who requests an item or service for the beneficiary for which payment may be made under the Medicare program. **Ordering physician:** A physician or, when appropriate, a non-physician practitioner who orders nonphysician services for the patient. See Pub. 100-02 Medicare Benefit Policy Manual, chapter 15 for non physician practitioner rules. Examples of services that might be ordered include diagnostic laboratory tests, clinical laboratory tests, pharmaceutical services, durable medical equipment, and services incident to that physician's or non-physician practitioner's service. The ordering/referring requirement became effective January 1, 1992, and is required by §1833(q) of the Act. **All claims** for Medicare covered services and items that are the result of a physician's order or referral shall include the ordering/referring physician's name. See Items 17a and 17b below for further guidance on reporting the referring/ordering provider's UPIN and/or NPI. The following services/situations require the submission of the referring/ordering provider information: • Medicare covered services and items that are the result of a physician's order or referral; • Parenteral and enteral nutrition; • Immunosuppressive drug claims; • Hepatitis B claims; • Diagnostic laboratory services • Diagnostic radiology services • Portable x-ray services • Consultative services; and • Durable medical equipment • When the ordering physician is also the performing physician (as often is the case with in-office clinical laboratory tests); • When a service is incident to the service of a physician or non-physician practitioner, the name of the physician or non-physician practitioner who performs the initial service and orders the non-physician service must appear in item 17; • When a physician extender or other limited licensed practitioner refers a patient for consultative service, submit the name of the physician who is supervising the limited licensed practitioner
17a	Enter the CMS assigned UPIN of the referring/ordering physician listed in item 17. The UPIN may be reported on the Form CMS-1500 until May 22, 2007, and MUST be reported if an NPI is not available. **NOTE**: Field17a and/or 17b is required when a service was ordered or referred by a physician. Effective May 23, 2007, and later, 17a is not to be reported but 17b MUST be reported when a service was ordered or referred by a physician. When a claim involves multiple referring and/or ordering physicians, a separate Form CMS-1500 shall be used for each ordering/referring physician. All physicians who order or refer Medicare beneficiaries or services must report either an NPI or UPIN or both prior to May 23, 2007. After that date, an NPI (but not a UPIN) must be reported even though they may never bill Medicare directly. A physician who has not been assigned a UPIN shall contact the Medicare carrier. Refer to Pub 100-08, Chapter 14, Section 14.6 for additional information regarding UPINs.

17b	Enter the NPI of the referring/ordering physician listed in item 17 as soon as it is available. The NPI may be reported on the Form CMS-1500 (08-05) as early as October 1, 2006. **NOTE**: Field17a and/or 17b is required when a service was ordered or referred by a physician. Effective May 23, 2007, and later, 17a is not to be reported but 17b MUST be reported when a service was ordered or referred by a physician.
18	Enter either a six-digit (MM | DD | YY) or eight-digit (MM | DD | CCYY) date when a medical service is furnished as a result of, or subsequent to, a related hospitalization.
19	Enter either a six-digit (MM | DD | YY) or eight-digit (MM | DD | CCYY) date patient was last seen and the UPIN of his/her attending physician when an independent physical or occupational therapist, or physician providing routine foot care submits claims. For physical therapy, occupational therapy or speech-language pathology services, effective for claims with dates of service on or after June 6, 2005, the date last seen and the UPIN/NPI of an ordering/referring/attending/certifying physician or non-physician practitioner are not required. If this information is submitted voluntarily, it must be correct or it will cause rejection or denial of the claim. However, when the therapy service is provided incident to the services of a physician or nonphysician practitioner, then incident to policies continue to apply. For example, for identification of the ordering physician who provided the initial service, see Item 17 and 17a, and for the identification of the supervisor, see item 24K of this section. Enter either a 6-digit (MM | DD | YY) or an 8-digit (MM | DD | CCYY) x-ray date for chiropractor services (if an x-ray, rather than a physical examination was the method used to demonstrate the subluxation). By entering an x-ray date and the initiation date for course of chiropractic treatment in item 14, the chiropractor is certifying that all the relevant information requirements (including level of subluxation) of Pub. 100-02, Medicare Benefit Policy Manual, chapter 15, are on file, along with the appropriate x-ray and all are available for carrier review. Enter the drug's name and dosage when submitting a claim for Not Otherwise Classified (NOC) drugs. Enter a concise description of an "unlisted procedure code" or a "not otherwise classified" (NOC) code if one can be given within the confines of this box. Otherwise an attachment must be submitted with the claim. Enter all applicable modifiers when modifier -99 (multiple modifiers) is entered in item 24d. If modifier -99 is entered on multiple line items of a single claim form, all applicable modifiers for each line item containing a -99 modifier should be listed as follows: 1= (mod), where the number 1 represents the line, and "mod" represents all modifiers applicable to the referenced line item.
19 cntd.	Enter the statement "homebound" when an independent laboratory renders an EKG tracing or obtains a specimen from a homebound or institutionalized patient. (See MCM §2051.1and §2070.1 respectively, for the definition of "homebound" and a more complete definition of a medically necessary laboratory service to a homebound or an institutional patient.) Enter the statement, "Patient refuses to assign benefits" when the beneficiary absolutely refuses to assign benefits to a participating provider. In this case, no payment may be made on the claim. Enter the statement, "Testing for hearing aid" when billing services involving the testing of a hearing aid(s) is used to obtain intentional denials when other payers are involved. When dental examinations are billed, enter the specific surgery for which the exam is being performed. Enter the specific name and dosage amount when low osmolar contrast material is billed, but only if HCPCS codes do not cover them. Enter the six-digit (MM | DD | YY) or eight-digit (MM | DD | CCYY) assumed and/or relinquished date for a global surgery claim when providers share post-operative care. Enter demonstration ID number "30" for all national emphysema treatment trial claims. Enter the pin (or NPI when effective) of the physician who is performing a purchased interpretation of a diagnostic test. (see Pub. 100-04, chapter 1, section 30.2.9.1 for additional information) Method II suppliers shall enter the most current HCT value for the injection of Aranesp for ESRD beneficiaries on dialysis. (See Pub. 100-04, chapter 8, section 60.7.2)

20	Complete this item when billing for diagnostic tests subject to purchase price limitations. Enter the purchase price under charges if the "yes" block is checked. A "yes" check indicates that an entity other than the entity billing for services performed the diagnostic test. A "no" check indicates that "o purchased tests are included on the claim. When "yes" is annotated, item 32 must be completed. When billing for multiple purchased diagnostic tests, each test must be submitted on a separate CMS-1500 claim form. Multiple purchased tests may be submitted on the ASC X12 837 electronic format as long as appropriate line level information is submitted when services are rendered at different service facility locations. Note: This is a required field when billing for diagnostic tests subject to purchase price limitations.
21	Enter the patient's diagnosis/condition. With the exception of claims submitted by ambulance suppliers (specialty type 59), all physician and nonphysician specialties (ie, PA, NP, CNS, CRNA) use an ICD-9-CM code number and code to the highest level of specificity for the date of service. Enter up to four codes in priority order (primary, secondary conditions). An independent laboratory must enter a diagnosis only for limited coverage procedures. All narrative diagnoses for non-physician specialties must be submitted on an attachment.
22	Leave blank. Not required by Medicare.
23	Enter the Quality Improvement Organization (QIO) prior authorization number for those procedures requiring QIO prior approval. Enter the Investigational Device Exemption (IDE) number when an investigational device is used in an FDA-approved clinical trial. Post Market Approval number should also be placed here when applicable. For physicians performing care plan oversight services, enter the 6-digit Medicare provider number (or NPI when effective) of the home health agency (HHA) or hospice when CPT code G0181 (HH) or G0182 (Hospice) is billed. Enter the 10-digit Clinical Laboratory Improvement (CLIA) certification number for laboratory services billed by an entity performing CLIA covered procedures. NOTE: Item 23 can contain only one condition. Any additional conditions should be reported on a separate Form CMS-1500.
24	The six service lines in section 24 have been divided horizontally to accommodate submission of both the NPI and legacy identifier during the NPI transition and to accommodate the submission of supplemental information to support the billed service. The top portion in each of the six service lines is shaded and is the location for reporting supplemental information. It is not intended to allow the billing of 12 service lines. At this time, the shaded area is not used by Medicare. Future guidance will be provided on when and how to use this shaded area for the submission of Medicare claims.
24a	Enter a 6-digit or 8-digit (MMDDCCYY) date for each procedure, service, or supply. When "from" and "to" dates are shown for a series of identical services, enter the number of days or units in column G. This is a required field. Return as unprocessable if a date of service extends more than one day and a valid "to" date is not present.
24b	Enter the appropriate place of service code(s) from the list provided in Section 10.5. Identify the location, using a place of service code, for each item used or service performed. This is a required field. NOTE: When a service is rendered to a hospital inpatient, use the "inpatient hospital" code.
24c	Medicare providers are not required to complete this item.
24d	Enter the procedures, services, or supplies using the Healthcare Common Procedure Coding System (HCPCS). When applicable, show HCPCS modifiers with the HCPCS code. The Form CMS-1500 (08-05) has the ability to capture up to four modifiers. Enter the specific procedure code without a narrative description. However, when reporting an "unlisted procedure code" or a "not otherwise classified" (NOC) code, include a narrative description in item 19 if a coherent description can be given within the confines of that box. Otherwise, an attachment shall be submitted with the claim. This is a required field. Return as unprocessable if an "unlisted procedure code" or an (NOC) code is indicated in item 24d, but an accompanying narrative is not present in item 19 or on an attachment.
24e	Enter the diagnostic code reference as shown in item 21, to relate the date of service and the procedures performed to the primary diagnosis. Enter only one reference number per line item. When multiple services are performed, enter the primary reference number of each service; either 1, 2, 3, 4. If a situation arises where two or more diagnoses are required for a procedure code (e.g., pap smears), you must reference only one of the diagnoses in item 21.
24f	Enter the charges for each listed service.

24g	Enter the number of days or units. This field is most commonly used for multiple visits, units of supplies, anesthesia minutes, or oxygen volume. If only one service is performed, the numeral 1 must be entered. Some services require that the actual number or quantity billed be clearly indicated on the claim form (e.g., multiple ostomy or urinary supplies, medication dosages, or allergy testing procedures). When multiple services are provided, enter the actual number provided. For anesthesia, show the elapsed time (minutes) in item 24g. Convert hours into minutes and enter the total minutes required for the procedure. NOTE: This field should contain at least 1 day or unit. The carrier should program their system to automatically default "1" unit when the information in this field is missing to avoid returning as unprocessable.
24h	Leave blank. Not required by Medicare.
24i	The Form CMS-1500 (08-05) has the ability to capture up to four modifiers.
24J	Prior to May 23, 2007, enter the rendering provider's PIN in the shaded portion. In the case of a service provided incident to the service of a physician or non-physician practitioner, when the person who ordered the service is not supervising, enter the PIN of the supervisor in the shaded portion. Effective May 23, 2007 and later, do not use the shaded portion. Beginning no earlier than October 1, 2006, enter the rendering provider's NPI number in the lower portion. In the case of a service provided incident to the service of a physician or non-physician practitioner, when the person who ordered the service is not supervising, enter the NPI of the supervisor in the lower portion.
24k	Enter the PIN (the NPI will be used when implemented) of the performing provider of service/supplier if the provider is a member of a group practice. When several different providers of service or suppliers within a group are billing on the same Form CMS-1500, show the individual PIN (or NPI when implemented) in the corresponding line item. In the case of a service provided incident to the service of a physician or non-physician practitioner, when the person who ordered the service is not supervising, enter the PIN (or NPI when implemented) of the supervisor in item 24k.
25	Enter your provider of service or supplier Federal Tax I.D. (Employer Identification Number) or Social Security number. The participating provider of service or supplier Federal Tax ID Number is required for a mandated Medigap transfer.
26	Enter the patient account number assigned by the service provider's or supplier's accounting system. This field is optional to assist you in patient identification. As a service, any account number entered here will be returned to the provider.
27	Check the appropriate block to indicate whether the provider of service or supplier accepts assignment of Medicare benefits. If Medigap is indicated in item 9 and Medigap payment authorization is given in item 13, the provider of service or supplier shall also be a Medicare participating provider of service or supplier and accept assignment of Medicare benefits for all covered charges for all patients. The following providers of service/suppliers and claims can only be paid on an assignment basis: • Clinical diagnostic laboratory services; • Physician services to individuals dually entitled to Medicare and Medicaid; • Services of physician assistants, nurse practitioners, clinical nurse specialists, nurse midwives, certified registered nurse anesthetists, clinical psychologists, and clinical social workers; • Ambulatory surgical center services for covered ASC procedures; • Home dialysis supplies and equipment paid under Method II; • Ambulance services; • Drugs and biologicals; and • Simplified Billing Roster for influenza virus vaccine and pneumococcal vaccine.
28	Enter total charges for the services (i.e., total of all charges in item 24f).
29	Enter the total amount the patient paid on the covered services only.
30	Leave blank. Not required by Medicare.

31	Enter the signature of provider of service or supplier, or his/her representative, and either the six-digit (MM | DD | YY), or eight-digit (MM | DD | CCYY) date, or alphanumeric date (e.g., January 1, 1998) for the date the form was signed.
	In the case of a service that is provided incident to the service of a physician or non-physician practitioner, when the ordering physician or non-physician practitioner is directly supervising the service as in 42 CFR 410.32, the signature of the ordering physician or non-physician practitioner shall be entered in item 31. When the ordering physician or non-physician practitioner is not supervising the service, then enter the signature of the physician or non-physician practitioner providing the direct supervision in item 31.
	NOTE: This is a required field, however the claim can be processed if the following is true. If a physician, supplier, or authorized person's signature is missing, but the signature is on file; or if any authorization is attached to the claim or if the signature field has "Signature on File" and/or a computer generated signature.
32	Enter the name and address, and ZIP code of the facility if the services were furnished in a hospital, clinic, laboratory, or facility other than the patient's home or physician's office. Effective for claims received on or after April 1, 2004, the name, address, and zip code of the service location for all services other than those furnished in place of service home – 12. Effective for claims received on or after April 1, 2004, on the Form CMS-1500, only one name, address and zip code may be entered in the block. If additional entries are needed, separate claim forms shall be submitted.
	Providers of service (namely physicians) shall identify the supplier's name, address, and ZIP code when billing for purchased diagnostic tests. When more than one supplier is used, a separate Form CMS-1500 should be used to bill for each supplier.
	For foreign claims, only the enrollee can file for Part B benefits rendered outside of the United States. These claims will not include a valid ZIP code. When a claim is received for these services on a beneficiary submitted Form CMS-1490S, before the claim is entered in the system, it should be determined if it is a foreign claim. If it is a foreign claim, follow instructions in chapter 1 for disposition of the claim. The carrier processing the foreign claim will have to make necessary accommodations to verify that the claim is not returned as unprocessable due to the lack of a ZIP code.
	For durable medical, orthotic, and prosthetic claims, the name and address of the location where the order was accepted must be entered (DMERC only). This field is required. When more than one supplier is used, a separate Form CMS-1500 should be used to bill for each supplier. This item is completed whether the supplier's personnel performs the work at the physician's office or at another location.
	If a modifier is billed, indicating the service was rendered in a Health Professional Shortage Area (HPSA) or Physician Scarcity Area (PSA), the physical location where the service was rendered shall be entered if other than home.
	Complete this item for all laboratory work performed outside a physician's office. If an independent laboratory is billing, enter the place where the test was performed.
32a	Enter the NPI of the service facility as soon as it is available. The NPI may be reported on the Form CMS-1500 (08-05) as early as October 1, 2006.
32b	Enter the ID qualifier 1C followed by one blank space and then the PIN of the service facility. Effective May 23, 2007, and later, 32b is not to be reported.
	Providers of service (namely physicians) shall identify the supplier's PIN when billing for purchased diagnostic tests.
	If the supplier is a certified mammography screening center, enter the 6-digit FDA approved certification number.
	For durable medical, orthotic, and prosthetic claims, enter the PIN (of the location where the order was accepted) if the name and address was not provided in item 32 (DMERC only).
33	Enter the provider of service/supplier's billing name, address, zip code, and telephone number.
	Enter the carrier-assigned PIN (not the CMS-assigned PIN), for the performing provider of service/supplier who is not a member of a group practice.
	Enter the group PIN (or NPI when implemented), for the performing provider of service/supplier who is a member of a group practice.
	Suppliers billing the DMERC will use the National Supplier Clearinghouse (NSC) number in this item.
	Enter the group UPIN, including the 2-digit location identifier, for the performing practitioner/supplier who is a member of a group practice.
33a	Effective May 23, 2007, and later, you MUST enter the NPI of the billing provider or group. The NPI may be reported on the Form CMS-1500 (08-05) as early as October 1, 2006. This is a required field.

33b	Enter the ID qualifier 1C followed by one blank space and then the PIN of the billing provider or group. Effective May 23, 2007, and later, 33b is not to be reported. Suppliers billing the DMERC will use the National Supplier Clearinghouse (NSC) number in this it em. Enter the PIN for the performing provider of service/supplier who is not a member of a group practice. Enter the group PIN for the performing provider of service/supplier who is a member of a group practice. Enter the group UPIN, including the 2-digit location identifier, for the performing practitioner/supplier who is a member of a group practice.

National POS Code Set

Place of Service Codes for Professional Claims Database

(last updated March 22th, 2006)

Listed below are place of service codes and descriptions. These codes should be used on professional claims to specify the entity where service(s) were rendered. Check with individual payers (e.g., Medicare, Medicaid, other private insurance) for reimbursement policies regarding these codes. If you would like to comment on a code(s) or description(s), please send your request to posinfo@cms.hhs.gov.

Place of Service Codes (POS) and Definitions (Rev. 121, 03-19-04) • HIPAA

- The Health Insurance Portability and Accountability Act of 1996 (HIPAA) became effective October 16, 2003, for all covered entities. Medicare is a covered entity under HIPAA.

- The final rule, "Health Insurance Reform: Standards for Electronic Transactions," published in the "Federal Register", August 17, 2000, adopts the standards to be used under HIPAA and names the implementation guides to be used for these standards. The ASC X12N 837 professional is the standard to be used for transmitting health care claims electronically, and its implementation guide requires the use of POS codes from the National POS code set, currently maintained by CMS.

- As a covered entity, Medicare must use the POS codes from the National POS code set for processing its electronically submitted claims. Medicare must also recognize as valid POS codes from the POS code set when these codes appear on such a claim.

Medicare must recognize and accept POS codes from the National POS code set in terms of HIPAA compliance. Note special considerations for Homeless Shelter (code 04) as well as Indian Health Service (codes 05, 06) and Tribal 638 (codes 07, 08) settings, described below. Where there is no National policy for a given POS code, carriers may work with their carrier medical directors to develop local policy regarding the services payable in a given setting, and this could include creating a crosswalk to an existing setting if desired. However, carriers must pay for the services at either the facility or the nonfacility rate as designated below. In addition, carriers, when developing policy, must ensure that they continue to pay appropriate rates for services rendered in the new setting; if they choose to create a crosswalk from one setting to another, they must crosswalk a facility rate designated code to another facility rate designated code, and a nonfacility rate designated code to another nonfacility rate designated code. For previously issued POS codes for which a crosswalk was mandated, and for which no other National Medicare directive has been issued, carriers may elect to continue to use the crosswalk or develop local policy regarding the services payable in the setting, including another crosswalk, if appropriate. If a carrier develops local policy for these settings, but later receives specific National instructions for these codes, the carriers shall defer to and comply with the newer instructions. (Note: While, effective January 1, 2003, codes 03 School, 04 Homeless Shelter, and 20 Urgent Care became part of the National POS code set and were to be crosswalked to 11 Office, this mandate to crosswalk has since been lifted as indicated above).

Place of Service Code(s)	Place of Service Name	Place of Service Description	Payment Rate Facility = F Nonfaciltiy = NF
01	Pharmacy**	A facility or location where drugs and other medically related items and services are sold, dispensed, or otherwise provided directly to patients.	
02	Unassigned	N/A	
03	School	A facility whose primary purpose is education.	NF

04	Homeless Shelter	A facility or location whose primary purpose is to provide temporary housing to homeless individuals (e.g., emergency shelters, individual or family shelters).	NF
05	Indian Health Service Free-standing Facility	A facility or location, owned and operated by the Indian Health Service, which provides diagnostic, therapeutic (surgical and non-surgical), and rehabilitation services to American Indians and Alaska Natives who do not require hospitalization.	Not applicable for adjudication of Medicare claims; systems must recognize for HIPAA
06	Indian Health Service Provider-based Facility	A facility or location, owned and operated by the Indian Health Service, which provides diagnostic, therapeutic (surgical and non-surgical), and rehabilitation services rendered by, or under the supervision of, physicians to American Indians and Alaska Natives admitted as inpatients or outpatients.	Not applicable for adjudication of Medicare claims; systems must recognize for HIPAA
07	Tribal 638 Free-standing Facility	A facility or location owned and operated by a federally recognized American Indian or Alaska Native tribe or tribal organization under a 638 agreement, which provides diagnostic, therapeutic (surgical and non-surgical), and rehabilitation services to tribal members who do not require hospitalization.	Not applicable for adjudication of Medicare claims; systems must recognize for HIPAA
08	Tribal 638 Provider-based Facility	A facility or location owned and operated by a federally recognized American Indian or Alaska Native tribe or tribal organization under a 638 agreement, which provides diagnostic, therapeutic (surgical and non-surgical), and rehabilitation services to tribal members admitted as inpatients or outpatients.	Not applicable for adjudication of Medicare claims; systems must recognize for HIPAA
09	Prison-Correctional Facility	A prison, jail, reformatory, work farm, detention center, or any other similar facility maintained by either Federal, State, or local authorities for the purpose of confinement or rehabilitation of adult or juvenile criminal offenders (effective 7/1/06)	
10	Unassigned	N/A	
11	Office	Location, other than a hospital, skilled nursing facility (SNF), military treatment facility, community health center, State or local public health clinic, or intermediate care facility (ICF), where the health professional routinely provides health examinations, diagnosis, and treatment of illness or injury on an ambulatory basis.	NF

12	Home	Location, other than a hospital or other facility, where the patient receives care in a private residence.	NF
13	Assisted Living Facility	Congregate residential facility with self-contained living units providing assessment of each resident's needs and on-site support 24 hours a day, 7 days a week, with the capacity to deliver or arrange for services including some health care and other services. (effective 10/1/03)	NF
14	Group Home *	A residence, with shared living areas, where clients receive supervision and other services such as social and/or behavioral services, custodial service, and minimal services (e.g., medication administration).	NF
15	Mobile Unit	A facility/unit that moves from place-to-place equipped to provide preventive, screening, diagnostic, and/or treatment services.	NF
16-19	Unassigned	N/A	
20	Urgent Care Facility	Location, distinct from a hospital emergency room, an office, or a clinic, whose purpose is to diagnose and treat illness or injury for unscheduled, ambulatory patients seeking immediate medical attention.	NF
21	Inpatient Hospital	A facility, other than psychiatric, which primarily provides diagnostic, therapeutic (both surgical and nonsurgical), and rehabilitation services by, or under, the supervision of physicians to patients admitted for a variety of medical conditions.	F
22	Outpatient Hospital	A portion of a hospital which provides diagnostic, therapeutic (both surgical and nonsurgical), and rehabilitation services to sick or injured persons who do not require hospitalization or institutionalization.	F
23	Emergency Room - Hospital	A portion of a hospital where emergency diagnosis and treatment of illness or injury is provided.	F
24	Ambulatory Surgical Center	A freestanding facility, other than a physician's office, where surgical and diagnostic services are provided on an ambulatory basis.	F (NOTE: pay at the nonfacility rate for payable procedures not on the ASC list)
25	Birthing Center	A facility, other than a hospital's maternity facilities or a physician's office, which provides a setting for labor, delivery, and immediate post-partum care as well as immediate care of new born infants.	NF

26	Military Treatment Facility	A medical facility operated by one or more of the Uniformed Services. Military Treatment Facility (MTF) also refers to certain former U.S. Public Health Service (USPHS) facilities now designated as Uniformed Service Treatment Facilities (USTF).	F
27-30	Unassigned	N/A	
31	Skilled Nursing Facility	A facility which primarily provides inpatient skilled nursing care and related services to patients who require medical, nursing, or rehabilitative services but does not provide the level of care or treatment available in a hospital.	F
32	Nursing Facility	A facility which primarily provides to residents skilled nursing care and related services for the rehabilitation of injured, disabled, or sick persons, or, on a regular basis, health-related care services above the level of custodial care to other than mentally retarded individuals.	NF
33	Custodial Care Facility	A facility which provides room, board and other personal assistance services, generally on a long-term basis, and which does not include a medical component.	NF
34	Hospice	A facility, other than a patient's home, in which palliative and supportive care for terminally ill patients and their families are provided.	F
35-40	Unassigned	N/A	
41	Ambulance - Land	A land vehicle specifically designed, equipped and staffed for lifesaving and transporting the sick or injured.	F
42	Ambulance - Air or Water	An air or water vehicle specifically designed, equipped and staffed for lifesaving and transporting the sick or injured.	F
43-48	Unassigned	N/A	
49	Independent Clinic	A location, not part of a hospital and not described by any other Place of Service code, that is organized and operated to provide preventive, diagnostic, therapeutic, rehabilitative, or palliative services to outpatients only. (effective 10/1/03)	NF
50	Federally Qualified Health Center	A facility located in a medically underserved area that provides Medicare beneficiaries preventive primary medical care under the general direction of a physician.	NF

51	Inpatient Psychiatric Facility	A facility that provides inpatient psychiatric services for the diagnosis and treatment of mental illness on a 24-hour basis, by or under the supervision of a physician.	F
52	Psychiatric Facility-Partial Hospitalization	A facility for the diagnosis and treatment of mental illness that provides a planned therapeutic program for patients who do not require full time hospitalization, but who need broader programs than are possible from outpatient visits to a hospital-based or hospital-affiliated facility.	F
53	Community Mental Health Center	A facility that provides the following services: outpatient services, including specialized outpatient services for children, the elderly, individuals who are chronically ill, and residents of the CMHC's mental health services area who have been discharged from inpatient treatment at a mental health facility; 24 hour a day emergency care services; day treatment, other partial hospitalization services, or psychosocial rehabilitation services; screening for patients being considered for admission to State mental health facilities to determine the appropriateness of such admission; and consultation and education services.	F
54	Intermediate Care Facility/Mentally Retarded	A facility which primarily provides health-related care and services above the level of custodial care to mentally retarded individuals but does not provide the level of care or treatment available in a hospital or SNF.	NF
55	Residential Substance Abuse treatment Facility	A facility which provides treatment for substance (alcohol and drug) abuse to live-in residents who do not require acute medical care. Services include individual and group therapy and counseling, family counseling, laboratory tests, drugs and supplies, psychological testing, and room and board.	NF
56	Psychiatric Residential Treatment Center	A facility or distinct part of a facility for psychiatric care which provides a total 24-hour therapeutically planned and professionally staffed group living and learning environment.	F
57	Non-residential Substance Abuse treatment Facility	A location which provides treatment for substance (alcohol and drug) abuse on an ambulatory basis. Services include individual and group therapy and counseling, family counseling, laboratory tests, drugs and supplies, and psychological testing. (effective 10/1/03)	NF

58-59	Unassigned	N/A	
60	Mass Immunization Center	A location where providers administer pneumococcal pneumonia and influenza virus vaccinations and submit these services as electronic media claims, paper claims, or using the roster billing method. This generally takes place in a mass immunization setting, such as, a public health center, pharmacy, or mall but may include a physician office setting.	NF
61	Comprehensive Inpatient Rehabilitation Facility	A facility that provides comprehensive rehabilitation services under the supervision of a physician to inpatients with physical disabilities. Services include physical therapy, occupational therapy, speech pathology, social or psychological services, and orthotics and prosthetics services.	F
62	Comprehensive Outpatient Rehabilitation Facility	A facility that provides comprehensive rehabilitation services under the supervision of a physician to outpatients with physical disabilities. Services include physical therapy, occupational therapy, and speech pathology services.	NF
63-64	Unassigned	N/A	
65	End-Stage Renal Disease Treatment Facility	A facility other than a hospital, which provides dialysis treatment, maintenance, and/or training to patients or care givers on an ambulatory or home-care basis.	NF
66-70	Unassigned	N/A	
71	Public Health Clinic	A facility maintained by either State or local health departments that provides ambulatory primary medical care under the general direction of a physician. (effective 10/1/03)	NF
72	Rural Health Clinic	A certified facility which is located in a rural medically underserved area that provides ambulatory primary medical care under the general direction of a physician.	NF
73-80	Unassigned	N/A	
81	Independent Laboratory	A laboratory certified to perform diagnostic and/or clinical tests independent of an institution or a physician's office.	NF
82-98	Unassigned	N/A	
99	Other Place of Service	Other place of service not identified above.	NF

		Medicare RVU	National Fee	PFR Fee Information 50%	75%	90%

Surgery

General

10021	Fine needle aspiration; without imaging guidance	3.51	128.09	202	240	297
10022	Fine needle aspiration; with imaging guidance	3.76	137.57	228	274	322

Integumentary System

Skin, Subcutaneous and Accessory Structures

Incision and Drainage

10040	Acne surgery (eg, marsupialization, opening or removal of multiple milia, comedones, cysts, pustules)	2.33	83.75	129	171	213
	(UNBUNDLING ALERT: 10060 and 10061 cannot be used with peripheral nerve anesthesia, 64450, by the same physician on the same day.)					
10060	Incision and drainage of abscess (eg, carbuncle, suppurative hidradenitis, cutaneous or subcutaneous abscess, cyst, furuncle, or paronychia); simple or single	2.60	93.99	162	191	227
10061	Incision and drainage of abscess (eg, carbuncle, suppurative hidradenitis, cutaneous or subcutaneous abscess, cyst, furuncle, or paronychia); complicated or multiple	4.57	164.10	339	437	544
10080	Incision and drainage of pilonidal cyst; simple	4.29	158.03	199	228	293
10081	Incision and drainage of pilonidal cyst; complicated	6.63	241.79	444	541	688
10120	Incision and removal of foreign body, subcutaneous tissues; simple	3.47	126.96	161	199	235
10121	Incision and removal of foreign body, subcutaneous tissues; complicated	6.55	238.00	394	470	630
10140	Incision and drainage of hematoma, seroma or fluid collection	3.63	131.50	204	238	293
10160	Puncture aspiration of abscess, hematoma, bulla, or cyst	3.02	109.90	146	178	202
	(To substantiate code 10180, the ICD-9-CM codes must indicate a postoperative wound infection, 998.59, in addition to the ICD-9-CM code for a complicated wound of the appropriate site.)					
10180	Incision and drainage, complex, postoperative wound infection	5.68	206.54	468	544	605

Excision-Debridement

	(UNBUNDLING ALERT: 11000 cannot be used with peripheral nerve anesthesia, 64450, by the same physician on the same day.)					
11000	Debridement of extensive eczematous or infected skin; up to 10% of body surface	1.29	46.61	132	182	239
✚ **11001**	Debridement of extensive eczematous or infected skin; each additional 10% of the body surface (List separately in addition to code for primary procedure)	0.57	20.46	89	131	195
11004	Debridement of skin, subcutaneous tissue, muscle and fascia for necrotizing soft tissue infection; external genitalia and perineum	15.20	534.73	1603	2150	2794
11005	Debridement of skin, subcutaneous tissue, muscle and fascia for necrotizing soft tissue infection; abdominal wall, with or without fascial closure	20.43	720.05	2183	2929	3806
11006	Debridement of skin, subcutaneous tissue, muscle and fascia for necrotizing soft tissue infection; external genitalia, perineum and abdominal wall, with or without fascial closure	18.97	668.89	2019	2708	3519
✚ **11008**	Removal of prosthetic material or mesh, abdominal wall for necrotizing soft tissue infection (List separately in addition to code for primary procedure)	7.47	264.15	822	1102	1433
11010	Debridement including removal of foreign material associated with open fracture(s) and/or dislocation(s); skin and subcutaneous tissues	11.68	426.73	895	1076	1203
11011	Debridement including removal of foreign material associated with open fracture(s) and/or dislocation(s); skin, subcutaneous tissue, muscle fascia, and muscle	13.56	494.94	1072	1285	1483

© PFR 2007

● = New Code ⊗ = Conscious Sedation ✚ = Add-on Code ∅ = Modifier '51' Exempt ▲ =Revised Code

		Medicare RVU	National Fee	PFR Fee Information 50%	75%	90%
11012	Debridement including removal of foreign material associated with open fracture(s) and/or dislocation(s); skin, subcutaneous tissue, muscle fascia, muscle, and bone	19.35	707.17	1589	1842	2125
	(UNBUNDLING ALERT: 11040 cannot be used with peripheral nerve anesthesia, 64450, by the same physician on the same day.)					
11040	Debridement; skin, partial thickness	1.12	40.55	118	192	263
	(UNBUNDLING ALERT: 11041 cannot be used with 11040 by the same physician on the same day.)					
11041	Debridement; skin, full thickness	1.38	50.02	211	297	402
	(UNBUNDLING ALERT: 11042 cannot be used with 11040-11401 or 64450 by the same physician on the same day.)					
11042	Debridement; skin, and subcutaneous tissue	1.90	68.97	334	418	527
	(UNBUNDLING ALERT: 11043 cannot be used with 11040-11042 or 64450 by the same physician on the same day.)					
11043	Debridement; skin, subcutaneous tissue, and muscle	6.81	246.33	601	738	833
	(UNBUNDLING ALERT: 11044 cannot be used with 11040-11043 or 64450, peripheral nerve anesthesia, by the same physician on the same day.)					
11044	Debridement; skin, subcutaneous tissue, muscle, and bone	9.12	330.09	750	879	963

Paring or Cutting

(When coding lesion removal in the Integumentary System chapter, be sure to indicate the number of lesions in the units box of the HCFA 1500 claim form.)

(See also HCPCS code S0390 for routine foot care; removal and/or trimming of corns, calluses and/or nails and preventive medicine in specific)

		Medicare RVU	National Fee	50%	75%	90%
11055	Paring or cutting of benign hyperkeratotic lesion (eg, corn or callus); single lesion	1.11	40.55	64	79	90
11056	Paring or cutting of benign hyperkeratotic lesion (eg, corn or callus); two to four lesions	1.38	50.02	82	100	124
11057	Paring or cutting of benign hyperkeratotic lesion (eg, corn or callus); more than four lesions	1.70	61.39	106	116	143

Biopsy

		Medicare RVU	National Fee	50%	75%	90%
11100	Biopsy of skin, subcutaneous tissue and/or mucous membrane (including simple closure), unless otherwise listed; single lesion	2.25	82.24	142	166	213
+ 11101	Biopsy of skin, subcutaneous tissue and/or mucous membrane (including simple closure), unless otherwise listed; each separate/additional lesion (List separately in addition to code for primary procedure)	0.78	28.04	85	107	139

Removal of Skin Tags

(UNBUNDLING ALERT: 11200 and 11201 cannot be used with the simple repair codes 12001-12018 by the same physician on the same day.)

		Medicare RVU	National Fee	50%	75%	90%
11200	Removal of skin tags, multiple fibrocutaneous tags, any area; up to and including 15 lesions	1.92	69.73	137	166	184
+ 11201	Removal of skin tags, multiple fibrocutaneous tags, any area; each additional ten lesions (List separately in addition to code for primary procedure)	0.47	16.67	80	105	160

Shaving of Epidermal or Dermal Lesions

(UNBUNDLING ALERT: 11300-11313 cannot be used with the simple repair codes 12001-12018 by the same physician on the same day.)

		Medicare RVU	National Fee	50%	75%	90%
11300	Shaving of epidermal or dermal lesion, single lesion, trunk, arms or legs; lesion diameter 0.5 cm or less	1.58	57.98	115	132	152
11301	Shaving of epidermal or dermal lesion, single lesion, trunk, arms or legs; lesion diameter 0.6 to 1.0 cm	2.10	76.17	148	166	199
11302	Shaving of epidermal or dermal lesion, single lesion, trunk, arms or legs; lesion diameter 1.1 to 2.0 cm	2.52	91.33	188	214	251
11303	Shaving of epidermal or dermal lesion, single lesion, trunk, arms or legs; lesion diameter over 2.0 cm	3.00	109.14	263	295	336
11305	Shaving of epidermal or dermal lesion, single lesion, scalp, neck, hands, feet, genitalia; lesion diameter 0.5 cm or less	1.65	59.88	132	156	189
11306	Shaving of epidermal or dermal lesion, single lesion, scalp, neck, hands, feet, genitalia; lesion diameter 0.6 to 1.0 cm	2.24	81.10	173	196	228
11307	Shaving of epidermal or dermal lesion, single lesion, scalp, neck, hands, feet, genitalia; lesion diameter 1.1 to 2.0 cm	2.61	94.74	206	233	262
11308	Shaving of epidermal or dermal lesion, single lesion, scalp, neck, hands, feet, genitalia; lesion diameter over 2.0 cm	3.07	111.04	288	316	358
11310	Shaving of epidermal or dermal lesion, single lesion, face, ears, eyelids, nose, lips, mucous membrane; lesion diameter 0.5 cm or less	1.95	71.25	145	161	189

● = New Code ⊗ = Conscious Sedation ✚ = Add-on Code ∅ = Modifier '51' Exempt ▲ =Revised Code

		Medicare RVU	National Fee	PFR Fee Information 50%	75%	90%
11311	Shaving of epidermal or dermal lesion, single lesion, face, ears, eyelids, nose, lips, mucous membrane; lesion diameter 0.6 to 1.0 cm	2.44	88.30	196	224	244
11312	Shaving of epidermal or dermal lesion, single lesion, face, ears, eyelids, nose, lips, mucous membrane; lesion diameter 1.1 to 2.0 cm	2.81	101.94	232	265	279
11313	Shaving of epidermal or dermal lesion, single lesion, face, ears, eyelids, nose, lips, mucous membrane; lesion diameter over 2.0 cm	3.62	131.13	325	358	377

Excision-Benign Lesions

(For excision of benign lesions requiring more than simple closure, i.e., requiring intermediate or complex closure, report 11400-11466 in addition to appropriate intermediate (12031-12057) or complex closure (13100-13153) codes. For reconstructive closure, see 14000-14300, 15000-15261, 15570-15770.)

(For electrosurgical and other methods, see 17000 et seq.)

(When coding excision of benign lesions, be sure that an ICD-9-CM code for a benign lesion is submitted. If the lesion is malignant, see the 11600 series of codes and submit an ICD-9-CM code for the malignant lesion.)

(When the excision of a lesion involves the use of microsurgery, be sure to add code 69990 for the use of an operating microscope.)

(UNBUNDLING ALERT: 11400-11446 cannot be used with the simple repair codes 12001-12018 by the same physician on the same day.)

		Medicare RVU	National Fee	50%	75%	90%
11400	Excision, benign lesion including margins, except skin tag (unless listed elsewhere), trunk, arms or legs; excised diameter 0.5 cm or less	2.89	106.11	158	184	210
11401	Excision, benign lesion including margins, except skin tag (unless listed elsewhere), trunk, arms or legs; excised diameter 0.6 to 1.0 cm	3.43	125.06	200	233	264
11402	Excision, benign lesion including margins, except skin tag (unless listed elsewhere), trunk, arms or legs; excised diameter 1.1 to 2.0 cm	3.81	139.08	266	322	394
11403	Excision, benign lesion including margins, except skin tag (unless listed elsewhere), trunk, arms or legs; excised diameter 2.1 to 3.0 cm	4.41	160.31	336	388	441
11404	Excision, benign lesion including margins, except skin tag (unless listed elsewhere), trunk, arms or legs; excised diameter 3.1 to 4.0 cm	5.03	182.67	454	510	558
11406	Excision, benign lesion including margins, except skin tag (unless listed elsewhere), trunk, arms or legs; excised diameter over 4.0 cm	6.96	250.50	638	739	874
11420	Excision, benign lesion including margins, except skin tag (unless listed elsewhere), scalp, neck, hands, feet, genitalia; excised diameter 0.5 cm or less	2.87	104.98	191	221	266
11421	Excision, benign lesion including margins, except skin tag (unless listed elsewhere), scalp, neck, hands, feet, genitalia; excised diameter 0.6 to 1.0 cm	3.67	133.78	234	274	319
11422	Excision, benign lesion including margins, except skin tag (unless listed elsewhere), scalp, neck, hands, feet, genitalia; excised diameter 1.1 to 2.0 cm	4.10	148.94	302	364	421
11423	Excision, benign lesion including margins, except skin tag (unless listed elsewhere), scalp, neck, hands, feet, genitalia; excised diameter 2.1 to 3.0 cm	4.83	175.47	406	486	606
11424	Excision, benign lesion including margins, except skin tag (unless listed elsewhere), scalp, neck, hands, feet, genitalia; excised diameter 3.1 to 4.0 cm	5.54	200.48	514	641	792
11426	Excision, benign lesion including margins, except skin tag (unless listed elsewhere), scalp, neck, hands, feet, genitalia; excised diameter over 4.0 cm	7.99	287.26	680	804	901
11440	Excision, other benign lesion including margins, except skin tag (unless listed elsewhere), face, ears, eyelids, nose, lips, mucous membrane; excised diameter 0.5 cm or less	3.25	119.38	210	250	286
11441	Excision, other benign lesion including margins, except skin tag (unless listed elsewhere), face, ears, eyelids, nose, lips, mucous membrane; excised diameter 0.6 to 1.0 cm	3.98	145.15	273	362	449
11442	Excision, other benign lesion including margins, except skin tag (unless listed elsewhere), face, ears, eyelids, nose, lips, mucous membrane; excised diameter 1.1 to 2.0 cm	4.46	162.20	357	450	554
11443	Excision, other benign lesion including margins, except skin tag (unless listed elsewhere), face, ears, eyelids, nose, lips, mucous membrane; excised diameter 2.1 to 3.0 cm	5.43	197.07	450	536	651
11444	Excision, other benign lesion including margins, except skin tag (unless listed elsewhere), face, ears, eyelids, nose, lips, mucous membrane; excised diameter 3.1 to 4.0 cm	6.88	248.61	578	679	824
11446	Excision, other benign lesion including margins, except skin tag (unless listed elsewhere), face, ears, eyelids, nose, lips, mucous membrane; excised diameter over 4.0 cm	9.23	331.60	810	902	1044

(UNBUNDLING ALERT: 11450, 11462 and 11470 cannot be used with the simple or intermediate repair codes, 12001-12018 and 12031-12057 by the same physician on the same day.)

11450	Excision of skin and subcutaneous tissue for hidradenitis, axillary; with simple or intermediate repair	8.54	311.52	964	1335	1523

(UNBUNDLING ALERT: 11451, 11463 and 11471 cannot be used with any repair codes from 12001-12018 and 12031-13300 by the same physician on the same day.)

11451	Excision of skin and subcutaneous tissue for hidradenitis, axillary; with complex repair	11.36	413.84	1329	1611	1943

● = New Code ⊗ = Conscious Sedation ✚ = Add-on Code ∅ = Modifier '51' Exempt ▲ =Revised Code

		Medicare RVU	National Fee	PFR Fee Information 50%	75%	90%
11462	Excision of skin and subcutaneous tissue for hidradenitis, inguinal; with simple or intermediate repair	8.40	307.35	914	1183	1360
11463	Excision of skin and subcutaneous tissue for hidradenitis, inguinal; with complex repair	11.66	425.21	1218	1493	1682
11470	Excision of skin and subcutaneous tissue for hidradenitis, perianal, perineal, or umbilical; with simple or intermediate repair	9.25	336.53	1259	1745	1911
11471	Excision of skin and subcutaneous tissue for hidradenitis, perianal, perineal, or umbilical; with complex repair	12.03	437.72	1094	1515	1840

Excision-Malignant Lesions

(For excision of malignant lesions requiring more than simple closure, i.e., requiring intermediate or complex closure, report 11600-11646 in addition to appropriate intermediate (12031-12057) or complex closure (13100-13153) codes. For reconstructive closure, see 14000-14300, 15000-15261, 15570-15770.)

(UNBUNDLING ALERT: 11600-11646 cannot be used with the simple repair codes, 12001-12018 by the same physician on the same day.)

		Medicare RVU	National Fee	PFR Fee Information 50%	75%	90%
11600	Excision, malignant lesion including margins, trunk, arms, or legs; excised diameter 0.5 cm or less	4.34	158.41	250	293	344
11601	Excision, malignant lesion including margins, trunk, arms, or legs; excised diameter 0.6 to 1.0 cm	5.03	183.04	309	356	464
11602	Excision, malignant lesion including margins, trunk, arms, or legs; excised diameter 1.1 to 2.0 cm	5.42	197.07	364	438	524
11603	Excision, malignant lesion including margins, trunk, arms, or legs; excised diameter 2.1 to 3.0 cm	6.25	226.25	494	570	669
11604	Excision, malignant lesion including margins, trunk, arms, or legs; excised diameter 3.1 to 4.0 cm	6.94	251.26	562	704	884
11606	Excision, malignant lesion including margins, trunk, arms, or legs; excised diameter over 4.0 cm	9.75	350.55	754	952	1059
11620	Excision, malignant lesion including margins, scalp, neck, hands, feet, genitalia; excised diameter 0.5 cm or less	4.34	158.41	323	363	442
11621	Excision, malignant lesion including margins, scalp, neck, hands, feet, genitalia; excised diameter 0.6 to 1.0 cm	5.05	183.80	407	484	561
11622	Excision, malignant lesion including margins, scalp, neck, hands, feet, genitalia; excised diameter 1.1 to 2.0 cm	5.70	206.92	505	595	666
11623	Excision, malignant lesion including margins, scalp, neck, hands, feet, genitalia; excised diameter 2.1 to 3.0 cm	6.79	245.58	661	704	786
11624	Excision, malignant lesion including margins, scalp, neck, hands, feet, genitalia; excised diameter 3.1 to 4.0 cm	7.76	280.44	744	842	1066
11626	Excision, malignant lesion including margins, scalp, neck, hands, feet, genitalia; excised diameter over 4.0 cm	9.72	350.93	906	1000	1187
11640	Excision, malignant lesion including margins, face, ears, eyelids, nose, lips; excised diameter 0.5 cm or less	4.48	163.72	369	442	521
11641	Excision, malignant lesion including margins, face, ears, eyelids, nose, lips; excised diameter 0.6 to 1.0 cm	5.46	198.96	497	577	649
11642	Excision, malignant lesion including margins, face, ears, eyelids, nose, lips; excised diameter 1.1 to 2.0 cm	6.32	229.66	634	719	843
11643	Excision, malignant lesion including margins, face, ears, eyelids, nose, lips; excised diameter 2.1 to 3.0 cm	7.55	273.24	748	874	1030
11644	Excision, malignant lesion including margins, face, ears, eyelids, nose, lips; excised diameter 3.1 to 4.0 cm	9.44	341.46	909	1030	1166
11646	Excision, malignant lesion including margins, face, ears, eyelids, nose, lips; excised diameter over 4.0 cm	12.60	454.01	1045	1214	1334

Nails

(See also HCPCS code S0390 for routine food care; removal and/or trimming of corns, calluses and/or nails and preventive medicine in specific)

		Medicare RVU	National Fee	PFR Fee Information 50%	75%	90%
11719	Trimming of nondystrophic nails, any number	0.47	17.05	40	48	54

(UNBUNDLING ALERT: 11720-11732 cannot be used with peripheral nerve anesthesia, 64450, by the same physician on the same day.)

		Medicare RVU	National Fee	PFR Fee Information 50%	75%	90%
11720	Debridement of nail(s) by any method(s); one to five	0.73	26.53	81	92	102
11721	Debridement of nail(s) by any method(s); six or more	1.08	39.03	111	122	137
11730	Avulsion of nail plate, partial or complete, simple; single	2.35	84.89	128	154	185
✚ 11732	Avulsion of nail plate, partial or complete, simple; each additional nail plate (List separately in addition to code for primary procedure)	1.11	39.79	79	112	134

● = New Code ⊗ = Conscious Sedation ✚ = Add-on Code ∅ = Modifier '51' Exempt ▲ =Revised Code

		Medicare RVU	National Fee	PFR Fee Information 50%	75%	90%
11740	Evacuation of subungual hematoma	1.02	37.14	94	117	172
	(UNBUNDLING ALERT: 11750 cannot be used with 11730 by the same physician on the same day.)					
11750	Excision of nail and nail matrix, partial or complete, (eg, ingrown or deformed nail) for permanent removal;	4.99	180.01	406	464	516
	(UNBUNDLING ALERT: 11752 cannot be used with 11730 or 11750 by the same physician on the same day.)					
11752	Excision of nail and nail matrix, partial or complete, (eg, ingrown or deformed nail) for permanent removal; with amputation of tuft of distal phalanx	7.11	256.19	575	741	834
11755	Biopsy of nail unit (eg, plate, bed, matrix, hyponychium, proximal and lateral nail folds) (separate procedure)	3.14	114.07	306	418	505
11760	Repair of nail bed	4.64	169.78	420	540	568
11762	Reconstruction of nail bed with graft	6.37	230.42	631	756	847
11765	Wedge excision of skin of nail fold (eg, for ingrown toenail)	2.80	103.46	198	308	385

Pilonidal Cyst

11770	Excision of pilonidal cyst or sinus; simple	6.44	234.21	694	852	921
11771	Excision of pilonidal cyst or sinus; extensive	12.62	455.53	1160	1340	1455
11772	Excision of pilonidal cyst or sinus; complicated	15.74	568.84	1368	1642	1806

Introduction

11900	Injection, intralesional; up to and including seven lesions	1.26	45.86	91	114	140
11901	Injection, intralesional; more than seven lesions	1.58	56.85	132	156	229
11920	Tattooing, intradermal introduction of insoluble opaque pigments to correct color defects of skin, including micropigmentation; 6.0 sq cm or less	5.23	192.14	583	725	882
11921	Tattooing, intradermal introduction of insoluble opaque pigments to correct color defects of skin, including micropigmentation; 6.1 to 20.0 sq cm	5.87	215.26	1028	1403	1717
✚ 11922	Tattooing, intradermal introduction of insoluble opaque pigments to correct color defects of skin, including micropigmentation; each additional 20.0 sq cm (List separately in addition to code for primary procedure)	1.65	60.64	690	828	963
11950	Subcutaneous injection of filling material (eg, collagen); 1 cc or less	1.97	71.63	279	319	390
11951	Subcutaneous injection of filling material (eg, collagen); 1.1 to 5.0 cc	2.72	98.53	433	544	640
11952	Subcutaneous injection of filling material (eg, collagen); 5.1 to 10.0 cc	3.68	133.02	679	844	981
11954	Subcutaneous injection of filling material (eg, collagen); over 10.0 cc	4.37	158.41	925	1143	1240
11960	Insertion of tissue expander(s) for other than breast, including subsequent expansion	22.80	822.00	2330	2971	3329
11970	Replacement of tissue expander with permanent prosthesis	15.10	542.31	2545	2909	3424
11971	Removal of tissue expander(s) without insertion of prosthesis	12.23	451.36	943	996	1108
	(Codes 11975 and 11977 do not include the cost of the implantable capsules. See HCPCS A4260 for Levonorgestrel contraceptive implants.)					
11975	Insertion, implantable contraceptive capsules	3.10	111.80	355	648	725
11976	Removal, implantable contraceptive capsules	3.71	133.78	309	370	412
11977	Removal with reinsertion, implantable contraceptive capsules	5.87	209.95	631	847	909
11980	Subcutaneous hormone pellet implantation (implantation of estradiol and/or testosterone pellets beneath the skin)	2.71	97.02	257	363	417
11981	Insertion, non-biodegradable drug delivery implant	3.36	121.65	349	461	524
11982	Removal, non-biodegradable drug delivery implant	3.92	141.74	399	525	597
11983	Removal with reinsertion, non-biodegradable drug delivery implant	5.91	211.47	635	834	948

		Medicare RVU	National Fee	PFR Fee Information 50%	75%	90%

Repair (Closure)

Repair-Simple

(Repairs of different anatomical sites can have a wide variety of reimbursement levels. Be sure to verify the anatomical site with the code being chosen and check the Surgery Section under the anatomical site for other possible codes.)

(Simple repair is included in the excision of lesions. If the excision site requires intermediate or complex repair, see 12031-13300. Intermediate or complex repair can be coded in addition to the excision.)

(For 12001-13000, basic debridement is included in the wound repair code. If the wound had extensive contamination, additional codes for further debridement may be appropriate. See the notes in the CPT book that precede this section for full details.)

(For 12001-13300, measure the length of all wounds to be repaired. Add the lengths of wounds in each repair classification and report as a single coded item. List the most complicated repair first and other repairs after, using a -51 modifier.)

(See also HCPCS code G0168 for wound closure utilizing tissue adhesive(s) only)

Code	Description	Medicare RVU	National Fee	50%	75%	90%
12001	Simple repair of superficial wounds of scalp, neck, axillae, external genitalia, trunk and/or extremities (including hands and feet); 2.5 cm or less	3.79	137.19	191	235	269
12002	Simple repair of superficial wounds of scalp, neck, axillae, external genitalia, trunk and/or extremities (including hands and feet); 2.6 cm to 7.5 cm	4.03	145.53	242	290	348
12004	Simple repair of superficial wounds of scalp, neck, axillae, external genitalia, trunk and/or extremities (including hands and feet); 7.6 cm to 12.5 cm	4.73	170.54	313	360	393
12005	Simple repair of superficial wounds of scalp, neck, axillae, external genitalia, trunk and/or extremities (including hands and feet); 12.6 cm to 20.0 cm	5.90	212.60	392	452	529
12006	Simple repair of superficial wounds of scalp, neck, axillae, external genitalia, trunk and/or extremities (including hands and feet); 20.1 cm to 30.0 cm	7.33	263.77	479	544	623
12007	Simple repair of superficial wounds of scalp, neck, axillae, external genitalia, trunk and/or extremities (including hands and feet); over 30.0 cm	8.29	298.25	593	696	757

(If the wound includes lid margins, tarsus and/or palpebral conjunctiva, see codes 67930-67935 for other possible codes to describe this service.)

Code	Description	Medicare RVU	National Fee	50%	75%	90%
12011	Simple repair of superficial wounds of face, ears, eyelids, nose, lips and/or mucous membranes; 2.5 cm or less	4.01	145.15	230	283	340
12013	Simple repair of superficial wounds of face, ears, eyelids, nose, lips and/or mucous membranes; 2.6 cm to 5.0 cm	4.41	159.55	289	343	393
12014	Simple repair of superficial wounds of face, ears, eyelids, nose, lips and/or mucous membranes; 5.1 cm to 7.5 cm	5.21	187.97	346	415	471
12015	Simple repair of superficial wounds of face, ears, eyelids, nose, lips and/or mucous membranes; 7.6 cm to 12.5 cm	6.54	235.72	430	522	595
12016	Simple repair of superficial wounds of face, ears, eyelids, nose, lips and/or mucous membranes; 12.6 cm to 20.0 cm	7.76	278.93	560	690	768
12017	Simple repair of superficial wounds of face, ears, eyelids, nose, lips and/or mucous membranes; 20.1 cm to 30.0 cm	6.98	246.71	784	916	1163
12018	Simple repair of superficial wounds of face, ears, eyelids, nose, lips and/or mucous membranes; over 30.0 cm	8.37	295.98	896	1100	1345
12020	Treatment of superficial wound dehiscence; simple closure	6.74	245.20	390	446	518
12021	Treatment of superficial wound dehiscence; with packing	3.93	141.74	365	475	630

Repair-Intermediate

Code	Description	Medicare RVU	National Fee	50%	75%	90%
12031	Layer closure of wounds of scalp, axillae, trunk and/or extremities (excluding hands and feet); 2.5 cm or less	5.03	182.29	255	314	371
12032	Layer closure of wounds of scalp, axillae, trunk and/or extremities (excluding hands and feet); 2.6 cm to 7.5 cm	6.84	249.74	345	422	486
12034	Layer closure of wounds of scalp, axillae, trunk and/or extremities (excluding hands and feet); 7.6 cm to 12.5 cm	6.73	243.68	414	475	608
12035	Layer closure of wounds of scalp, axillae, trunk and/or extremities (excluding hands and feet); 12.6 cm to 20.0 cm	9.04	329.33	523	610	710
12036	Layer closure of wounds of scalp, axillae, trunk and/or extremities (excluding hands and feet); 20.1 cm to 30.0 cm	10.12	367.98	660	774	923
12037	Layer closure of wounds of scalp, axillae, trunk and/or extremities (excluding hands and feet); over 30.0 cm	11.39	413.84	817	936	1130
12041	Layer closure of wounds of neck, hands, feet and/or external genitalia; 2.5 cm or less	5.45	197.45	298	343	415
12042	Layer closure of wounds of neck, hands, feet and/or external genitalia; 2.6 cm to 7.5 cm	6.50	235.72	350	409	462
12044	Layer closure of wounds of neck, hands, feet and/or external genitalia; 7.6 cm to 12.5 cm	7.17	259.60	450	510	600
12045	Layer closure of wounds of neck, hands, feet and/or external genitalia; 12.6 cm to 20.0 cm	9.27	337.29	573	664	741

© PFR 2007

● = New Code ⊗ = Conscious Sedation ✚ = Add-on Code ∅ = Modifier '51' Exempt ▲ =Revised Code

		Medicare RVU	National Fee	PFR Fee Information 50%	75%	90%
12046	Layer closure of wounds of neck, hands, feet and/or external genitalia; 20.1 cm to 30.0 cm	11.08	403.61	695	880	1006
12047	Layer closure of wounds of neck, hands, feet and/or external genitalia; over 30.0 cm	11.54	419.53	835	1006	1220
12051	Layer closure of wounds of face, ears, eyelids, nose, lips and/or mucous membranes; 2.5 cm or less	6.17	224.35	356	404	503
12052	Layer closure of wounds of face, ears, eyelids, nose, lips and/or mucous membranes; 2.6 cm to 5.0 cm	6.62	240.27	420	535	636
12053	Layer closure of wounds of face, ears, eyelids, nose, lips and/or mucous membranes; 5.1 cm to 7.5 cm	7.14	258.46	497	628	744
12054	Layer closure of wounds of face, ears, eyelids, nose, lips and/or mucous membranes; 7.6 cm to 12.5 cm	7.79	281.96	668	785	942
12055	Layer closure of wounds of face, ears, eyelids, nose, lips and/or mucous membranes; 12.6 cm to 20.0 cm	9.76	352.83	877	1060	1160
12056	Layer closure of wounds of face, ears, eyelids, nose, lips and/or mucous membranes; 20.1 cm to 30.0 cm	12.46	452.12	1030	1226	1439
12057	Layer closure of wounds of face, ears, eyelids, nose, lips and/or mucous membranes; over 30.0 cm	13.00	469.93	1109	1366	1456

Repair-Complex

(Documentation must be very specific to justify the use of complex repair codes. Repeated use of this series of codes can target a physician for audit.)

(Complex repair is synonymous with "reconstructive surgery".)

		Medicare RVU	National Fee	50%	75%	90%
13100	Repair, complex, trunk; 1.1 cm to 2.5 cm	7.55	274.00	376	448	548
13101	Repair, complex, trunk; 2.6 cm to 7.5 cm	9.18	332.74	541	648	793
✚ 13102	Repair, complex, trunk; each additional 5 cm or less (List separately in addition to code for primary procedure)	2.59	93.61	245	281	316
13120	Repair, complex, scalp, arms, and/or legs; 1.1 cm to 2.5 cm	7.84	284.61	429	522	596
13121	Repair, complex, scalp, arms, and/or legs; 2.6 cm to 7.5 cm	9.93	359.65	728	802	944
✚ 13122	Repair, complex, scalp, arms, and/or legs; each additional 5 cm or less (List separately in addition to code for primary procedure)	3.07	111.04	279	360	411
13131	Repair, complex, forehead, cheeks, chin, mouth, neck, axillae, genitalia, hands and/or feet; 1.1 cm to 2.5 cm	8.59	311.14	553	649	740
13132	Repair, complex, forehead, cheeks, chin, mouth, neck, axillae, genitalia, hands and/or feet; 2.6 cm to 7.5 cm	13.22	476.37	938	1087	1321
✚ 13133	Repair, complex, forehead, cheeks, chin, mouth, neck, axillae, genitalia, hands and/or feet; each additional 5 cm or less (List separately in addition to code for primary procedure)	4.09	146.66	378	467	533
13150	Repair, complex, eyelids, nose, ears and/or lips; 1.0 cm or less	8.99	326.30	532	628	696
13151	Repair, complex, eyelids, nose, ears and/or lips; 1.1 cm to 2.5 cm	9.76	352.83	721	811	902
13152	Repair, complex, eyelids, nose, ears and/or lips; 2.6 cm to 7.5 cm	13.16	474.48	1227	1472	1656
✚ 13153	Repair, complex, eyelids, nose, ears and/or lips; each additional 5 cm or less (List separately in addition to code for primary procedure)	4.58	164.48	316	573	712
13160	Secondary closure of surgical wound or dehiscence, extensive or complicated	20.53	732.94	1222	1484	1687

Adjacent Tissue Transfer or Rearrangement

		Medicare RVU	National Fee	50%	75%	90%
14000	Adjacent tissue transfer or rearrangement, trunk; defect 10 sq cm or less	15.56	563.54	1017	1168	1415
14001	Adjacent tissue transfer or rearrangement, trunk; defect 10.1 sq cm to 30.0 sq cm	20.28	731.80	1436	1731	1949
14020	Adjacent tissue transfer or rearrangement, scalp, arms and/or legs; defect 10 sq cm or less	17.28	625.69	1292	1500	1716
14021	Adjacent tissue transfer or rearrangement, scalp, arms and/or legs; defect 10.1 sq cm to 30.0 sq cm	22.62	814.80	1599	1862	2374
	(UNBUNDLING ALERT: 14040 cannot be used with 11420-11421, 11440-11441, 11630-11622, or 11640-11641 by the same physician on the same day.)					
14040	Adjacent tissue transfer or rearrangement, forehead, cheeks, chin, mouth, neck, axillae, genitalia, hands and/or feet; defect 10 sq cm or less	18.23	658.66	1467	1632	1765
14041	Adjacent tissue transfer or rearrangement, forehead, cheeks, chin, mouth, neck, axillae, genitalia, hands and/or feet; defect 10.1 sq cm to 30.0 sq cm	24.77	890.59	1951	2248	2700
	(UNBUNDLING ALERT: 14060 cannot be used with 11440-11441 or 11640-11641 by the same physician on the same day.)					
14060	Adjacent tissue transfer or rearrangement, eyelids, nose, ears and/or lips; defect 10 sq cm or less	18.77	676.85	1802	2075	2356

● = New Code ⊗ = Conscious Sedation ✚ = Add-on Code ∅ = Modifier '51' Exempt ▲ =Revised Code

		Medicare RVU	National Fee	PFR Fee Information 50%	75%	90%
14061	Adjacent tissue transfer or rearrangement, eyelids, nose, ears and/or lips; defect 10.1 sq cm to 30.0 sq cm	26.88	966.39	2568	3234	3621
14300	Adjacent tissue transfer or rearrangement, more than 30 sq cm, unusual or complicated, any area	26.19	942.13	2862	3468	3959
14350	Filleted finger or toe flap, including preparation of recipient site	19.28	689.36	1520	1762	1964

Skin Replacement Surgery and Skin Substitutes
Surgical Preparation

		Medicare RVU	National Fee	50%	75%	90%
● 15002	Surgical preparation or creation of recipient site by excision of open wounds, burn eschar, or scar (including subcutaneous tissues), or incisional release of scar contracture, trunk, arms, legs; first 100 sq cm or 1% of body area of infants and children	8.26	299.01	710	873	1075
✚● 15003	Surgical preparation or creation of recipient site by excision of open wounds, burn eschar, or scar (including subcutaneous tissues), or incisional release of scar contracture, trunk, arms, legs; each additional 100 sq cm or each additional 1% of body area of infants and children (List separately in addition to code for primary procedure)	1.83	66.32	157	194	238
● 15004	Surgical preparation or creation of recipient site by excision of open wounds, burn eschar, or scar (including subcutaneous tissues), or incisional release of scar contracture, face, scalp, eyelids, mouth, neck, ears, orbits, genitalia, hands, feet and/or multiple digits; first 100 sq cm or 1% of body area of infants and children	9.97	360.41	857	1054	1297
✚● 15005	Surgical preparation or creation of recipient site by excision of open wounds, burn eschar, or scar (including subcutaneous tissues), or incisional release of scar contracture, face, scalp, eyelids, mouth, neck, ears, orbits, genitalia, hands, feet and/or multiple digits; each additional 100 sq cm or each additional 1% of body area of infants and children (List separately in addition to code for primary procedure)	3.10	111.42	267	328	403

Grafts
Autograft/Tissue Cultured Autograft

		Medicare RVU	National Fee	50%	75%	90%
15040	Harvest of skin for tissue cultured skin autograft, 100 sq cm or less	6.63	243.68	620	799	953
15050	Pinch graft, single or multiple, to cover small ulcer, tip of digit, or other minimal open area (except on face), up to defect size 2 cm diameter	13.05	474.10	695	917	1195
15100	Split-thickness autograft, trunk, arms, legs; first 100 sq cm or less, or 1% of body area of infants and children (except 15050)	22.93	831.85	1419	1602	1812
✚ 15101	Split-thickness autograft, trunk, arms, legs; each additional 100 sq cm, or each additional 1% of body area of infants and children, or part thereof (List separately in addition to code for primary procedure)	5.39	197.82	729	875	1111
15110	Epidermal autograft, trunk, arms, legs; first 100 sq cm or less, or 1% of body area of infants and children	22.45	809.49	1960	2524	3011
✚ 15111	Epidermal autograft, trunk, arms, legs; each additional 100 sq cm, or each additional 1% of body area of infants and children, or part thereof (List separately in addition to code for primary procedure)	3.30	117.86	310	399	476
15115	Epidermal autograft, face, scalp, eyelids, mouth, neck, ears, orbits, genitalia, hands, feet, and/or multiple digits; first 100 sq cm or less, or 1% of body area of infants and children	21.58	775.00	1841	2371	2829
✚ 15116	Epidermal autograft, face, scalp, eyelids, mouth, neck, ears, orbits, genitalia, hands, feet, and/or multiple digits; each additional 100 sq cm, or each additional 1% of body area of infants and children, or part thereof (List separately in addition to code for primary procedure)	4.33	154.62	406	522	623
15120	Split-thickness autograft, face, scalp, eyelids, mouth, neck, ears, orbits, genitalia, hands, feet, and/or multiple digits; first 100 sq cm or less, or 1% of body area of infants and children (except 15050)	22.99	829.58	1764	2057	2446
✚ 15121	Split-thickness autograft, face, scalp, eyelids, mouth, neck, ears, orbits, genitalia, hands, feet, and/or multiple digits; each additional 100 sq cm, or each additional 1% of body area of infants and children, or part thereof (List separately in addition to code for primary procedure)	7.27	265.28	1005	1511	1686
15130	Dermal autograft, trunk, arms, legs; first 100 sq cm or less, or 1% of body area of infants and children	17.80	646.15	1627	2096	2500
✚ 15131	Dermal autograft, trunk, arms, legs; each additional 100 sq cm, or each additional 1% of body area of infants and children, or part thereof (List separately in addition to code for primary procedure)	2.69	96.26	258	333	397
15135	Dermal autograft, face, scalp, eyelids, mouth, neck, ears, orbits, genitalia, hands, feet, and/or multiple digits; first 100 sq cm or less, or 1% of body area of infants and children	21.93	789.40	1971	2538	3028
✚ 15136	Dermal autograft, face, scalp, eyelids, mouth, neck, ears, orbits, genitalia, hands, feet, and/or multiple digits; each additional 100 sq cm, or each additional 1% of body area of infants and children, or part thereof (List separately in addition to code for primary procedure)	2.54	90.58	241	310	370
15150	Tissue cultured epidermal autograft, trunk, arms, legs; first 25 sq cm or less	18.61	669.65	1628	2097	2502
✚ 15151	Tissue cultured epidermal autograft, trunk, arms, legs; additional 1 sq cm to 75 sq cm (List separately in addition to code for primary procedure)	3.49	124.68	334	429	513

© PFR 2007

● = New Code ⊗ = Conscious Sedation ✚ = Add-on Code ∅ = Modifier '51' Exempt ▲ =Revised Code

		Medicare RVU	National Fee	PFR Fee Information 50%	75%	90%
+ 15152	Tissue cultured epidermal autograft, trunk, arms, legs; each additional 100 sq cm, or each additional 1% of body area of infants and children, or part thereof (List separately in addition to code for primary procedure)	4.29	153.11	410	527	629
15155	Tissue cultured epidermal autograft, face, scalp, eyelids, mouth, neck, ears, orbits, genitalia, hands, feet, and/or multiple digits; first 25 sq cm or less	18.90	677.99	1630	2099	2505
+ 15156	Tissue cultured epidermal autograft, face, scalp, eyelids, mouth, neck, ears, orbits, genitalia, hands, feet, and/or multiple digits; additional 1 sq cm to 75 sq cm (List separately in addition to code for primary procedure)	4.58	162.96	429	553	661
+ 15157	Tissue cultured epidermal autograft, face, scalp, eyelids, mouth, neck, ears, orbits, genitalia, hands, feet, and/or multiple digits; each additional 100 sq cm, or each additional 1% of body area of infants and children, or part thereof (List separately in addition to code for primary procedure)	5.07	180.77	480	619	738

Acellular Dermal Replacement

		Medicare RVU	National Fee	PFR Fee Information 50%	75%	90%
15170	Acellular dermal replacement, trunk, arms, legs; first 100 sq cm or less, or 1% of body area of infants and children	10.33	368.74	1211	1492	1795
+ 15171	Acellular dermal replacement, trunk, arms, legs; each additional 100 sq cm, or each additional 1% of body area of infants and children, or part thereof (List separately in addition to code for primary procedure)	2.42	85.65	315	389	468
15175	Acellular dermal replacement, face, scalp, eyelids, mouth, neck, ears, orbits, genitalia, hands, feet, and/or multiple digits; first 100 sq cm or less, or 1% of body area of infants and children	14.21	508.21	1710	2107	2535
+ 15176	Acellular dermal replacement, face, scalp, eyelids, mouth, neck, ears, orbits, genitalia, hands, feet, and/or multiple digits; each additional 100 sq cm, or each additional 1% of body area of infants and children, or part thereof (List separately in addition to code for primary procedure)	3.84	136.05	502	618	743
15200	Full thickness graft, free, including direct closure of donor site, trunk; 20 sq cm or less	19.49	704.51	1136	1378	1723
+ 15201	Full thickness graft, free, including direct closure of donor site, trunk; each additional 20 sq cm (List separately in addition to code for primary procedure)	3.96	145.15	572	754	1033
15220	Full thickness graft, free, including direct closure of donor site, scalp, arms, and/or legs; 20 sq cm or less	18.29	662.83	1353	1491	1808
+ 15221	Full thickness graft, free, including direct closure of donor site, scalp, arms, and/or legs; each additional 20 sq cm (List separately in addition to code for primary procedure)	3.60	131.88	853	1022	1078
15240	Full thickness graft, free, including direct closure of donor site, forehead, cheeks, chin, mouth, neck, axillae, genitalia, hands, and/or feet; 20 sq cm or less	21.73	784.86	1683	2035	2365
+ 15241	Full thickness graft, free, including direct closure of donor site, forehead, cheeks, chin, mouth, neck, axillae, genitalia, hands, and/or feet; each additional 20 sq cm (List separately in addition to code for primary procedure)	4.56	165.61	832	989	1313
15260	Full thickness graft, free, including direct closure of donor site, nose, ears, eyelids, and/or lips; 20 sq cm or less	23.01	828.44	1889	2340	2647
+ 15261	Full thickness graft, free, including direct closure of donor site, nose, ears, eyelids, and/or lips; each additional 20 sq cm (List separately in addition to code for primary procedure)	5.20	188.73	875	1160	1349

Allograft/Tissue Cultured Allogeneic Skin Substitute

		Medicare RVU	National Fee	PFR Fee Information 50%	75%	90%
15300	Allograft skin for temporary wound closure, trunk, arms, legs; first 100 sq cm or less, or 1% of body area of infants and children	8.39	300.15	992	1222	1470
+ 15301	Allograft skin for temporary wound closure, trunk, arms, legs; each additional 100 sq cm, or each additional 1% of body area of infants and children, or part thereof (List separately in addition to code for primary procedure)	1.61	57.23	208	256	308
15320	Allograft skin for temporary wound closure, face, scalp, eyelids, mouth, neck, ears, orbits, genitalia, hands, feet, and/or multiple digits; first 100 sq cm or less, or 1% of body area of infants and children	9.60	343.35	1149	1416	1703
+ 15321	Allograft skin for temporary wound closure, face, scalp, eyelids, mouth, neck, ears, orbits, genitalia, hands, feet, and/or multiple digits; each additional 100 sq cm, or each additional 1% of body area of infants and children, or part thereof (List separately in addition to code for primary procedure)	2.40	85.27	310	381	459
15330	Acellular dermal allograft, trunk, arms, legs; first 100 sq cm or less, or 1% of body area of infants and children	7.66	275.14	990	1220	1468
+ 15331	Acellular dermal allograft, trunk, arms, legs; each additional 100 sq cm, or each additional 1% of body area of infants and children, or part thereof (List separately in addition to code for primary procedure)	1.60	56.85	206	254	306
15335	Acellular dermal allograft, face, scalp, eyelids, mouth, neck, ears, orbits, genitalia, hands, feet, and/or multiple digits; first 100 sq cm or less, or 1% of body area of infants and children	8.51	305.45	1100	1356	1631
+ 15336	Acellular dermal allograft, face, scalp, eyelids, mouth, neck, ears, orbits, genitalia, hands, feet, and/or multiple digits; each additional 100 sq cm, or each additional 1% of body area of infants and children, or part thereof (List separately in addition to code for primary procedure)	2.33	83.00	299	369	444
15340	Tissue cultured allogeneic skin substitute; first 25 sq cm or less	8.12	293.33	945	1165	1400
+ 15341	Tissue cultured allogeneic skin substitute; each additional 25 sq cm	1.20	43.58	151	186	224

● = New Code ⊗ = Conscious Sedation ✚ = Add-on Code ∅ = Modifier '51' Exempt ▲ =Revised Code

		Medicare RVU	National Fee	PFR Fee Information 50%	75%	90%
15360	Tissue cultured allogeneic dermal substitute, trunk, arms, legs; first 100 sq cm or less, or 1% of body area of infants and children	8.83	319.48	1132	1395	1679
+ 15361	Tissue cultured allogeneic dermal substitute, trunk, arms, legs; each additional 100 sq cm, or each additional 1% of body area of infants and children, or part thereof (List separately in addition to code for primary procedure)	1.87	66.32	241	297	358
15365	Tissue cultured allogeneic dermal substitute, face, scalp, eyelids, mouth, neck, ears, orbits, genitalia, hands, feet, and/or multiple digits; first 100 sq cm or less, or 1% of body area of infants and children	9.17	331.60	1183	1457	1753
+ 15366	Tissue cultured allogeneic dermal substitute, face, scalp, eyelids, mouth, neck, ears, orbits, genitalia, hands, feet, and/or multiple digits; each additional 100 sq cm, or each additional 1% of body area of infants and children, or part thereof (List separately in addition to code for primary procedure)	2.32	82.24	299	369	444

Xenograft

15400	Xenograft, skin (dermal), for temporary wound closure, trunk, arms, legs; first 100 sq cm or less, or 1% of body area of infants and children	9.10	328.19	597	860	1001
+ 15401	Xenograft, skin (dermal), for temporary wound closure, trunk, arms, legs; each additional 100 sq cm, or each additional 1% of body area of infants and children, or part thereof (List separately in addition to code for primary procedure)	2.81	102.70	159	194	254
15420	Xenograft skin (dermal), for temporary wound closure, face, scalp, eyelids, mouth, neck, ears, orbits, genitalia, hands, feet, and/or multiple digits; first 100 sq cm or less, or 1% of body area of infants and children	10.27	370.64	602	811	989
+ 15421	Xenograft skin (dermal), for temporary wound closure, face, scalp, eyelids, mouth, neck, ears, orbits, genitalia, hands, feet, and/or multiple digits; each additional 100 sq cm, or each additional 1% of body area of infants and children, or part thereof (List separately in addition to code for primary procedure)	3.00	108.01	198	268	326
15430	Acellular xenograft implant; first 100 sq cm or less, or 1% of body area of infants and children	13.54	490.39	871	1175	1434
+ 15431	Acellular xenograft implant; each additional 100 sq cm, or each additional 1% of body area of infants and children, or part thereof (List separately in addition to code for primary procedure)	-	-	450	607	740

Flaps (Skin and/or Deep Tissues)

15570	Formation of direct or tubed pedicle, with or without transfer; trunk	22.43	811.76	2125	2454	2746
15572	Formation of direct or tubed pedicle, with or without transfer; scalp, arms, or legs	20.73	747.72	2322	2626	2900
15574	Formation of direct or tubed pedicle, with or without transfer; forehead, cheeks, chin, mouth, neck, axillae, genitalia, hands or feet	22.36	807.22	2664	2901	3132
15576	Formation of direct or tubed pedicle, with or without transfer; eyelids, nose, ears, lips, or intraoral	19.85	717.02	2010	2741	3329
15600	Delay of flap or sectioning of flap (division and inset); at trunk	9.25	342.97	988	1098	1259
15610	Delay of flap or sectioning of flap (division and inset); at scalp, arms, or legs	7.73	283.47	990	1267	1426
15620	Delay of flap or sectioning of flap (division and inset); at forehead, cheeks, chin, neck, axillae, genitalia, hands, or feet	11.41	418.77	1272	1582	1673
15630	Delay of flap or sectioning of flap (division and inset); at eyelids, nose, ears, or lips	11.33	414.22	1340	1653	1898
15650	Transfer, intermediate, of any pedicle flap (eg, abdomen to wrist, Walking tube), any location	12.20	444.54	1246	1582	1821
● 15731	Forehead flap with preservation of vascular pedicle (eg, axial pattern flap, paramedian forehead flap)	27.53	989.50	3146	3670	3977
15732	Muscle, myocutaneous, or fasciocutaneous flap; head and neck (eg, temporalis, masseter muscle, sternocleidomastoid, levator scapulae)	38.97	1401.83	4068	4826	5153
15734	Muscle, myocutaneous, or fasciocutaneous flap; trunk	39.82	1434.42	4301	5092	5525
15736	Muscle, myocutaneous, or fasciocutaneous flap; upper extremity	36.55	1320.73	4701	5215	5639
15738	Muscle, myocutaneous, or fasciocutaneous flap; lower extremity	38.62	1391.60	4482	5363	5892

Other Flaps and Grafts

15740	Flap; island pedicle	23.21	835.64	2365	2764	3362
15750	Flap; neurovascular pedicle	23.19	830.33	2748	3282	3746
15756	Free muscle or myocutaneous flap with microvascular anastomosis	61.51	2190.85	7590	9089	10131
15757	Free skin flap with microvascular anastomosis	61.31	2182.52	7448	8918	9484
15758	Free fascial flap with microvascular anastomosis	61.35	2185.17	7658	8989	9655
15760	Graft; composite (eg, full thickness of external ear or nasal ala), including primary closure, donor area	20.63	745.06	2077	2521	2802

© PFR 2007

● = New Code ⊗ = Conscious Sedation ✚ = Add-on Code ∅ = Modifier '51' Exempt ▲ =Revised Code

		Medicare RVU	National Fee	PFR Fee Information 50%	75%	90%
15770	Graft; derma-fat-fascia	16.46	590.44	1791	2265	2412
	(Medicare fees for the code below are based on Non Facility RVUs. PFR information reflects fee when procedure is performed in a facility.)					
15775	Punch graft for hair transplant; 1 to 15 punch grafts	8.52	307.73	243	290	336
	(Medicare fees for the code below are based on Non Facility RVUs. PFR information reflects fee when procedure is performed in a facility.)					
15776	Punch graft for hair transplant; more than 15 punch grafts	11.24	404.75	408	541	741

Other Procedures

		Medicare RVU	National Fee	50%	75%	90%
15780	Dermabrasion; total face (eg, for acne scarring, fine wrinkling, rhytids, general keratosis)	20.77	754.54	1794	2707	3236
15781	Dermabrasion; segmental, face	12.60	458.94	832	1000	1349
15782	Dermabrasion; regional, other than face	14.50	532.84	687	820	981
15783	Dermabrasion; superficial, any site, (eg, tattoo removal)	11.80	430.52	636	797	884
15786	Abrasion; single lesion (eg, keratosis, scar)	5.63	205.40	305	401	487
✚ 15787	Abrasion; each additional four lesions or less (List separately in addition to code for primary procedure)	1.40	51.92	117	153	214
15788	Chemical peel, facial; epidermal	9.37	347.14	717	1254	1770
15789	Chemical peel, facial; dermal	13.49	492.67	1701	2159	2691
15792	Chemical peel, nonfacial; epidermal	9.02	334.63	451	596	667
15793	Chemical peel, nonfacial; dermal	10.11	368.74	638	876	974
15819	Cervicoplasty	18.51	661.69	1950	2247	2447
15820	Blepharoplasty, lower eyelid;	13.35	482.81	1508	2144	2300
15821	Blepharoplasty, lower eyelid; with extensive herniated fat pad	14.32	517.30	1417	1802	2308
15822	Blepharoplasty, upper eyelid;	10.60	384.66	1419	2295	2725
	(UNBUNDLING ALERT: 15823 cannot be used with 15822 by the same physician on the same day.)					
15823	Blepharoplasty, upper eyelid; with excessive skin weighting down lid	16.42	591.20	1634	2170	2523
15824	Rhytidectomy; forehead	-	-	2305	2546	3185
15825	Rhytidectomy; neck with platysmal tightening (platysmal flap, P-flap)	-	-	2893	3582	3897
15826	Rhytidectomy; glabellar frown lines	-	-	1816	2471	2884
15828	Rhytidectomy; cheek, chin, and neck	-	-	4826	7000	7870
15829	Rhytidectomy; superficial musculoaponeurotic system (SMAS) flap	-	-	5155	5734	6202
● 15830	Excision, excessive skin and subcutaneous tissue (includes lipectomy); abdomen, infraumbilical panniculectomy	29.98	1071.74	5024	5594	6243
15832	Excision, excessive skin and subcutaneous tissue (includes lipectomy); thigh	22.67	811.01	3761	4410	4998
15833	Excision, excessive skin and subcutaneous tissue (includes lipectomy); leg	21.14	756.43	3874	4139	4459
15834	Excision, excessive skin and subcutaneous tissue (includes lipectomy); hip	21.31	762.12	3636	4084	4459
15835	Excision, excessive skin and subcutaneous tissue (includes lipectomy); buttock	22.03	785.99	4021	4447	4797
15836	Excision, excessive skin and subcutaneous tissue (includes lipectomy); arm	18.62	665.86	2524	2778	3404
15837	Excision, excessive skin and subcutaneous tissue (includes lipectomy); forearm or hand	19.16	690.49	2013	2245	2499
15838	Excision, excessive skin and subcutaneous tissue (includes lipectomy); submental fat pad	14.44	516.54	1643	2289	2774
15839	Excision, excessive skin and subcutaneous tissue (includes lipectomy); other area	20.51	737.86	1795	2420	2806
15840	Graft for facial nerve paralysis; free fascia graft (including obtaining fascia)	25.75	919.77	3357	3804	4103
15841	Graft for facial nerve paralysis; free muscle graft (including obtaining graft)	42.82	1525.00	4076	4490	4616
15842	Graft for facial nerve paralysis; free muscle flap by microsurgical technique	68.21	2429.99	5701	6570	7644

● = New Code ⊗ = Conscious Sedation ✚ = Add-on Code ∅ = Modifier '51' Exempt ▲ =Revised Code

		Medicare RVU	National Fee	PFR Fee Information 50%	75%	90%
15845	Graft for facial nerve paralysis; regional muscle transfer	24.05	858.00	3589	3873	4404
✚● **15847**	Excision, excessive skin and subcutaneous tissue (includes lipectomy), abdomen (eg, abdominoplasty) (includes umbilical transposition and fascial plication) (List separately in addition to code for primary procedure)	-	-	IR	IR	IR
	(Removal of sutures under local anesthesia or without anesthesia, by the same physician who originally closed the wound, is included in the)					
	(See also HCPCS code S0630 for removal of sutures by a physician other than the physician who originally closed the wound.)					
15850	Removal of sutures under anesthesia (other than local), same surgeon	2.30	84.13	140	237	357
15851	Removal of sutures under anesthesia (other than local), other surgeon	2.51	91.71	135	258	342
15852	Dressing change (for other than burns) under anesthesia (other than local)	1.26	44.34	230	372	507
15860	Intravenous injection of agent (eg, fluorescein) to test vascular flow in flap or graft	2.98	105.36	372	406	439
15876	Suction assisted lipectomy; head and neck	-	-	1584	1740	2043
15877	Suction assisted lipectomy; trunk	-	-	2262	2620	2759
15878	Suction assisted lipectomy; upper extremity	-	-	1717	2081	2420
15879	Suction assisted lipectomy; lower extremity	-	-	2060	2369	2472

Pressure Ulcers (Decubitus Ulcers)

		Medicare RVU	National Fee	50%	75%	90%
15920	Excision, coccygeal pressure ulcer, with coccygectomy; with primary suture	14.82	530.56	1296	1492	1573
15922	Excision, coccygeal pressure ulcer, with coccygectomy; with flap closure	18.84	674.95	1957	2263	2554
15931	Excision, sacral pressure ulcer, with primary suture;	16.86	601.05	1350	1619	1798
15933	Excision, sacral pressure ulcer, with primary suture; with ostectomy	20.86	746.20	1971	2397	2754
15934	Excision, sacral pressure ulcer, with skin flap closure;	23.29	831.09	2525	2736	3029
15935	Excision, sacral pressure ulcer, with skin flap closure; with ostectomy	28.01	1002.01	2748	2980	3318
15936	Excision, sacral pressure ulcer, in preparation for muscle or myocutaneous flap or skin graft closure;	22.88	817.45	2207	2449	2783
15937	Excision, sacral pressure ulcer, in preparation for muscle or myocutaneous flap or skin graft closure; with ostectomy	26.72	955.40	2937	3430	3771
15940	Excision, ischial pressure ulcer, with primary suture;	17.53	625.69	1446	1817	2407
15941	Excision, ischial pressure ulcer, with primary suture; with ostectomy (ischiectomy)	23.15	830.71	2035	2407	2563
15944	Excision, ischial pressure ulcer, with skin flap closure;	22.48	805.32	2323	2548	2803
15945	Excision, ischial pressure ulcer, with skin flap closure; with ostectomy	24.99	895.14	2720	3130	3509
15946	Excision, ischial pressure ulcer, with ostectomy, in preparation for muscle or myocutaneous flap or skin graft closure	41.31	1474.97	3256	3647	4821
15950	Excision, trochanteric pressure ulcer, with primary suture;	14.37	514.27	1440	1623	1827
15951	Excision, trochanteric pressure ulcer, with primary suture; with ostectomy	20.82	745.44	1915	2236	2611
15952	Excision, trochanteric pressure ulcer, with skin flap closure;	21.53	769.70	1943	2305	2665
15953	Excision, trochanteric pressure ulcer, with skin flap closure; with ostectomy	24.25	867.85	2340	2720	3125
15956	Excision, trochanteric pressure ulcer, in preparation for muscle or myocutaneous flap or skin graft closure;	29.34	1048.62	3247	3620	3990
15958	Excision, trochanteric pressure ulcer, in preparation for muscle or myocutaneous flap or skin graft closure; with ostectomy	29.71	1063.02	3439	4215	4910
15999	Unlisted procedure, excision pressure ulcer	-	-	IR	IR	IR

Burns, Local Treatment

		Medicare RVU	National Fee	50%	75%	90%
16000	Initial treatment, first degree burn, when no more than local treatment is required	1.80	64.80	94	110	139
16020	Dressings and/or debridement of partial-thickness burns, initial or subsequent; small (less than 5% total body surface area)	2.13	77.69	104	130	150
16025	Dressings and/or debridement of partial-thickness burns, initial or subsequent; medium (eg, whole face or whole extremity, or 5% to 10% total body surface area)	3.76	135.29	174	252	328

		Medicare RVU	National Fee	PFR Fee Information 50%	75%	90%
16030	Dressings and/or debridement of partial-thickness burns, initial or subsequent; large (eg, more than one extremity, or greater than 10% total body surface area)	4.44	160.31	272	391	534
16035	Escharotomy; initial incision	5.71	201.99	784	866	985
✚ 16036	Escharotomy; each additional incision (List separately in addition to code for primary procedure)	2.27	80.34	304	373	411

Destruction

Destruction, Benign or Premalignant Lesions

(When coding destruction of benign lesions, be sure that the ICD-9-CM code for the benign lesion is submitted. If the lesion is malignant, see the 17260 series of codes and submit an ICD-9-CM code for the malignant lesion.)

		Medicare RVU	National Fee	50%	75%	90%
▲ 17000	Destruction (eg, laser surgery, electrosurgery, cryosurgery, chemosurgery, surgical curettement), premalignant lesions (eg, actinic keratoses); first lesion	1.73	63.29	102	119	152
✚ 17003	Destruction (eg, laser surgery, electrosurgery, cryosurgery, chemosurgery, surgical curettement), premalignant lesions (eg, actinic keratoses); second through 14 lesions, each (List separately in addition to code for first lesion)	0.19	6.82	43	56	78
⊘▲ 17004	Destruction (eg, laser surgery, electrosurgery, cryosurgery, chemosurgery, surgical curettement), premalignant lesions (eg, actinic keratoses), 15 or more lesions	4.26	154.62	445	556	706

(For 17106-17108, measure the area requiring destruction in square centimeters (determine the length of the two longest edges and multiply). Choose the code for the appropriate number of square centimeters (cm).)

		Medicare RVU	National Fee	50%	75%	90%
17106	Destruction of cutaneous vascular proliferative lesions (eg, laser technique); less than 10 sq cm	9.60	346.38	567	678	785
17107	Destruction of cutaneous vascular proliferative lesions (eg, laser technique); 10.0 to 50.0 sq cm	17.06	611.67	1124	1419	1538
17108	Destruction of cutaneous vascular proliferative lesions (eg, laser technique); over 50.0 sq cm	23.10	825.03	1714	2080	2446
▲ 17110	Destruction (eg, laser surgery, electrosurgery, cryosurgery, chemosurgery, surgical curettement), of benign lesions other than skin tags or cutaneous vascular lesions; up to 14 lesions	2.38	87.54	103	160	197
17111	Destruction (eg, laser surgery, electrosurgery, cryosurgery, chemosurgery, surgical curettement), of benign lesions other than skin tags or cutaneous vascular lesions; 15 or more lesions	2.82	103.46	153	189	247
17250	Chemical cauterization of granulation tissue (proud flesh, sinus or fistula)	1.81	66.70	107	152	207

Destruction, Malignant Lesions, Any Method

		Medicare RVU	National Fee	50%	75%	90%
17260	Destruction, malignant lesion (eg, laser surgery, electrosurgery, cryosurgery, chemosurgery, surgical curettement), trunk, arms or legs; lesion diameter 0.5 cm or less	2.29	83.37	173	239	278
17261	Destruction, malignant lesion (eg, laser surgery, electrosurgery, cryosurgery, chemosurgery, surgical curettement), trunk, arms or legs; lesion diameter 0.6 to 1.0 cm	3.08	112.18	223	273	354
17262	Destruction, malignant lesion (eg, laser surgery, electrosurgery, cryosurgery, chemosurgery, surgical curettement), trunk, arms or legs; lesion diameter 1.1 to 2.0 cm	3.79	137.57	283	322	363
17263	Destruction, malignant lesion (eg, laser surgery, electrosurgery, cryosurgery, chemosurgery, surgical curettement), trunk, arms or legs; lesion diameter 2.1 to 3.0 cm	4.19	151.97	342	373	413
17264	Destruction, malignant lesion (eg, laser surgery, electrosurgery, cryosurgery, chemosurgery, surgical curettement), trunk, arms or legs; lesion diameter 3.1 to 4.0 cm	4.53	164.10	384	454	556
17266	Destruction, malignant lesion (eg, laser surgery, electrosurgery, cryosurgery, chemosurgery, surgical curettement), trunk, arms or legs; lesion diameter over 4.0 cm	5.22	188.73	496	584	674
17270	Destruction, malignant lesion (eg, laser surgery, electrosurgery, cryosurgery, chemosurgery, surgical curettement), scalp, neck, hands, feet, genitalia; lesion diameter 0.5 cm or less	3.28	119.38	221	246	338
17271	Destruction, malignant lesion (eg, laser surgery, electrosurgery, cryosurgery, chemosurgery, surgical curettement), scalp, neck, hands, feet, genitalia; lesion diameter 0.6 to 1.0 cm	3.57	129.61	268	305	369
17272	Destruction, malignant lesion (eg, laser surgery, electrosurgery, cryosurgery, chemosurgery, surgical curettement), scalp, neck, hands, feet, genitalia; lesion diameter 1.1 to 2.0 cm	4.10	148.56	327	395	450
17273	Destruction, malignant lesion (eg, laser surgery, electrosurgery, cryosurgery, chemosurgery, surgical curettement), scalp, neck, hands, feet, genitalia; lesion diameter 2.1 to 3.0 cm	4.61	166.75	397	474	543
17274	Destruction, malignant lesion (eg, laser surgery, electrosurgery, cryosurgery, chemosurgery, surgical curettement), scalp, neck, hands, feet, genitalia; lesion diameter 3.1 to 4.0 cm	5.55	200.48	504	597	667

● = New Code ⊗ = Conscious Sedation ✚ = Add-on Code ⊘ = Modifier '51' Exempt ▲ =Revised Code

Code	Description	Medicare RVU	National Fee	PFR Fee Information 50%	75%	90%
17276	Destruction, malignant lesion (eg, laser surgery, electrosurgery, cryosurgery, chemosurgery, surgical curettement), scalp, neck, hands, feet, genitalia; lesion diameter over 4.0 cm	6.57	236.86	601	705	806
17280	Destruction, malignant lesion (eg, laser surgery, electrosurgery, cryosurgery, chemosurgery, surgical curettement), face, ears, eyelids, nose, lips, mucous membrane; lesion diameter 0.5 cm or less	3.04	110.66	236	264	316
17281	Destruction, malignant lesion (eg, laser surgery, electrosurgery, cryosurgery, chemosurgery, surgical curettement), face, ears, eyelids, nose, lips, mucous membrane; lesion diameter 0.6 to 1.0 cm	3.93	142.12	315	370	479
17282	Destruction, malignant lesion (eg, laser surgery, electrosurgery, cryosurgery, chemosurgery, surgical curettement), face, ears, eyelids, nose, lips, mucous membrane; lesion diameter 1.1 to 2.0 cm	4.55	164.48	408	470	520
17283	Destruction, malignant lesion (eg, laser surgery, electrosurgery, cryosurgery, chemosurgery, surgical curettement), face, ears, eyelids, nose, lips, mucous membrane; lesion diameter 2.1 to 3.0 cm	5.58	201.24	491	551	609
17284	Destruction, malignant lesion (eg, laser surgery, electrosurgery, cryosurgery, chemosurgery, surgical curettement), face, ears, eyelids, nose, lips, mucous membrane; lesion diameter 3.1 to 4.0 cm	6.56	236.48	567	710	869
17286	Destruction, malignant lesion (eg, laser surgery, electrosurgery, cryosurgery, chemosurgery, surgical curettement), face, ears, eyelids, nose, lips, mucous membrane; lesion diameter over 4.0 cm	8.55	306.97	749	994	1179

(To code 17304-17310 appropriately, all of the components of the Mohs' chemosurgery technique must be performed by the same surgeon.)

(UNBUNDLING ALERT: 17304-17310 cannot be used with surgical pathology codes, 88300-88309 and 88331-88332 by the same physician on the same day.)

(For 17304-17310, do not add a -51 modifier if multiple procedures are performed in this range. The multiple surgery rule is not applicable to these codes.)

Mohs' Micrographic Surgery

Code	Description	Medicare RVU	National Fee	50%	75%	90%
● 17311	Mohs micrographic technique, including removal of all gross tumor, surgical excision of tissue specimens, mapping, color coding of specimens, microscopic examination of specimens by the surgeon, and histopathologic preparation including routine stain(s) (eg, hematoxylin and eosin, toluidine blue), head, neck, hands, feet, genitalia, or any location with surgery directly involving muscle, cartilage, bone, tendon, major nerves, or vessels; first stage, up to 5 tissue blocks	17.23	629.48	943	1266	1658
✚● 17312	Mohs micrographic technique, including removal of all gross tumor, surgical excision of tissue specimens, mapping, color coding of specimens, microscopic examination of specimens by the surgeon, and histopathologic preparation including routine stain(s) (eg, hematoxylin and eosin, toluidine blue), head, neck, hands, feet, genitalia, or any location with surgery directly involving muscle, cartilage, bone, tendon, major nerves, or vessels; each additional stage after the first stage, up to 5 tissue blocks (List separately in addition to code for primary procedure)	10.35	379.73	567	761	996
● 17313	Mohs micrographic technique, including removal of all gross tumor, surgical excision of tissue specimens, mapping, color coding of specimens, microscopic examination of specimens by the surgeon, and histopathologic preparation including routine stain(s) (eg, hematoxylin and eosin, toluidine blue), of the trunk, arms, or legs; first stage, up to 5 tissue blocks	15.73	574.91	861	1156	1513
✚● 17314	Mohs micrographic technique, including removal of all gross tumor, surgical excision of tissue specimens, mapping, color coding of specimens, microscopic examination of specimens by the surgeon, and histopathologic preparation including routine stain(s) (eg, hematoxylin and eosin, toluidine blue), of the trunk, arms, or legs; each additional stage after the first stage, up to 5 tissue blocks (List separately in addition to code for primary procedure)	9.59	351.69	525	705	923
✚● 17315	Mohs micrographic technique, including removal of all gross tumor, surgical excision of tissue specimens, mapping, color coding of specimens, microscopic examination of specimens by the surgeon, and histopathologic preparation including routine stain(s) (eg, hematoxylin and eosin, toluidine blue), each additional block after the first 5 tissue blocks, any stage (List separately in addition to code for primary procedure)	2.05	74.28	112	151	197

Other Procedures

Code	Description	Medicare RVU	National Fee	50%	75%	90%
17340	Cryotherapy (CO2 slush, liquid N2) for acne	1.17	41.31	80	105	142
17360	Chemical exfoliation for acne (eg, acne paste, acid)	3.04	109.90	125	174	216
17380	Electrolysis epilation, each 30 minutes	-	-	94	144	166
17999	Unlisted procedure, skin, mucous membrane and subcutaneous tissue	-	-	IR	IR	IR

Breast

Incision

Code	Description	Medicare RVU	National Fee	50%	75%	90%
19000	Puncture aspiration of cyst of breast;	2.86	105.36	166	203	238
✚ 19001	Puncture aspiration of cyst of breast; each additional cyst (List separately in addition to code for primary procedure)	0.71	25.39	88	111	128
19020	Mastotomy with exploration or drainage of abscess, deep	10.58	386.55	583	752	970

● = New Code ⊗ = Conscious Sedation ✚ = Add-on Code ∅ = Modifier '51' Exempt ▲ =Revised Code

		Medicare RVU	National Fee	PFR Fee Information 50%	75%	90%
19030	Injection procedure only for mammary ductogram or galactogram	4.38	160.31	178	228	290

Excision

		Medicare RVU	National Fee	50%	75%	90%
19100	Biopsy of breast; percutaneous, needle core, not using imaging guidance (separate procedure)	3.50	127.71	257	297	347
	(A4550 (Disposable Surgical Tray) can be coded in addition to 19101 in the office setting. Payment is at carrier discretion.)					
19101	Biopsy of breast; open, incisional	8.04	292.57	812	969	1159
19102	Biopsy of breast; percutaneous, needle core, using imaging guidance	5.82	212.98	441	527	627
19103	Biopsy of breast; percutaneous, automated vacuum assisted or rotating biopsy device, using imaging guidance	15.00	554.44	780	947	1174
● 19105	Ablation, cryosurgical, of fibroadenoma, including ultrasound guidance, each fibroadenoma	49.92	1877.82	4402	5433	6107
19110	Nipple exploration, with or without excision of a solitary lactiferous duct or a papilloma lactiferous duct	10.85	394.51	1000	1243	1335
19112	Excision of lactiferous duct fistula	10.30	376.32	836	1060	1197
	(UNBUNDLING ALERT: 19120 cannot be used with breast biopsy codes, 19100-19101 by the same physician on the same day.)					
	(A4550 (Disposable Surgical Tray) can be coded in addition to 19120 in the office setting. Payment is at carrier discretion.)					
▲ 19120	Excision of cyst, fibroadenoma, or other benign or malignant tumor, aberrant breast tissue, duct lesion, nipple or areolar lesion (except 19300), open, male or female, one or more lesions	11.24	403.61	984	1262	1520
	(The excision of a breast lesion identified by a radiological marker is a three-part procedure. The surgeon normally codes 19125 (and 19126, if necessary) and the radiologist codes 19290 and 76096, placement of the marker under radiologic guidance.)					
	(A4550 (Disposable Surgical Tray) can be coded in addition to 19125 in the office setting. Payment is at carrier discretion.)					
19125	Excision of breast lesion identified by preoperative placement of radiological marker, open; single lesion	12.36	443.40	1135	1305	1420
	(A4550 (Disposable Surgical Tray) can be coded in addition to 19126 in the office setting. Payment is at carrier discretion.)					
✚ 19126	Excision of breast lesion identified by preoperative placement of radiological marker, open; each additional lesion separately identified by a preoperative radiological marker (List separately in addition to code for primary procedure)	4.25	150.07	719	812	1029
	(UNBUNDLING ALERT: 19160 cannot be used with breast biopsy or excision codes, 19100-19101 or 19120 by the same physician on the same day.)					
	(UNBUNDLING ALERT: 19162 cannot be used with 19100-19101, 19120, 19160, 38525 or 38745 by the same physician on the same day.)					
	(To code a breast prosthesis implanted at the time of mastectomy, code 19340 and L8600 (implant) on the same claim as 19180. For delayed insertion of the prosthesis, code 19342 and L8600.)					
	(UNBUNDLING ALERT: 19240 cannot be used with 19100-19101, 19120, 19160, 19180, 38525 or 38745 by the same physician on the same day.)					
19260	Excision of chest wall tumor including ribs	30.67	1095.24	2721	3086	3433
19271	Excision of chest wall tumor involving ribs, with plastic reconstruction; without mediastinal lymphadenectomy	41.92	1505.29	3816	4526	4852
19272	Excision of chest wall tumor involving ribs, with plastic reconstruction; with mediastinal lymphadenectomy	46.27	1658.77	4255	5400	5945

Introduction

		Medicare RVU	National Fee	50%	75%	90%
19290	Preoperative placement of needle localization wire, breast;	4.15	152.35	241	291	305
✚ 19291	Preoperative placement of needle localization wire, breast; each additional lesion (List separately in addition to code for primary procedure)	1.84	67.46	136	162	178
✚ 19295	Image guided placement, metallic localization clip, percutaneous, during breast biopsy (List separately in addition to code for primary procedure)	2.58	97.78	163	192	211
19296	Placement of radiotherapy afterloading balloon catheter into the breast for interstitial radioelement application following partial mastectomy, includes imaging guidance; on date separate from partial mastectomy	118.91	4492.37	11616	13779	14930
✚ 19297	Placement of radiotherapy afterloading balloon catheter into the breast for interstitial radioelement application following partial mastectomy, includes imaging guidance; concurrent with partial mastectomy (List separately in addition to code for primary procedure)	2.49	87.92	231	275	298
⊗ 19298	Placement of radiotherapy afterloading brachytherapy catheters (multiple tube and button type) into the breast for interstitial radioelement application following (at the time of or subsequent to) partial mastectomy, includes imaging guidance	43.82	1637.93	4362	5175	5607

● = New Code ⊗ = Conscious Sedation ✚ = Add-on Code ∅ = Modifier '51' Exempt ▲ =Revised Code

		Medicare RVU	National Fee	PFR Fee Information 50%	75%	90%

Mastectomy Procedures

		Medicare RVU	National Fee	50%	75%	90%
● **19300**	Mastectomy for gynecomastia	13.23	481.68	1655	2166	2567
● **19301**	Mastectomy, partial (eg, lumpectomy, tylectomy, quadrantectomy, segmentectomy);	10.29	366.85	1287	1685	1997
● **19302**	Mastectomy, partial (eg, lumpectomy, tylectomy, quadrantectomy, segmentectomy); with axillary lymphadenectomy	21.97	779.55	2749	3597	4263
● **19303**	Mastectomy, simple, complete	22.37	787.89	2799	3662	4341
● **19304**	Mastectomy, subcutaneous	13.65	487.36	1708	2235	2649
● **19305**	Mastectomy, radical, including pectoral muscles, axillary lymph nodes	27.17	964.11	3399	4448	5272
● **19306**	Mastectomy, radical, including pectoral muscles, axillary and internal mammary lymph nodes (Urban type operation)	28.26	1002.77	3536	4626	5484
● **19307**	Mastectomy, modified radical, including axillary lymph nodes, with or without pectoralis minor muscle, but excluding pectoralis major muscle	28.42	1008.45	3556	4653	5515

Repair and Reconstruction

		Medicare RVU	National Fee	50%	75%	90%
19316	Mastopexy	20.07	718.92	2594	3467	3803
19318	Reduction mammaplasty	29.78	1067.95	4044	5410	6654
19324	Mammaplasty, augmentation; without prosthetic implant	12.33	441.88	1692	1862	2253
19325	Mammaplasty, augmentation; with prosthetic implant	16.40	588.93	2059	2772	3157
19328	Removal of intact mammary implant	12.31	442.26	1203	1774	2242
19330	Removal of mammary implant material	15.76	565.43	1881	2387	2611
	(Payment for code 19340 by Medicare is restricted to the presence of the following ICD-9-CM codes: V10.3, 173.5, 174.0-174.9, 175.9, 198.2, 198.81, 216.5, 217, 232.5, 233.0, 238.3, 239.2, 239.3, 610.0-610.9.)					
19340	Immediate insertion of breast prosthesis following mastopexy, mastectomy or in reconstruction	10.45	371.77	2351	3058	3288
	(Payment for code 19342 by Medicare is restricted to the presence of the following ICD-9-CM codes: V10.3, 173.5, 174.0-174.9, 175.9, 198.2, 198.81, 216.5, 217, 232.5, 233.0, 238.3, 239.2, 239.3, 610.0-610.9.)					
19342	Delayed insertion of breast prosthesis following mastopexy, mastectomy or in reconstruction	23.24	833.37	2815	3379	4176
	(Payment for code 19350 by Medicare is restricted to the presence of the following ICD-9-CM codes: V10.3, 173.5, 174.0-174.9, 175.9, 198.2, 198.81, 216.5, 217, 232.5, 233.0, 238.3, 239.2, 239.3, 610.0-610.9.)					
19350	Nipple/areola reconstruction	23.30	848.90	2056	2767	3274
19355	Correction of inverted nipples	18.94	685.94	1486	2103	2721
	(Payment for code 19357 by Medicare is restricted to the presence of the following ICD-9-CM codes: V10.3, 173.5, 174.0-174.9, 175.9, 198.2, 198.81, 216.5, 217, 232.5, 233.0, 238.3, 239.2, 239.3, 610.0-610.9.)					
19357	Breast reconstruction, immediate or delayed, with tissue expander, including subsequent expansion	39.20	1407.13	4457	5412	5889
	(To code the breast implant, see HCPCS L8600.)					
	(Payment for code 19361 by Medicare is restricted to the presence of the following ICD-9-CM codes: V10.3, 173.5, 174.0-174.9, 175.9, 198.2, 198.81, 216.5, 217, 232.5, 233.0, 238.3, 239.2, 239.3, 610.0-610.9.)					
▲ **19361**	Breast reconstruction with latissimus dorsi flap, without prosthetic implant	39.75	1418.12	4989	6086	7094
	(Payment for code 19364 - 19396 by Medicare is restricted to the presence of the following ICD-9-CM codes: V10.3, 173.5, 174.0-174.9, 175.9, 198.2, 198.81, 216.5, 217, 232.5, 233.0, 238.3, 239.2, 239.3, 610.0-610.9.)					
19364	Breast reconstruction with free flap	72.19	2574.00	6304	7889	11097
	(Use also the appropriate CPT code for flap.)					
19366	Breast reconstruction with other technique	36.21	1289.65	4988	6073	8281
19367	Breast reconstruction with transverse rectus abdominis myocutaneous flap (TRAM), single pedicle, including closure of donor site;	47.09	1683.41	5836	8935	10417
19368	Breast reconstruction with transverse rectus abdominis myocutaneous flap (TRAM), single pedicle, including closure of donor site; with microvascular anastomosis (supercharging)	58.04	2071.48	7631	8280	9152
19369	Breast reconstruction with transverse rectus abdominis myocutaneous flap (TRAM), double pedicle, including closure of donor site	53.43	1906.62	7720	9325	11146
19370	Open periprosthetic capsulotomy, breast	17.21	618.11	2081	2579	3079

CPT® 2006 © American Medical Assoc. All rights reserved.

© PFR 2007

● = New Code ⊗ = Conscious Sedation ✚ = Add-on Code ∅ = Modifier '51' Exempt ▲ =Revised Code

		Medicare RVU	National Fee	PFR Fee Information 50%	75%	90%
19371	Periprosthetic capsulectomy, breast	19.89	713.99	2547	3111	3510
19380	Revision of reconstructed breast	19.39	695.80	2418	3027	3748
19396	Preparation of moulage for custom breast implant	4.42	159.17	531	852	1039

Other Procedures

19499	Unlisted procedure, breast	-	-	IR	IR	IR

Musculoskeletal System

General
Incision

20000	Incision of soft tissue abscess (eg, secondary to osteomyelitis); superficial	5.10	184.94	239	293	360
20005	Incision of soft tissue abscess (eg, secondary to osteomyelitis); deep or complicated	7.55	272.48	653	771	967

Wound Exploration-Trauma (eg. Penetrating Gunshot, Stab Wound)

20100	Exploration of penetrating wound (separate procedure); neck	15.80	559.37	1419	1704	2101
20101	Exploration of penetrating wound (separate procedure); chest	9.69	355.10	1054	1318	1618
20102	Exploration of penetrating wound (separate procedure); abdomen/flank/back	11.76	430.52	1272	1898	2567
20103	Exploration of penetrating wound (separate procedure); extremity	14.42	526.40	1103	1272	1701

Excision

20150	Excision of epiphyseal bar, with or without autogenous soft tissue graft obtained through same fascial incision *(For biopsy of skin, see codes 11100-11101.)* *(A4550 (Disposable Surgical Tray) can be coded in addition to 20200 in the office setting. Payment is at carrier discretion.)*	23.87	848.90	2289	2614	3404
20200	Biopsy, muscle; superficial	4.75	174.33	362	446	504
	(A4550 (Disposable Surgical Tray) can be coded in addition to 20205 in the office setting. Payment is at carrier discretion.)					
20205	Biopsy, muscle; deep	6.55	239.13	578	680	774
	(Medicare fees for the code below are based on Non Facility RVUs. PFR information reflects fee when procedure is performed in a facility.)					
20206	Biopsy, muscle, percutaneous needle	7.18	268.31	261	309	360
	(A4550 (Disposable Surgical Tray) can be coded in addition to 20220 in the office setting. Payment is at carrier discretion.)					
20220	Biopsy, bone, trocar, or needle; superficial (eg, ilium, sternum, spinous process, ribs)	5.42	200.48	323	407	478
	(Medicare fees for the code below are based on Non Facility RVUs. PFR information reflects fee when procedure is performed in a facility.) *(A4550 (Disposable Surgical Tray) can be coded in addition to 20225 in the office setting. Payment is at carrier discretion.)*					
20225	Biopsy, bone, trocar, or needle; deep (eg, vertebral body, femur)	23.58	886.42	702	847	915
	(A4550 (Disposable Surgical Tray) can be coded in addition to 20240 in the office setting. Payment is at carrier discretion.)					
20240	Biopsy, bone, open; superficial (eg, ilium, sternum, spinous process, ribs, trochanter of femur)	6.13	219.81	589	704	914
20245	Biopsy, bone, open; deep (eg, humerus, ischium, femur)	16.46	590.44	1002	1123	1242
20250	Biopsy, vertebral body, open; thoracic	9.74	349.41	2444	2988	3179
20251	Biopsy, vertebral body, open; lumbar or cervical	10.94	393.00	2108	2513	2703

Introduction or Removal

	(Medicare fees for the code below are based on Non Facility RVUs. PFR information reflects fee when procedure is performed in a facility.) *(For removal of foreign body of deep structures, see the CPT Index under Removal, Foreign Body, by specific site.)* *(For removal of foreign body from the skin, see 10120 - 10121.)*					
20500	Injection of sinus tract; therapeutic (separate procedure)	3.38	123.17	130	170	212

● = New Code ⊗ = Conscious Sedation ✚ = Add-on Code ∅ = Modifier '51' Exempt ▲ =Revised Code

		Medicare RVU	National Fee	PFR Fee Information 50%	75%	90%
20501	Injection of sinus tract; diagnostic (sinogram)	3.54	131.13	173	191	214
20520	Removal of foreign body in muscle or tendon sheath; simple	4.91	178.88	317	389	471
20525	Removal of foreign body in muscle or tendon sheath; deep or complicated	12.64	465.76	718	789	932
20526	Injection, therapeutic (eg, local anesthetic, corticosteroid), carpal tunnel	2.00	72.38	112	147	171
	(UNBUNDLING ALERT: 20550-20605 cannot be used with 10160 or 64450 by the same physician on the same day.)					
20550	Injection(s); single tendon sheath, or ligament, aponeurosis (eg, plantar "fascia")	1.53	54.95	118	146	181
20551	Injection(s); single tendon origin/insertion	1.50	53.81	121	156	182
20552	Injection(s); single or multiple trigger point(s), one or two muscle(s)	1.40	50.40	133	163	189
20553	Injection(s); single or multiple trigger point(s), three or more muscle(s)	1.57	56.47	130	166	195
	(For codes 20600-20612, if medication is injected, code the medication using the appropriate HCPCS code in the J Section.)					
20600	Arthrocentesis, aspiration and/or injection; small joint or bursa (eg, fingers, toes)	1.40	50.40	108	139	168
20605	Arthrocentesis, aspiration and/or injection; intermediate joint or bursa (eg, temporomandibular, acromioclavicular, wrist, elbow or ankle, olecranon bursa)	1.52	54.95	126	148	170
	(UNBUNDLING ALERT: 20610 cannot be used with 10160 by the same physician on the same day.)					
20610	Arthrocentesis, aspiration and/or injection; major joint or bursa (eg, shoulder, hip, knee joint, subacromial bursa)	1.88	68.22	141	175	187
20612	Aspiration and/or injection of ganglion cyst(s) any location	1.51	54.57	108	130	149
20615	Aspiration and injection for treatment of bone cyst	5.81	211.47	444	522	613
	(Removal of hardware by the same physician is included in the fee for the original procedure. For removal of hardware by a different physician, see 20670-20680.)					
20650	Insertion of wire or pin with application of skeletal traction, including removal (separate procedure)	4.96	179.26	411	468	533
⊘ 20660	Application of cranial tongs, caliper, or stereotactic frame, including removal (separate procedure)	6.24	227.01	801	884	1258
20661	Application of halo, including removal; cranial	11.47	414.98	1231	1327	1655
20662	Application of halo, including removal; pelvic	12.18	437.72	756	966	1221
20663	Application of halo, including removal; femoral	11.48	413.46	767	853	1237
20664	Application of halo, including removal, cranial, 6 or more pins placed, for thin skull osteology (eg, pediatric patients, hydrocephalus, osteogenesis imperfecta), requiring general anesthesia	18.94	680.26	1244	1439	1747
20665	Removal of tongs or halo applied by another physician	3.50	127.71	175	252	386
	(Medicare fees for the code below are based on Non Facility RVUs. PFR information reflects fee when procedure is performed in a facility.)					
20670	Removal of implant; superficial, (eg, buried wire, pin or rod) (separate procedure)	12.36	461.59	380	493	563
	(UNBUNDLING ALERT: 20680 cannot be used with 11040 or 11042 by the same physician on the same day.)					
20680	Removal of implant; deep (eg, buried wire, pin, screw, metal band, nail, rod or plate)	15.09	549.51	856	1012	1134
⊘ 20690	Application of a uniplane (pins or wires in one plane), unilateral, external fixation system	6.72	240.65	1071	1271	1487
⊘ 20692	Application of a multiplane (pins or wires in more than one plane), unilateral, external fixation system (eg, Ilizarov, Monticelli type)	11.10	396.41	1553	1805	2150
20693	Adjustment or revision of external fixation system requiring anesthesia (eg, new pin(s) or wire(s) and/or new ring(s) or bar(s))	12.17	438.47	929	1219	1578
20694	Removal, under anesthesia, of external fixation system	11.60	423.69	768	938	1092

Replantation

		Medicare RVU	National Fee	PFR Fee Information 50%	75%	90%
20802	Replantation, arm (includes surgical neck of humerus through elbow joint), complete amputation	68.03	2416.72	8810	11196	12335
20805	Replantation, forearm (includes radius and ulna to radial carpal joint), complete amputation	88.25	3149.66	10151	11420	13129
20808	Replantation, hand (includes hand through metacarpophalangeal joints), complete amputation	111.25	3976.96	10911	12677	14010

● = New Code ⊗ = Conscious Sedation ✚ = Add-on Code ⊘ = Modifier '51' Exempt ▲ =Revised Code

		Medicare RVU	National Fee	PFR Fee Information 50%	75%	90%
20816	Replantation, digit, excluding thumb (includes metacarpophalangeal joint to insertion of flexor sublimis tendon), complete amputation	70.77	2561.11	5609	6907	7675
20822	Replantation, digit, excluding thumb (includes distal tip to sublimis tendon insertion), complete amputation	62.19	2256.04	4972	6340	6835
20824	Replantation, thumb (includes carpometacarpal joint to MP joint), complete amputation	70.25	2541.41	5848	7756	9119
20827	Replantation, thumb (includes distal tip to MP joint), complete amputation	64.29	2332.59	5251	6282	7982
20838	Replantation, foot, complete amputation	63.77	2254.52	10108	10911	13298

Grafts (or Implants)

		Medicare RVU	National Fee	50%	75%	90%
∅ 20900	Bone graft, any donor area; minor or small (eg, dowel or button)	15.36	560.13	889	1032	1324
∅ 20902	Bone graft, any donor area; major or large	15.91	572.63	1509	1746	2099
∅ 20910	Cartilage graft; costochondral	11.18	403.23	963	1390	1776
∅ 20912	Cartilage graft; nasal septum	12.64	454.39	1184	1400	1500
∅ 20920	Fascia lata graft; by stripper	10.35	371.40	673	969	1241
∅ 20922	Fascia lata graft; by incision and area exposure, complex or sheet	15.09	545.72	1019	1319	1616
∅ 20924	Tendon graft, from a distance (eg, palmaris, toe extensor, plantaris)	13.30	479.02	1252	1487	1639
∅ 20926	Tissue grafts, other (eg, paratenon, fat, dermis)	11.24	404.37	905	1124	1259
	(Code harvesting of bone graft separately using codes 20930 - 20938. Code 20930 - 20938 only once, regardless of the number of arthrodesis procedures performed.)					
∅ 20930	Allograft for spine surgery only; morselized	-	-	513	804	960
∅ 20931	Allograft for spine surgery only; structural	3.11	111.04	504	644	876
∅ 20936	Autograft for spine surgery only (includes harvesting the graft); local (eg, ribs, spinous process, or laminar fragments) obtained from same incision	-	-	1150	1489	1733
∅ 20937	Autograft for spine surgery only (includes harvesting the graft); morselized (through separate skin or fascial incision)	4.70	167.51	1036	1292	1683
∅ 20938	Autograft for spine surgery only (includes harvesting the graft); structural, bicortical or tricortical (through separate skin or fascial incision)	5.13	183.04	1237	1453	1748

Other Procedures

		Medicare RVU	National Fee	50%	75%	90%
	(Medicare fees for the code below are based on Non Facility RVUs. PFR information reflects fee when procedure is performed in a facility.)					
20950	Monitoring of interstitial fluid pressure (includes insertion of device, eg, wick catheter technique, needle manometer technique) in detection of muscle compartment syndrome	7.63	284.23	264	300	321
20955	Bone graft with microvascular anastomosis; fibula	67.75	2414.83	8355	10477	11990
20956	Bone graft with microvascular anastomosis; iliac crest	71.75	2563.01	6326	8400	10352
20957	Bone graft with microvascular anastomosis; metatarsal	68.52	2435.29	6490	8617	10619
20962	Bone graft with microvascular anastomosis; other than fibula, iliac crest, or metatarsal	71.04	2542.92	7145	7930	9400
20969	Free osteocutaneous flap with microvascular anastomosis; other than iliac crest, metatarsal, or great toe	75.08	2673.29	7232	8334	8876
20970	Free osteocutaneous flap with microvascular anastomosis; iliac crest	75.05	2675.56	7125	10206	11816
20972	Free osteocutaneous flap with microvascular anastomosis; metatarsal	69.40	2461.44	7460	9505	11469
20973	Free osteocutaneous flap with microvascular anastomosis; great toe with web space	75.18	2670.26	7752	9114	11145
∅ 20974	Electrical stimulation to aid bone healing; noninvasive (nonoperative)	1.50	54.57	710	930	1237
∅ 20975	Electrical stimulation to aid bone healing; invasive (operative)	4.77	170.92	1242	1318	1503
20979	Low intensity ultrasound stimulation to aid bone healing, noninvasive (nonoperative)	1.46	53.06	109	137	174
⊗ 20982	Ablation, bone tumor(s) (eg, osteoid osteoma, metastasis) radiofrequency, percutaneous, including computed tomographic guidance	109.72	4130.45	IR	IR	IR
20999	Unlisted procedure, musculoskeletal system, general	-	-	IR	IR	IR

● = New Code ⊗ = Conscious Sedation ✚ = Add-on Code ∅ = Modifier '51' Exempt ▲ =Revised Code

	Medicare RVU	National Fee	PFR Fee Information 50%	75%	90%

Head
Incision

21010 Arthrotomy, temporomandibular joint — 18.82 | 671.54 | 2586 | 3258 | 3908

Excision

21015 Radical resection of tumor (eg, malignant neoplasm), soft tissue of face or scalp — 11.14 | 400.96 | 1429 | 1798 | 2364

21025 Excision of bone (eg, for osteomyelitis or bone abscess); mandible — 24.71 | 894.38 | 1469 | 1925 | 2443

21026 Excision of bone (eg, for osteomyelitis or bone abscess); facial bone(s) — 14.22 | 517.68 | 1532 | 1885 | 2335

21029 Removal by contouring of benign tumor of facial bone (eg, fibrous dysplasia) — 18.56 | 671.92 | 1663 | 2220 | 2791

21030 Excision of benign tumor or cyst of maxilla or zygoma by enucleation and curettage — 11.89 | 432.41 | 1311 | 1739 | 2097

21031 Excision of torus mandibularis — 9.11 | 332.74 | 611 | 762 | 949

21032 Excision of maxillary torus palatinus — 9.27 | 338.80 | 853 | 1092 | 1409

21034 Excision of malignant tumor of maxilla or zygoma — 34.16 | 1229.02 | 2803 | 3170 | 3250

21040 Excision of benign tumor or cyst of mandible, by enucleation and/or curettage — 11.95 | 434.68 | 1080 | 1414 | 1662

21044 Excision of malignant tumor of mandible; — 22.66 | 810.63 | 2505 | 2852 | 3276

21045 Excision of malignant tumor of mandible; radical resection — 31.46 | 1123.28 | 4152 | 5611 | 7222

21046 Excision of benign tumor or cyst of mandible; requiring intra-oral osteotomy (eg, locally aggressive or destructive lesion(s)) — 27.69 | 995.95 | 3261 | 4029 | 4745

21047 Excision of benign tumor or cyst of mandible; requiring extra-oral osteotomy and partial mandibulectomy (eg, locally aggressive or destructive lesion(s)) — 34.52 | 1232.81 | 3840 | 4826 | 5684

21048 Excision of benign tumor or cyst of maxilla; requiring intra-oral osteotomy (eg, locally aggressive or destructive lesion(s)) — 28.21 | 1013.76 | 3260 | 4024 | 4740

21049 Excision of benign tumor or cyst of maxilla; requiring extra-oral osteotomy and partial maxillectomy (eg, locally aggressive or destructive lesion(s)) — 32.75 | 1168.38 | 3703 | 4571 | 5385

21050 Condylectomy, temporomandibular joint (separate procedure) — 22.16 | 795.85 | 2928 | 3491 | 3880

21060 Meniscectomy, partial or complete, temporomandibular joint (separate procedure) — 20.65 | 740.90 | 3110 | 3673 | 4528

21070 Coronoidectomy (separate procedure) — 16.65 | 598.40 | 2432 | 2780 | 3074

Introduction or Removal

21076 Impression and custom preparation; surgical obturator prosthesis — 26.66 | 959.19 | 2024 | 2470 | 2762

21077 Impression and custom preparation; orbital prosthesis — 66.45 | 2389.82 | 4913 | 6015 | 8328

21079 Impression and custom preparation; interim obturator prosthesis — 45.07 | 1623.15 | 3577 | 5014 | 7432

21080 Impression and custom preparation; definitive obturator prosthesis — 51.20 | 1844.85 | 3752 | 5328 | 7330

21081 Impression and custom preparation; mandibular resection prosthesis — 46.50 | 1675.07 | 3498 | 4918 | 6121

21082 Impression and custom preparation; palatal augmentation prosthesis — 42.22 | 1520.45 | 3387 | 4480 | 5792

21083 Impression and custom preparation; palatal lift prosthesis — 39.95 | 1440.48 | 2411 | 2813 | 3619

21084 Impression and custom preparation; speech aid prosthesis — 45.59 | 1642.10 | 3251 | 4226 | 5994

21085 Impression and custom preparation; oral surgical splint — 18.20 | 655.63 | 1170 | 1521 | 2105

21086 Impression and custom preparation; auricular prosthesis — 49.64 | 1786.49 | 3581 | 4822 | 5805

21087 Impression and custom preparation; nasal prosthesis — 49.08 | 1765.27 | 3425 | 4761 | 6204

21088 Impression and custom preparation; facial prosthesis — - | - | 1585 | 2433 | 3281

Other Procedures

21089 Unlisted maxillofacial prosthetic procedure — - | - | IR | IR | IR

● = New Code ⊗ = Conscious Sedation ✚ = Add-on Code ∅ = Modifier '51' Exempt ▲ =Revised Code

		Medicare RVU	National Fee	PFR Fee Information 50%	75%	90%

Introduction or Removal

(Medicare fees for the code below are based on Non Facility RVUs. PFR information reflects fee when procedure is performed in a facility.)

Code	Description	Medicare RVU	National Fee	50%	75%	90%
21100	Application of halo type appliance for maxillofacial fixation, includes removal (separate procedure)	16.99	626.45	522	820	1146
21110	Application of interdental fixation device for conditions other than fracture or dislocation, includes removal	17.01	622.66	1181	1351	1637

(Medicare fees for the code below are based on Non Facility RVUs. PFR information reflects fee when procedure is performed in a facility.)

Code	Description	Medicare RVU	National Fee	50%	75%	90%
21116	Injection procedure for temporomandibular joint arthrography	4.71	175.47	169	240	341

Repair, Revision, and/or Reconstruction

Code	Description	Medicare RVU	National Fee	50%	75%	90%
21120	Genioplasty; augmentation (autograft, allograft, prosthetic material)	16.05	589.31	1806	2825	3093
21121	Genioplasty; sliding osteotomy, single piece	18.56	674.20	2173	2576	3157
21122	Genioplasty; sliding osteotomies, two or more osteotomies (eg, wedge excision or bone wedge reversal for asymmetrical chin)	18.06	651.84	2529	3100	3502
21123	Genioplasty; sliding, augmentation with interpositional bone grafts (includes obtaining autografts)	23.26	838.67	2799	3438	3878

(Medicare fees for the code below are based on Non Facility RVUs. PFR information reflects fee when procedure is performed in a facility.)

Code	Description	Medicare RVU	National Fee	50%	75%	90%
21125	Augmentation, mandibular body or angle; prosthetic material	70.02	2613.03	1913	2467	2812
21127	Augmentation, mandibular body or angle; with bone graft, onlay or interpositional (includes obtaining autograft)	67.67	2517.91	2480	2795	3100
21137	Reduction forehead; contouring only	18.85	675.71	2175	2581	3015
21138	Reduction forehead; contouring and application of prosthetic material or bone graft (includes obtaining autograft)	23.84	854.97	2703	3238	3662
21139	Reduction forehead; contouring and setback of anterior frontal sinus wall	26.50	947.44	3213	3864	4876
21141	Reconstruction midface, LeFort I; single piece, segment movement in any direction (eg, for Long Face Syndrome), without bone graft	34.79	1244.93	4450	5053	6570
21142	Reconstruction midface, LeFort I; two pieces, segment movement in any direction, without bone graft	34.65	1236.97	4695	5359	6964
21143	Reconstruction midface, LeFort I; three or more pieces, segment movement in any direction, without bone graft	35.34	1260.09	4880	5372	6016
21145	Reconstruction midface, LeFort I; single piece, segment movement in any direction, requiring bone grafts (includes obtaining autografts)	40.10	1429.49	5044	6908	8357
21146	Reconstruction midface, LeFort I; two pieces, segment movement in any direction, requiring bone grafts (includes obtaining autografts) (eg, ungrafted unilateral alveolar cleft)	41.43	1476.49	5241	7191	8259
21147	Reconstruction midface, LeFort I; three or more pieces, segment movement in any direction, requiring bone grafts (includes obtaining autografts) (eg, ungrafted bilateral alveolar cleft or multiple osteotomies)	42.72	1519.31	5559	6651	7881
21150	Reconstruction midface, LeFort II; anterior intrusion (eg, Treacher-Collins Syndrome)	44.17	1575.78	5877	7227	8273
21151	Reconstruction midface, LeFort II; any direction, requiring bone grafts (includes obtaining autografts)	51.26	1832.72	6811	7314	7821
21154	Reconstruction midface, LeFort III (extracranial), any type, requiring bone grafts (includes obtaining autografts); without LeFort I	56.33	2016.53	7064	8152	9136
21155	Reconstruction midface, LeFort III (extracranial), any type, requiring bone grafts (includes obtaining autografts); with LeFort I	62.88	2249.60	8183	9214	11398
21159	Reconstruction midface, LeFort III (extra and intracranial) with forehead advancement (eg, mono bloc), requiring bone grafts (includes obtaining autografts); without LeFort I	76.69	2742.64	10124	11358	14062
21160	Reconstruction midface, LeFort III (extra and intracranial) with forehead advancement (eg, mono bloc), requiring bone grafts (includes obtaining autografts); with LeFort I	77.73	2766.90	10396	11807	13219
21172	Reconstruction superior-lateral orbital rim and lower forehead, advancement or alteration, with or without grafts (includes obtaining autografts)	45.41	1614.05	6330	8597	10252
21175	Reconstruction, bifrontal, superior-lateral orbital rims and lower forehead, advancement or alteration (eg, plagiocephaly, trigonocephaly, brachycephaly), with or without grafts (includes obtaining autografts)	54.91	1953.62	7928	9504	10624
21179	Reconstruction, entire or majority of forehead and/or supraorbital rims; with grafts (allograft or prosthetic material)	38.73	1381.74	5932	7271	8769
21180	Reconstruction, entire or majority of forehead and/or supraorbital rims; with autograft (includes obtaining grafts)	43.68	1558.35	6195	7184	8225
21181	Reconstruction by contouring of benign tumor of cranial bones (eg, fibrous dysplasia), extracranial	18.87	676.47	2032	2872	3549

● = New Code ⊗ = Conscious Sedation ✚ = Add-on Code ∅ = Modifier '51' Exempt ▲ =Revised Code

		Medicare RVU	National Fee	PFR Fee Information 50%	75%	90%
21182	Reconstruction of orbital walls, rims, forehead, nasoethmoid complex following intra- and extracranial excision of benign tumor of cranial bone (eg, fibrous dysplasia), with multiple autografts (includes obtaining grafts); total area of bone grafting less than 40 sq cm	53.19	1892.22	7137	8576	9769
21183	Reconstruction of orbital walls, rims, forehead, nasoethmoid complex following intra- and extracranial excision of benign tumor of cranial bone (eg, fibrous dysplasia), with multiple autografts (includes obtaining grafts); total area of bone grafting greater than 40 sq cm but less than 80 sq cm	59.57	2121.88	7712	8928	10207
21184	Reconstruction of orbital walls, rims, forehead, nasoethmoid complex following intra- and extracranial excision of benign tumor of cranial bone (eg, fibrous dysplasia), with multiple autografts (includes obtaining grafts); total area of bone grafting greater than 80 sq cm	66.02	2355.33	8201	9791	11179
21188	Reconstruction midface, osteotomies (other than LeFort type) and bone grafts (includes obtaining autografts)	42.56	1525.37	5363	6262	7407
21193	Reconstruction of mandibular rami, horizontal, vertical, C, or L osteotomy; without bone graft	32.86	1174.06	4304	5176	6422
21194	Reconstruction of mandibular rami, horizontal, vertical, C, or L osteotomy; with bone graft (includes obtaining graft)	36.75	1310.50	5272	6460	7261
21195	Reconstruction of mandibular rami and/or body, sagittal split; without internal rigid fixation	35.00	1254.41	4692	5355	6382
21196	Reconstruction of mandibular rami and/or body, sagittal split; with internal rigid fixation	37.75	1352.18	4850	6081	7304
21198	Osteotomy, mandible, segmental;	29.25	1049.38	3118	3654	4089
21199	Osteotomy, mandible, segmental; with genioglossus advancement	26.58	944.03	3377	3958	4430
21206	Osteotomy, maxilla, segmental (eg, Wassmund or Schuchard)	28.98	1039.53	3279	4835	5778
21208	Osteoplasty, facial bones; augmentation (autograft, allograft, or prosthetic implant)	37.09	1363.17	2323	2948	3539
21209	Osteoplasty, facial bones; reduction	19.68	717.02	1967	2504	2774
21210	Graft, bone; nasal, maxillary or malar areas (includes obtaining graft)	42.28	1558.72	2954	3373	4157
21215	Graft, bone; mandible (includes obtaining graft)	66.42	2471.67	3236	3727	4941
21230	Graft; rib cartilage, autogenous, to face, chin, nose or ear (includes obtaining graft)	20.12	720.43	3265	4222	4760
21235	Graft; ear cartilage, autogenous, to nose or ear (includes obtaining graft)	17.77	645.39	2149	2524	2716
21240	Arthroplasty, temporomandibular joint, with or without autograft (includes obtaining graft)	29.47	1056.58	4062	4726	5327
21242	Arthroplasty, temporomandibular joint, with allograft	26.98	967.90	4009	4778	5895
21243	Arthroplasty, temporomandibular joint, with prosthetic joint replacement	43.91	1572.37	4740	5984	6949
21244	Reconstruction of mandible, extraoral, with transosteal bone plate (eg, mandibular staple bone plate)	26.44	951.23	3905	4980	6142
21245	Reconstruction of mandible or maxilla, subperiosteal implant; partial	28.24	1020.96	3752	4950	6174
21246	Reconstruction of mandible or maxilla, subperiosteal implant; complete	22.61	807.97	4780	6721	8063
21247	Reconstruction of mandibular condyle with bone and cartilage autografts (includes obtaining grafts) (eg, for hemifacial microsomia)	42.93	1535.23	4919	6433	8248
21248	Reconstruction of mandible or maxilla, endosteal implant (eg, blade, cylinder); partial	26.35	950.85	3584	5115	6610
21249	Reconstruction of mandible or maxilla, endosteal implant (eg, blade, cylinder); complete	37.66	1356.35	5553	6534	7345
21255	Reconstruction of zygomatic arch and glenoid fossa with bone and cartilage (includes obtaining autografts)	36.01	1295.72	4337	5277	5736
21256	Reconstruction of orbit with osteotomies (extracranial) and with bone grafts (includes obtaining autografts) (eg, micro-ophthalmia)	30.28	1081.22	5362	6461	7807
21260	Periorbital osteotomies for orbital hypertelorism, with bone grafts; extracranial approach	30.63	1093.34	5748	6891	7793
21261	Periorbital osteotomies for orbital hypertelorism, with bone grafts; combined intra- and extracranial approach	59.06	2109.37	7072	8780	9970
21263	Periorbital osteotomies for orbital hypertelorism, with bone grafts; with forehead advancement	51.15	1821.35	8780	10040	11138
21267	Orbital repositioning, periorbital osteotomies, unilateral, with bone grafts; extracranial approach	41.07	1478.38	7222	8310	10320
21268	Orbital repositioning, periorbital osteotomies, unilateral, with bone grafts; combined intra- and extracranial approach	49.61	1778.15	9831	11280	13572

● = New Code ⊗ = Conscious Sedation ✚ = Add-on Code ∅ = Modifier '51' Exempt ▲ =Revised Code

		Medicare RVU	National Fee	PFR Fee Information		
				50%	75%	90%
21270	Malar augmentation, prosthetic material	22.79	823.51	2801	4006	5462
21275	Secondary revision of orbitocraniofacial reconstruction	20.96	749.99	5252	6645	7316
21280	Medial canthopexy (separate procedure)	13.26	475.99	2089	2407	2836
21282	Lateral canthopexy	8.81	318.34	1662	1957	2318
21295	Reduction of masseter muscle and bone (eg, for treatment of benign masseteric hypertrophy); extraoral approach	4.53	164.85	2095	2723	3372
21296	Reduction of masseter muscle and bone (eg, for treatment of benign masseteric hypertrophy); intraoral approach	10.07	363.82	2248	2665	3164

Other Procedures

21299	Unlisted craniofacial and maxillofacial procedure	-	-	IR	IR	IR

Fracture and/or Dislocation

(When fractures are re-reduced by the same physician, add a -76 modifier to indicate that the procedure was repeated.)
(See also HCPCS codes A4580, A4590, Q4001-A4048 and Q4050 for cast supplies.)

21310	Closed treatment of nasal bone fracture without manipulation	2.83	104.98	298	370	412
21315	Closed treatment of nasal bone fracture; without stabilization	6.21	228.52	389	508	624
21320	Closed treatment of nasal bone fracture; with stabilization	5.99	219.81	755	884	983
21325	Open treatment of nasal fracture; uncomplicated	12.54	459.70	1137	1691	1953
21330	Open treatment of nasal fracture; complicated, with internal and/or external skeletal fixation	15.40	562.02	1987	2538	2828
21335	Open treatment of nasal fracture; with concomitant open treatment of fractured septum	18.83	679.50	2873	3327	4100
21336	Open treatment of nasal septal fracture, with or without stabilization	16.38	595.75	1378	1704	2377
21337	Closed treatment of nasal septal fracture, with or without stabilization	9.61	351.69	836	1370	1545
21338	Open treatment of nasoethmoid fracture; without external fixation	20.53	752.27	2102	2623	3071
21339	Open treatment of nasoethmoid fracture; with external fixation	22.48	820.10	2401	2960	3535
21340	Percutaneous treatment of nasoethmoid complex fracture, with splint, wire or headcap fixation, including repair of canthal ligaments and/or the nasolacrimal apparatus	20.58	736.73	2740	3560	4212
21343	Open treatment of depressed frontal sinus fracture	30.35	1096.37	2897	3446	3963
21344	Open treatment of complicated (eg, comminuted or involving posterior wall) frontal sinus fracture, via coronal or multiple approaches	39.52	1416.23	4040	4749	5333
21345	Closed treatment of nasomaxillary complex fracture (LeFort II type), with interdental wire fixation or fixation of denture or splint	19.61	709.44	2627	3171	3650
21346	Open treatment of nasomaxillary complex fracture (LeFort II type); with wiring and/or local fixation	24.37	880.36	3103	4023	4897
21347	Open treatment of nasomaxillary complex fracture (LeFort II type); requiring multiple open approaches	29.92	1082.73	3869	4645	5951
21348	Open treatment of nasomaxillary complex fracture (LeFort II type); with bone grafting (includes obtaining graft)	29.76	1061.51	3582	4609	4984
21355	Percutaneous treatment of fracture of malar area, including zygomatic arch and malar tripod, with manipulation	10.74	390.72	1032	1625	2137
21356	Open treatment of depressed zygomatic arch fracture (eg, Gillies approach)	12.21	444.92	1428	1721	2011
21360	Open treatment of depressed malar fracture, including zygomatic arch and malar tripod	13.56	486.98	1925	2431	2647
21365	Open treatment of complicated (eg, comminuted or involving cranial nerve foramina) fracture(s) of malar area, including zygomatic arch and malar tripod; with internal fixation and multiple surgical approaches	28.62	1021.72	3153	3780	4094
21366	Open treatment of complicated (eg, comminuted or involving cranial nerve foramina) fracture(s) of malar area, including zygomatic arch and malar tripod; with bone grafting (includes obtaining graft)	32.05	1144.13	3709	4462	5342
21385	Open treatment of orbital floor blowout fracture; transantral approach (Caldwell-Luc type operation)	18.39	660.93	2107	2771	2988
21386	Open treatment of orbital floor blowout fracture; periorbital approach	17.20	615.83	2614	2995	3194
21387	Open treatment of orbital floor blowout fracture; combined approach	19.64	706.03	3158	3536	4039

© PFR 2007

● = New Code ⊗ = Conscious Sedation ✚ = Add-on Code ∅ = Modifier '51' Exempt ▲ =Revised Code

		Medicare RVU	National Fee	PFR Fee Information 50%	75%	90%
21390	Open treatment of orbital floor blowout fracture; periorbital approach, with alloplastic or other implant	19.61	701.10	2953	3538	3954
21395	Open treatment of orbital floor blowout fracture; periorbital approach with bone graft (includes obtaining graft)	24.82	884.91	3315	4091	5445
21400	Closed treatment of fracture of orbit, except blowout; without manipulation	4.23	155.00	508	703	1051
21401	Closed treatment of fracture of orbit, except blowout; with manipulation	11.75	431.65	1469	1771	2296
21406	Open treatment of fracture of orbit, except blowout; without implant	13.89	498.35	2192	2787	2937
21407	Open treatment of fracture of orbit, except blowout; with implant	16.49	590.82	2570	3367	3570
21408	Open treatment of fracture of orbit, except blowout; with bone grafting (includes obtaining graft)	22.79	815.55	2869	3517	3979
21421	Closed treatment of palatal or maxillary fracture (LeFort I type), with interdental wire fixation or fixation of denture or splint	16.56	605.60	1744	2555	2984
21422	Open treatment of palatal or maxillary fracture (LeFort I type);	17.39	626.07	2443	3153	3545
21423	Open treatment of palatal or maxillary fracture (LeFort I type); complicated (comminuted or involving cranial nerve foramina), multiple approaches	20.82	748.10	2648	3185	3502
21431	Closed treatment of craniofacial separation (LeFort III type) using interdental wire fixation of denture or splint	17.93	649.94	2113	2423	3361
21432	Open treatment of craniofacial separation (LeFort III type); with wiring and/or internal fixation	17.43	627.20	2957	3454	4337
21433	Open treatment of craniofacial separation (LeFort III type); complicated (eg, comminuted or involving cranial nerve foramina), multiple surgical approaches	44.36	1581.46	4520	5203	5872
21435	Open treatment of craniofacial separation (LeFort III type); complicated, utilizing internal and/or external fixation techniques (eg, head cap, halo device, and/or intermaxillary fixation)	34.22	1220.68	4715	5569	7168
21436	Open treatment of craniofacial separation (LeFort III type); complicated, multiple surgical approaches, internal fixation, with bone grafting (includes obtaining graft)	50.39	1795.20	5534	6304	7204
21440	Closed treatment of mandibular or maxillary alveolar ridge fracture (separate procedure)	11.56	425.59	1317	1639	1737
21445	Open treatment of mandibular or maxillary alveolar ridge fracture (separate procedure)	17.26	630.99	1805	1956	2150
21450	Closed treatment of mandibular fracture; without manipulation	12.01	441.51	754	930	1053
21451	Closed treatment of mandibular fracture; with manipulation	16.34	598.40	1822	2282	2806
21452	Percutaneous treatment of mandibular fracture, with external fixation	15.26	569.60	1703	1991	2781
21453	Closed treatment of mandibular fracture with interdental fixation	18.89	691.63	1848	2681	2925
21454	Open treatment of mandibular fracture with external fixation	14.13	508.21	2289	2877	3469
21461	Open treatment of mandibular fracture; without interdental fixation	38.69	1431.77	2472	2943	3133
21462	Open treatment of mandibular fracture; with interdental fixation	43.34	1601.55	2999	3593	4215
21465	Open treatment of mandibular condylar fracture	23.84	854.21	2816	3378	3998
21470	Open treatment of complicated mandibular fracture by multiple surgical approaches including internal fixation, interdental fixation, and/or wiring of dentures or splints	30.79	1101.30	3898	4418	5011
21480	Closed treatment of temporomandibular dislocation; initial or subsequent	2.37	87.54	279	401	641
21485	Closed treatment of temporomandibular dislocation; complicated (eg, recurrent requiring intermaxillary fixation or splinting), initial or subsequent	14.30	524.50	735	940	1166
21490	Open treatment of temporomandibular dislocation	23.94	858.76	2485	2735	3137
21495	Open treatment of hyoid fracture	15.74	571.49	2008	2413	2627
21497	Interdental wiring, for condition other than fracture	14.28	524.12	1417	1738	1976

Other Procedures

21499	Unlisted musculoskeletal procedure, head	-	-	IR	IR	IR

Neck (Soft Tissues) and Thorax

Incision

21501	Incision and drainage, deep abscess or hematoma, soft tissues of neck or thorax;	10.71	391.10	777	935	1240
21502	Incision and drainage, deep abscess or hematoma, soft tissues of neck or thorax; with partial rib ostectomy	13.82	495.32	1047	1177	1446

© PFR 2007

● = New Code ⊗ = Conscious Sedation ✚ = Add-on Code ∅ = Modifier '51' Exempt ▲ =Revised Code

		Medicare RVU	National Fee	PFR Fee Information 50%	75%	90%
21510	Incision, deep, with opening of bone cortex (eg, for osteomyelitis or bone abscess), thorax	12.29	442.64	988	1221	1324

Excision

(For biopsy of skin, see codes 11100-11101.)

21550	Biopsy, soft tissue of neck or thorax	5.99	219.05	352	432	663
21555	Excision tumor, soft tissue of neck or thorax; subcutaneous	10.53	382.39	625	724	984
21556	Excision tumor, soft tissue of neck or thorax; deep, subfascial, intramuscular	10.36	371.02	1087	1271	1469
21557	Radical resection of tumor (eg, malignant neoplasm), soft tissue of neck or thorax	15.12	538.90	2867	3612	4954
21600	Excision of rib, partial	13.88	498.73	1237	1562	1697
21610	Costotransversectomy (separate procedure)	27.54	983.44	2833	3173	3463
21615	Excision first and/or cervical rib;	18.14	648.05	2779	3122	3384
21616	Excision first and/or cervical rib; with sympathectomy	22.21	793.95	2720	3248	3760
21620	Ostectomy of sternum, partial	13.84	497.22	2670	3238	3822
21627	Sternal debridement	14.34	516.16	1955	2255	2571
21630	Radical resection of sternum;	33.17	1184.68	3602	4298	5021
21632	Radical resection of sternum; with mediastinal lymphadenectomy	32.90	1172.55	4778	6101	7419

Repair, Revision, and/or Reconstruction

21685	Hyoid myotomy and suspension	25.43	906.89	2284	2690	3248
21700	Division of scalenus anticus; without resection of cervical rib	10.89	388.83	1587	1865	2216
21705	Division of scalenus anticus; with resection of cervical rib	16.62	592.34	2089	2485	3052
21720	Division of sternocleidomastoid for torticollis, open operation; without cast application	9.57	340.70	1335	1494	1764
21725	Division of sternocleidomastoid for torticollis, open operation; with cast application	13.54	486.22	1451	1654	1895
21740	Reconstructive repair of pectus excavatum or carinatum; open	28.44	1011.11	3518	4149	5200
21742	Reconstructive repair of pectus excavatum or carinatum; minimally invasive approach (Nuss procedure), without thoracoscopy	-	-	2705	3560	4210
21743	Reconstructive repair of pectus excavatum or carinatum; minimally invasive approach (Nuss procedure), with thoracoscopy	-	-	3095	3882	4627
21750	Closure of median sternotomy separation with or without debridement (separate procedure)	18.92	673.82	2140	2866	3322

Fracture and/or Dislocation

21800	Closed treatment of rib fracture, uncomplicated, each	2.41	87.54	182	225	272
21805	Open treatment of rib fracture without fixation, each	6.46	234.21	1433	1633	1910
21810	Treatment of rib fracture requiring external fixation (flail chest)	12.89	461.97	3294	3907	4588
21820	Closed treatment of sternum fracture	3.29	119.76	368	486	588
21825	Open treatment of sternum fracture with or without skeletal fixation	14.92	536.25	1488	1882	2363

Other Procedures

21899	Unlisted procedure, neck or thorax	-	-	IR	IR	IR

Back and Flank
Excision

(For biopsy of skin, see codes 11100-11101.)

21920	Biopsy, soft tissue of back or flank; superficial	5.79	211.47	423	470	592
21925	Biopsy, soft tissue of back or flank; deep	10.38	375.94	735	890	1046
21930	Excision, tumor, soft tissue of back or flank	11.51	416.87	1259	1847	2194
21935	Radical resection of tumor (eg, malignant neoplasm), soft tissue of back or flank	30.23	1075.53	2954	3725	5096

© PFR 2007

● = New Code ⊗ = Conscious Sedation ✚ = Add-on Code ∅ = Modifier '51' Exempt ▲ =Revised Code

	Medicare RVU	National Fee	PFR Fee Information 50%	75%	90%

Spine (Vertebral Column)

Incision

22010 Incision and drainage, open, of deep abscess (subfascial), posterior spine; cervical, thoracic, or cervicothoracic — 22.94 — 821.62 — 1786 — 2164 — 2725

22015 Incision and drainage, open, of deep abscess (subfascial), posterior spine; lumbar, sacral, or lumbosacral — 22.75 — 814.80 — 1770 — 2146 — 2701

Excision

22100 Partial excision of posterior vertebral component (eg, spinous process, lamina or facet) for intrinsic bony lesion, single vertebral segment; cervical — 20.61 — 739.76 — 1500 — 1774 — 2392

22101 Partial excision of posterior vertebral component (eg, spinous process, lamina or facet) for intrinsic bony lesion, single vertebral segment; thoracic — 20.61 — 739.76 — 1370 — 1722 — 2291

22102 Partial excision of posterior vertebral component (eg, spinous process, lamina or facet) for intrinsic bony lesion, single vertebral segment; lumbar — 20.66 — 741.65 — 1447 — 1809 — 2286

✚ 22103 Partial excision of posterior vertebral component (eg, spinous process, lamina or facet) for intrinsic bony lesion, single vertebral segment; each additional segment (List separately in addition to code for primary procedure) — 3.91 — 139.08 — 446 — 526 — 603

22110 Partial excision of vertebral body, for intrinsic bony lesion, without decompression of spinal cord or nerve root(s), single vertebral segment; cervical — 25.73 — 922.43 — 2055 — 2438 — 2796

22112 Partial excision of vertebral body, for intrinsic bony lesion, without decompression of spinal cord or nerve root(s), single vertebral segment; thoracic — 25.61 — 917.50 — 1880 — 2528 — 2943

22114 Partial excision of vertebral body, for intrinsic bony lesion, without decompression of spinal cord or nerve root(s), single vertebral segment; lumbar — 25.73 — 922.05 — 1802 — 2132 — 2684

✚ 22116 Partial excision of vertebral body, for intrinsic bony lesion, without decompression of spinal cord or nerve root(s), single vertebral segment; each additional vertebral segment (List separately in addition to code for primary procedure) — 3.92 — 139.84 — 506 — 642 — 727

Osteotomy

22210 Osteotomy of spine, posterior or posterolateral approach, one vertebral segment; cervical — 45.86 — 1642.10 — 5055 — 5694 — 6750

22212 Osteotomy of spine, posterior or posterolateral approach, one vertebral segment; thoracic — 37.74 — 1351.05 — 5034 — 5994 — 6867

22214 Osteotomy of spine, posterior or posterolateral approach, one vertebral segment; lumbar — 38.22 — 1369.24 — 4924 — 5280 — 6524

✚ 22216 Osteotomy of spine, posterior or posterolateral approach, one vertebral segment; each additional vertebral segment (List separately in addition to primary procedure) — 10.27 — 366.09 — 1506 — 1726 — 1976

22220 Osteotomy of spine, including discectomy, anterior approach, single vertebral segment; cervical — 41.38 — 1481.79 — 4937 — 5800 — 6418

22222 Osteotomy of spine, including discectomy, anterior approach, single vertebral segment; thoracic — 38.39 — 1367.72 — 4877 — 5504 — 6673

22224 Osteotomy of spine, including discectomy, anterior approach, single vertebral segment; lumbar — 41.01 — 1467.01 — 4835 — 5708 — 6340

✚ 22226 Osteotomy of spine, including discectomy, anterior approach, single vertebral segment; each additional vertebral segment (List separately in addition to code for primary procedure) — 10.18 — 362.68 — 1317 — 1572 — 1776

Fracture and/or Dislocation

22305 Closed treatment of vertebral process fracture(s) — 4.74 — 171.68 — 557 — 652 — 710

22310 Closed treatment of vertebral body fracture(s), without manipulation, requiring and including casting or bracing — 7.04 — 252.78 — 871 — 1079 — 1227

22315 Closed treatment of vertebral fracture(s) and/or dislocation(s) requiring casting or bracing, with and including casting and/or bracing, with or without anesthesia, by manipulation or traction — 21.49 — 776.52 — 1474 — 1744 — 2382

22318 Open treatment and/or reduction of odontoid fracture(s) and or dislocation(s) (including os odontoideum), anterior approach, including placement of internal fixation; without grafting — 41.23 — 1476.49 — 4009 — 5027 — 6030

22319 Open treatment and/or reduction of odontoid fracture(s) and or dislocation(s) (including os odontoideum), anterior approach, including placement of internal fixation; with grafting — 45.78 — 1639.07 — 4515 — 5740 — 6843

22325 Open treatment and/or reduction of vertebral fracture(s) and/or dislocation(s), posterior approach, one fractured vertebrae or dislocated segment; lumbar — 35.58 — 1273.73 — 3443 — 3880 — 4779

22326 Open treatment and/or reduction of vertebral fracture(s) and/or dislocation(s), posterior approach, one fractured vertebrae or dislocated segment; cervical — 37.66 — 1348.39 — 3899 — 4523 — 5118

22327 Open treatment and/or reduction of vertebral fracture(s) and/or dislocation(s), posterior approach, one fractured vertebrae or dislocated segment; thoracic — 36.87 — 1319.21 — 3672 — 4295 — 5061

✚ 22328 Open treatment and/or reduction of vertebral fracture(s) and/or dislocation(s), posterior approach, one fractured vertebrae or dislocated segment; each additional fractured vertebrae or dislocated segment (List separately in addition to code for primary procedure) — 7.69 — 274.00 — 967 — 1340 — 1941

● = New Code ⊗ = Conscious Sedation ✚ = Add-on Code ∅ = Modifier '51' Exempt ▲ =Revised Code

		Medicare RVU	National Fee	PFR Fee Information 50%	75%	90%

Manipulation

22505	Manipulation of spine requiring anesthesia, any region	3.20	114.07	389	542	604

Vertebral Body, Embolization or Injection

(Medicare fees for the code below are based on Non Facility RVUs. PFR information reflects fee when procedure is performed in a facility.)

22520	Percutaneous vertebroplasty, one vertebral body, unilateral or bilateral injection; thoracic	67.72	2531.55	3279	4200	5280

(Medicare fees for the code below are based on Non Facility RVUs. PFR information reflects fee when procedure is performed in a facility.)

22521	Percutaneous vertebroplasty, one vertebral body, unilateral or bilateral injection; lumbar	63.07	2357.22	2967	3899	4836
+ 22522	Percutaneous vertebroplasty, one vertebral body, unilateral or bilateral injection; each additional thoracic or lumbar vertebral body (List separately in addition to code for primary procedure)	6.71	238.00	531	751	837
22523	Percutaneous vertebral augmentation, including cavity creation (fracture reduction and bone biopsy included when performed) using mechanical device, one vertebral body, unilateral or bilateral cannulation (eg, kyphoplasty); thoracic	16.53	591.20	755	1004	1176
22524	Percutaneous vertebral augmentation, including cavity creation (fracture reduction and bone biopsy included when performed) using mechanical device, one vertebral body, unilateral or bilateral cannulation (eg, kyphoplasty); lumbar	15.81	565.43	724	962	1127
+ 22525	Percutaneous vertebral augmentation, including cavity creation (fracture reduction and bone biopsy included when performed) using mechanical device, one vertebral body, unilateral or bilateral cannulation (eg, kyphoplasty); each additional thoracic or lumbar vertebral body (List separately in addition to code for primary procedure)	7.41	263.77	347	461	539
⊗ ● 22526	Percutaneous intradiscal electrothermal annuloplasty, unilateral or bilateral including fluoroscopic guidance; single level	53.74	2013.49	2477	3292	3854
+ ● 22527	Percutaneous intradiscal electrothermal annuloplasty, unilateral or bilateral including fluoroscopic guidance; one or more additional levels (List separately in addition to code for primary procedure)	43.50	1637.17	2005	2665	3120

Arthrodesis
Lateral Extracavitary Approach Technique

22532	Arthrodesis, lateral extracavitary technique, including minimal discectomy to prepare interspace (other than for decompression); thoracic	44.76	1597.76	5676	6537	7728
22533	Arthrodesis, lateral extracavitary technique, including minimal discectomy to prepare interspace (other than for decompression); lumbar	41.34	1472.70	5396	6213	7345
+ 22534	Arthrodesis, lateral extracavitary technique, including minimal discectomy to prepare interspace (other than for decompression); thoracic or lumbar, each additional vertebral segment (List separately in addition to code for primary procedure)	10.10	360.03	1403	1616	1912

Anterior or Anterolateral Approach Technique

22548	Arthrodesis, anterior transoral or extraoral technique, clivus-C1-C2 (atlas-axis), with or without excision of odontoid process	48.15	1722.44	5208	6132	7063

(UNBUNDLING ALERT: 22554 cannot be used with 20902 by the same physician on the same day.)

22554	Arthrodesis, anterior interbody technique, including minimal discectomy to prepare interspace (other than for decompression); cervical below C2	33.97	1220.68	4898	5567	6550
22556	Arthrodesis, anterior interbody technique, including minimal discectomy to prepare interspace (other than for decompression); thoracic	43.19	1543.57	5195	6022	7260
22558	Arthrodesis, anterior interbody technique, including minimal discectomy to prepare interspace (other than for decompression); lumbar	39.35	1402.21	5038	5520	6309
+ 22585	Arthrodesis, anterior interbody technique, including minimal discectomy to prepare interspace (other than for decompression); each additional interspace (List separately in addition to code for primary procedure)	9.39	334.63	1479	1906	2450

Posterior, Posterolateral or Lateral Transverse Process Technique

22590	Arthrodesis, posterior technique, craniocervical (occiput-C2)	39.65	1420.40	6081	6565	7424
22595	Arthrodesis, posterior technique, atlas-axis (C1-C2)	37.66	1349.15	5291	6565	7159
22600	Arthrodesis, posterior or posterolateral technique, single level; cervical below C2 segment	32.17	1153.60	4591	5536	6494
22610	Arthrodesis, posterior or posterolateral technique, single level; thoracic (with or without lateral transverse technique)	31.91	1144.13	4326	5234	6010
22612	Arthrodesis, posterior or posterolateral technique, single level; lumbar (with or without lateral transverse technique)	41.68	1490.51	4840	5790	6693
+ 22614	Arthrodesis, posterior or posterolateral technique, single level; each additional vertebral segment (List separately in addition to code for primary procedure)	10.96	390.72	1624	1882	2172
22630	Arthrodesis, posterior interbody technique, including laminectomy and/or discectomy to prepare interspace (other than for decompression), single interspace; lumbar	40.01	1432.90	4727	5448	6093

		Medicare RVU	National Fee	PFR Fee Information 50%	75%	90%
✚ 22632	Arthrodesis, posterior interbody technique, including laminectomy and/or discectomy to prepare interspace (other than for decompression), single interspace; each additional interspace (List separately in addition to code for primary procedure)	8.89	316.82	1393	1555	1906

Spine Deformity (eg, Scoliosis, Kyphosis)

22800	Arthrodesis, posterior, for spinal deformity, with or without cast; up to 6 vertebral segments	35.44	1269.57	4951	5816	6019
22802	Arthrodesis, posterior, for spinal deformity, with or without cast; 7 to 12 vertebral segments	56.84	2032.44	6551	7801	9238
22804	Arthrodesis, posterior, for spinal deformity, with or without cast; 13 or more vertebral segments	65.90	2355.33	7207	8251	9503
22808	Arthrodesis, anterior, for spinal deformity, with or without cast; 2 to 3 vertebral segments	47.95	1712.97	5156	6151	7101
22810	Arthrodesis, anterior, for spinal deformity, with or without cast; 4 to 7 vertebral segments	53.97	1925.95	5805	6900	8081
22812	Arthrodesis, anterior, for spinal deformity, with or without cast; 8 or more vertebral segments	58.57	2090.05	6523	7902	9177
22818	Kyphectomy, circumferential exposure of spine and resection of vertebral segment(s) (including body and posterior elements); single or 2 segments	58.99	2105.21	6435	8044	9249
22819	Kyphectomy, circumferential exposure of spine and resection of vertebral segment(s) (including body and posterior elements); 3 or more segments	66.79	2381.86	6572	8214	9036

Exploration

(22830 is used for exploration of a non-union of a spinal fusion.)

22830	Exploration of spinal fusion	21.19	760.60	3773	4618	5141

Spinal Instrumentation

∅ 22840	Posterior non-segmental instrumentation (eg, Harrington rod technique, pedicle fixation across one interspace, atlantoaxial transarticular screw fixation, sublaminar wiring at C1, facet screw fixation)	21.41	763.63	5072	5705	6415
∅ 22841	Internal spinal fixation by wiring of spinous processes	-	-	2027	3349	3909
∅ 22842	Posterior segmental instrumentation (eg, pedicle fixation, dual rods with multiple hooks and sublaminar wires); 3 to 6 vertebral segments	21.42	764.01	4104	5015	5669
∅ 22843	Posterior segmental instrumentation (eg, pedicle fixation, dual rods with multiple hooks and sublaminar wires); 7 to 12 vertebral segments	22.58	804.56	4374	5445	5921
∅ 22844	Posterior segmental instrumentation (eg, pedicle fixation, dual rods with multiple hooks and sublaminar wires); 13 or more vertebral segments	27.81	991.40	4830	5982	6757
∅ 22845	Anterior instrumentation; 2 to 3 vertebral segments	20.51	731.80	5617	6089	6576
∅ 22846	Anterior instrumentation; 4 to 7 vertebral segments	21.31	760.22	5534	6070	6661
∅ 22847	Anterior instrumentation; 8 or more vertebral segments	23.40	834.12	5190	5920	6612
∅ 22848	Pelvic fixation (attachment of caudal end of instrumentation to pelvic bony structures) other than sacrum	10.12	360.78	1340	1670	1800
22849	Reinsertion of spinal fixation device	34.37	1229.77	3630	3974	4436
22850	Removal of posterior nonsegmental instrumentation (eg, Harrington rod)	18.67	670.41	2184	2784	3416
	(22851 is used with a corpectomy or vertebrectomy. It is not used with a graft.)					
∅ 22851	Application of intervertebral biomechanical device(s) (eg, synthetic cage(s), threaded bone dowel(s), methylmethacrylate) to vertebral defect or interspace	11.37	405.50	1910	2234	2495
22852	Removal of posterior segmental instrumentation	17.85	641.23	2593	3085	3602
	(For spinal cord monitoring, use 95925.)					
22855	Removal of anterior instrumentation	28.88	1034.22	3294	3627	4072
● 22857	Total disc arthroplasty (artificial disc), anterior approach, including discectomy to prepare interspace (other than for decompression), lumbar, single interspace	39.29	1386.29	5346	6326	7320
● 22862	Revision including replacement of total disc arthroplasty (artificial disc) anterior approach, lumbar, single interspace	47.86	1690.23	6512	7706	8916
● 22865	Removal of total disc arthroplasty (artificial disc), anterior approach, lumbar, single interspace	46.60	1645.89	6341	7503	8682

Other Procedures

22899	Unlisted procedure, spine	-	-	IR	IR	IR

Abdomen

Excision

22900	Excision, abdominal wall tumor, subfascial (eg, desmoid)	10.20	363.06	1218	1484	2090

		Medicare RVU	National Fee	PFR Fee Information 50%	75%	90%

Other Procedures

| 22999 | Unlisted procedure, abdomen, musculoskeletal system | - | - | IR | IR | IR |

Shoulder

Incision

23000	Removal of subdeltoid calcareous deposits, open	13.42	491.91	942	1154	1315
23020	Capsular contracture release (eg, Sever type procedure)	18.08	649.94	1777	2187	2567
23030	Incision and drainage, shoulder area; deep abscess or hematoma	11.12	408.16	643	720	891
23031	Incision and drainage, shoulder area; infected bursa	10.73	396.03	525	620	711
23035	Incision, bone cortex (eg, osteomyelitis or bone abscess), shoulder area	18.47	665.48	1592	1804	2125
23040	Arthrotomy, glenohumeral joint, including exploration, drainage, or removal of foreign body	18.83	676.85	1875	2379	2879
23044	Arthrotomy, acromioclavicular, sternoclavicular joint, including exploration, drainage, or removal of foreign body	14.94	537.77	1223	1420	1685

Excision

(For biopsy of skin, see codes 11100-11101.)

23065	Biopsy, soft tissue of shoulder area; superficial	5.08	183.80	384	452	518
23066	Biopsy, soft tissue of shoulder area; deep	12.50	457.80	715	874	976
23075	Excision, soft tissue tumor, shoulder area; subcutaneous	6.42	234.21	570	705	888
23076	Excision, soft tissue tumor, shoulder area; deep, subfascial, or intramuscular	14.40	516.16	1020	1381	1648
23077	Radical resection of tumor (eg, malignant neoplasm), soft tissue of shoulder area	30.54	1088.42	3226	4584	5428
23100	Arthrotomy, glenohumeral joint, including biopsy	12.66	456.66	1584	1976	2209
23101	Arthrotomy, acromioclavicular joint or sternoclavicular joint, including biopsy and/or excision of torn cartilage	11.73	422.94	1494	1851	2211
23105	Arthrotomy; glenohumeral joint, with synovectomy, with or without biopsy	16.66	599.54	2505	2807	3038
23106	Arthrotomy; sternoclavicular joint, with synovectomy, with or without biopsy	12.44	448.33	1711	1973	2146
23107	Arthrotomy, glenohumeral joint, with joint exploration, with or without removal of loose or foreign body	17.36	624.55	2285	2701	3014
23120	Claviculectomy; partial	14.68	528.67	1455	1681	1840
23125	Claviculectomy; total	18.41	661.31	2229	2659	3086
23130	Acromioplasty or acromionectomy, partial, with or without coracoacromial ligament release	15.81	569.98	1635	2050	2516
23140	Excision or curettage of bone cyst or benign tumor of clavicle or scapula;	13.21	473.72	1078	1296	1516
23145	Excision or curettage of bone cyst or benign tumor of clavicle or scapula; with autograft (includes obtaining graft)	17.81	639.71	1634	1982	2173
23146	Excision or curettage of bone cyst or benign tumor of clavicle or scapula; with allograft	16.14	581.35	1161	1347	1675
23150	Excision or curettage of bone cyst or benign tumor of proximal humerus;	16.82	604.09	1776	1979	2268
23155	Excision or curettage of bone cyst or benign tumor of proximal humerus; with autograft (includes obtaining graft)	20.62	740.52	2212	2590	2839
23156	Excision or curettage of bone cyst or benign tumor of proximal humerus; with allograft	17.64	634.40	1909	2224	2496
23170	Sequestrectomy (eg, for osteomyelitis or bone abscess), clavicle	14.01	504.04	1178	1428	1690
23172	Sequestrectomy (eg, for osteomyelitis or bone abscess), scapula	14.18	510.10	1275	1534	1853
23174	Sequestrectomy (eg, for osteomyelitis or bone abscess), humeral head to surgical neck	19.65	706.79	1957	2679	3175
23180	Partial excision (craterization, saucerization, or diaphysectomy) bone (eg, osteomyelitis), clavicle	18.84	680.26	1294	1550	1854
23182	Partial excision (craterization, saucerization, or diaphysectomy) bone (eg, osteomyelitis), scapula	17.98	649.18	1350	1672	1975
23184	Partial excision (craterization, saucerization, or diaphysectomy) bone (eg, osteomyelitis), proximal humerus	20.26	730.66	1895	2385	2751

		Medicare RVU	National Fee	PFR Fee Information 50%	75%	90%
23190	Ostectomy of scapula, partial (eg, superior medial angle)	14.52	522.23	1149	1444	1884
23195	Resection, humeral head	19.45	698.07	2120	2443	2773
23200	Radical resection for tumor; clavicle	23.05	825.03	1975	2526	3040
23210	Radical resection for tumor; scapula	24.00	859.52	2786	3308	3749
23220	Radical resection of bone tumor, proximal humerus;	28.25	1011.86	2748	3427	4154
23221	Radical resection of bone tumor, proximal humerus; with autograft (includes obtaining graft)	31.91	1139.20	3620	4550	5205
23222	Radical resection of bone tumor, proximal humerus; with prosthetic replacement	44.64	1594.73	3747	4547	5281

Introduction or Removal

23330	Removal of foreign body, shoulder; subcutaneous	5.71	209.19	475	684	807
23331	Removal of foreign body, shoulder; deep (eg, Neer hemiarthroplasty removal)	15.35	552.92	1425	1605	2198
23332	Removal of foreign body, shoulder; complicated (eg, total shoulder)	23.27	835.26	2994	3381	3903
23350	Injection procedure for shoulder arthrography or enhanced CT/MRI shoulder arthrography	4.29	158.79	186	289	383

Repair, Revision, and/or Reconstruction

23395	Muscle transfer, any type, shoulder or upper arm; single	33.71	1207.79	2829	3438	3987
23397	Muscle transfer, any type, shoulder or upper arm; multiple	30.33	1086.14	2869	3445	3909
23400	Scapulopexy (eg, Sprengels deformity or for paralysis)	25.73	922.80	2592	3378	4088
23405	Tenotomy, shoulder area; single tendon	16.57	595.75	1536	1812	2407
23406	Tenotomy, shoulder area; multiple tendons through same incision	20.78	745.82	1957	2450	2893
23410	Repair of ruptured musculotendinous cuff (eg, rotator cuff) open; acute	23.82	854.59	2427	2886	3192
23412	Repair of ruptured musculotendinous cuff (eg, rotator cuff) open; chronic	25.36	909.54	2854	3315	3733
23415	Coracoacromial ligament release, with or without acromioplasty	19.48	699.59	1666	2018	2661
	(UNBUNDLING ALERT: 23420 cannot be used with 23412 by the same physician on the same day.)					
23420	Reconstruction of complete shoulder (rotator) cuff avulsion, chronic (includes acromioplasty)	27.66	992.16	3415	3858	4511
23430	Tenodesis of long tendon of biceps	19.57	703.38	1941	2361	2712
23440	Resection or transplantation of long tendon of biceps	20.27	728.01	1894	2028	2430
23450	Capsulorrhaphy, anterior; Putti-Platt procedure or Magnuson type operation	25.35	908.78	2963	3495	4128
23455	Capsulorrhaphy, anterior; with labral repair (eg, Bankart procedure)	27.04	969.42	3163	3634	4045
23460	Capsulorrhaphy, anterior, any type; with bone block	29.23	1047.87	3097	3456	4012
23462	Capsulorrhaphy, anterior, any type; with coracoid process transfer	28.55	1022.47	3131	3645	4049
23465	Capsulorrhaphy, glenohumeral joint, posterior, with or without bone block	29.73	1064.92	3058	3626	4216
23466	Capsulorrhaphy, glenohumeral joint, any type multi-directional instability	29.08	1042.94	3684	4074	4383
23470	Arthroplasty, glenohumeral joint; hemiarthroplasty	32.49	1163.45	3538	4135	4472
	(UNBUNDLING ALERT: 23472 cannot be used with 23130 or 23412 by the same physician on the same day.)					
23472	Arthroplasty, glenohumeral joint; total shoulder (glenoid and proximal humeral replacement (eg, total shoulder))	40.03	1431.39	4994	5692	6315
23480	Osteotomy, clavicle, with or without internal fixation;	21.80	782.58	1660	1962	2257
23485	Osteotomy, clavicle, with or without internal fixation; with bone graft for nonunion or malunion (includes obtaining graft and/or necessary fixation)	25.64	919.01	2303	2820	3589
23490	Prophylactic treatment (nailing, pinning, plating or wiring) with or without methylmethacrylate; clavicle	21.67	775.38	1895	2320	2601
23491	Prophylactic treatment (nailing, pinning, plating or wiring) with or without methylmethacrylate; proximal humerus	27.14	973.59	2416	2938	3468

● = New Code ⊗ = Conscious Sedation ✚ = Add-on Code ∅ = Modifier '51' Exempt ▲ =Revised Code

Fracture and/or Dislocation

(For codes 23500-23680, read carefully. Codes for fractures and dislocations are intermixed in this section.)

Code	Description	Medicare RVU	National Fee	PFR 50%	PFR 75%	PFR 90%
23500	Closed treatment of clavicular fracture; without manipulation	5.24	190.62	350	411	489
23505	Closed treatment of clavicular fracture; with manipulation	8.66	313.79	589	699	763
23515	Open treatment of clavicular fracture, with or without internal or external fixation	15.07	542.69	1587	1867	2123
23520	Closed treatment of sternoclavicular dislocation; without manipulation	5.35	194.41	345	438	505
23525	Closed treatment of sternoclavicular dislocation; with manipulation	8.66	314.17	575	660	780
23530	Open treatment of sternoclavicular dislocation, acute or chronic;	14.34	515.41	1558	1800	2004
23532	Open treatment of sternoclavicular dislocation, acute or chronic; with fascial graft (includes obtaining graft)	16.21	583.62	1768	2005	2342
23540	Closed treatment of acromioclavicular dislocation; without manipulation	5.37	194.79	353	470	562
23545	Closed treatment of acromioclavicular dislocation; with manipulation	7.75	281.20	538	634	732
23550	Open treatment of acromioclavicular dislocation, acute or chronic;	14.89	535.87	2105	2365	2554
23552	Open treatment of acromioclavicular dislocation, acute or chronic; with fascial graft (includes obtaining graft)	17.22	619.25	2406	2556	2772
23570	Closed treatment of scapular fracture; without manipulation	5.60	203.51	392	501	581
23575	Closed treatment of scapular fracture; with manipulation, with or without skeletal traction (with or without shoulder joint involvement)	9.46	342.97	591	710	820
23585	Open treatment of scapular fracture (body, glenoid or acromion) with or without internal fixation	18.06	649.56	2182	2561	2883
23600	Closed treatment of proximal humeral (surgical or anatomical neck) fracture; without manipulation	7.91	288.40	566	656	831
23605	Closed treatment of proximal humeral (surgical or anatomical neck) fracture; with manipulation, with or without skeletal traction	11.75	426.35	968	1156	1627
23615	Open treatment of proximal humeral (surgical or anatomical neck) fracture, with or without internal or external fixation, with or without repair of tuberosity(s);	21.26	764.01	2265	2695	3213
23616	Open treatment of proximal humeral (surgical or anatomical neck) fracture, with or without internal or external fixation, with or without repair of tuberosity(s); with proximal humeral prosthetic replacement	38.89	1391.22	4274	5139	5871
23620	Closed treatment of greater humeral tuberosity fracture; without manipulation	6.42	233.83	524	637	715
23625	Closed treatment of greater humeral tuberosity fracture; with manipulation	9.48	344.11	640	880	1070
23630	Open treatment of greater humeral tuberosity fracture, with or without internal or external fixation	15.14	545.35	1647	1958	2211
23650	Closed treatment of shoulder dislocation, with manipulation; without anesthesia	7.39	266.80	510	610	693
23655	Closed treatment of shoulder dislocation, with manipulation; requiring anesthesia	9.50	342.21	705	825	955
23660	Open treatment of acute shoulder dislocation	15.04	541.18	2027	2303	2585
23665	Closed treatment of shoulder dislocation, with fracture of greater humeral tuberosity, with manipulation	10.46	378.98	755	889	1057
23670	Open treatment of shoulder dislocation, with fracture of greater humeral tuberosity, with or without internal or external fixation	15.98	574.91	2116	2498	2843
23675	Closed treatment of shoulder dislocation, with surgical or anatomical neck fracture, with manipulation	13.80	499.49	937	1160	1439
23680	Open treatment of shoulder dislocation, with surgical or anatomical neck fracture, with or without internal or external fixation	19.90	714.75	2502	2943	3396

Manipulation

Code	Description	Medicare RVU	National Fee	PFR 50%	PFR 75%	PFR 90%
23700	Manipulation under anesthesia, shoulder joint, including application of fixation apparatus (dislocation excluded)	5.09	183.04	645	748	821

Arthrodesis

Code	Description	Medicare RVU	National Fee	PFR 50%	PFR 75%	PFR 90%
23800	Arthrodesis, glenohumeral joint;	26.67	955.02	3254	3983	4518
23802	Arthrodesis, glenohumeral joint; with autogenous graft (includes obtaining graft)	31.28	1116.08	3516	4371	5359

Amputation

Code	Description	Medicare RVU	National Fee	PFR 50%	PFR 75%	PFR 90%
23900	Interthoracoscapular amputation (forequarter)	35.23	1256.68	3891	4650	5137

		Medicare RVU	National Fee	PFR Fee Information 50%	75%	90%
23920	Disarticulation of shoulder;	28.34	1013.00	3031	3634	3998
23921	Disarticulation of shoulder; secondary closure or scar revision	11.42	411.57	979	1167	1363

Other Procedures

23929	Unlisted procedure, shoulder	-	-	IR	IR	IR

Humerus (Upper Arm) and Elbow
Incision

23930	Incision and drainage, upper arm or elbow area; deep abscess or hematoma	9.37	343.73	674	886	1032
23931	Incision and drainage, upper arm or elbow area; bursa	7.60	281.20	605	794	981
23935	Incision, deep, with opening of bone cortex (eg, for osteomyelitis or bone abscess), humerus or elbow	13.04	470.31	1281	1455	1630
24000	Arthrotomy, elbow, including exploration, drainage, or removal of foreign body	12.22	440.37	1676	1884	2249
24006	Arthrotomy of the elbow, with capsular excision for capsular release (separate procedure)	18.61	668.51	1702	2074	2524

Excision

(For biopsy of skin, see codes 11100-11101.)

24065	Biopsy, soft tissue of upper arm or elbow area; superficial	5.72	208.82	354	414	493
24066	Biopsy, soft tissue of upper arm or elbow area; deep (subfascial or intramuscular)	14.82	541.56	759	978	1122
24075	Excision, tumor, soft tissue of upper arm or elbow area; subcutaneous	11.82	432.79	637	711	834
24076	Excision, tumor, soft tissue of upper arm or elbow area; deep (subfascial or intramuscular)	12.11	434.68	1120	1394	1828
24077	Radical resection of tumor (eg, malignant neoplasm), soft tissue of upper arm or elbow area	21.24	759.47	2622	3494	4188
24100	Arthrotomy, elbow; with synovial biopsy only	10.29	371.02	1176	1340	1513
24101	Arthrotomy, elbow; with joint exploration, with or without biopsy, with or without removal of loose or foreign body	12.94	466.90	1835	2121	2356
24102	Arthrotomy, elbow; with synovectomy	16.09	578.69	2230	2478	2775
24105	Excision, olecranon bursa	8.58	311.14	915	1119	1304
24110	Excision or curettage of bone cyst or benign tumor, humerus;	15.16	546.10	1689	1908	2355
24115	Excision or curettage of bone cyst or benign tumor, humerus; with autograft (includes obtaining graft)	18.80	674.20	1959	2459	2842
24116	Excision or curettage of bone cyst or benign tumor, humerus; with allograft	22.90	821.62	2028	2510	3004
24120	Excision or curettage of bone cyst or benign tumor of head or neck of radius or olecranon process;	13.56	488.12	1557	1774	1913
24125	Excision or curettage of bone cyst or benign tumor of head or neck of radius or olecranon process; with autograft (includes obtaining graft)	15.21	545.72	1934	2181	2488
24126	Excision or curettage of bone cyst or benign tumor of head or neck of radius or olecranon process; with allograft	16.49	592.34	1752	2184	2586
24130	Excision, radial head	13.15	474.48	1500	1760	1935
24134	Sequestrectomy (eg, for osteomyelitis or bone abscess), shaft or distal humerus	20.26	729.15	1893	2203	2581
24136	Sequestrectomy (eg, for osteomyelitis or bone abscess), radial head or neck	16.51	594.23	1701	2083	2312
24138	Sequestrectomy (eg, for osteomyelitis or bone abscess), olecranon process	17.19	619.62	1802	2031	2425
24140	Partial excision (craterization, saucerization, or diaphysectomy) bone (eg, osteomyelitis), humerus	19.58	706.03	1910	2396	2748
24145	Partial excision (craterization, saucerization, or diaphysectomy) bone (eg, osteomyelitis), radial head or neck	16.58	599.16	1496	1770	1903
24147	Partial excision (craterization, saucerization, or diaphysectomy) bone (eg, osteomyelitis), olecranon process	17.17	621.52	1346	1507	1747
24149	Radical resection of capsule, soft tissue, and heterotopic bone, elbow, with contracture release (separate procedure)	29.72	1065.68	2632	3127	3680
24150	Radical resection for tumor, shaft or distal humerus;	25.67	920.53	2992	3698	4130
24151	Radical resection for tumor, shaft or distal humerus; with autograft (includes obtaining graft)	29.77	1066.81	3412	4255	4848

● = New Code ⊗ = Conscious Sedation ✚ = Add-on Code ∅ = Modifier '51' Exempt ▲ = Revised Code

		Medicare RVU	National Fee	PFR Fee Information 50%	75%	90%
24152	Radical resection for tumor, radial head or neck;	19.11	685.19	2570	2930	3211
24153	Radical resection for tumor, radial head or neck; with autograft (includes obtaining graft)	17.87	632.51	2931	3371	3773
24155	Resection of elbow joint (arthrectomy)	22.11	792.44	2589	3191	3636

Introduction or Removal

24160	Implant removal; elbow joint	15.82	569.60	1540	1890	2228
24164	Implant removal; radial head	12.93	465.76	1473	1702	2049
24200	Removal of foreign body, upper arm or elbow area; subcutaneous	5.23	191.38	329	390	507
24201	Removal of foreign body, upper arm or elbow area; deep (subfascial or intramuscular)	14.65	537.77	877	985	1192
24220	Injection procedure for elbow arthrography	4.74	174.71	196	236	310

Repair, Revision, and/or Reconstruction

24300	Manipulation, elbow, under anesthesia	10.09	367.61	888	1020	1145
24301	Muscle or tendon transfer, any type, upper arm or elbow, single (excluding 24320-24331)	19.78	710.58	2104	2580	2738
24305	Tendon lengthening, upper arm or elbow, each tendon	15.12	544.21	1033	1293	1516
24310	Tenotomy, open, elbow to shoulder, each tendon	12.38	446.05	894	1115	1325
24320	Tenoplasty, with muscle transfer, with or without free graft, elbow to shoulder, single (Seddon-Brookes type procedure)	19.92	713.99	2450	2817	3061
24330	Flexor-plasty, elbow (eg, Steindler type advancement);	18.85	677.61	1934	2589	3095
24331	Flexor-plasty, elbow (eg, Steindler type advancement); with extensor advancement	20.76	745.44	2253	2647	3060
24332	Tenolysis, triceps	15.53	558.99	1290	1562	1899
24340	Tenodesis of biceps tendon at elbow (separate procedure)	16.06	578.32	1876	2123	2330
24341	Repair, tendon or muscle, upper arm or elbow, each tendon or muscle, primary or secondary (excludes rotator cuff)	18.43	663.21	1947	2370	2655
24342	Reinsertion of ruptured biceps or triceps tendon, distal, with or without tendon graft	20.78	746.58	2484	2770	3087
24343	Repair lateral collateral ligament, elbow, with local tissue	18.30	659.42	1738	2179	2521
24344	Reconstruction lateral collateral ligament, elbow, with tendon graft (includes harvesting of graft)	28.51	1023.23	2620	3194	3668
24345	Repair medial collateral ligament, elbow, with local tissue	18.20	655.63	1750	2177	2433
24346	Reconstruction medial collateral ligament, elbow, with tendon graft (includes harvesting of graft)	28.34	1016.79	2647	3217	3702
24350	Fasciotomy, lateral or medial (eg, tennis elbow or epicondylitis);	11.60	419.15	1000	1208	1465
24351	Fasciotomy, lateral or medial (eg, tennis elbow or epicondylitis); with extensor origin detachment	12.69	458.18	1142	1471	1743
24352	Fasciotomy, lateral or medial (eg, tennis elbow or epicondylitis); with annular ligament resection	13.54	488.50	1385	1650	1801
24354	Fasciotomy, lateral or medial (eg, tennis elbow or epicondylitis); with stripping	13.54	488.12	1270	1498	1703
24356	Fasciotomy, lateral or medial (eg, tennis elbow or epicondylitis); with partial ostectomy	13.92	501.76	1594	1902	2321
24360	Arthroplasty, elbow; with membrane (eg, fascial)	23.70	850.42	3234	3704	4200
24361	Arthroplasty, elbow; with distal humeral prosthetic replacement	26.61	953.88	3129	3801	4269
24362	Arthroplasty, elbow; with implant and fascia lata ligament reconstruction	27.66	990.26	3636	4139	4574
24363	Arthroplasty, elbow; with distal humerus and proximal ulnar prosthetic replacement (eg, total elbow)	38.86	1387.05	4997	5601	6471
24365	Arthroplasty, radial head;	16.81	604.47	1535	1837	2135
24366	Arthroplasty, radial head; with implant	18.01	647.29	1891	2398	2913
24400	Osteotomy, humerus, with or without internal fixation	21.67	778.41	2306	2655	2973
24410	Multiple osteotomies with realignment on intramedullary rod, humeral shaft (Sofield type procedure)	27.62	989.88	2644	3271	3635

		Medicare RVU	National Fee	PFR Fee Information 50%	75%	90%
24420	Osteoplasty, humerus (eg, shortening or lengthening) (excluding 64876)	25.89	929.25	2568	3178	3634
24430	Repair of nonunion or malunion, humerus; without graft (eg, compression technique)	26.93	962.98	2722	3449	3982
24435	Repair of nonunion or malunion, humerus; with iliac or other autograft (includes obtaining graft)	27.66	992.16	3286	3838	4220
24470	Hemiepiphyseal arrest (eg, cubitus varus or valgus, distal humerus)	17.69	636.68	1683	2025	2357
24495	Decompression fasciotomy, forearm, with brachial artery exploration	17.70	639.33	1851	2191	2477
24498	Prophylactic treatment (nailing, pinning, plating or wiring), with or without methylmethacrylate, humeral shaft	23.12	829.96	2142	2658	3246

Fracture and/or Dislocation

24500	Closed treatment of humeral shaft fracture; without manipulation	8.54	311.14	583	704	879
24505	Closed treatment of humeral shaft fracture; with manipulation, with or without skeletal traction	12.56	455.91	1002	1268	1457
24515	Open treatment of humeral shaft fracture with plate/screws, with or without cerclage	23.07	828.82	2304	2664	2978
24516	Treatment of humeral shaft fracture, with insertion of intramedullary implant, with or without cerclage and/or locking screws	22.87	820.86	2489	2861	3223
24530	Closed treatment of supracondylar or transcondylar humeral fracture, with or without intercondylar extension; without manipulation	9.22	335.77	636	751	900
24535	Closed treatment of supracondylar or transcondylar humeral fracture, with or without intercondylar extension; with manipulation, with or without skin or skeletal traction	15.73	569.60	1142	1331	1639
24538	Percutaneous skeletal fixation of supracondylar or transcondylar humeral fracture, with or without intercondylar extension	19.61	706.41	1835	2127	2625
24545	Open treatment of humeral supracondylar or transcondylar fracture, with or without internal or external fixation; without intercondylar extension	20.87	749.61	2438	2854	3206
24546	Open treatment of humeral supracondylar or transcondylar fracture, with or without internal or external fixation; with intercondylar extension	29.61	1061.13	2775	3321	3768
24560	Closed treatment of humeral epicondylar fracture, medial or lateral; without manipulation	7.68	280.06	521	654	746
24565	Closed treatment of humeral epicondylar fracture, medial or lateral; with manipulation	12.99	470.69	940	1116	1368
24566	Percutaneous skeletal fixation of humeral epicondylar fracture, medial or lateral, with manipulation	18.03	649.56	1394	1653	1856
24575	Open treatment of humeral epicondylar fracture, medial or lateral, with or without internal or external fixation	21.02	754.54	1737	2033	2458
24576	Closed treatment of humeral condylar fracture, medial or lateral; without manipulation	8.08	294.84	521	638	717
24577	Closed treatment of humeral condylar fracture, medial or lateral; with manipulation	13.52	490.01	915	1105	1347
24579	Open treatment of humeral condylar fracture, medial or lateral, with or without internal or external fixation	22.59	810.63	1950	2235	2617
24582	Percutaneous skeletal fixation of humeral condylar fracture, medial or lateral, with manipulation	20.26	730.28	1404	1718	1989
24586	Open treatment of periarticular fracture and/or dislocation of the elbow (fracture distal humerus and proximal ulna and/or proximal radius);	29.07	1042.18	2850	3326	3735
24587	Open treatment of periarticular fracture and/or dislocation of the elbow (fracture distal humerus and proximal ulna and/or proximal radius); with implant arthroplasty	28.80	1031.95	3417	3991	4380
24600	Treatment of closed elbow dislocation; without anesthesia	9.39	339.56	540	655	839
24605	Treatment of closed elbow dislocation; requiring anesthesia	11.65	420.66	733	868	1069
24615	Open treatment of acute or chronic elbow dislocation	18.84	676.85	1981	2217	2529
24620	Closed treatment of Monteggia type of fracture dislocation at elbow (fracture proximal end of ulna with dislocation of radial head), with manipulation	14.20	511.24	967	1173	1374
24635	Open treatment of Monteggia type of fracture dislocation at elbow (fracture proximal end of ulna with dislocation of radial head), with or without internal or external fixation	28.95	1045.59	2326	2830	3254
24640	Closed treatment of radial head subluxation in child, nursemaid elbow, with manipulation	3.09	112.56	230	316	405
24650	Closed treatment of radial head or neck fracture; without manipulation	6.26	228.90	451	532	653
24655	Closed treatment of radial head or neck fracture; with manipulation	10.94	397.54	733	875	1009
24665	Open treatment of radial head or neck fracture, with or without internal fixation or radial head excision;	16.90	609.01	1702	2031	2249
24666	Open treatment of radial head or neck fracture, with or without internal fixation or radial head excision; with radial head prosthetic replacement	19.17	689.36	1901	2256	2552

		Medicare RVU	National Fee	PFR Fee Information 50%	75%	90%
24670	Closed treatment of ulnar fracture, proximal end (olecranon process); without manipulation	7.03	256.57	454	554	662
24675	Closed treatment of ulnar fracture, proximal end (olecranon process); with manipulation	11.43	414.98	772	933	1054
24685	Open treatment of ulnar fracture proximal end (olecranon process), with or without internal or external fixation	17.71	637.06	1800	2209	2542

Arthrodesis

24800	Arthrodesis, elbow joint; local	21.38	767.42	2415	2852	3118
24802	Arthrodesis, elbow joint; with autogenous graft (includes obtaining graft)	26.50	950.09	2855	3365	3658

Amputation

24900	Amputation, arm through humerus; with primary closure	18.49	662.45	1842	2148	2492
24920	Amputation, arm through humerus; open, circular (guillotine)	18.46	661.31	1609	1974	2235
24925	Amputation, arm through humerus; secondary closure or scar revision	14.13	508.21	843	1106	1338
24930	Amputation, arm through humerus; re-amputation	19.31	690.87	1663	2013	2385
24931	Amputation, arm through humerus; with implant	21.62	768.56	2020	2407	2778
24935	Stump elongation, upper extremity	26.68	948.95	2612	3132	3591
24940	Cineplasty, upper extremity, complete procedure	-	-	2377	3072	3590

Other Procedures

24999	Unlisted procedure, humerus or elbow	-	-	IR	IR	IR

Forearm and Wrist

Incision

25000	Incision, extensor tendon sheath, wrist (eg, deQuervains disease)	10.41	381.25	1011	1206	1409
25001	Incision, flexor tendon sheath, wrist (eg, flexor carpi radialis)	8.37	303.18	785	917	1061
25020	Decompression fasciotomy, forearm and/or wrist, flexor OR extensor compartment; without debridement of nonviable muscle and/or nerve	15.80	576.04	1314	1544	1791
25023	Decompression fasciotomy, forearm and/or wrist, flexor OR extensor compartment; with debridement of nonviable muscle and/or nerve	29.82	1077.80	1603	1938	2390
25024	Decompression fasciotomy, forearm and/or wrist, flexor AND extensor compartment; without debridement of nonviable muscle and/or nerve	19.40	694.66	1543	1736	2010
25025	Decompression fasciotomy, forearm and/or wrist, flexor AND extensor compartment; with debridement of nonviable muscle and/or nerve	29.36	1044.83	1887	2295	2756
25028	Incision and drainage, forearm and/or wrist; deep abscess or hematoma	13.79	502.52	860	1148	1397
25031	Incision and drainage, forearm and/or wrist; bursa	12.12	443.40	591	740	875
25035	Incision, deep, bone cortex, forearm and/or wrist (eg, osteomyelitis or bone abscess)	21.19	774.25	1359	1733	2010
25040	Arthrotomy, radiocarpal or midcarpal joint, with exploration, drainage, or removal of foreign body	15.52	559.75	1432	1833	2028

Excision

25065	Biopsy, soft tissue of forearm and/or wrist; superficial	5.65	206.54	402	446	513
25066	Biopsy, soft tissue of forearm and/or wrist; deep (subfascial or intramuscular)	11.48	419.15	737	856	1040
25075	Excision, tumor, soft tissue of forearm and/or wrist area; subcutaneous	9.97	363.44	613	765	887
25076	Excision, tumor, soft tissue of forearm and/or wrist area; deep (subfascial or intramuscular)	14.59	533.98	1080	1302	1471
25077	Radical resection of tumor (eg, malignant neoplasm), soft tissue of forearm and/or wrist area	22.62	819.34	2594	2937	3534
25085	Capsulotomy, wrist (eg, contracture)	13.11	475.61	1581	1871	2211
25100	Arthrotomy, wrist joint; with biopsy	9.56	347.14	1292	1502	1686
25101	Arthrotomy, wrist joint; with joint exploration, with or without biopsy, with or without removal of loose or foreign body	11.12	403.23	1345	1526	1723
25105	Arthrotomy, wrist joint; with synovectomy	13.77	499.49	1651	1914	2158

		Medicare RVU	National Fee	PFR Fee Information 50%	75%	90%
25107	Arthrotomy, distal radioulnar joint including repair of triangular cartilage, complex	16.55	598.78	1568	1810	2118
● 25109	Excision of tendon, forearm and/or wrist, flexor or extensor, each	13.09	469.93	1541	1776	2016
25110	Excision, lesion of tendon sheath, forearm and/or wrist	11.19	408.91	769	927	1067
	(A4550 (Disposable Surgical Tray) can be coded in addition to 25111 in the office setting. Payment is at carrier discretion.)					
25111	Excision of ganglion, wrist (dorsal or volar); primary	8.52	309.62	1028	1304	1529
25112	Excision of ganglion, wrist (dorsal or volar); recurrent	10.36	375.19	1186	1379	1719
25115	Radical excision of bursa, synovia of wrist, or forearm tendon sheaths (eg, tenosynovitis, fungus, Tbc, or other granulomas, rheumatoid arthritis); flexors	24.29	883.01	1767	2250	2495
25116	Radical excision of bursa, synovia of wrist, or forearm tendon sheaths (eg, tenosynovitis, fungus, Tbc, or other granulomas, rheumatoid arthritis); extensors, with or without transposition of dorsal retinaculum	20.62	753.40	1840	2190	2570
25118	Synovectomy, extensor tendon sheath, wrist, single compartment;	10.57	383.90	1804	1984	2212
25119	Synovectomy, extensor tendon sheath, wrist, single compartment; with resection of distal ulna	14.23	516.16	1536	1754	2002
25120	Excision or curettage of bone cyst or benign tumor of radius or ulna (excluding head or neck of radius and olecranon process);	18.20	666.24	1588	1759	1953
25125	Excision or curettage of bone cyst or benign tumor of radius or ulna (excluding head or neck of radius and olecranon process); with autograft (includes obtaining graft)	20.43	745.44	1755	2065	2409
25126	Excision or curettage of bone cyst or benign tumor of radius or ulna (excluding head or neck of radius and olecranon process); with allograft	20.85	760.98	1720	2114	2493
25130	Excision or curettage of bone cyst or benign tumor of carpal bones;	12.24	443.40	1494	1857	2118
25135	Excision or curettage of bone cyst or benign tumor of carpal bones; with autograft (includes obtaining graft)	15.16	548.00	1926	2351	2656
25136	Excision or curettage of bone cyst or benign tumor of carpal bones; with allograft	13.39	484.33	1748	2198	2457
25145	Sequestrectomy (eg, for osteomyelitis or bone abscess), forearm and/or wrist	18.52	677.23	1786	2106	2431
25150	Partial excision (craterization, saucerization, or diaphysectomy) of bone (eg, for osteomyelitis); ulna	16.17	585.14	1447	1779	2128
25151	Partial excision (craterization, saucerization, or diaphysectomy) of bone (eg, for osteomyelitis); radius	20.42	745.06	1469	1711	1922
25170	Radical resection for tumor, radius or ulna	27.12	984.58	2590	2943	3279
25210	Carpectomy; one bone	13.38	484.33	1424	1567	1822
25215	Carpectomy; all bones of proximal row	17.49	632.13	2029	2442	2737
25230	Radial styloidectomy (separate procedure)	11.92	431.65	1078	1361	1684
25240	Excision distal ulna partial or complete (eg, Darrach type or matched resection)	12.57	456.29	1448	1631	1756

Introduction or Removal

25246	Injection procedure for wrist arthrography	4.76	174.71	230	262	304
25248	Exploration with removal of deep foreign body, forearm or wrist	13.95	508.96	973	1120	1332
25250	Removal of wrist prosthesis; (separate procedure)	13.59	489.64	1398	1648	1854
25251	Removal of wrist prosthesis; complicated, including total wrist	18.59	667.37	1813	2217	2653
25259	Manipulation, wrist, under anesthesia	10.06	366.47	781	938	1103

Repair, Revision, and/or Reconstruction

25260	Repair, tendon or muscle, flexor, forearm and/or wrist; primary, single, each tendon or muscle	21.38	780.31	1447	1742	2019
25263	Repair, tendon or muscle, flexor, forearm and/or wrist; secondary, single, each tendon or muscle	21.28	776.52	1511	1977	2270
25265	Repair, tendon or muscle, flexor, forearm and/or wrist; secondary, with free graft (includes obtaining graft), each tendon or muscle	24.68	897.41	1811	2239	2709
25270	Repair, tendon or muscle, extensor, forearm and/or wrist; primary, single, each tendon or muscle	18.01	659.42	1200	1411	1623
25272	Repair, tendon or muscle, extensor, forearm and/or wrist; secondary, single, each tendon or muscle	19.90	727.25	1318	1549	1787

● = New Code ⊗ = Conscious Sedation ✚ = Add-on Code ∅ = Modifier '51' Exempt ▲ =Revised Code

		Medicare RVU	National Fee	PFR Fee Information 50%	75%	90%
25274	Repair, tendon or muscle, extensor, forearm and/or wrist; secondary, with free graft (includes obtaining graft), each tendon or muscle	22.71	826.92	1611	2183	2423
25275	Repair, tendon sheath, extensor, forearm and/or wrist, with free graft (includes obtaining graft) (eg, for extensor carpi ulnaris subluxation)	17.46	627.96	1315	1647	1967
25280	Lengthening or shortening of flexor or extensor tendon, forearm and/or wrist, single, each tendon	19.96	728.77	1350	1630	1792
25290	Tenotomy, open, flexor or extensor tendon, forearm and/or wrist, single, each tendon	19.69	725.74	1008	1231	1486
25295	Tenolysis, flexor or extensor tendon, forearm and/or wrist, single, each tendon	18.77	686.32	1288	1510	1709
25300	Tenodesis at wrist; flexors of fingers	18.30	659.80	1889	2221	2520
25301	Tenodesis at wrist; extensors of fingers	17.51	631.37	1632	1999	2156
25310	Tendon transplantation or transfer, flexor or extensor, forearm and/or wrist, single; each tendon	21.46	781.83	1807	2229	2726
25312	Tendon transplantation or transfer, flexor or extensor, forearm and/or wrist, single; with tendon graft(s) (includes obtaining graft), each tendon	23.98	871.64	1997	2357	2745
25315	Flexor origin slide (eg, for cerebral palsy, Volkmann contracture), forearm and/or wrist;	25.46	924.70	2124	2529	2956
25316	Flexor origin slide (eg, for cerebral palsy, Volkmann contracture), forearm and/or wrist; with tendon(s) transfer	29.45	1067.57	2545	2901	3324
25320	Capsulorrhaphy or reconstruction, wrist, open (eg, capsulodesis, ligament repair, tendon transfer or graft) (includes synovectomy, capsulotomy and open reduction) for carpal instability	25.15	905.75	2410	3124	3765
25332	Arthroplasty, wrist, with or without interposition, with or without external or internal fixation	22.27	799.64	2464	2655	3192
25335	Centralization of wrist on ulna (eg, radial club hand)	25.64	921.29	3516	4148	4670
25337	Reconstruction for stabilization of unstable distal ulna or distal radioulnar joint, secondary by soft tissue stabilization (eg, tendon transfer, tendon graft or weave, or tenodesis) with or without open reduction of distal radioulnar joint	23.72	855.35	2165	2588	2819
25350	Osteotomy, radius; distal third	23.23	846.25	1765	2060	2388
25355	Osteotomy, radius; middle or proximal third	25.63	931.52	2182	2453	2718
25360	Osteotomy; ulna	22.71	827.68	1662	2043	2465
25365	Osteotomy; radius AND ulna	29.43	1066.81	2383	2731	3158
25370	Multiple osteotomies, with realignment on intramedullary rod (Sofield type procedure); radius OR ulna	31.26	1131.62	2360	2862	3204
25375	Multiple osteotomies, with realignment on intramedullary rod (Sofield type procedure); radius AND ulna	30.83	1117.22	2884	3357	3834
25390	Osteoplasty, radius OR ulna; shortening	25.66	932.28	2132	2804	3183
25391	Osteoplasty, radius OR ulna; lengthening with autograft	31.70	1147.54	2416	2999	3435
25392	Osteoplasty, radius AND ulna; shortening (excluding 64876)	31.49	1138.44	2514	3156	3686
25393	Osteoplasty, radius AND ulna; lengthening with autograft	35.74	1291.93	2877	3354	3840
25394	Osteoplasty, carpal bone, shortening	20.06	719.29	1659	2062	2493
25400	Repair of nonunion or malunion, radius OR ulna; without graft (eg, compression technique)	26.93	978.13	1997	2504	2981
25405	Repair of nonunion or malunion, radius OR ulna; with autograft (includes obtaining graft)	33.14	1199.08	2626	3191	3522
25415	Repair of nonunion or malunion, radius AND ulna; without graft (eg, compression technique)	30.98	1122.14	2340	2819	3273
25420	Repair of nonunion or malunion, radius AND ulna; with autograft (includes obtaining graft)	36.42	1315.80	2887	3442	3844
25425	Repair of defect with autograft; radius OR ulna	35.26	1284.35	2307	2762	3218
25426	Repair of defect with autograft; radius AND ulna	34.40	1241.52	2883	3368	3890
25430	Insertion of vascular pedicle into carpal bone (eg, Hori procedure)	18.12	650.32	1365	1758	2182
25431	Repair of nonunion of carpal bone (excluding carpal scaphoid (navicular)) (includes obtaining graft and necessary fixation), each bone	20.79	746.96	1514	1816	2181
25440	Repair of nonunion, scaphoid carpal (navicular) bone, with or without radial styloidectomy (includes obtaining graft and necessary fixation)	21.13	760.60	2371	2684	2927

● = New Code ⊗ = Conscious Sedation ✚ = Add-on Code ∅ = Modifier '51' Exempt ▲ =Revised Code

		Medicare RVU	National Fee	PFR Fee Information 50%	75%	90%
25441	Arthroplasty with prosthetic replacement; distal radius	24.89	893.24	2418	2885	3220
25442	Arthroplasty with prosthetic replacement; distal ulna	21.03	755.30	1943	2567	2927
25443	Arthroplasty with prosthetic replacement; scaphoid carpal (navicular)	20.14	723.08	2023	2461	2951
25444	Arthroplasty with prosthetic replacement; lunate	21.71	779.93	2191	2776	3390
25445	Arthroplasty with prosthetic replacement; trapezium	19.00	682.91	2146	2699	3402
25446	Arthroplasty with prosthetic replacement; distal radius and partial or entire carpus (total wrist)	31.08	1112.29	3734	4319	4768
25447	Arthroplasty, interposition, intercarpal or carpometacarpal joints	21.04	755.68	2507	2930	3225
25449	Revision of arthroplasty, including removal of implant, wrist joint	27.32	978.89	2064	2530	2932
25450	Epiphyseal arrest by epiphysiodesis or stapling; distal radius OR ulna	18.76	680.64	1189	1366	1658
25455	Epiphyseal arrest by epiphysiodesis or stapling; distal radius AND ulna	20.28	732.18	1691	2094	2412
25490	Prophylactic treatment (nailing, pinning, plating or wiring) with or without methylmethacrylate; radius	23.71	861.79	1824	2201	2533
25491	Prophylactic treatment (nailing, pinning, plating or wiring) with or without methylmethacrylate; ulna	24.90	905.37	1761	2143	2445
25492	Prophylactic treatment (nailing, pinning, plating or wiring) with or without methylmethacrylate; radius AND ulna	28.79	1043.32	2145	2625	3052

Fracture and/or Dislocation

		Medicare RVU	National Fee	50%	75%	90%
25500	Closed treatment of radial shaft fracture; without manipulation	6.37	231.93	484	600	748
25505	Closed treatment of radial shaft fracture; with manipulation	12.57	456.29	886	1082	1324
25515	Open treatment of radial shaft fracture, with or without internal or external fixation	18.25	656.01	1700	2064	2439
25520	Closed treatment of radial shaft fracture and closed treatment of dislocation of distal radioulnar joint (Galeazzi fracture/dislocation)	14.08	509.34	1399	1505	1647
25525	Open treatment of radial shaft fracture, with internal and/or external fixation and closed treatment of dislocation of distal radioulnar joint (Galeazzi fracture/dislocation), with or without percutaneous skeletal fixation	24.51	880.36	2254	2713	3031
25526	Open treatment of radial shaft fracture, with internal and/or external fixation and open treatment, with or without internal or external fixation of distal radioulnar joint (Galeazzi fracture/dislocation), includes repair of triangular fibrocartilage complex	28.32	1022.10	2444	2954	3292
25530	Closed treatment of ulnar shaft fracture; without manipulation	6.18	225.87	485	602	704
25535	Closed treatment of ulnar shaft fracture; with manipulation	12.04	436.20	835	1000	1210
25545	Open treatment of ulnar shaft fracture, with or without internal or external fixation	18.03	648.81	1791	2044	2386
25560	Closed treatment of radial and ulnar shaft fractures; without manipulation	6.46	235.34	521	670	776
25565	Closed treatment of radial and ulnar shaft fractures; with manipulation	13.16	477.13	1056	1318	1615
25574	Open treatment of radial AND ulnar shaft fractures, with internal or external fixation; of radius OR ulna	15.74	568.08	2323	2540	2725
25575	Open treatment of radial AND ulnar shaft fractures, with internal or external fixation; of radius AND ulna	23.23	834.50	2459	2812	3071
	(UNBUNDLING ALERT: 25600 cannot be used with 29125 by the same physician on the same day.)					
▲ 25600	Closed treatment of distal radial fracture (eg, Colles or Smith type) or epiphyseal separation, includes closed treatment of fracture of ulnar styloid, when performed; without manipulation	7.10	258.84	566	670	787
	(UNBUNDLING ALERT: 25605 cannot be used with 25600, 29075, or 29125 by the same physician on the same day.)					
25605	Closed treatment of distal radial fracture (eg, Colles or Smith type) or epiphyseal separation, includes closed treatment of fracture of ulnar styloid, when performed; with manipulation	15.17	548.00	922	1120	1273
● 25606	Percutaneous skeletal fixation of distal radial fracture or epiphyseal separation	17.77	642.74	1308	1610	1893
● 25607	Open treatment of distal radial extra-articular fracture or epiphyseal separation, with internal fixation	17.97	645.39	1322	1628	1914
● 25608	Open treatment of distal radial intra-articular fracture or epiphyseal separation; with internal fixation of 2 fragments	20.58	738.62	1514	1864	2192
● 25609	Open treatment of distal radial intra-articular fracture or epiphyseal separation; with internal fixation of 3 or more fragments	26.27	941.75	1933	2379	2798
25622	Closed treatment of carpal scaphoid (navicular) fracture; without manipulation	7.27	265.28	521	718	884

● = New Code ⊗ = Conscious Sedation ✚ = Add-on Code ∅ = Modifier '51' Exempt ▲ =Revised Code

		Medicare RVU	National Fee	PFR Fee Information 50%	75%	90%
25624	Closed treatment of carpal scaphoid (navicular) fracture; with manipulation	11.50	418.39	801	955	1087
25628	Open treatment of carpal scaphoid (navicular) fracture, with or without internal or external fixation	18.58	667.75	1686	2060	2380
25630	Closed treatment of carpal bone fracture (excluding carpal scaphoid (navicular)); without manipulation, each bone	7.47	271.73	515	617	748
25635	Closed treatment of carpal bone fracture (excluding carpal scaphoid (navicular)); with manipulation, each bone	11.01	400.20	786	923	1142
25645	Open treatment of carpal bone fracture (other than carpal scaphoid (navicular)), each bone	14.94	538.14	1284	1634	2008
25650	Closed treatment of ulnar styloid fracture	7.77	282.72	705	810	924
25651	Percutaneous skeletal fixation of ulnar styloid fracture	11.94	430.89	825	1001	1211
25652	Open treatment of ulnar styloid fracture	15.94	573.77	1289	1523	1891
25660	Closed treatment of radiocarpal or intercarpal dislocation, one or more bones, with manipulation	10.08	363.44	789	914	1246
25670	Open treatment of radiocarpal or intercarpal dislocation, one or more bones	16.01	576.42	1496	1760	1965
25671	Percutaneous skeletal fixation of distal radioulnar dislocation	13.32	480.54	945	1171	1437
25675	Closed treatment of distal radioulnar dislocation with manipulation	10.83	392.24	646	833	974
25676	Open treatment of distal radioulnar dislocation, acute or chronic	16.56	596.51	1462	1717	1978
25680	Closed treatment of trans-scaphoperilunar type of fracture dislocation, with manipulation	11.52	413.46	1014	1128	1336
25685	Open treatment of trans-scaphoperilunar type of fracture dislocation	19.11	686.32	2007	2386	2713
25690	Closed treatment of lunate dislocation, with manipulation	11.80	425.97	976	1178	1474
25695	Open treatment of lunate dislocation	16.60	596.89	1769	2017	2233

Arthrodesis

25800	Arthrodesis, wrist; complete, without bone graft (includes radiocarpal and/or intercarpal and/or carpometacarpal joints)	20.17	726.50	2308	2731	2973
25805	Arthrodesis, wrist; with sliding graft	23.15	832.99	2416	2918	3512
25810	Arthrodesis, wrist; with iliac or other autograft (includes obtaining graft)	23.01	827.30	2893	3502	3980
25820	Arthrodesis, wrist; limited, without bone graft (eg, intercarpal or radiocarpal)	16.21	585.52	2174	2485	2674
25825	Arthrodesis, wrist; with autograft (includes obtaining graft)	19.78	713.23	2742	3212	3651
25830	Arthrodesis, distal radioulnar joint with segmental resection of ulna, with or without bone graft (eg, Sauve-Kapandji procedure)	25.67	931.90	2354	2901	3286

Amputation

25900	Amputation, forearm, through radius and ulna;	22.50	816.69	1910	2256	2467
25905	Amputation, forearm, through radius and ulna; open, circular (guillotine)	22.22	806.08	1636	1952	2208
25907	Amputation, forearm, through radius and ulna; secondary closure or scar revision	19.85	721.95	966	1209	1605
25909	Amputation, forearm, through radius and ulna; re-amputation	22.11	802.67	1764	2023	2343
25915	Krukenberg procedure	36.51	1317.32	2442	3052	3498
25920	Disarticulation through wrist;	17.85	642.36	1619	1952	2228
25922	Disarticulation through wrist; secondary closure or scar revision	15.59	562.02	916	1182	1401
25924	Disarticulation through wrist; re-amputation	17.78	640.47	1554	1897	2131
25927	Transmetacarpal amputation;	21.17	768.18	1804	2051	2239
25929	Transmetacarpal amputation; secondary closure or scar revision	14.62	524.50	936	1265	1616
25931	Transmetacarpal amputation; re-amputation	19.82	720.81	1559	1948	2209

Other Procedures

25999	Unlisted procedure, forearm or wrist	-	-	IR	IR	IR

● = New Code ⊗ = Conscious Sedation ✚ = Add-on Code ∅ = Modifier '51' Exempt ▲ =Revised Code

		Medicare National		PFR Fee Information		
		RVU	Fee	50%	75%	90%

Hand and Fingers

Incision

(Medicare fees for the code below are based on Non Facility RVUs. PFR information reflects fee when procedure is performed in a facility.)

26010	Drainage of finger abscess; simple	6.91	255.81	227	304	401
26011	Drainage of finger abscess; complicated (eg, felon)	10.71	397.54	528	651	737
26020	Drainage of tendon sheath, digit and/or palm, each	10.91	394.51	975	1443	1673
26025	Drainage of palmar bursa; single, bursa	10.71	386.93	1107	1431	1674
26030	Drainage of palmar bursa; multiple bursa	12.63	455.15	1934	2188	2467
26034	Incision, bone cortex, hand or finger (eg, osteomyelitis or bone abscess)	13.66	493.05	1255	1729	1955
26035	Decompression fingers and/or hand, injection injury (eg, grease gun)	20.54	735.97	2141	2443	3152
26037	Decompressive fasciotomy, hand (excludes 26035)	14.74	530.19	1773	2154	2431
26040	Fasciotomy, palmar (eg, Dupuytren's contracture); percutaneous	7.86	284.99	766	1091	1449
26045	Fasciotomy, palmar (eg, Dupuytren's contracture); open, partial	12.01	433.55	1283	1443	1723

(UNBUNDLING ALERT: 26055 cannot be used with 29125 by the same physician on the same day.)

26055	Tendon sheath incision (eg, for trigger finger)	16.45	612.04	919	1128	1331
26060	Tenotomy, percutaneous, single, each digit	6.70	242.92	502	601	710
26070	Arthrotomy, with exploration, drainage, or removal of loose or foreign body; carpometacarpal joint	7.49	269.45	850	956	1058
26075	Arthrotomy, with exploration, drainage, or removal of loose or foreign body; metacarpophalangeal joint, each	8.05	290.29	1040	1251	1429
26080	Arthrotomy, with exploration, drainage, or removal of loose or foreign body; interphalangeal joint, each	9.75	352.83	877	1058	1221

Excision

26100	Arthrotomy with biopsy; carpometacarpal joint, each	8.24	298.25	890	985	1136
26105	Arthrotomy with biopsy; metacarpophalangeal joint, each	8.45	305.83	886	1072	1182
26110	Arthrotomy with biopsy; interphalangeal joint, each	8.04	291.05	753	868	938
26115	Excision, tumor or vascular malformation, soft tissue of hand or finger; subcutaneous	16.78	621.14	773	1060	1239
26116	Excision, tumor or vascular malformation, soft tissue of hand or finger; deep (subfascial or intramuscular)	12.29	444.54	1213	1449	1569
26117	Radical resection of tumor (eg, malignant neoplasm), soft tissue of hand or finger	16.75	601.81	2394	2865	3523
26121	Fasciectomy, palm only, with or without Z-plasty, other local tissue rearrangement, or skin grafting (includes obtaining graft)	15.50	558.23	2259	2691	3080
26123	Fasciectomy, partial palmar with release of single digit including proximal interphalangeal joint, with or without Z-plasty, other local tissue rearrangement, or skin grafting (includes obtaining graft);	20.78	746.96	2470	2929	3333
✚ 26125	Fasciectomy, partial palmar with release of single digit including proximal interphalangeal joint, with or without Z-plasty, other local tissue rearrangement, or skin grafting (includes obtaining graft); each additional digit (List separately in addition to code for primary procedure)	7.61	270.97	1075	1574	1927
26130	Synovectomy, carpometacarpal joint	11.65	420.66	1374	1613	1978
26135	Synovectomy, metacarpophalangeal joint including intrinsic release and extensor hood reconstruction, each digit	14.32	515.78	1512	1911	2322
26140	Synovectomy, proximal interphalangeal joint, including extensor reconstruction, each interphalangeal joint	12.99	468.41	1344	1743	2037
26145	Synovectomy, tendon sheath, radical (tenosynovectomy), flexor tendon, palm and/or finger, each tendon	13.20	475.99	1477	1774	2049
26160	Excision of lesion of tendon sheath or joint capsule (eg, cyst, mucous cyst, or ganglion), hand or finger	15.48	573.39	870	1001	1185
▲ 26170	Excision of tendon, palm, flexor or extensor, single, each tendon	10.32	372.91	856	1012	1200
▲ 26180	Excision of tendon, finger, flexor or extensor, each tendon	11.28	407.40	880	951	1297
26185	Sesamoidectomy, thumb or finger (separate procedure)	13.11	472.58	851	1024	1302

● = New Code ⊗ = Conscious Sedation ✚ = Add-on Code ∅ = Modifier '51' Exempt ▲ =Revised Code

		Medicare RVU	National Fee	PFR Fee Information 50%	75%	90%
26200	Excision or curettage of bone cyst or benign tumor of metacarpal;	11.60	418.39	1117	1263	1517
26205	Excision or curettage of bone cyst or benign tumor of metacarpal; with autograft (includes obtaining graft)	15.66	563.54	1557	1770	1944
26210	Excision or curettage of bone cyst or benign tumor of proximal, middle, or distal phalanx of finger;	11.26	407.02	993	1272	1463
26215	Excision or curettage of bone cyst or benign tumor of proximal, middle, or distal phalanx of finger; with autograft (includes obtaining graft)	14.27	513.51	1287	1664	1881
26230	Partial excision (craterization, saucerization, or diaphysectomy) bone (eg, osteomyelitis); metacarpal	13.09	471.82	1112	1418	1672
26235	Partial excision (craterization, saucerization, or diaphysectomy) bone (eg, osteomyelitis); proximal or middle phalanx of finger	12.80	461.21	991	1178	1376
26236	Partial excision (craterization, saucerization, or diaphysectomy) bone (eg, osteomyelitis); distal phalanx of finger	11.32	408.54	888	1098	1312
26250	Radical resection, metacarpal (eg, tumor);	14.81	532.08	1562	1859	2243
26255	Radical resection, metacarpal (eg, tumor); with autograft (includes obtaining graft)	23.65	847.39	2092	2489	2928
26260	Radical resection, proximal or middle phalanx of finger (eg, tumor);	14.09	507.07	1616	1835	1994
26261	Radical resection, proximal or middle phalanx of finger (eg, tumor); with autograft (includes obtaining graft)	16.81	601.81	1890	2312	2535
26262	Radical resection, distal phalanx of finger (eg, tumor)	11.77	424.07	1475	1648	1804

Introduction or Removal

26320	Removal of implant from finger or hand	8.80	318.34	828	1069	1186

Repair, Revision, and/or Reconstruction

26340	Manipulation, finger joint, under anesthesia, each joint	7.83	286.88	575	676	750
26350	Repair or advancement, flexor tendon, not in zone 2 digital flexor tendon sheath (eg, no man's land); primary or secondary without free graft, each tendon	20.33	747.34	1836	2330	2681
26352	Repair or advancement, flexor tendon, not in zone 2 digital flexor tendon sheath (eg, no man's land); secondary with free graft (includes obtaining graft), each tendon	22.91	838.67	2134	2647	2828
26356	Repair or advancement, flexor tendon, in zone 2 digital flexor tendon sheath (eg, no man's land); primary, without free graft, each tendon	28.65	1046.73	2244	2746	3062
26357	Repair or advancement, flexor tendon, in zone 2 digital flexor tendon sheath (eg, no man's land); secondary, without free graft, each tendon	24.27	886.80	2536	2838	3033
26358	Repair or advancement, flexor tendon, in zone 2 digital flexor tendon sheath (eg, no man's land); secondary, with free graft (includes obtaining graft), each tendon	25.79	942.13	2644	3138	3519
26370	Repair or advancement of profundus tendon, with intact superficialis tendon; primary, each tendon	22.00	806.46	1888	2176	2468
26372	Repair or advancement of profundus tendon, with intact superficialis tendon; secondary with free graft (includes obtaining graft), each tendon	25.32	925.84	2080	2482	2802
26373	Repair or advancement of profundus tendon, with intact superficialis tendon; secondary without free graft, each tendon	24.10	881.87	1909	2393	2885
26390	Excision flexor tendon, with implantation of synthetic rod for delayed tendon graft, hand or finger, each rod	22.95	834.12	1788	2201	2696
26392	Removal of synthetic rod and insertion of flexor tendon graft, hand or finger (includes obtaining graft), each rod	27.26	993.67	2001	2672	3007
26410	Repair, extensor tendon, hand, primary or secondary; without free graft, each tendon	16.26	598.40	1102	1375	1577
26412	Repair, extensor tendon, hand, primary or secondary; with free graft (includes obtaining graft), each tendon	19.43	712.09	1426	1721	2076
26415	Excision of extensor tendon, with implantation of synthetic rod for delayed tendon graft, hand or finger, each rod	19.90	721.95	1462	1712	2014
26416	Removal of synthetic rod and insertion of extensor tendon graft (includes obtaining graft), hand or finger, each rod	23.35	848.90	1770	2238	2690
26418	Repair, extensor tendon, finger, primary or secondary; without free graft, each tendon	16.26	599.54	1094	1450	1679
26420	Repair, extensor tendon, finger, primary or secondary; with free graft (includes obtaining graft) each tendon	20.31	743.55	1506	1732	1952
26426	Repair of extensor tendon, central slip, secondary (eg, boutonniere deformity); using local tissue(s), including lateral band(s), each finger	19.17	703.00	1520	1789	1972
26428	Repair of extensor tendon, central slip, secondary (eg, boutonniere deformity); with free graft (includes obtaining graft), each finger	21.09	771.59	1894	2113	2365
26432	Closed treatment of distal extensor tendon insertion, with or without percutaneous pinning (eg, mallet finger)	14.08	518.06	999	1196	1412

● = New Code ⊗ = Conscious Sedation ✚ = Add-on Code ∅ = Modifier '51' Exempt ▲ =Revised Code

Code	Description	Medicare RVU	National Fee	50%	75%	90%
26433	Repair of extensor tendon, distal insertion, primary or secondary; without graft (eg, mallet finger)	15.16	557.09	1319	1692	1856
26434	Repair of extensor tendon, distal insertion, primary or secondary; with free graft (includes obtaining graft)	17.71	647.67	1405	1553	1758
26437	Realignment of extensor tendon, hand, each tendon	17.38	636.30	1291	1515	1620
26440	Tenolysis, flexor tendon; palm OR finger, each tendon	18.00	662.83	1179	1424	1708
26442	Tenolysis, flexor tendon; palm AND finger, each tendon	25.57	932.66	1544	1822	2096
26445	Tenolysis, extensor tendon, hand OR finger, each tendon	16.89	623.41	1167	1385	1555
26449	Tenolysis, complex, extensor tendon, finger, including forearm, each tendon	24.06	879.98	1497	1769	1914
26450	Tenotomy, flexor, palm, open, each tendon	11.08	405.88	753	852	905
26455	Tenotomy, flexor, finger, open, each tendon	10.99	402.47	834	1010	1165
26460	Tenotomy, extensor, hand or finger, open, each tendon	10.66	390.72	742	954	1184
26471	Tenodesis; of proximal interphalangeal joint, each joint	17.02	623.03	1420	1661	1865
26474	Tenodesis; of distal joint, each joint	16.56	607.12	981	1156	1400
26476	Lengthening of tendon, extensor, hand or finger, each tendon	16.08	589.31	986	1189	1335
26477	Shortening of tendon, extensor, hand or finger, each tendon	16.19	593.85	995	1259	1507
26478	Lengthening of tendon, flexor, hand or finger, each tendon	17.55	642.74	1318	1554	1712
26479	Shortening of tendon, flexor, hand or finger, each tendon	17.32	634.40	1228	1529	1744
26480	Transfer or transplant of tendon, carpometacarpal area or dorsum of hand; without free graft, each tendon	21.46	787.51	1705	1952	2446
26483	Transfer or transplant of tendon, carpometacarpal area or dorsum of hand; with free tendon graft (includes obtaining graft), each tendon	23.80	870.13	1964	2293	2635
26485	Transfer or transplant of tendon, palmar; without free tendon graft, each tendon	22.93	839.43	2012	2510	2772
26489	Transfer or transplant of tendon, palmar; with free tendon graft (includes obtaining graft), each tendon	22.62	820.10	2177	2503	2935
26490	Opponensplasty; superficialis tendon transfer type, each tendon	21.54	784.10	1770	2294	2890
26492	Opponensplasty; tendon transfer with graft (includes obtaining graft), each tendon	23.76	863.31	2130	2548	2906
26494	Opponensplasty; hypothenar muscle transfer	21.80	793.57	2047	2309	2604
26496	Opponensplasty; other methods	23.41	850.42	2220	2588	2937
26497	Transfer of tendon to restore intrinsic function; ring and small finger	23.59	857.24	2145	2518	2870
26498	Transfer of tendon to restore intrinsic function; all four fingers	31.20	1128.59	2560	2800	3672
26499	Correction claw finger, other methods	22.38	813.66	2080	2478	2815
26500	Reconstruction of tendon pulley, each tendon; with local tissues (separate procedure)	17.46	638.57	1136	1347	1606
26502	Reconstruction of tendon pulley, each tendon; with tendon or fascial graft (includes obtaining graft) (separate procedure)	19.44	709.44	1415	1967	2294
26508	Release of thenar muscle(s) (eg, thumb contracture)	17.75	649.56	1302	1611	1942
26510	Cross intrinsic transfer, each tendon	16.68	611.29	1797	2205	2476
26516	Capsulodesis, metacarpophalangeal joint; single digit	19.54	712.85	1452	1786	2026
26517	Capsulodesis, metacarpophalangeal joint; two digits	22.82	830.71	1651	1982	2214
26518	Capsulodesis, metacarpophalangeal joint; three or four digits	22.85	831.09	2090	2462	2814
26520	Capsulectomy or capsulotomy; metacarpophalangeal joint, each joint	18.78	691.25	1479	1850	2092
26525	Capsulectomy or capsulotomy; interphalangeal joint, each joint	18.89	695.42	1450	1980	2353
26530	Arthroplasty, metacarpophalangeal joint; each joint	13.77	496.08	1616	1894	2162
26531	Arthroplasty, metacarpophalangeal joint; with prosthetic implant, each joint	16.06	578.32	1846	2148	2410
26535	Arthroplasty, interphalangeal joint; each joint	9.84	352.83	1483	1708	1901

© PFR 2007
● = New Code ⊗ = Conscious Sedation ✚ = Add-on Code ∅ = Modifier '51' Exempt ▲ =Revised Code

		Medicare RVU	National Fee	PFR Fee Information 50%	75%	90%
26536	Arthroplasty, interphalangeal joint; with prosthetic implant, each joint	16.93	616.97	1771	2175	2466
26540	Repair of collateral ligament, metacarpophalangeal or interphalangeal joint	18.39	672.30	1690	1956	2095
26541	Reconstruction, collateral ligament, metacarpophalangeal joint, single; with tendon or fascial graft (includes obtaining graft)	22.28	811.39	2001	2512	2918
26542	Reconstruction, collateral ligament, metacarpophalangeal joint, single; with local tissue (eg, adductor advancement)	18.92	690.87	1919	2212	2579
26545	Reconstruction, collateral ligament, interphalangeal joint, single, including graft, each joint	19.23	702.24	1513	1880	2221
26546	Repair non-union, metacarpal or phalanx, (includes obtaining bone graft with or without external or internal fixation)	26.11	949.33	1673	2031	2427
26548	Repair and reconstruction, finger, volar plate, interphalangeal joint	21.15	770.84	1817	2128	2274
26550	Pollicization of a digit	41.06	1473.83	3798	4769	5462
26551	Transfer, toe-to-hand with microvascular anastomosis; great toe wrap-around with bone graft	85.97	3074.25	8223	9719	12594
26553	Transfer, toe-to-hand with microvascular anastomosis; other than great toe, single	72.52	2565.66	7774	9488	10487
26554	Transfer, toe-to-hand with microvascular anastomosis; other than great toe, double	99.16	3541.52	9180	11349	12937
26555	Transfer, finger to another position without microvascular anastomosis	36.55	1320.73	2838	3390	3781
26556	Transfer, free toe joint, with microvascular anastomosis	81.46	2898.78	8004	9911	11403
26560	Repair of syndactyly (web finger) each web space; with skin flaps	15.41	563.16	1528	1852	2130
26561	Repair of syndactyly (web finger) each web space; with skin flaps and grafts	24.06	870.13	2120	2686	3271
26562	Repair of syndactyly (web finger) each web space; complex (eg, involving bone, nails)	35.03	1265.02	2718	3385	4083
26565	Osteotomy; metacarpal, each	18.79	686.32	1417	1938	2057
26567	Osteotomy; phalanx of finger, each	18.93	691.25	1373	1793	1990
26568	Osteoplasty, lengthening, metacarpal or phalanx	24.76	903.48	1998	2424	2863
26580	Repair cleft hand	34.86	1246.83	3060	3454	3715
26587	Reconstruction of polydactylous digit, soft tissue and bone	24.92	889.83	1701	1995	2713
26590	Repair macrodactylia, each digit	34.38	1232.43	2528	3031	3476
26591	Repair, intrinsic muscles of hand, each muscle	12.57	463.87	1600	1807	2014
26593	Release, intrinsic muscles of hand, each muscle	16.45	602.95	1429	1669	1849
26596	Excision of constricting ring of finger, with multiple Z-plasties	18.94	683.29	1658	1885	2253

Fracture and/or Dislocation

		Medicare RVU	National Fee	PFR Fee Information 50%	75%	90%
26600	Closed treatment of metacarpal fracture, single; without manipulation, each bone	6.45	234.96	394	487	586
26605	Closed treatment of metacarpal fracture, single; with manipulation, each bone	7.85	286.51	551	653	792
26607	Closed treatment of metacarpal fracture, with manipulation, with external fixation, each bone	12.20	441.88	992	1185	1350
26608	Percutaneous skeletal fixation of metacarpal fracture, each bone	12.32	446.05	1131	1435	1601
26615	Open treatment of metacarpal fracture, single, with or without internal or external fixation, each bone	11.41	411.95	1382	1674	1876
26641	Closed treatment of carpometacarpal dislocation, thumb, with manipulation	8.87	320.99	527	634	727
26645	Closed treatment of carpometacarpal fracture dislocation, thumb (Bennett fracture), with manipulation	10.17	368.36	661	799	906
26650	Percutaneous skeletal fixation of carpometacarpal fracture dislocation, thumb (Bennett fracture), with manipulation, with or without external fixation	13.17	477.13	1144	1333	1495
26665	Open treatment of carpometacarpal fracture dislocation, thumb (Bennett fracture), with or without internal or external fixation	15.06	541.18	1802	1982	2308
26670	Closed treatment of carpometacarpal dislocation, other than thumb, with manipulation, each joint; without anesthesia	8.21	296.74	461	576	717
26675	Closed treatment of carpometacarpal dislocation, other than thumb, with manipulation, each joint; requiring anesthesia	10.80	391.48	775	894	1102

● = New Code ⊗ = Conscious Sedation ✚ = Add-on Code ∅ = Modifier '51' Exempt ▲ =Revised Code

Code	Description	Medicare RVU	National Fee	PFR Fee Information 50%	75%	90%
26676	Percutaneous skeletal fixation of carpometacarpal dislocation, other than thumb, with manipulation, each joint	12.93	468.79	926	1145	1398
26685	Open treatment of carpometacarpal dislocation, other than thumb; with or without internal or external fixation, each joint	14.15	509.34	1330	1572	1906
26686	Open treatment of carpometacarpal dislocation, other than thumb; complex, multiple or delayed reduction	16.02	576.42	1564	1996	2331
26700	Closed treatment of metacarpophalangeal dislocation, single, with manipulation; without anesthesia	7.74	278.93	422	492	571
26705	Closed treatment of metacarpophalangeal dislocation, single, with manipulation; requiring anesthesia	10.12	367.23	613	744	895
26706	Percutaneous skeletal fixation of metacarpophalangeal dislocation, single, with manipulation	11.00	397.17	796	1056	1243
26715	Open treatment of metacarpophalangeal dislocation, single, with or without internal or external fixation	12.07	435.44	1166	1322	1522
26720	Closed treatment of phalangeal shaft fracture, proximal or middle phalanx, finger or thumb; without manipulation, each	4.67	170.54	306	382	461
26725	Closed treatment of phalangeal shaft fracture, proximal or middle phalanx, finger or thumb; with manipulation, with or without skin or skeletal traction, each	8.52	310.00	531	644	740
26727	Percutaneous skeletal fixation of unstable phalangeal shaft fracture, proximal or middle phalanx, finger or thumb, with manipulation, each	12.12	439.23	951	1113	1175
26735	Open treatment of phalangeal shaft fracture, proximal or middle phalanx, finger or thumb, with or without internal or external fixation, each	12.40	446.81	1205	1427	1548
26740	Closed treatment of articular fracture, involving metacarpophalangeal or interphalangeal joint; without manipulation, each	5.39	196.69	442	590	691
26742	Closed treatment of articular fracture, involving metacarpophalangeal or interphalangeal joint; with manipulation, each	9.31	338.05	623	778	890
26746	Open treatment of articular fracture, involving metacarpophalangeal or interphalangeal joint, with or without internal or external fixation, each	12.19	439.61	1401	1728	1991
26750	Closed treatment of distal phalangeal fracture, finger or thumb; without manipulation, each	4.38	159.17	271	342	431
26755	Closed treatment of distal phalangeal fracture, finger or thumb; with manipulation, each	7.84	284.99	397	547	634
26756	Percutaneous skeletal fixation of distal phalangeal fracture, finger or thumb, each	10.68	387.69	755	909	1067
26765	Open treatment of distal phalangeal fracture, finger or thumb, with or without internal or external fixation, each	9.17	331.60	882	1117	1245
26770	Closed treatment of interphalangeal joint dislocation, single, with manipulation; without anesthesia	6.64	239.89	326	409	549
26775	Closed treatment of interphalangeal joint dislocation, single, with manipulation; requiring anesthesia	9.35	339.94	479	564	697
26776	Percutaneous skeletal fixation of interphalangeal joint dislocation, single, with manipulation	11.40	413.46	680	848	1014
26785	Open treatment of interphalangeal joint dislocation, with or without internal or external fixation, single	9.35	338.05	901	1289	1521

Arthrodesis

Code	Description	Medicare RVU	National Fee	PFR Fee Information 50%	75%	90%
26820	Fusion in opposition, thumb, with autogenous graft (includes obtaining graft)	21.75	792.44	1863	2190	2540
26841	Arthrodesis, carpometacarpal joint, thumb, with or without internal fixation;	20.49	748.85	1660	1857	2006
26842	Arthrodesis, carpometacarpal joint, thumb, with or without internal fixation; with autograft (includes obtaining graft)	21.96	800.40	1916	2256	2535
26843	Arthrodesis, carpometacarpal joint, digit, other than thumb, each;	20.13	733.70	1535	1827	2124
26844	Arthrodesis, carpometacarpal joint, digit, other than thumb, each; with autograft (includes obtaining graft)	22.51	819.34	1770	2186	2526
26850	Arthrodesis, metacarpophalangeal joint, with or without internal fixation;	19.32	705.27	1442	1936	2331
26852	Arthrodesis, metacarpophalangeal joint, with or without internal fixation; with autograft (includes obtaining graft)	21.77	792.44	1652	1928	2203
26860	Arthrodesis, interphalangeal joint, with or without internal fixation;	15.77	579.45	1231	1455	1662
✚ 26861	Arthrodesis, interphalangeal joint, with or without internal fixation; each additional interphalangeal joint (List separately in addition to code for primary procedure)	2.89	102.70	586	686	786
26862	Arthrodesis, interphalangeal joint, with or without internal fixation; with autograft (includes obtaining graft)	19.98	728.77	1519	1797	2032
✚ 26863	Arthrodesis, interphalangeal joint, with or without internal fixation; with autograft (includes obtaining graft), each additional joint (List separately in addition to code for primary procedure)	6.44	229.28	785	936	1011

		Medicare RVU	National Fee	PFR Fee Information 50%	75%	90%

Amputation

26910	Amputation, metacarpal, with finger or thumb (ray amputation), single, with or without interosseous transfer	19.33	703.38	1500	1946	2138
26951	Amputation, finger or thumb, primary or secondary, any joint or phalanx, single, including neurectomies; with direct closure	16.27	594.23	998	1238	1445
26952	Amputation, finger or thumb, primary or secondary, any joint or phalanx, single, including neurectomies; with local advancement flaps (V-Y, hood)	18.06	660.17	1295	1560	1809

Other Procedures

26989	Unlisted procedure, hands or fingers	-	-	IR	IR	IR

Pelvis and Hip Joint

Incision

26990	Incision and drainage, pelvis or hip joint area; deep abscess or hematoma	16.04	577.94	978	1227	1541
26991	Incision and drainage, pelvis or hip joint area; infected bursa	18.59	677.99	865	1059	1359
26992	Incision, bone cortex, pelvis and/or hip joint (eg, osteomyelitis or bone abscess)	25.49	914.85	1721	2148	2791
27000	Tenotomy, adductor of hip, percutaneous (separate procedure)	11.74	423.32	633	830	1070
27001	Tenotomy, adductor of hip, open	14.17	510.10	987	1107	1352
27003	Tenotomy, adductor, subcutaneous, open, with obturator neurectomy	15.14	544.59	1140	1464	1673
27005	Tenotomy, hip flexor(s), open (separate procedure)	19.26	692.01	1290	1555	1789
27006	Tenotomy, abductors and/or extensor(s) of hip, open (separate procedure)	19.39	696.94	1231	1548	1725
27025	Fasciotomy, hip or thigh, any type	22.95	821.62	1773	1948	2455
27030	Arthrotomy, hip, with drainage (eg, infection)	25.08	898.93	2419	2760	3316
27033	Arthrotomy, hip, including exploration or removal of loose or foreign body	25.88	927.35	2417	2856	3260
27035	Denervation, hip joint, intrapelvic or extrapelvic intra-articular branches of sciatic, femoral, or obturator nerves	30.25	1080.84	2728	3248	3779
27036	Capsulectomy or capsulotomy, hip, with or without excision of heterotopic bone, with release of hip flexor muscles (ie, gluteus medius, gluteus minimus, tensor fascia latae, rectus femoris, sartorius, iliopsoas)	26.20	938.72	2359	2789	3409

Excision

27040	Biopsy, soft tissue of pelvis and hip area; superficial	8.33	304.70	430	534	638
27041	Biopsy, soft tissue of pelvis and hip area; deep, subfascial or intramuscular	17.83	637.44	828	1254	1641
27047	Excision, tumor, pelvis and hip area; subcutaneous tissue	15.64	563.91	804	1041	1316
27048	Excision, tumor, pelvis and hip area; deep, subfascial, intramuscular	12.12	434.68	1396	1592	2038
27049	Radical resection of tumor, soft tissue of pelvis and hip area (eg, malignant neoplasm)	25.63	913.33	3142	4317	5633
27050	Arthrotomy, with biopsy; sacroiliac joint	9.51	342.59	1033	1235	1424
27052	Arthrotomy, with biopsy; hip joint	14.18	509.72	2262	2692	2915
27054	Arthrotomy with synovectomy, hip joint	17.69	635.92	3093	3597	4212
27060	Excision; ischial bursa	10.97	393.76	994	1083	1218
27062	Excision; trochanteric bursa or calcification	11.64	419.53	960	1145	1354
27065	Excision of bone cyst or benign tumor; superficial (wing of ilium, symphysis pubis, or greater trochanter of femur) with or without autograft	12.81	460.83	1162	1390	1768
27066	Excision of bone cyst or benign tumor; deep, with or without autograft	21.06	756.06	1892	2189	2584
27067	Excision of bone cyst or benign tumor; with autograft requiring separate incision	26.63	953.50	2417	2843	3114
27070	Partial excision (craterization, saucerization) (eg, osteomyelitis or bone abscess); superficial (eg, wing of ilium, symphysis pubis, or greater trochanter of femur)	22.03	791.30	1407	2111	2652
27071	Partial excision (craterization, saucerization) (eg, osteomyelitis or bone abscess); deep (subfascial or intramuscular)	23.91	859.52	2346	2788	3102
27075	Radical resection of tumor or infection; wing of ilium, one pubic or ischial ramus or symphysis pubis	61.02	2172.28	3450	4006	4697

● = New Code ⊗ = Conscious Sedation ✚ = Add-on Code ∅ = Modifier '51' Exempt ▲ =Revised Code

		Medicare RVU	National Fee	PFR Fee Information 50%	75%	90%
27076	Radical resection of tumor or infection; ilium, including acetabulum, both pubic rami, or ischium and acetabulum	42.05	1501.12	4390	5407	6323
27077	Radical resection of tumor or infection; innominate bone, total	70.70	2517.15	5711	6854	8419
27078	Radical resection of tumor or infection; ischial tuberosity and greater trochanter of femur	26.44	946.68	2227	2768	3146
27079	Radical resection of tumor or infection; ischial tuberosity and greater trochanter of femur, with skin flaps	25.89	924.32	2675	3236	3708
27080	Coccygectomy, primary	12.54	449.46	1258	1479	1684

Introduction or Removal

27086	Removal of foreign body, pelvis or hip; subcutaneous tissue	6.49	238.75	313	345	405
27087	Removal of foreign body, pelvis or hip; deep (subfascial or intramuscular)	16.48	591.20	1052	1424	1794
27090	Removal of hip prosthesis; (separate procedure)	21.97	788.65	2089	2659	3028
	(UNBUNDLING ALERT: 27091 cannot be used with 27090 by the same physician on the same day.)					
27091	Removal of hip prosthesis; complicated, including total hip prosthesis, methylmethacrylate with or without insertion of spacer	41.77	1490.89	4923	5428	6762
27093	Injection procedure for hip arthrography; without anesthesia	5.52	204.27	299	356	401
27095	Injection procedure for hip arthrography; with anesthesia	6.83	253.16	434	534	682
	(See also HCPCS code G0259 for injection procedure for sacroiliac joint; arthrography) *(See also HCPCS code G0260 for injection procedure for sacroiliac joint; provision of anesthetic, steroid and/or other therapeutic agent and)*					
27096	Injection procedure for sacroiliac joint, arthrography and/or anesthetic/steroid	5.36	197.82	427	572	746

Repair, Revision, and/or Reconstruction

27097	Release or recession, hamstring, proximal	17.13	614.32	1867	1972	2240
27098	Transfer, adductor to ischium	16.64	595.37	2063	2324	2893
27100	Transfer external oblique muscle to greater trochanter including fascial or tendon extension (graft)	21.42	768.94	2467	2833	3358
27105	Transfer paraspinal muscle to hip (includes fascial or tendon extension graft)	22.49	806.84	2402	3160	3776
27110	Transfer iliopsoas; to greater trochanter of femur	24.82	888.70	2935	3530	4465
27111	Transfer iliopsoas; to femoral neck	23.30	835.64	2650	3293	3962
27120	Acetabuloplasty; (eg, Whitman, Colonna, Haygroves, or cup type)	33.78	1207.41	3812	4269	4890
27122	Acetabuloplasty; resection, femoral head (eg, Girdlestone procedure)	29.24	1047.49	3399	4241	4765
27125	Hemiarthroplasty, hip, partial (eg, femoral stem prosthesis, bipolar arthroplasty)	29.41	1051.66	4169	4778	5275
	(UNBUNDLING ALERT: 27130 cannot be used with 27120 by the same physician on the same day.)					
27130	Arthroplasty, acetabular and proximal femoral prosthetic replacement (total hip arthroplasty), with or without autograft or allograft	38.08	1360.90	5894	6882	7288
	(UNBUNDLING ALERT: 27132 cannot be used with 27120, 27125, or 27130 by the same physician on the same day.)					
27132	Conversion of previous hip surgery to total hip arthroplasty, with or without autograft or allograft	44.67	1595.86	6557	7796	8603
	(UNBUNDLING ALERT: 27134 cannot be used with 20680, 27090, 27120, 27125, or 27137 by the same physician on the same day.)					
27134	Revision of total hip arthroplasty; both components, with or without autograft or allograft	52.16	1861.90	7722	9027	10374
	(UNBUNDLING ALERT: 27137 cannot be used with 20680, 27120 or 27125 by the same physician on the same day.)					
27137	Revision of total hip arthroplasty; acetabular component only, with or without autograft or allograft	39.65	1416.61	5870	6967	7800
	(UNBUNDLING ALERT: 27138 cannot be used with 20680 or 27125 by the same physician on the same day.)					
27138	Revision of total hip arthroplasty; femoral component only, with or without allograft	41.27	1474.21	5952	6986	7899
27140	Osteotomy and transfer of greater trochanter of femur (separate procedure)	23.80	853.83	2056	2588	3089
27146	Osteotomy, iliac, acetabular or innominate bone;	33.48	1197.56	3186	3782	4390

● = New Code ⊗ = Conscious Sedation ✚ = Add-on Code ∅ = Modifier '51' Exempt ▲ =Revised Code

Code	Description	Medicare RVU	National Fee	PFR Fee Information 50%	75%	90%
27147	Osteotomy, iliac, acetabular or innominate bone; with open reduction of hip	38.40	1371.89	3991	4890	5408
27151	Osteotomy, iliac, acetabular or innominate bone; with femoral osteotomy	36.93	1308.22	3976	4662	5226
27156	Osteotomy, iliac, acetabular or innominate bone; with femoral osteotomy and with open reduction of hip	45.70	1632.62	4972	5952	6870
27158	Osteotomy, pelvis, bilateral (eg, congenital malformation)	34.07	1211.58	3964	4841	5735
27161	Osteotomy, femoral neck (separate procedure)	32.38	1159.66	3220	3709	4262
27165	Osteotomy, intertrochanteric or subtrochanteric including internal or external fixation and/or cast	35.80	1280.18	3752	4576	5482
27170	Bone graft, femoral head, neck, intertrochanteric or subtrochanteric area (includes obtaining bone graft)	31.22	1116.46	3836	4525	5219
27175	Treatment of slipped femoral epiphysis; by traction, without reduction	17.21	616.97	1784	2108	2747
27176	Treatment of slipped femoral epiphysis; by single or multiple pinning, in situ	23.84	854.59	2986	3284	3894
27177	Open treatment of slipped femoral epiphysis; single or multiple pinning or bone graft (includes obtaining graft)	29.16	1044.46	3557	4066	4530
27178	Open treatment of slipped femoral epiphysis; closed manipulation with single or multiple pinning	23.26	832.61	3214	3669	3933
27179	Open treatment of slipped femoral epiphysis; osteoplasty of femoral neck (Heyman type procedure)	25.73	922.43	2694	3173	3597
27181	Open treatment of slipped femoral epiphysis; osteotomy and internal fixation	27.67	987.61	3740	4304	4586
27185	Epiphyseal arrest by epiphysiodesis or stapling, greater trochanter of femur	19.39	698.07	1586	1918	2221
27187	Prophylactic treatment (nailing, pinning, plating or wiring) with or without methylmethacrylate, femoral neck and proximal femur	26.40	946.68	3900	4715	5355

Fracture and/or Dislocation

Code	Description	Medicare RVU	National Fee	PFR Fee Information 50%	75%	90%
27193	Closed treatment of pelvic ring fracture, dislocation, diastasis or subluxation; without manipulation	11.92	429.00	896	1064	1345
27194	Closed treatment of pelvic ring fracture, dislocation, diastasis or subluxation; with manipulation, requiring more than local anesthesia	19.13	686.70	1559	1691	1828
27200	Closed treatment of coccygeal fracture	4.34	157.27	376	434	503
27202	Open treatment of coccygeal fracture	23.74	872.02	1235	1650	1981
27215	Open treatment of iliac spine(s), tuberosity avulsion, or iliac wing fracture(s) (eg, pelvic fracture(s) which do not disrupt the pelvic ring), with internal fixation	19.38	694.66	2438	2889	3465
27216	Percutaneous skeletal fixation of posterior pelvic ring fracture and/or dislocation (includes ilium, sacroiliac joint and/or sacrum)	27.89	997.08	2172	2545	3158
27217	Open treatment of anterior ring fracture and/or dislocation with internal fixation (includes pubic symphysis and/or rami)	26.86	962.22	2921	3839	4642
27218	Open treatment of posterior ring fracture and/or dislocation with internal fixation (includes ilium, sacroiliac joint and/or sacrum)	35.83	1277.90	3522	4388	4993
27220	Closed treatment of acetabulum (hip socket) fracture(s); without manipulation	13.40	482.06	861	1117	1465
27222	Closed treatment of acetabulum (hip socket) fracture(s); with manipulation, with or without skeletal traction	25.78	923.56	1845	2082	2577
27226	Open treatment of posterior or anterior acetabular wall fracture, with internal fixation	26.06	928.87	2980	3604	4364
27227	Open treatment of acetabular fracture(s) involving anterior or posterior (one) column, or a fracture running transversely across the acetabulum, with internal fixation	44.20	1578.81	4255	5940	6439
27228	Open treatment of acetabular fracture(s) involving anterior and posterior (two) columns, includes T-fracture and both column fracture with complete articular detachment, or single column or transverse fracture with associated acetabular wall fracture, with internal fixation	50.79	1813.77	5670	6773	7783
27230	Closed treatment of femoral fracture, proximal end, neck; without manipulation	12.02	433.93	851	1110	1243
27232	Closed treatment of femoral fracture, proximal end, neck; with manipulation, with or without skeletal traction	20.40	728.77	1720	1933	2494
27235	Percutaneous skeletal fixation of femoral fracture, proximal end, neck	24.11	864.44	3160	3719	4110
	(UNBUNDLING ALERT: 27236 cannot be used with 27235 by the same physician on the same day.)					
27236	Open treatment of femoral fracture, proximal end, neck, internal fixation or prosthetic replacement	31.00	1108.50	3624	4208	4950
27238	Closed treatment of intertrochanteric, peritrochanteric, or subtrochanteric femoral fracture; without manipulation	11.56	416.49	930	1166	1481

● = New Code ⊗ = Conscious Sedation ✚ = Add-on Code ∅ = Modifier '51' Exempt ▲ =Revised Code

		Medicare RVU	National Fee	PFR Fee Information 50%	75%	90%
27240	Closed treatment of intertrochanteric, peritrochanteric, or subtrochanteric femoral fracture; with manipulation, with or without skin or skeletal traction	24.96	894.00	1810	2248	2786
27244	Treatment of intertrochanteric, peritrochanteric, or subtrochanteric femoral fracture; with plate/screw type implant, with or without cerclage	30.77	1100.92	3414	4105	4853
27245	Treatment of intertrochanteric, peritrochanteric, or subtrochanteric femoral fracture; with intramedullary implant, with or without interlocking screws and/or cerclage	37.81	1352.56	3825	4555	5050
27246	Closed treatment of greater trochanteric fracture, without manipulation	9.89	356.62	807	995	1176
27248	Open treatment of greater trochanteric fracture, with or without internal or external fixation	20.54	737.11	1827	2402	2984
27250	Closed treatment of hip dislocation, traumatic; without anesthesia	12.37	441.13	869	971	1205
27252	Closed treatment of hip dislocation, traumatic; requiring anesthesia	19.79	708.30	1297	1545	1808
27253	Open treatment of hip dislocation, traumatic, without internal fixation	25.12	900.82	2447	2959	3581
27254	Open treatment of hip dislocation, traumatic, with acetabular wall and femoral head fracture, with or without internal or external fixation	33.65	1203.62	3206	3729	4295
27256	Treatment of spontaneous hip dislocation (developmental, including congenital or pathological), by abduction, splint or traction; without anesthesia, without manipulation	7.95	284.99	1346	1636	1706
27257	Treatment of spontaneous hip dislocation (developmental, including congenital or pathological), by abduction, splint or traction; with manipulation, requiring anesthesia	8.79	312.65	1500	1800	2018
27258	Open treatment of spontaneous hip dislocation (developmental, including congenital or pathological), replacement of femoral head in acetabulum (including tenotomy, etc);	29.22	1046.35	2771	3363	3846
27259	Open treatment of spontaneous hip dislocation (developmental, including congenital or pathological), replacement of femoral head in acetabulum (including tenotomy, etc); with femoral shaft shortening	40.61	1451.10	3544	4132	4713
27265	Closed treatment of post hip arthroplasty dislocation; without anesthesia	10.34	372.15	834	1020	1276
27266	Closed treatment of post hip arthroplasty dislocation; requiring regional or general anesthesia	15.11	543.45	1236	1571	1980

Manipulation

27275	Manipulation, hip joint, requiring general anesthesia	4.73	170.54	532	604	669

Arthrodesis

27280	Arthrodesis, sacroiliac joint (including obtaining graft)	27.00	967.90	2569	3013	3357
27282	Arthrodesis, symphysis pubis (including obtaining graft)	21.55	771.97	2649	3207	3505
27284	Arthrodesis, hip joint (including obtaining graft);	43.14	1539.78	3990	4993	5625
27286	Arthrodesis, hip joint (including obtaining graft); with subtrochanteric osteotomy	43.33	1546.98	4028	5185	5703

Amputation

27290	Interpelviabdominal amputation (hindquarter amputation)	41.51	1480.28	5788	6583	7242
27295	Disarticulation of hip	33.44	1192.63	4426	5206	6003

Other Procedures

27299	Unlisted procedure, pelvis or hip joint	-	-	IR	IR	IR

Femur (Thigh Region) and Knee Joint

Incision

27301	Incision and drainage, deep abscess, bursa, or hematoma, thigh or knee region	17.31	630.61	993	1312	1641
27303	Incision, deep, with opening of bone cortex, femur or knee (eg, osteomyelitis or bone abscess)	16.71	600.68	1643	1834	2003
27305	Fasciotomy, iliotibial (tenotomy), open	12.14	436.96	1005	1224	1423
27306	Tenotomy, percutaneous, adductor or hamstring; single tendon (separate procedure)	10.07	363.82	661	775	867
27307	Tenotomy, percutaneous, adductor or hamstring; multiple tendons	12.25	441.51	1001	1334	1611
27310	Arthrotomy, knee, with exploration, drainage, or removal of foreign body (eg, infection)	18.89	678.37	1921	2336	2803

Excision

27323	Biopsy, soft tissue of thigh or knee area; superficial	6.20	226.25	352	432	516

● = New Code ⊗ = Conscious Sedation ✚ = Add-on Code ∅ = Modifier '51' Exempt ▲ =Revised Code

		Medicare RVU	National Fee	PFR Fee Information 50%	75%	90%
27324	Biopsy, soft tissue of thigh or knee area; deep (subfascial or intramuscular)	9.80	352.45	842	900	1052
● 27325	Neurectomy, hamstring muscle	13.26	475.61	1111	1344	1657
● 27326	Neurectomy, popliteal (gastrocnemius)	12.54	450.98	1051	1271	1567
27327	Excision, tumor, thigh or knee area; subcutaneous	11.16	405.88	661	836	1041
27328	Excision, tumor, thigh or knee area; deep, subfascial, or intramuscular	10.75	385.80	1157	1412	1708
27329	Radical resection of tumor (eg, malignant neoplasm), soft tissue of thigh or knee area	26.74	953.50	2924	3714	4865
27330	Arthrotomy, knee; with synovial biopsy only	10.34	372.53	1740	2188	2438
27331	Arthrotomy, knee; including joint exploration, biopsy, or removal of loose or foreign bodies	12.30	443.40	1994	2273	2563
27332	Arthrotomy, with excision of semilunar cartilage (meniscectomy) knee; medial OR lateral	16.65	599.16	2436	2850	3184
27333	Arthrotomy, with excision of semilunar cartilage (meniscectomy) knee; medial AND lateral	15.13	544.97	2741	3128	3862
27334	Arthrotomy, with synovectomy, knee; anterior OR posterior	17.77	638.95	2502	3023	3562
27335	Arthrotomy, with synovectomy, knee; anterior AND posterior including popliteal area	20.12	722.71	2778	3227	3591
27340	Excision, prepatellar bursa	9.38	339.18	1087	1205	1405
27345	Excision of synovial cyst of popliteal space (eg, Baker's cyst)	12.42	447.95	1459	1824	2134
27347	Excision of lesion of meniscus or capsule (eg, cyst, ganglion), knee	12.94	465.38	1163	1446	1804
27350	Patellectomy or hemipatellectomy	16.96	610.15	2208	2629	2947
27355	Excision or curettage of bone cyst or benign tumor of femur;	15.76	567.33	1807	2056	2239
27356	Excision or curettage of bone cyst or benign tumor of femur; with allograft	19.23	690.87	2152	2672	3084
27357	Excision or curettage of bone cyst or benign tumor of femur; with autograft (includes obtaining graft)	21.40	768.94	2347	2800	3151
✚ 27358	Excision or curettage of bone cyst or benign tumor of femur; with internal fixation (List in addition to code for primary procedure)	7.92	281.96	1533	1788	2056
27360	Partial excision (craterization, saucerization, or diaphysectomy) bone, femur, proximal tibia and/or fibula (eg, osteomyelitis or bone abscess)	22.38	804.94	2015	2402	2786
27365	Radical resection of tumor, bone, femur or knee	32.13	1149.43	3575	4087	4666

Introduction and/or Removal

27370	Injection procedure for knee arthrography	4.51	167.13	216	271	327
27372	Removal of foreign body, deep, thigh region or knee area	15.57	570.36	912	1034	1593

Repair, Revision, and/or Reconstruction

27380	Suture of infrapatellar tendon; primary	15.56	561.64	1651	1800	2085
27381	Suture of infrapatellar tendon; secondary reconstruction, including fascial or tendon graft	21.15	760.98	2354	2651	2880
27385	Suture of quadriceps or hamstring muscle rupture; primary	16.68	601.81	1981	2292	2506
27386	Suture of quadriceps or hamstring muscle rupture; secondary reconstruction, including fascial or tendon graft	21.98	790.92	2477	2818	3072
27390	Tenotomy, open, hamstring, knee to hip; single tendon	11.34	408.91	877	1125	1318
27391	Tenotomy, open, hamstring, knee to hip; multiple tendons, one leg	14.92	537.39	1180	1447	1633
27392	Tenotomy, open, hamstring, knee to hip; multiple tendons, bilateral	18.46	663.21	1833	2090	2297
27393	Lengthening of hamstring tendon; single tendon	13.23	476.75	1015	1171	1350
27394	Lengthening of hamstring tendon; multiple tendons, one leg	17.12	615.83	1401	1750	1985
27395	Lengthening of hamstring tendon; multiple tendons, bilateral	23.15	831.09	2055	2359	2667
27396	Transplant, hamstring tendon to patella; single tendon	16.12	580.21	1996	2196	2717
27397	Transplant, hamstring tendon to patella; multiple tendons	23.18	831.09	2134	2872	3158
27400	Transfer, tendon or muscle, hamstrings to femur (eg, Egger's type procedure)	17.51	628.34	1911	2040	2587

		Medicare RVU	National Fee	PFR Fee Information 50%	75%	90%
27403	Arthrotomy with meniscus repair, knee	16.86	606.36	2450	2755	3198
27405	Repair, primary, torn ligament and/or capsule, knee; collateral	17.70	636.68	2260	2592	2858
27407	Repair, primary, torn ligament and/or capsule, knee; cruciate	20.42	732.94	2718	3128	3374
27409	Repair, primary, torn ligament and/or capsule, knee; collateral and cruciate ligaments	25.40	910.68	3130	3929	4712
27412	Autologous chondrocyte implantation, knee	43.42	1551.90	5541	6309	7304
27415	Osteochondral allograft, knee, open	36.54	1309.36	4627	5268	6099
27418	Anterior tibial tubercleplasty (eg, Maquet type procedure)	21.94	787.89	3082	3380	3805
27420	Reconstruction of dislocating patella; (eg, Hauser type procedure)	19.69	707.55	2389	2898	3534
27422	Reconstruction of dislocating patella; with extensor realignment and/or muscle advancement or release (eg, Campbell, Goldwaite type procedure)	19.62	704.89	2611	3032	3411
27424	Reconstruction of dislocating patella; with patellectomy	19.63	705.27	2681	3012	3452
27425	Lateral retinacular release, open	11.50	415.74	2259	2643	2969
27427	Ligamentous reconstruction (augmentation), knee; extra-articular	18.83	676.85	2885	3550	4069
27428	Ligamentous reconstruction (augmentation), knee; intra-articular (open)	28.73	1030.43	3776	4044	4414
27429	Ligamentous reconstruction (augmentation), knee; intra-articular (open) and extra-articular	32.10	1150.95	4274	4909	5459
27430	Quadricepsplasty (eg, Bennett or Thompson type)	19.47	699.59	2251	2702	3118
27435	Capsulotomy, posterior capsular release, knee	20.67	742.79	1917	2237	2509
27437	Arthroplasty, patella; without prosthesis	17.30	621.90	2090	2554	3199
27438	Arthroplasty, patella; with prosthesis	22.04	790.54	2799	3409	4005
27440	Arthroplasty, knee, tibial plateau;	19.08	681.40	2888	3196	3448
27441	Arthroplasty, knee, tibial plateau; with debridement and partial synovectomy	20.23	723.08	2954	3508	4013
27442	Arthroplasty, femoral condyles or tibial plateau(s), knee;	22.99	824.65	3033	3687	4269
27443	Arthroplasty, femoral condyles or tibial plateau(s), knee; with debridement and partial synovectomy	21.60	775.38	3370	3804	4497
27445	Arthroplasty, knee, hinge prosthesis (eg, Walldius type)	33.52	1199.83	4469	5270	6060
27446	Arthroplasty, knee, condyle and plateau; medial OR lateral compartment	29.88	1070.23	4453	5138	5825
	(UNBUNDLING ALERT: 27447 cannot be used with 27425 or 27446 by the same physician on the same day.)					
27447	Arthroplasty, knee, condyle and plateau; medial AND lateral compartments with or without patella resurfacing (total knee arthroplasty)	40.98	1465.12	5551	6634	7717
27448	Osteotomy, femur, shaft or supracondylar; without fixation	21.75	780.69	2588	2935	3349
27450	Osteotomy, femur, shaft or supracondylar; with fixation	27.05	969.80	2916	3177	3730
27454	Osteotomy, multiple, with realignment on intramedullary rod, femoral shaft (eg, Sofield type procedure)	34.17	1222.57	3011	3533	4107
27455	Osteotomy, proximal tibia, including fibular excision or osteotomy (includes correction of genu varus (bowleg) or genu valgus (knock-knee)); before epiphyseal closure	25.01	897.41	2378	2742	3329
27457	Osteotomy, proximal tibia, including fibular excision or osteotomy (includes correction of genu varus (bowleg) or genu valgus (knock-knee)); after epiphyseal closure	25.78	923.94	2738	3379	3991
27465	Osteoplasty, femur; shortening (excluding 64876)	31.19	1111.53	3082	3548	3928
27466	Osteoplasty, femur; lengthening	31.33	1122.14	3769	4236	4696
27468	Osteoplasty, femur; combined, lengthening and shortening with femoral segment transfer	35.23	1259.71	4715	5516	6205
27470	Repair, nonunion or malunion, femur, distal to head and neck; without graft (eg, compression technique)	31.18	1116.84	3168	3798	4448
27472	Repair, nonunion or malunion, femur, distal to head and neck; with iliac or other autogenous bone graft (includes obtaining graft)	33.85	1211.96	3638	4333	5083
27475	Arrest, epiphyseal, any method (eg, epiphysiodesis); distal femur	17.31	622.28	2486	2985	3443
27477	Arrest, epiphyseal, any method (eg, epiphysiodesis); tibia and fibula, proximal	19.24	690.87	2596	3038	3519

● = New Code ⊗ = Conscious Sedation ✚ = Add-on Code ∅ = Modifier '51' Exempt ▲ =Revised Code

		Medicare RVU	National Fee	PFR Fee Information 50%	75%	90%
27479	Arrest, epiphyseal, any method (eg, epiphysiodesis); combined distal femur, proximal tibia and fibula	24.33	872.40	3141	3746	4187
27485	Arrest, hemiepiphyseal, distal femur or proximal tibia or fibula (eg, genu varus or valgus)	17.67	635.16	1813	2220	2687
27486	Revision of total knee arthroplasty, with or without allograft; one component	37.36	1336.27	4815	5474	6125
	(UNBUNDLING ALERT: 27487 cannot be used with 27447 or 27486 by the same physician on the same day.)					
27487	Revision of total knee arthroplasty, with or without allograft; femoral and entire tibial component	47.28	1689.09	6649	7666	8216
27488	Removal of prosthesis, including total knee prosthesis, methylmethacrylate with or without insertion of spacer, knee	31.52	1128.21	3392	3956	4500
27495	Prophylactic treatment (nailing, pinning, plating or wiring) with or without methylmethacrylate, femur	30.11	1078.56	3004	3683	4264
27496	Decompression fasciotomy, thigh and/or knee, one compartment (flexor or extensor or adductor);	13.11	471.44	987	1282	1498
27497	Decompression fasciotomy, thigh and/or knee, one compartment (flexor or extensor or adductor); with debridement of nonviable muscle and/or nerve	14.09	504.79	1271	1587	1950
27498	Decompression fasciotomy, thigh and/or knee, multiple compartments;	15.59	558.23	1610	1989	2123
27499	Decompression fasciotomy, thigh and/or knee, multiple compartments; with debridement of nonviable muscle and/or nerve	17.36	622.28	1656	2063	2398

Fracture and/or Dislocation

		Medicare RVU	National Fee	50%	75%	90%
27500	Closed treatment of femoral shaft fracture, without manipulation	13.18	475.99	1141	1449	1813
27501	Closed treatment of supracondylar or transcondylar femoral fracture with or without intercondylar extension, without manipulation	12.98	467.66	1387	1542	1748
27502	Closed treatment of femoral shaft fracture, with manipulation, with or without skin or skeletal traction	20.85	747.34	1698	2005	2375
27503	Closed treatment of supracondylar or transcondylar femoral fracture with or without intercondylar extension, with manipulation, with or without skin or skeletal traction	21.02	754.16	1835	2272	2596
	(UNBUNDLING ALERT: 27506 cannot be used with 27502 by the same physician on the same day.)					
27506	Open treatment of femoral shaft fracture, with or without external fixation, with insertion of intramedullary implant, with or without cerclage and/or locking screws	34.86	1247.21	3615	4438	5156
27507	Open treatment of femoral shaft fracture with plate/screws, with or without cerclage	26.26	940.24	3273	3712	4012
27508	Closed treatment of femoral fracture, distal end, medial or lateral condyle, without manipulation	13.32	481.68	1005	1183	1525
27509	Percutaneous skeletal fixation of femoral fracture, distal end, medial or lateral condyle, or supracondylar or transcondylar, with or without intercondylar extension, or distal femoral epiphyseal separation	16.97	612.42	1536	2052	2319
27510	Closed treatment of femoral fracture, distal end, medial or lateral condyle, with manipulation	18.30	656.76	1389	1744	2152
27511	Open treatment of femoral supracondylar or transcondylar fracture without intercondylar extension, with or without internal or external fixation	27.00	970.18	3173	3724	4242
27513	Open treatment of femoral supracondylar or transcondylar fracture with intercondylar extension, with or without internal or external fixation	35.96	1288.52	3561	4296	5053
27514	Open treatment of femoral fracture, distal end, medial or lateral condyle, with or without internal or external fixation	35.12	1258.20	3273	3922	4372
27516	Closed treatment of distal femoral epiphyseal separation; without manipulation	12.45	450.98	1056	1275	1400
27517	Closed treatment of distal femoral epiphyseal separation; with manipulation, with or without skin or skeletal traction	17.31	621.90	1442	1765	2120
27519	Open treatment of distal femoral epiphyseal separation, with or without internal or external fixation	29.53	1058.86	2879	3474	3986
27520	Closed treatment of patellar fracture, without manipulation	7.83	285.75	600	732	890
27524	Open treatment of patellar fracture, with internal fixation and/or partial or complete patellectomy and soft tissue repair	19.92	715.88	2234	2745	3184
27530	Closed treatment of tibial fracture, proximal (plateau); without manipulation	9.81	356.62	745	896	1039
27532	Closed treatment of tibial fracture, proximal (plateau); with or without manipulation, with skeletal traction	15.82	571.12	1078	1302	1663
27535	Open treatment of tibial fracture, proximal (plateau); unicondylar, with or without internal or external fixation	23.46	843.98	2464	2953	3537
27536	Open treatment of tibial fracture, proximal (plateau); bicondylar, with or without internal fixation	31.22	1117.60	2830	3432	4094

● = New Code ⊗ = Conscious Sedation ✚ = Add-on Code ∅ = Modifier '51' Exempt ▲ =Revised Code

		Medicare RVU	National Fee	PFR Fee Information 50%	75%	90%
27538	Closed treatment of intercondylar spine(s) and/or tuberosity fracture(s) of knee, with or without manipulation	11.77	427.10	837	1058	1351
27540	Open treatment of intercondylar spine(s) and/or tuberosity fracture(s) of the knee, with or without internal or external fixation	24.88	891.73	2357	2854	3270
27550	Closed treatment of knee dislocation; without anesthesia	12.44	449.09	649	845	1062
27552	Closed treatment of knee dislocation; requiring anesthesia	16.15	581.35	1073	1363	1618
27556	Open treatment of knee dislocation, with or without internal or external fixation; without primary ligamentous repair or augmentation/reconstruction	28.54	1024.75	2621	3146	3515
27557	Open treatment of knee dislocation, with or without internal or external fixation; with primary ligamentous repair	32.79	1176.72	3502	3932	4256
27558	Open treatment of knee dislocation, with or without internal or external fixation; with primary ligamentous repair, with augmentation/reconstruction	33.55	1202.87	3619	4306	4955
27560	Closed treatment of patellar dislocation; without anesthesia	8.89	322.13	423	549	687
27562	Closed treatment of patellar dislocation; requiring anesthesia	11.49	413.08	800	941	1298
27566	Open treatment of patellar dislocation, with or without partial or total patellectomy	23.68	849.28	1989	2409	2791

Manipulation

27570	Manipulation of knee joint under general anesthesia (includes application of traction or other fixation devices)	3.79	136.81	537	648	744

Arthrodesis

27580	Arthrodesis, knee, any technique	38.48	1378.71	3148	3762	4339

Amputation

(UNBUNDLING ALERT: 27590 cannot be used with 27596 by the same physician on the same day.)

27590	Amputation, thigh, through femur, any level;	21.63	768.94	2413	2849	3212
27591	Amputation, thigh, through femur, any level; immediate fitting technique including first cast	24.19	864.06	2505	2883	3211
27592	Amputation, thigh, through femur, any level; open, circular (guillotine)	18.31	652.59	2543	3078	3514
27594	Amputation, thigh, through femur, any level; secondary closure or scar revision	13.26	475.23	1005	1270	1463

(UNBUNDLING ALERT: 27596 cannot be used with 37618 by the same physician on the same day.)

27596	Amputation, thigh, through femur, any level; re-amputation	19.34	690.49	2206	2737	3167
27598	Disarticulation at knee	19.58	699.97	2393	2730	3258

Other Procedures

27599	Unlisted procedure, femur or knee	-	-	IR	IR	IR

Leg (Tibia and Fibula) and Ankle Joint

Incision

27600	Decompression fasciotomy, leg; anterior and/or lateral compartments only	11.16	400.20	1033	1301	1434
27601	Decompression fasciotomy, leg; posterior compartment(s) only	11.44	410.81	1015	1293	1438
27602	Decompression fasciotomy, leg; anterior and/or lateral, and posterior compartment(s)	13.75	491.53	1315	1578	1932
27603	Incision and drainage, leg or ankle; deep abscess or hematoma	13.23	481.68	891	1122	1461
27604	Incision and drainage, leg or ankle; infected bursa	11.38	414.22	545	605	727
27605	Tenotomy, percutaneous, Achilles tendon (separate procedure); local anesthesia	10.38	382.39	523	626	765
27606	Tenotomy, percutaneous, Achilles tendon (separate procedure); general anesthesia	8.03	288.40	817	928	1198
27607	Incision (eg, osteomyelitis or bone abscess), leg or ankle	15.90	569.98	1352	1592	1879
27610	Arthrotomy, ankle, including exploration, drainage, or removal of foreign body	17.21	617.73	1488	1787	2056
27612	Arthrotomy, posterior capsular release, ankle, with or without Achilles tendon lengthening	15.06	540.04	1592	1862	2145

● = New Code ⊗ = Conscious Sedation ✚ = Add-on Code ∅ = Modifier '51' Exempt ▲ =Revised Code

		Medicare RVU	National Fee	PFR Fee Information 50%	75%	90%

Excision

(For biopsy of skin, see codes 11100-11101.)

Code	Description	RVU	Fee	50%	75%	90%
27613	Biopsy, soft tissue of leg or ankle area; superficial	5.78	210.71	408	494	594
27614	Biopsy, soft tissue of leg or ankle area; deep (subfascial or intramuscular)	13.81	501.76	810	942	1074
27615	Radical resection of tumor (eg, malignant neoplasm), soft tissue of leg or ankle area	23.84	854.21	2664	3126	3470
27618	Excision, tumor, leg or ankle area; subcutaneous tissue	11.96	433.55	820	883	1060
27619	Excision, tumor, leg or ankle area; deep (subfascial or intramuscular)	19.37	701.86	1223	1461	1734
27620	Arthrotomy, ankle, with joint exploration, with or without biopsy, with or without removal of loose or foreign body	12.26	441.51	1619	1913	2203
27625	Arthrotomy, with synovectomy, ankle;	15.90	570.74	2108	2415	2712
27626	Arthrotomy, with synovectomy, ankle; including tenosynovectomy	17.15	615.83	1982	2402	2834
27630	Excision of lesion of tendon sheath or capsule (eg, cyst or ganglion), leg and/or ankle	13.25	483.57	863	1052	1267
27635	Excision or curettage of bone cyst or benign tumor, tibia or fibula;	15.70	564.67	1929	2226	2530
27637	Excision or curettage of bone cyst or benign tumor, tibia or fibula; with autograft (includes obtaining graft)	19.85	713.61	2152	2427	2682
27638	Excision or curettage of bone cyst or benign tumor, tibia or fibula; with allograft	20.69	742.79	2259	2660	3063
27640	Partial excision (craterization, saucerization, or diaphysectomy) bone (eg, osteomyelitis or exostosis); tibia	23.78	854.97	2350	2915	3410
27641	Partial excision (craterization, saucerization, or diaphysectomy) bone (eg, osteomyelitis or exostosis); fibula	19.15	688.60	1845	2214	2560
27645	Radical resection of tumor, bone; tibia	28.62	1028.16	2757	3220	3610
27646	Radical resection of tumor, bone; fibula	25.66	922.05	2321	2830	3160
27647	Radical resection of tumor, bone; talus or calcaneus	21.99	784.48	2436	3026	3407

Introduction or Removal

Code	Description	RVU	Fee	50%	75%	90%
27648	Injection procedure for ankle arthrography	4.34	160.69	218	258	308

Repair, Revision, and/or Reconstruction

Code	Description	RVU	Fee	50%	75%	90%
27650	Repair, primary, open or percutaneous, ruptured Achilles tendon;	18.75	672.68	1930	2205	2570
27652	Repair, primary, open or percutaneous, ruptured Achilles tendon; with graft (includes obtaining graft)	20.01	717.78	2342	2799	3218
27654	Repair, secondary, Achilles tendon, with or without graft	18.76	671.54	2286	2725	2903
27656	Repair, fascial defect of leg	13.72	502.52	938	1225	1571
27658	Repair, flexor tendon, leg; primary, without graft, each tendon	10.22	367.98	1144	1333	1470
27659	Repair, flexor tendon, leg; secondary, with or without graft, each tendon	13.54	486.60	1476	1806	2096
27664	Repair, extensor tendon, leg; primary, without graft, each tendon	9.80	353.58	1066	1245	1430
27665	Repair, extensor tendon, leg; secondary, with or without graft, each tendon	11.20	403.61	1216	1501	1807
27675	Repair, dislocating peroneal tendons; without fibular osteotomy	13.84	496.84	1155	1482	1759
27676	Repair, dislocating peroneal tendons; with fibular osteotomy	16.49	591.96	1306	1674	1977
27680	Tenolysis, flexor or extensor tendon, leg and/or ankle; single, each tendon	11.65	419.53	1012	1391	1750
27681	Tenolysis, flexor or extensor tendon, leg and/or ankle; multiple tendons (through separate incision(s))	13.72	493.43	1165	1411	1726
27685	Lengthening or shortening of tendon, leg or ankle; single tendon (separate procedure)	15.22	551.79	1252	1549	1833
27686	Lengthening or shortening of tendon, leg or ankle; multiple tendons (through same incision), each	15.10	543.07	1413	1776	2083
27687	Gastrocnemius recession (eg, Strayer procedure)	12.42	446.81	1185	1462	1689
27690	Transfer or transplant of single tendon (with muscle redirection or rerouting); superficial (eg, anterior tibial extensors into midfoot)	16.44	588.93	1628	1993	2212

Code	Description	Medicare RVU	National Fee	PFR Fee Information 50%	75%	90%
27691	Transfer or transplant of single tendon (with muscle redirection or rerouting); deep (eg, anterior tibial or posterior tibial through interosseous space, flexor digitorum longus, flexor hallucis longus, or peroneal tendon to midfoot or hindfoot)	19.43	697.31	1940	2291	2601
✚ 27692	Transfer or transplant of single tendon (with muscle redirection or rerouting); each additional tendon (List separately in addition to code for primary procedure)	3.07	109.14	426	529	613
27695	Repair, primary, disrupted ligament, ankle; collateral	13.29	478.65	1685	1948	2208
27696	Repair, primary, disrupted ligament, ankle; both collateral ligaments	15.93	571.49	2099	2481	2788
27698	Repair, secondary, disrupted ligament, ankle, collateral (eg, Watson-Jones procedure)	17.66	633.27	2429	2859	3245
27700	Arthroplasty, ankle;	16.40	585.14	2743	3032	3423
27702	Arthroplasty, ankle; with implant (total ankle)	26.70	957.29	4098	4703	5285
27703	Arthroplasty, ankle; revision, total ankle	30.47	1090.69	3862	4627	5740
27704	Removal of ankle implant	14.58	523.36	1610	2172	2542
27705	Osteotomy; tibia	20.42	732.94	2122	2602	2996
27707	Osteotomy; fibula	10.26	371.02	1136	1432	1753
27709	Osteotomy; tibia and fibula	27.66	982.30	2625	3021	3433
27712	Osteotomy; multiple, with realignment on intramedullary rod (eg, Sofield type procedure)	28.51	1020.58	2601	3045	3295
27715	Osteoplasty, tibia and fibula, lengthening or shortening	28.20	1009.97	3468	4030	4594
27720	Repair of nonunion or malunion, tibia; without graft, (eg, compression technique)	23.32	837.16	3036	3942	4277
27722	Repair of nonunion or malunion, tibia; with sliding graft	23.24	833.74	2866	3527	3937
27724	Repair of nonunion or malunion, tibia; with iliac or other autograft (includes obtaining graft)	34.22	1223.71	3304	4034	4641
27725	Repair of nonunion or malunion, tibia; by synostosis, with fibula, any method	31.46	1126.69	3542	4080	4744
27727	Repair of congenital pseudarthrosis, tibia	27.05	969.04	2688	3398	4099
27730	Arrest, epiphyseal (epiphysiodesis), open; distal tibia	15.47	557.47	1601	1896	2172
27732	Arrest, epiphyseal (epiphysiodesis), open; distal fibula	11.01	396.79	1261	1646	1869
27734	Arrest, epiphyseal (epiphysiodesis), open; distal tibia and fibula	16.34	585.90	1999	2605	3031
27740	Arrest, epiphyseal (epiphysiodesis), any method, combined, proximal and distal tibia and fibula;	18.77	675.33	2579	2962	3331
27742	Arrest, epiphyseal (epiphysiodesis), any method, combined, proximal and distal tibia and fibula; and distal femur	17.94	639.71	2917	3453	3920
27745	Prophylactic treatment (nailing, pinning, plating or wiring) with or without methylmethacrylate, tibia	20.02	719.29	2552	2931	3252

Fracture and/or Dislocation

Code	Description	Medicare RVU	National Fee	PFR Fee Information 50%	75%	90%
27750	Closed treatment of tibial shaft fracture (with or without fibular fracture); without manipulation	8.46	308.11	744	935	1158
27752	Closed treatment of tibial shaft fracture (with or without fibular fracture); with manipulation, with or without skeletal traction	13.64	493.43	1192	1460	1692
27756	Percutaneous skeletal fixation of tibial shaft fracture (with or without fibular fracture) (eg, pins or screws)	14.79	532.46	1915	2329	2727
27758	Open treatment of tibial shaft fracture, (with or without fibular fracture) with plate/screws, with or without cerclage	23.35	837.53	2902	3644	4155
27759	Treatment of tibial shaft fracture (with or without fibular fracture) by intramedullary implant, with or without interlocking screws and/or cerclage	26.62	954.26	3117	3689	4155
27760	Closed treatment of medial malleolus fracture; without manipulation	8.15	297.12	581	737	881
27762	Closed treatment of medial malleolus fracture; with manipulation, with or without skin or skeletal traction	12.32	446.43	829	1007	1168
27766	Open treatment of medial malleolus fracture, with or without internal or external fixation	17.16	616.97	1681	2134	2438
27780	Closed treatment of proximal fibula or shaft fracture; without manipulation	7.24	264.15	455	604	710
27781	Closed treatment of proximal fibula or shaft fracture; with manipulation	10.56	383.14	750	960	1087

● = New Code ⊗ = Conscious Sedation ✚ = Add-on Code ∅ = Modifier '51' Exempt ▲ =Revised Code

Code	Description	Medicare RVU	National Fee	PFR Fee Information 50%	75%	90%
27784	Open treatment of proximal fibula or shaft fracture, with or without internal or external fixation	14.90	536.25	1455	1723	1932
27786	Closed treatment of distal fibular fracture (lateral malleolus); without manipulation	7.73	281.96	549	657	827
27788	Closed treatment of distal fibular fracture (lateral malleolus); with manipulation	10.74	389.97	751	867	1020
27792	Open treatment of distal fibular fracture (lateral malleolus), with or without internal or external fixation	15.94	573.77	1686	2086	2422
27808	Closed treatment of bimalleolar ankle fracture, (including Potts); without manipulation	8.07	294.84	651	778	967
27810	Closed treatment of bimalleolar ankle fracture, (including Potts); with manipulation	12.07	437.72	1157	1437	1652
27814	Open treatment of bimalleolar ankle fracture, with or without internal or external fixation	21.21	761.36	2181	2566	3046
27816	Closed treatment of trimalleolar ankle fracture; without manipulation	7.68	279.68	688	905	1018
27818	Closed treatment of trimalleolar ankle fracture; with manipulation	12.53	453.63	1230	1406	1615
27822	Open treatment of trimalleolar ankle fracture, with or without internal or external fixation, medial and/or lateral malleolus; without fixation of posterior lip	24.25	872.78	2487	2944	3458
27823	Open treatment of trimalleolar ankle fracture, with or without internal or external fixation, medial and/or lateral malleolus; with fixation of posterior lip	27.51	988.37	2838	3347	3770
27824	Closed treatment of fracture of weight bearing articular portion of distal tibia (eg, pilon or tibial plafond), with or without anesthesia; without manipulation	7.63	277.03	695	830	946
27825	Closed treatment of fracture of weight bearing articular portion of distal tibia (eg, pilon or tibial plafond), with or without anesthesia; with skeletal traction and/or requiring manipulation	14.04	507.07	1352	1729	1955
27826	Open treatment of fracture of weight bearing articular surface/portion of distal tibia (eg, pilon or tibial plafond), with internal or external fixation; of fibula only	18.81	678.74	2419	2853	3280
27827	Open treatment of fracture of weight bearing articular surface/portion of distal tibia (eg, pilon or tibial plafond), with internal or external fixation; of tibia only	30.47	1094.86	2854	3436	3972
27828	Open treatment of fracture of weight bearing articular surface/portion of distal tibia (eg, pilon or tibial plafond), with internal or external fixation; of both tibia and fibula	34.56	1240.39	3225	3989	4544
27829	Open treatment of distal tibiofibular joint (syndesmosis) disruption, with or without internal or external fixation	13.10	474.86	1641	1974	2253
27830	Closed treatment of proximal tibiofibular joint dislocation; without anesthesia	8.76	317.20	533	664	816
27831	Closed treatment of proximal tibiofibular joint dislocation; requiring anesthesia	9.70	350.17	682	821	941
27832	Open treatment of proximal tibiofibular joint dislocation, with or without internal or external fixation, or with excision of proximal fibula	13.52	486.98	1280	1516	1707
27840	Closed treatment of ankle dislocation; without anesthesia	8.84	317.20	469	634	879
27842	Closed treatment of ankle dislocation; requiring anesthesia, with or without percutaneous skeletal fixation	12.41	446.05	790	914	1173
27846	Open treatment of ankle dislocation, with or without percutaneous skeletal fixation; without repair or internal fixation	19.54	701.86	1993	2379	2942
27848	Open treatment of ankle dislocation, with or without percutaneous skeletal fixation; with repair or internal or external fixation	22.73	817.45	2268	2604	2939

Manipulation

Code	Description	Medicare RVU	National Fee	50%	75%	90%
27860	Manipulation of ankle under general anesthesia (includes application of traction or other fixation apparatus)	4.66	167.51	382	466	578

Arthrodesis

Code	Description	Medicare RVU	National Fee	50%	75%	90%
27870	Arthrodesis, ankle, open	27.78	994.81	3022	3574	4054
27871	Arthrodesis, tibiofibular joint, proximal or distal	18.33	658.66	2080	2443	2786

Amputation

Code	Description	Medicare RVU	National Fee	50%	75%	90%
27880	Amputation, leg, through tibia and fibula;	24.04	853.07	2417	2950	3469
27881	Amputation, leg, through tibia and fibula; with immediate fitting technique including application of first cast	23.81	851.56	2523	3069	3543
27882	Amputation, leg, through tibia and fibula; open, circular (guillotine)	17.20	615.08	1944	2449	2840
27884	Amputation, leg, through tibia and fibula; secondary closure or scar revision	15.45	552.55	1313	1549	1851
27886	Amputation, leg, through tibia and fibula; re-amputation	17.60	629.48	2215	2649	3042
27888	Amputation, ankle, through malleoli of tibia and fibula (eg, Syme, Pirogoff type procedures), with plastic closure and resection of nerves	18.93	678.37	2056	2549	2955

● = New Code ⊗ = Conscious Sedation ✚ = Add-on Code ∅ = Modifier '51' Exempt ▲ =Revised Code

		Medicare RVU	National Fee	PFR Fee Information 50%	75%	90%
27889	Ankle disarticulation	18.37	655.25	2049	2497	2806

Other Procedures

27892	Decompression fasciotomy, leg; anterior and/or lateral compartments only, with debridement of nonviable muscle and/or nerve	14.33	513.13	1461	1773	2034
27893	Decompression fasciotomy, leg; posterior compartment(s) only, with debridement of nonviable muscle and/or nerve	14.26	510.86	1340	1822	2122
27894	Decompression fasciotomy, leg; anterior and/or lateral, and posterior compartment(s), with debridement of nonviable muscle and/or nerve	21.74	776.52	1738	2086	2416
27899	Unlisted procedure, leg or ankle	-	-	IR	IR	IR

Foot and Toes
Incision

28001	Incision and drainage, bursa, foot	6.33	229.28	401	424	453
28002	Incision and drainage below fascia, with or without tendon sheath involvement, foot; single bursal space	11.83	426.35	723	835	981
28003	Incision and drainage below fascia, with or without tendon sheath involvement, foot; multiple areas	16.71	599.16	997	1225	1517
28005	Incision, bone cortex (eg, osteomyelitis or bone abscess), foot	16.38	585.14	1074	1316	1690
28008	Fasciotomy, foot and/or toe	10.04	363.44	737	822	986
28010	Tenotomy, percutaneous, toe; single tendon	5.75	206.92	428	500	808
28011	Tenotomy, percutaneous, toe; multiple tendons	8.22	295.60	527	651	777
28020	Arthrotomy, including exploration, drainage, or removal of loose or foreign body; intertarsal or tarsometatarsal joint	12.18	442.26	986	1242	1453
28022	Arthrotomy, including exploration, drainage, or removal of loose or foreign body; metatarsophalangeal joint	10.97	397.92	767	935	1146
28024	Arthrotomy, including exploration, drainage, or removal of loose or foreign body; interphalangeal joint	10.60	384.66	673	746	832
28035	Release, tarsal tunnel (posterior tibial nerve decompression)	12.11	439.23	1528	1889	2126

Excision

28043	Excision, tumor, foot; subcutaneous tissue	8.11	293.71	566	678	849
28045	Excision, tumor, foot; deep, subfascial, intramuscular	11.21	406.64	1005	1215	1391
28046	Radical resection of tumor (eg, malignant neoplasm), soft tissue of foot	21.11	759.84	1781	2374	2802
28050	Arthrotomy with biopsy; intertarsal or tarsometatarsal joint	10.30	374.05	948	1113	1273
28052	Arthrotomy with biopsy; metatarsophalangeal joint	9.81	356.62	723	860	1053
28054	Arthrotomy with biopsy; interphalangeal joint	9.05	329.71	609	680	759
● **28055**	Neurectomy, intrinsic musculature of foot	10.56	376.70	839	1013	1190
28060	Fasciectomy, plantar fascia; partial (separate procedure)	11.89	430.52	1019	1204	1448
28062	Fasciectomy, plantar fascia; radical (separate procedure)	14.28	516.16	1782	2039	2335
28070	Synovectomy; intertarsal or tarsometatarsal joint, each	11.61	420.28	955	1169	1326
28072	Synovectomy; metatarsophalangeal joint, each	11.36	412.70	713	831	1052
28080	Excision, interdigital (Morton) neuroma, single, each	10.89	394.89	858	1066	1225
28086	Synovectomy, tendon sheath, foot; flexor	13.53	494.18	1141	1370	1525
28088	Synovectomy, tendon sheath, foot; extensor	10.57	385.80	896	1019	1141
28090	Excision of lesion, tendon, tendon sheath, or capsule (including synovectomy) (eg, cyst or ganglion); foot	10.62	385.42	789	907	1028
28092	Excision of lesion, tendon, tendon sheath, or capsule (including synovectomy) (eg, cyst or ganglion); toe(s), each	9.73	354.72	628	714	814
28100	Excision or curettage of bone cyst or benign tumor, talus or calcaneus;	14.57	530.19	1266	1517	1725
28102	Excision or curettage of bone cyst or benign tumor, talus or calcaneus; with iliac or other autograft (includes obtaining graft)	14.65	525.64	1628	1915	2245

● = New Code ⊗ = Conscious Sedation ➕ = Add-on Code ∅ = Modifier '51' Exempt ▲ =Revised Code

		Medicare RVU	National Fee	PFR Fee Information 50%	75%	90%
28103	Excision or curettage of bone cyst or benign tumor, talus or calcaneus; with allograft	11.98	429.00	1444	1726	1954
28104	Excision or curettage of bone cyst or benign tumor, tarsal or metatarsal, except talus or calcaneus;	11.81	427.86	1053	1278	1450
28106	Excision or curettage of bone cyst or benign tumor, tarsal or metatarsal, except talus or calcaneus; with iliac or other autograft (includes obtaining graft)	12.65	451.74	1300	1629	1860
28107	Excision or curettage of bone cyst or benign tumor, tarsal or metatarsal, except talus or calcaneus; with allograft	13.23	479.78	1076	1381	1775
28108	Excision or curettage of bone cyst or benign tumor, phalanges of foot	9.79	355.10	848	931	1076
28110	Ostectomy, partial excision, fifth metatarsal head (bunionette) (separate procedure)	10.33	375.56	863	1010	1161
28111	Ostectomy, complete excision; first metatarsal head	12.28	446.05	1113	1359	1542
28112	Ostectomy, complete excision; other metatarsal head (second, third or fourth)	11.33	411.95	898	1100	1295
28113	Ostectomy, complete excision; fifth metatarsal head	13.17	476.75	927	1151	1410
28114	Ostectomy, complete excision; all metatarsal heads, with partial proximal phalangectomy, excluding first metatarsal (eg, Clayton type procedure)	25.10	906.89	2034	2517	2965
28116	Ostectomy, excision of tarsal coalition	17.46	627.58	1426	1841	2074
28118	Ostectomy, calcaneus;	13.54	490.01	1201	1470	1650
	(UNBUNDLING ALERT: 28119 cannot be used with 28118 by the same physician on the same day.)					
28119	Ostectomy, calcaneus; for spur, with or without plantar fascial release	12.04	435.44	1174	1358	1594
28120	Partial excision (craterization, saucerization, sequestrectomy, or diaphysectomy) bone (eg, osteomyelitis or bossing); talus or calcaneus	13.91	505.55	1167	1423	1537
28122	Partial excision (craterization, saucerization, sequestrectomy, or diaphysectomy) bone (eg, osteomyelitis or bossing); tarsal or metatarsal bone, except talus or calcaneus	15.81	570.36	1041	1347	1584
28124	Partial excision (craterization, saucerization, sequestrectomy, or diaphysectomy) bone (eg, osteomyelitis or bossing); phalanx of toe	10.94	396.03	801	1038	1178
28126	Resection, partial or complete, phalangeal base, each toe	8.67	314.93	727	900	1099
28130	Talectomy (astragalectomy)	17.08	611.67	1672	1947	2417
28140	Metatarsectomy	15.34	554.44	1206	1439	1658
28150	Phalangectomy, toe, each toe	9.91	359.65	749	921	1070
28153	Resection, condyle(s), distal end of phalanx, each toe	8.97	325.92	765	965	1158
28160	Hemiphalangectomy or interphalangeal joint excision, toe, proximal end of phalanx, each	9.31	338.42	761	909	1162
28171	Radical resection of tumor, bone; tarsal (except talus or calcaneus)	16.60	591.58	1604	2010	2379
28173	Radical resection of tumor, bone; metatarsal	18.09	651.08	1303	1702	2188
28175	Radical resection of tumor, bone; phalanx of toe	12.98	468.41	921	1179	1395

Introduction or Removal

28190	Removal of foreign body, foot; subcutaneous	5.75	210.33	400	539	713
28192	Removal of foreign body, foot; deep	11.10	402.85	706	892	1050
28193	Removal of foreign body, foot; complicated	12.57	454.39	930	1218	1424

Repair, Revision, and/or Reconstruction

28200	Repair, tendon, flexor, foot; primary or secondary, without free graft, each tendon	10.82	392.24	1125	1350	1503
28202	Repair, tendon, flexor, foot; secondary with free graft, each tendon (includes obtaining graft)	15.29	552.92	1466	1819	2203
28208	Repair, tendon, extensor, foot; primary or secondary, each tendon	10.29	373.29	737	978	1347
28210	Repair, tendon, extensor, foot; secondary with free graft, each tendon (includes obtaining graft)	13.78	497.97	881	1136	1368
28220	Tenolysis, flexor, foot; single tendon	10.27	371.77	845	1025	1175
28222	Tenolysis, flexor, foot; multiple tendons	12.03	434.31	1083	1337	1562
28225	Tenolysis, extensor, foot; single tendon	8.89	322.89	576	643	745

● = New Code ⊗ = Conscious Sedation ✚ = Add-on Code ∅ = Modifier '51' Exempt ▲ =Revised Code

		Medicare RVU	National Fee	PFR Fee Information 50%	75%	90%
28226	Tenolysis, extensor, foot; multiple tendons	10.51	380.87	716	789	954
28230	Tenotomy, open, tendon flexor; foot, single or multiple tendon(s) (separate procedure)	9.92	359.65	614	745	891
28232	Tenotomy, open, tendon flexor; toe, single tendon (separate procedure)	8.76	318.72	458	579	672
28234	Tenotomy, open, extensor, foot or toe, each tendon	8.96	326.30	464	610	696
28238	Reconstruction (advancement), posterior tibial tendon with excision of accessory tarsal navicular bone (eg, Kidner type procedure)	16.45	593.47	1493	1613	1944
28240	Tenotomy, lengthening, or release, abductor hallucis muscle	10.07	364.95	670	747	825
28250	Division of plantar fascia and muscle (eg, Steindler stripping) (separate procedure)	12.88	465.38	1052	1334	1518
28260	Capsulotomy, midfoot; medial release only (separate procedure)	16.13	580.59	1511	1856	2153
28261	Capsulotomy, midfoot; with tendon lengthening	23.65	847.01	1752	2056	2599
28262	Capsulotomy, midfoot; extensive, including posterior talotibial capsulotomy and tendon(s) lengthening (eg, resistant clubfoot deformity)	33.68	1211.58	2852	3486	4086
28264	Capsulotomy, midtarsal (eg, Heyman type procedure)	20.49	736.35	1990	2410	2666
28270	Capsulotomy; metatarsophalangeal joint, with or without tenorrhaphy, each joint (separate procedure)	10.86	393.38	659	777	879
28272	Capsulotomy; interphalangeal joint, each joint (separate procedure)	8.91	322.89	573	681	779
28280	Syndactylization, toes (eg, webbing or Kelikian type procedure)	12.50	453.63	776	930	1065
	(UNBUNDLING ALERT: 28285 cannot be used with 28153 or 28160 by the same physician on the same day.)					
28285	Correction, hammertoe (eg, interphalangeal fusion, partial or total phalangectomy)	10.58	383.14	849	1091	1220
28286	Correction, cock-up fifth toe, with plastic skin closure (eg, Ruiz-Mora type procedure)	10.41	377.08	929	1202	1314
28288	Ostectomy, partial, exostectomy or condylectomy, metatarsal head, each metatarsal head	13.08	473.72	944	1164	1317
28289	Hallux rigidus correction with cheilectomy, debridement and capsular release of the first metatarsophalangeal joint	17.50	632.13	936	1253	1504
	(A4550 (Disposable Surgical Tray) can be coded in addition to 28290 in the office setting. Payment is at carrier discretion.)					
28290	Correction, hallux valgus (bunion), with or without sesamoidectomy; simple exostectomy (eg, Silver type procedure)	13.29	481.68	1200	1375	1561
	(UNBUNDLING ALERT: 28292 cannot be used with 28270, 28288 or 28290 by the same physician on the same day.)					
	(A4550 (Disposable Surgical Tray) can be coded in addition to 28292 in the office setting. Payment is at carrier discretion.)					
28292	Correction, hallux valgus (bunion), with or without sesamoidectomy; Keller, McBride, or Mayo type procedure	17.84	642.74	1478	1819	2227
	(A4550 (Disposable Surgical Tray) can be coded in addition to 28293 in the office setting. Payment is at carrier discretion.)					

● = New Code ⊗ = Conscious Sedation ✚ = Add-on Code ∅ = Modifier '51' Exempt ▲ =Revised Code

		Medicare RVU	National Fee	PFR Fee Information 50%	75%	90%
28293	Correction, hallux valgus (bunion), with or without sesamoidectomy; resection of joint with implant	23.95	865.20	1877	2037	2368
	(A4550 (Disposable Surgical Tray) can be coded in addition to 28294 in the office setting. Payment is at carrier discretion.)					
28294	Correction, hallux valgus (bunion), with or without sesamoidectomy; with tendon transplants (eg, Joplin type procedure)	17.60	634.03	1702	2033	2357
	(UNBUNDLING ALERT: 28296 cannot be used with 28270, 28290, 28292, or 28298 by the same physician on the same day.)					
	(A4550 (Disposable Surgical Tray) can be coded in addition to 28296 in the office setting. Payment is at carrier discretion.)					
28296	Correction, hallux valgus (bunion), with or without sesamoidectomy; with metatarsal osteotomy (eg, Mitchell, Chevron, or concentric type procedures)	19.04	685.94	2024	2620	3041
	(A4550 (Disposable Surgical Tray) can be coded in addition to 28297 in the office setting. Payment is at carrier discretion.)					
28297	Correction, hallux valgus (bunion), with or without sesamoidectomy; Lapidus-type procedure	19.97	721.19	1843	2232	2626
	(A4550 (Disposable Surgical Tray) can be coded in addition to 28298 in the office setting. Payment is at carrier discretion.)					
28298	Correction, hallux valgus (bunion), with or without sesamoidectomy; by phalanx osteotomy	16.80	605.98	1572	1864	2152
	(A4550 (Disposable Surgical Tray) can be coded in addition to 28299 in the office setting. Payment is at carrier discretion.)					
28299	Correction, hallux valgus (bunion), with or without sesamoidectomy; by double osteotomy	22.00	790.16	1994	2331	2673
28300	Osteotomy; calcaneus (eg, Dwyer or Chambers type procedure), with or without internal fixation	17.96	643.88	1611	1955	2340
28302	Osteotomy; talus	17.65	632.13	1699	1999	2214
28304	Osteotomy, tarsal bones, other than calcaneus or talus;	18.92	681.78	1503	1714	1967
28305	Osteotomy, tarsal bones, other than calcaneus or talus; with autograft (includes obtaining graft) (eg, Fowler type)	18.37	655.63	1693	2143	2647
28306	Osteotomy, with or without lengthening, shortening or angular correction, metatarsal; first metatarsal	13.97	507.07	1263	1532	1785
28307	Osteotomy, with or without lengthening, shortening or angular correction, metatarsal; first metatarsal with autograft (other than first toe)	17.94	655.63	1414	1752	2082
28308	Osteotomy, with or without lengthening, shortening or angular correction, metatarsal; other than first metatarsal, each	12.36	447.95	1049	1284	1470
28309	Osteotomy, with or without lengthening, shortening or angular correction, metatarsal; multiple (eg, Swanson type cavus foot procedure)	23.94	854.21	1662	2101	2575
28310	Osteotomy, shortening, angular or rotational correction; proximal phalanx, first toe (separate procedure)	12.38	448.33	899	1230	1374
28312	Osteotomy, shortening, angular or rotational correction; other phalanges, any toe	11.16	405.50	717	862	1004
28313	Reconstruction, angular deformity of toe, soft tissue procedures only (eg, overlapping second toe, fifth toe, curly toes)	11.59	419.90	802	938	1053
28315	Sesamoidectomy, first toe (separate procedure)	10.90	394.51	890	1149	1320
28320	Repair, nonunion or malunion; tarsal bones	17.17	615.46	1401	1789	2277
28322	Repair, nonunion or malunion; metatarsal, with or without bone graft (includes obtaining graft)	19.07	690.49	1087	1488	1790
28340	Reconstruction, toe, macrodactyly; soft tissue resection	14.74	531.70	1277	1529	1837
28341	Reconstruction, toe, macrodactyly; requiring bone resection	17.00	611.29	1560	1838	2092
28344	Reconstruction, toe(s); polydactyly	10.83	394.13	930	1169	1452
28345	Reconstruction, toe(s); syndactyly, with or without skin graft(s), each web	13.38	484.33	1349	1457	1552
28360	Reconstruction, cleft foot	26.41	944.78	2234	3084	3695

Fracture and/or Dislocation

28400	Closed treatment of calcaneal fracture; without manipulation	6.14	224.35	553	728	841
28405	Closed treatment of calcaneal fracture; with manipulation	10.12	365.71	880	1014	1119
28406	Percutaneous skeletal fixation of calcaneal fracture, with manipulation	14.07	508.58	1260	1573	1744
28415	Open treatment of calcaneal fracture, with or without internal or external fixation;	32.92	1180.89	2180	2581	2947

● = New Code ⊗ = Conscious Sedation ✚ = Add-on Code ∅ = Modifier '51' Exempt ▲ =Revised Code

		Medicare RVU	National Fee	PFR Fee Information 50%	75%	90%
28420	Open treatment of calcaneal fracture, with or without internal or external fixation; with primary iliac or other autogenous bone graft (includes obtaining graft)	32.13	1152.46	2582	2947	3448
28430	Closed treatment of talus fracture; without manipulation	5.78	210.71	513	625	688
28435	Closed treatment of talus fracture; with manipulation	7.86	284.61	743	932	1076
28436	Percutaneous skeletal fixation of talus fracture, with manipulation	11.28	409.29	965	1153	1348
28445	Open treatment of talus fracture, with or without internal or external fixation	30.38	1086.14	2064	2332	2582
28450	Treatment of tarsal bone fracture (except talus and calcaneus); without manipulation, each	5.30	193.28	450	548	594
28455	Treatment of tarsal bone fracture (except talus and calcaneus); with manipulation, each	7.08	256.19	669	746	869
28456	Percutaneous skeletal fixation of tarsal bone fracture (except talus and calcaneus), with manipulation, each	7.21	262.63	816	996	1216
28465	Open treatment of tarsal bone fracture (except talus and calcaneus), with or without internal or external fixation, each	14.24	512.37	1337	1725	1987
28470	Closed treatment of metatarsal fracture; without manipulation, each	5.34	194.79	430	544	591
28475	Closed treatment of metatarsal fracture; with manipulation, each	6.70	242.54	599	712	834
28476	Percutaneous skeletal fixation of metatarsal fracture, with manipulation, each	8.83	321.37	898	1054	1226
28485	Open treatment of metatarsal fracture, with or without internal or external fixation, each	11.83	426.35	1248	1458	1657
28490	Closed treatment of fracture great toe, phalanx or phalanges; without manipulation	3.30	120.89	228	314	348
28495	Closed treatment of fracture great toe, phalanx or phalanges; with manipulation	4.07	148.18	351	439	500
28496	Percutaneous skeletal fixation of fracture great toe, phalanx or phalanges, with manipulation	10.74	397.92	595	667	738
28505	Open treatment of fracture great toe, phalanx or phalanges, with or without internal or external fixation	12.37	454.01	840	1013	1245
28510	Closed treatment of fracture, phalanx or phalanges, other than great toe; without manipulation, each	2.83	103.08	199	237	287
28515	Closed treatment of fracture, phalanx or phalanges, other than great toe; with manipulation, each	3.66	133.02	283	341	395
28525	Open treatment of fracture, phalanx or phalanges, other than great toe, with or without internal or external fixation, each	11.22	412.32	774	923	1091
28530	Closed treatment of sesamoid fracture	2.71	98.53	297	410	473
28531	Open treatment of sesamoid fracture, with or without internal fixation	9.76	360.41	579	690	913
28540	Closed treatment of tarsal bone dislocation, other than talotarsal; without anesthesia	4.86	176.22	353	452	578
28545	Closed treatment of tarsal bone dislocation, other than talotarsal; requiring anesthesia	5.47	197.82	536	634	750
28546	Percutaneous skeletal fixation of tarsal bone dislocation, other than talotarsal, with manipulation	10.90	400.58	705	790	926
28555	Open treatment of tarsal bone dislocation, with or without internal or external fixation	17.34	632.51	1275	1546	1805
28570	Closed treatment of talotarsal joint dislocation; without anesthesia	4.40	160.31	411	461	541
28575	Closed treatment of talotarsal joint dislocation; requiring anesthesia	7.83	283.85	574	680	778
28576	Percutaneous skeletal fixation of talotarsal joint dislocation, with manipulation	9.31	335.77	737	980	1232
28585	Open treatment of talotarsal joint dislocation, with or without internal or external fixation	17.40	628.34	1521	1833	2048
28600	Closed treatment of tarsometatarsal joint dislocation; without anesthesia	5.08	184.94	382	493	543
28605	Closed treatment of tarsometatarsal joint dislocation; requiring anesthesia	6.46	234.21	529	633	704
28606	Percutaneous skeletal fixation of tarsometatarsal joint dislocation, with manipulation	10.39	374.81	974	1150	1321
28615	Open treatment of tarsometatarsal joint dislocation, with or without internal or external fixation	18.05	649.94	1293	1715	2002
28630	Closed treatment of metatarsophalangeal joint dislocation; without anesthesia	3.59	129.61	271	304	360
28635	Closed treatment of metatarsophalangeal joint dislocation; requiring anesthesia	4.28	155.00	392	456	561

● = New Code ⊗ = Conscious Sedation ✚ = Add-on Code ∅ = Modifier '51' Exempt ▲ =Revised Code

Code	Description	Medicare RVU	National Fee	PFR Fee Information 50%	75%	90%
28636	Percutaneous skeletal fixation of metatarsophalangeal joint dislocation, with manipulation	7.19	261.87	525	651	821
28645	Open treatment of metatarsophalangeal joint dislocation, with or without internal or external fixation	10.28	373.29	726	862	1026
28660	Closed treatment of interphalangeal joint dislocation; without anesthesia	2.65	95.50	217	275	326
28665	Closed treatment of interphalangeal joint dislocation; requiring anesthesia	3.74	134.16	312	388	462
28666	Percutaneous skeletal fixation of interphalangeal joint dislocation, with manipulation	5.51	198.58	490	634	755
28675	Open treatment of interphalangeal joint dislocation, with or without internal or external fixation	10.45	384.66	650	823	929

Arthrodesis

Code	Description	Medicare RVU	National Fee	PFR Fee Information 50%	75%	90%
28705	Arthrodesis; pantalar	35.25	1259.33	3211	3879	4400
28715	Arthrodesis; triple	26.03	931.52	2826	3503	3885
28725	Arthrodesis; subtalar	21.77	779.55	2235	2566	2887
28730	Arthrodesis, midtarsal or tarsometatarsal, multiple or transverse;	22.24	796.23	2004	2501	2803
28735	Arthrodesis, midtarsal or tarsometatarsal, multiple or transverse; with osteotomy (eg, flatfoot correction)	21.35	763.26	2213	2603	3008
28737	Arthrodesis, with tendon lengthening and advancement, midtarsal, tarsal navicular-cuneiform (eg, Miller type procedure)	18.95	676.85	1956	2358	2644
28740	Arthrodesis, midtarsal or tarsometatarsal, single joint	21.20	768.94	1456	1912	2254
28750	Arthrodesis, great toe; metatarsophalangeal joint	21.15	769.70	1362	1661	1953
28755	Arthrodesis, great toe; interphalangeal joint	11.84	430.52	1009	1239	1479
28760	Arthrodesis, with extensor hallucis longus transfer to first metatarsal neck, great toe, interphalangeal joint (eg, Jones type procedure)	18.48	666.24	1079	1340	1692

Amputation

Code	Description	Medicare RVU	National Fee	PFR Fee Information 50%	75%	90%
28800	Amputation, foot; midtarsal (eg, Chopart type procedure)	15.42	551.41	1724	1988	2201
28805	Amputation, foot; transmetatarsal	19.47	690.11	1901	2217	2418
28810	Amputation, metatarsal, with toe, single	11.77	421.04	1121	1329	1556
28820	Amputation, toe; metatarsophalangeal joint	13.10	477.89	887	1029	1225
28825	Amputation, toe; interphalangeal joint	11.25	412.32	752	958	1238

Other Procedures

Code	Description	Medicare RVU	National Fee	PFR Fee Information 50%	75%	90%
28890	Extracorporeal shock wave, high energy, performed by a physician, requiring anesthesia other than local, including ultrasound guidance, involving the plantar fascia	9.25	337.67	926	1079	1252
28899	Unlisted procedure, foot or toes	-	-	IR	IR	IR

Application of Casts and Strapping
Body and Upper Extremity
Casts

(See also HCPCS codes A4580, A4590, Q4001-A4048 and Q4050 for cast supplies.)

Code	Description	Medicare RVU	National Fee	PFR Fee Information 50%	75%	90%
29000	Application of halo type body cast (see 20661-20663 for insertion)	6.06	220.94	646	753	853
29010	Application of Risser jacket, localizer, body; only	5.81	212.23	487	573	702
29015	Application of Risser jacket, localizer, body; including head	5.76	209.19	618	715	821
29020	Application of turnbuckle jacket, body; only	5.73	209.19	510	590	666
29025	Application of turnbuckle jacket, body; including head	6.10	222.08	580	664	750
29035	Application of body cast, shoulder to hips;	5.68	208.44	367	471	567
29040	Application of body cast, shoulder to hips; including head, Minerva type	5.33	193.66	504	626	709
29044	Application of body cast, shoulder to hips; including one thigh	6.43	235.72	403	504	591
29046	Application of body cast, shoulder to hips; including both thighs	6.30	229.66	470	573	650

© PFR 2007

● = New Code ⊗ = Conscious Sedation ✚ = Add-on Code ∅ = Modifier '51' Exempt ▲ =Revised Code

		Medicare RVU	National Fee	PFR Fee Information 50%	75%	90%
29049	Application, cast; figure-of-eight	2.28	83.00	166	209	268
29055	Application, cast; shoulder spica	5.04	184.18	340	409	492
29058	Application, cast; plaster Velpeau	2.96	107.25	182	222	260
29065	Application, cast; shoulder to hand (long arm)	2.34	85.27	183	239	312
29075	Application, cast; elbow to finger (short arm)	2.15	78.45	145	175	216
29085	Application, cast; hand and lower forearm (gauntlet)	2.29	83.37	143	190	216
29086	Application, cast; finger (eg, contracture)	1.67	61.01	106	133	163

Splints

29105	Application of long arm splint (shoulder to hand)	2.19	79.58	120	149	188
29125	Application of short arm splint (forearm to hand); static	1.67	61.01	96	122	143
29126	Application of short arm splint (forearm to hand); dynamic	2.00	72.76	132	161	196
29130	Application of finger splint; static	1.02	36.76	68	86	103
29131	Application of finger splint; dynamic	1.29	46.61	119	144	168

Strapping-Any Age

29200	Strapping; thorax	1.38	49.65	75	97	119
29220	Strapping; low back	1.37	49.65	85	106	122
29240	Strapping; shoulder (eg, Velpeau)	1.58	57.23	82	96	124
29260	Strapping; elbow or wrist	1.32	47.75	67	84	109
29280	Strapping; hand or finger	1.31	47.75	74	94	101

Lower Extremity
Casts

29305	Application of hip spica cast; one leg	5.73	209.57	459	572	628
29325	Application of hip spica cast; one and one-half spica or both legs	6.29	229.66	499	579	712
29345	Application of long leg cast (thigh to toes);	3.38	122.79	251	312	360
	(UNBUNDLING ALERT: 29355 cannot be used with 29345 by the same physician on the same day.)					
29355	Application of long leg cast (thigh to toes); walker or ambulatory type	3.48	126.20	260	309	360
29358	Application of long leg cast brace	3.74	136.43	405	477	563
29365	Application of cylinder cast (thigh to ankle)	3.02	109.90	222	259	302
29405	Application of short leg cast (below knee to toes);	2.22	80.72	208	257	281
	(UNBUNDLING ALERT: 29425 cannot be used with 29405 by the same physician on the same day.)					
29425	Application of short leg cast (below knee to toes); walking or ambulatory type	2.39	86.79	233	273	294
29435	Application of patellar tendon bearing (PTB) cast	2.93	106.49	279	343	386
29440	Adding walker to previously applied cast	1.32	47.75	69	92	108
29445	Application of rigid total contact leg cast	3.81	137.57	379	415	460
29450	Application of clubfoot cast with molding or manipulation, long or short leg	3.84	137.57	174	207	242

Splints

(See also HCPCS codes A4570, Q4049, Q4051 and S8450-S8452 for splint supplies.)

29505	Application of long leg splint (thigh to ankle or toes)	1.92	70.11	143	188	219
29515	Application of short leg splint (calf to foot)	1.71	62.15	114	145	174

Strapping-Any Age

29520	Strapping; hip	1.38	50.40	95	118	141

© PFR 2007

● = New Code ⊗ = Conscious Sedation ✚ = Add-on Code ∅ = Modifier '51' Exempt ▲ =Revised Code

		Medicare RVU	National Fee	PFR Fee Information 50%	75%	90%
29530	Strapping; knee	1.37	49.65	87	99	124
29540	Strapping; ankle and/or foot	1.02	36.76	65	81	102
29550	Strapping; toes	0.99	35.62	58	72	84
29580	Strapping; Unna boot	1.29	46.61	94	130	152
29590	Denis-Browne splint strapping	1.39	49.65	86	126	167

Removal or Repair

29700	Removal or bivalving; gauntlet, boot or body cast	1.56	56.85	81	117	155
29705	Removal or bivalving; full arm or full leg cast	1.70	61.39	92	109	140
29710	Removal or bivalving; shoulder or hip spica, Minerva, or Risser jacket, etc.	3.05	110.66	160	201	239
29715	Removal or bivalving; turnbuckle jacket	2.19	79.58	124	141	192

(Medicare fees for the code below are based on Non Facility RVUs. PFR information reflects fee when procedure is performed in a facility.)

29720	Repair of spica, body cast or jacket	1.96	71.63	80	112	170
29730	Windowing of cast	1.67	60.26	78	104	132
29740	Wedging of cast (except clubfoot casts)	2.43	87.92	126	144	175
29750	Wedging of clubfoot cast	2.50	89.82	104	129	148

Other Procedures

29799	Unlisted procedure, casting or strapping	-	-	IR	IR	IR

Endoscopy/Arthroscopy

29800	Arthroscopy, temporomandibular joint, diagnostic, with or without synovial biopsy (separate procedure)	14.19	512.00	1357	1837	2502
29804	Arthroscopy, temporomandibular joint, surgical	17.23	619.62	2413	2893	3226
29805	Arthroscopy, shoulder, diagnostic, with or without synovial biopsy (separate procedure)	12.40	447.19	1101	1448	1938

(See also HCPCS code S2300 for arthroscopy, shoulder, surgical; with thermally-induced capsulorrhaphy.)

29806	Arthroscopy, shoulder, surgical; capsulorrhaphy	28.18	1011.11	3423	3956	4151
29807	Arthroscopy, shoulder, surgical; repair of SLAP lesion	27.47	985.71	3209	3751	4241
29819	Arthroscopy, shoulder, surgical; with removal of loose body or foreign body	15.51	558.61	2087	2472	2590
29820	Arthroscopy, shoulder, surgical; synovectomy, partial	14.31	515.03	2223	2399	2670
29821	Arthroscopy, shoulder, surgical; synovectomy, complete	15.64	563.16	2506	2952	3298
29822	Arthroscopy, shoulder, surgical; debridement, limited	15.20	547.62	2358	2692	2951
29823	Arthroscopy, shoulder, surgical; debridement, extensive	16.59	597.26	2732	3171	3574
29824	Arthroscopy, shoulder, surgical; distal claviculectomy including distal articular surface (Mumford procedure)	17.54	630.99	2232	2445	2781
29825	Arthroscopy, shoulder, surgical; with lysis and resection of adhesions, with or without manipulation	15.49	557.85	2370	2734	3089
29826	Arthroscopy, shoulder, surgical; decompression of subacromial space with partial acromioplasty, with or without coracoacromial release	17.81	640.47	2787	3196	3501
29827	Arthroscopy, shoulder, surgical; with rotator cuff repair	29.12	1044.83	2960	3372	3837
29830	Arthroscopy, elbow, diagnostic, with or without synovial biopsy (separate procedure)	11.93	430.14	1215	1479	1679
29834	Arthroscopy, elbow, surgical; with removal of loose body or foreign body	13.01	468.79	2142	2666	3132
29835	Arthroscopy, elbow, surgical; synovectomy, partial	13.32	479.78	2221	2749	3118
29836	Arthroscopy, elbow, surgical; synovectomy, complete	15.32	551.41	2477	2706	2941
29837	Arthroscopy, elbow, surgical; debridement, limited	14.00	504.04	2128	2653	3024
29838	Arthroscopy, elbow, surgical; debridement, extensive	15.67	564.29	2292	2711	2959

© PFR 2007

● = New Code ⊗ = Conscious Sedation ✚ = Add-on Code ∅ = Modifier '51' Exempt ▲ =Revised Code

		Medicare RVU	National Fee	PFR Fee Information 50%	75%	90%
29840	Arthroscopy, wrist, diagnostic, with or without synovial biopsy (separate procedure)	11.59	418.01	1252	1504	1739
29843	Arthroscopy, wrist, surgical; for infection, lavage and drainage	12.43	447.95	1600	1858	2078
29844	Arthroscopy, wrist, surgical; synovectomy, partial	13.07	470.69	1957	2224	2456
29845	Arthroscopy, wrist, surgical; synovectomy, complete	14.81	532.46	2196	2571	3116
29846	Arthroscopy, wrist, surgical; excision and/or repair of triangular fibrocartilage and/or joint debridement	13.69	493.05	2385	2754	3053
29847	Arthroscopy, wrist, surgical; internal fixation for fracture or instability	14.16	509.34	2223	2611	2890
29848	Endoscopy, wrist, surgical, with release of transverse carpal ligament	12.63	454.77	1656	1988	2138
29850	Arthroscopically aided treatment of intercondylar spine(s) and/or tuberosity fracture(s) of the knee, with or without manipulation; without internal or external fixation (includes arthroscopy)	14.53	519.57	2034	2524	2959
29851	Arthroscopically aided treatment of intercondylar spine(s) and/or tuberosity fracture(s) of the knee, with or without manipulation; with internal or external fixation (includes arthroscopy)	24.85	891.73	2628	2989	3250
29855	Arthroscopically aided treatment of tibial fracture, proximal (plateau); unicondylar, with or without internal or external fixation (includes arthroscopy)	20.87	750.37	2427	2730	2912
29856	Arthroscopically aided treatment of tibial fracture, proximal (plateau); bicondylar, with or without internal or external fixation (includes arthroscopy)	26.71	958.43	2604	3125	3612
29860	Arthroscopy, hip, diagnostic with or without synovial biopsy (separate procedure)	16.99	610.15	1492	1641	1941
29861	Arthroscopy, hip, surgical; with removal of loose body or foreign body	18.71	671.16	2067	2521	2941
29862	Arthroscopy, hip, surgical; with debridement/shaving of articular cartilage (chondroplasty), abrasion arthroplasty, and/or resection of labrum	20.92	751.13	2508	2864	3261
29863	Arthroscopy, hip, surgical; with synovectomy	20.66	741.28	2381	2723	3131
29866	Arthroscopy, knee, surgical; osteochondral autograft(s) (eg, mosaicplasty) (includes harvesting of the autograft)	27.79	997.84	3171	3531	3984
29867	Arthroscopy, knee, surgical; osteochondral allograft (eg, mosaicplasty)	33.71	1208.17	3715	4526	5229
29868	Arthroscopy, knee, surgical; meniscal transplantation (includes arthrotomy for meniscal insertion), medial or lateral	45.34	1623.53	4988	6124	7111
29870	Arthroscopy, knee, diagnostic, with or without synovial biopsy (separate procedure)	10.68	385.42	1207	1423	1582
	(See also HCPCS code S2112 for arthroscopy, knee, surgical for harvesting of cartilage (chondrocyte cells).)					
	(See also CPT Category III code 0012T for arthroscopy, knee, surgical, implantation of osteochondral graft(s) for treatment of articular sur)					
	(See also CPT Category III code 0013T for arthroscopy, knee, surgical, implantation of osteochondral graft(s) for treatment of articular sur)					
29871	Arthroscopy, knee, surgical; for infection, lavage and drainage	13.40	482.81	1856	2212	2491

● = New Code ⊗ = Conscious Sedation ✚ = Add-on Code ∅ = Modifier '51' Exempt ▲ =Revised Code

Code	Description	Medicare RVU	National Fee	PFR Fee Information 50%	75%	90%
29873	Arthroscopy, knee, surgical; with lateral release	13.46	486.98	2119	2526	2842
	(UNBUNDLING ALERT: 29874 cannot be used with 20610 or 29870 by the same physician on the same day.)					
	(See also HCPCS code G0289 for arthroscopy, surgical of knee for removal of loose body or foreign body at the time of other surgical knee ar)					
29874	Arthroscopy, knee, surgical; for removal of loose body or foreign body (eg, osteochondritis dissecans fragmentation, chondral fragmentation)	14.06	505.93	2249	2593	2887
	(UNBUNDLING ALERT: 29875 cannot be used with 20610 or 29870 by the same physician on the same day.)					
29875	Arthroscopy, knee, surgical; synovectomy, limited (eg, plica or shelf resection) (separate procedure)	13.07	471.07	2292	2636	2988
	(UNBUNDLING ALERT: 29876 cannot be used with 20610, 29870, 29874 or 29875 by the same physician on the same day.)					
29876	Arthroscopy, knee, surgical; synovectomy, major, two or more compartments (eg, medial or lateral)	16.92	607.88	2669	3151	3398
	(UNBUNDLING ALERT: 29877 cannot be used with 20610, 29870, 29874 or 29875 by the same physician on the same day.)					
29877	Arthroscopy, knee, surgical; debridement/shaving of articular cartilage (chondroplasty)	15.99	574.91	2479	2859	3037
	(UNBUNDLING ALERT: 29879 cannot be used with 20610, 29870, 29874, 29875 or 29877 by the same physician on the same day.)					
29879	Arthroscopy, knee, surgical; abrasion arthroplasty (includes chondroplasty where necessary) or multiple drilling or microfracture	17.14	615.83	2664	3158	3435
	(UNBUNDLING ALERT: 29880 cannot be used with 20610, 29870, 29874, 29875, or 29881 by the same physician on the same day.)					
29880	Arthroscopy, knee, surgical; with meniscectomy (medial AND lateral, including any meniscal shaving)	17.91	643.12	3272	3920	4583
	(UNBUNDLING ALERT: 29881 cannot be used with 20610, 29870, 29874 or 29875 by the same physician on the same day.)					
29881	Arthroscopy, knee, surgical; with meniscectomy (medial OR lateral, including any meniscal shaving)	16.67	599.16	2754	3235	3636
29882	Arthroscopy, knee, surgical; with meniscus repair (medial OR lateral)	18.01	646.53	3067	3633	4125
29883	Arthroscopy, knee, surgical; with meniscus repair (medial AND lateral)	22.25	798.88	3659	4588	5314
29884	Arthroscopy, knee, surgical; with lysis of adhesions, with or without manipulation (separate procedure)	15.93	572.63	2408	2735	3064
29885	Arthroscopy, knee, surgical; drilling for osteochondritis dissecans with bone grafting, with or without internal fixation (including debridement of base of lesion)	19.36	695.42	2777	3193	3561
29886	Arthroscopy, knee, surgical; drilling for intact osteochondritis dissecans lesion	16.30	585.90	2577	2988	3222
29887	Arthroscopy, knee, surgical; drilling for intact osteochondritis dissecans lesion with internal fixation	19.26	692.01	3007	3619	3978
29888	Arthroscopically aided anterior cruciate ligament repair/augmentation or reconstruction	26.31	943.27	4734	5372	5953
29889	Arthroscopically aided posterior cruciate ligament repair/augmentation or reconstruction	31.96	1145.64	4678	5660	6403
29891	Arthroscopy, ankle, surgical, excision of osteochondral defect of talus and/or tibia, including drilling of the defect	18.17	652.59	2416	2907	3460
29892	Arthroscopically aided repair of large osteochondritis dissecans lesion, talar dome fracture, or tibial plafond fracture, with or without internal fixation (includes arthroscopy)	18.94	679.50	2461	2924	3426
29893	Endoscopic plantar fasciotomy	13.65	494.18	1212	1562	1870
29894	Arthroscopy, ankle (tibiotalar and fibulotalar joints), surgical; with removal of loose body or foreign body	13.70	491.53	2233	2608	2935
29895	Arthroscopy, ankle (tibiotalar and fibulotalar joints), surgical; synovectomy, partial	13.40	480.92	2173	2634	3059
29897	Arthroscopy, ankle (tibiotalar and fibulotalar joints), surgical; debridement, limited	14.06	505.17	2126	2630	3007
29898	Arthroscopy, ankle (tibiotalar and fibulotalar joints), surgical; debridement, extensive	15.64	560.88	2846	3424	3685
29899	Arthroscopy, ankle (tibiotalar and fibulotalar joints), surgical; with ankle arthrodesis	27.86	997.84	IR	IR	IR
29900	Arthroscopy, metacarpophalangeal joint, diagnostic, includes synovial biopsy	12.28	443.40	1576	1749	1978
29901	Arthroscopy, metacarpophalangeal joint, surgical; with debridement	13.60	490.77	1721	1910	2159
29902	Arthroscopy, metacarpophalangeal joint, surgical; with reduction of displaced ulnar collateral ligament (eg, Stener lesion)	13.97	502.52	1865	2070	2341
29999	Unlisted procedure, arthroscopy	-	-	IR	IR	IR

● = New Code ⊗ = Conscious Sedation ✚ = Add-on Code ∅ = Modifier '51' Exempt ▲ =Revised Code

	Medicare RVU	National Fee	PFR Fee Information 50%	75%	90%

Respiratory System

Nose

Incision

30000 Drainage abscess or hematoma, nasal, internal approach	5.55	204.65	259	336	408
30020 Drainage abscess or hematoma, nasal septum	4.99	183.42	273	329	390

Excision

30100 Biopsy, intranasal	3.09	113.69	171	225	267
30110 Excision, nasal polyp(s), simple	5.13	187.97	336	405	487
30115 Excision, nasal polyp(s), extensive	10.49	380.87	814	1050	1176
30117 Excision or destruction (eg, laser), intranasal lesion; internal approach	17.55	652.97	699	888	1099
30118 Excision or destruction (eg, laser), intranasal lesion; external approach (lateral rhinotomy)	19.45	699.59	1840	2244	2584
30120 Excision or surgical planing of skin of nose for rhinophyma	12.43	450.98	1627	2064	2494
30124 Excision dermoid cyst, nose; simple, skin, subcutaneous	7.01	253.53	593	794	922
30125 Excision dermoid cyst, nose; complex, under bone or cartilage	15.84	572.63	1680	2385	2823
30130 Excision inferior turbinate, partial or complete, any method	9.24	337.29	684	835	1072
30140 Submucous resection inferior turbinate, partial or complete, any method	10.12	370.26	991	1201	1454
30150 Rhinectomy; partial	20.79	751.89	1815	2077	2440
30160 Rhinectomy; total	20.47	738.24	2358	2490	2848

Introduction

30200 Injection into turbinate(s), therapeutic	2.53	92.85	120	137	151
30210 Displacement therapy (Proetz type)	3.35	122.79	164	192	224
30220 Insertion, nasal septal prosthesis (button)	6.21	229.28	393	493	622

Removal of Foreign Body

(Medicare fees for the code below are based on Non Facility RVUs. PFR information reflects fee when procedure is performed in a facility.)

30300 Removal foreign body, intranasal; office type procedure	5.65	209.95	178	213	245
30310 Removal foreign body, intranasal; requiring general anesthesia	5.15	187.59	463	634	768
30320 Removal foreign body, intranasal; by lateral rhinotomy	11.73	427.10	1233	1381	1574

Repair

(30400 - 30450 may be reimbursable by Medicare for nasal fracture, benign or malignant tumor or deviated septum with complications.)

30400 Rhinoplasty, primary; lateral and alar cartilages and/or elevation of nasal tip	26.69	971.31	2599	3406	3620
30410 Rhinoplasty, primary; complete, external parts including bony pyramid, lateral and alar cartilages, and/or elevation of nasal tip	32.53	1180.51	3182	3784	4099
30420 Rhinoplasty, primary; including major septal repair	35.24	1272.22	3950	4857	5268
30430 Rhinoplasty, secondary; minor revision (small amount of nasal tip work)	23.96	877.71	1507	1789	1993
30435 Rhinoplasty, secondary; intermediate revision (bony work with osteotomies)	31.90	1161.56	2186	2700	3324
30450 Rhinoplasty, secondary; major revision (nasal tip work and osteotomies)	41.86	1512.49	3289	3905	4488
30460 Rhinoplasty for nasal deformity secondary to congenital cleft lip and/or palate, including columellar lengthening; tip only	20.54	739.38	2141	2476	2792
30462 Rhinoplasty for nasal deformity secondary to congenital cleft lip and/or palate, including columellar lengthening; tip, septum, osteotomies	41.48	1495.44	4179	4685	5037
30465 Repair of nasal vestibular stenosis (eg, spreader grafting, lateral nasal wall reconstruction)	24.84	894.76	2603	3255	3907

● = New Code ⊗ = Conscious Sedation ✚ = Add-on Code ∅ = Modifier '51' Exempt ▲ =Revised Code

		Medicare RVU	National Fee	PFR Fee Information 50%	75%	90%
30520	Septoplasty or submucous resection, with or without cartilage scoring, contouring or replacement with graft	14.16	510.48	2167	2939	3273
30540	Repair choanal atresia; intranasal	17.20	621.90	1826	2222	2536
30545	Repair choanal atresia; transpalatine	24.67	890.97	2632	3282	3787
	(Medicare fees for the code below are based on Non Facility RVUs. PFR information reflects fee when procedure is performed in a facility.)					
30560	Lysis intranasal synechia	6.19	229.66	241	312	382
30580	Repair fistula; oromaxillary (combine with 31030 if antrotomy is included)	15.53	562.78	1492	1851	2405
30600	Repair fistula; oronasal	14.29	518.44	1539	1784	1948
30620	Septal or other intranasal dermatoplasty (does not include obtaining graft)	15.27	555.58	2329	2722	3118
30630	Repair nasal septal perforations	15.54	561.64	1794	2185	2455

Destruction

		Medicare RVU	National Fee	50%	75%	90%
30801	Cautery and/or ablation, mucosa of inferior turbinates, unilateral or bilateral, any method; superficial	5.30	196.69	254	299	360
30802	Cautery and/or ablation, mucosa of inferior turbinates, unilateral or bilateral, any method; intramural	6.82	250.50	419	514	716

Other Procedures

		Medicare RVU	National Fee	50%	75%	90%
30901	Control nasal hemorrhage, anterior, simple (limited cautery and/or packing) any method	2.64	95.50	175	219	251
30903	Control nasal hemorrhage, anterior, complex (extensive cautery and/or packing) any method	4.47	163.72	251	307	368
30905	Control nasal hemorrhage, posterior, with posterior nasal packs and/or cautery, any method; initial	5.71	208.82	452	541	629
30906	Control nasal hemorrhage, posterior, with posterior nasal packs and/or cautery, any method; subsequent	6.56	239.13	394	512	605
30915	Ligation arteries; ethmoidal	14.43	518.82	1627	1921	2210
30920	Ligation arteries; internal maxillary artery, transantral	20.62	739.38	2424	2767	3079
30930	Fracture nasal inferior turbinate(s), therapeutic	3.00	108.77	333	424	525
30999	Unlisted procedure, nose	-	-	IR	IR	IR

Accessory Sinuses
Incision

		Medicare RVU	National Fee	50%	75%	90%
31000	Lavage by cannulation; maxillary sinus (antrum puncture or natural ostium)	4.14	152.35	186	223	258
31002	Lavage by cannulation; sphenoid sinus	5.14	187.59	264	295	320
31020	Sinusotomy, maxillary (antrotomy); intranasal	11.70	432.03	724	836	1064
31030	Sinusotomy, maxillary (antrotomy); radical (Caldwell-Luc) without removal of antrochoanal polyps	17.62	645.02	1931	2173	2428
31032	Sinusotomy, maxillary (antrotomy); radical (Caldwell-Luc) with removal of antrochoanal polyps	14.26	515.41	2000	2332	2662
31040	Pterygomaxillary fossa surgery, any approach	19.72	710.58	2567	3269	3809
31050	Sinusotomy, sphenoid, with or without biopsy;	12.11	438.85	1524	2069	2911
31051	Sinusotomy, sphenoid, with or without biopsy; with mucosal stripping or removal of polyp(s)	15.90	575.28	1914	2336	3142
31070	Sinusotomy frontal; external, simple (trephine operation)	10.58	384.66	1295	1437	1584
31075	Sinusotomy frontal; transorbital, unilateral (for mucocele or osteoma, Lynch type)	19.60	706.79	2229	2626	2947
31080	Sinusotomy frontal; obliterative without osteoplastic flap, brow incision (includes ablation)	26.54	958.05	2456	2975	3347
31081	Sinusotomy frontal; obliterative, without osteoplastic flap, coronal incision (includes ablation)	30.66	1108.50	2618	3193	3650
31084	Sinusotomy frontal; obliterative, with osteoplastic flap, brow incision	29.06	1045.21	3240	3642	4204
31085	Sinusotomy frontal; obliterative, with osteoplastic flap, coronal incision	30.90	1112.29	3676	4063	4368
31086	Sinusotomy frontal; nonobliterative, with osteoplastic flap, brow incision	28.15	1013.00	2786	3446	4031

● = New Code ⊗ = Conscious Sedation ✚ = Add-on Code ∅ = Modifier '51' Exempt ▲ =Revised Code

Code	Description	Medicare RVU	National Fee	PFR Fee Information 50%	PFR Fee Information 75%	PFR Fee Information 90%
31087	Sinusotomy frontal; nonobliterative, with osteoplastic flap, coronal incision	27.94	1003.90	2828	3374	3699
31090	Sinusotomy, unilateral, three or more paranasal sinuses (frontal, maxillary, ethmoid, sphenoid)	24.33	880.74	3449	4337	5302

Excision

Code	Description	Medicare RVU	National Fee	50%	75%	90%
31200	Ethmoidectomy; intranasal, anterior	14.09	514.65	1156	1353	1510
31201	Ethmoidectomy; intranasal, total	18.27	660.17	1792	2112	2808
31205	Ethmoidectomy; extranasal, total	22.45	811.01	2050	2511	2823
31225	Maxillectomy; without orbital exenteration	45.53	1624.67	4020	4950	5876
31230	Maxillectomy; with orbital exenteration (en bloc)	51.18	1823.25	4874	5605	6636

Endoscopy

Code	Description	Medicare RVU	National Fee	50%	75%	90%
31231	Nasal endoscopy, diagnostic, unilateral or bilateral (separate procedure)	4.56	168.64	261	355	474
31233	Nasal/sinus endoscopy, diagnostic with maxillary sinusoscopy (via inferior meatus or canine fossa puncture)	6.59	241.41	562	690	911
31235	Nasal/sinus endoscopy, diagnostic with sphenoid sinusoscopy (via puncture of sphenoidal face or cannulation of ostium)	7.66	280.06	712	813	929
31237	Nasal/sinus endoscopy, surgical; with biopsy, polypectomy or debridement (separate procedure)	8.29	302.80	755	930	1168
31238	Nasal/sinus endoscopy, surgical; with control of nasal hemorrhage	8.57	312.28	884	1021	1183
31239	Nasal/sinus endoscopy, surgical; with dacryocystorhinostomy	17.44	625.69	2179	2730	2965
31240	Nasal/sinus endoscopy, surgical; with concha bullosa resection	4.44	158.41	770	918	1216
31254	Nasal/sinus endoscopy, surgical; with ethmoidectomy, partial (anterior)	7.66	272.48	1354	1850	2193
31255	Nasal/sinus endoscopy, surgical; with ethmoidectomy, total (anterior and posterior)	11.37	404.37	2110	2455	2916
31256	Nasal/sinus endoscopy, surgical, with maxillary antrostomy;	5.54	197.45	1153	1545	1821
31267	Nasal/sinus endoscopy, surgical, with maxillary antrostomy; with removal of tissue from maxillary sinus	8.96	318.72	1638	1905	2369
31276	Nasal/sinus endoscopy, surgical with frontal sinus exploration, with or without removal of tissue from frontal sinus	14.34	509.72	1803	2459	3142
31287	Nasal/sinus endoscopy, surgical, with sphenoidotomy;	6.52	232.31	1306	1455	2073
31288	Nasal/sinus endoscopy, surgical, with sphenoidotomy; with removal of tissue from the sphenoid sinus	7.57	269.45	1500	1819	2558
31290	Nasal/sinus endoscopy, surgical, with repair of cerebrospinal fluid leak; ethmoid region	30.99	1103.95	3398	3878	4455
31291	Nasal/sinus endoscopy, surgical, with repair of cerebrospinal fluid leak; sphenoid region	32.69	1164.59	3545	4158	4648
31292	Nasal/sinus endoscopy, surgical; with medial or inferior orbital wall decompression	26.80	955.40	2909	3343	3668
31293	Nasal/sinus endoscopy, surgical; with medial orbital wall and inferior orbital wall decompression	29.18	1039.53	3058	3615	4013
31294	Nasal/sinus endoscopy, surgical; with optic nerve decompression	33.61	1196.80	3364	3903	4387

Other Procedures

Code	Description	Medicare RVU	National Fee	50%	75%	90%
31299	Unlisted procedure, accessory sinuses	-	-	IR	IR	IR

Larynx
Excision

Code	Description	Medicare RVU	National Fee	50%	75%	90%
31300	Laryngotomy (thyrotomy, laryngofissure); with removal of tumor or laryngocele, cordectomy	31.51	1134.27	2938	3352	3981
31320	Laryngotomy (thyrotomy, laryngofissure); diagnostic	16.11	588.93	1221	1594	1811
31360	Laryngectomy; total, without radical neck dissection	48.07	1709.18	4117	4913	5712
31365	Laryngectomy; total, with radical neck dissection	60.95	2163.19	5660	6691	7651
31367	Laryngectomy; subtotal supraglottic, without radical neck dissection	53.56	1914.58	4492	5294	6119
31368	Laryngectomy; subtotal supraglottic, with radical neck dissection	60.79	2174.56	6020	7440	8449

© PFR 2007

● = New Code ⊗ = Conscious Sedation ✚ = Add-on Code ∅ = Modifier '51' Exempt ▲ =Revised Code

		Medicare RVU	National Fee	PFR Fee Information 50%	75%	90%
31370	Partial laryngectomy (hemilaryngectomy); horizontal	50.77	1820.22	4297	5061	5659
31375	Partial laryngectomy (hemilaryngectomy); laterovertical	47.52	1702.73	3841	4062	4390
31380	Partial laryngectomy (hemilaryngectomy); anterovertical	47.18	1691.74	3830	4527	5191
31382	Partial laryngectomy (hemilaryngectomy); antero-latero-vertical	51.29	1836.13	3862	4579	5310
31390	Pharyngolaryngectomy, with radical neck dissection; without reconstruction	68.61	2439.46	5575	6694	7654
31395	Pharyngolaryngectomy, with radical neck dissection; with reconstruction	73.67	2626.30	7192	8235	9249
31400	Arytenoidectomy or arytenoidopexy, external approach	25.52	923.56	2787	3531	4242
31420	Epiglottidectomy	21.29	763.63	2340	3038	3370

Introduction

		Medicare RVU	National Fee	50%	75%	90%
∅ 31500	Intubation, endotracheal, emergency procedure	3.02	105.73	309	372	433
31502	Tracheotomy tube change prior to establishment of fistula tract	0.96	33.73	174	231	298

Endoscopy

		Medicare RVU	National Fee	50%	75%	90%
31505	Laryngoscopy, indirect; diagnostic (separate procedure)	2.08	76.55	145	214	246
31510	Laryngoscopy, indirect; with biopsy	5.30	193.66	328	392	491
31511	Laryngoscopy, indirect; with removal of foreign body	5.38	195.55	372	431	512
31512	Laryngoscopy, indirect; with removal of lesion	5.33	194.04	462	522	578
31513	Laryngoscopy, indirect; with vocal cord injection	3.61	128.85	636	761	926
31515	Laryngoscopy direct, with or without tracheoscopy; for aspiration	5.36	196.31	371	412	537
31520	Laryngoscopy direct, with or without tracheoscopy; diagnostic, newborn	4.21	149.70	468	611	717
31525	Laryngoscopy direct, with or without tracheoscopy; diagnostic, except newborn	6.38	231.93	572	718	821
31526	Laryngoscopy direct, with or without tracheoscopy; diagnostic, with operating microscope or telescope	4.35	155.00	788	912	1282
31527	Laryngoscopy direct, with or without tracheoscopy; with insertion of obturator	5.26	186.83	1003	1237	1530
31528	Laryngoscopy direct, with or without tracheoscopy; with dilation, initial	3.90	138.70	702	840	971
31529	Laryngoscopy direct, with or without tracheoscopy; with dilation, subsequent	4.46	158.79	651	773	832
31530	Laryngoscopy, direct, operative, with foreign body removal;	5.46	194.04	879	986	1148
31531	Laryngoscopy, direct, operative, with foreign body removal; with operating microscope or telescope	5.93	211.09	1081	1409	1651
31535	Laryngoscopy, direct, operative, with biopsy;	5.24	186.46	875	1008	1191
	(UNBUNDLING ALERT: 31536 cannot be used with 31535 by the same physician on the same day.)					
31536	Laryngoscopy, direct, operative, with biopsy; with operating microscope or telescope	5.88	209.19	1127	1194	1432
31540	Laryngoscopy, direct, operative, with excision of tumor and/or stripping of vocal cords or epiglottis;	6.75	240.27	1058	1214	1530
	(UNBUNDLING ALERT: 31541 cannot be used with 31525 or 31540 by the same physician on the same day.)					
31541	Laryngoscopy, direct, operative, with excision of tumor and/or stripping of vocal cords or epiglottis; with operating microscope or telescope	7.40	263.39	1294	1447	1681
31545	Laryngoscopy, direct, operative, with operating microscope or telescope, with submucosal removal of non-neoplastic lesion(s) of vocal cord; reconstruction with local tissue flap(s)	9.84	349.04	1621	1866	2198
31546	Laryngoscopy, direct, operative, with operating microscope or telescope, with submucosal removal of non-neoplastic lesion(s) of vocal cord; reconstruction with graft(s) (includes obtaining autograft)	15.18	538.14	2451	2820	3324
31560	Laryngoscopy, direct, operative, with arytenoidectomy;	8.72	309.62	1752	2315	2572
31561	Laryngoscopy, direct, operative, with arytenoidectomy; with operating microscope or telescope	9.53	338.42	2045	2379	2740
31570	Laryngoscopy, direct, with injection into vocal cord(s), therapeutic;	9.41	341.84	1264	1339	1439

● = New Code ⊗ = Conscious Sedation ✚ = Add-on Code ∅ = Modifier '51' Exempt ▲ =Revised Code

		Medicare RVU	National Fee	PFR Fee Information 50%	75%	90%
31571	Laryngoscopy, direct, with injection into vocal cord(s), therapeutic; with operating microscope or telescope	6.97	247.85	1248	1473	1598
31575	Laryngoscopy, flexible fiberoptic; diagnostic	3.01	109.90	291	385	435
31576	Laryngoscopy, flexible fiberoptic; with biopsy	5.68	207.68	575	648	828
31577	Laryngoscopy, flexible fiberoptic; with removal of foreign body	6.31	229.66	790	1074	1296
31578	Laryngoscopy, flexible fiberoptic; with removal of lesion	7.20	261.87	1051	1250	1496
31579	Laryngoscopy, flexible or rigid fiberoptic, with stroboscopy	5.94	216.39	585	694	840

Repair

31580	Laryngoplasty; for laryngeal web, two stage, with keel insertion and removal	30.77	1111.15	2872	3332	3886
31582	Laryngoplasty; for laryngeal stenosis, with graft or core mold, including tracheotomy	49.11	1773.98	3680	4143	4438
31584	Laryngoplasty; with open reduction of fracture	39.26	1410.17	3511	4036	4564
31587	Laryngoplasty, cricoid split	25.05	891.73	2533	3174	3713
31588	Laryngoplasty, not otherwise specified (eg, for burns, reconstruction after partial laryngectomy)	28.75	1033.84	2999	3634	3955
31590	Laryngeal reinnervation by neuromuscular pedicle	23.14	847.77	2545	3417	3667

Destruction

31595	Section recurrent laryngeal nerve, therapeutic (separate procedure), unilateral	19.58	708.68	2241	2731	3132

Other Procedures

31599	Unlisted procedure, larynx	-	-	IR	IR	IR

Trachea and Bronchi

Incision

(Do not code 31600 separately when a planned tracheostomy is performed as a surgical approach to another organ or as the first part of another more extensive procedure. In this case, the tracheostomy is the incision for a larger procedure.)

31600	Tracheostomy, planned (separate procedure);	10.92	386.55	1043	1234	1297
31601	Tracheostomy, planned (separate procedure); younger than two years	7.05	250.12	1373	1484	1535
31603	Tracheostomy, emergency procedure; transtracheal	6.15	217.15	1088	1217	1392
31605	Tracheostomy, emergency procedure; cricothyroid membrane	5.07	178.50	894	1050	1250
31610	Tracheostomy, fenestration procedure with skin flaps	18.07	649.56	1671	2055	2468
31611	Construction of tracheoesophageal fistula and subsequent insertion of an alaryngeal speech prosthesis (eg, voice button, Blom-Singer prosthesis)	13.30	481.30	1611	2028	2303
31612	Tracheal puncture, percutaneous with transtracheal aspiration and/or injection	2.08	75.42	233	258	322
31613	Tracheostoma revision; simple, without flap rotation	10.99	398.68	799	936	1139
31614	Tracheostoma revision; complex, with flap rotation	17.81	642.74	1727	1931	2113

Endoscopy

⊗ 31615	Tracheobronchoscopy through established tracheostomy incision	4.75	172.05	507	620	721
✚ 31620	Endobronchial ultrasound (EBUS) during bronchoscopic diagnostic or therapeutic intervention(s) (List separately in addition to code for primary procedure(s))	7.24	269.07	698	797	908
⊗ 31622	Bronchoscopy, rigid or flexible, with or without fluoroscopic guidance; diagnostic, with or without cell washing (separate procedure)	8.51	311.90	683	782	847
⊗ 31623	Bronchoscopy, rigid or flexible, with or without fluoroscopic guidance; with brushing or protected brushings	9.33	342.59	683	786	847

● = New Code   ⊗ = Conscious Sedation   ✚ = Add-on Code   ∅ = Modifier '51' Exempt   ▲ = Revised Code

		Medicare RVU	National Fee	PFR Fee Information 50%	75%	90%
⊗ 31624	Bronchoscopy, rigid or flexible, with or without fluoroscopic guidance; with bronchial alveolar lavage	8.68	317.96	729	837	953
	(UNBUNDLING ALERT: 31625 cannot be used with 31622 by the same physician on the same day.)					
⊗ 31625	Bronchoscopy, rigid or flexible, with or without fluoroscopic guidance; with bronchial or endobronchial biopsy(s), single or multiple sites	9.27	338.42	781	852	1013
	(UNBUNDLING ALERT: 31628 cannot be used with 31622 or 31625 by the same physician on the same day.)					
⊗ 31628	Bronchoscopy, rigid or flexible, with or without fluoroscopic guidance; with transbronchial lung biopsy(s), single lobe	11.00	402.47	883	962	1090
⊗ 31629	Bronchoscopy, rigid or flexible, with or without fluoroscopic guidance; with transbronchial needle aspiration biopsy(s), trachea, main stem and/or lobar bronchus(i)	17.95	664.72	892	1041	1224
31630	Bronchoscopy, rigid or flexible, with or without fluoroscopic guidance; with tracheal/bronchial dilation or closed reduction of fracture	5.74	203.13	851	992	1058
31631	Bronchoscopy, rigid or flexible, with or without fluoroscopic guidance; with placement of tracheal stent(s) (includes tracheal/bronchial dilation as required)	6.37	224.73	1002	1118	1241
✚ 31632	Bronchoscopy, rigid or flexible, with or without fluoroscopic guidance; with transbronchial lung biopsy(s), each additional lobe (List separately in addition to code for primary procedure)	2.04	73.52	250	285	326
✚ 31633	Bronchoscopy, rigid or flexible, with or without fluoroscopic guidance; with transbronchial needle aspiration biopsy(s), each additional lobe (List separately in addition to code for primary procedure)	2.42	86.79	276	352	420
⊗ 31635	Bronchoscopy, rigid or flexible, with or without fluoroscopic guidance; with removal of foreign body	9.79	356.99	974	1162	1405
31636	Bronchoscopy, rigid or flexible, with or without fluoroscopic guidance; with placement of bronchial stent(s) (includes tracheal/bronchial dilation as required), initial bronchus	6.28	221.70	926	1172	1433
✚ 31637	Bronchoscopy, rigid or flexible, with or without fluoroscopic guidance; each additional major bronchus stented (List separately in addition to code for primary procedure)	2.24	78.83	271	348	445
31638	Bronchoscopy, rigid or flexible, with or without fluoroscopic guidance; with revision of tracheal or bronchial stent inserted at previous session (includes tracheal/bronchial dilation as required)	6.97	245.58	1173	1457	1643
31640	Bronchoscopy, rigid or flexible, with or without fluoroscopic guidance; with excision of tumor	7.33	258.84	1247	1490	1679
31641	Bronchoscopy, (rigid or flexible); with destruction of tumor or relief of stenosis by any method other than excision (eg, laser therapy, cryotherapy)	7.16	252.02	1517	1749	2020
31643	Bronchoscopy, (rigid or flexible); with placement of catheter(s) for intracavitary radioelement application	4.88	171.68	639	771	878
	(UNBUNDLING ALERT: 31645 cannot be used with 31622 by the same physician on the same day.)					
⊗ 31645	Bronchoscopy, (rigid or flexible); with therapeutic aspiration of tracheobronchial tree, initial (eg, drainage of lung abscess)	8.37	305.07	727	840	932
⊗ 31646	Bronchoscopy, (rigid or flexible); with therapeutic aspiration of tracheobronchial tree, subsequent	7.62	278.55	679	776	870
⊗ 31656	Bronchoscopy, (rigid or flexible); with injection of contrast material for segmental bronchography (fiberscope only)	9.11	336.91	585	733	774

Introduction

(Medicare fees for the code below are based on Non Facility RVUs. PFR information reflects fee when procedure is performed in a facility.)

31715	Transtracheal injection for bronchography	1.51	53.06	156	191	230
31717	Catheterization with bronchial brush biopsy	9.91	367.61	231	268	338
31720	Catheter aspiration (separate procedure); nasotracheal	1.44	50.40	141	170	203
⊗ 31725	Catheter aspiration (separate procedure); tracheobronchial with fiberscope, bedside	2.65	92.85	325	436	519
31730	Transtracheal (percutaneous) introduction of needle wire dilator/stent or indwelling tube for oxygen therapy	11.04	407.40	510	675	869

Repair

31750	Tracheoplasty; cervical	33.46	1210.07	3029	3143	3596
31755	Tracheoplasty; tracheopharyngeal fistulization, each stage	42.45	1543.19	3230	3772	4187
31760	Tracheoplasty; intrathoracic	36.78	1304.81	3613	3944	4319
31766	Carinal reconstruction	49.21	1744.42	4040	4839	5402
31770	Bronchoplasty; graft repair	36.20	1282.45	3670	4163	4660

● = New Code ⊗ = Conscious Sedation ✚ = Add-on Code ∅ = Modifier '51' Exempt ▲ =Revised Code

		Medicare RVU	National Fee	PFR Fee Information 50%	75%	90%
31775	Bronchoplasty; excision stenosis and anastomosis	38.60	1369.24	3861	4551	4906
31780	Excision tracheal stenosis and anastomosis; cervical	31.67	1125.18	3560	3943	4334
31781	Excision tracheal stenosis and anastomosis; cervicothoracic	38.43	1362.04	3957	4561	4952
31785	Excision of tracheal tumor or carcinoma; cervical	28.92	1026.26	3018	3774	4385
31786	Excision of tracheal tumor or carcinoma; thoracic	40.91	1453.75	3871	4460	5049
31800	Suture of tracheal wound or injury; cervical	17.90	647.67	2317	2652	2996
31805	Suture of tracheal wound or injury; intrathoracic	22.16	789.03	2659	3192	3635
31820	Surgical closure tracheostomy or fistula; without plastic repair	10.57	383.14	875	994	1088
31825	Surgical closure tracheostomy or fistula; with plastic repair	14.97	540.80	1020	1375	1552
31830	Revision of tracheostomy scar	10.71	388.45	892	1066	1247

Other Procedures

31899	Unlisted procedure, trachea, bronchi	-	-	IR	IR	IR

Lungs and Pleura

Incision

(A4550 (Disposable Surgical Tray) can be coded in addition to 32000 in the office setting. Payment is at carrier discretion.)

∅ 32000	Thoracentesis, puncture of pleural cavity for aspiration, initial or subsequent	4.48	164.10	272	332	386
∅ 32002	Thoracentesis with insertion of tube with or without water seal (eg, for pneumothorax) (separate procedure)	5.40	196.31	492	521	647
32005	Chemical pleurodesis (eg, for recurrent or persistent pneumothorax)	8.52	314.55	393	506	659
⊗ 32019	Insertion of indwelling tunneled pleural catheter with cuff	23.35	868.99	1683	2260	2914
∅ 32020	Tube thoracostomy with or without water seal (eg, for abscess, hemothorax, empyema) (separate procedure)	4.97	175.84	622	745	861
32035	Thoracostomy; with rib resection for empyema	18.37	653.35	1545	1836	2143
32036	Thoracostomy; with open flap drainage for empyema	20.06	713.61	1960	2388	2714
32095	Thoracotomy, limited, for biopsy of lung or pleura	16.60	590.82	1851	2374	2837
	(UNBUNDLING ALERT: 32100 cannot be used with 32020 by the same physician on the same day.)					
32100	Thoracotomy, major; with exploration and biopsy	25.95	922.05	2625	2986	3418
32110	Thoracotomy, major; with control of traumatic hemorrhage and/or repair of lung tear	38.92	1379.09	2876	3518	3924
32120	Thoracotomy, major; for postoperative complications	22.92	814.04	2594	3001	3394
32124	Thoracotomy, major; with open intrapleural pneumonolysis	24.40	866.34	2526	3090	3672
32140	Thoracotomy, major; with cyst(s) removal, with or without a pleural procedure	26.13	927.35	2892	3451	3885
32141	Thoracotomy, major; with excision-plication of bullae, with or without any pleural procedure	37.36	1312.39	2940	3436	3974
32150	Thoracotomy, major; with removal of intrapleural foreign body or fibrin deposit	26.29	932.66	2706	3395	3970
32151	Thoracotomy, major; with removal of intrapulmonary foreign body	27.05	961.08	2469	2907	3302
32160	Thoracotomy, major; with cardiac massage	19.74	698.45	2715	2996	3272
32200	Pneumonostomy; with open drainage of abscess or cyst	29.27	1038.77	2213	2787	3265
	(Medicare fees for the code below are based on Non Facility RVUs. PFR information reflects fee when procedure is performed in a facility.)					
⊗ 32201	Pneumonostomy; with percutaneous drainage of abscess or cyst	24.44	911.06	626	783	939
32215	Pleural scarification for repeat pneumothorax	21.39	761.36	2484	2941	3247
32220	Decortication, pulmonary (separate procedure); total	42.71	1517.79	3459	3773	4719
32225	Decortication, pulmonary (separate procedure); partial	26.32	934.17	2614	2984	3485

● = New Code ⊗ = Conscious Sedation ✚ = Add-on Code ∅ = Modifier '51' Exempt ▲ =Revised Code

		Medicare RVU	National Fee	PFR Fee Information 50%	75%	90%

Excision

32310	Pleurectomy, parietal (separate procedure)	24.44	868.23	2887	3398	3915
32320	Decortication and parietal pleurectomy	42.57	1510.22	4099	4749	5406
32400	Biopsy, pleura; percutaneous needle	3.95	142.87	334	434	500
32402	Biopsy, pleura; open	14.99	534.35	1541	1858	2218
32405	Biopsy, lung or mediastinum, percutaneous needle	2.68	94.36	497	596	709

Removal

32420	Pneumocentesis, puncture of lung for aspiration	2.96	103.84	364	444	501
32440	Removal of lung, total pneumonectomy;	43.30	1537.50	4447	5061	5821
32442	Removal of lung, total pneumonectomy; with resection of segment of trachea followed by broncho-tracheal anastomosis (sleeve pneumonectomy)	75.93	2662.68	4744	5331	5734
32445	Removal of lung, total pneumonectomy; extrapleural	83.62	2926.44	4541	5060	5440
	(UNBUNDLING ALERT: 32480 cannot be used with 32020 or 32100 by the same physician on the same day.)					
32480	Removal of lung, other than total pneumonectomy; single lobe (lobectomy)	40.84	1449.58	4103	4739	5293
32482	Removal of lung, other than total pneumonectomy; two lobes (bilobectomy)	43.43	1542.05	4394	4961	5587
32484	Removal of lung, other than total pneumonectomy; single segment (segmentectomy)	39.29	1392.35	3891	4568	5117
32486	Removal of lung, other than total pneumonectomy; with circumferential resection of segment of bronchus followed by broncho-bronchial anastomosis (sleeve lobectomy)	60.05	2112.41	4367	5109	5656
32488	Removal of lung, other than total pneumonectomy; all remaining lung following previous removal of a portion of lung (completion pneumonectomy)	60.90	2144.62	4641	5598	6034
32491	Removal of lung, other than total pneumonectomy; excision-plication of emphysematous lung(s) (bullous or non-bullous) for lung volume reduction, sternal split or transthoracic approach, with or without any pleural procedure	40.21	1428.36	4047	4672	5005
	(UNBUNDLING ALERT: 32500 cannot be used with 32020 or 32100 by the same physician on the same day.)					
32500	Removal of lung, other than total pneumonectomy; wedge resection, single or multiple	39.60	1407.51	3358	3813	4331
✚ 32501	Resection and repair of portion of bronchus (bronchoplasty) when performed at time of lobectomy or segmentectomy (List separately in addition to code for primary procedure)	6.83	241.03	933	1114	1309
32503	Resection of apical lung tumor (eg, Pancoast tumor), including chest wall resection, rib(s) resection(s), neurovascular dissection, when performed; without chest wall reconstruction(s)	50.36	1788.00	5888	6697	7698
32504	Resection of apical lung tumor (eg, Pancoast tumor), including chest wall resection, rib(s) resection(s), neurovascular dissection, when performed; with chest wall reconstruction	57.43	2037.75	6735	7659	8805
32540	Extrapleural enucleation of empyema (empyemectomy)	42.57	1498.09	3498	3786	4282

Endoscopy

32601	Thoracoscopy, diagnostic (separate procedure); lungs and pleural space, without biopsy	8.54	302.80	1020	1132	1212
32602	Thoracoscopy, diagnostic (separate procedure); lungs and pleural space, with biopsy	9.27	328.57	1160	1424	1819
32603	Thoracoscopy, diagnostic (separate procedure); pericardial sac, without biopsy	11.96	423.69	1308	1584	1702
32604	Thoracoscopy, diagnostic (separate procedure); pericardial sac, with biopsy	13.37	473.34	1424	1903	2160
32605	Thoracoscopy, diagnostic (separate procedure); mediastinal space, without biopsy	10.73	380.11	1119	1277	1562
32606	Thoracoscopy, diagnostic (separate procedure); mediastinal space, with biopsy	12.86	455.53	1594	1813	2261
32650	Thoracoscopy, surgical; with pleurodesis (eg, mechanical or chemical)	18.74	669.27	2146	2591	2931
32651	Thoracoscopy, surgical; with partial pulmonary decortication	27.93	987.23	2491	3064	3705
32652	Thoracoscopy, surgical; with total pulmonary decortication, including intrapleural pneumonolysis	42.14	1486.34	3392	4002	4662
32653	Thoracoscopy, surgical; with removal of intrapleural foreign body or fibrin deposit	27.08	957.29	2523	2931	3208
32654	Thoracoscopy, surgical; with control of traumatic hemorrhage	29.71	1047.87	2690	3143	3717

		Medicare RVU	National Fee	PFR Fee Information 50%	75%	90%
32655	Thoracoscopy, surgical; with excision-plication of bullae, including any pleural procedure	25.18	892.87	2852	3303	3740
32656	Thoracoscopy, surgical; with parietal pleurectomy	22.54	803.81	2876	3333	3802
32657	Thoracoscopy, surgical; with wedge resection of lung, single or multiple	22.13	789.78	2941	3576	4376
32658	Thoracoscopy, surgical; with removal of clot or foreign body from pericardial sac	20.27	723.84	2702	3242	3782
32659	Thoracoscopy, surgical; with creation of pericardial window or partial resection of pericardial sac for drainage	20.55	733.70	2755	3261	3807
32660	Thoracoscopy, surgical; with total pericardiectomy	28.76	1022.47	3661	4503	5198
32661	Thoracoscopy, surgical; with excision of pericardial cyst, tumor, or mass	22.59	805.70	3145	3572	3820
32662	Thoracoscopy, surgical; with excision of mediastinal cyst, tumor, or mass	25.38	904.99	3180	3882	4280
32663	Thoracoscopy, surgical; with lobectomy, total or segmental	37.73	1336.27	3887	4625	5468
32664	Thoracoscopy, surgical; with thoracic sympathectomy	23.87	850.42	2859	3331	3786
32665	Thoracoscopy, surgical; with esophagomyotomy (Heller type)	31.87	1125.93	3168	3770	4102

Repair

		Medicare RVU	National Fee	50%	75%	90%
32800	Repair lung hernia through chest wall	24.91	884.53	2348	3031	3423
32810	Closure of chest wall following open flap drainage for empyema (Clagett type procedure)	24.19	860.27	2102	2572	3177
32815	Open closure of major bronchial fistula	66.04	2312.88	3880	4721	5299
32820	Major reconstruction, chest wall (posttraumatic)	36.94	1314.66	3850	4685	5333

Lung Transplantation

		Medicare RVU	National Fee	50%	75%	90%
32850	Donor pneumonectomy(s) (including cold preservation), from cadaver donor	-	-	2091	2821	3166
32851	Lung transplant, single; without cardiopulmonary bypass	72.49	2591.05	6473	8923	10072
32852	Lung transplant, single; with cardiopulmonary bypass	81.47	2917.35	7166	9633	11802
32853	Lung transplant, double (bilateral sequential or en bloc); without cardiopulmonary bypass	86.82	3099.26	8034	11515	13496
32854	Lung transplant, double (bilateral sequential or en bloc); with cardiopulmonary bypass	93.78	3348.62	9340	11853	13929
32855	Backbench standard preparation of cadaver donor lung allograft prior to transplantation, including dissection of allograft from surrounding soft tissues to prepare pulmonary venous/atrial cuff, pulmonary artery, and bronchus; unilateral	-	-	IR	IR	IR
32856	Backbench standard preparation of cadaver donor lung allograft prior to transplantation, including dissection of allograft from surrounding soft tissues to prepare pulmonary venous/atrial cuff, pulmonary artery, and bronchus; bilateral	-	-	IR	IR	IR

Surgical Collapse Therapy; Thoracoplasty

		Medicare RVU	National Fee	50%	75%	90%
32900	Resection of ribs, extrapleural, all stages	36.49	1292.68	2277	2948	3396
32905	Thoracoplasty, Schede type or extrapleural (all stages);	36.33	1288.52	2864	3582	4269
32906	Thoracoplasty, Schede type or extrapleural (all stages); with closure of bronchopleural fistula	45.04	1595.48	3751	4819	5637
32940	Pneumonolysis, extraperiosteal, including filling or packing procedures	33.37	1183.92	2246	2660	3219
32960	Pneumothorax, therapeutic, intrapleural injection of air	3.68	132.26	237	287	310

Other Procedures

		Medicare RVU	National Fee	50%	75%	90%
32997	Total lung lavage (unilateral)	9.76	341.84	828	965	1201
● 32998	Ablation therapy for reduction or eradication of one or more pulmonary tumor(s) including pleura or chest wall when involved by tumor extension, percutaneous, radiofrequency, unilateral	74.68	2808.58	5490	6758	7959
32999	Unlisted procedure, lungs and pleura	-	-	IR	IR	IR

● = New Code ⊗ = Conscious Sedation ✚ = Add-on Code ∅ = Modifier '51' Exempt ▲ =Revised Code

		Medicare RVU	National Fee	PFR Fee Information 50%	75%	90%

Cardiovascular System

Heart and Pericardium

Pericardium

		RVU	Fee	50%	75%	90%
⊗ **33010**	Pericardiocentesis; initial	3.23	113.69	412	492	555
⊗ **33011**	Pericardiocentesis; subsequent	3.28	115.59	363	420	485
33015	Tube pericardiostomy	14.07	501.00	829	1085	1408
33020	Pericardiotomy for removal of clot or foreign body (primary procedure)	23.38	829.20	2537	3042	3433
33025	Creation of pericardial window or partial resection for drainage	21.71	770.84	2848	3196	3668
33030	Pericardiectomy, subtotal or complete; without cardiopulmonary bypass	34.56	1224.85	3912	4622	5270
33031	Pericardiectomy, subtotal or complete; with cardiopulmonary bypass	38.45	1360.52	4909	5967	7064
33050	Excision of pericardial cyst or tumor	26.78	950.47	2985	3394	3808

Cardiac Tumor

		RVU	Fee	50%	75%	90%
33120	Excision of intracardiac tumor, resection with cardiopulmonary bypass	42.40	1502.64	6185	7339	8406
33130	Resection of external cardiac tumor	37.01	1310.87	3942	4769	5442

Transmyocardial Revascularization

		RVU	Fee	50%	75%	90%
33140	Transmyocardial laser revascularization, by thoracotomy; (separate procedure)	41.94	1481.79	3556	4635	5853
✚ **33141**	Transmyocardial laser revascularization, by thoracotomy; performed at the time of other open cardiac procedure(s) (List separately in addition to code for primary procedure)	4.62	165.23	867	1208	1419

Pacemaker or Pacing Cardioverter Defibrillator

		RVU	Fee	50%	75%	90%
● **33202**	Insertion of epicardial electrode(s); open incision (eg, thoracotomy, median sternotomy, subxiphoid approach)	21.08	748.85	3691	4338	5001
● **33203**	Insertion of epicardial electrode(s); endoscopic approach (eg, thoracoscopy, pericardioscopy)	21.60	765.53	3782	4445	5124
	(Some pacemaker insertion codes do allow for co-surgery or team-surgery. A modifier -62 is used by each co-surgeon. Each physician's participation must be documented in the operative report.)					
⊗ **33206**	Insertion or replacement of permanent pacemaker with transvenous electrode(s); atrial	12.47	444.54	2163	2508	2886
	(UNBUNDLING ALERT: 33207 cannot be used with 33206 by the same physician on the same day.)					
⊗ **33207**	Insertion or replacement of permanent pacemaker with transvenous electrode(s); ventricular	14.59	518.44	2282	2716	3049
	(UNBUNDLING ALERT: 33208 cannot be used with 33206 or 33207 by the same physician on the same day.)					
⊗ **33208**	Insertion or replacement of permanent pacemaker with transvenous electrode(s); atrial and ventricular	13.63	485.47	2686	3103	3444
⊗ **33210**	Insertion or replacement of temporary transvenous single chamber cardiac electrode or pacemaker catheter (separate procedure)	4.85	171.30	841	1010	1241
⊗ **33211**	Insertion or replacement of temporary transvenous dual chamber pacing electrodes (separate procedure)	5.01	176.98	921	1080	1193
⊗ **33212**	Insertion or replacement of pacemaker pulse generator only; single chamber, atrial or ventricular	9.40	335.39	1301	1437	1705
⊗ **33213**	Insertion or replacement of pacemaker pulse generator only; dual chamber	10.68	380.49	1414	1523	1801
⊗ **33214**	Upgrade of implanted pacemaker system, conversion of single chamber system to dual chamber system (includes removal of previously placed pulse generator, testing of existing lead, insertion of new lead, insertion of new pulse generator)	13.39	477.89	1746	2262	3432
33215	Repositioning of previously implanted transvenous pacemaker or pacing cardioverter-defibrillator (right atrial or right ventricular) electrode	8.53	304.70	1035	1213	1471
⊗ **33216**	Insertion of a transvenous electrode; single chamber (one electrode) permanent pacemaker or single chamber pacing cardioverter-defibrillator	10.48	375.19	1290	1513	2036
⊗ **33217**	Insertion of a transvenous electrode; dual chamber (two electrodes) permanent pacemaker or dual chamber pacing cardioverter-defibrillator	10.48	375.19	1357	1570	2105
⊗ **33218**	Repair of single transvenous electrode for a single chamber, permanent pacemaker or single chamber pacing cardioverter-defibrillator	10.78	385.80	1045	1262	1654

● = New Code ⊗ = Conscious Sedation ✚ = Add-on Code ∅ = Modifier '51' Exempt ▲ =Revised Code

		Medicare RVU	National Fee	PFR Fee Information 50%	75%	90%
⊗ 33220	Repair of two transvenous electrodes for a dual chamber permanent pacemaker or dual chamber pacing cardioverter-defibrillator	10.86	388.45	1099	1297	1405
⊗ 33222	Revision or relocation of skin pocket for pacemaker	9.74	350.17	1185	1441	1560
⊗ 33223	Revision of skin pocket for single or dual chamber pacing cardioverter-defibrillator	11.64	416.49	1177	1373	1643
33224	Insertion of pacing electrode, cardiac venous system, for left ventricular pacing, with attachment to previously placed pacemaker or pacing cardioverter-defibrillator pulse generator (including revision of pocket, removal, insertion, and/or replacement of generator)	13.86	490.77	1570	1928	2316
✚ 33225	Insertion of pacing electrode, cardiac venous system, for left ventricular pacing, at time of insertion of pacing cardioverter-defibrillator or pacemaker pulse generator (including upgrade to dual chamber system) (List separately in addition to code for primary procedure)	12.35	436.20	1403	1787	2152
33226	Repositioning of previously implanted cardiac venous system (left ventricular) electrode (including removal, insertion and/or replacement of generator)	13.37	473.72	1525	1863	2133
⊗ 33233	Removal of permanent pacemaker pulse generator	6.84	246.71	778	995	1168
⊗ 33234	Removal of transvenous pacemaker electrode(s); single lead system, atrial or ventricular	13.49	481.30	1123	1422	1705
⊗ 33235	Removal of transvenous pacemaker electrode(s); dual lead system	17.62	629.86	1372	1582	1836
33236	Removal of permanent epicardial pacemaker and electrodes by thoracotomy; single lead system, atrial or ventricular	21.57	769.32	2430	3220	4072
33237	Removal of permanent epicardial pacemaker and electrodes by thoracotomy; dual lead system	23.10	823.13	2791	3523	3990
33238	Removal of permanent transvenous electrode(s) by thoracotomy	25.54	909.54	2771	3294	3826
⊗ 33240	Insertion of single or dual chamber pacing cardioverter-defibrillator pulse generator	12.81	456.29	1431	1612	1895
⊗ 33241	Subcutaneous removal of single or dual chamber pacing cardioverter-defibrillator pulse generator	6.43	231.17	804	1060	1319
33243	Removal of single or dual chamber pacing cardioverter-defibrillator electrode(s); by thoracotomy	36.87	1307.84	3005	3725	4319
⊗ 33244	Removal of single or dual chamber pacing cardioverter-defibrillator electrode(s); by transvenous extraction	23.91	853.45	2071	2766	3411
	(The Automatic Implantable Defibrillator Cardioverter (AICD) is covered by Medicare only when used as a treatment of last resort for life-threatening ventricular tachycardia or cardiac arrest not associated with myocardial infarction.)					
⊗ 33249	Insertion or repositioning of electrode lead(s) for single or dual chamber pacing cardioverter-defibrillator and insertion of pulse generator	24.68	878.09	3546	4033	5133

Electrophysiologic Operative Procedures

Incision

33250	Operative ablation of supraventricular arrhythmogenic focus or pathway (eg, Wolff-Parkinson-White, atrioventricular node re-entry), tract(s) and/or focus (foci); without cardiopulmonary bypass	39.77	1409.03	3454	4188	5164
33251	Operative ablation of supraventricular arrhythmogenic focus or pathway (eg, Wolff-Parkinson-White, atrioventricular node re-entry), tract(s) and/or focus (foci); with cardiopulmonary bypass	43.92	1554.56	4931	6081	7315
● 33254	Operative tissue ablation and reconstruction of atria, limited (eg, modified maze procedure)	36.87	1307.46	3790	4701	5461
● 33255	Operative tissue ablation and reconstruction of atria, extensive (eg, maze procedure); without cardiopulmonary bypass	44.42	1573.13	4566	5664	6579
● 33256	Operative tissue ablation and reconstruction of atria, extensive (eg, maze procedure); with cardiopulmonary bypass	53.09	1879.34	5457	6769	7863
33261	Operative ablation of ventricular arrhythmogenic focus with cardiopulmonary bypass	43.91	1554.18	4798	6092	6496

Endoscopy

● 33265	Endoscopy, surgical; operative tissue ablation and reconstruction of atria, limited (eg, modified maze procedure), without cardiopulmonary bypass	36.87	1307.46	3790	4701	5461
● 33266	Endoscopy, surgical; operative tissue ablation and reconstruction of atria, extensive (eg, maze procedure), without cardiopulmonary bypass	50.51	1788.76	5192	6440	7481

Patient-Activated Event Recorder

33282	Implantation of patient-activated cardiac event recorder	9.03	324.40	1014	1203	1393
33284	Removal of an implantable, patient-activated cardiac event recorder	6.68	241.41	731	968	1144

Wounds of The Heart and Great Vessels

33300	Repair of cardiac wound; without bypass	58.38	2041.16	3536	4288	5104

● = New Code ⊗ = Conscious Sedation ✚ = Add-on Code ∅ = Modifier '51' Exempt ▲ =Revised Code

		Medicare RVU	National Fee	PFR Fee Information 50%	75%	90%
33305	Repair of cardiac wound; with cardiopulmonary bypass	94.24	3278.51	4536	5894	6795
33310	Cardiotomy, exploratory (includes removal of foreign body, atrial or ventricular thrombus); without bypass	32.20	1143.37	3594	4105	4358
33315	Cardiotomy, exploratory (includes removal of foreign body, atrial or ventricular thrombus); with cardiopulmonary bypass	40.10	1420.40	5298	6294	7226
33320	Suture repair of aorta or great vessels; without shunt or cardiopulmonary bypass	28.88	1023.99	3847	4576	5100
33321	Suture repair of aorta or great vessels; with shunt bypass	33.53	1191.88	4424	5166	5702
33322	Suture repair of aorta or great vessels; with cardiopulmonary bypass	37.38	1324.14	4514	6214	7253
33330	Insertion of graft, aorta or great vessels; without shunt, or cardiopulmonary bypass	38.12	1348.77	5277	5923	6546
33332	Insertion of graft, aorta or great vessels; with shunt bypass	37.77	1338.16	5135	6130	6999
33335	Insertion of graft, aorta or great vessels; with cardiopulmonary bypass	51.31	1815.67	6233	8003	8694

Cardiac Valves
Aortic Valve

33400	Valvuloplasty, aortic valve; open, with cardiopulmonary bypass	61.02	2154.85	5729	6507	7566
33401	Valvuloplasty, aortic valve; open, with inflow occlusion	40.55	1443.52	5386	6768	7706
33403	Valvuloplasty, aortic valve; using transventricular dilation, with cardiopulmonary bypass	42.29	1506.05	5560	6915	7964
33404	Construction of apical-aortic conduit	49.54	1758.44	6618	7681	8666
33405	Replacement, aortic valve, with cardiopulmonary bypass; with prosthetic valve other than homograft or stentless valve	64.10	2272.33	7197	8148	8964
33406	Replacement, aortic valve, with cardiopulmonary bypass; with allograft valve (freehand)	77.03	2718.77	7088	8357	9225
33410	Replacement, aortic valve, with cardiopulmonary bypass; with stentless tissue valve	67.63	2386.41	6930	8255	9081
33411	Replacement, aortic valve; with aortic annulus enlargement, noncoronary cusp	86.86	3055.68	7552	8977	10031
33412	Replacement, aortic valve; with transventricular aortic annulus enlargement (Konno procedure)	69.58	2470.16	7632	9161	10044
33413	Replacement, aortic valve; by translocation of autologous pulmonary valve with allograft replacement of pulmonary valve (Ross procedure)	87.02	3070.08	9688	11134	12211
33414	Repair of left ventricular outflow tract obstruction by patch enlargement of the outflow tract	58.26	2058.21	6887	8056	9082
33415	Resection or incision of subvalvular tissue for discrete subvalvular aortic stenosis	53.59	1889.19	5541	7117	8716
33416	Ventriculomyotomy (-myectomy) for idiopathic hypertrophic subaortic stenosis (eg, asymmetric septal hypertrophy)	54.52	1927.47	6309	7274	8926
33417	Aortoplasty (gusset) for supravalvular stenosis	46.50	1651.19	6346	7616	8442

Mitral Valve

33420	Valvotomy, mitral valve; closed heart	36.91	1301.02	5031	5990	6615
33422	Valvotomy, mitral valve; open heart, with cardiopulmonary bypass	46.90	1664.46	6263	7547	8641
33425	Valvuloplasty, mitral valve, with cardiopulmonary bypass;	68.16	2393.23	6388	7485	8576
33426	Valvuloplasty, mitral valve, with cardiopulmonary bypass; with prosthetic ring	65.04	2300.38	7004	8218	9077
33427	Valvuloplasty, mitral valve, with cardiopulmonary bypass; radical reconstruction, with or without ring	69.32	2456.52	7189	8398	9352
33430	Replacement, mitral valve, with cardiopulmonary bypass	73.56	2594.08	7181	8433	9012

Tricuspid Valve

33460	Valvectomy, tricuspid valve, with cardiopulmonary bypass	60.42	2119.61	5764	6746	7658
33463	Valvuloplasty, tricuspid valve; without ring insertion	75.44	2641.83	6122	7663	8822
33464	Valvuloplasty, tricuspid valve; with ring insertion	62.84	2211.70	6362	7357	8993
33465	Replacement, tricuspid valve, with cardiopulmonary bypass	69.14	2427.33	6470	7658	8507
33468	Tricuspid valve repositioning and plication for Ebstein anomaly	50.97	1806.57	7584	8997	10126

● = New Code ⊗ = Conscious Sedation ✚ = Add-on Code ∅ = Modifier '51' Exempt ▲ =Revised Code

		Medicare RVU	National Fee	PFR Fee Information 50%	75%	90%

Pulmonary Valve

33470	Valvotomy, pulmonary valve, closed heart; transventricular	32.54	1152.08	4828	5655	6476
33471	Valvotomy, pulmonary valve, closed heart; via pulmonary artery	35.46	1256.68	4807	5828	7033
33472	Valvotomy, pulmonary valve, open heart; with inflow occlusion	37.15	1320.73	4924	6014	7035
33474	Valvotomy, pulmonary valve, open heart; with cardiopulmonary bypass	54.96	1933.15	5953	7194	8348
33475	Replacement, pulmonary valve	62.66	2213.59	6731	8470	9590
33476	Right ventricular resection for infundibular stenosis, with or without commissurotomy	40.66	1440.10	6270	7447	8518
33478	Outflow tract augmentation (gusset), with or without commissurotomy or infundibular resection	43.80	1555.69	6513	7793	8972

Other Valvular Procedures

| 33496 | Repair of non-structural prosthetic valve dysfunction with cardiopulmonary bypass (separate procedure) | 46.26 | 1639.82 | 6340 | 7489 | 8660 |

Coronary Artery Anomalies

33500	Repair of coronary arteriovenous or arteriocardiac chamber fistula; with cardiopulmonary bypass	43.05	1525.37	5112	6256	7109
33501	Repair of coronary arteriovenous or arteriocardiac chamber fistula; without cardiopulmonary bypass	29.62	1048.62	3591	4664	5564
33502	Repair of anomalous coronary artery from pulmonary artery origin; by ligation	35.31	1255.54	3694	4521	5130
33503	Repair of anomalous coronary artery from pulmonary artery origin; by graft, without cardiopulmonary bypass	34.03	1204.76	4681	5537	6482
33504	Repair of anomalous coronary artery from pulmonary artery origin; by graft, with cardiopulmonary bypass	40.05	1421.16	5834	7138	7827
33505	Repair of anomalous coronary artery from pulmonary artery origin; with construction of intrapulmonary artery tunnel (Takeuchi procedure)	53.29	1873.27	6180	7552	9137
33506	Repair of anomalous coronary artery from pulmonary artery origin; by translocation from pulmonary artery to aorta	57.27	2026.38	6253	7639	9243
33507	Repair of anomalous (eg, intramural) aortic origin of coronary artery by unroofing or translocation	48.58	1721.68	6124	7516	8752

Endoscopy

| + 33508 | Endoscopy, surgical, including video-assisted harvest of vein(s) for coronary artery bypass procedure (List separately in addition to code for primary procedure) | 0.45 | 15.92 | 59 | 71 | 92 |

Venous Grafting Only For Coronary Artery Bypass

(UNBUNDLING ALERT: 33510 cannot be used with 32020, 32100, 33210, 37720, or 37730 by the same physician on the same day.)

(For separate procurement of graft by a physician other than an assistant, add modifier -62, Services rendered by two surgeons.)

| 33510 | Coronary artery bypass, vein only; single coronary venous graft | 54.83 | 1944.90 | 6417 | 7042 | 7667 |

(UNBUNDLING ALERT: 33511 cannot be used with 32020, 32100, 33210, 33510, 37720, or 37730 by the same physician on the same day.)

| 33511 | Coronary artery bypass, vein only; two coronary venous grafts | 59.32 | 2101.80 | 7033 | 7669 | 8316 |

(UNBUNDLING ALERT: 33512 cannot be used with 32020, 32100, 33210, 33510, 33511, 37720, or 37730 by the same physician on the same day.)

| 33512 | Coronary artery bypass, vein only; three coronary venous grafts | 65.80 | 2326.53 | 7709 | 8563 | 9438 |

(UNBUNDLING ALERT: 33513 cannot be used with 32020, 32100, 33210, 33510, 33511, 33512, 37720, or 37730 by the same physician on the same day.)

| 33513 | Coronary artery bypass, vein only; four coronary venous grafts | 67.68 | 2392.47 | 8190 | 9179 | 10007 |

(UNBUNDLING ALERT: 33514 cannot be used with 32020, 32100, 33210, 33510, 33511, 33512, 33513, 37720, or 37730 by the same physician on the same day.)

| 33514 | Coronary artery bypass, vein only; five coronary venous grafts | 70.69 | 2495.93 | 9472 | 10083 | 11557 |

(UNBUNDLING ALERT: 33516 cannot be used with 32020, 32100, 33210, 33510, 33511, 33512, 33513, 33514, 37720, or 37730 by the same physician on the same day.)

| 33516 | Coronary artery bypass, vein only; six or more coronary venous grafts | 73.52 | 2597.12 | 9910 | 10938 | 12048 |

Combined Arterial-Venous Grafting For Coronary Bypass

| ∅ 33517 | Coronary artery bypass, using venous graft(s) and arterial graft(s); single vein graft (List separately in addition to code for arterial graft) | 4.91 | 172.43 | 771 | 1042 | 1230 |

© PFR 2007

		Medicare RVU	National Fee	PFR Fee Information 50%	75%	90%
∅ 33518	Coronary artery bypass, using venous graft(s) and arterial graft(s); two venous grafts (List separately in addition to code for arterial graft)	10.45	365.71	1290	1604	2036
∅ 33519	Coronary artery bypass, using venous graft(s) and arterial graft(s); three venous grafts (List separately in addition to code for arterial graft)	14.07	493.05	1577	2068	2668
∅ 33521	Coronary artery bypass, using venous graft(s) and arterial graft(s); four venous grafts (List separately in addition to code for arterial graft)	17.23	604.84	2194	2480	3053
∅ 33522	Coronary artery bypass, using venous graft(s) and arterial graft(s); five venous grafts (List separately in addition to code for arterial graft)	19.86	698.83	2715	3189	3616
∅ 33523	Coronary artery bypass, using venous graft(s) and arterial graft(s); six or more venous grafts (List separately in addition to code for arterial graft)	22.85	804.56	3495	4333	4685
	(This code for the repeat operation of coronary bypass surgery should not be coded as a multiple procedure. List it separately without a modifier.)					
✚ 33530	Reoperation, coronary artery bypass procedure or valve procedure, more than one month after original operation (List separately in addition to code for primary procedure)	13.22	462.35	1458	1776	2220

Arterial Grafting For Coronary Artery Bypass

33533	Coronary artery bypass, using arterial graft(s); single arterial graft	53.75	1908.90	6568	7648	8889
33534	Coronary artery bypass, using arterial graft(s); two coronary arterial grafts	61.50	2179.11	7312	8765	9980
33535	Coronary artery bypass, using arterial graft(s); three coronary arterial grafts	67.42	2384.89	8140	10082	11984
33536	Coronary artery bypass, using arterial graft(s); four or more coronary arterial grafts	71.87	2539.51	8534	9820	11094
33542	Myocardial resection (eg, ventricular aneurysmectomy)	66.58	2339.79	6500	7531	8267
33545	Repair of postinfarction ventricular septal defect, with or without myocardial resection	78.99	2776.37	7733	10003	12260
33548	Surgical ventricular restoration procedure, includes prosthetic patch, when performed (eg, ventricular remodeling, SVR, SAVER, DOR procedures)	78.97	2786.98	8682	10182	11511

Coronary Endarterectomy

	(This code for a Coronary Endarterectomy(s) should be listed along with the primary procedure. Use along with 33510 - 33516 and 33533 - 33536. Do not use "Multiple Procedure" modifier -51 with this code.)					
✚ 33572	Coronary endarterectomy, open, any method, of left anterior descending, circumflex, or right coronary artery performed in conjunction with coronary artery bypass graft procedure, each vessel (List separately in addition to primary procedure)	6.51	229.66	1068	1226	1487

Single Ventricle and Other Complex Cardiac Anomalies

33600	Closure of atrioventricular valve (mitral or tricuspid) by suture or patch	47.07	1669.01	6691	7987	8743
33602	Closure of semilunar valve (aortic or pulmonary) by suture or patch	45.73	1621.63	6374	7650	8781
33606	Anastomosis of pulmonary artery to aorta (Damus-Kaye-Stansel procedure)	49.06	1739.50	6829	8041	8987
33608	Repair of complex cardiac anomaly other than pulmonary atresia with ventricular septal defect by construction or replacement of conduit from right or left ventricle to pulmonary artery	50.39	1788.76	7417	9142	10979
33610	Repair of complex cardiac anomalies (eg, single ventricle with subaortic obstruction) by surgical enlargement of ventricular septal defect	48.82	1731.16	7289	9120	10967
33611	Repair of double outlet right ventricle with intraventricular tunnel repair;	53.60	1896.01	7895	10414	11977
33612	Repair of double outlet right ventricle with intraventricular tunnel repair; with repair of right ventricular outflow tract obstruction	56.38	1997.58	7614	9073	10440
33615	Repair of complex cardiac anomalies (eg, tricuspid atresia) by closure of atrial septal defect and anastomosis of atria or vena cava to pulmonary artery (simple Fontan procedure)	53.07	1874.79	7422	8780	10125
33617	Repair of complex cardiac anomalies (eg, single ventricle) by modified Fontan procedure	60.72	2152.58	7855	9680	11708
33619	Repair of single ventricle with aortic outflow obstruction and aortic arch hypoplasia (hypoplastic left heart syndrome) (eg, Norwood procedure)	75.22	2665.33	9082	11026	13537

Septal Defect

33641	Repair atrial septal defect, secundum, with cardiopulmonary bypass, with or without patch	42.66	1504.15	5180	5982	7122
33645	Direct or patch closure, sinus venosus, with or without anomalous pulmonary venous drainage	43.34	1535.99	5827	6752	7619
33647	Repair of atrial septal defect and ventricular septal defect, with direct or patch closure	46.09	1634.90	6718	8108	9669
33660	Repair of incomplete or partial atrioventricular canal (ostium primum atrial septal defect), with or without atrioventricular valve repair	49.21	1744.04	6535	7469	8679

● = New Code ⊗ = Conscious Sedation ✚ = Add-on Code ∅ = Modifier '51' Exempt ▲ =Revised Code

		Medicare RVU	National Fee	PFR Fee Information 50%	75%	90%
33665	Repair of intermediate or transitional atrioventricular canal, with or without atrioventricular valve repair	52.25	1847.50	6869	8586	9204
33670	Repair of complete atrioventricular canal, with or without prosthetic valve	54.17	1913.44	7249	8999	11675
● 33675	Closure of multiple ventricular septal defects;	58.64	2085.50	7973	9648	11403
● 33676	Closure of multiple ventricular septal defects; with pulmonary valvotomy or infundibular resection (acyanotic)	60.48	2151.44	8223	9951	11761
● 33677	Closure of multiple ventricular septal defects; with removal of pulmonary artery band, with or without gusset	62.87	2236.33	8548	10344	12226
▲ 33681	Closure of single ventricular septal defect, with or without patch;	50.93	1807.33	6665	7871	8932
33684	Closure of single ventricular septal defect, with or without patch; with pulmonary valvotomy or infundibular resection (acyanotic)	52.81	1870.62	6781	7917	8976
33688	Closure of single ventricular septal defect, with or without patch; with removal of pulmonary artery band, with or without gusset	49.61	1747.83	6640	8039	9506
33690	Banding of pulmonary artery	31.94	1133.51	3104	3822	4390
33692	Complete repair tetralogy of Fallot without pulmonary atresia;	48.70	1725.85	6854	8514	9667
33694	Complete repair tetralogy of Fallot without pulmonary atresia; with transannular patch	53.95	1909.28	7341	8946	10642
33697	Complete repair tetralogy of Fallot with pulmonary atresia including construction of conduit from right ventricle to pulmonary artery and closure of ventricular septal defect	58.22	2063.52	7659	9299	10273

Sinus of Valsalva

33702	Repair sinus of Valsalva fistula, with cardiopulmonary bypass;	43.08	1529.16	6097	7854	9370
33710	Repair sinus of Valsalva fistula, with cardiopulmonary bypass; with repair of ventricular septal defect	48.09	1706.90	6832	8592	10112
33720	Repair sinus of Valsalva aneurysm, with cardiopulmonary bypass	42.96	1524.62	6578	7722	8531
33722	Closure of aortico-left ventricular tunnel	42.90	1515.14	6646	8254	9751

Venous Anomalies

● 33724	Repair of isolated partial anomalous pulmonary venous return (eg, Scimitar Syndrome)	42.11	1490.89	5602	6712	7736
● 33726	Repair of pulmonary venous stenosis	55.53	1963.09	7388	8851	10202
33730	Complete repair of anomalous pulmonary venous return (supracardiac, intracardiac, or infracardiac types)	54.95	1945.28	7034	8518	9883
33732	Repair of cor triatriatum or supravalvular mitral ring by resection of left atrial membrane	46.22	1641.72	6382	7569	8670

Shunting Procedures

33735	Atrial septectomy or septostomy; closed heart (Blalock-Hanlon type operation)	33.04	1168.00	4402	5501	6300
33736	Atrial septectomy or septostomy; open heart with cardiopulmonary bypass	38.82	1379.09	4945	6145	7193
33737	Atrial septectomy or septostomy; open heart, with inflow occlusion	35.67	1266.53	4578	5528	6884
33750	Shunt; subclavian to pulmonary artery (Blalock-Taussig type operation)	33.73	1194.15	4012	4904	6339
33755	Shunt; ascending aorta to pulmonary artery (Waterston type operation)	34.25	1212.34	4301	4990	5922
33762	Shunt; descending aorta to pulmonary artery (Potts-Smith type operation)	34.98	1240.01	4141	4882	6191
33764	Shunt; central, with prosthetic graft	35.42	1256.68	4037	5118	6494
33766	Shunt; superior vena cava to pulmonary artery for flow to one lung (classical Glenn procedure)	38.00	1350.67	4534	5333	6125
33767	Shunt; superior vena cava to pulmonary artery for flow to both lungs (bidirectional Glenn procedure)	40.11	1424.19	4621	5563	6428
✚ 33768	Anastomosis, cavopulmonary, second superior vena cava (List separately in addition to primary procedure)	11.74	414.60	1549	1842	2271

Transposition of The Great Vessels

33770	Repair of transposition of the great arteries with ventricular septal defect and subpulmonary stenosis; without surgical enlargement of ventricular septal defect	58.41	2064.66	7172	8595	10933
33771	Repair of transposition of the great arteries with ventricular septal defect and subpulmonary stenosis; with surgical enlargement of ventricular septal defect	58.18	2050.25	7717	9323	11197
33774	Repair of transposition of the great arteries, atrial baffle procedure (eg, Mustard or Senning type) with cardiopulmonary bypass;	50.44	1791.41	6891	8518	9821

● = New Code ⊗ = Conscious Sedation ✚ = Add-on Code ∅ = Modifier '51' Exempt ▲ = Revised Code

		Medicare RVU	National Fee	PFR Fee Information 50%	75%	90%
33775	Repair of transposition of the great arteries, atrial baffle procedure (eg, Mustard or Senning type) with cardiopulmonary bypass; with removal of pulmonary band	51.59	1830.07	7430	8762	11047
33776	Repair of transposition of the great arteries, atrial baffle procedure (eg, Mustard or Senning type) with cardiopulmonary bypass; with closure of ventricular septal defect	54.80	1945.28	7712	9341	11110
33777	Repair of transposition of the great arteries, atrial baffle procedure (eg, Mustard or Senning type) with cardiopulmonary bypass; with repair of subpulmonic obstruction	53.63	1902.83	8051	9113	10900
33778	Repair of transposition of the great arteries, aortic pulmonary artery reconstruction (eg, Jatene type);	65.29	2311.75	8004	9516	11242
33779	Repair of transposition of the great arteries, aortic pulmonary artery reconstruction (eg, Jatene type); with removal of pulmonary band	60.44	2126.05	8130	9678	11596
33780	Repair of transposition of the great arteries, aortic pulmonary artery reconstruction (eg, Jatene type); with closure of ventricular septal defect	64.76	2287.11	8169	9935	13332
33781	Repair of transposition of the great arteries, aortic pulmonary artery reconstruction (eg, Jatene type); with repair of subpulmonic obstruction	62.67	2210.56	7866	9578	13465

Truncus Arteriosus

33786	Total repair, truncus arteriosus (Rastelli type operation)	62.84	2222.31	7636	9356	10608
33788	Reimplantation of an anomalous pulmonary artery	42.68	1513.63	5184	6308	7458

Aortic Anomalies

33800	Aortic suspension (aortopexy) for tracheal decompression (eg, for tracheomalacia) (separate procedure)	27.60	980.41	3336	4060	4768
33802	Division of aberrant vessel (vascular ring);	29.31	1041.42	3542	4173	4807
33803	Division of aberrant vessel (vascular ring); with reanastomosis	32.68	1161.56	4086	4839	5879
33813	Obliteration of aortopulmonary septal defect; without cardiopulmonary bypass	34.78	1236.97	4188	5241	6556
33814	Obliteration of aortopulmonary septal defect; with cardiopulmonary bypass	42.35	1504.15	5719	6660	8299
33820	Repair of patent ductus arteriosus; by ligation	27.33	972.45	3139	4145	4854
33822	Repair of patent ductus arteriosus; by division, younger than 18 years	28.51	1013.38	3766	4707	5250
33824	Repair of patent ductus arteriosus; by division, 18 years and older	32.62	1159.66	3997	4625	5288
33840	Excision of coarctation of aorta, with or without associated patent ductus arteriosus; with direct anastomosis	33.33	1182.40	4169	4851	6004
33845	Excision of coarctation of aorta, with or without associated patent ductus arteriosus; with graft	36.90	1311.63	5521	7020	7643
33851	Excision of coarctation of aorta, with or without associated patent ductus arteriosus; repair using either left subclavian artery or prosthetic material as gusset for enlargement	35.32	1255.17	5323	7252	8407
33852	Repair of hypoplastic or interrupted aortic arch using autogenous or prosthetic material; without cardiopulmonary bypass	37.42	1325.65	5451	6578	7028
33853	Repair of hypoplastic or interrupted aortic arch using autogenous or prosthetic material; with cardiopulmonary bypass	51.20	1817.19	7116	8429	9680

Thoracic Aortic Aneurysm

33860	Ascending aorta graft, with cardiopulmonary bypass, with or without valve suspension;	82.57	2902.95	7221	8510	9738
33861	Ascending aorta graft, with cardiopulmonary bypass, with or without valve suspension; with coronary reconstruction	67.61	2394.74	7970	9607	11012
33863	Ascending aorta graft, with cardiopulmonary bypass, with or without valve suspension; with aortic root replacement using composite prosthesis and coronary reconstruction	84.31	2971.16	8017	9533	11075
33870	Transverse arch graft, with cardiopulmonary bypass	70.50	2496.69	8711	10124	12180
33875	Descending thoracic aorta graft, with or without bypass	54.42	1926.33	6965	8394	9733
33877	Repair of thoracoabdominal aortic aneurysm with graft, with or without cardiopulmonary bypass	92.46	3241.37	8525	10016	12535

Endovascular Repair of Descending Thoracic Aorta

33880	Endovascular repair of descending thoracic aorta (eg, aneurysm, pseudoaneurysm, dissection, penetrating ulcer, intramural hematoma, or traumatic disruption); involving coverage of left subclavian artery origin, initial endoprosthesis plus descending thoracic aortic extension(s), if required, to level of celiac artery origin	49.96	1761.85	6043	7150	8328
33881	Endovascular repair of descending thoracic aorta (eg, aneurysm, pseudoaneurysm, dissection, penetrating ulcer, intramural hematoma, or traumatic disruption); not involving coverage of left subclavian artery origin, initial endoprosthesis plus descending thoracic aortic extension(s), if required, to level of celiac artery origin	43.10	1520.83	5192	6143	7154

● = New Code ⊗ = Conscious Sedation ✚ = Add-on Code ∅ = Modifier '51' Exempt ▲ =Revised Code

		Medicare RVU	National Fee	PFR Fee Information 50%	75%	90%
33883	Placement of proximal extension prosthesis for endovascular repair of descending thoracic aorta (eg, aneurysm, pseudoaneurysm, dissection, penetrating ulcer, intramural hematoma, or traumatic disruption); initial extension	31.72	1122.14	3627	4290	4997
+ 33884	Placement of proximal extension prosthesis for endovascular repair of descending thoracic aorta (eg, aneurysm, pseudoaneurysm, dissection, penetrating ulcer, intramural hematoma, or traumatic disruption); each additional proximal extension (List separately in addition to code for primary procedure)	11.49	404.37	1495	1768	2060
33886	Placement of distal extension prosthesis(s) delayed after endovascular repair of descending thoracic aorta	27.51	973.97	3318	3926	4572
33889	Open subclavian to carotid artery transposition performed in conjunction with endovascular repair of descending thoracic aorta, by neck incision, unilateral	23.02	811.76	2857	3380	3937
33891	Bypass graft, with other than vein, transcervical retropharyngeal carotid-carotid, performed in conjunction with endovascular repair of descending thoracic aorta, by neck incision	29.53	1042.94	3644	4312	5022

Pulmonary Artery

33910	Pulmonary artery embolectomy; with cardiopulmonary bypass	44.68	1580.33	5337	6766	8023
33915	Pulmonary artery embolectomy; without cardiopulmonary bypass	35.85	1263.88	3822	4677	5719
33916	Pulmonary endarterectomy, with or without embolectomy, with cardiopulmonary bypass	43.19	1528.79	5926	7315	8619
33917	Repair of pulmonary artery stenosis by reconstruction with patch or graft	40.57	1441.62	5877	7316	8626
33920	Repair of pulmonary atresia with ventricular septal defect, by construction or replacement of conduit from right or left ventricle to pulmonary artery	50.16	1776.63	7210	8535	9560
33922	Transection of pulmonary artery with cardiopulmonary bypass	38.23	1357.11	5153	6253	7020
+ 33924	Ligation and takedown of a systemic-to-pulmonary artery shunt, performed in conjunction with a congenital heart procedure (List separately in addition to code for primary procedure)	8.23	291.05	974	1393	1571
33925	Repair of pulmonary artery arborization anomalies by unifocalization; without cardiopulmonary bypass	49.40	1753.14	6539	8198	9518
33926	Repair of pulmonary artery arborization anomalies by unifocalization; with cardiopulmonary bypass	67.74	2397.02	8834	11075	12858

Heart/lung Transplantation

33930	Donor cardiectomy-pneumonectomy (including cold preservation)	-	-	5331	5942	7024
33933	Backbench standard preparation of cadaver donor heart/lung allograft prior to transplantation, including dissection of allograft from surrounding soft tissues to prepare aorta, superior vena cava, inferior vena cava, and trachea for implantation	-	-	IR	IR	IR
33935	Heart-lung transplant with recipient cardiectomy-pneumonectomy	98.13	3483.54	14201	17493	19745
33940	Donor cardiectomy (including cold preservation)	-	-	2757	4741	5907
33944	Backbench standard preparation of cadaver donor heart allograft prior to transplantation, including dissection of allograft from surrounding soft tissues to prepare aorta, superior vena cava, inferior vena cava, pulmonary artery, and left atrium for implantation	-	-	IR	IR	IR
33945	Heart transplant, with or without recipient cardiectomy	119.08	4173.27	12343	14799	16863

Cardiac Assist

33960	Prolonged extracorporeal circulation for cardiopulmonary insufficiency; initial 24 hours	27.09	953.12	2699	3288	4022
+ 33961	Prolonged extracorporeal circulation for cardiopulmonary insufficiency; each additional 24 hours (List separately in addition to code for primary procedure)	15.24	535.87	1973	2317	2878
33967	Insertion of intra-aortic balloon assist device, percutaneous	7.19	253.91	878	1068	1280
33968	Removal of intra-aortic balloon assist device, percutaneous	0.95	33.73	90	113	132
	(These codes are used for the placement and removal of balloon assist devices through the femoral artery.)					
33970	Insertion of intra-aortic balloon assist device through the femoral artery, open approach	9.91	349.79	1902	2146	2556
	(Use these codes for placement of the assist device through the ascending aorta.)					
33971	Removal of intra-aortic balloon assist device including repair of femoral artery, with or without graft	19.18	681.40	1813	2193	2935
33973	Insertion of intra-aortic balloon assist device through the ascending aorta	14.47	511.24	1876	2181	2379
33974	Removal of intra-aortic balloon assist device from the ascending aorta, including repair of the ascending aorta, with or without graft	24.53	872.78	2136	2831	3338
33975	Insertion of ventricular assist device; extracorporeal, single ventricle	30.41	1072.50	3745	4492	5137

● = New Code ⊗ = Conscious Sedation ✚ = Add-on Code ∅ = Modifier '51' Exempt ▲ =Revised Code

		Medicare RVU	National Fee	PFR Fee Information 50%	75%	90%
33976	Insertion of ventricular assist device; extracorporeal, biventricular	33.87	1196.05	4957	5868	6749
33977	Removal of ventricular assist device; extracorporeal, single ventricle	33.52	1193.77	3583	4400	5162
33978	Removal of ventricular assist device; extracorporeal, biventricular	37.25	1326.03	4134	4835	5463
33979	Insertion of ventricular assist device, implantable intracorporeal, single ventricle	67.69	2390.20	5041	6321	7687
33980	Removal of ventricular assist device, implantable intracorporeal, single ventricle	98.62	3490.36	4415	5755	7083

Other Procedures

33999	Unlisted procedure, cardiac surgery	-	-	IR	IR	IR

Arteries and Veins
Embolectomy/Thrombectomy
Arterial, With or Without Catheter

34001	Embolectomy or thrombectomy, with or without catheter; carotid, subclavian or innominate artery, by neck incision	26.32	929.63	2428	2709	3016
34051	Embolectomy or thrombectomy, with or without catheter; innominate, subclavian artery, by thoracic incision	26.68	946.68	2838	3117	3394
34101	Embolectomy or thrombectomy, with or without catheter; axillary, brachial, innominate, subclavian artery, by arm incision	17.37	616.97	2204	2462	3250
34111	Embolectomy or thrombectomy, with or without catheter; radial or ulnar artery, by arm incision	17.38	617.35	2393	3201	3882
34151	Embolectomy or thrombectomy, with or without catheter; renal, celiac, mesentery, aortoiliac artery, by abdominal incision	39.97	1413.96	3176	3777	4368
	(UNBUNDLING ALERT: 34201 cannot be used with 36000 or 36140 by the same physician on the same day.)					
34201	Embolectomy or thrombectomy, with or without catheter; femoropopliteal, aortoiliac artery, by leg incision	26.58	933.42	2461	2955	3814
34203	Embolectomy or thrombectomy, with or without catheter; popliteal-tibio-peroneal artery, by leg incision	27.77	984.96	2626	3012	3431

Venous, Direct or With Catheter

34401	Thrombectomy, direct or with catheter; vena cava, iliac vein, by abdominal incision	39.90	1411.30	2665	2986	3286
34421	Thrombectomy, direct or with catheter; vena cava, iliac, femoropopliteal vein, by leg incision	20.86	739.76	2145	2486	2835
34451	Thrombectomy, direct or with catheter; vena cava, iliac, femoropopliteal vein, by abdominal and leg incision	43.25	1530.68	2995	3416	3858
34471	Thrombectomy, direct or with catheter; subclavian vein, by neck incision	28.07	983.82	2150	2468	2700
34490	Thrombectomy, direct or with catheter; axillary and subclavian vein, by arm incision	17.42	618.87	1876	2278	2627

Venous Reconstruction

34501	Valvuloplasty, femoral vein	27.19	966.77	2166	2705	2884
34502	Reconstruction of vena cava, any method	43.40	1538.64	5075	5645	5948
34510	Venous valve transposition, any vein donor	31.00	1099.41	2573	3232	3778
34520	Cross-over vein graft to venous system	29.99	1063.78	3105	3479	3751
34530	Saphenopopliteal vein anastomosis	27.94	991.02	2866	3365	4111

Endovascular Repair of Abdominal Aortic Aneurysm

34800	Endovascular repair of infrarenal abdominal aortic aneurysm or dissection; using aorto-aortic tube prosthesis	32.64	1155.12	2987	3652	4189
34802	Endovascular repair of infrarenal abdominal aortic aneurysm or dissection; using modular bifurcated prosthesis (one docking limb)	35.42	1251.75	3523	4159	4738
34803	Endovascular repair of infrarenal abdominal aortic aneurysm or dissection; using modular bifurcated prosthesis (two docking limbs)	36.43	1286.24	3552	4289	4856
34804	Endovascular repair of infrarenal abdominal aortic aneurysm or dissection; using unibody bifurcated prosthesis	35.38	1250.24	3503	4278	4757
34805	Endovascular repair of infrarenal abdominal aortic aneurysm or dissection; using aorto-uniiliac or aorto-unifemoral prosthesis	33.64	1188.84	3310	3997	4524
✚ 34808	Endovascular placement of iliac artery occlusion device (List separately in addition to code for primary procedure)	6.01	212.23	720	836	912

● = New Code ⊗ = Conscious Sedation ✚ = Add-on Code ∅ = Modifier '51' Exempt ▲ =Revised Code

		Medicare RVU	National Fee	PFR Fee Information 50%	75%	90%
34812	Open femoral artery exposure for delivery of endovascular prosthesis, by groin incision, unilateral	10.02	353.96	1003	1251	1414
✚ 34813	Placement of femoral-femoral prosthetic graft during endovascular aortic aneurysm repair (List separately in addition to code for primary procedure)	6.94	244.82	822	976	1103
34820	Open iliac artery exposure for delivery of endovascular prosthesis or iliac occlusion during endovascular therapy, by abdominal or retroperitoneal incision, unilateral	14.28	504.04	1574	1860	2151
34825	Placement of proximal or distal extension prosthesis for endovascular repair of infrarenal abdominal aortic or iliac aneurysm, false aneurysm, or dissection; initial vessel	19.89	705.27	1998	2452	2700
✚ 34826	Placement of proximal or distal extension prosthesis for endovascular repair of infrarenal abdominal aortic or iliac aneurysm, false aneurysm, or dissection; each additional vessel (List separately in addition to code for primary procedure)	5.87	206.92	610	764	880
34830	Open repair of infrarenal aortic aneurysm or dissection, plus repair of associated arterial trauma, following unsuccessful endovascular repair; tube prosthesis	52.61	1860.01	4587	5864	6803
34831	Open repair of infrarenal aortic aneurysm or dissection, plus repair of associated arterial trauma, following unsuccessful endovascular repair; aorto-bi-iliac prosthesis	54.56	1923.30	5085	6216	7100
34832	Open repair of infrarenal aortic aneurysm or dissection, plus repair of associated arterial trauma, following unsuccessful endovascular repair; aorto-bifemoral prosthesis	56.57	1999.47	5187	6340	7113
34833	Open iliac artery exposure with creation of conduit for delivery of aortic or iliac endovascular prosthesis, by abdominal or retroperitoneal incision, unilateral	17.83	629.86	1805	2219	2526
34834	Open brachial artery exposure to assist in the deployment of aortic or iliac endovascular prosthesis by arm incision, unilateral	8.14	288.02	950	1169	1331

Endovascular Repair of Iliac Aneurysm

		Medicare RVU	National Fee	50%	75%	90%
34900	Endovascular graft placement for repair of iliac artery (eg, aneurysm, pseudoaneurysm, arteriovenous malformation, trauma)	26.01	921.67	2943	3620	4187

Direct Repair of Aneurysm or Excision (Partial or Total) and Graft Insertion For Aneurysm, False Aneurysm, Ruptured Aneurysm, and Associated Occlusive Disease

		Medicare RVU	National Fee	50%	75%	90%
35001	Direct repair of aneurysm, pseudoaneurysm, or excision (partial or total) and graft insertion, with or without patch graft; for aneurysm and associated occlusive disease, carotid, subclavian artery, by neck incision	32.58	1155.87	3749	4044	4456
35002	Direct repair of aneurysm, pseudoaneurysm, or excision (partial or total) and graft insertion, with or without patch graft; for ruptured aneurysm, carotid, subclavian artery, by neck incision	34.34	1216.89	3884	4333	4907
35005	Direct repair of aneurysm, pseudoaneurysm, or excision (partial or total) and graft insertion, with or without patch graft; for aneurysm, pseudoaneurysm, and associated occlusive disease, vertebral artery	29.47	1043.70	3294	4420	4961
35011	Direct repair of aneurysm, pseudoaneurysm, or excision (partial or total) and graft insertion, with or without patch graft; for aneurysm and associated occlusive disease, axillary-brachial artery, by arm incision	28.64	1014.90	3150	3565	3777
35013	Direct repair of aneurysm, pseudoaneurysm, or excision (partial or total) and graft insertion, with or without patch graft; for ruptured aneurysm, axillary-brachial artery, by arm incision	35.44	1255.17	3529	4007	4679
35021	Direct repair of aneurysm, pseudoaneurysm, or excision (partial or total) and graft insertion, with or without patch graft; for aneurysm, pseudoaneurysm, and associated occlusive disease, innominate, subclavian artery, by thoracic incision	34.19	1211.58	3844	4396	5035
35022	Direct repair of aneurysm, pseudoaneurysm, or excision (partial or total) and graft insertion, with or without patch graft; for ruptured aneurysm, innominate, subclavian artery, by thoracic incision	38.54	1362.79	4217	4904	5418
35045	Direct repair of aneurysm, pseudoaneurysm, or excision (partial or total) and graft insertion, with or without patch graft; for aneurysm, pseudoaneurysm, and associated occlusive disease, radial or ulnar artery *(UNBUNDLING ALERT: 35081 cannot be used with 44005 or 49000 by the same physician on the same day.)*	27.65	979.65	3257	4159	4624
35081	Direct repair of aneurysm, pseudoaneurysm, or excision (partial or total) and graft insertion, with or without patch graft; for aneurysm, pseudoaneurysm, and associated occlusive disease, abdominal aorta *(UNBUNDLING ALERT: 35082 cannot be used with 44005 or 49000 by the same physician on the same day.)*	48.74	1719.79	5062	5679	6353
35082	Direct repair of aneurysm, pseudoaneurysm, or excision (partial or total) and graft insertion, with or without patch graft; for ruptured aneurysm, abdominal aorta	62.12	2194.27	5852	6968	7283
35091	Direct repair of aneurysm, pseudoaneurysm, or excision (partial or total) and graft insertion, with or without patch graft; for aneurysm, pseudoaneurysm, and associated occlusive disease, abdominal aorta involving visceral vessels (mesenteric, celiac, renal)	53.26	1883.51	5747	6565	7777

● = New Code ⊗ = Conscious Sedation ✚ = Add-on Code ∅ = Modifier '51' Exempt ▲ =Revised Code

		Medicare RVU	National Fee	PFR Fee Information 50%	75%	90%
35092	Direct repair of aneurysm, pseudoaneurysm, or excision (partial or total) and graft insertion, with or without patch graft; for ruptured aneurysm, abdominal aorta involving visceral vessels (mesenteric, celiac, renal)	74.19	2617.96	6902	7569	8723
	(UNBUNDLING ALERT: 35102 cannot be used with 44005 or 49000 by the same physician on the same day.)					
35102	Direct repair of aneurysm, pseudoaneurysm, or excision (partial or total) and graft insertion, with or without patch graft; for aneurysm, pseudoaneurysm, and associated occlusive disease, abdominal aorta involving iliac vessels (common, hypogastric, external)	53.02	1870.62	5625	6467	7297
35103	Direct repair of aneurysm, pseudoaneurysm, or excision (partial or total) and graft insertion, with or without patch graft; for ruptured aneurysm, abdominal aorta involving iliac vessels (common, hypogastric, external)	64.44	2276.12	5821	6837	7855
35111	Direct repair of aneurysm, pseudoaneurysm, or excision (partial or total) and graft insertion, with or without patch graft; for aneurysm, pseudoaneurysm, and associated occlusive disease, splenic artery	39.63	1402.21	3811	4587	4894
35112	Direct repair of aneurysm, pseudoaneurysm, or excision (partial or total) and graft insertion, with or without patch graft; for ruptured aneurysm, splenic artery	48.11	1699.70	3673	4258	4996
35121	Direct repair of aneurysm, pseudoaneurysm, or excision (partial or total) and graft insertion, with or without patch graft; for aneurysm, pseudoaneurysm, and associated occlusive disease, hepatic, celiac, renal, or mesenteric artery	47.60	1684.16	4564	5260	5783
35122	Direct repair of aneurysm, pseudoaneurysm, or excision (partial or total) and graft insertion, with or without patch graft; for ruptured aneurysm, hepatic, celiac, renal, or mesenteric artery	55.88	1973.70	4934	5861	6648
35131	Direct repair of aneurysm, pseudoaneurysm, or excision (partial or total) and graft insertion, with or without patch graft; for aneurysm, pseudoaneurysm, and associated occlusive disease, iliac artery (common, hypogastric, external)	40.37	1429.87	4465	4890	5598
35132	Direct repair of aneurysm, pseudoaneurysm, or excision (partial or total) and graft insertion, with or without patch graft; for ruptured aneurysm, iliac artery (common, hypogastric, external)	48.59	1717.89	4326	4885	5429
	(UNBUNDLING ALERT: 35141 cannot be used with 35371, 35372, or 35381 by the same physician on the same day.)					
35141	Direct repair of aneurysm, pseudoaneurysm, or excision (partial or total) and graft insertion, with or without patch graft; for aneurysm, pseudoaneurysm, and associated occlusive disease, common femoral artery (profunda femoris, superficial femoral)	32.19	1140.34	3588	4096	4376
35142	Direct repair of aneurysm, pseudoaneurysm, or excision (partial or total) and graft insertion, with or without patch graft; for ruptured aneurysm, common femoral artery (profunda femoris, superficial femoral)	38.26	1354.46	4018	4530	5042
35151	Direct repair of aneurysm, pseudoaneurysm, or excision (partial or total) and graft insertion, with or without patch graft; for aneurysm, pseudoaneurysm, and associated occlusive disease, popliteal artery	36.31	1285.86	3822	4166	4719
35152	Direct repair of aneurysm, pseudoaneurysm, or excision (partial or total) and graft insertion, with or without patch graft; for ruptured aneurysm, popliteal artery	41.93	1484.07	3666	4377	5089

Repair Arteriovenous Fistula

35180	Repair, congenital arteriovenous fistula; head and neck	22.65	801.15	2953	3602	4147
35182	Repair, congenital arteriovenous fistula; thorax and abdomen	48.47	1716.38	3710	4624	4939
35184	Repair, congenital arteriovenous fistula; extremities	29.20	1035.36	3310	3927	4250
35188	Repair, acquired or traumatic arteriovenous fistula; head and neck	24.49	870.88	2943	3602	3998
35189	Repair, acquired or traumatic arteriovenous fistula; thorax and abdomen	45.35	1604.96	3881	5102	5546
35190	Repair, acquired or traumatic arteriovenous fistula; extremities	21.31	756.81	3434	3772	4187

Repair Blood Vessel Other Than For Fistula, With or Without Patch Angioplasty

35201	Repair blood vessel, direct; neck	26.78	950.85	3295	4013	4617
35206	Repair blood vessel, direct; upper extremity	21.89	777.28	3056	3587	3954
35207	Repair blood vessel, direct; hand, finger	19.52	698.45	3418	3777	4046
35211	Repair blood vessel, direct; intrathoracic, with bypass	38.18	1353.70	4490	5402	6012
35216	Repair blood vessel, direct; intrathoracic, without bypass	49.32	1730.02	4096	4535	4954
35221	Repair blood vessel, direct; intra-abdominal	39.49	1395.39	3966	4816	5727
35226	Repair blood vessel, direct; lower extremity	24.29	862.55	2987	4190	4521
35231	Repair blood vessel with vein graft; neck	33.22	1178.61	3719	4280	4547

© PFR 2007

● = New Code ⊗ = Conscious Sedation ✚ = Add-on Code ∅ = Modifier '51' Exempt ▲ =Revised Code

		Medicare RVU	National Fee	PFR Fee Information 50%	75%	90%
35236	Repair blood vessel with vein graft; upper extremity	27.91	989.50	3914	4934	5491
35241	Repair blood vessel with vein graft; intrathoracic, with bypass	39.85	1412.82	4685	5310	6256
35246	Repair blood vessel with vein graft; intrathoracic, without bypass	43.58	1544.32	4071	4850	5553
35251	Repair blood vessel with vein graft; intra-abdominal	47.25	1669.38	4522	5582	6422
35256	Repair blood vessel with vein graft; lower extremity	29.53	1046.73	3611	4430	5151
35261	Repair blood vessel with graft other than vein; neck	29.30	1038.39	3430	3964	4393
35266	Repair blood vessel with graft other than vein; upper extremity	24.53	869.75	3453	3946	4706
35271	Repair blood vessel with graft other than vein; intrathoracic, with bypass	37.96	1345.36	4385	5832	6727
35276	Repair blood vessel with graft other than vein; intrathoracic, without bypass	40.01	1418.12	3841	4515	5291
35281	Repair blood vessel with graft other than vein; intra-abdominal	45.12	1595.86	4193	4716	5368
35286	Repair blood vessel with graft other than vein; lower extremity	27.06	960.32	3587	4049	4575

Thromboendarterectomy

(UNBUNDLING ALERT: 35301 cannot be used with 37720 or 37730 by the same physician on the same day.)

		Medicare RVU	National Fee	PFR Fee Information 50%	75%	90%
▲ 35301	Thromboendarterectomy, including patch graft, if performed; carotid, vertebral, subclavian, by neck incision	30.25	1072.12	3708	4238	4705
● 35302	Thromboendarterectomy, including patch graft, if performed; superficial femoral artery	31.39	1108.50	3547	4161	4718
● 35303	Thromboendarterectomy, including patch graft, if performed; popliteal artery	34.50	1217.65	3898	4573	5185
● 35304	Thromboendarterectomy, including patch graft, if performed; tibioperoneal trunk artery	35.90	1266.91	4056	4759	5395
● 35305	Thromboendarterectomy, including patch graft, if performed; tibial or peroneal artery, initial vessel	34.50	1217.65	3898	4573	5185
✚● 35306	Thromboendarterectomy, including patch graft, if performed; each additional tibial or peroneal artery (List separately in addition to code for primary procedure)	12.97	456.29	1465	1719	1949
35311	Thromboendarterectomy, including patch graft, if performed; subclavian, innominate, by thoracic incision	43.16	1526.89	3842	4737	5499
35321	Thromboendarterectomy, including patch graft, if performed; axillary-brachial	25.79	914.47	3510	3944	4467
35331	Thromboendarterectomy, including patch graft, if performed; abdominal aorta	42.11	1490.51	4444	5016	5730
35341	Thromboendarterectomy, including patch graft, if performed; mesenteric, celiac, or renal	40.16	1422.29	4270	4954	6053
35351	Thromboendarterectomy, including patch graft, if performed; iliac	37.06	1310.87	3810	4542	5017
35355	Thromboendarterectomy, including patch graft, if performed; iliofemoral	30.14	1066.81	3875	4826	5236
35361	Thromboendarterectomy, including patch graft, if performed; combined aortoiliac	45.46	1607.99	4405	5473	5842
35363	Thromboendarterectomy, including patch graft, if performed; combined aortoiliofemoral	48.62	1719.79	4618	5470	6068

(UNBUNDLING ALERT: 35371 cannot be used with 35456, 37720 or 37730 by the same physician on the same day.)

		Medicare RVU	National Fee	PFR Fee Information 50%	75%	90%
35371	Thromboendarterectomy, including patch graft, if performed; common femoral	23.95	849.66	3118	3476	4193
35372	Thromboendarterectomy, including patch graft, if performed; deep (profunda) femoral	28.74	1018.68	3290	3909	4307

(UNBUNDLING ALERT: 35381 cannot be used with 35456, 37720 or 37730 by the same physician on the same day.)

		Medicare RVU	National Fee	PFR Fee Information 50%	75%	90%
✚ 35390	Reoperation, carotid, thromboendarterectomy, more than one month after original operation (List separately in addition to code for primary procedure)	4.66	164.48	693	904	1242

Angioscopy

		Medicare RVU	National Fee	PFR Fee Information 50%	75%	90%
✚ 35400	Angioscopy (non-coronary vessels or grafts) during therapeutic intervention (List separately in addition to code for primary procedure)	4.45	157.27	545	612	727

Transluminal Angioplasty

Open

		Medicare RVU	National Fee	PFR Fee Information 50%	75%	90%
35450	Transluminal balloon angioplasty, open; renal or other visceral artery	14.77	521.47	2408	2850	3399
35452	Transluminal balloon angioplasty, open; aortic	10.32	364.95	2147	2761	3476
35454	Transluminal balloon angioplasty, open; iliac	9.09	321.37	2146	2618	3282

● = New Code ⊗ = Conscious Sedation ✚ = Add-on Code ∅ = Modifier '51' Exempt ▲ =Revised Code

		Medicare RVU	National Fee	PFR Fee Information 50%	75%	90%
35456	Transluminal balloon angioplasty, open; femoral-popliteal	11.02	389.59	2203	2633	3082
35458	Transluminal balloon angioplasty, open; brachiocephalic trunk or branches, each vessel	14.07	497.22	2163	2636	2993
35459	Transluminal balloon angioplasty, open; tibioperoneal trunk and branches	12.84	453.63	2091	2396	2750
35460	Transluminal balloon angioplasty, open; venous	9.01	318.34	1276	1541	1677

Percutaneous

(Medicare fees for the code below are based on Non Facility RVUs. PFR information reflects fee when procedure is performed in a facility.)

		Medicare RVU	National Fee	50%	75%	90%
⊗ 35470	Transluminal balloon angioplasty, percutaneous; tibioperoneal trunk or branches, each vessel	91.09	3419.11	1970	2344	2797

(Medicare fees for the code below are based on Non Facility RVUs. PFR information reflects fee when procedure is performed in a facility.)

⊗ 35471	Transluminal balloon angioplasty, percutaneous; renal or visceral artery	102.32	3839.40	2322	2864	3335

(Medicare fees for the code below are based on Non Facility RVUs. PFR information reflects fee when procedure is performed in a facility.)

⊗ 35472	Transluminal balloon angioplasty, percutaneous; aortic	67.53	2533.07	2116	2708	3161

(Medicare fees for the code below are based on Non Facility RVUs. PFR information reflects fee when procedure is performed in a facility.)

⊗ 35473	Transluminal balloon angioplasty, percutaneous; iliac	62.94	2362.15	1791	1984	2437

(Medicare fees for the code below are based on Non Facility RVUs. PFR information reflects fee when procedure is performed in a facility.)

⊗ 35474	Transluminal balloon angioplasty, percutaneous; femoral-popliteal	88.62	3330.43	1947	2349	2466

(Medicare fees for the code below are based on Non Facility RVUs. PFR information reflects fee when procedure is performed in a facility.)

⊗ 35475	Transluminal balloon angioplasty, percutaneous; brachiocephalic trunk or branches, each vessel	64.05	2391.33	2209	2515	2797

(Medicare fees for the code below are based on Non Facility RVUs. PFR information reflects fee when procedure is performed in a facility.)

⊗ 35476	Transluminal balloon angioplasty, percutaneous; venous	48.82	1827.04	1340	1542	1753

Transluminal Atherectomy
Open

		Medicare RVU	National Fee	50%	75%	90%
35480	Transluminal peripheral atherectomy, open; renal or other visceral artery	16.37	578.32	2759	3294	3596
35481	Transluminal peripheral atherectomy, open; aortic	11.51	407.40	2718	3100	3625
35482	Transluminal peripheral atherectomy, open; iliac	9.98	352.83	1871	2320	2799
35483	Transluminal peripheral atherectomy, open; femoral-popliteal	12.20	431.65	2304	2645	3116
35484	Transluminal peripheral atherectomy, open; brachiocephalic trunk or branches, each vessel	15.28	539.28	2374	2786	3116
35485	Transluminal peripheral atherectomy, open; tibioperoneal trunk and branches	14.23	503.28	2110	2597	2899

Percutaneous

35490	Transluminal peripheral atherectomy, percutaneous; renal or other visceral artery	16.88	597.64	2503	2953	3360
35491	Transluminal peripheral atherectomy, percutaneous; aortic	11.80	418.39	2293	2986	4005
35492	Transluminal peripheral atherectomy, percutaneous; iliac	10.37	367.61	1920	2297	2918
35493	Transluminal peripheral atherectomy, percutaneous; femoral-popliteal	12.54	444.54	2048	2453	2846
35494	Transluminal peripheral atherectomy, percutaneous; brachiocephalic trunk or branches, each vessel	15.65	553.30	2169	2763	3010
35495	Transluminal peripheral atherectomy, percutaneous; tibioperoneal trunk and branches	14.62	518.06	2010	2349	2725

Bypass Graft
Vein

✚ 35500	Harvest of upper extremity vein, one segment, for lower extremity or coronary artery bypass procedure (List separately in addition to code for primary procedure)	9.31	328.19	923	1048	1172
▲ 35501	Bypass graft, with vein; common carotid-ipsilateral internal carotid	42.31	1492.78	3630	4122	4473
▲ 35506	Bypass graft, with vein; carotid-subclavian or subclavian-carotid	37.31	1317.70	3773	4409	4796

● = New Code ⊗ = Conscious Sedation ✚ = Add-on Code ∅ = Modifier '51' Exempt ▲ =Revised Code

		Medicare RVU	National Fee	PFR Fee Information 50%	75%	90%
35508	Bypass graft, with vein; carotid-vertebral	38.12	1345.74	3917	4452	4901
▲ 35509	Bypass graft, with vein; carotid-contralateral carotid	41.15	1452.61	3846	4158	4307
35510	Bypass graft, with vein; carotid-brachial	35.98	1271.08	4258	4795	5257
35511	Bypass graft, with vein; subclavian-subclavian	33.86	1198.70	3532	3953	4489
35512	Bypass graft, with vein; subclavian-brachial	35.28	1246.45	4054	4566	5006
35515	Bypass graft, with vein; subclavian-vertebral	37.83	1334.75	3699	4197	4597
35516	Bypass graft, with vein; subclavian-axillary	33.49	1177.10	3606	4114	4703
35518	Bypass graft, with vein; axillary-axillary	34.20	1210.07	3881	4666	5214
35521	Bypass graft, with vein; axillary-femoral	36.53	1293.06	3964	4363	4743
35522	Bypass graft, with vein; axillary-brachial	34.35	1213.86	3976	4478	4910
35525	Bypass graft, with vein; brachial-brachial	32.52	1150.19	3758	4334	4843
35526	Bypass graft, with vein; aortosubclavian or carotid	49.07	1739.50	4060	4773	5632
35531	Bypass graft, with vein; aortoceliac or aortomesenteric	57.99	2049.12	4535	5139	5860
35533	Bypass graft, with vein; axillary-femoral-femoral	44.92	1588.66	4678	5731	6726
35536	Bypass graft, with vein; splenorenal	50.56	1788.00	4538	5398	6102
● 35537	Bypass graft, with vein; aortoiliac	60.69	2140.83	6023	6965	7872
● 35538	Bypass graft, with vein; aortobi-iliac	67.81	2391.33	6729	7782	8795
● 35539	Bypass graft, with vein; aortofemoral	63.73	2247.70	6324	7314	8266
● 35540	Bypass graft, with vein; aortobifemoral	71.06	2505.40	7052	8155	9217
35548	Bypass graft, with vein; aortoiliofemoral, unilateral	34.58	1224.47	3941	4560	4957
35549	Bypass graft, with vein; aortoiliofemoral, bilateral	37.71	1336.27	4933	5826	6727
35551	Bypass graft, with vein; aortofemoral-popliteal	42.55	1506.80	4539	5684	6489
	(UNBUNDLING ALERT: 35556 cannot be used with 37720 or 37730 by the same physician on the same day.)					
35556	Bypass graft, with vein; femoral-popliteal	39.23	1385.15	4055	4572	5337
35558	Bypass graft, with vein; femoral-femoral	35.17	1245.31	3756	4278	4999
35560	Bypass graft, with vein; aortorenal	51.32	1815.67	4171	5043	5519
35563	Bypass graft, with vein; ilioiliac	39.54	1399.55	3664	4718	5456
35565	Bypass graft, with vein; iliofemoral	38.01	1344.98	3870	4610	5228
35566	Bypass graft, with vein; femoral-anterior tibial, posterior tibial, peroneal artery or other distal vessels	47.12	1662.94	4556	5132	5842
35571	Bypass graft, with vein; popliteal-tibial, -peroneal artery or other distal vessels	39.05	1383.26	4348	5055	5552
✚ 35572	Harvest of femoropopliteal vein, one segment, for vascular reconstruction procedure (eg, aortic, vena caval, coronary, peripheral artery) (List separately in addition to code for primary procedure)	9.95	350.93	1226	1518	1769

In-Situ Vein

		Medicare RVU	National Fee	PFR Fee Information 50%	75%	90%
	(UNBUNDLING ALERT: 35583 cannot be used with 37720 or 37730 by the same physician on the same day.)					
35583	In-situ vein bypass; femoral-popliteal	40.64	1434.80	4417	4739	5294
	(UNBUNDLING ALERT: 35585 cannot be used with 37720 or 37730 by the same physician on the same day.)					
35585	In-situ vein bypass; femoral-anterior tibial, posterior tibial, or peroneal artery	47.98	1695.53	4898	5630	6555
35587	In-situ vein bypass; popliteal-tibial, peroneal	40.35	1429.87	4573	5042	5719

Other Than Vein

		Medicare RVU	National Fee	PFR Fee Information 50%	75%	90%
⊘ 35600	Harvest of upper extremity artery, one segment, for coronary artery bypass procedure	7.27	256.57	896	1105	1325
▲ 35601	Bypass graft, with other than vein; common carotid-ipsilateral internal carotid	39.80	1405.24	3739	3884	4548

● = New Code ⊗ = Conscious Sedation ✚ = Add-on Code ⊘ = Modifier '51' Exempt ▲ = Revised Code

Code	Description	Medicare RVU	National Fee	PFR Fee Information 50%	75%	90%
35606	Bypass graft, with other than vein; carotid-subclavian	33.73	1193.01	3760	4246	4808
35612	Bypass graft, with other than vein; subclavian-subclavian	26.30	933.04	3515	4008	4533
35616	Bypass graft, with other than vein; subclavian-axillary	31.79	1121.77	3329	3899	4519
35621	Bypass graft, with other than vein; axillary-femoral	32.12	1137.30	3737	4375	4759
35623	Bypass graft, with other than vein; axillary-popliteal or -tibial	39.27	1390.08	3895	4714	5473
35626	Bypass graft, with other than vein; aortosubclavian or carotid	44.67	1582.22	4006	5041	5727
35631	Bypass graft, with other than vein; aortoceliac, aortomesenteric, aortorenal	53.98	1908.90	4266	4941	5556
35636	Bypass graft, with other than vein; splenorenal (splenic to renal arterial anastomosis)	47.41	1676.21	4036	4493	4869
● 35637	Bypass graft, with other than vein; aortoiliac	48.28	1704.25	4619	5456	6144
● 35638	Bypass graft, with other than vein; aortobi-iliac	49.05	1731.16	4693	5543	6242
35642	Bypass graft, with other than vein; carotid-vertebral	29.56	1048.24	3508	4132	4525
35645	Bypass graft, with other than vein; subclavian-vertebral	28.87	1023.99	3445	3991	4217
35646	Bypass graft, with other than vein; aortobifemoral	49.79	1761.85	4977	5547	6165
35647	Bypass graft, with other than vein; aortofemoral	44.88	1587.91	4626	5288	5848
35650	Bypass graft, with other than vein; axillary-axillary	30.76	1089.17	3500	4206	4670
35651	Bypass graft, with other than vein; aortofemoral-popliteal	39.57	1400.69	4084	4946	5979
35654	Bypass graft, with other than vein; axillary-femoral-femoral	39.82	1409.41	4722	5453	5778
35656	Bypass graft, with other than vein; femoral-popliteal	31.40	1112.29	3897	4394	5090
35661	Bypass graft, with other than vein; femoral-femoral	31.45	1114.94	3741	4216	4937
35663	Bypass graft, with other than vein; ilioiliac	36.41	1289.27	3529	4252	4764
35665	Bypass graft, with other than vein; iliofemoral	34.21	1211.58	3942	4246	4750
35666	Bypass graft, with other than vein; femoral-anterior tibial, posterior tibial, or peroneal artery	36.85	1306.71	3809	4426	4972
35671	Bypass graft, with other than vein; popliteal-tibial or -peroneal artery	32.43	1150.19	3745	4541	4940

Composite Grafts

Code	Description	Medicare RVU	National Fee	PFR Fee Information 50%	75%	90%
✚ 35681	Bypass graft; composite, prosthetic and vein (List separately in addition to code for primary procedure)	2.33	82.24	1122	1582	1990
✚ 35682	Bypass graft; autogenous composite, two segments of veins from two locations (List separately in addition to code for primary procedure)	10.45	368.74	1175	1312	1520
✚ 35683	Bypass graft; autogenous composite, three or more segments of vein from two or more locations (List separately in addition to code for primary procedure)	12.33	435.06	1470	1679	1922

Adjuvant Techniques

Code	Description	Medicare RVU	National Fee	PFR Fee Information 50%	75%	90%
✚ 35685	Placement of vein patch or cuff at distal anastomosis of bypass graft, synthetic conduit (List separately in addition to code for primary procedure)	5.88	207.30	549	737	912
✚ 35686	Creation of distal arteriovenous fistula during lower extremity bypass surgery (non-hemodialysis) (List separately in addition to code for primary procedure)	4.87	171.68	513	629	733

Arterial Transposition

Code	Description	Medicare RVU	National Fee	PFR Fee Information 50%	75%	90%
35691	Transposition and/or reimplantation; vertebral to carotid artery	28.78	1020.96	3769	4187	4523
35693	Transposition and/or reimplantation; vertebral to subclavian artery	25.16	894.00	3220	3945	4659
35694	Transposition and/or reimplantation; subclavian to carotid artery	29.98	1063.02	3455	4082	4590
35695	Transposition and/or reimplantation; carotid to subclavian artery	30.77	1089.93	3451	4068	4569
✚ 35697	Reimplantation, visceral artery to infrarenal aortic prosthesis, each artery (List separately in addition to code for primary procedure)	4.37	154.24	646	738	828

Exploration/Revision

Code	Description	Medicare RVU	National Fee	PFR Fee Information 50%	75%	90%
✚ 35700	Reoperation, femoral-popliteal or femoral (popliteal)-anterior tibial, posterior tibial, peroneal artery, or other distal vessels, more than one month after original operation (List separately in addition to code for primary procedure)	4.49	158.41	823	910	989
35701	Exploration (not followed by surgical repair), with or without lysis of artery; carotid artery	15.16	539.66	1681	2061	2401

		Medicare RVU	National Fee	PFR Fee Information 50%	75%	90%
35721	Exploration (not followed by surgical repair), with or without lysis of artery; femoral artery	12.95	461.59	1418	1681	2030
35741	Exploration (not followed by surgical repair), with or without lysis of artery; popliteal artery	14.22	505.93	1545	1842	1984
35761	Exploration (not followed by surgical repair), with or without lysis of artery; other vessels	10.47	374.43	1500	1826	2167
35800	Exploration for postoperative hemorrhage, thrombosis or infection; neck	13.42	478.27	1554	1827	2170
35820	Exploration for postoperative hemorrhage, thrombosis or infection; chest	47.46	1658.39	2158	2765	3112
35840	Exploration for postoperative hemorrhage, thrombosis or infection; abdomen	17.39	617.73	2140	2582	2801
35860	Exploration for postoperative hemorrhage, thrombosis or infection; extremity	11.39	405.88	1630	1851	2244
35870	Repair of graft-enteric fistula	36.77	1300.64	4951	5588	6281
35875	Thrombectomy of arterial or venous graft (other than hemodialysis graft or fistula);	17.03	604.84	2200	2572	2906
35876	Thrombectomy of arterial or venous graft (other than hemodialysis graft or fistula); with revision of arterial or venous graft	27.30	967.14	2588	3138	3534
35879	Revision, lower extremity arterial bypass, without thrombectomy, open; with vein patch angioplasty	26.86	951.99	3001	3538	4033
35881	Revision, lower extremity arterial bypass, without thrombectomy, open; with segmental vein interposition	29.95	1061.89	3234	4056	4627
● 35883	Revision, femoral anastomosis of synthetic arterial bypass graft in groin, open; with nonautogenous patch graft (eg, Dacron, ePTFE, bovine pericardium)	35.22	1246.83	3869	4704	5365
● 35884	Revision, femoral anastomosis of synthetic arterial bypass graft in groin, open; with autogenous vein patch graft	37.41	1324.14	4110	4997	5698
35901	Excision of infected graft; neck	14.46	516.54	1857	2252	2848
35903	Excision of infected graft; extremity	16.53	590.44	2195	2552	2999
35905	Excision of infected graft; thorax	50.40	1782.70	2591	3201	3963
35907	Excision of infected graft; abdomen	55.50	1961.57	3470	3977	4371

Vascular Injection Procedures

Intravenous

		Medicare RVU	National Fee	50%	75%	90%
36000	Introduction of needle or intracatheter, vein	0.73	26.91	114	147	181
36002	Injection procedures (eg, thrombin) for percutaneous treatment of extremity pseudoaneurysm	4.81	174.71	427	508	614
	(Medicare fees for the code below are based on Non Facility RVUs. PFR information reflects fee when procedure is performed in a facility.)					
36005	Injection procedure for extremity venography (including introduction of needle or intracatheter)	8.80	329.71	196	222	293
	(Medicare fees for the code below are based on Non Facility RVUs. PFR information reflects fee when procedure is performed in a facility.)					
36010	Introduction of catheter, superior or inferior vena cava	19.80	741.28	558	707	816
	(Medicare fees for the code below are based on Non Facility RVUs. PFR information reflects fee when procedure is performed in a facility.)					
	(To code for the supply of the implantable vascular access port, see HCPCS code A4300.)					
36011	Selective catheter placement, venous system; first order branch (eg, renal vein, jugular vein)	29.03	1088.04	522	644	778
	(Medicare fees for the code below are based on Non Facility RVUs. PFR information reflects fee when procedure is performed in a facility.)					
36012	Selective catheter placement, venous system; second order, or more selective, branch (eg, left adrenal vein, petrosal sinus)	22.83	851.94	681	803	924
	(Medicare fees for the code below are based on Non Facility RVUs. PFR information reflects fee when procedure is performed in a facility.)					
36013	Introduction of catheter, right heart or main pulmonary artery	23.55	883.01	588	795	975
	(Medicare fees for the code below are based on Non Facility RVUs. PFR information reflects fee when procedure is performed in a facility.)					
36014	Selective catheter placement, left or right pulmonary artery	22.83	853.83	593	660	850
	(Medicare fees for the code below are based on Non Facility RVUs. PFR information reflects fee when procedure is performed in a facility.)					
36015	Selective catheter placement, segmental or subsegmental pulmonary artery	25.86	966.77	666	813	941

		Medicare RVU	National Fee	PFR Fee Information 50%	75%	90%

Intra-Arterial—-Intra-Aortic

36100	Introduction of needle or intracatheter, carotid or vertebral artery	15.12	561.64	575	689	853
36120	Introduction of needle or intracatheter; retrograde brachial artery	12.44	463.87	544	711	811

(Medicare fees for the code below are based on Non Facility RVUs. PFR information reflects fee when procedure is performed in a facility.)

36140	Introduction of needle or intracatheter; extremity artery	14.32	535.11	444	510	707
36145	Introduction of needle or intracatheter; arteriovenous shunt created for dialysis (cannula, fistula, or graft)	13.99	522.61	553	705	909
36160	Introduction of needle or intracatheter, aortic, translumbar	15.77	588.17	603	687	920

(Medicare fees for the code below are based on Non Facility RVUs. PFR information reflects fee when procedure is performed in a facility.)

36200	Introduction of catheter, aorta	18.96	707.17	592	706	818

(Medicare fees for the code below are based on Non Facility RVUs. PFR information reflects fee when procedure is performed in a facility.)

36215	Selective catheter placement, arterial system; each first order thoracic or brachiocephalic branch, within a vascular family	31.53	1177.10	703	816	1037

(Medicare fees for the code below are based on Non Facility RVUs. PFR information reflects fee when procedure is performed in a facility.)

36216	Selective catheter placement, arterial system; initial second order thoracic or brachiocephalic branch, within a vascular family	34.15	1274.11	782	964	1091

(Medicare fees for the code below are based on Non Facility RVUs. PFR information reflects fee when procedure is performed in a facility.)

36217	Selective catheter placement, arterial system; initial third order or more selective thoracic or brachiocephalic branch, within a vascular family	59.38	2226.48	1005	1324	1604
✚ 36218	Selective catheter placement, arterial system; additional second order, third order, and beyond, thoracic or brachiocephalic branch, within a vascular family (List in addition to code for initial second or third order vessel as appropriate)	5.80	216.02	240	279	343

(Medicare fees for the code below are based on Non Facility RVUs. PFR information reflects fee when procedure is performed in a facility.)

36245	Selective catheter placement, arterial system; each first order abdominal, pelvic, or lower extremity artery branch, within a vascular family	36.15	1352.18	740	824	967

(Medicare fees for the code below are based on Non Facility RVUs. PFR information reflects fee when procedure is performed in a facility.)

36246	Selective catheter placement, arterial system; initial second order abdominal, pelvic, or lower extremity artery branch, within a vascular family	34.83	1299.88	796	930	1065

(Medicare fees for the code below are based on Non Facility RVUs. PFR information reflects fee when procedure is performed in a facility.)

36247	Selective catheter placement, arterial system; initial third order or more selective abdominal, pelvic, or lower extremity artery branch, within a vascular family	54.98	2059.73	1040	1157	1396
✚ 36248	Selective catheter placement, arterial system; additional second order, third order, and beyond, abdominal, pelvic, or lower extremity artery branch, within a vascular family (List in addition to code for initial second or third order vessel as appropriate)	4.89	181.53	215	275	358
36260	Insertion of implantable intra-arterial infusion pump (eg, for chemotherapy of liver)	15.98	568.08	2011	2218	2463
36261	Revision of implanted intra-arterial infusion pump	9.79	349.79	873	1108	1555
36262	Removal of implanted intra-arterial infusion pump	7.32	261.87	683	901	1056
36299	Unlisted procedure, vascular injection	-	-	IR	IR	IR

Venous

36400	Venipuncture, younger than age 3 years, necessitating physician's skill, not to be used for routine venipuncture; femoral or jugular vein	0.70	25.01	59	73	94
36405	Venipuncture, younger than age 3 years, necessitating physician's skill, not to be used for routine venipuncture; scalp vein	0.61	21.98	85	92	111
36406	Venipuncture, younger than age 3 years, necessitating physician's skill, not to be used for routine venipuncture; other vein	0.48	17.43	69	90	99
36410	Venipuncture, age 3 years or older, necessitating physician's skill (separate procedure), for diagnostic or therapeutic purposes (not to be used for routine venipuncture)	0.49	17.81	56	83	110

(Commercial insurance carriers may accept 36415 for routine venipuncture. Medicare requires the use of HCPCS code G0001.)

36415	Collection of venous blood by venipuncture	-	-	16	21	27
36416	Collection of capillary blood specimen (eg, finger, heel, ear stick)	-	-	15	19	22
36420	Venipuncture, cutdown; younger than age 1 year	1.34	46.99	178	215	299

● = New Code ⊗ = Conscious Sedation ✚ = Add-on Code ∅ = Modifier '51' Exempt ▲ =Revised Code

Code	Description	Medicare RVU	National Fee	50%	75%	90%
36425	Venipuncture, cutdown; age 1 or over	1.04	36.38	160	226	328
36430	Transfusion, blood or blood components	1.05	39.79	116	146	167
36440	Push transfusion, blood, 2 years or younger	1.46	51.54	204	244	272
36450	Exchange transfusion, blood; newborn	3.17	111.80	832	870	926
36455	Exchange transfusion, blood; other than newborn	3.53	124.68	676	906	1041
36460	Transfusion, intrauterine, fetal	9.47	333.88	1176	1509	2003
36468	Single or multiple injections of sclerosing solutions, spider veins (telangiectasia); limb or trunk	-	-	215	341	408
36469	Single or multiple injections of sclerosing solutions, spider veins (telangiectasia); face	-	-	173	207	237
36470	Injection of sclerosing solution; single vein	3.83	140.98	182	252	309
36471	Injection of sclerosing solution; multiple veins, same leg	4.73	173.19	277	323	380
36475	Endovenous ablation therapy of incompetent vein, extremity, inclusive of all imaging guidance and monitoring, percutaneous, radiofrequency; first vein treated	54.66	2045.71	4738	6036	7410
✚ 36476	Endovenous ablation therapy of incompetent vein, extremity, inclusive of all imaging guidance and monitoring, percutaneous, radiofrequency; second and subsequent veins treated in a single extremity, each through separate access sites (List separately in addition to code for primary procedure)	10.95	402.09	955	1216	1492
36478	Endovenous ablation therapy of incompetent vein, extremity, inclusive of all imaging guidance and monitoring, percutaneous, laser; first vein treated	49.94	1866.83	4407	5614	6893
✚ 36479	Endovenous ablation therapy of incompetent vein, extremity, inclusive of all imaging guidance and monitoring, percutaneous, laser; second and subsequent veins treated in a single extremity, each through separate access sites (List separately in addition to code for primary procedure)	11.15	409.67	946	1204	1478
36481	Percutaneous portal vein catheterization by any method	9.99	352.07	1204	1527	1715

(Code 36488-36491 can be used to code the insertion of a venous access device. Some common names for these devices are: Hickman, Broviac, Raaf, Corcath and Groshong.)

Code	Description	Medicare RVU	National Fee	50%	75%	90%
36500	Venous catheterization for selective organ blood sampling	5.03	177.36	458	514	602
36510	Catheterization of umbilical vein for diagnosis or therapy, newborn	4.38	161.82	248	301	339
36511	Therapeutic apheresis; for white blood cells	2.51	88.30	333	401	481
36512	Therapeutic apheresis; for red blood cells	2.53	89.06	339	410	490
36513	Therapeutic apheresis; for platelets	2.59	91.33	335	407	486

(Medicare fees for the code below are based on Non Facility RVUs. PFR information reflects fee when procedure is performed in a facility.)

Code	Description	Medicare RVU	National Fee	50%	75%	90%
36514	Therapeutic apheresis; for plasma pheresis	17.15	643.12	339	410	490

(Medicare fees for the code below are based on Non Facility RVUs. PFR information reflects fee when procedure is performed in a facility.)

Code	Description	Medicare RVU	National Fee	50%	75%	90%
36515	Therapeutic apheresis; with extracorporeal immunoadsorption and plasma reinfusion	62.74	2370.87	339	410	490

(Medicare fees for the code below are based on Non Facility RVUs. PFR information reflects fee when procedure is performed in a facility.)

Code	Description	Medicare RVU	National Fee	50%	75%	90%
36516	Therapeutic apheresis; with extracorporeal selective adsorption or selective filtration and plasma reinfusion	76.67	2901.05	339	410	490

(Medicare fees for the code below are based on Non Facility RVUs. PFR information reflects fee when procedure is performed in a facility.)

Code	Description	Medicare RVU	National Fee	50%	75%	90%
36522	Photopheresis, extracorporeal	34.82	1313.15	522	620	777
36540	Collection of blood specimen from a completely implantable venous access device	-	-	42	55	73
36550	Declotting by thrombolytic agent of implanted vascular access device or catheter	0.74	28.04	121	143	180

Central Venous Access Procedures
Insertion of Central Venous Access Device

Code	Description	Medicare RVU	National Fee	50%	75%	90%
⊗ 36555	Insertion of non-tunneled centrally inserted central venous catheter; younger than 5 years of age	8.13	297.87	771	938	1224

		Medicare RVU	National Fee	PFR Fee Information 50%	75%	90%
36556	Insertion of non-tunneled centrally inserted central venous catheter; age 5 years or older	7.62	279.30	744	906	1181
	(Medicare fees for the code below are based on Non Facility RVUs. PFR information reflects fee when procedure is performed in a facility.)					
⊗ 36557	Insertion of tunneled centrally inserted central venous catheter, without subcutaneous port or pump; younger than 5 years of age	25.11	932.28	954	1091	1211
	(Medicare fees for the code below are based on Non Facility RVUs. PFR information reflects fee when procedure is performed in a facility.)					
⊗ 36558	Insertion of tunneled centrally inserted central venous catheter, without subcutaneous port or pump; age 5 years or older	24.75	919.77	933	1068	1184
⊗ 36560	Insertion of tunneled centrally inserted central venous access device, with subcutaneous port; younger than 5 years of age	34.27	1274.87	1785	2043	2264
⊗ 36561	Insertion of tunneled centrally inserted central venous access device, with subcutaneous port; age 5 years or older	34.21	1273.73	1769	2026	2244
⊗ 36563	Insertion of tunneled centrally inserted central venous access device with subcutaneous pump	32.81	1219.92	3619	4169	4630
⊗ 36565	Insertion of tunneled centrally inserted central venous access device, requiring two catheters via two separate venous access sites; without subcutaneous port or pump (eg, Tesio type catheter)	29.47	1094.10	1466	1678	1860
⊗ 36566	Insertion of tunneled centrally inserted central venous access device, requiring two catheters via two separate venous access sites; with subcutaneous port(s)	54.25	2031.31	1532	1754	1944
⊗ 36568	Insertion of peripherally inserted central venous catheter (PICC), without subcutaneous port or pump; younger than 5 years of age	9.06	336.15	1002	1219	1590
36569	Insertion of peripherally inserted central venous catheter (PICC), without subcutaneous port or pump; age 5 years or older	8.56	317.58	910	1106	1444
⊗ 36570	Insertion of peripherally inserted central venous access device, with subcutaneous port; younger than 5 years of age	36.37	1357.87	1929	2208	2448
⊗ 36571	Insertion of peripherally inserted central venous access device, with subcutaneous port; age 5 years or older	36.88	1377.57	1916	2194	2431

Repair of Central Venous Access Device

36575	Repair of tunneled or non-tunneled central venous access catheter, without subcutaneous port or pump, central or peripheral insertion site	4.71	175.84	438	559	641
⊗ 36576	Repair of central venous access device, with subcutaneous port or pump, central or peripheral insertion site	10.03	367.98	1091	1360	1598

Partial Replacement of Central venous Access Device (Catheter Only)

⊗ 36578	Replacement, catheter only, of central venous access device, with subcutaneous port or pump, central or peripheral insertion site	14.22	525.64	1389	1729	2034

Complete Replacement of Central Venous Access Device Through Same Venous Access Site

36580	Replacement, complete, of a non-tunneled centrally inserted central venous catheter, without subcutaneous port or pump, through same venous access	7.66	285.37	799	972	1268
⊗ 36581	Replacement, complete, of a tunneled centrally inserted central venous catheter, without subcutaneous port or pump, through same venous access	21.97	819.34	1643	2045	2405
⊗ 36582	Replacement, complete, of a tunneled centrally inserted central venous access device, with subcutaneous port, through same venous access	29.91	1113.81	3079	3832	4508
⊗ 36583	Replacement, complete, of a tunneled centrally inserted central venous access device, with subcutaneous pump, through same venous access	29.98	1116.08	2115	2633	3098
36584	Replacement, complete, of a peripherally inserted central venous catheter (PICC), without subcutaneous port or pump, through same venous access	7.55	281.58	815	1017	1195
⊗ 36585	Replacement, complete, of a peripherally inserted central venous access device, with subcutaneous port, through same venous access	31.29	1167.62	3103	3864	4545

Removal of Central Venous Access Device

36589	Removal of tunneled central venous catheter, without subcutaneous port or pump	4.64	167.13	421	528	619
⊗ 36590	Removal of tunneled central venous access device, with subcutaneous port or pump, central or peripheral insertion	7.18	259.60	978	1167	1538

Mechanical Removal of Obstructive Material

36595	Mechanical removal of pericatheter obstructive material (eg, fibrin sheath) from central venous device via separate venous access	19.30	717.78	1750	2114	2532
36596	Mechanical removal of intraluminal (intracatheter) obstructive material from central venous device through device lumen	4.18	155.38	382	461	552

Other Central Venous Access Procedures

36597	Repositioning of previously placed central venous catheter under fluoroscopic guidance	3.56	130.37	322	405	464

● = New Code ⊗ = Conscious Sedation ✚ = Add-on Code ∅ = Modifier '51' Exempt ▲ =Revised Code

		Medicare RVU	National Fee	PFR Fee Information 50%	75%	90%
36598	Contrast injection(s) for radiologic evaluation of existing central venous access device, including fluoroscopy, image documentation and report	3.31	122.79	356	448	513

Arterial

(Arterial puncture can be coded in addition to the laboratory tests on arterial blood, if performed by the physician. 36600 cannot be used with codes 36620, 36625, 35540, 36660, or 75894.)

36600	Arterial puncture, withdrawal of blood for diagnosis	0.83	30.32	74	100	141

(Percutaneous arterial cannulation is the normal method of establishing an arterial line. Other methods are covered by Medicare only when percutaneous attempts are unsuccessful or the patient's condition will not allow the percutaneous method.)

∅ 36620	Arterial catheterization or cannulation for sampling, monitoring or transfusion (separate procedure); percutaneous	1.44	50.02	227	278	336

(Arterial cannulation by cutdown is considered appropriate in the critically ill, severe trauma cases or in small children.)

36625	Arterial catheterization or cannulation for sampling, monitoring or transfusion (separate procedure); cutdown	2.89	101.57	351	386	461
36640	Arterial catheterization for prolonged infusion therapy (chemotherapy), cutdown	3.32	117.86	429	556	695
∅ 36660	Catheterization, umbilical artery, newborn, for diagnosis or therapy	1.92	67.46	301	350	428

Intraosseous

36680	Placement of needle for intraosseous infusion	1.76	62.15	233	290	343

Hemodialysis Access, Intervascular Cannulation for Extracorporeal Circulation, or Shunt Insertion

36800	Insertion of cannula for hemodialysis, other purpose (separate procedure); vein to vein	4.42	158.41	586	766	960
36810	Insertion of cannula for hemodialysis, other purpose (separate procedure); arteriovenous, external (Scribner type)	6.01	212.60	1124	1259	1501
36815	Insertion of cannula for hemodialysis, other purpose (separate procedure); arteriovenous, external revision, or closure	4.11	145.91	816	947	1127
36818	Arteriovenous anastomosis, open; by upper arm cephalic vein transposition	19.44	691.63	2367	2791	3473
36819	Arteriovenous anastomosis, open; by upper arm basilic vein transposition	22.43	795.09	2152	2530	3450
36820	Arteriovenous anastomosis, open; by forearm vein transposition	22.45	795.85	2758	3242	4421
36821	Arteriovenous anastomosis, open; direct, any site (eg, Cimino type) (separate procedure)	14.87	528.67	2008	2346	2780
36822	Insertion of cannula(s) for prolonged extracorporeal circulation for cardiopulmonary insufficiency (ECMO) (separate procedure)	10.53	378.22	1660	1967	2433
36823	Insertion of arterial and venous cannula(s) for isolated extracorporeal circulation including regional chemotherapy perfusion to an extremity, with or without hyperthermia, with removal of cannula(s) and repair of arteriotomy and venotomy sites	34.94	1236.97	2508	3146	3745
36825	Creation of arteriovenous fistula by other than direct arteriovenous anastomosis (separate procedure); autogenous graft	16.22	576.42	2650	3080	3573
36830	Creation of arteriovenous fistula by other than direct arteriovenous anastomosis (separate procedure); nonautogenous graft (eg, biological collagen, thermoplastic graft)	18.64	660.55	2752	3052	3329
36831	Thrombectomy, open, arteriovenous fistula without revision, autogenous or nonautogenous dialysis graft (separate procedure)	12.87	457.04	1463	1747	1872
36832	Revision, open, arteriovenous fistula; without thrombectomy, autogenous or nonautogenous dialysis graft (separate procedure)	16.44	582.86	2199	2441	3052
36833	Revision, open, arteriovenous fistula; with thrombectomy, autogenous or nonautogenous dialysis graft (separate procedure)	18.56	657.90	1902	2575	3034
36834	Plastic repair of arteriovenous aneurysm (separate procedure)	17.16	607.88	2052	2460	2861
36835	Insertion of Thomas shunt (separate procedure)	12.62	449.84	1836	2418	2854
36838	Distal revascularization and interval ligation (DRIL), upper extremity hemodialysis access (steal syndrome)	33.42	1184.30	3924	4677	5486
36860	External cannula declotting (separate procedure); without balloon catheter	4.28	154.62	403	501	647
36861	External cannula declotting (separate procedure); with balloon catheter	4.21	150.07	702	936	1198
⊗ 36870	Thrombectomy, percutaneous, arteriovenous fistula, autogenous or nonautogenous graft (includes mechanical thrombus extraction and intra-graft thrombolysis)	55.00	2064.66	3472	3974	4478

● = New Code ⊗ = Conscious Sedation ✚ = Add-on Code ∅ = Modifier '51' Exempt ▲ =Revised Code

		Medicare RVU	National Fee	PFR Fee Information 50%	75%	90%

Portal Decompression Procedures

		Medicare RVU	National Fee	50%	75%	90%
37140	Venous anastomosis, open; portocaval	37.21	1314.29	4400	5487	6680
37145	Venous anastomosis, open; renoportal	39.80	1408.65	4348	5508	6424
37160	Venous anastomosis, open; caval-mesenteric	34.92	1235.08	4327	5436	6493
37180	Venous anastomosis, open; splenorenal, proximal	39.44	1395.01	4458	5479	6414
37181	Venous anastomosis, open; splenorenal, distal (selective decompression of esophagogastric varices, any technique)	42.25	1493.54	5065	6048	6878
37182	Insertion of transvenous intrahepatic portosystemic shunt(s) (TIPS) (includes venous access, hepatic and portal vein catheterization, portography with hemodynamic evaluation, intrahepatic tract formation/dilatation, stent placement and all associated imaging guidance and documentation)	23.79	836.78	3153	3849	4608
37183	Revision of transvenous intrahepatic portosystemic shunt(s) (TIPS) (includes venous access, hepatic and portal vein catheterization, portography with hemodynamic evaluation, intrahepatic tract recanulization/dilatation, stent placement and all associated imaging guidance and documentation)	11.35	399.82	1479	1806	2162

Venous Mechanical Thrombectomy

Transcatheter Procedures

		Medicare RVU	National Fee	50%	75%	90%
⊗ 37184	Primary percutaneous transluminal mechanical thrombectomy, noncoronary, arterial or arterial bypass graft, including fluoroscopic guidance and intraprocedural pharmacological thrombolytic injection(s); initial vessel	74.83	2802.90	10797	13386	15836
⊗ ✚ 37185	Primary percutaneous transluminal mechanical thrombectomy, noncoronary, arterial or arterial bypass graft, including fluoroscopic guidance and intraprocedural pharmacological thrombolytic injection(s); second and all subsequent vessel(s) within the same vascular family (List separately in addition to code for primary mechanical thrombectomy procedure)	24.50	915.98	3555	4406	5213
⊗ ✚ 37186	Secondary percutaneous transluminal thrombectomy (eg, nonprimary mechanical, snare basket, suction technique), noncoronary, arterial or arterial bypass graft, including fluoroscopic guidance and intraprocedural pharmacological thrombolytic injections, provided in conjunction with another percutaneous intervention other than primary mechanical thrombectomy (List separately in addition to code for primary procedure)	50.42	1892.22	7363	9128	10799

Venous Mechanical Thrombectomy

		Medicare RVU	National Fee	50%	75%	90%
⊗ 37187	Percutaneous transluminal mechanical thrombectomy, vein(s), including intraprocedural pharmacological thrombolytic injections and fluoroscopic guidance	72.75	2726.35	10506	13024	15408
⊗ 37188	Percutaneous transluminal mechanical thrombectomy, vein(s), including intraprocedural pharmacological thrombolytic injections and fluoroscopic guidance, repeat treatment on subsequent day during course of thrombolytic therapy	62.67	2353.43	9173	11371	13453

Other Procedures

		Medicare RVU	National Fee	50%	75%	90%
37195	Thrombolysis, cerebral, by intravenous infusion	-	-	797	872	958
37200	Transcatheter biopsy	6.28	220.56	743	1129	1619
37201	Transcatheter therapy, infusion for thrombolysis other than coronary	7.75	274.76	1254	1479	1673
37202	Transcatheter therapy, infusion other than for thrombolysis, any type (eg, spasmolytic, vasoconstrictive)	9.23	328.19	983	1110	1300
	(Medicare fees for the code below are based on Non Facility RVUs. PFR information reflects fee when procedure is performed in a facility.)					
⊗ 37203	Transcatheter retrieval, percutaneous, of intravascular foreign body (eg, fractured venous or arterial catheter)	37.18	1389.70	946	1121	1531
37204	Transcatheter occlusion or embolization (eg, for tumor destruction, to achieve hemostasis, to occlude a vascular malformation), percutaneous, any method, non-central nervous system, non-head or neck	25.34	891.35	3067	3737	4122
37205	Transcatheter placement of an intravascular stent(s), (except coronary, carotid, and vertebral vessel), percutaneous; initial vessel	12.64	447.57	1830	2141	2586
✚ 37206	Transcatheter placement of an intravascular stent(s), (except coronary, carotid, and vertebral vessel), percutaneous; each additional vessel (List separately in addition to code for primary procedure)	5.89	207.68	844	946	1063
37207	Transcatheter placement of an intravascular stent(s), (non-coronary vessel), open; initial vessel	12.42	439.23	1715	2293	2687
✚ 37208	Transcatheter placement of an intravascular stent(s), (non-coronary vessel), open; each additional vessel (List separately in addition to code for primary procedure)	6.01	212.23	887	1139	1266
37209	Exchange of a previously placed intravascular catheter during thrombolytic therapy	3.14	110.28	334	393	450

● = New Code ⊗ = Conscious Sedation ✚ = Add-on Code ∅ = Modifier '51' Exempt ▲ =Revised Code

		Medicare RVU	National Fee	PFR Fee Information 50%	75%	90%
⊗ ● **37210**	Uterine fibroid embolization (UFE, embolization of the uterine arteries to treat uterine fibroids, leiomyomata), percutaneous approach inclusive of vascular access, vessel selection, embolization, and all radiological supervision and interpretation, intraprocedural roadmapping, and imaging guidance necessary to complete the procedure	57.23	2128.32	7426	9120	10384
⊗ **37215**	Transcatheter placement of intravascular stent(s), cervical carotid artery, percutaneous; with distal embolic protection	30.01	1062.65	3910	4761	5484
⊗ **37216**	Transcatheter placement of intravascular stent(s), cervical carotid artery, percutaneous; without distal embolic protection	27.94	986.85	3766	4586	5282

Intravascular Ultrasound Services

		Medicare RVU	National Fee	50%	75%	90%
✚ **37250**	Intravascular ultrasound (non-coronary vessel) during diagnostic evaluation and/or therapeutic intervention; initial vessel (List separately in addition to code for primary procedure)	3.08	108.77	300	358	383
✚ **37251**	Intravascular ultrasound (non-coronary vessel) during diagnostic evaluation and/or therapeutic intervention; each additional vessel (List separately in addition to code for primary procedure)	2.33	82.24	214	266	296

Endoscopy

		Medicare RVU	National Fee	50%	75%	90%
37500	Vascular endoscopy, surgical, with ligation of perforator veins, subfascial (SEPS)	19.57	697.69	2106	2579	3174
37501	Unlisted vascular endoscopy procedure	-	-	IR	IR	IR

Ligation

		Medicare RVU	National Fee	50%	75%	90%
37565	Ligation, internal jugular vein	18.79	666.62	1405	1942	2171
37600	Ligation; external carotid artery	19.93	708.30	1542	1850	2104
37605	Ligation; internal or common carotid artery	22.76	808.35	1558	1797	2038
37606	Ligation; internal or common carotid artery, with gradual occlusion, as with Selverstone or Crutchfield clamp	14.59	519.57	1529	1891	2187
37607	Ligation or banding of angioaccess arteriovenous fistula	10.48	373.67	1191	1263	1471
	(A4550 (Disposable Surgical Tray) can be coded in addition to 37609 in the office setting. Payment is at carrier discretion.)					
37609	Ligation or biopsy, temporal artery	7.81	284.61	620	759	861
37615	Ligation, major artery (eg, post-traumatic, rupture); neck	12.49	443.78	1365	1752	1878
37616	Ligation, major artery (eg, post-traumatic, rupture); chest	29.26	1036.88	2610	2896	3233
37617	Ligation, major artery (eg, post-traumatic, rupture); abdomen	35.54	1256.30	2549	2767	3131
37618	Ligation, major artery (eg, post-traumatic, rupture); extremity	10.17	362.68	1428	1608	1751
37620	Interruption, partial or complete, of inferior vena cava by suture, ligation, plication, clip, extravascular, intravascular (umbrella device)	17.92	635.16	2337	2587	3080
37650	Ligation of femoral vein	13.98	497.59	1154	1311	1638
37660	Ligation of common iliac vein	33.48	1184.30	2074	2360	2577
37700	Ligation and division of long saphenous vein at saphenofemoral junction, or distal interruptions	6.99	250.50	1003	1099	1212
37718	Ligation, division, and stripping, short saphenous vein	11.11	394.13	1367	1525	1833
37722	Ligation, division, and stripping, long (greater) saphenous veins from saphenofemoral junction to knee or below	13.19	469.17	1612	1799	2162
37735	Ligation and division and complete stripping of long or short saphenous veins with radical excision of ulcer and skin graft and/or interruption of communicating veins of lower leg, with excision of deep fascia	17.58	624.93	2547	2793	3387
37760	Ligation of perforator veins, subfascial, radical (Linton type), with or without skin graft, open	17.27	613.56	2651	2853	3332
37765	Stab phlebectomy of varicose veins, one extremity; 10-20 stab incisions	12.47	443.40	1849	2077	2472
37766	Stab phlebectomy of varicose veins, one extremity; more than 20 incisions	15.07	534.73	2247	2524	3003
37780	Ligation and division of short saphenous vein at saphenopopliteal junction (separate procedure)	7.16	256.57	650	736	854
37785	Ligation, division, and/or excision of varicose vein cluster(s), one leg	9.53	346.38	723	866	1168

Other Procedures

		Medicare RVU	National Fee	50%	75%	90%
37788	Penile revascularization, artery, with or without vein graft	35.32	1250.24	3823	4487	4923

● = New Code   ⊗ = Conscious Sedation   ✚ = Add-on Code   ∅ = Modifier '51' Exempt   ▲ =Revised Code

		Medicare RVU	National Fee	PFR Fee Information 50%	75%	90%
37790	Penile venous occlusive procedure	13.52	480.54	1530	1843	2100
37799	Unlisted procedure, vascular surgery	-	-	IR	IR	IR

Hemic and Lymphatic Systems

Spleen
Excision

38100	Splenectomy; total (separate procedure)	27.74	977.00	2599	2962	3448
38101	Splenectomy; partial (separate procedure)	28.24	995.95	3022	3448	3983
✚ 38102	Splenectomy; total, en bloc for extensive disease, in conjunction with other procedure (List in addition to code for primary procedure)	6.97	245.95	1389	1995	2411

Repair

38115	Repair of ruptured spleen (splenorrhaphy) with or without partial splenectomy	30.76	1082.73	2663	3011	3711

Laparoscopy

38120	Laparoscopy, surgical, splenectomy	26.49	939.10	2947	3810	4329
38129	Unlisted laparoscopy procedure, spleen	-	-	IR	IR	IR

Introduction

38200	Injection procedure for splenoportography	3.69	129.61	416	524	638

General
Bone Marrow or Stem Cell Transplantation Services/Procedures

38204	Management of recipient hematopoietic progenitor cell donor search and cell acquisition	2.97	104.98	IR	IR	IR
38205	Blood-derived hematopoietic progenitor cell harvesting for transplantation, per collection; allogenic	2.21	78.07	474	636	777
38206	Blood-derived hematopoietic progenitor cell harvesting for transplantation, per collection; autologous	2.21	78.07	474	636	777
38207	Transplant preparation of hematopoietic progenitor cells; cryopreservation and storage	1.31	46.23	IR	IR	IR
38208	Transplant preparation of hematopoietic progenitor cells; thawing of previously frozen harvest, without washing	0.83	29.18	IR	IR	IR
38209	Transplant preparation of hematopoietic progenitor cells; thawing of previously frozen harvest, with washing	0.36	12.89	IR	IR	IR
38210	Transplant preparation of hematopoietic progenitor cells; specific cell depletion within harvest, T-cell depletion	2.32	81.86	IR	IR	IR
38211	Transplant preparation of hematopoietic progenitor cells; tumor cell depletion	2.09	73.90	IR	IR	IR
38212	Transplant preparation of hematopoietic progenitor cells; red blood cell removal	1.39	49.27	IR	IR	IR
38213	Transplant preparation of hematopoietic progenitor cells; platelet depletion	0.36	12.89	IR	IR	IR
38214	Transplant preparation of hematopoietic progenitor cells; plasma (volume) depletion	1.19	42.07	IR	IR	IR
38215	Transplant preparation of hematopoietic progenitor cells; cell concentration in plasma, mononuclear, or buffy coat layer	1.39	49.27	IR	IR	IR
38220	Bone marrow; aspiration only	4.59	169.78	214	305	411
38221	Bone marrow; biopsy, needle or trocar	5.08	187.21	247	337	404
38230	Bone marrow harvesting for transplantation	8.40	300.15	1130	1519	1805
38240	Bone marrow or blood-derived peripheral stem cell transplantation; allogenic	3.36	118.62	769	891	1159
38241	Bone marrow or blood-derived peripheral stem cell transplantation; autologous	3.37	119.00	910	1435	1936
38242	Bone marrow or blood-derived peripheral stem cell transplantation; allogeneic donor lymphocyte infusions	2.55	90.20	645	765	878

Lymph Nodes and Lymphatic Channels
Incision

38300	Drainage of lymph node abscess or lymphadenitis; simple	6.65	243.30	269	375	451

● = New Code ⊗ = Conscious Sedation ✚ = Add-on Code ∅ = Modifier '51' Exempt ▲ =Revised Code

		Medicare RVU	National Fee	PFR Fee Information 50%	75%	90%
38305	Drainage of lymph node abscess or lymphadenitis; extensive	11.61	414.98	657	783	930
38308	Lymphangiotomy or other operations on lymphatic channels	11.27	401.33	860	932	1159
38380	Suture and/or ligation of thoracic duct; cervical approach	14.52	518.44	1418	1646	1838
38381	Suture and/or ligation of thoracic duct; thoracic approach	21.85	777.28	2539	2993	3658
38382	Suture and/or ligation of thoracic duct; abdominal approach	17.56	625.31	2165	2625	2986

Excision

(A4550 (Disposable Surgical Tray) can be coded in addition to 38500 in the office setting. Payment is at carrier discretion.)

38500	Biopsy or excision of lymph node(s); open, superficial	7.95	286.88	567	649	775
38505	Biopsy or excision of lymph node(s); by needle, superficial (eg, cervical, inguinal, axillary)	3.27	119.76	330	457	627
38510	Biopsy or excision of lymph node(s); open, deep cervical node(s)	12.87	462.35	814	926	1091
38520	Biopsy or excision of lymph node(s); open, deep cervical node(s) with excision scalene fat pad	11.75	418.77	906	1015	1242
38525	Biopsy or excision of lymph node(s); open, deep axillary node(s)	10.48	372.91	1050	1272	1600
38530	Biopsy or excision of lymph node(s); open, internal mammary node(s)	13.70	487.74	1106	1369	1469
38542	Dissection, deep jugular node(s)	10.98	393.00	1109	1325	1544
38550	Excision of cystic hygroma, axillary or cervical; without deep neurovascular dissection	11.86	422.94	1174	1326	1438
38555	Excision of cystic hygroma, axillary or cervical; with deep neurovascular dissection	25.40	903.86	2422	2736	3202

Limited Lymphadenectomy For Staging

38562	Limited lymphadenectomy for staging (separate procedure); pelvic and para-aortic	17.89	636.30	2322	2958	3572
38564	Limited lymphadenectomy for staging (separate procedure); retroperitoneal (aortic and/or splenic)	17.85	633.27	2435	2855	3416

Laparoscopy

38570	Laparoscopy, surgical; with retroperitoneal lymph node sampling (biopsy), single or multiple	14.39	510.10	2369	2775	3042
38571	Laparoscopy, surgical; with bilateral total pelvic lymphadenectomy	21.82	770.84	2734	3344	3925
38572	Laparoscopy, surgical; with bilateral total pelvic lymphadenectomy and peri-aortic lymph node sampling (biopsy), single or multiple	25.63	906.89	2812	3396	3714
38589	Unlisted laparoscopy procedure, lymphatic system	-	-	IR	IR	IR

Radical Lymphadenectomy (Radical Resection of Lymph Nodes)

38700	Suprahyoid lymphadenectomy	19.58	693.52	2148	2574	3008
38720	Cervical lymphadenectomy (complete)	32.28	1140.34	3483	4030	4946
38724	Cervical lymphadenectomy (modified radical neck dissection)	34.87	1230.91	3530	3858	4473
38740	Axillary lymphadenectomy; superficial	16.85	598.40	1695	1846	1953
38745	Axillary lymphadenectomy; complete	21.52	763.26	2449	2724	2893
+ 38746	Thoracic lymphadenectomy, regional, including mediastinal and peritracheal nodes (List separately in addition to code for primary procedure)	7.17	253.16	911	1147	1404
+ 38747	Abdominal lymphadenectomy, regional, including celiac, gastric, portal, peripancreatic, with or without para-aortic and vena caval nodes (List separately in addition to code for primary procedure)	7.09	250.12	1063	1232	1603
38760	Inguinofemoral lymphadenectomy, superficial, including Cloquets node (separate procedure)	21.30	755.68	1816	2352	2596
38765	Inguinofemoral lymphadenectomy, superficial, in continuity with pelvic lymphadenectomy, including external iliac, hypogastric, and obturator nodes (separate procedure)	33.03	1168.76	3386	3858	4492
38770	Pelvic lymphadenectomy, including external iliac, hypogastric, and obturator nodes (separate procedure)	21.43	758.71	2846	3614	3958
38780	Retroperitoneal transabdominal lymphadenectomy, extensive, including pelvic, aortic, and renal nodes (separate procedure)	27.61	979.27	4391	5298	6015

© PFR 2007

● = New Code ⊗ = Conscious Sedation ✚ = Add-on Code ∅ = Modifier '51' Exempt ▲ =Revised Code

		Medicare RVU	National Fee	PFR Fee Information 50%	75%	90%

Introduction

| 38790 | Injection procedure; lymphangiography | 2.17 | 77.31 | 537 | 724 | 839 |

(PFR research shows that fees for code 38792 may vary widely.)

| ∅ 38792 | Injection procedure; for identification of sentinel node | 1.03 | 37.14 | 453 | 534 | 648 |
| 38794 | Cannulation, thoracic duct | 8.13 | 291.05 | 707 | 774 | 827 |

Other Procedures

| 38999 | Unlisted procedure, hemic or lymphatic system | - | - | IR | IR | IR |

Mediastinum and Diaphragm

Mediastinum
Incision

| 39000 | Mediastinotomy with exploration, drainage, removal of foreign body, or biopsy; cervical approach | 12.95 | 462.35 | 1471 | 1776 | 2474 |
| 39010 | Mediastinotomy with exploration, drainage, removal of foreign body, or biopsy; transthoracic approach, including either transthoracic or median sternotomy | 22.06 | 785.99 | 2604 | 3099 | 3617 |

Excision

| 39200 | Excision of mediastinal cyst | 24.28 | 862.93 | 2870 | 3359 | 3782 |
| 39220 | Excision of mediastinal tumor | 30.97 | 1099.41 | 3329 | 3719 | 4457 |

Endoscopy

| 39400 | Mediastinoscopy, with or without biopsy | 13.50 | 481.30 | 1303 | 1494 | 1834 |

Other Procedures

| 39499 | Unlisted procedure, mediastinum | - | - | IR | IR | IR |

Diaphragm
Repair

| 39501 | Repair, laceration of diaphragm, any approach | 21.99 | 780.31 | 2616 | 3141 | 3585 |
| 39502 | Repair, paraesophageal hiatus hernia, transabdominal, with or without fundoplasty, vagotomy, and/or pyloroplasty, except neonatal | 26.27 | 930.38 | 3059 | 3385 | 3981 |

(Medicare fees for the code below are based on Non Facility RVUs. PFR information reflects fee when procedure is performed in a facility.)

39503	Repair, neonatal diaphragmatic hernia, with or without chest tube insertion and with or without creation of ventral hernia	152.38	5360.60	4162	6586	8999
39520	Repair, diaphragmatic hernia (esophageal hiatal); transthoracic	26.63	945.92	3002	3483	3912
39530	Repair, diaphragmatic hernia (esophageal hiatal); combined, thoracoabdominal	25.28	896.28	3230	3401	3869
39531	Repair, diaphragmatic hernia (esophageal hiatal); combined, thoracoabdominal, with dilation of stricture (with or without gastroplasty)	26.63	943.65	2912	3513	3859
39540	Repair, diaphragmatic hernia (other than neonatal), traumatic; acute	22.38	792.82	3513	3858	4475
39541	Repair, diaphragmatic hernia (other than neonatal), traumatic; chronic	24.08	852.69	3215	3551	4512
39545	Imbrication of diaphragm for eventration, transthoracic or transabdominal, paralytic or nonparalytic	23.88	849.28	3330	3605	3832
39560	Resection, diaphragm; with simple repair (eg, primary suture)	20.66	733.70	1858	2347	2920
39561	Resection, diaphragm; with complex repair (eg, prosthetic material, local muscle flap)	31.54	1119.87	2947	3537	4129

Other Procedures

| 39599 | Unlisted procedure, diaphragm | - | - | IR | IR | IR |

Digestive System

Lips
Excision

| 40490 | Biopsy of lip | 3.02 | 109.90 | 178 | 235 | 288 |

● = New Code ⊗ = Conscious Sedation ✚ = Add-on Code ∅ = Modifier '51' Exempt ▲ =Revised Code

Code	Description	Medicare RVU	National Fee	PFR Fee Information 50%	75%	90%
40500	Vermilionectomy (lip shave), with mucosal advancement	11.85	432.41	1345	1608	1874
40510	Excision of lip; transverse wedge excision with primary closure	11.83	430.14	1459	1729	2132
40520	Excision of lip; V-excision with primary direct linear closure	12.61	460.08	1111	1462	1680
40525	Excision of lip; full thickness, reconstruction with local flap (eg, Estlander or fan)	14.52	521.09	2760	3182	3322
40527	Excision of lip; full thickness, reconstruction with cross lip flap (Abbe-Estlander)	17.18	615.83	2954	3328	3700
40530	Resection of lip, more than one-fourth, without reconstruction	13.70	498.35	1301	1632	1885

Repair (Cheiloplasty)

Code	Description	Medicare RVU	National Fee	PFR Fee Information 50%	75%	90%
40650	Repair lip, full thickness; vermilion only	10.65	389.59	1058	1277	1389
40652	Repair lip, full thickness; up to half vertical height	12.41	454.01	1129	1326	1500
40654	Repair lip, full thickness; over one-half vertical height, or complex	14.45	527.15	1407	1536	1680
40700	Plastic repair of cleft lip/nasal deformity; primary, partial or complete, unilateral	24.05	858.00	2467	2782	3518
40701	Plastic repair of cleft lip/nasal deformity; primary bilateral, one stage procedure	30.04	1073.64	3612	4224	4566
40702	Plastic repair of cleft lip/nasal deformity; primary bilateral, one of two stages	23.34	830.71	2608	2876	3317
40720	Plastic repair of cleft lip/nasal deformity; secondary, by recreation of defect and reclosure	26.06	932.28	2570	3103	3384
40761	Plastic repair of cleft lip/nasal deformity; with cross lip pedicle flap (Abbe-Estlander type), including sectioning and inserting of pedicle	27.60	986.09	3123	3481	3921

Other Procedures

Code	Description	Medicare RVU	National Fee	PFR Fee Information 50%	75%	90%
40799	Unlisted procedure, lips	-	-	IR	IR	IR

Vestibule of Mouth

Incision

Code	Description	Medicare RVU	National Fee	PFR Fee Information 50%	75%	90%
40800	Drainage of abscess, cyst, hematoma, vestibule of mouth; simple	4.50	165.99	184	283	323
40801	Drainage of abscess, cyst, hematoma, vestibule of mouth; complicated	7.11	259.60	476	715	894
40804	Removal of embedded foreign body, vestibule of mouth; simple	4.82	177.74	239	296	354
40805	Removal of embedded foreign body, vestibule of mouth; complicated	7.68	280.82	647	772	935
40806	Incision of labial frenum (frenotomy)	2.32	86.79	260	332	476

Excision, Destruction

Code	Description	Medicare RVU	National Fee	PFR Fee Information 50%	75%	90%
40808	Biopsy, vestibule of mouth	3.95	145.91	201	263	324
40810	Excision of lesion of mucosa and submucosa, vestibule of mouth; without repair	4.51	165.99	269	340	450
40812	Excision of lesion of mucosa and submucosa, vestibule of mouth; with simple repair	6.53	238.75	359	472	575
40814	Excision of lesion of mucosa and submucosa, vestibule of mouth; with complex repair	8.97	326.68	749	919	1073
40816	Excision of lesion of mucosa and submucosa, vestibule of mouth; complex, with excision of underlying muscle	9.43	343.35	982	1195	1433
40818	Excision of mucosa of vestibule of mouth as donor graft	8.25	302.42	520	646	771
40819	Excision of frenum, labial or buccal (frenumectomy, frenulectomy, frenectomy)	7.02	256.57	396	475	532
40820	Destruction of lesion or scar of vestibule of mouth by physical methods (eg, laser, thermal, cryo, chemical)	5.64	208.82	250	435	550

Repair

Code	Description	Medicare RVU	National Fee	PFR Fee Information 50%	75%	90%
40830	Closure of laceration, vestibule of mouth; 2.5 cm or less	5.78	212.23	265	292	346
40831	Closure of laceration, vestibule of mouth; over 2.5 cm or complex	7.63	279.68	503	582	676
	(40840 - 40845 may be reimbursable by Medicare for injury or tumor. It is not reimbursable if dental-related.)					
40840	Vestibuloplasty; anterior	19.96	721.95	1536	1779	1970
40842	Vestibuloplasty; posterior, unilateral	20.10	727.25	1467	1613	1798

© PFR 2007

● = New Code ⊗ = Conscious Sedation ✚ = Add-on Code ∅ = Modifier '51' Exempt ▲ =Revised Code

		Medicare RVU	National Fee	PFR Fee Information 50%	75%	90%
40843	Vestibuloplasty; posterior, bilateral	25.93	934.55	2111	2405	2664
40844	Vestibuloplasty; entire arch	34.11	1229.39	2648	3011	3172
40845	Vestibuloplasty; complex (including ridge extension, muscle repositioning)	37.78	1359.00	2923	3530	4435

Other Procedures

40899	Unlisted procedure, vestibule of mouth	-	-	IR	IR	IR

Tongue and Floor of Mouth
Incision

41000	Intraoral incision and drainage of abscess, cyst, or hematoma of tongue or floor of mouth; lingual	3.80	139.08	237	272	347
41005	Intraoral incision and drainage of abscess, cyst, or hematoma of tongue or floor of mouth; sublingual, superficial	4.95	182.67	254	311	404
41006	Intraoral incision and drainage of abscess, cyst, or hematoma of tongue or floor of mouth; sublingual, deep, supramylohyoid	8.55	311.52	548	693	959
41007	Intraoral incision and drainage of abscess, cyst, or hematoma of tongue or floor of mouth; submental space	8.64	315.31	667	772	864
41008	Intraoral incision and drainage of abscess, cyst, or hematoma of tongue or floor of mouth; submandibular space	8.69	316.44	590	765	887
41009	Intraoral incision and drainage of abscess, cyst, or hematoma of tongue or floor of mouth; masticator space	9.28	337.67	696	850	1032
41010	Incision of lingual frenum (frenotomy)	4.56	168.64	262	378	474
41015	Extraoral incision and drainage of abscess, cyst, or hematoma of floor of mouth; sublingual	10.07	366.47	646	852	1022
41016	Extraoral incision and drainage of abscess, cyst, or hematoma of floor of mouth; submental	10.39	378.22	719	849	982
41017	Extraoral incision and drainage of abscess, cyst, or hematoma of floor of mouth; submandibular	10.45	380.49	678	902	1066
41018	Extraoral incision and drainage of abscess, cyst, or hematoma of floor of mouth; masticator space	12.06	437.34	766	949	1098

Excision

41100	Biopsy of tongue; anterior two-thirds	4.00	146.28	218	275	345
41105	Biopsy of tongue; posterior one-third	3.94	144.01	282	322	382
41108	Biopsy of floor of mouth	3.32	121.65	212	240	310
41110	Excision of lesion of tongue without closure	4.76	174.71	309	418	500
41112	Excision of lesion of tongue with closure; anterior two-thirds	7.68	280.44	553	749	907
41113	Excision of lesion of tongue with closure; posterior one-third	8.48	309.24	755	963	1135
41114	Excision of lesion of tongue with closure; with local tongue flap	16.44	589.69	1599	2126	2276
41115	Excision of lingual frenum (frenectomy)	5.47	200.48	380	470	614
41116	Excision, lesion of floor of mouth	7.29	266.80	683	857	1160
41120	Glossectomy; less than one-half tongue	26.51	962.98	1670	2033	2440
41130	Glossectomy; hemiglossectomy	32.25	1163.07	2037	2589	3065
41135	Glossectomy; partial, with unilateral radical neck dissection	54.17	1939.22	3952	4789	5415
41140	Glossectomy; complete or total, with or without tracheostomy, without radical neck dissection	56.47	2030.17	3815	4159	4734
41145	Glossectomy; complete or total, with or without tracheostomy, with unilateral radical neck dissection	69.70	2498.20	4636	5548	6492
41150	Glossectomy; composite procedure with resection floor of mouth and mandibular resection, without radical neck dissection	55.34	1984.69	4180	5047	6148
41153	Glossectomy; composite procedure with resection floor of mouth, with suprahyoid neck dissection	59.59	2131.36	4447	5304	5984
41155	Glossectomy; composite procedure with resection floor of mouth, mandibular resection, and radical neck dissection (Commando type)	72.78	2590.67	5641	6678	7651

	Medicare RVU	National Fee	PFR Fee Information 50%	75%	90%

Repair

41250 Repair of laceration 2.5 cm or less; floor of mouth and/or anterior two-thirds of tongue	5.11	186.46	279	430	518
41251 Repair of laceration 2.5 cm or less; posterior one-third of tongue	5.75	209.19	390	477	615
41252 Repair of laceration of tongue, floor of mouth, over 2.6 cm or complex	7.29	264.90	644	904	1042

Other Procedures

41500 Fixation of tongue, mechanical, other than suture (eg, K-wire)	11.26	412.32	740	774	867
41510 Suture of tongue to lip for micrognathia (Douglas type procedure)	11.36	417.25	1154	1366	1476
41520 Frenoplasty (surgical revision of frenum, eg, with Z-plasty)	7.94	290.29	593	752	922
41599 Unlisted procedure, tongue, floor of mouth	-	-	IR	IR	IR

Dentoalveolar Structures

Incision

41800 Drainage of abscess, cyst, hematoma from dentoalveolar structures	4.46	164.48	229	272	332
41805 Removal of embedded foreign body from dentoalveolar structures; soft tissues	4.59	169.02	262	305	345
41806 Removal of embedded foreign body from dentoalveolar structures; bone	7.26	264.90	353	597	720

Excision, Destruction

(41820 - 41821 may be reimbursable by Medicare for trauma or if related to a tumor.)

41820 Gingivectomy, excision gingiva, each quadrant	-	-	545	686	824
41821 Operculectomy, excision pericoronal tissues	-	-	126	167	190

(41822 - 41823 may be reimbursable by Medicare for benign or malignant tumors, if there is interference with speech, swallowing or ability to close mouth.)

41822 Excision of fibrous tuberosities, dentoalveolar structures	6.74	246.33	378	479	632
41823 Excision of osseous tuberosities, dentoalveolar structures	9.90	361.16	634	756	886
41825 Excision of lesion or tumor (except listed above), dentoalveolar structures; without repair	4.70	172.81	310	397	452
41826 Excision of lesion or tumor (except listed above), dentoalveolar structures; with simple repair	5.75	208.82	520	596	698
41827 Excision of lesion or tumor (except listed above), dentoalveolar structures; with complex repair	9.86	359.65	734	840	1206

(41828 - 41830 may be reimbursable by Medicare for trauma or if related to a tumor.)

41828 Excision of hyperplastic alveolar mucosa, each quadrant (specify)	7.43	269.83	688	841	935
41830 Alveolectomy, including curettage of osteitis or sequestrectomy	9.05	330.09	632	857	998

(41850 may be reimbursable by Medicare if related to a tumor.)

41850 Destruction of lesion (except excision), dentoalveolar structures	-	-	177	241	378

Other Procedures

(41870 may be reimbursable by Medicare if related to a tumor.)

41870 Periodontal mucosal grafting	-	-	675	844	928

(41872 - 41874 may be reimbursable by Medicare for trauma or if related to a tumor.)

41872 Gingivoplasty, each quadrant (specify)	8.44	308.86	709	869	1059
41874 Alveoloplasty, each quadrant (specify)	8.65	316.07	583	817	968
41899 Unlisted procedure, dentoalveolar structures	-	-	IR	IR	IR

Palate and Uvula

Incision

42000 Drainage of abscess of palate, uvula	3.88	142.12	230	278	368

Excision, Destruction

42100 Biopsy of palate, uvula	3.57	130.37	252	318	390
42104 Excision, lesion of palate, uvula; without closure	4.58	167.13	388	504	592

● = New Code ⊗ = Conscious Sedation ✚ = Add-on Code ∅ = Modifier '51' Exempt ▲ =Revised Code

		Medicare RVU	National Fee	PFR Fee Information 50%	75%	90%
42106	Excision, lesion of palate, uvula; with simple primary closure	5.89	215.26	520	619	852
42107	Excision, lesion of palate, uvula; with local flap closure	10.79	391.86	1076	1665	1818
42120	Resection of palate or extensive resection of lesion	23.93	862.17	2058	2244	2647
42140	Uvulectomy, excision of uvula	5.63	206.92	422	520	724
42145	Palatopharyngoplasty (eg, uvulopalatopharyngoplasty, uvulopharyngoplasty)	17.61	630.61	2389	2764	3200
42160	Destruction of lesion, palate or uvula (thermal, cryo or chemical)	6.09	223.97	371	478	525

Repair

42180	Repair, laceration of palate; up to 2 cm	5.84	211.85	388	497	589
42182	Repair, laceration of palate; over 2 cm or complex	8.16	294.46	755	849	1068
42200	Palatoplasty for cleft palate, soft and/or hard palate only	23.40	839.43	2676	3351	4014
42205	Palatoplasty for cleft palate, with closure of alveolar ridge; soft tissue only	24.60	880.36	3027	3563	4190
42210	Palatoplasty for cleft palate, with closure of alveolar ridge; with bone graft to alveolar ridge (includes obtaining graft)	28.14	1009.59	3654	4831	5774
42215	Palatoplasty for cleft palate; major revision	18.83	679.88	2626	3261	4035
42220	Palatoplasty for cleft palate; secondary lengthening procedure	14.59	526.02	2619	2953	3670
42225	Palatoplasty for cleft palate; attachment pharyngeal flap	26.35	961.84	2766	3041	3671
42226	Lengthening of palate, and pharyngeal flap	25.14	913.71	3120	3723	4344
42227	Lengthening of palate, with island flap	24.89	905.75	2740	3269	3727
42235	Repair of anterior palate, including vomer flap	20.12	732.18	2303	2847	3366
42260	Repair of nasolabial fistula	21.42	773.11	1389	1698	1985
42280	Maxillary impression for palatal prosthesis	3.78	137.19	283	325	417
42281	Insertion of pin-retained palatal prosthesis	4.80	174.33	335	414	480

Other Procedures

42299	Unlisted procedure, palate, uvula	-	-	IR	IR	IR

Salivary Gland and Ducts

Incision

42300	Drainage of abscess; parotid, simple	4.96	180.39	313	337	381
42305	Drainage of abscess; parotid, complicated	11.21	400.96	655	847	1298
42310	Drainage of abscess; submaxillary or sublingual, intraoral	3.95	143.63	303	357	418
42320	Drainage of abscess; submaxillary, external	5.92	215.26	466	564	615
42330	Sialolithotomy; submandibular (submaxillary), sublingual or parotid, uncomplicated, intraoral	5.58	203.13	333	426	559
42335	Sialolithotomy; submandibular (submaxillary), complicated, intraoral	8.68	316.07	650	862	1004
42340	Sialolithotomy; parotid, extraoral or complicated intraoral	11.17	405.50	1105	1344	1565

Excision

42400	Biopsy of salivary gland; needle	2.55	93.61	201	268	351
42405	Biopsy of salivary gland; incisional	7.53	272.86	489	571	663
42408	Excision of sublingual salivary cyst (ranula)	10.99	399.06	856	1014	1305
42409	Marsupialization of sublingual salivary cyst (ranula)	7.78	283.85	684	862	1024
42410	Excision of parotid tumor or parotid gland; lateral lobe, without nerve dissection	16.28	580.97	1621	1995	2325
42415	Excision of parotid tumor or parotid gland; lateral lobe, with dissection and preservation of facial nerve	29.53	1050.52	3442	3700	4432

		Medicare RVU	National Fee	PFR Fee Information 50%	75%	90%
42420	Excision of parotid tumor or parotid gland; total, with dissection and preservation of facial nerve	33.98	1208.17	3917	4463	5121
42425	Excision of parotid tumor or parotid gland; total, en bloc removal with sacrifice of facial nerve	22.36	796.61	2694	3298	4031
42426	Excision of parotid tumor or parotid gland; total, with unilateral radical neck dissection	36.35	1291.55	4859	5700	6792
42440	Excision of submandibular (submaxillary) gland	12.12	432.41	2186	2365	2833
42450	Excision of sublingual gland	10.98	398.30	1354	1619	1925

Repair

42500	Plastic repair of salivary duct, sialodochoplasty; primary or simple	10.47	380.11	1133	1368	1554
42505	Plastic repair of salivary duct, sialodochoplasty; secondary or complicated	13.82	499.87	1637	1793	2208
42507	Parotid duct diversion, bilateral (Wilke type procedure);	13.04	470.69	1843	2045	2272
42508	Parotid duct diversion, bilateral (Wilke type procedure); with excision of one submandibular gland	18.41	662.45	2318	2602	3160
42509	Parotid duct diversion, bilateral (Wilke type procedure); with excision of both submandibular glands	22.41	804.94	2834	3163	3473
42510	Parotid duct diversion, bilateral (Wilke type procedure); with ligation of both submandibular (Wharton's) ducts	16.37	588.93	2144	2622	2924

Other Procedures

42550	Injection procedure for sialography	4.25	156.14	177	217	266
42600	Closure salivary fistula	11.85	430.52	1314	1506	1908
42650	Dilation salivary duct	1.97	71.63	125	149	184
42660	Dilation and catheterization of salivary duct, with or without injection	2.59	93.99	186	220	299
42665	Ligation salivary duct, intraoral	7.11	259.60	362	483	539
42699	Unlisted procedure, salivary glands or ducts	-	-	IR	IR	IR

Pharynx, Adenoids, and Tonsils
Incision

42700	Incision and drainage abscess; peritonsillar	4.45	162.58	301	376	458
42720	Incision and drainage abscess; retropharyngeal or parapharyngeal, intraoral approach	11.46	410.43	545	725	811
42725	Incision and drainage abscess; retropharyngeal or parapharyngeal, external approach	21.03	749.99	1138	1529	1860

Excision, Destruction

42800	Biopsy; oropharynx	3.73	136.05	235	269	332
42802	Biopsy; hypopharynx	6.21	229.28	280	333	387
42804	Biopsy; nasopharynx, visible lesion, simple	5.00	184.56	281	318	349
42806	Biopsy; nasopharynx, survey for unknown primary lesion	5.67	208.82	361	440	517
42808	Excision or destruction of lesion of pharynx, any method	5.58	202.75	531	593	685
42809	Removal of foreign body from pharynx	4.27	155.00	279	340	415
42810	Excision branchial cleft cyst or vestige, confined to skin and subcutaneous tissues	9.31	340.32	768	879	1153
42815	Excision branchial cleft cyst, vestige, or fistula, extending beneath subcutaneous tissues and/or into pharynx	14.09	506.31	1849	2219	2583
42820	Tonsillectomy and adenoidectomy; younger than age 12	7.59	271.73	840	1043	1323
42821	Tonsillectomy and adenoidectomy; age 12 or over	7.97	285.75	896	1167	1285
42825	Tonsillectomy, primary or secondary; younger than age 12	6.69	240.27	774	873	1014
42826	Tonsillectomy, primary or secondary; age 12 or over	6.56	235.72	839	978	1168
42830	Adenoidectomy, primary; younger than age 12	5.28	190.25	592	744	884
42831	Adenoidectomy, primary; age 12 or over	5.71	205.78	628	837	889

● = New Code ⊗ = Conscious Sedation ✚ = Add-on Code ∅ = Modifier '51' Exempt ▲ =Revised Code

		Medicare RVU	National Fee	PFR Fee Information 50%	75%	90%
42835	Adenoidectomy, secondary; younger than age 12	4.83	174.33	509	574	643
42836	Adenoidectomy, secondary; age 12 or over	6.30	226.63	604	703	816
42842	Radical resection of tonsil, tonsillar pillars, and/or retromolar trigone; without closure	23.74	853.83	2322	2829	4309
42844	Radical resection of tonsil, tonsillar pillars, and/or retromolar trigone; closure with local flap (eg, tongue, buccal)	34.45	1238.49	3395	4106	4736
42845	Radical resection of tonsil, tonsillar pillars, and/or retromolar trigone; closure with other flap	56.55	2019.94	4620	5184	5913
42860	Excision of tonsil tags	4.76	171.68	511	606	698
42870	Excision or destruction lingual tonsil, any method (separate procedure)	14.31	521.47	778	991	1276
42890	Limited pharyngectomy	34.08	1219.54	2410	2744	3161
42892	Resection of lateral pharyngeal wall or pyriform sinus, direct closure by advancement of lateral and posterior pharyngeal walls	44.33	1581.84	2952	3486	3757
42894	Resection of pharyngeal wall requiring closure with myocutaneous flap	57.34	2044.95	4457	5069	5908

Repair

42900	Suture pharynx for wound or injury	9.19	328.19	925	1169	1451
42950	Pharyngoplasty (plastic or reconstructive operation on pharynx)	20.36	740.52	2072	2243	2743
42953	Pharyngoesophageal repair	26.45	966.77	2411	2905	3517

Other Procedures

42955	Pharyngostomy (fistulization of pharynx, external for feeding)	19.06	692.01	1211	1378	1608
42960	Control oropharyngeal hemorrhage, primary or secondary (eg, post-tonsillectomy); simple	4.41	158.03	308	393	458
42961	Control oropharyngeal hemorrhage, primary or secondary (eg, post-tonsillectomy); complicated, requiring hospitalization	10.90	391.48	546	650	841
42962	Control oropharyngeal hemorrhage, primary or secondary (eg, post-tonsillectomy); with secondary surgical intervention	13.52	484.33	838	1088	1684
42970	Control of nasopharyngeal hemorrhage, primary or secondary (eg, postadenoidectomy); simple, with posterior nasal packs, with or without anterior packs and/or cautery	10.17	363.44	529	657	816
42971	Control of nasopharyngeal hemorrhage, primary or secondary (eg, postadenoidectomy); complicated, requiring hospitalization	11.93	427.10	720	924	1077
42972	Control of nasopharyngeal hemorrhage, primary or secondary (eg, postadenoidectomy); with secondary surgical intervention	13.55	484.71	861	1189	1435
42999	Unlisted procedure, pharynx, adenoids, or tonsils	-	-	IR	IR	IR

Esophagus

Incision

43020	Esophagotomy, cervical approach, with removal of foreign body	14.16	505.55	1851	2057	2347
43030	Cricopharyngeal myotomy	13.78	491.91	2025	2348	2761
43045	Esophagotomy, thoracic approach, with removal of foreign body	34.83	1237.35	3050	3419	3771

Excision

43100	Excision of lesion, esophagus, with primary repair; cervical approach	16.42	585.90	2250	2494	3170
43101	Excision of lesion, esophagus, with primary repair; thoracic or abdominal approach	27.03	959.56	3046	3525	4077
43107	Total or near total esophagectomy, without thoracotomy; with pharyngogastrostomy or cervical esophagogastrostomy, with or without pyloroplasty (transhiatal)	67.05	2373.52	5240	5866	6369
43108	Total or near total esophagectomy, without thoracotomy; with colon interposition or small intestine reconstruction, including intestine mobilization, preparation and anastomosis(es)	103.83	3619.59	6049	6773	7598
43112	Total or near total esophagectomy, with thoracotomy; with pharyngogastrostomy or cervical esophagogastrostomy, with or without pyloroplasty	71.87	2543.30	6001	7204	8491
43113	Total or near total esophagectomy, with thoracotomy; with colon interposition or small intestine reconstruction, including intestine mobilization, preparation, and anastomosis(es)	102.57	3582.83	6353	7599	8308
43116	Partial esophagectomy, cervical, with free intestinal graft, including microvascular anastomosis, obtaining the graft and intestinal reconstruction	115.59	4026.99	6310	7528	8720

● = New Code ⊗ = Conscious Sedation ✚ = Add-on Code ∅ = Modifier '51' Exempt ▲ =Revised Code

		Medicare RVU	National Fee	PFR Fee Information 50%	75%	90%
43117	Partial esophagectomy, distal two-thirds, with thoracotomy and separate abdominal incision, with or without proximal gastrectomy; with thoracic esophagogastrostomy, with or without pyloroplasty (Ivor Lewis)	65.49	2315.92	6227	6447	7102
43118	Partial esophagectomy, distal two-thirds, with thoracotomy and separate abdominal incision, with or without proximal gastrectomy; with colon interposition or small intestine reconstruction, including intestine mobilization, preparation, and anastomosis(es)	86.65	3028.77	6081	7283	8122
43121	Partial esophagectomy, distal two-thirds, with thoracotomy only, with or without proximal gastrectomy, with thoracic esophagogastrostomy, with or without pyloroplasty	69.95	2455.76	5322	6315	6999
43122	Partial esophagectomy, thoracoabdominal or abdominal approach, with or without proximal gastrectomy; with esophagogastrostomy, with or without pyloroplasty	66.37	2347.75	5531	6148	7026
43123	Partial esophagectomy, thoracoabdominal or abdominal approach, with or without proximal gastrectomy; with colon interposition or small intestine reconstruction, including intestine mobilization, preparation, and anastomosis(es)	104.12	3629.82	6089	6967	7626
43124	Total or partial esophagectomy, without reconstruction (any approach), with cervical esophagostomy	88.37	3086.75	4733	5625	6511
43130	Diverticulectomy of hypopharynx or esophagus, with or without myotomy; cervical approach	20.74	738.62	2382	2765	3299
43135	Diverticulectomy of hypopharynx or esophagus, with or without myotomy; thoracic approach	37.00	1302.92	2987	3199	3855

Endoscopy

(A4550 (Disposable Surgical Tray) can be coded in addition to 43200 in the office setting. Payment is at carrier discretion.)

		Medicare RVU	National Fee	PFR Fee Information 50%	75%	90%
⊗ **43200**	Esophagoscopy, rigid or flexible; diagnostic, with or without collection of specimen(s) by brushing or washing (separate procedure)	5.70	209.95	591	705	826
⊗ **43201**	Esophagoscopy, rigid or flexible; with directed submucosal injection(s), any substance	7.10	261.11	633	746	873

(A4550 (Disposable Surgical Tray) can be coded in addition to 43202 in the office setting. Payment is at carrier discretion.)

		Medicare RVU	National Fee	PFR Fee Information 50%	75%	90%
⊗ **43202**	Esophagoscopy, rigid or flexible; with biopsy, single or multiple	7.48	276.27	649	755	882
⊗ **43204**	Esophagoscopy, rigid or flexible; with injection sclerosis of esophageal varices	5.69	201.24	895	1050	1225
⊗ **43205**	Esophagoscopy, rigid or flexible; with band ligation of esophageal varices	5.72	202.37	819	1009	1136
⊗ **43215**	Esophagoscopy, rigid or flexible; with removal of foreign body	4.04	143.25	825	931	1077
⊗ **43216**	Esophagoscopy, rigid or flexible; with removal of tumor(s), polyp(s), or other lesion(s) by hot biopsy forceps or bipolar cautery	4.15	148.18	738	899	1253
⊗ **43217**	Esophagoscopy, rigid or flexible; with removal of tumor(s), polyp(s), or other lesion(s) by snare technique	10.01	368.36	852	1035	1312
⊗ **43219**	Esophagoscopy, rigid or flexible; with insertion of plastic tube or stent	4.44	157.65	819	1023	1190

(A4550 (Disposable Surgical Tray) can be coded in addition to 43220 in the office setting. Payment is at carrier discretion.)

		Medicare RVU	National Fee	PFR Fee Information 50%	75%	90%
⊗ **43220**	Esophagoscopy, rigid or flexible; with balloon dilation (less than 30 mm diameter)	3.28	116.35	692	815	983

(A4550 (Disposable Surgical Tray) can be coded in addition to 43226 in the office setting. Payment is at carrier discretion.)

		Medicare RVU	National Fee	PFR Fee Information 50%	75%	90%
⊗ **43226**	Esophagoscopy, rigid or flexible; with insertion of guide wire followed by dilation over guide wire	3.63	128.47	646	702	853
⊗ **43227**	Esophagoscopy, rigid or flexible; with control of bleeding (eg, injection, bipolar cautery, unipolar cautery, laser, heater probe, stapler, plasma coagulator)	5.42	191.76	874	1058	1207
⊗ **43228**	Esophagoscopy, rigid or flexible; with ablation of tumor(s), polyp(s), or other lesion(s), not amenable to removal by hot biopsy forceps, bipolar cautery or snare technique	5.73	202.75	856	1067	1135
⊗ **43231**	Esophagoscopy, rigid or flexible; with endoscopic ultrasound examination	4.84	171.30	734	809	1017
⊗ **43232**	Esophagoscopy, rigid or flexible; with transendoscopic ultrasound-guided intramural or transmural fine needle aspiration/biopsy(s)	6.77	239.51	846	1022	1253

(A4550 (Disposable Surgical Tray) can be coded in addition to 43234 in the office setting. Payment is at carrier discretion.)

		Medicare RVU	National Fee	PFR Fee Information 50%	75%	90%
⊗ **43234**	Upper gastrointestinal endoscopy, simple primary examination (eg, with small diameter flexible endoscope) (separate procedure)	7.41	273.24	560	636	705

(UNBUNDLING ALERT: 43235 cannot be used with 43200 or 43234 by the same physician on the same day.)

(A4550 (Disposable Surgical Tray) can be coded in addition to 43235 in the office setting. Payment is at carrier discretion.)

		Medicare RVU	National Fee	PFR Fee Information 50%	75%	90%
⊗ **43235**	Upper gastrointestinal endoscopy including esophagus, stomach, and either the duodenum and/or jejunum as appropriate; diagnostic, with or without collection of specimen(s) by brushing or washing (separate procedure)	7.77	285.37	653	742	873

© PFR 2007

● = New Code   ⊗ = Conscious Sedation   ✚ = Add-on Code   ∅ = Modifier '51' Exempt   ▲ =Revised Code

		Medicare RVU	National Fee	PFR Fee Information 50%	75%	90%
⊗ **43236**	Upper gastrointestinal endoscopy including esophagus, stomach, and either the duodenum and/or jejunum as appropriate; with directed submucosal injection(s), any substance	9.60	352.83	1018	1183	1406
⊗ **43237**	Upper gastrointestinal endoscopy including esophagus, stomach, and either the duodenum and/or jejunum as appropriate; with endoscopic ultrasound examination limited to the esophagus	6.15	217.91	713	820	937
⊗ **43238**	Upper gastrointestinal endoscopy including esophagus, stomach, and either the duodenum and/or jejunum as appropriate; with transendoscopic ultrasound-guided intramural or transmural fine needle aspiration/biopsy(s), esophagus (includes endoscopic ultrasound examination limited to the esophagus)	7.56	267.18	857	987	1129

(UNBUNDLING ALERT: 43239 cannot be used with 43200, 43202, 43234, or 43235 by the same physician on the same day.)

(A4550 (Disposable Surgical Tray) can be coded in addition to 43239 in the office setting. Payment is at carrier discretion.)

⊗ **43239**	Upper gastrointestinal endoscopy including esophagus, stomach, and either the duodenum and/or jejunum as appropriate; with biopsy, single or multiple	8.88	325.54	744	828	942
⊗ **43240**	Upper gastrointestinal endoscopy including esophagus, stomach, and either the duodenum and/or jejunum as appropriate; with transmural drainage of pseudocyst	10.23	361.54	1061	1297	1415
⊗ **43241**	Upper gastrointestinal endoscopy including esophagus, stomach, and either the duodenum and/or jejunum as appropriate; with transendoscopic intraluminal tube or catheter placement	3.98	140.98	871	1002	1139
⊗ **43242**	Upper gastrointestinal endoscopy including esophagus, stomach, and either the duodenum and/or jejunum as appropriate; with transendoscopic ultrasound-guided intramural or transmural fine needle aspiration/biopsy(s) (includes endoscopic ultrasound examination of the esophagus, stomach, and either the duodenum and/or jejunum as appropriate)	10.81	382.01	924	1007	1093
⊗ **43243**	Upper gastrointestinal endoscopy including esophagus, stomach, and either the duodenum and/or jejunum as appropriate; with injection sclerosis of esophageal and/or gastric varices	6.83	241.41	955	1111	1297
⊗ **43244**	Upper gastrointestinal endoscopy including esophagus, stomach, and either the duodenum and/or jejunum as appropriate; with band ligation of esophageal and/or gastric varices	7.55	266.80	908	1019	1145

(A4550 (Disposable Surgical Tray) can be coded in addition to 43245 in the office setting. Payment is at carrier discretion.)

⊗ **43245**	Upper gastrointestinal endoscopy including esophagus, stomach, and either the duodenum and/or jejunum as appropriate; with dilation of gastric outlet for obstruction (eg, balloon, guide wire, bougie)	4.83	170.92	812	950	1063

(UNBUNDLING ALERT: 43246 cannot be used with 43200, 43202, 43234, 43235, 43241, 43750 or 43760 by the same physician on the same day.)

⊗ **43246**	Upper gastrointestinal endoscopy including esophagus, stomach, and either the duodenum and/or jejunum as appropriate; with directed placement of percutaneous gastrostomy tube	6.46	228.52	1104	1193	1378

(UNBUNDLING ALERT: 43247 cannot be used with 43200, 43202, 43215, 43234, 43235 by the same physician on the same day.)

(A4550 (Disposable Surgical Tray) can be coded in addition to 43247 in the office setting. Payment is at carrier discretion.)

⊗ **43247**	Upper gastrointestinal endoscopy including esophagus, stomach, and either the duodenum and/or jejunum as appropriate; with removal of foreign body	5.13	181.53	825	941	1059
⊗ **43248**	Upper gastrointestinal endoscopy including esophagus, stomach, and either the duodenum and/or jejunum as appropriate; with insertion of guide wire followed by dilation of esophagus over guide wire	4.81	170.16	750	840	930
⊗ **43249**	Upper gastrointestinal endoscopy including esophagus, stomach, and either the duodenum and/or jejunum as appropriate; with balloon dilation of esophagus (less than 30 mm diameter)	4.44	157.27	752	912	958

(A4550 (Disposable Surgical Tray) can be coded in addition to 43250 in the office setting. Payment is at carrier discretion.)

⊗ **43250**	Upper gastrointestinal endoscopy including esophagus, stomach, and either the duodenum and/or jejunum as appropriate; with removal of tumor(s), polyp(s), or other lesion(s) by hot biopsy forceps or bipolar cautery	4.86	172.05	873	1002	1230

(A4550 (Disposable Surgical Tray) can be coded in addition to 43251 in the office setting. Payment is at carrier discretion.)

⊗ **43251**	Upper gastrointestinal endoscopy including esophagus, stomach, and either the duodenum and/or jejunum as appropriate; with removal of tumor(s), polyp(s), or other lesion(s) by snare technique	5.58	197.45	953	1079	1195

(UNBUNDLING ALERT: 43255 cannot be used with 43200, 43202, 43204, 43234, 43235 by the same physician on the same day.)

⊗ **43255**	Upper gastrointestinal endoscopy including esophagus, stomach, and either the duodenum and/or jejunum as appropriate; with control of bleeding, any method	7.21	255.05	965	1115	1257
⊗ **43256**	Upper gastrointestinal endoscopy including esophagus, stomach, and either the duodenum and/or jejunum as appropriate; with transendoscopic stent placement (includes predilation)	6.51	230.04	778	890	994

● = New Code ⊗ = Conscious Sedation ✚ = Add-on Code ∅ = Modifier '51' Exempt ▲ =Revised Code

		Medicare RVU	National Fee	PFR Fee Information 50%	75%	90%
⊗ **43257**	Upper gastrointestinal endoscopy including esophagus, stomach, and either the duodenum and/or jejunum as appropriate; with delivery of thermal energy to the muscle of lower esophageal sphincter and/or gastric cardia, for treatment of gastroesophageal reflux disease	8.02	283.09	1266	1526	1819
	(A4550 (Disposable Surgical Tray) can be coded in addition to 43258 in the office setting. Payment is at carrier discretion.)					
⊗ **43258**	Upper gastrointestinal endoscopy including esophagus, stomach, and either the duodenum and/or jejunum as appropriate; with ablation of tumor(s), polyp(s), or other lesion(s) not amenable to removal by hot biopsy forceps, bipolar cautery or snare technique	6.81	240.65	989	1191	1378
⊗ **43259**	Upper gastrointestinal endoscopy including esophagus, stomach, and either the duodenum and/or jejunum as appropriate; with endoscopic ultrasound examination, including the esophagus, stomach, and either the duodenum and/or jejunum as appropriate	7.71	272.48	883	961	1131
	(UNBUNDLING ALERT: 43260 cannot be used with 43200, 43234, or 43235 by the same physician on the same day.)					
⊗ **43260**	Endoscopic retrograde cholangiopancreatography (ERCP); diagnostic, with or without collection of specimen(s) by brushing or washing (separate procedure)	8.87	313.41	1093	1241	1452
⊗ **43261**	Endoscopic retrograde cholangiopancreatography (ERCP); with biopsy, single or multiple	9.33	329.71	1269	1439	1581
	(UNBUNDLING ALERT: 43262 cannot be used with 43200, 43234, 43235, or 43260 by the same physician on the same day.)					
⊗ **43262**	Endoscopic retrograde cholangiopancreatography (ERCP); with sphincterotomy/papillotomy	10.95	386.93	1540	1801	2274
⊗ **43263**	Endoscopic retrograde cholangiopancreatography (ERCP); with pressure measurement of sphincter of Oddi (pancreatic duct or common bile duct)	10.84	383.14	1324	1654	1767
	(UNBUNDLING ALERT: 43264 cannot be used with 43200, 43215, 43234, 43235, or 43260 by the same physician on the same day.)					
⊗ **43264**	Endoscopic retrograde cholangiopancreatography (ERCP); with endoscopic retrograde removal of calculus/calculi from biliary and/or pancreatic ducts	13.15	464.62	1712	2057	2438
⊗ **43265**	Endoscopic retrograde cholangiopancreatography (ERCP); with endoscopic retrograde destruction, lithotripsy of calculus/calculi, any method	14.76	521.09	1577	1889	2186
⊗ **43267**	Endoscopic retrograde cholangiopancreatography (ERCP); with endoscopic retrograde insertion of nasobiliary or nasopancreatic drainage tube	10.93	386.18	1408	1684	1957
	(UNBUNDLING ALERT: 43268 cannot be used with 43200, 43234, 43235, or 43260 by the same physician on the same day.)					
⊗ **43268**	Endoscopic retrograde cholangiopancreatography (ERCP); with endoscopic retrograde insertion of tube or stent into bile or pancreatic duct	11.07	391.48	1553	1781	2103
⊗ **43269**	Endoscopic retrograde cholangiopancreatography (ERCP); with endoscopic retrograde removal of foreign body and/or change of tube or stent	12.15	429.38	1398	1626	1821
⊗ **43271**	Endoscopic retrograde cholangiopancreatography (ERCP); with endoscopic retrograde balloon dilation of ampulla, biliary and/or pancreatic duct(s)	10.95	386.93	1486	1813	2112
⊗ **43272**	Endoscopic retrograde cholangiopancreatography (ERCP); with ablation of tumor(s), polyp(s), or other lesion(s) not amenable to removal by hot biopsy forceps, bipolar cautery or snare technique	10.97	387.69	1237	1407	1568
Laparoscopy						
43280	Laparoscopy, surgical, esophagogastric fundoplasty (eg, Nissen, Toupet procedures)	27.41	970.18	3060	3490	3986
43289	Unlisted laparoscopy procedure, esophagus	-	-	IR	IR	IR
Repair						
43300	Esophagoplasty (plastic repair or reconstruction), cervical approach; without repair of tracheoesophageal fistula	16.41	586.65	2500	2877	3253
43305	Esophagoplasty (plastic repair or reconstruction), cervical approach; with repair of tracheoesophageal fistula	29.45	1047.49	3259	3639	4062
43310	Esophagoplasty (plastic repair or reconstruction), thoracic approach; without repair of tracheoesophageal fistula	40.61	1439.35	3826	4483	5037
43312	Esophagoplasty (plastic repair or reconstruction), thoracic approach; with repair of tracheoesophageal fistula	44.65	1580.70	4198	4829	5371
43313	Esophagoplasty for congenital defect (plastic repair or reconstruction), thoracic approach; without repair of congenital tracheoesophageal fistula	72.07	2547.47	6086	7252	8117
43314	Esophagoplasty for congenital defect (plastic repair or reconstruction), thoracic approach; with repair of congenital tracheoesophageal fistula	78.78	2782.81	6876	8020	8876
43320	Esophagogastrostomy (cardioplasty), with or without vagotomy and pyloroplasty, transabdominal or transthoracic approach	35.03	1239.25	3246	3677	4121
43324	Esophagogastric fundoplasty (eg, Nissen, Belsey IV, Hill procedures)	34.29	1212.34	3290	3692	3947
43325	Esophagogastric fundoplasty; with fundic patch (Thal-Nissen procedure)	33.75	1193.39	3023	3722	4461

● = New Code ⊗ = Conscious Sedation ✚ = Add-on Code ∅ = Modifier '51' Exempt ▲ =Revised Code

		Medicare RVU	National Fee	PFR Fee Information 50%	75%	90%
43326	Esophagogastric fundoplasty; with gastroplasty (eg, Collis)	34.30	1215.37	3366	3903	4347
43330	Esophagomyotomy (Heller type); abdominal approach	33.15	1172.17	2863	3497	4081
43331	Esophagomyotomy (Heller type); thoracic approach	35.59	1261.23	3002	3624	4136
43340	Esophagojejunostomy (without total gastrectomy); abdominal approach	34.31	1213.10	3225	3645	4474
43341	Esophagojejunostomy (without total gastrectomy); thoracic approach	37.05	1312.39	3579	4193	4624
43350	Esophagostomy, fistulization of esophagus, external; abdominal approach	29.07	1028.16	2231	2729	3026
43351	Esophagostomy, fistulization of esophagus, external; thoracic approach	34.08	1208.17	2274	2866	3339
43352	Esophagostomy, fistulization of esophagus, external; cervical approach	28.07	996.33	2115	2709	3207
43360	Gastrointestinal reconstruction for previous esophagectomy, for obstructing esophageal lesion or fistula, or for previous esophageal exclusion; with stomach, with or without pyloroplasty	60.13	2126.81	4600	5953	7323
43361	Gastrointestinal reconstruction for previous esophagectomy, for obstructing esophageal lesion or fistula, or for previous esophageal exclusion; with colon interposition or small intestine reconstruction, including intestine mobilization, preparation, and anastomosis(es)	66.88	2361.01	5718	6892	7718
43400	Ligation, direct, esophageal varices	37.94	1340.81	2942	3735	4402
43401	Transection of esophagus with repair, for esophageal varices	38.88	1373.03	2921	3646	4328
43405	Ligation or stapling at gastroesophageal junction for pre-existing esophageal perforation	37.17	1315.04	2953	3650	4506
43410	Suture of esophageal wound or injury; cervical approach	25.61	908.40	2290	2578	2852
43415	Suture of esophageal wound or injury; transthoracic or transabdominal approach	44.02	1558.72	2936	3671	4152
43420	Closure of esophagostomy or fistula; cervical approach	25.37	898.17	1846	2253	2636
43425	Closure of esophagostomy or fistula; transthoracic or transabdominal approach	38.01	1345.36	2566	3286	3972

Manipulation

		Medicare RVU	National Fee	50%	75%	90%
43450	Dilation of esophagus, by unguided sound or bougie, single or multiple passes	4.13	151.21	233	286	379
⊗ 43453	Dilation of esophagus, over guide wire	7.74	287.64	366	423	469
⊗ 43456	Dilation of esophagus, by balloon or dilator, retrograde	16.32	608.63	624	730	818
⊗ 43458	Dilation of esophagus with balloon (30 mm diameter or larger) for achalasia	10.02	367.98	584	739	1069
43460	Esophagogastric tamponade, with balloon (Sengstaaken type)	5.65	199.72	610	705	764

Other Procedures

		Medicare RVU	National Fee	50%	75%	90%
43496	Free jejunum transfer with microvascular anastomosis	-	-	4001	5020	5987
43499	Unlisted procedure, esophagus	-	-	IR	IR	IR

Stomach

Incision

		Medicare RVU	National Fee	50%	75%	90%
43500	Gastrotomy; with exploration or foreign body removal	19.20	679.12	1873	2206	2627
43501	Gastrotomy; with suture repair of bleeding ulcer	33.38	1179.37	2526	3248	3854
43502	Gastrotomy; with suture repair of pre-existing esophagogastric laceration (eg, Mallory-Weiss)	38.00	1342.71	2525	3202	3430
43510	Gastrotomy; with esophageal dilation and insertion of permanent intraluminal tube (eg, Celestin or Mousseaux-Barbin)	23.14	819.72	1869	2295	2642
43520	Pyloromyotomy, cutting of pyloric muscle (Fredet-Ramstedt type operation)	17.72	628.72	1760	1969	2172

Excision

		Medicare RVU	National Fee	50%	75%	90%
43600	Biopsy of stomach; by capsule, tube, peroral (one or more specimens)	2.75	97.02	254	304	343
43605	Biopsy of stomach; by laparotomy	20.54	726.50	1959	2347	2851
43610	Excision, local; ulcer or benign tumor of stomach	24.33	859.89	2293	2650	3100
43611	Excision, local; malignant tumor of stomach	30.17	1066.06	2497	3067	3591

● = New Code ⊗ = Conscious Sedation ✚ = Add-on Code ∅ = Modifier '51' Exempt ▲ =Revised Code

		Medicare RVU	National Fee	PFR Fee Information 50%	75%	90%
43620	Gastrectomy, total; with esophagoenterostomy	49.49	1746.32	4238	5077	5760
43621	Gastrectomy, total; with Roux-en-Y reconstruction	55.54	1954.75	4898	5625	6313
43622	Gastrectomy, total; with formation of intestinal pouch, any type	56.79	2000.23	4988	5748	6332
43631	Gastrectomy, partial, distal; with gastroduodenostomy	36.39	1286.24	3310	3693	4165
43632	Gastrectomy, partial, distal; with gastrojejunostomy	47.70	1674.31	3278	3905	4376
43633	Gastrectomy, partial, distal; with Roux-en-Y reconstruction	45.78	1609.13	3810	4201	4715
43634	Gastrectomy, partial, distal; with formation of intestinal pouch	50.37	1769.81	4644	5655	6451
	(UNBUNDLING ALERT: 43635 cannot be used with 38100, 38500, 43610, 43630, 43640, 43750, 43760, 43825, 43830, 43832, 43840, 43860, 44005, 44600, 44950, 49000, or 49255 by the same physician on the same day.)					
✚ 43635	Vagotomy when performed with partial distal gastrectomy (List separately in addition to code(s) for primary procedure)	2.99	105.36	1092	1292	1539
	(UNBUNDLING ALERT: 43640 cannot be used with 38100, 43750, 43760, 43825, 43920, 43832, 43840, 44005, 44300, 44950, 49000, 49255 by the same physician on the same day.)					
43640	Vagotomy including pyloroplasty, with or without gastrostomy; truncal or selective	28.97	1023.99	2694	3375	3769
43641	Vagotomy including pyloroplasty, with or without gastrostomy; parietal cell (highly selective)	29.38	1038.39	2919	3302	3571

Laparoscopy

		Medicare RVU	National Fee	50%	75%	90%
43644	Laparoscopy, surgical, gastric restrictive procedure; with gastric bypass and Roux-en-Y gastroenterostomy (roux limb 150 cm or less)	43.37	1532.20	5077	6124	7162
43645	Laparoscopy, surgical, gastric restrictive procedure; with gastric bypass and small intestine reconstruction to limit absorption	46.70	1650.06	5475	6389	7508
● 43647	Laparoscopy, surgical; implantation or replacement of gastric neurostimulator electrodes, antrum	-	-	IR	IR	IR
● 43648	Laparoscopy, surgical; revision or removal of gastric neurostimulator electrodes, antrum	-	-	IR	IR	IR
43651	Laparoscopy, surgical; transection of vagus nerves, truncal	16.19	574.91	1750	2145	2528
43652	Laparoscopy, surgical; transection of vagus nerves, selective or highly selective	19.29	684.81	2482	2862	3405
43653	Laparoscopy, surgical; gastrostomy, without construction of gastric tube (eg, Stamm procedure) (separate procedure)	13.62	484.33	1698	2001	2386
43659	Unlisted laparoscopy procedure, stomach	-	-	IR	IR	IR

Introduction

		Medicare RVU	National Fee	50%	75%	90%
	(UNBUNDLING ALERT: 43750 cannot be used with 43234 or 43760 by the same physician on the same day.)					
⊗ 43750	Percutaneous placement of gastrostomy tube	7.17	254.29	1040	1257	1566
	(See also HCPCS code G0272 for Naso/orogastric tube placement, requiring physician skill and fluoroscopic guidance (includes fluoroscopy ima)					
43752	Naso- or oro-gastric tube placement, requiring physician's skill and fluoroscopic guidance (includes fluoroscopy, image documentation and report)	1.08	37.90	175	289	381
43760	Change of gastrostomy tube	5.96	221.70	194	243	295
43761	Repositioning of the gastric feeding tube, any method, through the duodenum for enteric nutrition	3.25	115.59	288	362	420

Bariatric Surgery

		Medicare RVU	National Fee	50%	75%	90%
43770	Laparoscopy, surgical, gastric restrictive procedure; placement of adjustable gastric band (gastric band and subcutaneous port components)	27.69	981.17	3170	3699	4348
43771	Laparoscopy, surgical, gastric restrictive procedure; revision of adjustable gastric band component only	31.67	1121.39	3650	4259	5006
43772	Laparoscopy, surgical, gastric restrictive procedure; removal of adjustable gastric band component only	23.86	844.74	2782	3246	3815
43773	Laparoscopy, surgical, gastric restrictive procedure; removal and replacement of adjustable gastric band component only	31.68	1121.77	3651	4261	5007
43774	Laparoscopy, surgical, gastric restrictive procedure; removal of adjustable gastric band and subcutaneous port components	23.97	848.53	2789	3254	3825

Other Procedures

		Medicare RVU	National Fee	50%	75%	90%
43800	Pyloroplasty	23.06	815.55	2148	2315	2642
43810	Gastroduodenostomy	24.94	881.12	2221	2765	3132

© PFR 2007

● = New Code   ⊗ = Conscious Sedation   ✚ = Add-on Code   ∅ = Modifier '51' Exempt   ▲ =Revised Code

		Medicare RVU	National Fee	PFR Fee Information 50%	75%	90%
43820	Gastrojejunostomy; without vagotomy	31.28	1100.16	2430	2830	3269
43825	Gastrojejunostomy; with vagotomy, any type	32.16	1136.17	2905	3378	3816
	(UNBUNDLING ALERT: 43830 cannot be used with 43750 or 43760 by the same physician on the same day.)					
43830	Gastrostomy, open; without construction of gastric tube (eg, Stamm procedure) (separate procedure)	16.93	600.68	1751	2181	2401
43831	Gastrostomy, open; neonatal, for feeding	14.08	501.76	1573	1709	1860
	(UNBUNDLING ALERT: 43832 cannot be used with 38500, 43750, 43760, 43830, 44005, or 44300 by the same physician on the same day.)					
43832	Gastrostomy, open; with construction of gastric tube (eg, Janeway procedure)	26.16	925.46	2221	2732	3219
	(UNBUNDLING ALERT: 43840 cannot be used with 38500, 43750, 43760, 44005, 44600, 44950, 49000, 49010, or 49255 by the same physician on the same day.)					
43840	Gastrorrhaphy, suture of perforated duodenal or gastric ulcer, wound, or injury	31.89	1122.14	2132	2663	3100
43842	Gastric restrictive procedure, without gastric bypass, for morbid obesity; vertical-banded gastroplasty	30.88	1090.69	3483	3956	4270
43843	Gastric restrictive procedure, without gastric bypass, for morbid obesity; other than vertical-banded gastroplasty	31.31	1106.23	3499	3990	4264
43845	Gastric restrictive procedure with partial gastrectomy, pylorus-preserving duodenoileostomy and ileoileostomy (50 to 100 cm common channel) to limit absorption (biliopancreatic diversion with duodenal switch)	48.37	1706.90	5134	6650	8056
43846	Gastric restrictive procedure, with gastric bypass for morbid obesity; with short limb (150 cm or less) Roux-en-Y gastroenterostomy	40.45	1429.11	4592	5651	6919
43847	Gastric restrictive procedure, with gastric bypass for morbid obesity; with small intestine reconstruction to limit absorption	44.50	1571.61	5097	6398	8097
43848	Revision, open, of gastric restrictive procedure for morbid obesity, other than adjustable gastric band (separate procedure)	48.15	1700.46	4440	5604	6436
43850	Revision of gastroduodenal anastomosis (gastroduodenostomy) with reconstruction; without vagotomy	40.45	1428.36	3103	4200	5004
43855	Revision of gastroduodenal anastomosis (gastroduodenostomy) with reconstruction; with vagotomy	42.22	1491.27	3560	4214	4682
43860	Revision of gastrojejunal anastomosis (gastrojejunostomy) with reconstruction, with or without partial gastrectomy or intestine resection; without vagotomy	40.92	1445.03	3236	4209	4960
43865	Revision of gastrojejunal anastomosis (gastrojejunostomy) with reconstruction, with or without partial gastrectomy or intestine resection; with vagotomy	42.84	1513.25	3463	4275	5200
43870	Closure of gastrostomy, surgical	17.27	611.29	1491	1720	2248
43880	Closure of gastrocolic fistula	40.08	1415.85	2736	3360	3727
● 43881	Implantation or replacement of gastric neurostimulator electrodes, antrum, open	-	-	IR	IR	IR
● 43882	Revision or removal of gastric neurostimulator electrodes, antrum, open	-	-	IR	IR	IR
43886	Gastric restrictive procedure, open; revision of subcutaneous port component only	7.98	284.99	685	852	1018
43887	Gastric restrictive procedure, open; removal of subcutaneous port component only	7.56	270.21	671	835	998
43888	Gastric restrictive procedure, open; removal and replacement of subcutaneous port component only	10.83	386.18	951	1184	1416
43999	Unlisted procedure, stomach	-	-	IR	IR	IR

Intestines (Except Rectum)

Incision

	(UNBUNDLING ALERT: 44005 cannot be used with 38500, 44950, 49000, or 49255 by the same physician on the same day.)					
44005	Enterolysis (freeing of intestinal adhesion) (separate procedure)	27.22	961.46	2383	2702	3165
44010	Duodenotomy, for exploration, biopsy(s), or foreign body removal	21.29	752.64	2229	2616	3167
✚ 44015	Tube or needle catheter jejunostomy for enteral alimentation, intraoperative, any method (List separately in addition to primary procedure)	3.80	134.16	1123	1445	1995
44020	Enterotomy, small intestine, other than duodenum; for exploration, biopsy(s), or foreign body removal	23.96	846.63	2197	2579	2955
44021	Enterotomy, small intestine, other than duodenum; for decompression (eg, Baker tube)	24.15	853.45	2046	2462	2898
44025	Colotomy, for exploration, biopsy(s), or foreign body removal	24.39	861.79	2303	2769	3060
44050	Reduction of volvulus, intussusception, internal hernia, by laparotomy	23.23	821.62	2080	2614	3203

● = New Code ⊗ = Conscious Sedation ✚ = Add-on Code ∅ = Modifier '51' Exempt ▲ =Revised Code

		Medicare RVU	National Fee	PFR Fee Information 50%	75%	90%
44055	Correction of malrotation by lysis of duodenal bands and/or reduction of midgut volvulus (eg, Ladd procedure)	37.12	1309.36	2683	3154	3646

Excision

44100	Biopsy of intestine by capsule, tube, peroral (one or more specimens)	2.94	103.84	419	477	535
44110	Excision of one or more lesions of small or large intestine not requiring anastomosis, exteriorization, or fistulization; single enterotomy	20.82	735.97	2237	2575	2891
44111	Excision of one or more lesions of small or large intestine not requiring anastomosis, exteriorization, or fistulization; multiple enterotomies	24.43	863.31	2991	3285	3831
	(UNBUNDLING ALERT: 44120 cannot be used with 38500, 44005, 44020, 44130, 44600, 44950, 49000, or 49255 by the same physician on the same day.)					
44120	Enterectomy, resection of small intestine; single resection and anastomosis	30.10	1061.51	2816	3346	3731
✚ 44121	Enterectomy, resection of small intestine; each additional resection and anastomosis (List separately in addition to code for primary procedure)	6.45	227.38	909	1159	1702
44125	Enterectomy, resection of small intestine; with enterostomy	29.41	1038.77	3030	3653	4215
44126	Enterectomy, resection of small intestine for congenital atresia, single resection and anastomosis of proximal segment of intestine; without tapering	60.77	2142.72	5565	6544	7998
44127	Enterectomy, resection of small intestine for congenital atresia, single resection and anastomosis of proximal segment of intestine; with tapering	70.34	2478.50	6556	7334	8935
✚ 44128	Enterectomy, resection of small intestine for congenital atresia, single resection and anastomosis of proximal segment of intestine; each additional resection and anastomosis (List separately in addition to code for primary procedure)	6.46	227.76	790	883	1077
	(UNBUNDLING ALERT: 44130 cannot be used with 44005, 44600, 44950, 49000, or 49255 by the same physician on the same day.)					
44130	Enteroenterostomy, anastomosis of intestine, with or without cutaneous enterostomy (separate procedure)	30.52	1072.88	2730	2919	3293
44132	Donor enterectomy (including cold preservation), open; from cadaver donor	-	-	IR	IR	IR
44133	Donor enterectomy (including cold preservation), open; partial, from living donor	-	-	IR	IR	IR
44135	Intestinal allotransplantation; from cadaver donor	-	-	IR	IR	IR
44136	Intestinal allotransplantation; from living donor	-	-	IR	IR	IR
44137	Removal of transplanted intestinal allograft, complete	-	-	IR	IR	IR
✚ 44139	Mobilization (take-down) of splenic flexure performed in conjunction with partial colectomy (List separately in addition to primary procedure)	3.22	113.69	463	571	707
	(UNBUNDLING ALERT: 44140 cannot be used with 38500, 44005, 44130, 44600, 44950, 49000, 49010, or 49255 by the same physician on the same day.)					
44140	Colectomy, partial; with anastomosis	33.69	1191.12	3069	3414	3747
	(UNBUNDLING ALERT: 44141 cannot be used with 38500, 44005, 44140, 44320, 44600, 44950, 49000, 49010, or 49255 by the same physician on the same day.)					
44141	Colectomy, partial; with skin level cecostomy or colostomy	42.79	1508.32	3153	3728	4290
	(UNBUNDLING ALERT: 44143 cannot be used with 38500, 44005, 44600, 44950, 49000, 49010, or 49255 by the same physician on the same day.)					
44143	Colectomy, partial; with end colostomy and closure of distal segment (Hartmann type procedure)	41.28	1459.05	3205	3610	4038
	(UNBUNDLING ALERT: 44144 cannot be used with 38500, 44005, 44141, 44320, 44600, 44950, 49000, 49010, or 49255 by the same physician on the same day.)					
44144	Colectomy, partial; with resection, with colostomy or ileostomy and creation of mucofistula	42.49	1496.95	3317	3902	4472
	(UNBUNDLING ALERT: 44145 cannot be used with 38500, 44005, 44140, 44600, 44950, 49000, 49010, or 49255 by the same physician on the same day.)					
44145	Colectomy, partial; with coloproctostomy (low pelvic anastomosis)	42.24	1492.40	3606	4114	4613
44146	Colectomy, partial; with coloproctostomy (low pelvic anastomosis), with colostomy	51.54	1819.08	3941	4710	5436
44147	Colectomy, partial; abdominal and transanal approach	45.39	1592.07	4248	4777	5306
	(UNBUNDLING ALERT: 44150 cannot be used with 38500, 44005, 44130, 44140, 44141, 44144, 44600, 44950, 49000, 49010, or 49255 by the same physician on the same day.)					
44150	Colectomy, total, abdominal, without proctectomy; with ileostomy or ileoproctostomy	45.22	1599.27	3992	4757	5282
44151	Colectomy, total, abdominal, without proctectomy; with continent ileostomy	51.79	1830.45	4776	5571	6305
44155	Colectomy, total, abdominal, with proctectomy; with ileostomy	50.88	1797.86	4860	5868	6850
44156	Colectomy, total, abdominal, with proctectomy; with continent ileostomy	56.15	1985.83	5183	6302	7540

● = New Code ⊗ = Conscious Sedation ✚ = Add-on Code ∅ = Modifier '51' Exempt ▲ =Revised Code

		Medicare RVU	National Fee	PFR Fee Information 50%	75%	90%
● 44157	Colectomy, total, abdominal, with proctectomy; with ileoanal anastomosis, includes loop ileostomy, and rectal mucosectomy, when performed	55.09	1952.48	4943	5848	6701
● 44158	Colectomy, total, abdominal, with proctectomy; with ileoanal anastomosis, creation of ileal reservoir (S or J), includes loop ileostomy, and rectal mucosectomy, when performed	56.52	2002.88	5072	6000	6875
	(UNBUNDLING ALERT: 44160 cannot be used with 38500, 44005, 44140, 44141, 44144, 44600, 44950, 49000, 49010, or 49255 by the same physician on the same day.)					
44160	Colectomy, partial, with removal of terminal ileum with ileocolostomy	30.85	1089.93	3444	4099	4752

Laparoscopy

44180	Laparoscopy, surgical, enterolysis (freeing of intestinal adhesion) (separate procedure)	23.14	818.96	2212	2687	3066

Enterostomy-External Fistulization of Intestines

44186	Laparoscopy, surgical; jejunostomy (eg, for decompression or feeding)	16.27	577.18	1540	1871	2135
44187	Laparoscopy, surgical; ileostomy or jejunostomy, non-tube	27.48	975.48	2545	3091	3528
44188	Laparoscopy, surgical, colostomy or skin level cecostomy	30.26	1073.64	2792	3391	3870

Excision

44202	Laparoscopy, surgical; enterectomy, resection of small intestine, single resection and anastomosis	34.89	1233.56	3227	3963	4185
✚ 44203	Laparoscopy, surgical; each additional small intestine resection and anastomosis (List separately in addition to code for primary procedure)	6.42	226.25	768	1018	1394
44204	Laparoscopy, surgical; colectomy, partial, with anastomosis	39.11	1382.12	3202	4090	4426
44205	Laparoscopy, surgical; colectomy, partial, with removal of terminal ileum with ileocolostomy	34.21	1209.31	2971	3566	4358
44206	Laparoscopy, surgical; colectomy, partial, with end colostomy and closure of distal segment (Hartmann type procedure)	44.17	1561.00	4125	4886	5392
44207	Laparoscopy, surgical; colectomy, partial, with anastomosis, with coloproctostomy (low pelvic anastomosis)	46.63	1645.89	4515	5347	5902
44208	Laparoscopy, surgical; colectomy, partial, with anastomosis, with coloproctostomy (low pelvic anastomosis) with colostomy	50.63	1789.52	4881	5782	6382
44210	Laparoscopy, surgical; colectomy, total, abdominal, without proctectomy, with ileostomy or ileoproctostomy	45.02	1592.07	4322	5119	5650
▲ 44211	Laparoscopy, surgical; colectomy, total, abdominal, with proctectomy, with ileoanal anastomosis, creation of ileal reservoir (S or J), with loop ileostomy, includes rectal mucosectomy, when performed	55.51	1963.09	5529	6548	7227
44212	Laparoscopy, surgical; colectomy, total, abdominal, with proctectomy, with ileostomy	51.73	1829.31	5065	5999	6622
✚ 44213	Laparoscopy, surgical, mobilization (take-down) of splenic flexure performed in conjunction with partial colectomy (List separately in addition to primary procedure)	5.08	179.26	507	616	703

Repair

44227	Laparoscopy, surgical, closure of enterostomy, large or small intestine, with resection and anastomosis	42.23	1491.65	3940	4786	5462

Other Procedures

44238	Unlisted laparoscopy procedure, intestine (except rectum)	-	-	IR	IR	IR

Enterostomy-External Fistulization of Intestines

44300	Enterostomy or cecostomy, tube (eg, for decompression or feeding) (separate procedure)	20.76	734.83	1834	2153	2857
44310	Ileostomy or jejunostomy, non-tube	26.11	922.80	2144	2738	3241
44312	Revision of ileostomy; simple (release of superficial scar) (separate procedure)	14.41	510.48	1108	1412	1820
44314	Revision of ileostomy; complicated (reconstruction in-depth) (separate procedure)	24.99	883.77	2233	2714	3224
44316	Continent ileostomy (Kock procedure) (separate procedure)	34.58	1221.06	3232	3766	4286
	(UNBUNDLING ALERT: 44320 cannot be used with 38500, 44005, 44300, 44950, 49000, or 49255 by the same physician on the same day.)					
44320	Colostomy or skin level cecostomy;	29.66	1048.62	2004	2536	3011
44322	Colostomy or skin level cecostomy; with multiple biopsies (eg, for congenital megacolon) (separate procedure)	23.47	839.43	2188	2552	3312
44340	Revision of colostomy; simple (release of superficial scar) (separate procedure)	14.55	516.54	774	927	1045
44345	Revision of colostomy; complicated (reconstruction in-depth) (separate procedure)	25.93	917.50	1782	2136	2473

● = New Code ⊗ = Conscious Sedation ✚ = Add-on Code ∅ = Modifier '51' Exempt ▲ =Revised Code

		Medicare RVU	National Fee	PFR Fee Information 50%	75%	90%
44346	Revision of colostomy; with repair of paracolostomy hernia (separate procedure)	29.03	1025.89	1983	2365	2823

Endoscopy, Small Intestine and Stomal

		Medicare RVU	National Fee	50%	75%	90%
⊗ 44360	Small intestinal endoscopy, enteroscopy beyond second portion of duodenum, not including ileum; diagnostic, with or without collection of specimen(s) by brushing or washing (separate procedure)	3.99	141.36	799	887	1082
⊗ 44361	Small intestinal endoscopy, enteroscopy beyond second portion of duodenum, not including ileum; with biopsy, single or multiple	4.40	155.76	836	1019	1177
⊗ 44363	Small intestinal endoscopy, enteroscopy beyond second portion of duodenum, not including ileum; with removal of foreign body	5.29	187.21	842	1027	1162
⊗ 44364	Small intestinal endoscopy, enteroscopy beyond second portion of duodenum, not including ileum; with removal of tumor(s), polyp(s), or other lesion(s) by snare technique	5.63	198.96	941	1101	1254
⊗ 44365	Small intestinal endoscopy, enteroscopy beyond second portion of duodenum, not including ileum; with removal of tumor(s), polyp(s), or other lesion(s) by hot biopsy forceps or bipolar cautery	5.02	177.74	948	1109	1288
⊗ 44366	Small intestinal endoscopy, enteroscopy beyond second portion of duodenum, not including ileum; with control of bleeding (eg, injection, bipolar cautery, unipolar cautery, laser, heater probe, stapler, plasma coagulator)	6.62	234.21	1088	1334	1459
⊗ 44369	Small intestinal endoscopy, enteroscopy beyond second portion of duodenum, not including ileum; with ablation of tumor(s), polyp(s), or other lesion(s) not amenable to removal by hot biopsy forceps, bipolar cautery or snare technique	6.75	238.75	1075	1225	1415
⊗ 44370	Small intestinal endoscopy, enteroscopy beyond second portion of duodenum, not including ileum; with transendoscopic stent placement (includes predilation)	7.28	257.70	828	1039	1245
⊗ 44372	Small intestinal endoscopy, enteroscopy beyond second portion of duodenum, not including ileum; with placement of percutaneous jejunostomy tube	6.59	233.07	940	1275	1468
⊗ 44373	Small intestinal endoscopy, enteroscopy beyond second portion of duodenum, not including ileum; with conversion of percutaneous gastrostomy tube to percutaneous jejunostomy tube	5.26	186.08	882	1032	1171
⊗ 44376	Small intestinal endoscopy, enteroscopy beyond second portion of duodenum, including ileum; diagnostic, with or without collection of specimen(s) by brushing or washing (separate procedure)	7.81	275.89	898	1184	1334
⊗ 44377	Small intestinal endoscopy, enteroscopy beyond second portion of duodenum, including ileum; with biopsy, single or multiple	8.23	290.67	1078	1145	1280
⊗ 44378	Small intestinal endoscopy, enteroscopy beyond second portion of duodenum, including ileum; with control of bleeding (eg, injection, bipolar cautery, unipolar cautery, laser, heater probe, stapler, plasma coagulator)	10.56	372.91	1338	1609	1690
⊗ 44379	Small intestinal endoscopy, enteroscopy beyond second portion of duodenum, including ileum; with transendoscopic stent placement (includes predilation)	11.10	392.24	1186	1468	1657
⊗ 44380	Ileoscopy, through stoma; diagnostic, with or without collection of specimen(s) by brushing or washing (separate procedure)	1.73	61.39	527	607	696
⊗ 44382	Ileoscopy, through stoma; with biopsy, single or multiple	2.06	73.14	627	716	936
⊗ 44383	Ileoscopy, through stoma; with transendoscopic stent placement (includes predilation)	4.51	159.55	717	892	1017
⊗ 44385	Endoscopic evaluation of small intestinal (abdominal or pelvic) pouch; diagnostic, with or without collection of specimen(s) by brushing or washing (separate procedure)	5.70	209.19	645	760	846
⊗ 44386	Endoscopic evaluation of small intestinal (abdominal or pelvic) pouch; with biopsy, single or multiple	8.98	332.36	731	843	965
⊗ 44388	Colonoscopy through stoma; diagnostic, with or without collection of specimen(s) by brushing or washing (separate procedure)	8.42	308.49	763	907	1140
⊗ 44389	Colonoscopy through stoma; with biopsy, single or multiple	10.13	372.15	827	1099	1316
⊗ 44390	Colonoscopy through stoma; with removal of foreign body	11.46	419.90	921	1035	1118
⊗ 44391	Colonoscopy through stoma; with control of bleeding (eg, injection, bipolar cautery, unipolar cautery, laser, heater probe, stapler, plasma coagulator)	13.43	492.67	1053	1325	1503
⊗ 44392	Colonoscopy through stoma; with removal of tumor(s), polyp(s), or other lesion(s) by hot biopsy forceps or bipolar cautery	10.93	399.82	1172	1333	1612
⊗ 44393	Colonoscopy through stoma; with ablation of tumor(s), polyp(s), or other lesion(s) not amenable to removal by hot biopsy forceps, bipolar cautery or snare technique	12.39	450.98	1238	1348	1540
⊗ 44394	Colonoscopy through stoma; with removal of tumor(s), polyp(s), or other lesion(s) by snare technique	12.77	467.28	1045	1313	1545
⊗ 44397	Colonoscopy through stoma; with transendoscopic stent placement (includes predilation)	7.02	248.23	1001	1468	1947

Introduction

		Medicare RVU	National Fee	50%	75%	90%
∅ 44500	Introduction of long gastrointestinal tube (eg, Miller-Abbott) (separate procedure)	0.68	23.88	112	141	163

● = New Code ⊗ = Conscious Sedation ✚ = Add-on Code ∅ = Modifier '51' Exempt ▲ =Revised Code

		Medicare RVU	National Fee	PFR Fee Information 50%	75%	90%

Repair

44602	Suture of small intestine (enterorrhaphy) for perforated ulcer, diverticulum, wound, injury or rupture; single perforation	33.48	1174.82	2116	2409	2825
44603	Suture of small intestine (enterorrhaphy) for perforated ulcer, diverticulum, wound, injury or rupture; multiple perforations	38.17	1339.68	2505	2923	3381
44604	Suture of large intestine (colorrhaphy) for perforated ulcer, diverticulum, wound, injury or rupture (single or multiple perforations); without colostomy	26.55	937.21	2441	2887	3545
44605	Suture of large intestine (colorrhaphy) for perforated ulcer, diverticulum, wound, injury or rupture (single or multiple perforations); with colostomy	32.80	1159.28	2600	3082	3557
44615	Intestinal stricturoplasty (enterotomy and enterorrhaphy) with or without dilation, for intestinal obstruction	26.81	947.06	2439	2908	3415
44620	Closure of enterostomy, large or small intestine;	21.24	750.37	1823	2195	2672
	(UNBUNDLING ALERT: 44625 cannot be used with 44005, 44620, or 49000 by the same physician on the same day.)					
44625	Closure of enterostomy, large or small intestine; with resection and anastomosis other than colorectal	25.34	894.76	2639	3110	3523
44626	Closure of enterostomy, large or small intestine; with resection and colorectal anastomosis (eg, closure of Hartmann type procedure)	40.70	1436.32	3155	3943	4842
44640	Closure of intestinal cutaneous fistula	35.36	1247.96	2202	2468	3147
44650	Closure of enteroenteric or enterocolic fistula	36.73	1296.47	2408	3008	3588
44660	Closure of enterovesical fistula; without intestinal or bladder resection	34.67	1222.95	2313	2841	3159
44661	Closure of enterovesical fistula; with intestine and/or bladder resection	39.61	1397.28	3624	4022	4859
44680	Intestinal plication (separate procedure)	26.36	930.76	2720	3085	3345

Other Procedures

44700	Exclusion of small intestine from pelvis by mesh or other prosthesis, or native tissue (eg, bladder or omentum)	25.81	911.81	2548	2786	3048
✛ 44701	Intraoperative colonic lavage (List separately in addition to code for primary procedure)	4.46	157.27	448	490	536
44715	Backbench standard preparation of cadaver or living donor intestine allograft prior to transplantation, including mobilization and fashioning of the superior mesenteric artery and vein	-	-	IR	IR	IR
44720	Backbench reconstruction of cadaver or living donor intestine allograft prior to transplantation; venous anastomosis, each	6.97	245.20	728	795	870
44721	Backbench reconstruction of cadaver or living donor intestine allograft prior to transplantation; arterial anastomosis, each	10.22	360.78	1065	1163	1274
44799	Unlisted procedure, intestine	-	-	IR	IR	IR

Meckel's Diverticulum and The Mesentery
Excision

44800	Excision of Meckel's diverticulum (diverticulectomy) or omphalomesenteric duct	18.83	668.13	1799	2154	2667
44820	Excision of lesion of mesentery (separate procedure)	20.74	734.07	1837	2054	2641

Suture

44850	Suture of mesentery (separate procedure)	18.43	652.59	1710	2046	2326

Other Procedures

44899	Unlisted procedure, Meckel's diverticulum and the mesentery	-	-	IR	IR	IR

Appendix
Incision

44900	Incision and drainage of appendiceal abscess; open	18.55	655.63	1363	1619	1884
	(Medicare fees for the code below are based on Non Facility RVUs. PFR information reflects fee when procedure is performed in a facility.)					
⊗ 44901	Incision and drainage of appendiceal abscess; percutaneous	29.20	1093.72	620	711	809

● = New Code ⊗ = Conscious Sedation ✛ = Add-on Code ∅ = Modifier '51' Exempt ▲ =Revised Code

	Medicare RVU	National Fee	PFR Fee Information		
			50%	**75%**	**90%**

Excision

(The ICD-9-CM code must indicate that the appendix has not ruptured, code 541.)

(Code 44950 cannot be reported when a normal appendix is removed at the time of another major abdominal procedure. This is considered an incidental appendectomy and is not coded separately.)

44950 Appendectomy;	16.08	569.22	1560	1843	2075

(UNBUNDLING ALERT: 44955 cannot be used with 44950 by the same physician on the same day.)

✚ 44955 Appendectomy; when done for indicated purpose at time of other major procedure (not as separate procedure) (List separately in addition to code for primary procedure)	2.24	79.21	880	1100	1225

(UNBUNDLING ALERT: 44960 cannot be used with 44950 by the same physician on the same day.)

(The ICD-9-CM code must indicate that the appendix has ruptured, 540.0.)

44960 Appendectomy; for ruptured appendix with abscess or generalized peritonitis	21.38	755.30	1992	2423	3166

Laparoscopy

44970 Laparoscopy, surgical, appendectomy	14.60	517.68	1887	2211	2831
44979 Unlisted laparoscopy procedure, appendix	-	-	IR	IR	IR

Rectum

Incision

45000 Transrectal drainage of pelvic abscess	9.82	348.66	738	910	1090
45005 Incision and drainage of submucosal abscess, rectum	6.27	230.04	426	581	750
45020 Incision and drainage of deep supralevator, pelvirectal, or retrorectal abscess	12.56	443.78	806	958	1147

(See also 46050, 46060.)

Excision

45100 Biopsy of anorectal wall, anal approach (eg, congenital megacolon)	6.88	245.58	667	752	821
45108 Anorectal myomectomy	8.47	301.66	1121	1221	1434

(UNBUNDLING ALERT: 45110 cannot be used with 38500, 44005, 44141, 44143, 44144, 44145, 44146, 44150, 44155, 44160, 44320, 44345, 44600, 44620, 44625, 44950, 45170, 45180, 49000, 49010, 49255 by the same physician on the same day.)

45110 Proctectomy; complete, combined abdominoperineal, with colostomy	46.22	1634.90	4208	4928	5689
45111 Proctectomy; partial resection of rectum, transabdominal approach	27.09	958.43	3081	3739	4332
45112 Proctectomy, combined abdominoperineal, pull-through procedure (eg, colo-anal anastomosis)	47.91	1689.85	4245	5088	5725
45113 Proctectomy, partial, with rectal mucosectomy, ileoanal anastomosis, creation of ileal reservoir (S or J), with or without loop ileostomy	48.94	1728.50	4573	5780	6874
45114 Proctectomy, partial, with anastomosis; abdominal and transsacral approach	44.75	1579.19	3864	4856	5355
45116 Proctectomy, partial, with anastomosis; transsacral approach only (Kraske type)	40.32	1423.05	3224	3944	4604
45119 Proctectomy, combined abdominoperineal pull-through procedure (eg, colo-anal anastomosis), with creation of colonic reservoir (eg, J-pouch), with diverting enterostomy when performed	49.00	1729.64	4502	5243	6192
45120 Proctectomy, complete (for congenital megacolon), abdominal and perineal approach; with pull-through procedure and anastomosis (eg, Swenson, Duhamel, or Soave type operation)	39.11	1382.12	4168	5438	6352
45121 Proctectomy, complete (for congenital megacolon), abdominal and perineal approach; with subtotal or total colectomy, with multiple biopsies	43.09	1522.72	4114	5224	5866
45123 Proctectomy, partial, without anastomosis, perineal approach	27.48	970.18	2733	3225	3692
45126 Pelvic exenteration for colorectal malignancy, with proctectomy (with or without colostomy), with removal of bladder and ureteral transplantations, and/or hysterectomy, or cervicectomy, with or without removal of tube(s), with or without removal of ovary(s), or any combination thereof	71.97	2541.03	6550	7704	8607
45130 Excision of rectal procidentia, with anastomosis; perineal approach	26.94	950.85	2578	3152	3583
45135 Excision of rectal procidentia, with anastomosis; abdominal and perineal approach	33.16	1172.17	3698	4260	4935
45136 Excision of ileoanal reservoir with ileostomy	45.82	1619.74	4018	4799	5458
45150 Division of stricture of rectum	9.46	336.53	1035	1283	1545

		Medicare RVU	National Fee	PFR Fee Information 50%	75%	90%
45160	Excision of rectal tumor by proctotomy, transsacral or transcoccygeal approach	24.48	865.96	2628	2962	3376
45170	Excision of rectal tumor, transanal approach	19.11	676.47	1322	1623	2150

Destruction

45190	Destruction of rectal tumor (eg, electrodessication, electrosurgery, laser ablation, laser resection, cryosurgery) transanal approach	16.29	577.94	1296	1493	1637

Endoscopy

(UNBUNDLING ALERT: 45300 cannot be used with 46600 by the same physician on the same day.)

45300	Proctosigmoidoscopy, rigid; diagnostic, with or without collection of specimen(s) by brushing or washing (separate procedure)	2.05	76.17	136	169	234

(Medicare fees for the code below are based on Non Facility RVUs. PFR information reflects fee when procedure is performed in a facility.)

⊗ 45303	Proctosigmoidoscopy, rigid; with dilation (eg, balloon, guide wire, bougie)	19.35	731.80	191	220	257
⊗ 45305	Proctosigmoidoscopy, rigid; with biopsy, single or multiple	3.90	144.01	212	310	386
⊗ 45307	Proctosigmoidoscopy, rigid; with removal of foreign body	4.15	153.86	351	401	499
⊗ 45308	Proctosigmoidoscopy, rigid; with removal of single tumor, polyp, or other lesion by hot biopsy forceps or bipolar cautery	3.23	119.38	376	413	492
⊗ 45309	Proctosigmoidoscopy, rigid; with removal of single tumor, polyp, or other lesion by snare technique	5.28	192.52	376	439	556
⊗ 45315	Proctosigmoidoscopy, rigid; with removal of multiple tumors, polyps, or other lesions by hot biopsy forceps, bipolar cautery or snare technique	4.59	168.64	494	597	692
⊗ 45317	Proctosigmoidoscopy, rigid; with control of bleeding (eg, injection, bipolar cautery, unipolar cautery, laser, heater probe, stapler, plasma coagulator)	4.34	158.79	483	585	677
⊗ 45320	Proctosigmoidoscopy, rigid; with ablation of tumor(s), polyp(s), or other lesion(s) not amenable to removal by hot biopsy forceps, bipolar cautery or snare technique (eg, laser)	4.91	180.01	441	645	728
⊗ 45321	Proctosigmoidoscopy, rigid; with decompression of volvulus	1.88	66.70	407	535	632
⊗ 45327	Proctosigmoidoscopy, rigid; with transendoscopic stent placement (includes predilation)	2.53	89.44	266	386	478

(UNBUNDLING ALERT: 45330 cannot be used with 45300 or 46600 by the same physician on the same day.)

(See also HCPCS code G0104 for colorectal cancer screening; flexible sigmoidoscopy.)

45330	Sigmoidoscopy, flexible; diagnostic, with or without collection of specimen(s) by brushing or washing (separate procedure)	3.37	123.92	246	296	371

(UNBUNDLING ALERT: 45331 cannot be used with 45300, 45305 or 45330 by the same physician on the same day.)

45331	Sigmoidoscopy, flexible; with biopsy, single or multiple	4.35	160.31	336	403	479
⊗ 45332	Sigmoidoscopy, flexible; with removal of foreign body	7.10	262.25	419	513	590
⊗ 45333	Sigmoidoscopy, flexible; with removal of tumor(s), polyp(s), or other lesion(s) by hot biopsy forceps or bipolar cautery	7.00	258.46	520	668	790
⊗ 45334	Sigmoidoscopy, flexible; with control of bleeding (eg, injection, bipolar cautery, unipolar cautery, laser, heater probe, stapler, plasma coagulator)	4.17	147.80	583	660	770
⊗ 45335	Sigmoidoscopy, flexible; with directed submucosal injection(s), any substance	5.31	195.55	419	508	590
⊗ 45337	Sigmoidoscopy, flexible; with decompression of volvulus, any method	3.63	128.47	639	804	870
⊗ 45338	Sigmoidoscopy, flexible; with removal of tumor(s), polyp(s), or other lesion(s) by snare technique	7.90	290.29	543	649	795
⊗ 45339	Sigmoidoscopy, flexible; with ablation of tumor(s), polyp(s), or other lesion(s) not amenable to removal by hot biopsy forceps, bipolar cautery or snare technique	7.43	269.45	628	770	905
⊗ 45340	Sigmoidoscopy, flexible; with dilation by balloon, 1 or more strictures	9.22	342.21	670	810	945
⊗ 45341	Sigmoidoscopy, flexible; with endoscopic ultrasound examination	3.96	140.22	467	532	592
⊗ 45342	Sigmoidoscopy, flexible; with transendoscopic ultrasound guided intramural or transmural fine needle aspiration/biopsy(s)	6.06	214.12	530	608	697
⊗ 45345	Sigmoidoscopy, flexible; with transendoscopic stent placement (includes predilation)	4.41	156.14	395	498	543

● = New Code ⊗ = Conscious Sedation ✚ = Add-on Code ∅ = Modifier '51' Exempt ▲ =Revised Code

		Medicare RVU	National Fee	PFR Fee Information 50%	75%	90%
⊗ **45355**	Colonoscopy, rigid or flexible, transabdominal via colotomy, single or multiple	5.30	187.59	512	700	800
	(UNBUNDLING ALERT: 45378 cannot be used with 45300 or 45330 by the same physician on the same day.)					
	(A4550 (Disposable Surgical Tray) can be coded in addition to 45378 in the office setting. Payment is at carrier discretion.)					
	(See also HCPCS code G0105 for colorectal cancer screening ; colonscopy on individual at high risk.)					
	(See also HCPCS code G0121 for colorectal cancer screening ; colonscopy on individual not meeting criteria for high risk.)					
⊗ **45378**	Colonoscopy, flexible, proximal to splenic flexure; diagnostic, with or without collection of specimen(s) by brushing or washing, with or without colon decompression (separate procedure)	10.19	372.15	876	985	1106
	(A4550 (Disposable Surgical Tray) can be coded in addition to 45379 in the office setting. Payment is at carrier discretion.)					
⊗ **45379**	Colonoscopy, flexible, proximal to splenic flexure; with removal of foreign body	12.85	469.17	1055	1148	1385
	(UNBUNDLING ALERT: 45380 cannot be used with 45300, 45305, 45330, 45331, 45378 or 46600 by the same physician on the same day.)					
	(A4550 (Disposable Surgical Tray) can be coded in addition to 45380 in the office setting. Payment is at carrier discretion.)					
⊗ **45380**	Colonoscopy, flexible, proximal to splenic flexure; with biopsy, single or multiple	12.11	441.88	958	1190	1375
⊗ **45381**	Colonoscopy, flexible, proximal to splenic flexure; with directed submucosal injection(s), any substance	11.75	429.38	916	1107	1306
	(A4550 (Disposable Surgical Tray) can be coded in addition to 45382 in the office setting. Payment is at carrier discretion.)					
⊗ **45382**	Colonoscopy, flexible, proximal to splenic flexure; with control of bleeding (eg, injection, bipolar cautery, unipolar cautery, laser, heater probe, stapler, plasma coagulator)	16.13	589.69	1114	1234	1538
	(UNBUNDLING ALERT: 45383 cannot be used with 45300, 45302, 45310, 45320, 45330, 45331, 45333, 45336, 45355, 45378 or 46600 by the same physician on the same day.)					
	(A4550 (Disposable Surgical Tray) can be coded in addition to 45383 in the office setting. Payment is at carrier discretion.)					
⊗ **45383**	Colonoscopy, flexible, proximal to splenic flexure; with ablation of tumor(s), polyp(s), or other lesion(s) not amenable to removal by hot biopsy forceps, bipolar cautery or snare technique	14.42	524.12	1193	1372	1631
	(A4550 (Disposable Surgical Tray) can be coded in addition to 45384 in the office setting. Payment is at carrier discretion.)					
⊗ **45384**	Colonoscopy, flexible, proximal to splenic flexure; with removal of tumor(s), polyp(s), or other lesion(s) by hot biopsy forceps or bipolar cautery	11.97	435.82	1213	1400	1558
	(UNBUNDLING ALERT: 45385 cannot be used with 45300, 45330, 45333, or 45378 by the same physician on the same day.)					
	(A4550 (Disposable Surgical Tray) can be coded in addition to 45385 in the office setting. Payment is at carrier discretion.)					
⊗ **45385**	Colonoscopy, flexible, proximal to splenic flexure; with removal of tumor(s), polyp(s), or other lesion(s) by snare technique	13.66	497.59	1275	1602	1815
⊗ **45386**	Colonoscopy, flexible, proximal to splenic flexure; with dilation by balloon, 1 or more strictures	17.33	639.33	1674	2023	2385
⊗ **45387**	Colonoscopy, flexible, proximal to splenic flexure; with transendoscopic stent placement (includes predilation)	8.87	313.79	1137	1528	2004
⊗ **45391**	Colonoscopy, flexible, proximal to splenic flexure; with endoscopic ultrasound examination	7.64	270.21	716	862	1033
⊗ **45392**	Colonoscopy, flexible, proximal to splenic flexure; with transendoscopic ultrasound guided intramural or transmural fine needle aspiration/biopsy(s)	9.61	339.18	904	1088	1305

Laparoscopy
Excision

45395	Laparoscopy, surgical; proctectomy, complete, combined abdominoperineal, with colostomy	49.93	1767.16	4475	5363	6386
45397	Laparoscopy, surgical; proctectomy, combined abdominoperineal pull-through procedure (eg, colo-anal anastomosis), with creation of colonic reservoir (eg, J-pouch), with diverting enterostomy, when performed	54.07	1910.79	4861	5826	6937

Repair

45400	Laparoscopy, surgical; proctopexy (for prolapse)	29.02	1026.26	2588	3101	3693
45402	Laparoscopy, surgical; proctopexy (for prolapse), with sigmoid resection	38.91	1374.16	3542	4245	5054
45499	Unlisted laparoscopy procedure, rectum	-	-	IR	IR	IR

● = New Code ⊗ = Conscious Sedation ✚ = Add-on Code ∅ = Modifier '51' Exempt ▲ =Revised Code

		Medicare RVU	National Fee	PFR Fee Information 50%	75%	90%

Repair

45500	Proctoplasty; for stenosis	12.14	430.89	1511	1619	1829
45505	Proctoplasty; for prolapse of mucous membrane	13.23	470.31	1523	1653	1814
45520	Perirectal injection of sclerosing solution for prolapse	2.59	95.88	133	146	161
45540	Proctopexy (eg, for prolapse); abdominal approach	26.42	932.66	2572	3038	3296
45541	Proctopexy (eg, for prolapse); perineal approach	22.38	792.06	2377	2702	2978
45550	Proctopexy (eg, for prolapse); with sigmoid resection, abdominal approach	36.46	1287.76	3080	3628	4205
	(Code 45560 has been historically miscoded)					
45560	Repair of rectocele (separate procedure)	17.73	628.34	1300	1509	1925
45562	Exploration, repair, and presacral drainage for rectal injury;	26.94	953.12	2274	2596	2877
45563	Exploration, repair, and presacral drainage for rectal injury; with colostomy	39.95	1413.96	3035	3579	4040
45800	Closure of rectovesical fistula;	29.93	1057.34	2681	3127	3466
45805	Closure of rectovesical fistula; with colostomy	34.66	1225.23	2923	3371	3847
45820	Closure of rectourethral fistula;	29.88	1055.07	2605	3056	3355
45825	Closure of rectourethral fistula; with colostomy	36.45	1289.65	2868	3348	3641

Manipulation

45900	Reduction of procidentia (separate procedure) under anesthesia	4.81	170.92	324	389	445
45905	Dilation of anal sphincter (separate procedure) under anesthesia other than local	4.08	145.91	294	348	377
45910	Dilation of rectal stricture (separate procedure) under anesthesia other than local	4.82	172.05	359	448	485
45915	Removal of fecal impaction or foreign body (separate procedure) under anesthesia	7.76	281.96	379	456	551

Other Procedures

| 45990 | Anorectal exam, surgical, requiring anesthesia (general, spinal, or epidural), diagnostic | 2.76 | 97.78 | 147 | 178 | 214 |
| 45999 | Unlisted procedure, rectum | - | - | IR | IR | IR |

Anus
Incision

46020	Placement of seton	5.81	208.82	408	588	756
46030	Removal of anal seton, other marker	2.86	103.84	259	308	384
46040	Incision and drainage of ischiorectal and/or perirectal abscess (separate procedure)	11.63	420.66	669	793	907
46045	Incision and drainage of intramural, intramuscular, or submucosal abscess, transanal, under anesthesia	9.48	337.29	667	807	1035
46050	Incision and drainage, perianal abscess, superficial	4.05	148.94	251	306	422
46060	Incision and drainage of ischiorectal or intramural abscess, with fistulectomy or fistulotomy, submuscular, with or without placement of seton	10.45	372.15	1525	1857	2079
46070	Incision, anal septum (infant)	5.06	181.15	368	454	556
46080	Sphincterotomy, anal, division of sphincter (separate procedure)	5.33	192.52	690	890	1038
46083	Incision of thrombosed hemorrhoid, external	4.05	148.18	227	298	381

Excision

46200	Fissurectomy, with or without sphincterotomy	8.33	302.42	829	1013	1262
46210	Cryptectomy; single	8.36	306.59	340	394	488
46211	Cryptectomy; multiple (separate procedure)	10.62	386.18	881	968	1087

● = New Code ⊗ = Conscious Sedation ✚ = Add-on Code ∅ = Modifier '51' Exempt ▲ =Revised Code

		Medicare RVU	National Fee	PFR Fee Information 50%	75%	90%
46220	Papillectomy or excision of single tag, anus (separate procedure)	4.21	153.48	245	339	398
	(If a hemorrhoidectomy by simple ligature is performed at the time of an E/M code, add a -25 modifier to code 46221.)					
46221	Hemorrhoidectomy, by simple ligature (eg, rubber band)	5.45	197.82	293	382	510
46230	Excision of external hemorrhoid tags and/or multiple papillae	6.07	220.18	368	444	584
46250	Hemorrhoidectomy, external, complete	10.11	367.23	834	1009	1340
46255	Hemorrhoidectomy, internal and external, simple;	11.43	414.60	1155	1378	1538
46257	Hemorrhoidectomy, internal and external, simple; with fissurectomy	9.43	335.77	1239	1439	1733
46258	Hemorrhoidectomy, internal and external, simple; with fistulectomy, with or without fissurectomy	10.42	371.02	1393	1548	1733
	(UNBUNDLING ALERT: 46260 cannot be used with 46221, 46255, 46600, or 46934 by the same physician on the same day.)					
46260	Hemorrhoidectomy, internal and external, complex or extensive;	10.81	384.28	1594	1754	1938
46261	Hemorrhoidectomy, internal and external, complex or extensive; with fissurectomy	12.21	433.55	1515	1823	2162
46262	Hemorrhoidectomy, internal and external, complex or extensive; with fistulectomy, with or without fissurectomy	12.60	447.95	1635	1952	2213
46270	Surgical treatment of anal fistula (fistulectomy/fistulotomy); subcutaneous	10.58	382.76	797	946	1068
46275	Surgical treatment of anal fistula (fistulectomy/fistulotomy); submuscular	10.95	394.89	1282	1455	1806
46280	Surgical treatment of anal fistula (fistulectomy/fistulotomy); complex or multiple, with or without placement of seton	10.45	372.15	1509	1783	2146
46285	Surgical treatment of anal fistula (fistulectomy/fistulotomy); second stage	10.20	366.47	528	700	827
46288	Closure of anal fistula with rectal advancement flap	12.40	440.75	1367	1661	1882
46320	Enucleation or excision of external thrombotic hemorrhoid	3.99	145.15	246	348	391

Introduction

46500	Injection of sclerosing solution, hemorrhoids	4.28	156.14	165	204	245
46505	Chemodenervation of internal anal sphincter	6.37	229.66	563	684	806

Endoscopy

(Anoscopy performed at the time of an Evaluation and Management service should not be coded separately. The anoscopy is considered part of the diagnostic portion of the E&M service.)

46600	Anoscopy; diagnostic, with or without collection of specimen(s) by brushing or washing (separate procedure)	2.08	76.93	89	117	130

(Medicare fees for the code below are based on Non Facility RVUs. PFR information reflects fee when procedure is performed in a facility.)

(If 46604-46615 are performed at the time of an Evaluation and Management service, add a -25 modifier to the procedure code to indicate that this additional service was provided.)

46604	Anoscopy; with dilation (eg, balloon, guide wire, bougie)	11.40	427.10	168	215	282

(Medicare fees for the code below are based on Non Facility RVUs. PFR information reflects fee when procedure is performed in a facility.)

46606	Anoscopy; with biopsy, single or multiple	4.71	175.47	173	219	328
46608	Anoscopy; with removal of foreign body	5.95	219.81	244	289	365
46610	Anoscopy; with removal of single tumor, polyp, or other lesion by hot biopsy forceps or bipolar cautery	5.52	204.27	263	359	443
46611	Anoscopy; with removal of single tumor, polyp, or other lesion by snare technique	5.20	190.25	304	366	435
46612	Anoscopy; with removal of multiple tumors, polyps, or other lesions by hot biopsy forceps, bipolar cautery or snare technique	7.82	287.26	415	514	592
46614	Anoscopy; with control of bleeding (eg, injection, bipolar cautery, unipolar cautery, laser, heater probe, stapler, plasma coagulator)	4.59	166.37	355	410	478
46615	Anoscopy; with ablation of tumor(s), polyp(s), or other lesion(s) not amenable to removal by hot biopsy forceps, bipolar cautery or snare technique	5.44	195.93	461	524	610

Repair

46700	Anoplasty, plastic operation for stricture; adult	15.07	534.35	1399	1626	1972

● = New Code ⊗ = Conscious Sedation ✚ = Add-on Code ∅ = Modifier '51' Exempt ▲ =Revised Code

		Medicare RVU	National Fee	PFR Fee Information 50%	75%	90%
46705	Anoplasty, plastic operation for stricture; infant	12.00	426.73	1411	1652	1802
46706	Repair of anal fistula with fibrin glue	3.99	142.12	399	469	562
46710	Repair of ileoanal pouch fistula/sinus (eg, perineal or vaginal), pouch advancement; transperineal approach	26.16	926.59	2568	3003	3483
46712	Repair of ileoanal pouch fistula/sinus (eg, perineal or vaginal), pouch advancement; combined transperineal and transabdominal approach	54.84	1939.97	5385	6296	7304
46715	Repair of low imperforate anus; with anoperineal fistula (cut-back procedure)	12.07	428.62	1456	1611	1875
46716	Repair of low imperforate anus; with transposition of anoperineal or anovestibular fistula	27.10	961.84	1962	2364	3093
46730	Repair of high imperforate anus without fistula; perineal or sacroperineal approach	44.54	1572.75	3242	4038	5214
46735	Repair of high imperforate anus without fistula; combined transabdominal and sacroperineal approaches	52.43	1850.91	3832	4927	6023
46740	Repair of high imperforate anus with rectourethral or rectovaginal fistula; perineal or sacroperineal approach	49.40	1744.80	3957	4837	5274
46742	Repair of high imperforate anus with rectourethral or rectovaginal fistula; combined transabdominal and sacroperineal approaches	59.92	2119.61	4727	5516	6674
46744	Repair of cloacal anomaly by anorectovaginoplasty and urethroplasty, sacroperineal approach	86.04	3037.86	5884	7112	8306
46746	Repair of cloacal anomaly by anorectovaginoplasty and urethroplasty, combined abdominal and sacroperineal approach;	96.41	3406.23	6447	7942	9101
46748	Repair of cloacal anomaly by anorectovaginoplasty and urethroplasty, combined abdominal and sacroperineal approach; with vaginal lengthening by intestinal graft or pedicle flaps	97.27	3416.08	7248	8616	9908
46750	Sphincteroplasty, anal, for incontinence or prolapse; adult	18.37	650.32	1622	1926	2327
46751	Sphincteroplasty, anal, for incontinence or prolapse; child	15.29	544.59	1629	1894	2317
46753	Graft (Thiersch operation) for rectal incontinence and/or prolapse	13.79	488.88	1250	1486	1739
46754	Removal of Thiersch wire or suture, anal canal	6.69	242.54	312	391	460
46760	Sphincteroplasty, anal, for incontinence, adult; muscle transplant	26.17	926.21	2054	2462	2764
46761	Sphincteroplasty, anal, for incontinence, adult; levator muscle imbrication (Park posterior anal repair)	22.72	803.05	2221	2661	3055
46762	Sphincteroplasty, anal, for incontinence, adult; implantation artificial sphincter	21.75	768.56	2606	3242	4008

Destruction

(For destruction of lesions of surrounding skin, see 17100.)

		Medicare RVU	National Fee	PFR Fee Information 50%	75%	90%
46900	Destruction of lesion(s), anus (eg, condyloma, papilloma, molluscum contagiosum, herpetic vesicle), simple; chemical	4.92	179.26	206	264	358
46910	Destruction of lesion(s), anus (eg, condyloma, papilloma, molluscum contagiosum, herpetic vesicle), simple; electrodesiccation	5.22	190.62	313	401	470
46916	Destruction of lesion(s), anus (eg, condyloma, papilloma, molluscum contagiosum, herpetic vesicle), simple; cryosurgery	5.30	193.66	316	431	479
46917	Destruction of lesion(s), anus (eg, condyloma, papilloma, molluscum contagiosum, herpetic vesicle), simple; laser surgery	11.09	413.08	705	839	1054
46922	Destruction of lesion(s), anus (eg, condyloma, papilloma, molluscum contagiosum, herpetic vesicle), simple; surgical excision	5.58	204.27	392	490	598
46924	Destruction of lesion(s), anus (eg, condyloma, papilloma, molluscum contagiosum, herpetic vesicle), extensive (eg, laser surgery, electrosurgery, cryosurgery, chemosurgery)	11.95	442.26	835	980	1248
46934	Destruction of hemorrhoids, any method; internal	9.26	336.53	484	602	689
46935	Destruction of hemorrhoids, any method; external	6.19	225.11	447	623	773
46936	Destruction of hemorrhoids, any method; internal and external	9.23	335.77	809	976	1162
46937	Cryosurgery of rectal tumor; benign	5.96	215.64	454	535	587
46938	Cryosurgery of rectal tumor; malignant	9.72	350.55	715	812	919
46940	Curettage or cautery of anal fissure, including dilation of anal sphincter (separate procedure); initial	4.76	171.68	264	339	507
46942	Curettage or cautery of anal fissure, including dilation of anal sphincter (separate procedure); subsequent	4.31	155.38	214	268	320

● = New Code ⊗ = Conscious Sedation ✚ = Add-on Code ∅ = Modifier '51' Exempt ▲ =Revised Code

		Medicare RVU	National Fee	PFR Fee Information 50%	75%	90%
Suture						
46945	Ligation of internal hemorrhoids; single procedure	5.97	218.29	310	367	441
46946	Ligation of internal hemorrhoids; multiple procedures	6.82	248.61	438	500	603
46947	Hemorrhoidopexy (eg, for prolapsing internal hemorrhoids) by stapling	9.05	322.13	540	627	756
Other Procedures						
46999	Unlisted procedure, anus	-	-	IR	IR	IR
Liver						
Incision						
47000	Biopsy of liver, needle; percutaneous	6.14	225.49	417	503	618
✚ 47001	Biopsy of liver, needle; when done for indicated purpose at time of other major procedure (List separately in addition to code for primary procedure)	2.76	97.40	313	380	444
47010	Hepatotomy; for open drainage of abscess or cyst, one or two stages	29.41	1041.04	2152	2365	2517
⊗ 47011	Hepatotomy; for percutaneous drainage of abscess or cyst, one or two stages	5.08	178.50	571	638	706
47015	Laparotomy, with aspiration and/or injection of hepatic parasitic (eg, amoebic or echinococcal) cyst(s) or abscess(es)	27.77	982.30	1776	2192	2564
Excision						
47100	Biopsy of liver, wedge	20.42	724.98	1457	1815	2196
47120	Hepatectomy, resection of liver; partial lobectomy	58.36	2063.52	3668	4615	5474
47122	Hepatectomy, resection of liver; trisegmentectomy	87.35	3084.10	5158	6366	7352
47125	Hepatectomy, resection of liver; total left lobectomy	78.28	2765.00	5154	6068	6999
47130	Hepatectomy, resection of liver; total right lobectomy	84.26	2975.71	5476	6799	7583
Liver Transplantation						
47133	Donor hepatectomy (including cold preservation), from cadaver donor	-	-	IR	IR	IR
	(Payment for code 47134 by Medicare is restricted to the presence of the following ICD-9-CM codes: 275.0, 275.1, 277.6, 571.2, 571.5, 571.6, 576.1.)					
	(Payment for codes 47135 - 47136 by Medicare is restricted to the presence of the following ICD-9-CM codes: 275.0, 275.1, 277.6, 571.2, 571.5, 571.6, 576.1.)					
47135	Liver allotransplantation; orthotopic, partial or whole, from cadaver or living donor, any age	123.84	4375.65	12830	17169	22553
47136	Liver allotransplantation; heterotopic, partial or whole, from cadaver or living donor, any age	105.03	3712.06	10814	14039	17978
47140	Donor hepatectomy (including cold preservation), from living donor; left lateral segment only (segments II and III)	86.55	3054.16	8354	11010	14281
47141	Donor hepatectomy (including cold preservation), from living donor; total left lobectomy (segments II, III and IV)	103.01	3632.10	10089	13297	17248
47142	Donor hepatectomy (including cold preservation), from living donor; total right lobectomy (segments V, VI, VII and VIII)	113.38	3994.78	11220	14787	19182
47143	Backbench standard preparation of cadaver donor whole liver graft prior to allotransplantation, including cholecystectomy, if necessary, and dissection and removal of surrounding soft tissues to prepare the vena cava, portal vein, hepatic artery, and common bile duct for implantation; without trisegment or lobe split	-	-	IR	IR	IR
47144	Backbench standard preparation of cadaver donor whole liver graft prior to allotransplantation, including cholecystectomy, if necessary, and dissection and removal of surrounding soft tissues to prepare the vena cava, portal vein, hepatic artery, and common bile duct for implantation; with trisegment split of whole liver graft into two partial liver grafts (ie, left lateral segment (segments II and III) and right trisegment (segments I and IV through VIII))	-	-	IR	IR	IR
47145	Backbench standard preparation of cadaver donor whole liver graft prior to allotransplantation, including cholecystectomy, if necessary, and dissection and removal of surrounding soft tissues to prepare the vena cava, portal vein, hepatic artery, and common bile duct for implantation; with lobe split of whole liver graft into two partial liver grafts (ie, left lobe (segments II, III, and IV) and right lobe (segments I and V through VIII))	-	-	IR	IR	IR
47146	Backbench reconstruction of cadaver or living donor liver graft prior to allotransplantation; venous anastomosis, each	8.75	308.86	913	1204	1561
47147	Backbench reconstruction of cadaver or living donor liver graft prior to allotransplantation; arterial anastomosis, each	10.21	360.41	1066	1404	1822

● = New Code ⊗ = Conscious Sedation ✚ = Add-on Code ∅ = Modifier '51' Exempt ▲ =Revised Code

		Medicare RVU	National Fee	PFR Fee Information 50%	75%	90%

Repair

Code	Description	Medicare RVU	National Fee	50%	75%	90%
47300	Marsupialization of cyst or abscess of liver	27.33	967.14	2238	2406	2975
47350	Management of liver hemorrhage; simple suture of liver wound or injury	33.82	1196.42	2322	2976	3893
47360	Management of liver hemorrhage; complex suture of liver wound or injury, with or without hepatic artery ligation	46.08	1627.32	3194	3925	4686
47361	Management of liver hemorrhage; exploration of hepatic wound, extensive debridement, coagulation and/or suture, with or without packing of liver	76.43	2696.41	4546	5673	6895
47362	Management of liver hemorrhage; re-exploration of hepatic wound for removal of packing	34.78	1228.64	1999	2456	2919

Laparoscopy

Code	Description	Medicare RVU	National Fee	50%	75%	90%
47370	Laparoscopy, surgical, ablation of one or more liver tumor(s); radiofrequency	31.25	1105.47	2044	2586	3110
47371	Laparoscopy, surgical, ablation of one or more liver tumor(s); cryosurgical	31.42	1111.91	2014	2544	3111
47379	Unlisted laparoscopic procedure, liver	-	-	IR	IR	IR

Other Procedures

Code	Description	Medicare RVU	National Fee	50%	75%	90%
47380	Ablation, open, of one or more liver tumor(s); radiofrequency	36.44	1287.76	2565	3035	3778
47381	Ablation, open, of one or more liver tumor(s); cryosurgical	37.01	1308.22	2511	2971	3698
47382	Ablation, one or more liver tumor(s), percutaneous, radiofrequency	21.98	775.00	1544	1940	2501
47399	Unlisted procedure, liver	-	-	IR	IR	IR

Biliary Tract

Incision

Code	Description	Medicare RVU	National Fee	50%	75%	90%
47400	Hepaticotomy or hepaticostomy with exploration, drainage, or removal of calculus	52.66	1857.74	3510	3959	4391
47420	Choledochotomy or choledochostomy with exploration, drainage, or removal of calculus, with or without cholecystotomy; without transduodenal sphincterotomy or sphincteroplasty	33.27	1177.10	2730	3351	3797
47425	Choledochotomy or choledochostomy with exploration, drainage, or removal of calculus, with or without cholecystotomy; with transduodenal sphincterotomy or sphincteroplasty	33.57	1187.71	3336	3946	4398
47460	Transduodenal sphincterotomy or sphincteroplasty, with or without transduodenal extraction of calculus (separate procedure)	31.14	1102.44	2971	3365	3767
47480	Cholecystotomy or cholecystostomy with exploration, drainage, or removal of calculus (separate procedure)	20.63	731.80	1945	2214	2647
47490	Percutaneous cholecystostomy	13.80	492.29	996	1183	1492

Introduction

Code	Description	Medicare RVU	National Fee	50%	75%	90%
47500	Injection procedure for percutaneous transhepatic cholangiography	2.70	94.74	431	580	700
47505	Injection procedure for cholangiography through an existing catheter (eg, percutaneous transhepatic or T-tube)	1.04	36.38	250	294	330
47510	Introduction of percutaneous transhepatic catheter for biliary drainage	13.16	468.41	883	1126	1365
47511	Introduction of percutaneous transhepatic stent for internal and external biliary drainage *(Medicare fees for the code below are based on Non Facility RVUs. PFR information reflects fee when procedure is performed in a facility.)*	16.23	574.15	1146	1447	1654
47525	Change of percutaneous biliary drainage catheter *(Medicare fees for the code below are based on Non Facility RVUs. PFR information reflects fee when procedure is performed in a facility.)*	20.68	762.50	573	664	824
47530	Revision and/or reinsertion of transhepatic tube	38.89	1451.10	651	753	960

Endoscopy

Code	Description	Medicare RVU	National Fee	50%	75%	90%
✚ 47550	Biliary endoscopy, intraoperative (choledochoscopy) (List separately in addition to code for primary procedure)	4.38	154.62	594	739	775
47552	Biliary endoscopy, percutaneous via T-tube or other tract; diagnostic, with or without collection of specimen(s) by brushing and/or washing (separate procedure)	8.75	308.49	742	996	1143
47553	Biliary endoscopy, percutaneous via T-tube or other tract; with biopsy, single or multiple	8.72	306.21	950	1049	1324
47554	Biliary endoscopy, percutaneous via T-tube or other tract; with removal of calculus/calculi	13.25	467.66	1262	1464	1690

● = New Code   ⊗ = Conscious Sedation   ✚ = Add-on Code   ∅ = Modifier '51' Exempt   ▲ =Revised Code

		Medicare RVU	National Fee	PFR Fee Information 50%	75%	90%
47555	Biliary endoscopy, percutaneous via T-tube or other tract; with dilation of biliary duct stricture(s) without stent	10.40	365.33	915	1138	1372
47556	Biliary endoscopy, percutaneous via T-tube or other tract; with dilation of biliary duct stricture(s) with stent	11.75	412.70	1079	1238	1595

Laparoscopy

47560	Laparoscopy, surgical; with guided transhepatic cholangiography, without biopsy	7.10	250.50	891	1291	1637
47561	Laparoscopy, surgical; with guided transhepatic cholangiography with biopsy	7.65	270.21	1130	1455	1723
47562	Laparoscopy, surgical; cholecystectomy	18.15	643.50	2623	2987	3366
47563	Laparoscopy, surgical; cholecystectomy with cholangiography	18.85	668.51	2797	3301	3709
47564	Laparoscopy, surgical; cholecystectomy with exploration of common duct	21.92	776.52	3065	3539	3864
47570	Laparoscopy, surgical; cholecystoenterostomy	19.49	690.87	2472	2886	3311
47579	Unlisted laparoscopy procedure, biliary tract	-	-	IR	IR	IR

Excision

(UNBUNDLING ALERT: 47600 cannot be used with 38500, 44005, 44950, 47480, 49000, or 49255 by the same physician on the same day.)

47600	Cholecystectomy;	25.55	901.96	2300	2672	2931

(UNBUNDLING ALERT: 47605 cannot be used with 48500, 44005, 44950, 47420, 47480, 47600, 49000, or 49255 by the same physician on the same day.)

47605	Cholecystectomy; with cholangiography	24.32	861.03	2357	2556	3278

(UNBUNDLING ALERT: 47610 cannot be used with 48500, 44005, 44950, 47420, 47480, 47600, 47605, or 49000 by the same physician on the same day.)

47610	Cholecystectomy with exploration of common duct;	31.20	1102.82	2804	3293	3715

(UNBUNDLING ALERT: 47612 cannot be used with 38500, 44005, 44020, 44950, 47420, 47480, 47600, 47605, 47610, or 49000 by the same physician on the same day.)

47612	Cholecystectomy with exploration of common duct; with choledochoenterostomy	31.45	1111.15	3628	4333	5027

(UNBUNDLING ALERT: 47620 cannot be used with 38500, 44005, 44950, 47420, 47480, 47600, 47605, 47610, or 49000 by the same physician on the same day.)

47620	Cholecystectomy with exploration of common duct; with transduodenal sphincterotomy or sphincteroplasty, with or without cholangiography	34.17	1207.41	3142	3879	4510
47630	Biliary duct stone extraction, percutaneous via T-tube tract, basket, or snare (eg, Burhenne technique)	14.93	529.43	1164	1483	1718
47700	Exploration for congenital atresia of bile ducts, without repair, with or without liver biopsy, with or without cholangiography	25.83	916.36	2317	2617	3351
47701	Portoenterostomy (eg, Kasai procedure)	43.43	1536.74	4097	4894	5401
47711	Excision of bile duct tumor, with or without primary repair of bile duct; extrahepatic	38.65	1366.58	3630	4164	4865
47712	Excision of bile duct tumor, with or without primary repair of bile duct; intrahepatic	49.72	1756.17	4035	4825	5611
47715	Excision of choledochal cyst	32.37	1145.26	2810	3460	4005

Repair

● 47719	Anastomosis, choledochal cyst, without excision	29.07	1028.92	2258	2687	3322
47720	Cholecystoenterostomy; direct	27.85	986.09	2357	2758	3450
47721	Cholecystoenterostomy; with gastroenterostomy	32.96	1165.73	2965	3449	4473
47740	Cholecystoenterostomy; Roux-en-Y	31.92	1129.35	2765	3402	4178
47741	Cholecystoenterostomy; Roux-en-Y with gastroenterostomy	36.18	1279.42	3311	4261	5128
47760	Anastomosis, of extrahepatic biliary ducts and gastrointestinal tract	52.97	1861.90	3416	4050	5066
47765	Anastomosis, of intrahepatic ducts and gastrointestinal tract	67.64	2365.18	3725	4216	5028
47780	Anastomosis, Roux-en-Y, of extrahepatic biliary ducts and gastrointestinal tract	57.57	2021.07	4119	4621	5622
47785	Anastomosis, Roux-en-Y, of intrahepatic biliary ducts and gastrointestinal tract	74.27	2601.28	4545	5412	6228
47800	Reconstruction, plastic, of extrahepatic biliary ducts with end-to-end anastomosis	39.10	1382.50	3311	3978	4606
47801	Placement of choledochal stent	26.64	942.89	2133	2534	2907

● = New Code ⊗ = Conscious Sedation ✚ = Add-on Code ∅ = Modifier '51' Exempt ▲ =Revised Code

		Medicare RVU	National Fee	PFR Fee Information 50%	75%	90%
47802	U-tube hepaticoenterostomy	37.28	1318.45	3402	4031	4661
47900	Suture of extrahepatic biliary duct for pre-existing injury (separate procedure)	33.79	1195.67	2908	3349	3793

Other Procedures

47999	Unlisted procedure, biliary tract	-	-	IR	IR	IR

Pancreas
Incision

48000	Placement of drains, peripancreatic, for acute pancreatitis;	46.64	1646.27	2421	2849	3682
48001	Placement of drains, peripancreatic, for acute pancreatitis; with cholecystostomy, gastrostomy, and jejunostomy	57.83	2040.78	4123	4788	5558
48020	Removal of pancreatic calculus	28.47	1006.56	2672	3143	3461

Excision

48100	Biopsy of pancreas, open (eg, fine needle aspiration, needle core biopsy, wedge biopsy)	21.66	765.91	2156	2509	2813
48102	Biopsy of pancreas, percutaneous needle	13.17	481.30	609	741	898
● 48105	Resection or debridement of pancreas and peripancreatic tissue for acute necrotizing pancreatitis	71.02	2504.65	6392	7640	8972
48120	Excision of lesion of pancreas (eg, cyst, adenoma)	27.29	964.49	2782	3354	3871
48140	Pancreatectomy, distal subtotal, with or without splenectomy; without pancreaticojejunostomy	38.71	1367.34	3451	4179	5012
48145	Pancreatectomy, distal subtotal, with or without splenectomy; with pancreaticojejunostomy	40.24	1421.16	3750	4538	5480
48146	Pancreatectomy, distal, near-total with preservation of duodenum (Child-type procedure)	45.87	1622.39	4308	5172	5991
48148	Excision of ampulla of Vater	30.28	1070.23	3211	3770	4485
48150	Pancreatectomy, proximal subtotal with total duodenectomy, partial gastrectomy, choledochoenterostomy and gastrojejunostomy (Whipple-type procedure); with pancreatojejunostomy	78.09	2758.94	6742	7841	9123
48152	Pancreatectomy, proximal subtotal with total duodenectomy, partial gastrectomy, choledochoenterostomy and gastrojejunostomy (Whipple-type procedure); without pancreatojejunostomy	72.07	2546.33	6008	7023	8044
48153	Pancreatectomy, proximal subtotal with near-total duodenectomy, choledochoenterostomy and duodenojejunostomy (pylorus-sparing, Whipple-type procedure); with pancreatojejunostomy	78.06	2757.80	6361	7692	9196
48154	Pancreatectomy, proximal subtotal with near-total duodenectomy, choledochoenterostomy and duodenojejunostomy (pylorus-sparing, Whipple-type procedure); without pancreatojejunostomy	72.45	2559.98	6021	7467	8894
48155	Pancreatectomy, total	44.27	1566.30	5246	6392	7842
48160	Pancreatectomy, total or subtotal, with autologous transplantation of pancreas or pancreatic islet cells	-	-	IR	IR	IR

Introduction

✚ 48400	Injection procedure for intraoperative pancreatography (List separately in addition to code for primary procedure)	2.79	98.15	304	353	394

Repair

48500	Marsupialization of pancreatic cyst	27.56	975.86	2313	2865	3424
48510	External drainage, pseudocyst of pancreas; open	26.35	933.42	2812	3497	4021

(Medicare fees for the code below are based on Non Facility RVUs. PFR information reflects fee when procedure is performed in a facility.)

⊗ 48511	External drainage, pseudocyst of pancreas; percutaneous	24.66	919.39	796	975	1273
48520	Internal anastomosis of pancreatic cyst to gastrointestinal tract; direct	26.85	948.57	2607	3432	4354
48540	Internal anastomosis of pancreatic cyst to gastrointestinal tract; Roux-en-Y	32.49	1147.92	3118	3729	4327
48545	Pancreatorrhaphy for injury	32.49	1147.16	2815	3207	3564
48547	Duodenal exclusion with gastrojejunostomy for pancreatic injury	44.10	1556.07	4696	5499	6192
● 48548	Pancreaticojejunostomy, side-to-side anastomosis (Puestow-type operation)	41.33	1459.81	3990	4815	5636

● = New Code   ⊗ = Conscious Sedation   ✚ = Add-on Code   ∅ = Modifier '51' Exempt   ▲ =Revised Code

		Medicare RVU	National Fee	PFR Fee Information 50%	75%	90%

Pancreas Transplantation

48550	Donor pancreatectomy (including cold preservation), with or without duodenal segment for transplantation	-	-	IR	IR	IR
48551	Backbench standard preparation of cadaver donor pancreas allograft prior to transplantation, including dissection of allograft from surrounding soft tissues, splenectomy, duodenotomy, ligation of bile duct, ligation of mesenteric vessels, and Y-graft arterial anastomoses from iliac artery to superior mesenteric artery and to splenic artery	-	-	IR	IR	IR
48552	Backbench reconstruction of cadaver donor pancreas allograft prior to transplantation, venous anastomosis, each	5.99	210.71	560	684	752
48554	Transplantation of pancreatic allograft	60.04	2134.01	5108	6244	6978
48556	Removal of transplanted pancreatic allograft	29.72	1052.79	2736	3345	3831

Other Procedures

48999	Unlisted procedure, pancreas	-	-	IR	IR	IR

Abdomen, Peritoneum, and Omentum
Incision

49000	Exploratory laparotomy, exploratory celiotomy with or without biopsy(s) (separate procedure)	19.29	683.67	1970	2370	2653
49002	Reopening of recent laparotomy	24.29	853.45	1821	2191	2587
49010	Exploration, retroperitoneal area with or without biopsy(s) (separate procedure)	23.49	829.20	2033	2352	2846
49020	Drainage of peritoneal abscess or localized peritonitis, exclusive of appendiceal abscess; open	39.41	1392.73	1755	2131	2543
⊗ 49021	Drainage of peritoneal abscess or localized peritonitis, exclusive of appendiceal abscess; percutaneous	24.00	896.65	1130	1428	1623
49040	Drainage of subdiaphragmatic or subphrenic abscess; open	24.55	867.85	1844	2273	3317
	(Medicare fees for the code below are based on Non Facility RVUs. PFR information reflects fee when procedure is performed in a facility.)					
⊗ 49041	Drainage of subdiaphragmatic or subphrenic abscess; percutaneous	23.56	877.71	732	814	977
49060	Drainage of retroperitoneal abscess; open	27.53	973.21	1913	2328	2743
	(Medicare fees for the code below are based on Non Facility RVUs. PFR information reflects fee when procedure is performed in a facility.)					
⊗ 49061	Drainage of retroperitoneal abscess; percutaneous	23.29	868.61	630	708	778
49062	Drainage of extraperitoneal lymphocele to peritoneal cavity, open	18.88	669.27	1734	1978	2199
	(A4550 (Disposable Surgical Tray) can be coded in addition to 49080 in the office setting. Payment is at carrier discretion.)					
49080	Peritoneocentesis, abdominal paracentesis, or peritoneal lavage (diagnostic or therapeutic); initial	5.06	186.46	272	353	404
	(A4550 (Disposable Surgical Tray) can be coded in addition to 49081 in the office setting. Payment is at carrier discretion.)					
49081	Peritoneocentesis, abdominal paracentesis, or peritoneal lavage (diagnostic or therapeutic); subsequent	4.00	146.66	230	300	371

Excision, Destruction

49180	Biopsy, abdominal or retroperitoneal mass, percutaneous needle	4.72	172.43	539	650	837
49200	Excision or destruction, open, intra-abdominal or retroperitoneal tumors or cysts or endometriomas;	17.16	608.63	2283	2596	2822
	(UNBUNDLING ALERT: 49201 cannot be used with 38500, 44005, 44950, 49000, 49200 or 49255 by the same physician on the same day.)					
49201	Excision or destruction, open, intra-abdominal or retroperitoneal tumors or cysts or endometriomas; extensive	24.43	865.96	3116	3631	4164
49215	Excision of presacral or sacrococcygeal tumor	55.76	1969.53	3575	4126	4610
49220	Staging laparotomy for Hodgkins disease or lymphoma (includes splenectomy, needle or open biopsies of both liver lobes, possibly also removal of abdominal nodes, abdominal node and/or bone marrow biopsies, ovarian repositioning)	24.12	854.21	3033	3755	4646
49250	Umbilectomy, omphalectomy, excision of umbilicus (separate procedure)	14.28	507.07	1281	1403	1582
49255	Omentectomy, epiploectomy, resection of omentum (separate procedure)	19.45	689.73	1576	1839	2142

● = New Code ⊗ = Conscious Sedation ✚ = Add-on Code ∅ = Modifier '51' Exempt ▲ =Revised Code

		Medicare RVU	National Fee	PFR Fee Information 50%	75%	90%

Laparoscopy

49320	Laparoscopy, abdomen, peritoneum, and omentum, diagnostic, with or without collection of specimen(s) by brushing or washing (separate procedure)	8.33	296.36	1404	1707	1961
49321	Laparoscopy, surgical; with biopsy (single or multiple)	8.71	309.62	1687	1823	2142
49322	Laparoscopy, surgical; with aspiration of cavity or cyst (eg, ovarian cyst) (single or multiple)	9.57	339.94	1687	1875	2235
49323	Laparoscopy, surgical; with drainage of lymphocele to peritoneal cavity	15.87	562.78	1564	1912	2237
● 49324	Laparoscopy, surgical; with insertion of intraperitoneal cannula or catheter, permanent	9.80	347.52	1561	1790	2097
● 49325	Laparoscopy, surgical; with revision of previously placed intraperitoneal cannula or catheter, with removal of intraluminal obstructive material if performed	10.56	374.43	1682	1929	2259
✚● 49326	Laparoscopy, surgical; with omentopexy (omental tacking procedure) (List separately in addition to code for primary procedure)	4.86	170.92	774	888	1040
49329	Unlisted laparoscopy procedure, abdomen, peritoneum and omentum	-	-	IR	IR	IR

Introduction, Revision, and/or Removal

49400	Injection of air or contrast into peritoneal cavity (separate procedure)	4.91	178.88	243	304	340
● 49402	Removal of peritoneal foreign body from peritoneal cavity	21.14	747.72	2045	2479	3068
49419	Insertion of intraperitoneal cannula or catheter, with subcutaneous reservoir, permanent (ie, totally implantable)	11.36	403.61	1212	1470	1769
49420	Insertion of intraperitoneal cannula or catheter for drainage or dialysis; temporary	3.54	125.82	467	604	871
49421	Insertion of intraperitoneal cannula or catheter for drainage or dialysis; permanent	9.76	347.52	1283	1537	1974
49422	Removal of permanent intraperitoneal cannula or catheter	9.91	351.69	1037	1278	1401
	(Medicare fees for the code below are based on Non Facility RVUs. PFR information reflects fee when procedure is performed in a facility.)					
49423	Exchange of previously placed abscess or cyst drainage catheter under radiological guidance (separate procedure)	15.22	571.12	249	316	349
	(Medicare fees for the code below are based on Non Facility RVUs. PFR information reflects fee when procedure is performed in a facility.)					
49424	Contrast injection for assessment of abscess or cyst via previously placed drainage catheter or tube (separate procedure)	4.31	160.31	162	178	185
49425	Insertion of peritoneal-venous shunt	19.18	680.64	1998	2408	3012
49426	Revision of peritoneal-venous shunt	16.31	578.69	1690	2126	2636
49427	Injection procedure (eg, contrast media) for evaluation of previously placed peritoneal-venous shunt	1.25	43.96	196	220	252
49428	Ligation of peritoneal-venous shunt	11.30	402.47	513	665	820
49429	Removal of peritoneal-venous shunt	11.74	416.49	1179	1425	1671
✚● 49435	Insertion of subcutaneous extension to intraperitoneal cannula or catheter with remote chest exit site (List separately in addition to code for primary procedure)	3.13	109.90	303	367	454
● 49436	Delayed creation of exit site from embedded subcutaneous segment of intraperitoneal cannula or catheter	4.60	164.10	445	540	668

Repair

Hernioplasty, Herniorrhaphy, Herniotomy

49491	Repair, initial inguinal hernia, preterm infant (younger than 37 weeks gestation at birth), performed from birth up to 50 weeks postconception age, with or without hydrocelectomy; reducible	18.97	671.54	1973	2316	2902
49492	Repair, initial inguinal hernia, preterm infant (younger than 37 weeks gestation at birth), performed from birth up to 50 weeks postconception age, with or without hydrocelectomy; incarcerated or strangulated	23.17	819.72	2026	2415	3152
49495	Repair, initial inguinal hernia, full term infant younger than age 6 months, or preterm infant older than 50 weeks postconception age and younger than age 6 months at the time of surgery, with or without hydrocelectomy; reducible	9.85	349.79	1521	1814	2091
49496	Repair, initial inguinal hernia, full term infant younger than age 6 months, or preterm infant older than 50 weeks postconception age and younger than age 6 months at the time of surgery, with or without hydrocelectomy; incarcerated or strangulated	14.68	520.71	1697	1895	2454
49500	Repair initial inguinal hernia, age 6 months to younger than 5 years, with or without hydrocelectomy; reducible	9.71	346.00	1270	1392	1608

		Medicare RVU	National Fee	PFR Fee Information 50%	75%	90%
49501	Repair initial inguinal hernia, age 6 months to younger than 5 years, with or without hydrocelectomy; incarcerated or strangulated	14.61	518.44	1554	1724	2435
	(UNBUNDLING ALERT: 49505 cannot be used with 38500 by the same physician on the same day.)					
49505	Repair initial inguinal hernia, age 5 years or older; reducible	12.69	450.98	1457	1620	1849
49507	Repair initial inguinal hernia, age 5 years or older; incarcerated or strangulated	15.70	557.09	1734	2027	2473
	(UNBUNDLING ALERT: 49520 cannot be used with 38500, 44005 or 49505 by the same physician on the same day.)					
49520	Repair recurrent inguinal hernia, any age; reducible	15.61	553.68	1806	1918	2238
49521	Repair recurrent inguinal hernia, any age; incarcerated or strangulated	19.13	677.99	1903	2229	2785
49525	Repair inguinal hernia, sliding, any age	14.07	499.49	1497	1697	2044
49540	Repair lumbar hernia	16.75	594.23	1590	1941	2297
49550	Repair initial femoral hernia, any age; reducible	14.17	502.90	1464	1708	1886
49553	Repair initial femoral hernia, any age; incarcerated or strangulated	15.49	549.51	1603	1932	2355
49555	Repair recurrent femoral hernia; reducible	14.76	523.74	1605	1917	2344
49557	Repair recurrent femoral hernia; incarcerated or strangulated	17.96	636.68	1799	2234	2602
	(For 49560-49566, code implantation of surgical mesh separately using CPT code 49568.)					
49560	Repair initial incisional or ventral hernia; reducible	18.44	653.73	1843	2212	2452
49561	Repair initial incisional or ventral hernia; incarcerated or strangulated	23.19	820.48	2041	2433	2981
	(UNBUNDLING ALERT: 49565 cannot be used with 44005 or 49560 by the same physician on the same day.)					
49565	Repair recurrent incisional or ventral hernia; reducible	19.00	673.06	2238	2595	2965
49566	Repair recurrent incisional or ventral hernia; incarcerated or strangulated	23.42	828.82	2499	2889	3391
✚ 49568	Implantation of mesh or other prosthesis for incisional or ventral hernia repair (List separately in addition to code for the incisional or ventral hernia repair)	7.09	250.12	804	982	1043
49570	Repair epigastric hernia (eg, preperitoneal fat); reducible (separate procedure)	9.93	353.58	1192	1451	2159
49572	Repair epigastric hernia (eg, preperitoneal fat); incarcerated or strangulated	12.23	433.93	1464	1754	2244
49580	Repair umbilical hernia, younger than age 5 years; reducible	7.62	272.10	1133	1333	1586
49582	Repair umbilical hernia, younger than age 5 years; incarcerated or strangulated	11.43	406.26	1358	1650	2222
49585	Repair umbilical hernia, age 5 years or older; reducible	10.68	380.11	1387	1670	1938
49587	Repair umbilical hernia, age 5 years or older; incarcerated or strangulated	12.72	451.74	1533	1791	2107
49590	Repair spigelian hernia	14.04	498.35	1458	1807	2116
49600	Repair of small omphalocele, with primary closure	18.08	641.60	1674	2008	2294
	(PFR research shows that fees for code 38792 may vary widely.)					
49605	Repair of large omphalocele or gastroschisis; with or without prosthesis	124.23	4376.78	5107	8892	12449
49606	Repair of large omphalocele or gastroschisis; with removal of prosthesis, final reduction and closure, in operating room	28.80	1019.44	2436	3047	3544
49610	Repair of omphalocele (Gross type operation); first stage	16.97	601.81	1684	2173	2523
49611	Repair of omphalocele (Gross type operation); second stage	16.18	577.94	1738	2166	2519

Laparoscopy

49650	Laparoscopy, surgical; repair initial inguinal hernia	10.46	372.53	1582	1994	2282
49651	Laparoscopy, surgical; repair recurrent inguinal hernia	13.52	480.92	1741	2119	2302
49659	Unlisted laparoscopy procedure, hernioplasty, herniorrhaphy, herniotomy	-	-	IR	IR	IR

Suture

49900	Suture, secondary, of abdominal wall for evisceration or dehiscence	20.12	715.88	1550	1900	2433

		Medicare RVU	National Fee	PFR Fee Information 50%	75%	90%

Other Procedures

49904	Omental flap, extra-abdominal (eg, for reconstruction of sternal and chest wall defects)	39.35	1406.76	4550	5350	5975
✚ 49905	Omental flap, intra-abdominal (List separately in addition to code for primary procedure)	9.45	333.12	1360	1601	1788
49906	Free omental flap with microvascular anastomosis	-	-	3615	4276	5032
49999	Unlisted procedure, abdomen, peritoneum and omentum	-	-	IR	IR	IR

Urinary System

Kidney
Incision

50010	Renal exploration, not necessitating other specific procedures	18.70	662.45	2176	2491	2861
50020	Drainage of perirenal or renal abscess; open	27.15	960.70	2258	2688	3147
	(Medicare fees for the code below are based on Non Facility RVUs. PFR information reflects fee when procedure is performed in a facility.)					
⊗ 50021	Drainage of perirenal or renal abscess; percutaneous	24.80	926.97	568	686	776
50040	Nephrostomy, nephrotomy with drainage	24.84	878.46	2453	2770	3094
50045	Nephrotomy, with exploration	24.99	883.39	2658	3094	3512
50060	Nephrolithotomy; removal of calculus	30.84	1089.55	3028	3534	4001
50065	Nephrolithotomy; secondary surgical operation for calculus	31.27	1100.54	3297	3927	4166
50070	Nephrolithotomy; complicated by congenital kidney abnormality	32.21	1138.06	3562	4205	4814
50075	Nephrolithotomy; removal of large staghorn calculus filling renal pelvis and calyces (including anatrophic pyelolithotomy)	39.63	1399.18	3737	4461	5077
50080	Percutaneous nephrostolithotomy or pyelostolithotomy, with or without dilation, endoscopy, lithotripsy, stenting, or basket extraction; up to 2 cm	23.53	832.23	3076	3476	3930
50081	Percutaneous nephrostolithotomy or pyelostolithotomy, with or without dilation, endoscopy, lithotripsy, stenting, or basket extraction; over 2 cm	34.54	1219.92	3731	4174	4895
50100	Transection or repositioning of aberrant renal vessels (separate procedure)	27.01	957.67	2123	2619	3031
50120	Pyelotomy; with exploration	25.57	903.86	2593	3172	3601
50125	Pyelotomy; with drainage, pyelostomy	26.81	948.57	2834	3197	3555
50130	Pyelotomy; with removal of calculus (pyelolithotomy, pelviolithotomy, including coagulum pyelolithotomy)	27.82	983.06	2850	3331	3655
50135	Pyelotomy; complicated (eg, secondary operation, congenital kidney abnormality)	30.34	1071.74	3479	3990	4537

Excision

50200	Renal biopsy; percutaneous, by trocar or needle	4.03	142.87	549	655	731
50205	Renal biopsy; by surgical exposure of kidney	18.65	660.17	1554	1921	2688
50220	Nephrectomy, including partial ureterectomy, any open approach including rib resection;	27.74	980.79	2916	3605	4419
50225	Nephrectomy, including partial ureterectomy, any open approach including rib resection; complicated because of previous surgery on same kidney	32.15	1135.41	3608	4247	5116
	(UNBUNDLING ALERT: 50230 cannot be used with 32020, 35761, 38100, 49010, 49255, 50080, 50081, 50220, 50370, 50526, or 50780 by the same physician on the same day.)					
50230	Nephrectomy, including partial ureterectomy, any open approach including rib resection; radical, with regional lymphadenectomy and/or vena caval thrombectomy	34.65	1222.95	4173	5116	6035
50234	Nephrectomy with total ureterectomy and bladder cuff; through same incision	35.20	1243.04	3866	4691	5280
50236	Nephrectomy with total ureterectomy and bladder cuff; through separate incision	39.76	1404.86	4038	4731	5541
50240	Nephrectomy, partial	35.54	1255.17	3419	4131	4935
50250	Ablation, open, one or more renal mass lesion(s), cryosurgical, including intraoperative ultrasound, if performed	33.01	1166.86	3551	4282	5067
50280	Excision or unroofing of cyst(s) of kidney	25.50	901.96	2414	3107	3852

● = New Code ⊗ = Conscious Sedation ✚ = Add-on Code ∅ = Modifier '51' Exempt ▲ =Revised Code

		Medicare RVU	National Fee	PFR Fee Information 50%	75%	90%
50290	Excision of perinephric cyst	24.32	860.65	2477	3166	3792

Renal Transplantation

		Medicare RVU	National Fee	50%	75%	90%
50300	Donor nephrectomy (including cold preservation); from cadaver donor, unilateral or bilateral	-	-	2827	3398	3884
50320	Donor nephrectomy (including cold preservation); open, from living donor	35.74	1269.57	4137	4742	5325
50323	Backbench standard preparation of cadaver donor renal allograft prior to transplantation, including dissection and removal of perinephric fat, diaphragmatic and retroperitoneal attachments, excision of adrenal gland, and preparation of ureter(s), renal vein(s), and renal artery(s), ligating branches, as necessary	-	-	IR	IR	IR
50325	Backbench standard preparation of living donor renal allograft (open or laparoscopic) prior to transplantation, including dissection and removal of perinephric fat and preparation of ureter(s), renal vein(s), and renal artery(s), ligating branches, as necessary	-	-	IR	IR	IR
50327	Backbench reconstruction of cadaver or living donor renal allograft prior to transplantation; venous anastomosis, each	5.58	196.31	682	832	979
50328	Backbench reconstruction of cadaver or living donor renal allograft prior to transplantation; arterial anastomosis, each	4.89	172.05	597	729	858
50329	Backbench reconstruction of cadaver or living donor renal allograft prior to transplantation; ureteral anastomosis, each	4.68	164.48	571	697	820
50340	Recipient nephrectomy (separate procedure)	22.29	792.06	2701	3335	3885
50360	Renal allotransplantation, implantation of graft; without recipient nephrectomy	60.59	2141.97	5988	7418	8590
50365	Renal allotransplantation, implantation of graft; with recipient nephrectomy	68.64	2426.96	6601	8245	9048
50370	Removal of transplanted renal allograft	28.04	991.40	2622	3231	3653
50380	Renal autotransplantation, reimplantation of kidney	45.29	1603.44	4203	4972	6137

Introduction
Renal Pelvis Catheter Procedures
Internally Dwelling

		Medicare RVU	National Fee	50%	75%	90%
⊗ **50382**	Removal (via snare/capture) and replacement of internally dwelling ureteral stent via percutaneous approach, including radiological supervision and interpretation	39.14	1462.46	5281	6536	7895
⊗ **50384**	Removal (via snare/capture) of internally dwelling ureteral stent via percutaneous approach, including radiological supervision and interpretation	36.61	1368.48	5102	6313	7627

Externally Accessible

		Medicare RVU	National Fee	50%	75%	90%
⊗ **50387**	Removal and replacement of externally accessible transnephric ureteral stent (eg, external/internal stent) requiring fluoroscopic guidance, including radiological supervision and interpretation	18.78	704.14	2559	3167	3826
50389	Removal of nephrostomy tube, requiring fluoroscopic guidance (eg, with concurrent indwelling ureteral stent)	12.32	462.73	1752	2168	2619

Other Introduction Procedures

		Medicare RVU	National Fee	50%	75%	90%
50390	Aspiration and/or injection of renal cyst or pelvis by needle, percutaneous	2.70	94.74	468	600	773
50391	Instillation(s) of therapeutic agent into renal pelvis and/or ureter through established nephrostomy, pyelostomy or ureterostomy tube (eg, anticarcinogenic or antifungal agent)	3.66	131.13	418	505	580
50392	Introduction of intracatheter or catheter into renal pelvis for drainage and/or injection, percutaneous	5.03	177.74	646	799	963
50393	Introduction of ureteral catheter or stent into ureter through renal pelvis for drainage and/or injection, percutaneous	6.11	215.64	704	885	995
50394	Injection procedure for pyelography (as nephrostogram, pyelostogram, antegrade pyeloureterograms) through nephrostomy or pyelostomy tube, or indwelling ureteral catheter	3.26	120.51	212	274	338
50395	Introduction of guide into renal pelvis and/or ureter with dilation to establish nephrostomy tract, percutaneous	5.05	178.50	778	905	967
50396	Manometric studies through nephrostomy or pyelostomy tube, or indwelling ureteral catheter	3.26	115.59	189	222	279
	(Medicare fees for the code below are based on Non Facility RVUs. PFR information reflects fee when procedure is performed in a facility.)					
50398	Change of nephrostomy or pyelostomy tube	16.61	623.79	224	285	375

● = New Code ⊗ = Conscious Sedation ✚ = Add-on Code ∅ = Modifier '51' Exempt ▲ =Revised Code

		Medicare RVU	National Fee	PFR Fee Information 50%	75%	90%
Repair						
50400	Pyeloplasty (Foley Y-pyeloplasty), plastic operation on renal pelvis, with or without plastic operation on ureter, nephropexy, nephrostomy, pyelostomy, or ureteral splinting; simple	31.22	1102.82	3240	3884	4490
50405	Pyeloplasty (Foley Y-pyeloplasty), plastic operation on renal pelvis, with or without plastic operation on ureter, nephropexy, nephrostomy, pyelostomy, or ureteral splinting; complicated (congenital kidney abnormality, secondary pyeloplasty, solitary kidney, calycoplasty)	37.57	1326.03	3727	4365	4975
50500	Nephrorrhaphy, suture of kidney wound or injury	31.71	1121.39	2905	3569	4164
50520	Closure of nephrocutaneous or pyelocutaneous fistula	28.17	996.33	2699	3113	3604
50525	Closure of nephrovisceral fistula (eg, renocolic), including visceral repair; abdominal approach	35.56	1255.17	3344	4211	5063
50526	Closure of nephrovisceral fistula (eg, renocolic), including visceral repair; thoracic approach	37.53	1322.62	3331	4312	5050
50540	Symphysiotomy for horseshoe kidney with or without pyeloplasty and/or other plastic procedure, unilateral or bilateral (one operation)	31.28	1105.47	3702	4543	5065
Laparoscopy						
50541	Laparoscopy, surgical; ablation of renal cysts	24.97	882.25	2391	2921	3343
50542	Laparoscopy, surgical; ablation of renal mass lesion(s)	31.50	1113.05	3065	3737	4271
50543	Laparoscopy, surgical; partial nephrectomy	40.23	1421.16	3816	4604	5368
50544	Laparoscopy, surgical; pyeloplasty	34.16	1205.90	3082	3790	4433
50545	Laparoscopy, surgical; radical nephrectomy (includes removal of Gerota's fascia and surrounding fatty tissue, removal of regional lymph nodes, and adrenalectomy)	36.65	1293.82	3365	3899	4245
50546	Laparoscopy, surgical; nephrectomy, including partial ureterectomy	32.41	1145.64	3285	3725	4397
50547	Laparoscopy, surgical; donor nephrectomy (including cold preservation), from living donor	40.51	1435.18	4587	5106	5612
50548	Laparoscopy, surgical; nephrectomy with total ureterectomy	36.98	1305.19	3276	4033	5121
50549	Unlisted laparoscopy procedure, renal	-	-	IR	IR	IR
Endoscopy						
50551	Renal endoscopy through established nephrostomy or pyelostomy, with or without irrigation, instillation, or ureteropyelography, exclusive of radiologic service;	10.25	367.23	758	855	1072
50553	Renal endoscopy through established nephrostomy or pyelostomy, with or without irrigation, instillation, or ureteropyelography, exclusive of radiologic service; with ureteral catheterization, with or without dilation of ureter	10.72	383.52	729	845	1273
50555	Renal endoscopy through established nephrostomy or pyelostomy, with or without irrigation, instillation, or ureteropyelography, exclusive of radiologic service; with biopsy	11.86	424.45	878	1087	1520
50557	Renal endoscopy through established nephrostomy or pyelostomy, with or without irrigation, instillation, or ureteropyelography, exclusive of radiologic service; with fulguration and/or incision, with or without biopsy	11.84	423.69	856	1167	1712
50561	Renal endoscopy through established nephrostomy or pyelostomy, with or without irrigation, instillation, or ureteropyelography, exclusive of radiologic service; with removal of foreign body or calculus	13.37	477.89	1323	1559	1880
50562	Renal endoscopy through established nephrostomy or pyelostomy, with or without irrigation, instillation, or ureteropyelography, exclusive of radiologic service; with resection of tumor	16.23	573.39	1223	1481	1935
50570	Renal endoscopy through nephrotomy or pyelotomy, with or without irrigation, instillation, or ureteropyelography, exclusive of radiologic service;	13.70	482.81	875	1221	1402
50572	Renal endoscopy through nephrotomy or pyelotomy, with or without irrigation, instillation, or ureteropyelography, exclusive of radiologic service; with ureteral catheterization, with or without dilation of ureter	14.97	527.91	1490	1926	2283
50574	Renal endoscopy through nephrotomy or pyelotomy, with or without irrigation, instillation, or ureteropyelography, exclusive of radiologic service; with biopsy	15.78	555.96	1448	1977	2427
50575	Renal endoscopy through nephrotomy or pyelotomy, with or without irrigation, instillation, or ureteropyelography, exclusive of radiologic service; with endopyelotomy (includes cystoscopy, ureteroscopy, dilation of ureter and ureteral pelvic junction, incision of ureteral pelvic junction and insertion of endopyelotomy stent)	19.96	703.38	2022	2451	2776
50576	Renal endoscopy through nephrotomy or pyelotomy, with or without irrigation, instillation, or ureteropyelography, exclusive of radiologic service; with fulguration and/or incision, with or without biopsy	15.73	554.44	1638	2033	2304

© PFR 2007

● = New Code ⊗ = Conscious Sedation ✚ = Add-on Code ∅ = Modifier '51' Exempt ▲ =Revised Code

		Medicare RVU	National Fee	PFR Fee Information 50%	75%	90%
50580	Renal endoscopy through nephrotomy or pyelotomy, with or without irrigation, instillation, or ureteropyelography, exclusive of radiologic service; with removal of foreign body or calculus	16.95	597.26	1778	2255	2366

Other Procedures

50590	Lithotripsy, extracorporeal shock wave	23.89	868.61	2892	3571	4282
⊗ **50592**	Ablation, one or more renal tumor(s), percutaneous, unilateral, radiofrequency	137.36	5179.83	15522	19836	22908

Ureter
Incision

50600	Ureterotomy with exploration or drainage (separate procedure)	25.34	895.52	2349	2787	3190
50605	Ureterotomy for insertion of indwelling stent, all types	25.17	890.21	1948	2408	2634
50610	Ureterolithotomy; upper one-third of ureter	26.08	923.18	2630	2935	3852
50620	Ureterolithotomy; middle one-third of ureter	24.39	862.17	2485	3067	3610
50630	Ureterolithotomy; lower one-third of ureter	23.97	847.01	2658	3253	4052

Excision

50650	Ureterectomy, with bladder cuff (separate procedure)	27.88	985.34	2671	3114	3552
50660	Ureterectomy, total, ectopic ureter, combination abdominal, vaginal and/or perineal approach	30.96	1093.72	3023	3439	3920

Introduction

(Medicare fees for the code below are based on Non Facility RVUs. PFR information reflects fee when procedure is performed in a facility.)

50684	Injection procedure for ureterography or ureteropyelography through ureterostomy or indwelling ureteral catheter	5.54	206.92	142	157	186

(Medicare fees for the code below are based on Non Facility RVUs. PFR information reflects fee when procedure is performed in a facility.)

50686	Manometric studies through ureterostomy or indwelling ureteral catheter	4.71	172.81	115	139	181
50688	Change of ureterostomy tube or externally accessible ureteral stent via ileal conduit	2.26	81.10	162	180	206
50690	Injection procedure for visualization of ileal conduit and/or ureteropyelography, exclusive of radiologic service	2.94	106.87	151	175	217

Repair

50700	Ureteroplasty, plastic operation on ureter (eg, stricture)	25.25	894.00	2710	2921	3344
50715	Ureterolysis, with or without repositioning of ureter for retroperitoneal fibrosis	31.36	1110.40	2734	3319	3936
50722	Ureterolysis for ovarian vein syndrome	27.57	977.00	2342	2518	2748
50725	Ureterolysis for retrocaval ureter, with reanastomosis of upper urinary tract or vena cava	30.04	1061.89	3174	3856	4385
50727	Revision of urinary-cutaneous anastomosis (any type urostomy);	13.43	477.89	1690	1918	2361
50728	Revision of urinary-cutaneous anastomosis (any type urostomy); with repair of fascial defect and hernia	18.98	673.44	2244	2697	2948
50740	Ureteropyelostomy, anastomosis of ureter and renal pelvis	29.96	1059.61	3019	3459	3919
50750	Ureterocalycostomy, anastomosis of ureter to renal calyx	30.91	1091.07	3266	3725	4364
50760	Ureteroureterostomy	29.70	1049.76	3196	3587	4003
50770	Transureteroureterostomy, anastomosis of ureter to contralateral ureter	31.21	1102.44	3412	3911	4366
50780	Ureteroneocystostomy; anastomosis of single ureter to bladder	29.56	1044.83	3123	3567	4042
50782	Ureteroneocystostomy; anastomosis of duplicated ureter to bladder	29.83	1056.20	3324	3870	4102
50783	Ureteroneocystostomy; with extensive ureteral tailoring	31.20	1104.33	3361	4018	4652
50785	Ureteroneocystostomy; with vesico-psoas hitch or bladder flap	32.58	1150.57	3635	4195	4670
50800	Ureteroenterostomy, direct anastomosis of ureter to intestine	24.62	871.26	3088	3515	4072
50810	Ureterosigmoidostomy, with creation of sigmoid bladder and establishment of abdominal or perineal colostomy, including intestine anastomosis	33.92	1200.21	4076	5079	6691

● = New Code ⊗ = Conscious Sedation ✚ = Add-on Code ∅ = Modifier '51' Exempt ▲ =Revised Code

		Medicare RVU	National Fee	PFR Fee Information 50%	75%	90%
50815	Ureterocolon conduit, including intestine anastomosis	32.87	1161.56	4333	5294	6082
50820	Ureteroileal conduit (ileal bladder), including intestine anastomosis (Bricker operation)	35.30	1246.83	4208	5443	6347
50825	Continent diversion, including intestine anastomosis using any segment of small and/or large intestine (Kock pouch or Camey enterocystoplasty)	44.72	1578.43	5425	6045	8053
50830	Urinary undiversion (eg, taking down of ureteroileal conduit, ureterosigmoidostomy or ureteroenterostomy with ureteroureterostomy or ureteroneocystostomy)	49.10	1732.67	5293	5921	6732
50840	Replacement of all or part of ureter by intestine segment, including intestine anastomosis	33.00	1166.11	3726	4405	4857
50845	Cutaneous appendico-vesicostomy	33.59	1188.47	3480	4435	5379
50860	Ureterostomy, transplantation of ureter to skin	25.47	900.82	2561	2938	3399
50900	Ureterorrhaphy, suture of ureter (separate procedure)	22.67	802.29	2439	2856	3172
50920	Closure of ureterocutaneous fistula	23.72	839.05	2643	3019	3259
50930	Closure of ureterovisceral fistula (including visceral repair)	29.89	1056.20	3122	3814	4349
50940	Deligation of ureter	23.91	845.87	2532	3104	3693

Laparoscopy

50945	Laparoscopy, surgical; ureterolithotomy	26.73	944.78	2342	2862	3123
50947	Laparoscopy, surgical; ureteroneocystostomy with cystoscopy and ureteral stent placement	38.22	1350.67	3139	3910	4572
50948	Laparoscopy, surgical; ureteroneocystostomy without cystoscopy and ureteral stent placement	34.96	1234.70	2843	3537	4065
50949	Unlisted laparoscopy procedure, ureter	-	-	IR	IR	IR

Endoscopy

50951	Ureteral endoscopy through established ureterostomy, with or without irrigation, instillation, or ureteropyelography, exclusive of radiologic service;	10.68	382.39	627	710	915
50953	Ureteral endoscopy through established ureterostomy, with or without irrigation, instillation, or ureteropyelography, exclusive of radiologic service; with ureteral catheterization, with or without dilation of ureter	11.22	401.33	600	731	840
50955	Ureteral endoscopy through established ureterostomy, with or without irrigation, instillation, or ureteropyelography, exclusive of radiologic service; with biopsy	13.34	479.78	706	831	907
50957	Ureteral endoscopy through established ureterostomy, with or without irrigation, instillation, or ureteropyelography, exclusive of radiologic service; with fulguration and/or incision, with or without biopsy	12.02	429.76	759	891	1046
50961	Ureteral endoscopy through established ureterostomy, with or without irrigation, instillation, or ureteropyelography, exclusive of radiologic service; with removal of foreign body or calculus	10.92	390.72	890	998	1246
50970	Ureteral endoscopy through ureterotomy, with or without irrigation, instillation, or ureteropyelography, exclusive of radiologic service;	10.33	364.19	760	936	1112
50972	Ureteral endoscopy through ureterotomy, with or without irrigation, instillation, or ureteropyelography, exclusive of radiologic service; with ureteral catheterization, with or without dilation of ureter	9.98	352.07	749	856	910
50974	Ureteral endoscopy through ureterotomy, with or without irrigation, instillation, or ureteropyelography, exclusive of radiologic service; with biopsy	13.12	462.35	1068	1342	1508
50976	Ureteral endoscopy through ureterotomy, with or without irrigation, instillation, or ureteropyelography, exclusive of radiologic service; with fulguration and/or incision, with or without biopsy	12.91	454.77	1005	1249	1489
50980	Ureteral endoscopy through ureterotomy, with or without irrigation, instillation, or ureteropyelography, exclusive of radiologic service; with removal of foreign body or calculus	9.88	348.28	915	1076	1209

Bladder

Incision

51000	Aspiration of bladder by needle	2.52	92.47	122	148	192

(Medicare fees for the code below are based on Non Facility RVUs. PFR information reflects fee when procedure is performed in a facility.)

51005	Aspiration of bladder; by trocar or intracatheter	5.25	195.17	174	220	289
51010	Aspiration of bladder; with insertion of suprapubic catheter	9.94	360.41	459	550	676
51020	Cystotomy or cystostomy; with fulguration and/or insertion of radioactive material	12.26	435.82	1814	2007	2124

● = New Code ⊗ = Conscious Sedation ✚ = Add-on Code ∅ = Modifier '51' Exempt ▲ =Revised Code

Code	Description	Medicare RVU	National Fee	PFR Fee Information 50%	75%	90%
51030	Cystotomy or cystostomy; with cryosurgical destruction of intravesical lesion	12.45	442.64	1728	1982	2228
51040	Cystostomy, cystotomy with drainage	7.75	276.65	1570	1840	2278
51045	Cystotomy, with insertion of ureteral catheter or stent (separate procedure)	12.46	443.02	1613	1988	2325
51050	Cystolithotomy, cystotomy with removal of calculus, without vesical neck resection	12.45	441.88	1895	2207	2785
51060	Transvesical ureterolithotomy	15.44	547.62	2502	2714	2928
51065	Cystotomy, with calculus basket extraction and/or ultrasonic or electrohydraulic fragmentation of ureteral calculus	15.32	543.07	2154	2519	2787
51080	Drainage of perivesical or prevesical space abscess	10.77	383.14	1544	1789	1996

Excision

Code	Description	Medicare RVU	National Fee	PFR Fee Information 50%	75%	90%
51500	Excision of urachal cyst or sinus, with or without umbilical hernia repair	17.17	609.01	1990	2245	2474
51520	Cystotomy; for simple excision of vesical neck (separate procedure)	15.92	565.05	1974	2347	2664
51525	Cystotomy; for excision of bladder diverticulum, single or multiple (separate procedure)	23.06	815.55	2637	3002	3329
51530	Cystotomy; for excision of bladder tumor	20.78	735.59	2222	2557	2840
51535	Cystotomy for excision, incision, or repair of ureterocele	21.48	761.36	2226	2713	2920
51550	Cystectomy, partial; simple	25.70	908.78	2728	3074	3669
51555	Cystectomy, partial; complicated (eg, postradiation, previous surgery, difficult location)	34.13	1205.52	3410	3825	4524
51565	Cystectomy, partial, with reimplantation of ureter(s) into bladder (ureteroneocystostomy)	34.90	1233.18	3723	4444	5371
51570	Cystectomy, complete; (separate procedure)	39.72	1401.07	4604	5316	5825
51575	Cystectomy, complete; with bilateral pelvic lymphadenectomy, including external iliac, hypogastric, and obturator nodes	49.44	1744.04	5300	6306	7319
51580	Cystectomy, complete, with ureterosigmoidostomy or ureterocutaneous transplantations;	51.22	1806.95	5409	6175	6957
51585	Cystectomy, complete, with ureterosigmoidostomy or ureterocutaneous transplantations; with bilateral pelvic lymphadenectomy, including external iliac, hypogastric, and obturator nodes	57.15	2015.77	6175	7455	8800
51590	Cystectomy, complete, with ureteroileal conduit or sigmoid bladder, including intestine anastomosis; *(UNBUNDLING ALERT: 51595 cannot be used with 44130, 51590, 51840, or 51841 by the same physician on the same day.)*	52.31	1844.47	7117	8020	9861
51595	Cystectomy, complete, with ureteroileal conduit or sigmoid bladder, including intestine anastomosis; with bilateral pelvic lymphadenectomy, including external iliac, hypogastric, and obturator nodes	59.33	2091.56	7771	8758	10930
51596	Cystectomy, complete, with continent diversion, any open technique, using any segment of small and/or large intestine to construct neobladder	63.62	2243.15	8533	9555	10544
51597	Pelvic exenteration, complete, for vesical, prostatic or urethral malignancy, with removal of bladder and ureteral transplantations, with or without hysterectomy and/or abdominoperineal resection of rectum and colon and colostomy, or any combination thereof	61.64	2173.42	9614	10745	12986

Introduction

(Medicare fees for the code below are based on Non Facility RVUs. PFR information reflects fee when procedure is performed in a facility.)
(UNBUNDLING ALERT: 51600 cannot be used with 53670 by the same physician on the same day.)

Code	Description	Medicare RVU	National Fee	PFR Fee Information 50%	75%	90%
51600	Injection procedure for cystography or voiding urethrocystography	5.75	214.50	151	181	225

(Medicare fees for the code below are based on Non Facility RVUs. PFR information reflects fee when procedure is performed in a facility.)
(UNBUNDLING ALERT: 51605 cannot be used with 53670 by the same physician on the same day.)

Code	Description	Medicare RVU	National Fee	PFR Fee Information 50%	75%	90%
51605	Injection procedure and placement of chain for contrast and/or chain urethrocystography	1.05	37.52	139	154	180
51610	Injection procedure for retrograde urethrocystography	3.30	120.89	180	203	230

● = New Code ⊗ = Conscious Sedation ✚ = Add-on Code ∅ = Modifier '51' Exempt ▲ =Revised Code

Code	Description	Medicare RVU	National Fee	PFR Fee Information 50%	75%	90%
51700	Bladder irrigation, simple, lavage and/or instillation	2.52	92.09	125	149	180
	(See also HCPCS code P9612 for catheterization for collection of specimen, single patient, all places of service.)					
	(See also HCPCS codes A4310-A4355 for urinary catheterization supplies.)					
51701	Insertion of non-indwelling bladder catheter (eg, straight catheterization for residual urine)	1.99	73.52	108	135	173
51702	Insertion of temporary indwelling bladder catheter; simple (eg, Foley)	2.48	92.09	150	196	241
51703	Insertion of temporary indwelling bladder catheter; complicated (eg, altered anatomy, fractured catheter/balloon)	4.19	153.11	221	271	370
51705	Change of cystostomy tube; simple	3.31	121.65	134	152	176
51710	Change of cystostomy tube; complicated	4.79	175.84	319	380	453
51715	Endoscopic injection of implant material into the submucosal tissues of the urethra and/or bladder neck	8.06	291.05	803	923	999
	(UNBUNDLING ALERT: 51720 cannot be used with 51700, 53670, or 53675 by the same physician on the same day.)					
▲ 51720	Bladder instillation of anticarcinogenic agent (including retention time)	3.36	121.65	211	253	276

Urodynamics

Code	Description	Medicare RVU	National Fee	PFR Fee Information 50%	75%	90%
51725	Simple cystometrogram (CMG) (eg, spinal manometer)	6.93	256.95	331	415	490
-26		2.14	75.42	116	145	171
	(UNBUNDLING ALERT: 51726 cannot be used with 51725, or 53670 by the same physician on the same day.)					
51726	Complex cystometrogram (eg, calibrated electronic equipment)	9.30	346.00	424	561	725
-26		2.43	85.65	127	168	217
51736	Simple uroflowmetry (UFR) (eg, stop-watch flow rate, mechanical uroflowmeter)	1.34	48.51	103	165	184
-26		0.87	30.70	72	115	129
51741	Complex uroflowmetry (eg, calibrated electronic equipment)	2.16	77.69	162	203	237
-26		1.62	57.23	130	162	190
51772	Urethral pressure profile studies (UPP) (urethral closure pressure profile), any technique	7.25	268.69	325	408	478
-26		2.31	81.48	114	143	167
51784	Electromyography studies (EMG) of anal or urethral sphincter, other than needle, any technique	5.64	208.06	270	318	358
-26		2.16	76.17	108	127	143
51785	Needle electromyography studies (EMG) of anal or urethral sphincter, any technique	6.14	227.01	263	325	402
-26		2.16	76.17	105	130	161
	(Medicare fees for the code below are based on Non Facility RVUs. PFR information reflects fee when procedure is performed in a facility.)					
51792	Stimulus evoked response (eg, measurement of bulbocavernosus reflex latency time)	7.04	262.63	294	482	690
-26		1.58	55.71	74	120	172
	(Medicare fees for the code below are based on Non Facility RVUs. PFR information reflects fee when procedure is performed in a facility.)					
51795	Voiding pressure studies (VP); bladder voiding pressure, any technique	8.90	331.60	344	473	508
-26		2.17	76.55	86	118	127
51797	Voiding pressure studies (VP); intra-abdominal voiding pressure (AP) (rectal, gastric, intraperitoneal)	7.32	271.35	314	346	410
-26		2.27	79.96	110	121	143
51798	Measurement of post-voiding residual urine and/or bladder capacity by ultrasound, non-imaging	0.48	18.19	42	74	104

Repair

Code	Description	Medicare RVU	National Fee	PFR Fee Information 50%	75%	90%
51800	Cystoplasty or cystourethroplasty, plastic operation on bladder and/or vesical neck (anterior Y-plasty, vesical fundus resection), any procedure, with or without wedge resection of posterior vesical neck	28.28	1000.12	2999	3299	4067

● = New Code ⊗ = Conscious Sedation ✚ = Add-on Code ∅ = Modifier '51' Exempt ▲ =Revised Code

		Medicare RVU	National Fee	PFR Fee Information 50%	75%	90%
51820	Cystourethroplasty with unilateral or bilateral ureteroneocystostomy	30.03	1064.16	3641	4092	5103
	(UNBUNDLING ALERT: 51840 cannot be used with 49000, 53660, 53661, 57240, or 57289 by the same physician on the same day.)					
51840	Anterior vesicourethropexy, or urethropexy (eg, Marshall-Marchetti-Krantz, Burch); simple	17.96	637.81	2388	2639	3180
51841	Anterior vesicourethropexy, or urethropexy (eg, Marshall-Marchetti-Krantz, Burch); complicated (eg, secondary repair)	21.34	756.81	2749	2952	3420
	(UNBUNDLING ALERT: 51845 cannot be used with 49000, 53660, 53661, 57240, or 57289 by the same physician on the same day.)					
51845	Abdomino-vaginal vesical neck suspension, with or without endoscopic control (eg, Stamey, Raz, modified Pereyra)	15.90	564.29	2492	2922	3192
51860	Cystorrhaphy, suture of bladder wound, injury or rupture; simple	19.68	698.07	2069	2438	2703
51865	Cystorrhaphy, suture of bladder wound, injury or rupture; complicated	24.06	851.94	2711	3235	3588
51880	Closure of cystostomy (separate procedure)	12.68	450.60	1315	1602	1888
51900	Closure of vesicovaginal fistula, abdominal approach	22.26	788.27	3110	3629	3998
51920	Closure of vesicouterine fistula;	20.63	731.42	2534	2976	3309
51925	Closure of vesicouterine fistula; with hysterectomy	28.44	1011.48	3023	3744	4273
51940	Closure, exstrophy of bladder	44.56	1572.37	4409	4933	5616
51960	Enterocystoplasty, including intestinal anastomosis	37.38	1320.35	4753	5257	5988
51980	Cutaneous vesicostomy	19.17	679.12	2456	2943	3255

Laparoscopy

51990	Laparoscopy, surgical; urethral suspension for stress incontinence	20.75	735.97	2357	2834	3332
51992	Laparoscopy, surgical; sling operation for stress incontinence (eg, fascia or synthetic)	22.50	796.23	2419	2689	3184
51999	Unlisted laparoscopy procedure, bladder	-	-	IR	IR	IR

Endoscopy—-Cystoscopy, Urethroscopy, Cystourethroscopy

	(UNBUNDLING ALERT: 52000 cannot be used with HCPCS G0002 or CPT 53670 by the same physician on the same day.)					
52000	Cystourethroscopy (separate procedure)	5.77	210.33	412	483	558
	(Medicare fees for the code below are based on Non Facility RVUs. PFR information reflects fee when procedure is performed in a facility.)					
52001	Cystourethroscopy with irrigation and evacuation of multiple obstructing clots	10.92	393.00	446	520	623
	(UNBUNDLING ALERT: 52005 cannot be used with 51700, 52000, or 53670 by the same physician on the same day.)					
	(A4550 (Disposable Surgical Tray) can be coded in addition to 52005 in the office setting. Payment is at carrier discretion.)					
52005	Cystourethroscopy, with ureteral catheterization, with or without irrigation, instillation, or ureteropyelography, exclusive of radiologic service;	8.15	299.77	590	684	707
	(Medicare fees for the code below are based on Non Facility RVUs. PFR information reflects fee when procedure is performed in a facility.)					
	(UNBUNDLING ALERT: 52007 cannot be used with 51700, 52000, or 52005 by the same physician on the same day.)					
	(A4550 (Disposable Surgical Tray) can be coded in addition to 52007 in the office setting. Payment is at carrier discretion.)					
52007	Cystourethroscopy, with ureteral catheterization, with or without irrigation, instillation, or ureteropyelography, exclusive of radiologic service; with brush biopsy of ureter and/or renal pelvis	18.25	680.26	674	761	877
	(A4550 (Disposable Surgical Tray) can be coded in addition to 52010 in the office setting. Payment is at carrier discretion.)					
52010	Cystourethroscopy, with ejaculatory duct catheterization, with or without irrigation, instillation, or duct radiography, exclusive of radiologic service	13.33	493.80	564	686	814

● = New Code ⊗ = Conscious Sedation   ✚ = Add-on Code   ∅ = Modifier '51' Exempt   ▲ =Revised Code

		Medicare RVU	National Fee	PFR Fee Information 50%	75%	90%

Transurethral Surgery Urethra and Bladder

(Medicare fees for the code below are based on Non Facility RVUs. PFR information reflects fee when procedure is performed in a facility.)

(UNBUNDLING ALERT: 52204 cannot be used with 53670 by the same physician on the same day.)

(A4550 (Disposable Surgical Tray) can be coded in addition to 52204 in the office setting. Payment is at carrier discretion.)

▲ **52204** Cystourethroscopy, with biopsy(s) — 15.73 | 586.27 | 610 | 756 | 867

(Medicare fees for the code below are based on Non Facility RVUs. PFR information reflects fee when procedure is performed in a facility.)

(A4550 (Disposable Surgical Tray) can be coded in addition to 52214 in the office setting. Payment is at carrier discretion.)

52214 Cystourethroscopy, with fulguration (including cryosurgery or laser surgery) of trigone, bladder neck, prostatic fossa, urethra, or periurethral glands — 37.51 | 1407.51 | 712 | 767 | 831

(Medicare fees for the code below are based on Non Facility RVUs. PFR information reflects fee when procedure is performed in a facility.)

(A4550 (Disposable Surgical Tray) can be coded in addition to 52224 in the office setting. Payment is at carrier discretion.)

52224 Cystourethroscopy, with fulguration (including cryosurgery or laser surgery) or treatment of MINOR (less than 0.5 cm) lesion(s) with or without biopsy — 35.47 | 1332.10 | 685 | 806 | 935

(A4550 (Disposable Surgical Tray) can be coded in addition to 52234 in the office setting. Payment is at carrier discretion.)

52234 Cystourethroscopy, with fulguration (including cryosurgery or laser surgery) and/or resection of; SMALL bladder tumor(s) (0.5 up to 2.0 cm) — 6.78 | 239.51 | 1015 | 1153 | 1335

(A4550 (Disposable Surgical Tray) can be coded in addition to 52235 in the office setting. Payment is at carrier discretion.)

(UNBUNDLING ALERT: 52235 cannot be used with 51700, 52214, 52224, or 52234 by the same physician on the same day.)

52235 Cystourethroscopy, with fulguration (including cryosurgery or laser surgery) and/or resection of; MEDIUM bladder tumor(s) (2.0 to 5.0 cm) — 7.96 | 280.82 | 1587 | 1937 | 2250

(UNBUNDLING ALERT: 52240 cannot be used with 51700, 52214, 52224, or 52234 by the same physician on the same day.)

(A4550 (Disposable Surgical Tray) can be coded in addition to 52240 in the office setting. Payment is at carrier discretion.)

52240 Cystourethroscopy, with fulguration (including cryosurgery or laser surgery) and/or resection of; LARGE bladder tumor(s) — 14.00 | 493.43 | 2305 | 2705 | 3187

(A4550 (Disposable Surgical Tray) can be coded in addition to 52250 in the office setting. Payment is at carrier discretion.)

52250 Cystourethroscopy with insertion of radioactive substance, with or without biopsy or fulguration — 6.64 | 234.59 | 761 | 919 | 1058

(A4550 (Disposable Surgical Tray) can be coded in addition to 52260 in the office setting. Payment is at carrier discretion.)

52260 Cystourethroscopy, with dilation of bladder for interstitial cystitis; general or conduction (spinal) anesthesia — 5.76 | 203.51 | 620 | 757 | 888

(Medicare fees for the code below are based on Non Facility RVUs. PFR information reflects fee when procedure is performed in a facility.)

52265 Cystourethroscopy, with dilation of bladder for interstitial cystitis; local anesthesia — 15.09 | 560.50 | 576 | 643 | 677

(A4550 (Disposable Surgical Tray) can be coded in addition to 52270 in the office setting. Payment is at carrier discretion.)

52270 Cystourethroscopy, with internal urethrotomy; female — 13.64 | 504.04 | 760 | 837 | 906

(A4550 (Disposable Surgical Tray) can be coded in addition to 52275 in the office setting. Payment is at carrier discretion.)

52275 Cystourethroscopy, with internal urethrotomy; male — 19.02 | 703.00 | 804 | 978 | 1140

(UNBUNDLING ALERT: 52276 cannot be used with 51700, 53600, 53620, or 53660 by the same physician on the same day.)

(A4550 (Disposable Surgical Tray) can be coded in addition to 52276 in the office setting. Payment is at carrier discretion.)

52276 Cystourethroscopy with direct vision internal urethrotomy — 7.30 | 257.70 | 1186 | 1313 | 1543

(A4550 (Disposable Surgical Tray) can be coded in addition to 52277 in the office setting. Payment is at carrier discretion.)

52277 Cystourethroscopy, with resection of external sphincter (sphincterotomy) — 9.00 | 317.58 | 1000 | 1208 | 1413

(UNBUNDLING ALERT: 52281 cannot be used with 51700, 52000, 53600, or 53601 by the same physician on the same day.)

52281 Cystourethroscopy, with calibration and/or dilation of urethral stricture or stenosis, with or without meatotomy, with or without injection procedure for cystography, male or female — 9.65 | 355.10 | 601 | 778 | 986

● = New Code   ⊗ = Conscious Sedation   ✚ = Add-on Code   ∅ = Modifier '51' Exempt   ▲ = Revised Code

		Medicare RVU	National Fee	PFR Fee Information 50%	75%	90%
52282	Cystourethroscopy, with insertion of urethral stent	9.28	327.43	929	1184	1492
	(A4550 (Disposable Surgical Tray) can be coded in addition to 52283 in the office setting. Payment is at carrier discretion.)					
52283	Cystourethroscopy, with steroid injection into stricture	7.98	288.02	573	675	772
52285	Cystourethroscopy for treatment of the female urethral syndrome with any or all of the following: urethral meatotomy, urethral dilation, internal urethrotomy, lysis of urethrovaginal septal fibrosis, lateral incisions of the bladder neck, and fulguration of polyp(s) of urethra, bladder neck, and/or trigone	7.97	288.40	688	798	991
	(A4550 (Disposable Surgical Tray) can be coded in addition to 52290 in the office setting. Payment is at carrier discretion.)					
52290	Cystourethroscopy; with ureteral meatotomy, unilateral or bilateral	6.72	237.24	671	856	1030
	(A4550 (Disposable Surgical Tray) can be coded in addition to 52300 in the office setting. Payment is at carrier discretion.)					
52300	Cystourethroscopy; with resection or fulguration of orthotopic ureterocele(s), unilateral or bilateral	7.78	274.76	916	1066	1270
52301	Cystourethroscopy; with resection or fulguration of ectopic ureterocele(s), unilateral or bilateral	7.99	281.96	931	1119	1278
	(A4550 (Disposable Surgical Tray) can be coded in addition to 52305 in the office setting. Payment is at carrier discretion.)					
52305	Cystourethroscopy; with incision or resection of orifice of bladder diverticulum, single or multiple	7.71	272.10	870	1090	1268
	(A4550 (Disposable Surgical Tray) can be coded in addition to 52310 in the office setting. Payment is at carrier discretion.)					
52310	Cystourethroscopy, with removal of foreign body, calculus, or ureteral stent from urethra or bladder (separate procedure); simple	7.54	275.14	687	819	917
	(A4550 (Disposable Surgical Tray) can be coded in addition to 52315 in the office setting. Payment is at carrier discretion.)					
52315	Cystourethroscopy, with removal of foreign body, calculus, or ureteral stent from urethra or bladder (separate procedure); complicated	13.74	501.00	1147	1417	1661
52317	Litholapaxy: crushing or fragmentation of calculus by any means in bladder and removal of fragments; simple or small (less than 2.5 cm)	33.18	1231.67	1369	1527	1807
52318	Litholapaxy: crushing or fragmentation of calculus by any means in bladder and removal of fragments; complicated or large (over 2.5 cm)	13.19	465.00	1712	2110	2468

Ureter and Pelvis

		Medicare RVU	National Fee	50%	75%	90%
52320	Cystourethroscopy (including ureteral catheterization); with removal of ureteral calculus	6.81	240.27	1130	1344	1498
52325	Cystourethroscopy (including ureteral catheterization); with fragmentation of ureteral calculus (eg, ultrasonic or electro-hydraulic technique)	8.90	313.79	1611	1958	2190
	(Medicare fees for the code below are based on Non Facility RVUs. PFR information reflects fee when procedure is performed in a facility.)					
52327	Cystourethroscopy (including ureteral catheterization); with subureteric injection of implant material	33.87	1263.88	1060	1315	1511
	(Medicare fees for the code below are based on Non Facility RVUs. PFR information reflects fee when procedure is performed in a facility.)					
52330	Cystourethroscopy (including ureteral catheterization); with manipulation, without removal of ureteral calculus	39.62	1482.17	918	1036	1275
52332	Cystourethroscopy, with insertion of indwelling ureteral stent (eg, Gibbons or double-J type)	10.46	385.80	876	978	1150
52334	Cystourethroscopy with insertion of ureteral guide wire through kidney to establish a percutaneous nephrostomy, retrograde	7.06	249.37	817	954	1073
52341	Cystourethroscopy; with treatment of ureteral stricture (eg, balloon dilation, laser, electrocautery, and incision)	8.98	317.20	1114	1401	1649
52342	Cystourethroscopy; with treatment of ureteropelvic junction stricture (eg, balloon dilation, laser, electrocautery, and incision)	9.66	341.08	1194	1531	1887
52343	Cystourethroscopy; with treatment of intra-renal stricture (eg, balloon dilation, laser, electrocautery, and incision)	10.66	375.94	1322	1649	1957
52344	Cystourethroscopy with ureteroscopy; with treatment of ureteral stricture (eg, balloon dilation, laser, electrocautery, and incision)	11.45	403.99	1357	1742	2222
52345	Cystourethroscopy with ureteroscopy; with treatment of ureteropelvic junction stricture (eg, balloon dilation, laser, electrocautery, and incision)	12.16	429.00	1461	1895	2364
52346	Cystourethroscopy with ureteroscopy; with treatment of intra-renal stricture (eg, balloon dilation, laser, electrocautery, and incision)	13.61	480.16	1677	2096	2524
52351	Cystourethroscopy, with ureteroscopy and/or pyeloscopy; diagnostic	8.62	304.32	1229	1528	1746
52352	Cystourethroscopy, with ureteroscopy and/or pyeloscopy; with removal or manipulation of calculus (ureteral catheterization is included)	10.13	357.75	2064	2680	3097

● = New Code ⊗ = Conscious Sedation ✚ = Add-on Code ∅ = Modifier '51' Exempt ▲ =Revised Code

		Medicare RVU	National Fee	PFR Fee Information 50%	75%	90%
52353	Cystourethroscopy, with ureteroscopy and/or pyeloscopy; with lithotripsy (ureteral catheterization is included)	11.67	411.95	2585	3025	3421
52354	Cystourethroscopy, with ureteroscopy and/or pyeloscopy; with biopsy and/or fulguration of ureteral or renal pelvic lesion	10.79	380.87	1467	1920	2208
52355	Cystourethroscopy, with ureteroscopy and/or pyeloscopy; with resection of ureteral or renal pelvic tumor	12.88	454.39	1674	2091	2539

Vesical Neck and Prostrate

52400	Cystourethroscopy with incision, fulguration, or resection of congenital posterior urethral valves, or congenital obstructive hypertrophic mucosal folds	14.92	527.15	1670	2074	2294
52402	Cystourethroscopy with transurethral resection or incision of ejaculatory ducts	7.51	264.52	914	1084	1219
52450	Transurethral incision of prostate	12.32	437.72	1274	1564	1655
52500	Transurethral resection of bladder neck (separate procedure)	14.51	514.27	1604	1754	2108
52510	Transurethral balloon dilation of the prostatic urethra	11.55	409.29	1402	1782	1924
52601	Transurethral electrosurgical resection of prostate, including control of postoperative bleeding, complete (vasectomy, meatotomy, cystourethroscopy, urethral calibration and/or dilation, and internal urethrotomy are included)	21.99	775.76	2487	2756	3271
52606	Transurethral fulguration for postoperative bleeding occurring after the usual follow-up time	13.48	477.13	891	972	1216
52612	Transurethral resection of prostate; first stage of two-stage resection (partial resection)	13.93	493.43	2303	2483	2804
52614	Transurethral resection of prostate; second stage of two-stage resection (resection completed)	12.17	431.27	1389	1542	1707
52620	Transurethral resection; of residual obstructive tissue after 90 days postoperative	11.07	392.24	1265	1444	1671
52630	Transurethral resection; of regrowth of obstructive tissue longer than one year postoperative	11.78	417.25	2364	2635	2937
52640	Transurethral resection; of postoperative bladder neck contracture	10.71	379.73	1566	2047	2164
	(Medicare fees for the code below are based on Non Facility RVUs. PFR information reflects fee when procedure is performed in a facility.)					
52647	Laser coagulation of prostate, including control of postoperative bleeding, complete (vasectomy, meatotomy, cystourethroscopy, urethral calibration and/or dilation, and internal urethrotomy are included if performed)	77.85	2907.88	2091	2460	2803
52648	Laser vaporization of prostate, including control of postoperative bleeding, complete (vasectomy, meatotomy, cystourethroscopy, urethral calibration and/or dilation, internal urethrotomy and transurethral resection of prostate are included if performed)	78.89	2943.88	2333	2783	3135
52700	Transurethral drainage of prostatic abscess	11.52	408.54	1205	1293	1574

Urethra

Incision

53000	Urethrotomy or urethrostomy, external (separate procedure); pendulous urethra	4.07	145.53	435	528	643
53010	Urethrotomy or urethrostomy, external (separate procedure); perineal urethra, external	7.73	276.27	897	1008	1160
53020	Meatotomy, cutting of meatus (separate procedure); except infant	2.65	93.61	353	431	502
	(Medicare fees for the code below are based on Non Facility RVUs. PFR information reflects fee when procedure is performed in a facility.)					
53025	Meatotomy, cutting of meatus (separate procedure); infant	1.80	64.05	188	284	355
53040	Drainage of deep periurethral abscess	10.63	378.22	691	902	1363
53060	Drainage of Skene's gland abscess or cyst	4.99	178.88	318	372	432
53080	Drainage of perineal urinary extravasation; uncomplicated (separate procedure)	13.05	468.41	742	996	1240
53085	Drainage of perineal urinary extravasation; complicated	18.67	665.48	1740	1985	2267

Excision

53200	Biopsy of urethra	4.21	149.70	408	560	619
53210	Urethrectomy, total, including cystostomy; female	20.82	737.11	2113	2319	2875
53215	Urethrectomy, total, including cystostomy; male	25.12	888.32	2652	3068	3473
53220	Excision or fulguration of carcinoma of urethra	12.07	428.62	1491	1617	1774

● = New Code ⊗ = Conscious Sedation ✚ = Add-on Code ∅ = Modifier '51' Exempt ▲ =Revised Code

		Medicare RVU	National Fee	PFR Fee Information 50%	75%	90%
53230	Excision of urethral diverticulum (separate procedure); female	16.21	574.91	1902	2258	2482
53235	Excision of urethral diverticulum (separate procedure); male	17.02	603.71	1916	2152	2410
53240	Marsupialization of urethral diverticulum, male or female	11.35	403.61	934	1010	1342
53250	Excision of bulbourethral gland (Cowper's gland)	10.57	375.94	1346	1492	1579
53260	Excision or fulguration; urethral polyp(s), distal urethra	5.55	198.96	437	573	632
53265	Excision or fulguration; urethral caruncle	6.16	221.32	544	628	712
53270	Excision or fulguration; Skene's glands	5.64	201.99	517	613	694
53275	Excision or fulguration; urethral prolapse	7.25	257.32	618	726	875

Repair

		Medicare RVU	National Fee	50%	75%	90%
53400	Urethroplasty; first stage, for fistula, diverticulum, or stricture (eg, Johannsen type)	21.55	763.26	1685	2056	2647
53405	Urethroplasty; second stage (formation of urethra), including urinary diversion	23.61	835.64	2062	2440	2901
53410	Urethroplasty, one-stage reconstruction of male anterior urethra	26.47	936.45	2519	2900	3209
53415	Urethroplasty, transpubic or perineal, one stage, for reconstruction or repair of prostatic or membranous urethra	30.20	1066.06	2966	3402	3792
53420	Urethroplasty, two-stage reconstruction or repair of prostatic or membranous urethra; first stage	22.36	790.16	2602	3196	3547
53425	Urethroplasty, two-stage reconstruction or repair of prostatic or membranous urethra; second stage	25.59	905.37	2672	3308	3574
53430	Urethroplasty, reconstruction of female urethra	25.90	915.60	2411	3050	3313
53431	Urethroplasty with tubularization of posterior urethra and/or lower bladder for incontinence (eg, Tenago, Leadbetter procedure)	31.28	1105.09	2992	3640	4144
53440	Sling operation for correction of male urinary incontinence (eg, fascia or synthetic)	23.13	818.21	2870	3485	3809
53442	Removal or revision of sling for male urinary incontinence (eg, fascia or synthetic)	20.32	719.29	1150	1383	1663
53444	Insertion of tandem cuff (dual cuff)	21.45	759.47	2145	2609	2971
53445	Insertion of inflatable urethral/bladder neck sphincter, including placement of pump, reservoir, and cuff	23.75	842.08	4272	5211	6453
53446	Removal of inflatable urethral/bladder neck sphincter, including pump, reservoir, and cuff	17.31	614.32	2448	2978	3389
53447	Removal and replacement of inflatable urethral/bladder neck sphincter including pump, reservoir, and cuff at the same operative session	22.06	782.20	2355	2817	3209
53448	Removal and replacement of inflatable urethral/bladder neck sphincter including pump, reservoir, and cuff through an infected field at the same operative session including irrigation and debridement of infected tissue	34.71	1226.74	4007	4875	5548
53449	Repair of inflatable urethral/bladder neck sphincter, including pump, reservoir, and cuff	16.34	579.45	1730	2017	2297
53450	Urethromeatoplasty, with mucosal advancement	10.78	383.14	809	1013	1303
53460	Urethromeatoplasty, with partial excision of distal urethral segment (Richardson type procedure)	12.22	433.93	826	953	1391
53500	Urethrolysis, transvaginal, secondary, open, including cystourethroscopy (eg, postsurgical obstruction, scarring)	20.30	720.43	2347	2704	3038
53502	Urethrorrhaphy, suture of urethral wound or injury, female	13.04	463.11	1430	1750	1898
53505	Urethrorrhaphy, suture of urethral wound or injury; penile	12.97	460.45	1448	1706	1867
53510	Urethrorrhaphy, suture of urethral wound or injury; perineal	17.15	608.63	1878	2180	2538
53515	Urethrorrhaphy, suture of urethral wound or injury; prostatomembranous	21.57	763.63	2563	2974	3286
53520	Closure of urethrostomy or urethrocutaneous fistula, male (separate procedure)	14.87	527.91	1190	1416	1715

Manipulation

		Medicare RVU	National Fee	50%	75%	90%
53600	Dilation of urethral stricture by passage of sound or urethral dilator, male; initial	2.45	88.30	147	206	262
53601	Dilation of urethral stricture by passage of sound or urethral dilator, male; subsequent	2.35	85.27	133	192	209
53605	Dilation of urethral stricture or vesical neck by passage of sound or urethral dilator, male, general or conduction (spinal) anesthesia	1.81	63.67	202	240	282

© PFR 2007

● = New Code ⊗ = Conscious Sedation ✚ = Add-on Code ∅ = Modifier '51' Exempt ▲ =Revised Code

		Medicare RVU	National Fee	PFR Fee Information 50%	75%	90%
53620	Dilation of urethral stricture by passage of filiform and follower, male; initial	3.65	132.26	220	291	344
53621	Dilation of urethral stricture by passage of filiform and follower, male; subsequent	3.46	125.82	158	200	246
53660	Dilation of female urethra including suppository and/or instillation; initial	2.07	75.80	121	174	188
53661	Dilation of female urethra including suppository and/or instillation; subsequent	2.07	75.80	129	152	167
53665	Dilation of female urethra, general or conduction (spinal) anesthesia	1.08	37.90	178	217	233

Other Procedures

(Medicare fees for the code below are based on Non Facility RVUs. PFR information reflects fee when procedure is performed in a facility.)

53850	Transurethral destruction of prostate tissue; by microwave thermotherapy	93.52	3506.28	3859	4630	5253

(Medicare fees for the code below are based on Non Facility RVUs. PFR information reflects fee when procedure is performed in a facility.)

53852	Transurethral destruction of prostate tissue; by radiofrequency thermotherapy	89.58	3354.31	3624	4455	4896
53853	Transurethral destruction of prostate tissue; by water-induced thermotherapy	54.70	2051.77	IR	IR	IR
53899	Unlisted procedure, urinary system	-	-	IR	IR	IR

Male Genital System

Penis
Incision

54000	Slitting of prepuce, dorsal or lateral (separate procedure); newborn	4.53	165.61	202	258	306
54001	Slitting of prepuce, dorsal or lateral (separate procedure); except newborn	5.51	200.48	302	368	385
54015	Incision and drainage of penis, deep	8.43	299.01	491	561	739

Destruction

54050	Destruction of lesion(s), penis (eg, condyloma, papilloma, molluscum contagiosum, herpetic vesicle), simple; chemical	3.11	112.93	155	184	219
54055	Destruction of lesion(s), penis (eg, condyloma, papilloma, molluscum contagiosum, herpetic vesicle), simple; electrodesiccation	2.99	108.77	252	328	381
54056	Destruction of lesion(s), penis (eg, condyloma, papilloma, molluscum contagiosum, herpetic vesicle), simple; cryosurgery	3.18	115.59	225	301	368
54057	Destruction of lesion(s), penis (eg, condyloma, papilloma, molluscum contagiosum, herpetic vesicle), simple; laser surgery	3.66	133.78	564	664	753
54060	Destruction of lesion(s), penis (eg, condyloma, papilloma, molluscum contagiosum, herpetic vesicle), simple; surgical excision	5.18	188.73	428	504	551
54065	Destruction of lesion(s), penis (eg, condyloma, papilloma, molluscum contagiosum, herpetic vesicle), extensive (eg, laser surgery, electrosurgery, cryosurgery, chemosurgery)	5.37	194.04	752	986	1191

Excision

54100	Biopsy of penis; (separate procedure)	4.94	180.01	253	297	361
54105	Biopsy of penis; deep structures	7.98	289.16	393	524	579
54110	Excision of penile plaque (Peyronie disease);	16.74	593.10	1493	1785	2281
54111	Excision of penile plaque (Peyronie disease); with graft to 5 cm in length	21.63	765.15	2207	2634	3006
54112	Excision of penile plaque (Peyronie disease); with graft greater than 5 cm in length	25.42	899.31	2427	2945	3426
54115	Removal foreign body from deep penile tissue (eg, plastic implant)	12.00	428.62	1021	1212	1340
54120	Amputation of penis; partial	16.79	594.99	1546	1974	2270
54125	Amputation of penis; complete	21.83	772.35	2323	2845	3402
54130	Amputation of penis, radical; with bilateral inguinofemoral lymphadenectomy	32.20	1137.68	3581	4118	4583

● = New Code ⊗ = Conscious Sedation ✚ = Add-on Code ∅ = Modifier '51' Exempt ▲ =Revised Code

		Medicare RVU	National Fee	PFR Fee Information 50%	75%	90%
54135	Amputation of penis, radical; in continuity with bilateral pelvic lymphadenectomy, including external iliac, hypogastric and obturator nodes	41.12	1451.47	4293	5115	5849
	(Medicare fees for the code below are based on Non Facility RVUs. PFR information reflects fee when procedure is performed in a facility.)					
▲ 54150	Circumcision, using clamp or other device with regional dorsal penile or ring block	3.56	127.71	223	297	418
▲ 54160	Circumcision, surgical excision other than clamp, device, or dorsal slit; neonate (28 days of age or less)	6.72	245.20	399	479	550
▲ 54161	Circumcision, surgical excision other than clamp, device, or dorsal slit; older than 28 days of age	5.25	186.46	598	713	783
54162	Lysis or excision of penile post-circumcision adhesions	7.97	289.54	476	597	665
54163	Repair incomplete circumcision	5.71	203.89	454	570	638
54164	Frenulotomy of penis	4.99	178.50	402	505	564

Introduction

		Medicare RVU	National Fee	50%	75%	90%
54200	Injection procedure for Peyronie disease;	3.01	109.90	145	180	231
54205	Injection procedure for Peyronie disease; with surgical exposure of plaque	14.46	514.27	1163	1467	1702
54220	Irrigation of corpora cavernosa for priapism	6.31	230.04	389	516	748
54230	Injection procedure for corpora cavernosography	2.59	93.23	285	323	366
54231	Dynamic cavernosometry, including intracavernosal injection of vasoactive drugs (eg, papaverine, phentolamine)	3.70	132.26	445	518	602
54235	Injection of corpora cavernosa with pharmacologic agent(s) (eg, papaverine, phentolamine)	2.34	84.13	174	230	268
54240	Penile plethysmography	2.64	95.12	225	308	370
-26		1.87	65.94	191	262	314
54250	Nocturnal penile tumescence and/or rigidity test	3.40	120.51	290	405	434
-26		3.14	110.66	246	344	369

Repair

		Medicare RVU	National Fee	50%	75%	90%
54300	Plastic operation of penis for straightening of chordee (eg, hypospadias), with or without mobilization of urethra	17.72	629.48	1574	1992	2274
54304	Plastic operation on penis for correction of chordee or for first stage hypospadias repair with or without transplantation of prepuce and/or skin flaps	20.77	737.11	2066	2439	2913
54308	Urethroplasty for second stage hypospadias repair (including urinary diversion); less than 3 cm	19.71	699.21	2140	2516	2913
54312	Urethroplasty for second stage hypospadias repair (including urinary diversion); greater than 3 cm	23.01	817.45	2411	2856	3333
54316	Urethroplasty for second stage hypospadias repair (including urinary diversion) with free skin graft obtained from site other than genitalia	27.62	978.51	2715	3216	3571
54318	Urethroplasty for third stage hypospadias repair to release penis from scrotum (eg, third stage Cecil repair)	19.57	694.66	1649	1934	2358
54322	One stage distal hypospadias repair (with or without chordee or circumcision); with simple meatal advancement (eg, Magpi, V-flap)	21.61	766.29	1875	2252	2650
54324	One stage distal hypospadias repair (with or without chordee or circumcision); with urethroplasty by local skin flaps (eg, flip-flap, prepucial flap)	26.99	956.53	2412	2979	3581
54326	One stage distal hypospadias repair (with or without chordee or circumcision); with urethroplasty by local skin flaps and mobilization of urethra	26.25	930.38	2687	3256	3686
54328	One stage distal hypospadias repair (with or without chordee or circumcision); with extensive dissection to correct chordee and urethroplasty with local skin flaps, skin graft patch, and/or island flap	25.62	907.27	2951	3383	3770
54332	One stage proximal penile or penoscrotal hypospadias repair requiring extensive dissection to correct chordee and urethroplasty by use of skin graft tube and/or island flap	27.80	984.20	2980	3492	3987
54336	One stage perineal hypospadias repair requiring extensive dissection to correct chordee and urethroplasty by use of skin graft tube and/or island flap	34.37	1220.68	3406	4078	4524
54340	Repair of hypospadias complications (ie, fistula, stricture, diverticula); by closure, incision, or excision, simple	15.61	555.20	1610	1782	1931
54344	Repair of hypospadias complications (ie, fistula, stricture, diverticula); requiring mobilization of skin flaps and urethroplasty with flap or patch graft	26.74	948.95	2526	3226	3819
54348	Repair of hypospadias complications (ie, fistula, stricture, diverticula); requiring extensive dissection and urethroplasty with flap, patch or tubed graft (includes urinary diversion)	27.24	962.98	2732	3247	3988

© PFR 2007

● = New Code ⊗ = Conscious Sedation ✚ = Add-on Code ∅ = Modifier '51' Exempt ▲ =Revised Code

Code	Description	Medicare RVU	National Fee	PFR Fee Information 50%	75%	90%
54352	Repair of hypospadias cripple requiring extensive dissection and excision of previously constructed structures including re-release of chordee and reconstruction of urethra and penis by use of local skin as grafts and island flaps and skin brought in as flaps or grafts	40.05	1418.88	4012	4847	5424
54360	Plastic operation on penis to correct angulation	19.91	706.41	2024	2286	2549
54380	Plastic operation on penis for epispadias distal to external sphincter;	21.33	754.92	1933	2572	3094
54385	Plastic operation on penis for epispadias distal to external sphincter; with incontinence	25.53	904.99	2869	3230	3517
54390	Plastic operation on penis for epispadias distal to external sphincter; with exstrophy of bladder	33.03	1165.73	3361	3924	4464
54400	Insertion of penile prosthesis; non-inflatable (semi-rigid)	14.45	513.13	2342	2728	2993
54401	Insertion of penile prosthesis; inflatable (self-contained)	17.35	618.49	2412	2829	3031
54405	Insertion of multi-component, inflatable penile prosthesis, including placement of pump, cylinders, and reservoir	21.85	773.11	3553	4094	4558
54406	Removal of all components of a multi-component, inflatable penile prosthesis without replacement of prosthesis	19.63	695.42	2010	2417	2782
54408	Repair of component(s) of a multi-component, inflatable penile prosthesis	21.02	744.31	2000	2401	2766
54410	Removal and replacement of all component(s) of a multi-component, inflatable penile prosthesis at the same operative session	24.93	881.87	2250	2702	3113
54411	Removal and replacement of all components of a multi-component inflatable penile prosthesis through an infected field at the same operative session, including irrigation and debridement of infected tissue	27.20	961.84	2474	2973	3425
54415	Removal of non-inflatable (semi-rigid) or inflatable (self-contained) penile prosthesis, without replacement of prosthesis	14.00	497.22	1462	1756	2024
54416	Removal and replacement of non-inflatable (semi-rigid) or inflatable (self-contained) penile prosthesis at the same operative session	18.67	662.45	1729	2236	2494
54417	Removal and replacement of non-inflatable (semi-rigid) or inflatable (self-contained) penile prosthesis through an infected field at the same operative session, including irrigation and debridement of infected tissue	23.89	844.74	2216	2661	3066
54420	Corpora cavernosa-saphenous vein shunt (priapism operation), unilateral or bilateral	19.16	679.50	1966	2616	3063
54430	Corpora cavernosa-corpus spongiosum shunt (priapism operation), unilateral or bilateral	17.24	611.67	1760	2215	2707
54435	Corpora cavernosa-glans penis fistulization (eg, biopsy needle, Winter procedure, rongeur, or punch) for priapism	11.10	394.89	1050	1204	1419
54440	Plastic operation of penis for injury	-	-	2428	2657	2904

Manipulation

Code	Description	Medicare RVU	National Fee	50%	75%	90%
54450	Foreskin manipulation including lysis of preputial adhesions and stretching	2.13	76.55	214	304	420

Testis
Excision

Code	Description	Medicare RVU	National Fee	50%	75%	90%
54500	Biopsy of testis, needle (separate procedure)	2.03	72.01	214	259	320
54505	Biopsy of testis, incisional (separate procedure)	5.78	205.78	575	719	819
54512	Excision of extraparenchymal lesion of testis	14.43	511.62	896	1195	1345
54520	Orchiectomy, simple (including subcapsular), with or without testicular prosthesis, scrotal or inguinal approach	8.78	312.65	1098	1288	1527
54522	Orchiectomy, partial	16.14	573.01	1521	1905	2034
54530	Orchiectomy, radical, for tumor; inguinal approach	14.69	521.09	1550	1852	1977
54535	Orchiectomy, radical, for tumor; with abdominal exploration	20.08	711.34	1862	2279	2627
54550	Exploration for undescended testis (inguinal or scrotal area)	13.11	465.00	1246	1611	1794
54560	Exploration for undescended testis with abdominal exploration	18.32	648.81	1698	2047	2407

Repair

Code	Description	Medicare RVU	National Fee	50%	75%	90%
54600	Reduction of torsion of testis, surgical, with or without fixation of contralateral testis	12.01	426.35	1312	1599	1931
54620	Fixation of contralateral testis (separate procedure)	8.18	290.29	745	890	1013
54640	Orchiopexy, inguinal approach, with or without hernia repair	12.37	439.99	1600	1901	2212

● = New Code ⊗ = Conscious Sedation ✚ = Add-on Code ∅ = Modifier '51' Exempt ▲ =Revised Code

		Medicare RVU	National Fee	PFR Fee Information 50%	75%	90%
54650	Orchiopexy, abdominal approach, for intra-abdominal testis (eg, Fowler-Stephens)	19.40	688.60	1845	2164	2661
54660	Insertion of testicular prosthesis (separate procedure)	9.44	336.15	737	865	971
54670	Suture or repair of testicular injury	10.91	388.45	1190	1466	1657
54680	Transplantation of testis(es) to thigh (because of scrotal destruction)	21.64	767.05	1532	1989	2463

Laparoscopy

54690	Laparoscopy, surgical; orchiectomy	17.88	633.27	1746	2190	2545
54692	Laparoscopy, surgical; orchiopexy for intra-abdominal testis	20.94	741.65	1788	2253	2617
54699	Unlisted laparoscopy procedure, testis	-	-	IR	IR	IR

Epididymis
Incision

54700	Incision and drainage of epididymis, testis and/or scrotal space (eg, abscess or hematoma)	5.77	205.40	458	555	673

Excision

54800	Biopsy of epididymis, needle	3.49	123.55	244	312	383
54830	Excision of local lesion of epididymis	9.71	345.63	854	1020	1160
54840	Excision of spermatocele, with or without epididymectomy	8.64	307.35	1215	1437	1619
54860	Epididymectomy; unilateral	11.02	391.48	1139	1470	1708
54861	Epididymectomy; bilateral	15.02	532.84	1594	1918	2114

Exploration

● 54865	Exploration of epididymis, with or without biopsy	9.36	333.12	951	1164	1333

Repair

54900	Epididymovasostomy, anastomosis of epididymis to vas deferens; unilateral	20.62	728.01	1979	2403	2739
54901	Epididymovasostomy, anastomosis of epididymis to vas deferens; bilateral	28.03	990.26	2702	3118	3549

Tunica Vaginalis
Incision

55000	Puncture aspiration of hydrocele, tunica vaginalis, with or without injection of medication	3.55	129.23	181	246	307

Excision

55040	Excision of hydrocele; unilateral	8.99	320.23	1155	1503	1769
55041	Excision of hydrocele; bilateral	13.43	476.75	1833	2197	2589

Repair

55060	Repair of tunica vaginalis hydrocele (Bottle type)	9.94	353.58	1018	1275	1447

Scrotum
Incision

55100	Drainage of scrotal wall abscess	6.20	225.87	334	406	481
55110	Scrotal exploration	10.14	360.41	945	1180	1304
55120	Removal of foreign body in scrotum	9.30	330.85	574	755	937

Excision

55150	Resection of scrotum	12.83	455.53	1313	1536	1758

Repair

55175	Scrotoplasty; simple	9.49	337.67	1126	1257	1507
55180	Scrotoplasty; complicated	18.40	652.97	1765	2142	2322

● = New Code ⊗ = Conscious Sedation ✚ = Add-on Code ∅ = Modifier '51' Exempt ▲ =Revised Code

		Medicare RVU	National Fee	PFR Fee Information		
				50%	75%	90%

Vas Deferens
Incision

(Medicare fees for the code below are based on Non Facility RVUs. PFR information reflects fee when procedure is performed in a facility.)

55200	Vasotomy, cannulization with or without incision of vas, unilateral or bilateral (separate procedure)	16.12	593.85	651	831	926

Excision

55250	Vasectomy, unilateral or bilateral (separate procedure), including postoperative semen examination(s)	14.10	521.85	671	822	912

Introduction

55300	Vasotomy for vasograms, seminal vesiculograms, or epididymograms, unilateral or bilateral	5.14	181.53	648	741	821

Repair

55400	Vasovasostomy, vasovasorrhaphy	13.60	482.81	2616	3169	3731

Suture

55450	Ligation (percutaneous) of vas deferens, unilateral or bilateral (separate procedure)	11.41	415.74	593	706	827

Spermatic Cord
Excision

55500	Excision of hydrocele of spermatic cord, unilateral (separate procedure)	10.05	357.37	1000	1217	1403
55520	Excision of lesion of spermatic cord (separate procedure)	10.70	380.49	1015	1176	1289
55530	Excision of varicocele or ligation of spermatic veins for varicocele; (separate procedure)	9.44	336.15	1365	1590	1919
55535	Excision of varicocele or ligation of spermatic veins for varicocele; abdominal approach	11.33	402.47	1439	1702	2082
55540	Excision of varicocele or ligation of spermatic veins for varicocele; with hernia repair	13.06	463.87	1501	1801	2060

Laparoscopy

55550	Laparoscopy, surgical, with ligation of spermatic veins for varicocele	11.29	400.96	1339	1787	2090
55559	Unlisted laparoscopy procedure, spermatic cord	-	-	IR	IR	IR

Seminal Vesicles
Incision

55600	Vesiculotomy;	11.27	400.58	1099	1360	1507
55605	Vesiculotomy; complicated	13.72	486.98	1614	1835	2101

Excision

55650	Vesiculectomy, any approach	19.23	681.02	2705	3189	3523
55680	Excision of Mullerian duct cyst	9.26	329.71	2556	2794	3251

Prostate
Incision

55700	Biopsy, prostate; needle or punch, single or multiple, any approach	6.77	246.71	372	470	550
55705	Biopsy, prostate; incisional, any approach	7.35	261.11	1089	1298	1561
55720	Prostatotomy, external drainage of prostatic abscess, any approach; simple	12.70	452.12	1180	1482	1675
55725	Prostatotomy, external drainage of prostatic abscess, any approach; complicated	15.55	551.41	1661	2041	2282

Excision

55801	Prostatectomy, perineal, subtotal (including control of postoperative bleeding, vasectomy, meatotomy, urethral calibration and/or dilation, and internal urethrotomy)	29.36	1038.01	2788	3321	3827
55810	Prostatectomy, perineal radical;	35.60	1257.06	3688	4330	4948
55812	Prostatectomy, perineal radical; with lymph node biopsy(s) (limited pelvic lymphadenectomy)	43.78	1545.84	4151	5043	5850

© PFR 2007

● = New Code ⊗ = Conscious Sedation ✚ = Add-on Code ∅ = Modifier '51' Exempt ▲ =Revised Code

		Medicare RVU	National Fee	PFR Fee Information 50%	75%	90%
55815	Prostatectomy, perineal radical; with bilateral pelvic lymphadenectomy, including external iliac, hypogastric and obturator nodes	48.01	1694.78	5426	6211	6853
55821	Prostatectomy (including control of postoperative bleeding, vasectomy, meatotomy, urethral calibration and/or dilation, and internal urethrotomy); suprapubic, subtotal, one or two stages	23.51	831.47	2945	3510	4052
55831	Prostatectomy (including control of postoperative bleeding, vasectomy, meatotomy, urethral calibration and/or dilation, and internal urethrotomy); retropubic, subtotal	25.51	901.58	3084	3680	4273
55840	Prostatectomy, retropubic radical, with or without nerve sparing;	36.25	1280.56	3775	4686	5306
55842	Prostatectomy, retropubic radical, with or without nerve sparing; with lymph node biopsy(s) (limited pelvic lymphadenectomy)	38.87	1372.65	3912	4806	5697
55845	Prostatectomy, retropubic radical, with or without nerve sparing; with bilateral pelvic lymphadenectomy, including external iliac, hypogastric, and obturator nodes	44.56	1572.37	4948	5834	6675
55860	Exposure of prostate, any approach, for insertion of radioactive substance;	23.73	839.43	1773	2248	2753
55862	Exposure of prostate, any approach, for insertion of radioactive substance; with lymph node biopsy(s) (limited pelvic lymphadenectomy)	30.00	1061.13	2562	3183	3910
55865	Exposure of prostate, any approach, for insertion of radioactive substance; with bilateral pelvic lymphadenectomy, including external iliac, hypogastric and obturator nodes	36.24	1280.56	3684	4391	5091

Laparoscopy

55866	Laparoscopy, surgical prostatectomy, retropubic radical, including nerve sparing	47.29	1669.38	4181	4918	5743

Other Procedures

55870	Electroejaculation	4.51	161.06	282	357	489
55873	Cryosurgical ablation of the prostate (includes ultrasonic guidance for interstitial cryosurgical probe placement)	31.22	1105.85	2904	3492	4002
● 55875	Transperineal placement of needles or catheters into prostate for interstitial radioelement application, with or without cystoscopy	20.58	729.15	1601	1965	2435
● 55876	Placement of interstitial device(s) for radiation therapy guidance (eg, fiducial markers, dosimeter), prostate (via needle, any approach), single or multiple	4.05	147.04	315	387	479
55899	Unlisted procedure, male genital system	-	-	IR	IR	IR

Intersex Surgery

55970	Intersex surgery; male to female	-	-	IR	IR	IR
55980	Intersex surgery; female to male	-	-	IR	IR	IR

Female Genital System

Vulva, Perineum, and Introitus
Incision

56405	Incision and drainage of vulva or perineal abscess	2.92	104.98	272	323	374
56420	Incision and drainage of Bartholin's gland abscess	3.65	133.02	259	330	397
56440	Marsupialization of Bartholin's gland cyst	4.88	173.95	763	949	1122
56441	Lysis of labial adhesions	3.98	143.25	442	541	652
● 56442	Hymenotomy, simple incision	1.27	45.48	137	169	200

Destruction

56501	Destruction of lesion(s), vulva; simple (eg, laser surgery, electrosurgery, cryosurgery, chemosurgery)	3.47	125.44	241	326	411
56515	Destruction of lesion(s), vulva; extensive (eg, laser surgery, electrosurgery, cryosurgery, chemosurgery)	5.86	210.71	825	991	1177

Excision

56605	Biopsy of vulva or perineum (separate procedure); one lesion	2.26	81.48	226	291	332
✚ 56606	Biopsy of vulva or perineum (separate procedure); each separate additional lesion (List separately in addition to code for primary procedure)	1.08	38.66	127	166	209
56620	Vulvectomy simple; partial	14.04	499.87	1880	2364	2745
56625	Vulvectomy simple; complete	15.75	560.50	2507	2916	3242

		Medicare RVU	National Fee	PFR Fee Information 50%	75%	90%
56630	Vulvectomy, radical, partial;	22.86	810.25	3039	3654	4042
56631	Vulvectomy, radical, partial; with unilateral inguinofemoral lymphadenectomy	29.31	1039.15	3889	4866	5732
56632	Vulvectomy, radical, partial; with bilateral inguinofemoral lymphadenectomy	33.47	1186.19	4551	5652	6554
56633	Vulvectomy, radical, complete;	29.85	1056.96	3711	4539	5337
56634	Vulvectomy, radical, complete; with unilateral inguinofemoral lymphadenectomy	31.77	1125.93	4348	5448	6382
56637	Vulvectomy, radical, complete; with bilateral inguinofemoral lymphadenectomy	37.80	1338.92	4818	6160	7283
56640	Vulvectomy, radical, complete, with inguinofemoral, iliac, and pelvic lymphadenectomy	37.77	1337.40	4832	5948	7015
56700	Partial hymenectomy or revision of hymenal ring	4.90	175.09	594	707	802
56740	Excision of Bartholin's gland or cyst	7.89	280.44	888	1094	1191

Repair

56800	Plastic repair of introitus	6.48	230.80	913	1128	1330
56805	Clitoroplasty for intersex state	31.29	1110.40	2348	2972	3467
56810	Perineoplasty, repair of perineum, nonobstetrical (separate procedure)	6.98	248.23	937	1212	1733

Endoscopy

56820	Colposcopy of the vulva;	2.96	106.49	265	313	370
56821	Colposcopy of the vulva; with biopsy(s)	3.99	143.25	334	396	466

Vagina
Incision

57000	Colpotomy; with exploration	5.02	178.88	831	961	1180
57010	Colpotomy; with drainage of pelvic abscess	11.26	400.96	1021	1343	1530
57020	Colpocentesis (separate procedure)	2.57	91.71	227	363	450
57022	Incision and drainage of vaginal hematoma; obstetrical/postpartum	4.44	158.03	408	500	601
57023	Incision and drainage of vaginal hematoma; non-obstetrical (eg, post-trauma, spontaneous bleeding)	8.24	292.57	440	536	632

Destruction

57061	Destruction of vaginal lesion(s); simple (eg, laser surgery, electrosurgery, cryosurgery, chemosurgery)	3.03	109.90	326	526	665
57065	Destruction of vaginal lesion(s); extensive (eg, laser surgery, electrosurgery, cryosurgery, chemosurgery)	5.16	185.70	886	1190	1488

Excision

57100	Biopsy of vaginal mucosa; simple (separate procedure)	2.38	85.65	231	289	358
57105	Biopsy of vaginal mucosa; extensive, requiring suture (including cysts)	3.65	131.88	566	761	856
57106	Vaginectomy, partial removal of vaginal wall;	12.28	437.34	1221	1480	1663
57107	Vaginectomy, partial removal of vaginal wall; with removal of paravaginal tissue (radical vaginectomy)	37.27	1319.21	3114	3892	4560
57109	Vaginectomy, partial removal of vaginal wall; with removal of paravaginal tissue (radical vaginectomy) with bilateral total pelvic lymphadenectomy and para-aortic lymph node sampling (biopsy)	42.50	1503.01	3683	4925	6124
57110	Vaginectomy, complete removal of vaginal wall;	24.13	855.73	2573	3444	4227
57111	Vaginectomy, complete removal of vaginal wall; with removal of paravaginal tissue (radical vaginectomy)	43.45	1539.02	3570	4570	5436
57112	Vaginectomy, complete removal of vaginal wall; with removal of paravaginal tissue (radical vaginectomy) with bilateral total pelvic lymphadenectomy and para-aortic lymph node sampling (biopsy)	45.44	1606.10	4393	5889	6443
57120	Colpocleisis (Le Fort type)	13.56	482.81	2023	2436	2642
57130	Excision of vaginal septum	4.84	173.95	847	1037	1192
57135	Excision of vaginal cyst or tumor	5.19	186.46	706	799	900

● = New Code ⊗ = Conscious Sedation ✚ = Add-on Code ∅ = Modifier '51' Exempt ▲ =Revised Code

		Medicare RVU	National Fee	PFR Fee Information 50%	75%	90%

Introduction

(When medication is applied, code the medication using the appropriate HCPCS code in the J section.)

57150	Irrigation of vagina and/or application of medicament for treatment of bacterial, parasitic, or fungoid disease	1.59	57.98	102	123	156
57155	Insertion of uterine tandems and/or vaginal ovoids for clinical brachytherapy	11.52	410.81	1256	1599	1875

(To code the pessary in addition to 57160 for the insertion, see HCPCS code A4561-A4562.)

57160	Fitting and insertion of pessary or other intravaginal support device	2.01	72.76	119	149	180
57170	Diaphragm or cervical cap fitting with instructions	2.27	82.62	104	133	165
57180	Introduction of any hemostatic agent or pack for spontaneous or traumatic nonobstetrical vaginal hemorrhage (separate procedure)	3.87	140.60	284	359	426

Repair

57200	Colporrhaphy, suture of injury of vagina (nonobstetrical)	7.70	275.14	940	1120	1342
57210	Colpoperineorrhaphy, suture of injury of vagina and/or perineum (nonobstetrical)	9.64	343.73	1140	1408	1689
57220	Plastic operation on urethral sphincter, vaginal approach (eg, Kelly urethral plication)	8.36	298.63	1218	1419	1648
57230	Plastic repair of urethrocele	10.25	364.57	1179	1380	1515
57240	Anterior colporrhaphy, repair of cystocele with or without repair of urethrocele	16.26	572.63	1444	1805	2160
57250	Posterior colporrhaphy, repair of rectocele with or without perineorrhaphy	16.00	562.78	1489	1672	1930
57260	Combined anteroposterior colporrhaphy;	20.41	718.92	2024	2509	2894
57265	Combined anteroposterior colporrhaphy; with enterocele repair	23.28	821.62	2508	2957	3471
✚ 57267	Insertion of mesh or other prosthesis for repair of pelvic floor defect, each site (anterior, posterior compartment), vaginal approach (List separately in addition to code for primary procedure)	7.38	261.11	954	1143	1320
57268	Repair of enterocele, vaginal approach (separate procedure)	12.47	444.16	1678	2003	2337
57270	Repair of enterocele, abdominal approach (separate procedure)	21.09	747.34	2186	2653	3045
57280	Colpopexy, abdominal approach	25.57	905.75	2401	2938	3331
57282	Colpopexy, vaginal; extra-peritoneal approach (sacrospinous, iliococcygeus)	13.34	475.61	2463	2951	3301
57283	Colpopexy, vaginal; intra-peritoneal approach (uterosacral, levator myorrhaphy)	18.34	651.08	2166	2554	2991
57284	Paravaginal defect repair (including repair of cystocele, stress urinary incontinence, and/or incomplete vaginal prolapse)	21.96	780.69	2622	2990	3371
57287	Removal or revision of sling for stress incontinence (eg, fascia or synthetic)	18.12	642.74	1841	2324	2760
57288	Sling operation for stress incontinence (eg, fascia or synthetic)	21.34	755.30	2702	3292	3792
57289	Pereyra procedure, including anterior colporrhaphy	19.98	708.68	2241	2653	3071
57291	Construction of artificial vagina; without graft	14.25	507.45	2107	2697	3300
57292	Construction of artificial vagina; with graft	22.20	788.27	3258	3547	4212
57295	Revision (including removal) of prosthetic vaginal graft; vaginal approach	12.98	462.35	1706	2051	2429
● 57296	Revision (including removal) of prosthetic vaginal graft; open abdominal approach	24.89	880.36	3349	3981	4742
57300	Closure of rectovaginal fistula; vaginal or transanal approach	13.78	489.64	1939	2326	2567
57305	Closure of rectovaginal fistula; abdominal approach	23.21	821.62	2533	3079	3485
57307	Closure of rectovaginal fistula; abdominal approach, with concomitant colostomy	26.04	922.05	2757	3324	3801
57308	Closure of rectovaginal fistula; transperineal approach, with perineal body reconstruction, with or without levator plication	16.66	591.58	2256	2437	2679
57310	Closure of urethrovaginal fistula;	12.24	435.06	1906	2375	2730
57311	Closure of urethrovaginal fistula; with bulbocavernosus transplant	13.85	491.15	2169	2764	3353
57320	Closure of vesicovaginal fistula; vaginal approach	14.09	500.63	2375	2759	3075
57330	Closure of vesicovaginal fistula; transvesical and vaginal approach	20.26	717.78	2528	3077	3499

● = New Code ⊗ = Conscious Sedation ✚ = Add-on Code ∅ = Modifier '51' Exempt ▲ =Revised Code

		Medicare RVU	National Fee	PFR Fee Information 50%	75%	90%
57335	Vaginoplasty for intersex state	30.82	1092.21	2977	3535	4211

Manipulation

57400	Dilation of vagina under anesthesia	3.61	128.09	374	422	484
57410	Pelvic examination under anesthesia	2.83	100.43	322	400	516
57415	Removal of impacted vaginal foreign body (separate procedure) under anesthesia	4.12	146.66	376	451	510

Endoscopy

57420	Colposcopy of the entire vagina, with cervix if present;	3.11	111.80	273	323	381
57421	Colposcopy of the entire vagina, with cervix if present; with biopsy(s) of vagina/cervix	4.25	152.73	366	434	512
57425	Laparoscopy, surgical, colpopexy (suspension of vaginal apex)	25.40	898.17	2272	2690	3172

Cervix Uteri
Endoscopy

(See also CPT Category III code 0003T for cervicography (photographs of cervix).)
(See also CPT Category III codes 0031T - 0032T for Speculoscopy (chemiluminescent light exam of cervix to detect dysplasia).)

57452	Colposcopy of the cervix including upper/adjacent vagina;	2.93	105.36	257	314	366
57454	Colposcopy of the cervix including upper/adjacent vagina; with biopsy(s) of the cervix and endocervical curettage	4.19	150.07	362	467	507
57455	Colposcopy of the cervix including upper/adjacent vagina; with biopsy(s) of the cervix	3.89	139.84	324	385	449
57456	Colposcopy of the cervix including upper/adjacent vagina; with endocervical curettage	3.67	131.88	307	364	429
57460	Colposcopy of the cervix including upper/adjacent vagina; with loop electrode biopsy(s) of the cervix	8.62	316.07	867	1047	1275
57461	Colposcopy of the cervix including upper/adjacent vagina; with loop electrode conization of the cervix	9.55	348.66	925	1098	1296

Excision

57500	Biopsy, single or multiple, or local excision of lesion, with or without fulguration (separate procedure)	3.72	136.43	218	272	420
57505	Endocervical curettage (not done as part of a dilation and curettage)	2.72	98.53	218	274	354
57510	Cautery of cervix; electro or thermal	3.63	130.37	248	332	411
57511	Cautery of cervix; cryocautery, initial or repeat	3.91	140.98	284	367	401
57513	Cautery of cervix; laser ablation	3.83	137.95	904	1030	1185

(A4550 (Disposable Surgical Tray) can be coded in addition to 57520 in the office setting. Payment is at carrier discretion.)

57520	Conization of cervix, with or without fulguration, with or without dilation and curettage, with or without repair; cold knife or laser	8.34	300.53	1018	1238	1547

(For LEEP without conization, see CPT code 57460.)

57522	Conization of cervix, with or without fulguration, with or without dilation and curettage, with or without repair; loop electrode excision	7.08	254.67	964	1220	1380
57530	Trachelectomy (cervicectomy), amputation of cervix (separate procedure)	9.08	324.40	955	1146	1273
57531	Radical trachelectomy, with bilateral total pelvic lymphadenectomy and para-aortic lymph node sampling biopsy, with or without removal of tube(s), with or without removal of ovary(s)	45.68	1617.84	4336	5311	5932
57540	Excision of cervical stump, abdominal approach;	20.76	736.35	1903	2386	2774
57545	Excision of cervical stump, abdominal approach; with pelvic floor repair	22.08	783.34	2105	2533	2855
57550	Excision of cervical stump, vaginal approach;	10.68	380.87	1508	1867	2036
57555	Excision of cervical stump, vaginal approach; with anterior and/or posterior repair	15.93	566.19	2142	2537	2739
57556	Excision of cervical stump, vaginal approach; with repair of enterocele	14.98	532.46	2110	2664	3064
● 57558	Dilation and curettage of cervical stump	3.33	119.76	462	568	629

Repair

57700	Cerclage of uterine cervix, nonobstetrical	7.77	278.55	933	1100	1355

● = New Code ⊗ = Conscious Sedation ✚ = Add-on Code ∅ = Modifier '51' Exempt ▲ =Revised Code

		Medicare RVU	National Fee	PFR Fee Information 50%	75%	90%
57720	Trachelorrhaphy, plastic repair of uterine cervix, vaginal approach	8.07	288.40	941	1111	1237

Manipulation

57800	Dilation of cervical canal, instrumental (separate procedure)	1.61	57.98	220	258	318

Corpus Uteri
Excision

(See also HCPCS code S2250 for uterine artery embolization for uterine fibroids.)

58100	Endometrial sampling (biopsy) with or without endocervical sampling (biopsy), without cervical dilation, any method (separate procedure)	2.98	107.25	219	282	367
✚ 58110	Endometrial sampling (biopsy) performed in conjunction with colposcopy (List separately in addition to code for primary procedure)	1.37	48.89	161	194	234

(In addition to 58120, code the cervical block (64435), if performed.)

(A4550 (Disposable Surgical Tray) can be coded in addition to 58120 in the office setting. Payment is at carrier discretion.)

(This code excludes a Dilation and Curettage performed for hydatidiform mole. For uterine evacuation and curettage for hydatidiform mole, see 59870.)

58120	Dilation and curettage, diagnostic and/or therapeutic (nonobstetrical)	6.33	226.25	796	927	1093
58140	Myomectomy, excision of fibroid tumor(s) of uterus, 1 to 4 intramural myoma(s) with total weight of 250 g or less and/or removal of surface myomas; abdominal approach	24.39	864.44	2529	3137	3708
58145	Myomectomy, excision of fibroid tumor(s) of uterus, 1 to 4 intramural myoma(s) with total weight of 250 g or less and/or removal of surface myomas; vaginal approach	14.43	513.13	2123	2518	3029
58146	Myomectomy, excision of fibroid tumor(s) of uterus, 5 or more intramural myomas and/or intramural myomas with total weight greater than 250 g, abdominal approach	31.15	1103.20	3231	4039	4784

Hysterectomy Procedures

58150	Total abdominal hysterectomy (corpus and cervix), with or without removal of tube(s), with or without removal of ovary(s);	26.31	931.52	2869	3400	3979
58152	Total abdominal hysterectomy (corpus and cervix), with or without removal of tube(s), with or without removal of ovary(s); with colpo-urethrocystopexy (eg, Marshall-Marchetti-Krantz, Burch)	33.63	1191.50	3686	4379	4926
58180	Supracervical abdominal hysterectomy (subtotal hysterectomy), with or without removal of tube(s), with or without removal of ovary(s)	25.31	896.28	2912	3390	3715
58200	Total abdominal hysterectomy, including partial vaginectomy, with para-aortic and pelvic lymph node sampling, with or without removal of tube(s), with or without removal of ovary(s)	35.09	1242.28	3968	4659	5390
58210	Radical abdominal hysterectomy, with bilateral total pelvic lymphadenectomy and para-aortic lymph node sampling (biopsy), with or without removal of tube(s), with or without removal of ovary(s)	46.73	1653.85	5842	6913	7548
58240	Pelvic exenteration for gynecologic malignancy, with total abdominal hysterectomy or cervicectomy, with or without removal of tube(s), with or without removal of ovary(s), with removal of bladder and ureteral transplantations, and/or abdominoperineal resection of rectum and colon and colostomy, or any combination thereof	70.90	2500.10	6795	8568	9613
58260	Vaginal hysterectomy, for uterus 250 g or less;	22.05	782.20	2734	3264	3697
58262	Vaginal hysterectomy, for uterus 250 g or less; with removal of tube(s), and/or ovary(s)	24.71	876.19	3010	3626	3942
58263	Vaginal hysterectomy, for uterus 250 g or less; with removal of tube(s), and/or ovary(s), with repair of enterocele	26.62	943.65	3481	4061	4414
58267	Vaginal hysterectomy, for uterus 250 g or less; with colpo-urethrocystopexy (Marshall-Marchetti-Krantz type, Pereyra type) with or without endoscopic control	28.33	1004.28	3578	4148	4640
58270	Vaginal hysterectomy, for uterus 250 g or less; with repair of enterocele	23.72	840.95	3211	3725	4187
58275	Vaginal hysterectomy, with total or partial vaginectomy;	26.31	932.66	3345	3910	4407
58280	Vaginal hysterectomy, with total or partial vaginectomy; with repair of enterocele	28.22	1000.12	3417	4057	4608
58285	Vaginal hysterectomy, radical (Schauta type operation)	35.48	1255.92	3623	4572	5323
58290	Vaginal hysterectomy, for uterus greater than 250 g;	31.16	1103.95	3668	4455	5108
58291	Vaginal hysterectomy, for uterus greater than 250 g; with removal of tube(s) and/or ovary(s)	33.85	1199.08	3954	4789	5536
58292	Vaginal hysterectomy, for uterus greater than 250 g; with removal of tube(s) and/or ovary(s), with repair of enterocele	35.77	1266.91	4147	4914	5684
58293	Vaginal hysterectomy, for uterus greater than 250 g; with colpo-urethrocystopexy (Marshall-Marchetti-Krantz type, Pereyra type) with or without endoscopic control	37.13	1314.66	4351	5251	6050
58294	Vaginal hysterectomy, for uterus greater than 250 g; with repair of enterocele	32.82	1161.94	4008	4651	5205

● = New Code ⊗ = Conscious Sedation ✚ = Add-on Code ∅ = Modifier '51' Exempt ▲ =Revised Code

	Medicare National		PFR Fee Information		
	RVU	Fee	50%	75%	90%

Introduction

(For 58300, if a copper intrauterine device is inserted, code HCPCS code J7300.)

58300	Insertion of intrauterine device (IUD)	2.35	85.27	258	333	448
58301	Removal of intrauterine device (IUD)	2.67	96.26	153	223	269
58321	Artificial insemination; intra-cervical	2.12	76.93	206	255	301
58322	Artificial insemination; intra-uterine	2.39	86.41	236	266	321
58323	Sperm washing for artificial insemination	0.70	25.77	152	203	224

(Code 58340 is a two-part procedure, with the OB/GYN physician normally coding 58340 and the radiologist coding 74740.)

58340	Catheterization and introduction of saline or contrast material for saline infusion sonohysterography (SIS) or hysterosalpingography	3.87	143.25	247	345	403

(Code 58345 is a two-part procedure, with the OB/GYN physician normally coding 58345 and the radiologist coding 74742.)

58345	Transcervical introduction of fallopian tube catheter for diagnosis and/or re-establishing patency (any method), with or without hysterosalpingography	7.41	263.01	909	1140	1342
58346	Insertion of Heyman capsules for clinical brachytherapy	11.93	423.69	1269	1504	1769
58350	Chromotubation of oviduct, including materials	2.60	94.74	318	347	437

(Medicare fees for the code below are based on Non Facility RVUs. PFR information reflects fee when procedure is performed in a facility.)

58353	Endometrial ablation, thermal, without hysteroscopic guidance	36.41	1366.20	791	933	1017

(Medicare fees for the code below are based on Non Facility RVUs. PFR information reflects fee when procedure is performed in a facility.)

58356	Endometrial cryoablation with ultrasonic guidance, including endometrial curettage, when performed	63.98	2400.43	1294	1524	1825

Repair

58400	Uterine suspension, with or without shortening of round ligaments, with or without shortening of sacrouterine ligaments; (separate procedure)	11.71	416.87	1712	2039	2483
58410	Uterine suspension, with or without shortening of round ligaments, with or without shortening of sacrouterine ligaments; with presacral sympathectomy	21.44	760.22	2326	2903	3450
58520	Hysterorrhaphy, repair of ruptured uterus (nonobstetrical)	20.74	734.83	1656	1983	2306
58540	Hysteroplasty, repair of uterine anomaly (Strassman type)	24.16	856.10	2468	3006	3436

Laparoscopy/Hysteroscopy

● 58541	Laparoscopy, surgical, supracervical hysterectomy, for uterus 250 g or less;	22.39	792.82	2460	3061	3613
● 58542	Laparoscopy, surgical, supracervical hysterectomy, for uterus 250 g or less; with removal of tube(s) and/or ovary(s)	24.78	876.57	2723	3388	3999
● 58543	Laparoscopy, surgical, supracervical hysterectomy, for uterus greater than 250 g;	25.20	891.35	2769	3445	4066
● 58544	Laparoscopy, surgical, supracervical hysterectomy, for uterus greater than 250 g; with removal of tube(s) and/or ovary(s)	27.29	964.87	2999	3731	4404
58545	Laparoscopy, surgical, myomectomy, excision; 1 to 4 intramural myomas with total weight of 250 g or less and/or removal of surface myomas	24.10	854.59	2535	3277	3893
58546	Laparoscopy, surgical, myomectomy, excision; 5 or more intramural myomas and/or intramural myomas with total weight greater than 250 g	30.61	1084.25	3507	4207	4934
● 58548	Laparoscopy, surgical, with radical hysterectomy, with bilateral total pelvic lymphadenectomy and para-aortic lymph node sampling (biopsy), with removal of tube(s) and ovary(s), if performed	47.71	1688.33	5242	6522	7699
58550	Laparoscopy, surgical, with vaginal hysterectomy, for uterus 250 g or less;	23.71	841.32	3205	3447	3958
58552	Laparoscopy, surgical, with vaginal hysterectomy, for uterus 250 g or less; with removal of tube(s) and/or ovary(s)	26.17	927.73	3053	3699	4332
58553	Laparoscopy, surgical, with vaginal hysterectomy, for uterus greater than 250 g;	30.74	1088.80	3320	4098	4686
58554	Laparoscopy, surgical, with vaginal hysterectomy, for uterus greater than 250 g; with removal of tube(s) and/or ovary(s)	35.14	1244.17	3760	4799	5678
58555	Hysteroscopy, diagnostic (separate procedure)	6.05	216.77	835	1035	1190
58558	Hysteroscopy, surgical; with sampling (biopsy) of endometrium and/or polypectomy, with or without D & C	7.83	278.55	1246	1520	1753
58559	Hysteroscopy, surgical; with lysis of intrauterine adhesions (any method)	9.46	335.01	1461	1853	2125
58560	Hysteroscopy, surgical; with division or resection of intrauterine septum (any method)	10.71	379.35	1644	2023	2323

● = New Code ⊗ = Conscious Sedation ✚ = Add-on Code ∅ = Modifier '51' Exempt ▲ =Revised Code

		Medicare RVU	National Fee	PFR Fee Information 50%	75%	90%
58561	Hysteroscopy, surgical; with removal of leiomyomata	15.20	538.14	1993	2450	2833
58562	Hysteroscopy, surgical; with removal of impacted foreign body	8.46	300.91	1165	1388	1634
58563	Hysteroscopy, surgical; with endometrial ablation (eg, endometrial resection, electrosurgical ablation, thermoablation)	58.28	2185.17	2415	2751	3056
58565	Hysteroscopy, surgical; with bilateral fallopian tube cannulation to induce occlusion by placement of permanent implants	53.93	2016.90	2450	2852	3360
58578	Unlisted laparoscopy procedure, uterus	-	-	IR	IR	IR
58579	Unlisted hysteroscopy procedure, uterus	-	-	IR	IR	IR

Oviduct/Ovary

Incision

58600	Ligation or transection of fallopian tube(s), abdominal or vaginal approach, unilateral or bilateral	9.75	347.14	1413	1578	1696
58605	Ligation or transection of fallopian tube(s), abdominal or vaginal approach, postpartum, unilateral or bilateral, during same hospitalization (separate procedure)	8.84	314.93	1158	1468	1710
✚ 58611	Ligation or transection of fallopian tube(s) when done at the time of cesarean delivery or intra-abdominal surgery (not a separate procedure) (List separately in addition to code for primary procedure)	2.16	76.17	704	998	1414
58615	Occlusion of fallopian tube(s) by device (eg, band, clip, Falope ring) vaginal or suprapubic approach	6.90	246.71	1286	1529	1904

Laparoscopy

58660	Laparoscopy, surgical; with lysis of adhesions (salpingolysis, ovariolysis) (separate procedure)	18.01	638.57	2080	2716	3180
58661	Laparoscopy, surgical; with removal of adnexal structures (partial or total oophorectomy and/or salpingectomy)	17.48	619.25	2226	2851	3255
58662	Laparoscopy, surgical; with fulguration or excision of lesions of the ovary, pelvic viscera, or peritoneal surface by any method	19.04	675.33	2274	2888	3423
58670	Laparoscopy, surgical; with fulguration of oviducts (with or without transection)	9.72	346.00	1513	1786	2147
58671	Laparoscopy, surgical; with occlusion of oviducts by device (eg, band, clip, or Falope ring)	9.73	346.38	1479	1786	2040
58672	Laparoscopy, surgical; with fimbrioplasty	20.30	720.05	2519	3164	3523
58673	Laparoscopy, surgical; with salpingostomy (salpingoneostomy)	21.92	777.28	2486	3241	3657
58679	Unlisted laparoscopy procedure, oviduct, ovary	-	-	IR	IR	IR

Excision

58700	Salpingectomy, complete or partial, unilateral or bilateral (separate procedure)	20.22	717.40	1930	2250	2581
58720	Salpingo-oophorectomy, complete or partial, unilateral or bilateral (separate procedure)	19.07	676.47	2179	2600	2963

Repair

58740	Lysis of adhesions (salpingolysis, ovariolysis)	23.38	829.58	2115	2730	3277
58750	Tubotubal anastomosis	24.45	867.09	3273	4096	4609
58752	Tubouterine implantation	24.08	853.07	3121	3521	3978
58760	Fimbrioplasty	22.09	784.48	2926	3452	3880
58770	Salpingostomy (salpingoneostomy)	23.05	817.45	2949	3425	3809

Ovary

Incision

58800	Drainage of ovarian cyst(s), unilateral or bilateral, (separate procedure); vaginal approach	8.48	303.94	978	1257	1501
58805	Drainage of ovarian cyst(s), unilateral or bilateral, (separate procedure); abdominal approach	10.51	374.05	1686	2009	2234
58820	Drainage of ovarian abscess; vaginal approach, open	8.33	298.25	1177	1421	1762

		Medicare RVU	National Fee	PFR Fee Information 50%	75%	90%
58822	Drainage of ovarian abscess; abdominal approach	18.04	638.95	1911	2287	2772
	(Medicare fees for the code below are based on Non Facility RVUs. PFR information reflects fee when procedure is performed in a facility.)					
⊗ 58823	Drainage of pelvic abscess, transvaginal or transrectal approach, percutaneous (eg, ovarian, pericolic)	24.36	910.30	714	806	890
58825	Transposition, ovary(s)	18.61	660.55	1915	2309	2719

Excision

58900	Biopsy of ovary, unilateral or bilateral (separate procedure)	10.73	382.01	1871	2123	2564
58920	Wedge resection or bisection of ovary, unilateral or bilateral	18.79	667.00	2066	2748	3179
58925	Ovarian cystectomy, unilateral or bilateral	19.32	685.19	2222	2865	3369
58940	Oophorectomy, partial or total, unilateral or bilateral;	13.12	466.14	2184	2662	3206
58943	Oophorectomy, partial or total, unilateral or bilateral; for ovarian, tubal or primary peritoneal malignancy, with para-aortic and pelvic lymph node biopsies, peritoneal washings, peritoneal biopsies, diaphragmatic assessments, with or without salpingectomy(s), with or without omentectomy	29.94	1060.75	3686	4214	4678
▲ 58950	Resection (initial) of ovarian, tubal or primary peritoneal malignancy with bilateral salpingo-oophorectomy and omentectomy;	28.42	1007.69	3607	4261	4778
58951	Resection (initial) of ovarian, tubal or primary peritoneal malignancy with bilateral salpingo-oophorectomy and omentectomy; with total abdominal hysterectomy, pelvic and limited para-aortic lymphadenectomy	36.78	1301.78	5041	5851	6656
58952	Resection (initial) of ovarian, tubal or primary peritoneal malignancy with bilateral salpingo-oophorectomy and omentectomy; with radical dissection for debulking (ie, radical excision or destruction, intra-abdominal or retroperitoneal tumors)	41.46	1467.77	5469	6720	7600
58953	Bilateral salpingo-oophorectomy with omentectomy, total abdominal hysterectomy and radical dissection for debulking;	51.64	1827.42	6417	7342	8153
58954	Bilateral salpingo-oophorectomy with omentectomy, total abdominal hysterectomy and radical dissection for debulking; with pelvic lymphadenectomy and limited para-aortic lymphadenectomy	56.07	1983.93	6709	7677	8526
58956	Bilateral salpingo-oophorectomy with total omentectomy, total abdominal hysterectomy for malignancy	36.55	1298.75	4431	5069	5629
● 58957	Resection (tumor debulking) of recurrent ovarian, tubal, primary peritoneal, uterine malignancy (intra-abdominal, retroperitoneal tumors), with omentectomy, if performed;	38.64	1365.07	4510	5377	6245
● 58958	Resection (tumor debulking) of recurrent ovarian, tubal, primary peritoneal, uterine malignancy (intra-abdominal, retroperitoneal tumors), with omentectomy, if performed; with pelvic lymphadenectomy and limited para-aortic lymphadenectomy	42.79	1510.97	4994	5954	6916
58960	Laparotomy, for staging or restaging of ovarian, tubal, or primary peritoneal malignancy (second look), with or without omentectomy, peritoneal washing, biopsy of abdominal and pelvic peritoneum, diaphragmatic assessment with pelvic and limited para-aortic lymphadenectomy	24.57	871.26	3630	4257	4608

In Vitro Fertilization

58970	Follicle puncture for oocyte retrieval, any method	6.14	219.43	1296	1788	2652
58974	Embryo transfer, intrauterine	-	-	511	711	1109
58976	Gamete, zygote, or embryo intrafallopian transfer, any method	6.78	242.54	1380	1592	1804

Other Procedures

58999	Unlisted procedure, female genital system (nonobstetrical)	-	-	IR	IR	IR

Maternity Care and Delivery

Antepartum Services

(For codes 59000-59051, use the diagnosis codes V22.0 or V22.1 for non-complicated pregnancies only. In complicated pregnancy cases, code complications instead of the V Code.)

(For codes 59000-59051, do not use V22.2 (Incidental Pregnancy). V22.2 is meant to be used when other conditions or injuries are treated and the pregnancy is present but not involved or affected by the condition or treatment.)

59000	Amniocentesis; diagnostic	3.59	131.13	339	384	464
59001	Amniocentesis; therapeutic amniotic fluid reduction (includes ultrasound guidance)	5.04	179.63	499	569	674
59012	Cordocentesis (intrauterine), any method	5.70	202.75	644	750	840
59015	Chorionic villus sampling, any method	4.24	152.35	373	416	540

● = New Code ⊗ = Conscious Sedation ✚ = Add-on Code ∅ = Modifier '51' Exempt ▲ =Revised Code

		Medicare RVU	National Fee	PFR Fee Information 50%	75%	90%
59020	Fetal contraction stress test	1.77	64.43	184	221	260
-26		1.06	37.52	156	188	221
59025	Fetal non-stress test	1.17	42.45	135	168	200
-26		0.86	30.70	115	143	170
59030	Fetal scalp blood sampling	3.18	112.93	196	240	267
59050	Fetal monitoring during labor by consulting physician (ie, non-attending physician) with written report; supervision and interpretation	1.43	50.78	215	280	306
59051	Fetal monitoring during labor by consulting physician (ie, non-attending physician) with written report; interpretation only	1.18	42.07	104	137	166
59070	Transabdominal amnioinfusion, including ultrasound guidance	10.47	376.70	1131	1336	1582
59072	Fetal umbilical cord occlusion, including ultrasound guidance	12.21	428.62	1309	1548	1830
59074	Fetal fluid drainage (eg, vesicocentesis, thoracocentesis, paracentesis), including ultrasound guidance	9.91	355.48	1056	1248	1477
59076	Fetal shunt placement, including ultrasound guidance	12.09	424.07	1309	1548	1830

Excision

59100	Hysterotomy, abdominal (eg, for hydatidiform mole, abortion)	22.50	802.29	1927	2222	2579
59120	Surgical treatment of ectopic pregnancy; tubal or ovarian, requiring salpingectomy and/or oophorectomy, abdominal or vaginal approach	21.33	760.60	2091	2504	2681
59121	Surgical treatment of ectopic pregnancy; tubal or ovarian, without salpingectomy and/or oophorectomy	21.51	767.05	1979	2407	3023
59130	Surgical treatment of ectopic pregnancy; abdominal pregnancy	23.48	832.61	2003	2511	3057
59135	Surgical treatment of ectopic pregnancy; interstitial, uterine pregnancy requiring total hysterectomy	24.81	883.77	2336	2773	3443
59136	Surgical treatment of ectopic pregnancy; interstitial, uterine pregnancy with partial resection of uterus	23.67	843.22	2174	2582	2992
59140	Surgical treatment of ectopic pregnancy; cervical, with evacuation	9.53	338.80	1392	1692	2085
59150	Laparoscopic treatment of ectopic pregnancy; without salpingectomy and/or oophorectomy	20.78	740.90	2012	2519	2706
59151	Laparoscopic treatment of ectopic pregnancy; with salpingectomy and/or oophorectomy	20.51	731.42	2228	2754	3221
59160	Curettage, postpartum	6.33	229.66	668	782	894

Introduction

59200	Insertion of cervical dilator (eg, laminaria, prostaglandin) (separate procedure)	2.11	76.93	237	320	357

Repair

59300	Episiotomy or vaginal repair, by other than attending physician	5.16	186.46	492	573	676
59320	Cerclage of cervix, during pregnancy; vaginal	4.25	151.59	1018	1314	1530
59325	Cerclage of cervix, during pregnancy; abdominal	6.67	237.24	1221	1559	1808
59350	Hysterorrhaphy of ruptured uterus	7.86	278.93	1919	2113	2370

Vaginal Delivery, Antepartum and Postpartum Care

(59400 is coded once after the six week postpartum office visit and is inclusive of all care during the antepartum state, delivery, and postpartum state. Code any care for complications separately.)

(59400 is for vaginal delivery of newborn. For cesarean delivery of newborn, see 59510-59515.)

(When coding obstetrical care for multiple gestation pregnancies, code the first birth using the global code (59400 to 59510) and add 59409 or 59514 for each additional birth.)

59400	Routine obstetric care including antepartum care, vaginal delivery (with or without episiotomy, and/or forceps) and postpartum care	47.36	1692.50	3009	3694	4590
59409	Vaginal delivery only (with or without episiotomy and/or forceps);	21.61	767.42	1772	2245	3082
59410	Vaginal delivery only (with or without episiotomy and/or forceps); including postpartum care	24.77	880.36	1968	2702	3297
59412	External cephalic version, with or without tocolysis	2.88	102.70	504	607	760
59414	Delivery of placenta (separate procedure)	2.58	91.71	437	541	649

● = New Code ⊗ = Conscious Sedation ✚ = Add-on Code ∅ = Modifier '51' Exempt ▲ =Revised Code

		Medicare RVU	National Fee	PFR Fee Information 50%	75%	90%
59425	Antepartum care only; 4-6 visits	11.57	414.60	656	739	913
59426	Antepartum care only; 7 or more visits	20.62	739.38	1140	1347	1515
59430	Postpartum care only (separate procedure)	3.82	136.81	234	291	345

Cesarean Delivery

59510	Routine obstetric care including antepartum care, cesarean delivery, and postpartum care	53.51	1912.31	3455	4277	4870
59514	Cesarean delivery only;	25.53	906.89	2281	2861	3297
59515	Cesarean delivery only; including postpartum care	29.82	1060.37	2346	2889	3227
✚ 59525	Subtotal or total hysterectomy after cesarean delivery (List separately in addition to code for primary procedure)	13.55	480.92	1367	1867	2598

Delivery After Previous Cesarean Delivery

59610	Routine obstetric care including antepartum care, vaginal delivery (with or without episiotomy, and/or forceps) and postpartum care, after previous cesarean delivery	49.60	1772.09	3326	3909	4670
59612	Vaginal delivery only, after previous cesarean delivery (with or without episiotomy and/or forceps);	24.23	861.03	2080	2596	3137
59614	Vaginal delivery only, after previous cesarean delivery (with or without episiotomy and/or forceps); including postpartum care	26.97	958.81	2253	2697	3208
59618	Routine obstetric care including antepartum care, cesarean delivery, and postpartum care, following attempted vaginal delivery after previous cesarean delivery	56.13	2005.91	3817	4263	4682
59620	Cesarean delivery only, following attempted vaginal delivery after previous cesarean delivery;	27.94	992.16	2398	2936	3246
59622	Cesarean delivery only, following attempted vaginal delivery after previous cesarean delivery; including postpartum care	32.34	1150.57	2547	2991	3358

Abortion

(See also HCPCS code S0199 for medically induced abortion by oral ingestion of medication.)

59812	Treatment of incomplete abortion, any trimester, completed surgically	8.02	287.26	800	899	999
59820	Treatment of missed abortion, completed surgically; first trimester	9.96	359.65	806	1000	1206
59821	Treatment of missed abortion, completed surgically; second trimester	10.18	366.85	936	1115	1256

(Code 59830 should not be used to code treatment of septic abortion by hysterectomy. See codes 58150-58294 for the appropriate approach and method.)

59830	Treatment of septic abortion, completed surgically	11.80	422.56	1038	1225	1386

(See also HCPCS code S2260 for induced abortion, 17 to 24 weeks, any surgical method.)
(See also HCPCS code S2262 for abortion for maternal indication, 25 weeks or greater.)
(See also HCPCS code S2265 for abortion for fetal indication 25 to 28 weeks.)
(See also HCPCS code S2266 for abortion for fetal indication, 29 to 31 weeks.)
(See also HCPCS code S2267 for abortion for fetal indication, 32 weeks or greater.)

59840	Induced abortion, by dilation and curettage	5.81	208.82	889	1105	1237
59841	Induced abortion, by dilation and evacuation	10.22	366.09	1159	1361	1538
59850	Induced abortion, by one or more intra-amniotic injections (amniocentesis-injections), including hospital admission and visits, delivery of fetus and secundines;	10.28	367.23	1222	1579	1810
59851	Induced abortion, by one or more intra-amniotic injections (amniocentesis-injections), including hospital admission and visits, delivery of fetus and secundines; with dilation and curettage and/or evacuation	10.83	387.69	1425	1740	1996
59852	Induced abortion, by one or more intra-amniotic injections (amniocentesis-injections), including hospital admission and visits, delivery of fetus and secundines; with hysterotomy (failed intra-amniotic injection)	14.77	528.29	1533	1984	2186
59855	Induced abortion, by one or more vaginal suppositories (eg, prostaglandin) with or without cervical dilation (eg, laminaria), including hospital admission and visits, delivery of fetus and secundines;	11.23	401.33	1124	1379	1780
59856	Induced abortion, by one or more vaginal suppositories (eg, prostaglandin) with or without cervical dilation (eg, laminaria), including hospital admission and visits, delivery of fetus and secundines; with dilation and curettage and/or evacuation	13.54	483.57	1300	1648	2012
59857	Induced abortion, by one or more vaginal suppositories (eg, prostaglandin) with or without cervical dilation (eg, laminaria), including hospital admission and visits, delivery of fetus and secundines; with hysterotomy (failed medical evacuation)	15.64	557.09	1668	1867	2035

Other Procedures

59866	Multifetal pregnancy reduction(s) (MPR)	6.59	234.59	677	813	994

© PFR 2007

● = New Code ⊗ = Conscious Sedation ✚ = Add-on Code ∅ = Modifier '51' Exempt ▲ =Revised Code

		Medicare RVU	National Fee	PFR Fee Information 50%	75%	90%
59870	Uterine evacuation and curettage for hydatidiform mole	12.25	439.99	916	1204	1547
59871	Removal of cerclage suture under anesthesia (other than local)	3.71	132.64	408	476	510
59897	Unlisted fetal invasive procedure, including ultrasound guidance	-	-	IR	IR	IR
59898	Unlisted laparoscopy procedure, maternity care and delivery	-	-	IR	IR	IR
59899	Unlisted procedure, maternity care and delivery	-	-	IR	IR	IR

Endocrine System

Thyroid Gland
Incision

60000	Incision and drainage of thyroglossal duct cyst, infected	3.88	140.22	269	300	341

Excision

60001	Aspiration and/or injection, thyroid cyst	2.56	93.23	204	246	278
60100	Biopsy thyroid, percutaneous core needle	3.01	108.01	248	318	424
60200	Excision of cyst or adenoma of thyroid, or transection of isthmus	16.72	595.75	1586	1872	2139
60210	Partial thyroid lobectomy, unilateral; with or without isthmusectomy	17.87	634.78	2420	2636	2955
60212	Partial thyroid lobectomy, unilateral; with contralateral subtotal lobectomy, including isthmusectomy	25.72	912.57	2781	3246	3399
60220	Total thyroid lobectomy, unilateral; with or without isthmusectomy	19.57	694.66	2336	2697	3263
60225	Total thyroid lobectomy, unilateral; with contralateral subtotal lobectomy, including isthmusectomy	23.53	835.64	2760	3484	4191
60240	Thyroidectomy, total or complete	25.27	895.90	2942	3408	3923
60252	Thyroidectomy, total or subtotal for malignancy; with limited neck dissection	33.86	1199.83	3815	4409	5012
60254	Thyroidectomy, total or subtotal for malignancy; with radical neck dissection	44.12	1564.03	4660	5537	6233
60260	Thyroidectomy, removal of all remaining thyroid tissue following previous removal of a portion of thyroid	28.36	1005.42	2570	3084	3384
60270	Thyroidectomy, including substernal thyroid; sternal split or transthoracic approach	35.48	1256.68	3395	4082	4613
60271	Thyroidectomy, including substernal thyroid; cervical approach	27.43	972.83	3000	3431	3881
60280	Excision of thyroglossal duct cyst or sinus;	11.12	398.30	1906	2301	2708
60281	Excision of thyroglossal duct cyst or sinus; recurrent	14.98	534.35	1863	2256	2611

Parathyroid, Thymus, Adrenal Glands, Pancreas, and Carotid Body
Excision

60500	Parathyroidectomy or exploration of parathyroid(s);	25.93	919.01	2874	3427	3926
60502	Parathyroidectomy or exploration of parathyroid(s); re-exploration	32.68	1158.53	3205	3979	4528
60505	Parathyroidectomy or exploration of parathyroid(s); with mediastinal exploration, sternal split or transthoracic approach	36.06	1279.42	3531	4383	5126
✚ 60512	Parathyroid autotransplantation (List separately in addition to code for primary procedure)	6.48	228.52	704	860	993
60520	Thymectomy, partial or total; transcervical approach (separate procedure)	27.22	966.39	3112	3802	4459
60521	Thymectomy, partial or total; sternal split or transthoracic approach, without radical mediastinal dissection (separate procedure)	31.15	1107.74	3253	3808	4182
60522	Thymectomy, partial or total; sternal split or transthoracic approach, with radical mediastinal dissection (separate procedure)	37.53	1333.23	3872	4531	5345
60540	Adrenalectomy, partial or complete, or exploration of adrenal gland with or without biopsy, transabdominal, lumbar or dorsal (separate procedure);	27.38	969.42	2962	3625	4382
60545	Adrenalectomy, partial or complete, or exploration of adrenal gland with or without biopsy, transabdominal, lumbar or dorsal (separate procedure); with excision of adjacent retroperitoneal tumor	31.52	1115.32	3600	4371	5043
60600	Excision of carotid body tumor; without excision of carotid artery	37.60	1329.82	3030	3706	4310

● = New Code ⊗ = Conscious Sedation ✚ = Add-on Code ∅ = Modifier '51' Exempt ▲ =Revised Code

		Medicare RVU	National Fee	PFR Fee Information 50%	75%	90%
60605	Excision of carotid body tumor; with excision of carotid artery	46.61	1644.75	3543	4367	4964

Laparoscopy

60650	Laparoscopy, surgical, with adrenalectomy, partial or complete, or exploration of adrenal gland with or without biopsy, transabdominal, lumbar or dorsal	30.96	1094.48	3048	3875	4383
60659	Unlisted laparoscopy procedure, endocrine system	-	-	IR	IR	IR

Other Procedures

60699	Unlisted procedure, endocrine system	-	-	IR	IR	IR

Nervous System

Skull, Meninges, and Brain

Injection, Drainage or Aspiration

61000	Subdural tap through fontanelle, or suture, infant, unilateral or bilateral; initial	2.73	97.40	343	380	401
61001	Subdural tap through fontanelle, or suture, infant, unilateral or bilateral; subsequent taps	2.75	98.53	275	342	401
61020	Ventricular puncture through previous burr hole, fontanelle, suture, or implanted ventricular catheter/reservoir; without injection	3.25	117.48	388	483	571
61026	Ventricular puncture through previous burr hole, fontanelle, suture, or implanted ventricular catheter/reservoir; with injection of medication or other substance for diagnosis or treatment	3.44	123.92	444	508	582
61050	Cisternal or lateral cervical (C1-C2) puncture; without injection (separate procedure)	2.85	102.32	373	406	458
61055	Cisternal or lateral cervical (C1-C2) puncture; with injection of medication or other substance for diagnosis or treatment (eg, C1-C2)	3.64	129.99	533	667	741
61070	Puncture of shunt tubing or reservoir for aspiration or injection procedure	2.11	76.55	302	390	452

Twist Drill, Burr Hole(s) or Trephine

61105	Twist drill hole for subdural or ventricular puncture	10.90	392.62	1600	1916	2102
∅ ▲ 61107	Twist drill hole(s) for subdural, intracerebral, or ventricular puncture; for implanting ventricular catheter, pressure recording device, or other intracerebral monitoring device	8.65	308.86	2048	2287	2576
61108	Twist drill hole(s) for subdural, intracerebral, or ventricular puncture; for evacuation and/or drainage of subdural hematoma	21.64	776.14	2897	3352	3793
61120	Burr hole(s) for ventricular puncture (including injection of gas, contrast media, dye, or radioactive material)	17.80	638.19	1650	1975	2226
61140	Burr hole(s) or trephine; with biopsy of brain or intracranial lesion	31.26	1119.49	3434	4056	4408
61150	Burr hole(s) or trephine; with drainage of brain abscess or cyst	33.62	1202.49	3554	3931	4446
61151	Burr hole(s) or trephine; with subsequent tapping (aspiration) of intracranial abscess or cyst	24.43	874.67	1241	1634	1913
61154	Burr hole(s) with evacuation and/or drainage of hematoma, extradural or subdural	30.96	1108.88	3895	4614	5046
61156	Burr hole(s); with aspiration of hematoma or cyst, intracerebral	31.48	1126.69	3621	4487	5093
∅ ▲ 61210	Burr hole(s); for implanting ventricular catheter, reservoir, EEG electrode(s), pressure recording device, or other cerebral monitoring device (separate procedure)	10.07	359.27	2128	2711	3201
61215	Insertion of subcutaneous reservoir, pump or continuous infusion system for connection to ventricular catheter	11.40	410.05	1851	2470	2856
61250	Burr hole(s) or trephine, supratentorial, exploratory, not followed by other surgery	21.23	760.98	2072	2678	3080
61253	Burr hole(s) or trephine, infratentorial, unilateral or bilateral	23.79	850.42	3169	3785	4341

Craniectomy or Craniotomy

61304	Craniectomy or craniotomy, exploratory; supratentorial	41.76	1493.92	4969	5778	6464
61305	Craniectomy or craniotomy, exploratory; infratentorial (posterior fossa)	49.91	1782.70	5623	6687	7583
61312	Craniectomy or craniotomy for evacuation of hematoma, supratentorial; extradural or subdural	51.60	1840.68	5691	6700	7571
61313	Craniectomy or craniotomy for evacuation of hematoma, supratentorial; intracerebral	49.42	1766.40	5968	7233	8265
61314	Craniectomy or craniotomy for evacuation of hematoma, infratentorial; extradural or subdural	45.43	1623.53	6078	6799	7778

© PFR 2007

● = New Code ⊗ = Conscious Sedation ✚ = Add-on Code ∅ = Modifier '51' Exempt ▲ =Revised Code

		Medicare RVU	National Fee	PFR Fee Information 50%	75%	90%
61315	Craniectomy or craniotomy for evacuation of hematoma, infratentorial; intracerebellar	52.64	1882.37	6731	7254	8138
✚ 61316	Incision and subcutaneous placement of cranial bone graft (List separately in addition to code for primary procedure)	2.32	82.62	320	362	406
61320	Craniectomy or craniotomy, drainage of intracranial abscess; supratentorial	48.63	1738.74	5414	6594	7554
61321	Craniectomy or craniotomy, drainage of intracranial abscess; infratentorial	53.26	1902.45	5218	6574	7776
61322	Craniectomy or craniotomy, decompressive, with or without duraplasty, for treatment of intracranial hypertension, without evacuation of associated intraparenchymal hematoma; without lobectomy	57.97	2066.93	5835	6836	7678
61323	Craniectomy or craniotomy, decompressive, with or without duraplasty, for treatment of intracranial hypertension, without evacuation of associated intraparenchymal hematoma; with lobectomy	59.34	2115.82	6465	7389	8183
61330	Decompression of orbit only, transcranial approach	40.80	1450.34	4547	5259	5909
61332	Exploration of orbit (transcranial approach); with biopsy	48.44	1726.99	5080	5853	6608
61333	Exploration of orbit (transcranial approach); with removal of lesion	48.16	1714.10	5276	6145	7014
61334	Exploration of orbit (transcranial approach); with removal of foreign body	31.54	1121.01	4300	5251	5515
61340	Subtemporal cranial decompression (pseudotumor cerebri, slit ventricle syndrome)	36.08	1291.17	3736	4507	4968
61343	Craniectomy, suboccipital with cervical laminectomy for decompression of medulla and spinal cord, with or without dural graft (eg, Arnold-Chiari malformation)	56.07	2004.02	7611	9288	9976
61345	Other cranial decompression, posterior fossa	51.55	1842.58	4089	5017	5813
61440	Craniotomy for section of tentorium cerebelli (separate procedure)	49.65	1772.85	4108	5012	5675
61450	Craniectomy, subtemporal, for section, compression, or decompression of sensory root of gasserian ganglion	47.31	1687.58	5044	6380	7158
61458	Craniectomy, suboccipital; for exploration or decompression of cranial nerves	51.18	1830.07	6292	7603	8290
61460	Craniectomy, suboccipital; for section of one or more cranial nerves	52.30	1867.21	6162	7577	8640
61470	Craniectomy, suboccipital; for medullary tractotomy	47.14	1681.51	5186	6119	7024
61480	Craniectomy, suboccipital; for mesencephalic tractotomy or pedunculotomy	48.17	1719.03	5085	6361	7271
61490	Craniotomy for lobotomy, including cingulotomy	48.42	1731.54	3787	4739	5380
61500	Craniectomy; with excision of tumor or other bone lesion of skull	33.95	1213.86	5203	6330	7129
61501	Craniectomy; for osteomyelitis	28.76	1028.16	4420	5304	6236
61510	Craniectomy, trephination, bone flap craniotomy; for excision of brain tumor, supratentorial, except meningioma	54.83	1961.20	7081	8533	9889
61512	Craniectomy, trephination, bone flap craniotomy; for excision of meningioma, supratentorial	65.54	2342.82	7275	8980	9995
61514	Craniectomy, trephination, bone flap craniotomy; for excision of brain abscess, supratentorial	48.15	1721.30	6202	7439	8423
61516	Craniectomy, trephination, bone flap craniotomy; for excision or fenestration of cyst, supratentorial	47.12	1684.92	6007	7244	8142
✚ 61517	Implantation of brain intracavitary chemotherapy agent (List separately in addition to code for primary procedure)	2.34	83.37	303	381	430
61518	Craniectomy for excision of brain tumor, infratentorial or posterior fossa; except meningioma, cerebellopontine angle tumor, or midline tumor at base of skull	70.35	2514.88	7329	9020	10541
61519	Craniectomy for excision of brain tumor, infratentorial or posterior fossa; meningioma	76.18	2722.18	7821	9648	10606
61520	Craniectomy for excision of brain tumor, infratentorial or posterior fossa; cerebellopontine angle tumor	97.37	3473.31	8150	9971	11914
61521	Craniectomy for excision of brain tumor, infratentorial or posterior fossa; midline tumor at base of skull	82.02	2929.86	8259	10116	12025
61522	Craniectomy, infratentorial or posterior fossa; for excision of brain abscess	55.28	1975.22	5975	7190	8396
61524	Craniectomy, infratentorial or posterior fossa; for excision or fenestration of cyst	52.67	1882.75	6272	7557	8850
61526	Craniectomy, bone flap craniotomy, transtemporal (mastoid) for excision of cerebellopontine angle tumor;	88.62	3153.07	7460	8399	9712
61530	Craniectomy, bone flap craniotomy, transtemporal (mastoid) for excision of cerebellopontine angle tumor; combined with middle/posterior fossa craniotomy/craniectomy	75.02	2669.88	7269	8818	10113

© PFR 2007

● = New Code ⊗ = Conscious Sedation ✚ = Add-on Code ∅ = Modifier '51' Exempt ▲ =Revised Code

		Medicare RVU	National Fee	PFR Fee Information 50%	75%	90%
61531	Subdural implantation of strip electrodes through one or more burr or trephine hole(s) for long term seizure monitoring	29.51	1056.20	3789	4524	5014
61533	Craniotomy with elevation of bone flap; for subdural implantation of an electrode array, for long term seizure monitoring	38.11	1362.79	5035	6003	6569
61534	Craniotomy with elevation of bone flap; for excision of epileptogenic focus without electrocorticography during surgery	40.73	1456.40	5066	5776	6977
61535	Craniotomy with elevation of bone flap; for removal of epidural or subdural electrode array, without excision of cerebral tissue (separate procedure)	23.89	855.73	3460	3927	4486
61536	Craniotomy with elevation of bone flap; for excision of cerebral epileptogenic focus, with electrocorticography during surgery (includes removal of electrode array)	66.33	2370.49	6441	7936	9303
61537	Craniotomy with elevation of bone flap; for lobectomy, temporal lobe, without electrocorticography during surgery	58.80	2089.67	5808	6955	7977
61538	Craniotomy with elevation of bone flap; for lobectomy, temporal lobe, with electrocorticography during surgery	62.55	2220.41	6586	7772	8815
61539	Craniotomy with elevation of bone flap; for lobectomy, other than temporal lobe, partial or total, with electrocorticography during surgery	59.73	2133.25	6497	7741	8600
61540	Craniotomy with elevation of bone flap; for lobectomy, other than temporal lobe, partial or total, without electrocorticography during surgery	56.59	2025.24	6418	7735	8540
61541	Craniotomy with elevation of bone flap; for transection of corpus callosum	53.65	1915.72	6641	7697	8203
61542	Craniotomy with elevation of bone flap; for total hemispherectomy	58.54	2092.70	6901	7937	8843
61543	Craniotomy with elevation of bone flap; for partial or subtotal (functional) hemispherectomy	55.17	1971.81	6345	7677	8600
61544	Craniotomy with elevation of bone flap; for excision or coagulation of choroid plexus	47.25	1686.82	5455	6653	7695
61545	Craniotomy with elevation of bone flap; for excision of craniopharyngioma	80.70	2882.10	8291	10074	11658
61546	Craniotomy for hypophysectomy or excision of pituitary tumor, intracranial approach	58.32	2083.23	6636	8227	9050
61548	Hypophysectomy or excision of pituitary tumor, transnasal or transseptal approach, nonstereotactic	39.18	1396.14	5958	7251	8418
61550	Craniectomy for craniosynostosis; single cranial suture	23.03	814.04	3814	4754	5581
61552	Craniectomy for craniosynostosis; multiple cranial sutures	29.82	1052.79	4598	5628	6510
61556	Craniotomy for craniosynostosis; frontal or parietal bone flap	40.41	1440.10	4577	5611	6295
61557	Craniotomy for craniosynostosis; bifrontal bone flap	42.65	1528.03	5293	6323	7355
61558	Extensive craniectomy for multiple cranial suture craniosynostosis (eg, cloverleaf skull); not requiring bone grafts	40.39	1430.25	5636	6549	7286
61559	Extensive craniectomy for multiple cranial suture craniosynostosis (eg, cloverleaf skull); recontouring with multiple osteotomies and bone autografts (eg, barrel-stave procedure) (includes obtaining grafts)	61.66	2207.91	6737	8187	9368
61563	Excision, intra and extracranial, benign tumor of cranial bone (eg, fibrous dysplasia); without optic nerve decompression	48.59	1733.43	5685	6898	7993
61564	Excision, intra and extracranial, benign tumor of cranial bone (eg, fibrous dysplasia); with optic nerve decompression	61.21	2187.82	7224	8704	10089
61566	Craniotomy with elevation of bone flap; for selective amygdalohippocampectomy	56.82	2030.17	6608	8145	9585
61567	Craniotomy with elevation of bone flap; for multiple subpial transections, with electrocorticography during surgery	63.16	2253.01	7550	9593	11096
61570	Craniectomy or craniotomy; with excision of foreign body from brain	46.29	1653.85	6182	7407	8255
61571	Craniectomy or craniotomy; with treatment of penetrating wound of brain	50.29	1797.86	6723	7964	8920
61575	Transoral approach to skull base, brain stem or upper spinal cord for biopsy, decompression or excision of lesion;	60.47	2152.96	6273	7395	8214
61576	Transoral approach to skull base, brain stem or upper spinal cord for biopsy, decompression or excision of lesion; requiring splitting of tongue and/or mandible (including tracheostomy)	93.30	3325.88	6901	8395	9799

Surgery of Skull Base
Approach Procedures
Anterior Cranial Fossa

		Medicare RVU	National Fee	50%	75%	90%
61580	Craniofacial approach to anterior cranial fossa; extradural, including lateral rhinotomy, ethmoidectomy, sphenoidectomy, without maxillectomy or orbital exenteration	62.15	2224.58	5720	6918	7926
61581	Craniofacial approach to anterior cranial fossa; extradural, including lateral rhinotomy, orbital exenteration, ethmoidectomy, sphenoidectomy and/or maxillectomy	66.69	2379.21	6144	7656	8760

● = New Code ⊗ = Conscious Sedation ✚ = Add-on Code ∅ = Modifier '51' Exempt ▲ =Revised Code

		Medicare RVU	National Fee	PFR Fee Information 50%	75%	90%
61582	Craniofacial approach to anterior cranial fossa; extradural, including unilateral or bifrontal craniotomy, elevation of frontal lobe(s), osteotomy of base of anterior cranial fossa	70.28	2530.42	5998	7512	8829
61583	Craniofacial approach to anterior cranial fossa; intradural, including unilateral or bifrontal craniotomy, elevation or resection of frontal lobe, osteotomy of base of anterior cranial fossa	72.98	2619.48	6396	7815	8657
61584	Orbitocranial approach to anterior cranial fossa, extradural, including supraorbital ridge osteotomy and elevation of frontal and/or temporal lobe(s); without orbital exenteration	70.63	2533.45	5958	7371	7922
61585	Orbitocranial approach to anterior cranial fossa, extradural, including supraorbital ridge osteotomy and elevation of frontal and/or temporal lobe(s); with orbital exenteration	75.65	2705.12	6617	8079	8904
61586	Bicoronal, transzygomatic and/or LeFort I osteotomy approach to anterior cranial fossa with or without internal fixation, without bone graft	54.63	1966.50	4257	5403	6555

Middle Cranial Fossa

61590	Infratemporal pre-auricular approach to middle cranial fossa (parapharyngeal space, infratemporal and midline skull base, nasopharynx), with or without disarticulation of the mandible, including parotidectomy, craniotomy, decompression and/or mobilization of the facial nerve and/or petrous carotid artery	79.54	2835.49	7811	9605	10989
61591	Infratemporal post-auricular approach to middle cranial fossa (internal auditory meatus, petrous apex, tentorium, cavernous sinus, parasellar area, infratemporal fossa) including mastoidectomy, resection of sigmoid sinus, with or without decompression and/or mobilization of contents of auditory canal or petrous carotid artery	80.73	2880.59	7988	9909	11496
61592	Orbitocranial zygomatic approach to middle cranial fossa (cavernous sinus and carotid artery, clivus, basilar artery or petrous apex) including osteotomy of zygoma, craniotomy, extra- or intradural elevation of temporal lobe	79.90	2864.29	7331	8841	9901

Posterior Cranial Fossa

61595	Transtemporal approach to posterior cranial fossa, jugular foramen or midline skull base, including mastoidectomy, decompression of sigmoid sinus and/or facial nerve, with or without mobilization	59.21	2115.82	5777	6938	7952
61596	Transcochlear approach to posterior cranial fossa, jugular foramen or midline skull base, including labyrinthectomy, decompression, with or without mobilization of facial nerve and/or petrous carotid artery	65.74	2341.69	6131	7647	8672
61597	Transcondylar (far lateral) approach to posterior cranial fossa, jugular foramen or midline skull base, including occipital condylectomy, mastoidectomy, resection of C1-C3 vertebral body(s), decompression of vertebral artery, with or without mobilization	72.60	2595.98	7247	8767	9692
61598	Transpetrosal approach to posterior cranial fossa, clivus or foramen magnum, including ligation of superior petrosal sinus and/or sigmoid sinus	64.86	2319.33	5972	7416	8891

Definitive Procedures

Base of Anterior Cranial Fossa

61600	Resection or excision of neoplastic, vascular or infectious lesion of base of anterior cranial fossa; extradural	53.11	1899.04	5214	6306	7218
61601	Resection or excision of neoplastic, vascular or infectious lesion of base of anterior cranial fossa; intradural, including dural repair, with or without graft	58.68	2105.59	5501	6818	8096

Base of Middle Cranial Fossa

61605	Resection or excision of neoplastic, vascular or infectious lesion of infratemporal fossa, parapharyngeal space, petrous apex; extradural	56.21	2006.67	5902	7321	8570
61606	Resection or excision of neoplastic, vascular or infectious lesion of infratemporal fossa, parapharyngeal space, petrous apex; intradural, including dural repair, with or without graft	75.93	2717.63	7634	9243	10453
61607	Resection or excision of neoplastic, vascular or infectious lesion of parasellar area, cavernous sinus, clivus or midline skull base; extradural	70.79	2527.01	7128	8601	9922
61608	Resection or excision of neoplastic, vascular or infectious lesion of parasellar area, cavernous sinus, clivus or midline skull base; intradural, including dural repair, with or without graft	82.86	2967.00	8444	10246	12349
+ 61609	Transection or ligation, carotid artery in cavernous sinus; without repair (List separately in addition to code for primary procedure)	17.03	607.88	2139	2597	2940
+ 61610	Transection or ligation, carotid artery in cavernous sinus; with repair by anastomosis or graft (List separately in addition to code for primary procedure)	50.02	1782.70	6140	7167	8098
+ 61611	Transection or ligation, carotid artery in petrous canal; without repair (List separately in addition to code for primary procedure)	12.88	459.70	1462	1787	2081
+ 61612	Transection or ligation, carotid artery in petrous canal; with repair by anastomosis or graft (List separately in addition to code for primary procedure)	44.22	1569.71	5792	6840	7487
61613	Obliteration of carotid aneurysm, arteriovenous malformation, or carotid-cavernous fistula by dissection within cavernous sinus	80.05	2862.40	8131	9988	11599

© PFR 2007

● = New Code ⊗ = Conscious Sedation ✚ = Add-on Code ∅ = Modifier '51' Exempt ▲ =Revised Code

		Medicare RVU	National Fee	PFR Fee Information 50%	75%	90%

Base of Posterior Cranial Fossa

61615 Resection or excision of neoplastic, vascular or infectious lesion of base of posterior cranial fossa, jugular foramen, foramen magnum, or C1-C3 vertebral bodies; extradural — 62.30 | 2225.34 | 6288 | 7511 | 8630

61616 Resection or excision of neoplastic, vascular or infectious lesion of base of posterior cranial fossa, jugular foramen, foramen magnum, or C1-C3 vertebral bodies; intradural, including dural repair, with or without graft — 83.08 | 2970.79 | 8517 | 10054 | 11341

Repair and/or Reconstruction of Surgical Defects of Skull Base

61618 Secondary repair of dura for cerebrospinal fluid leak, anterior, middle or posterior cranial fossa following surgery of the skull base; by free tissue graft (eg, pericranium, fascia, tensor fascia lata, adipose tissue, homologous or synthetic grafts) — 32.69 | 1168.00 | 3833 | 4492 | 5025

61619 Secondary repair of dura for cerebrospinal fluid leak, anterior, middle or posterior cranial fossa following surgery of the skull base; by local or regionalized vascularized pedicle flap or myocutaneous flap (including galea, temporalis, frontalis or occipitalis muscle) — 37.93 | 1353.70 | 4724 | 6564 | 7803

Endovascular Therapy

61623 Endovascular temporary balloon arterial occlusion, head or neck (extracranial/intracranial) including selective catheterization of vessel to be occluded, positioning and inflation of occlusion balloon, concomitant neurological monitoring, and radiologic supervision and interpretation of all angiography required for balloon occlusion and to exclude vascular injury post occlusion — 14.85 | 524.88 | 2266 | 2614 | 2882

61624 Transcatheter permanent occlusion or embolization (eg, for tumor destruction, to achieve hemostasis, to occlude a vascular malformation), percutaneous, any method; central nervous system (intracranial, spinal cord) — 28.82 | 1015.65 | 4557 | 5388 | 6121

61626 Transcatheter permanent occlusion or embolization (eg, for tumor destruction, to achieve hemostasis, to occlude a vascular malformation), percutaneous, any method; non-central nervous system, head or neck (extracranial, brachiocephalic branch) — 23.20 | 815.93 | 3500 | 4179 | 4678

61630 Balloon angioplasty, intracranial (eg, atherosclerotic stenosis), percutaneous — 35.07 | 1244.93 | 3300 | 3807 | 4196

61635 Transcatheter placement of intravascular stent(s), intracranial (eg, atherosclerotic stenosis), including balloon angioplasty, if performed — 38.38 | 1362.04 | 4243 | 4895 | 5395

61640 Balloon dilatation of intracranial vasospasm, percutaneous; initial vessel — 15.88 | 554.82 | 1814 | 2094 | 2308

✚ 61641 Balloon dilatation of intracranial vasospasm, percutaneous; each additional vessel in same vascular family (List separately in addition to code for primary procedure) — 5.58 | 194.79 | 946 | 1091 | 1203

✚ 61642 Balloon dilatation of intracranial vasospasm, percutaneous; each additional vessel in different vascular family (List separately in addition to code for primary procedure) — 11.16 | 389.97 | 1179 | 1361 | 1500

Surgery For Aneurysm, Arteriovenous Malformation or Vascular Disease

61680 Surgery of intracranial arteriovenous malformation; supratentorial, simple — 57.70 | 2063.14 | 7484 | 9009 | 10200

61682 Surgery of intracranial arteriovenous malformation; supratentorial, complex — 110.32 | 3939.45 | 10028 | 11325 | 13759

61684 Surgery of intracranial arteriovenous malformation; infratentorial, simple — 73.50 | 2627.43 | 8709 | 10192 | 11763

61686 Surgery of intracranial arteriovenous malformation; infratentorial, complex — 117.77 | 4206.62 | 10761 | 13429 | 15085

61690 Surgery of intracranial arteriovenous malformation; dural, simple — 54.69 | 1953.62 | 6629 | 8084 | 8999

61692 Surgery of intracranial arteriovenous malformation; dural, complex — 94.73 | 3382.35 | 8566 | 9690 | 10845

61697 Surgery of complex intracranial aneurysm, intracranial approach; carotid circulation — 104.40 | 3715.47 | 8857 | 10205 | 11718

61698 Surgery of complex intracranial aneurysm, intracranial approach; vertebrobasilar circulation — 109.87 | 3898.89 | 8695 | 10115 | 11593

61700 Surgery of simple intracranial aneurysm, intracranial approach; carotid circulation — 90.41 | 3234.17 | 8765 | 10655 | 12382

61702 Surgery of simple intracranial aneurysm, intracranial approach; vertebrobasilar circulation — 97.28 | 3458.53 | 8932 | 10602 | 12248

61703 Surgery of intracranial aneurysm, cervical approach by application of occluding clamp to cervical carotid artery (Selverstone-Crutchfield type) — 33.35 | 1192.63 | 3727 | 4125 | 4862

61705 Surgery of aneurysm, vascular malformation or carotid-cavernous fistula; by intracranial and cervical occlusion of carotid artery — 65.75 | 2346.99 | 7246 | 9390 | 10811

61708 Surgery of aneurysm, vascular malformation or carotid-cavernous fistula; by intracranial electrothrombosis — 54.16 | 1911.17 | 6238 | 7698 | 9082

61710 Surgery of aneurysm, vascular malformation or carotid-cavernous fistula; by intra-arterial embolization, injection procedure, or balloon catheter — 49.13 | 1742.91 | 4322 | 5644 | 7620

61711 Anastomosis, arterial, extracranial-intracranial (eg, middle cerebral/cortical) arteries — 67.09 | 2397.40 | 6822 | 8421 | 9562

● = New Code ⊗ = Conscious Sedation ✚ = Add-on Code ∅ = Modifier '51' Exempt ▲ =Revised Code

		Medicare RVU	National Fee	PFR Fee Information 50%	75%	90%

Stereotaxis

Code	Description	Medicare RVU	National Fee	50%	75%	90%
61720	Creation of lesion by stereotactic method, including burr hole(s) and localizing and recording techniques, single or multiple stages; globus pallidus or thalamus	29.85	1064.54	5369	6280	6843
61735	Creation of lesion by stereotactic method, including burr hole(s) and localizing and recording techniques, single or multiple stages; subcortical structure(s) other than globus pallidus or thalamus	36.94	1315.04	5360	6124	6676
61750	Stereotactic biopsy, aspiration, or excision, including burr hole(s), for intracranial lesion;	35.19	1258.58	4981	5644	6193
61751	Stereotactic biopsy, aspiration, or excision, including burr hole(s), for intracranial lesion; with computed tomography and/or magnetic resonance guidance	34.21	1225.23	5802	6689	7331
61760	Stereotactic implantation of depth electrodes into the cerebrum for long term seizure monitoring	37.22	1325.65	5037	6448	7378
61770	Stereotactic localization, including burr hole(s), with insertion of catheter(s) or probe(s) for placement of radiation source	38.34	1365.07	5110	6560	7545
61790	Creation of lesion by stereotactic method, percutaneous, by neurolytic agent (eg, alcohol, thermal, electrical, radiofrequency); gasserian ganglion	20.72	741.28	3606	4543	5383
61791	Creation of lesion by stereotactic method, percutaneous, by neurolytic agent (eg, alcohol, thermal, electrical, radiofrequency); trigeminal medullary tract	27.32	977.00	3901	4800	5520
61793	Stereotactic radiosurgery (particle beam, gamma ray or linear accelerator), one or more sessions	32.29	1155.87	5925	7254	8403
✚ 61795	Stereotactic computer-assisted volumetric (navigational) procedure, intracranial, extracranial, or spinal (List separately in addition to code for primary procedure)	6.69	238.00	1518	1856	2076

Neurostimulators (Intracranial)

Code	Description	Medicare RVU	National Fee	50%	75%	90%
61850	Twist drill or burr hole(s) for implantation of neurostimulator electrodes, cortical	23.64	845.49	3202	3846	4499
61860	Craniectomy or craniotomy for implantation of neurostimulator electrodes, cerebral, cortical	39.00	1393.49	4183	4816	5396
61863	Twist drill, burr hole, craniotomy, or craniectomy with stereotactic implantation of neurostimulator electrode array in subcortical site (eg, thalamus, globus pallidus, subthalamic nucleus, periventricular, periaqueductal gray), without use of intraoperative microelectrode recording; first array	37.98	1360.90	4103	4837	5557
✚ 61864	Twist drill, burr hole, craniotomy, or craniectomy with stereotactic implantation of neurostimulator electrode array in subcortical site (eg, thalamus, globus pallidus, subthalamic nucleus, periventricular, periaqueductal gray), without use of intraoperative microelectrode recording; each additional array (List separately in addition to primary procedure)	12.06	439.99	1224	1444	1660
61867	Twist drill, burr hole, craniotomy, or craniectomy with stereotactic implantation of neurostimulator electrode array in subcortical site (eg, thalamus, globus pallidus, subthalamic nucleus, periventricular, periaqueductal gray), with use of intraoperative microelectrode recording; first array	56.06	1999.09	5490	6743	7829
✚ 61868	Twist drill, burr hole, craniotomy, or craniectomy with stereotactic implantation of neurostimulator electrode array in subcortical site (eg, thalamus, globus pallidus, subthalamic nucleus, periventricular, periaqueductal gray), with use of intraoperative microelectrode recording; each additional array (List separately in addition to primary procedure)	17.10	617.73	1877	2311	2741
61870	Craniectomy for implantation of neurostimulator electrodes, cerebellar; cortical	29.58	1059.24	3112	3976	4690
61875	Craniectomy for implantation of neurostimulator electrodes, cerebellar; subcortical	27.07	963.35	3247	3608	4155
61880	Revision or removal of intracranial neurostimulator electrodes	13.34	479.40	2164	2725	3076
61885	Insertion or replacement of cranial neurostimulator pulse generator or receiver, direct or inductive coupling; with connection to a single electrode array	14.81	533.22	1161	1485	1710
61886	Insertion or replacement of cranial neurostimulator pulse generator or receiver, direct or inductive coupling; with connection to two or more electrode arrays	18.67	670.41	1623	1981	2391
61888	Revision or removal of cranial neurostimulator pulse generator or receiver	10.19	366.47	955	1210	1426

Repair

Code	Description	Medicare RVU	National Fee	50%	75%	90%
62000	Elevation of depressed skull fracture; simple, extradural	20.84	737.11	3282	3884	4447
62005	Elevation of depressed skull fracture; compound or comminuted, extradural	30.40	1085.38	4203	4762	5038
62010	Elevation of depressed skull fracture; with repair of dura and/or debridement of brain	38.24	1368.10	5052	6111	7007
62100	Craniotomy for repair of dural/cerebrospinal fluid leak, including surgery for rhinorrhea/otorrhea	40.84	1458.67	5466	6997	8136
62115	Reduction of craniomegalic skull (eg, treated hydrocephalus); not requiring bone grafts or cranioplasty	40.49	1448.06	4004	5188	6213
62116	Reduction of craniomegalic skull (eg, treated hydrocephalus); with simple cranioplasty	44.39	1587.53	4394	5402	6595

● = New Code ⊗ = Conscious Sedation ✚ = Add-on Code ∅ = Modifier '51' Exempt ▲ =Revised Code

		Medicare RVU	National Fee	PFR Fee Information 50%	75%	90%
62117	Reduction of craniomegalic skull (eg, treated hydrocephalus); requiring craniotomy and reconstruction with or without bone graft (includes obtaining grafts)	48.05	1713.35	5123	6086	6924
62120	Repair of encephalocele, skull vault, including cranioplasty	45.23	1621.26	4687	5697	6615
62121	Craniotomy for repair of encephalocele, skull base	42.24	1513.25	4813	5727	6633
62140	Cranioplasty for skull defect; up to 5 cm diameter	26.34	943.27	3794	5086	6070
62141	Cranioplasty for skull defect; larger than 5 cm diameter	28.87	1033.09	4848	5781	6629
62142	Removal of bone flap or prosthetic plate of skull	21.66	776.14	3293	3662	4063
62143	Replacement of bone flap or prosthetic plate of skull	25.67	919.39	3818	4865	5556
62145	Cranioplasty for skull defect with reparative brain surgery	35.25	1259.71	4858	5780	6548
62146	Cranioplasty with autograft (includes obtaining bone grafts); up to 5 cm diameter	30.33	1083.87	3925	4704	5554
62147	Cranioplasty with autograft (includes obtaining bone grafts); larger than 5 cm diameter	36.05	1287.76	5019	5739	6455
✚ 62148	Incision and retrieval of subcutaneous cranial bone graft for cranioplasty (List separately in addition to code for primary procedure)	3.32	118.24	479	516	571

Neuroendoscopy

		Medicare RVU	National Fee	50%	75%	90%
✚ 62160	Neuroendoscopy, intracranial, for placement or replacement of ventricular catheter and attachment to shunt system or external drainage (List separately in addition to code for primary procedure)	5.21	186.08	545	632	736
62161	Neuroendoscopy, intracranial; with dissection of adhesions, fenestration of septum pellucidum or intraventricular cysts (including placement, replacement, or removal of ventricular catheter)	38.43	1376.06	4892	5685	6461
62162	Neuroendoscopy, intracranial; with fenestration or excision of colloid cyst, including placement of external ventricular catheter for drainage	47.23	1688.33	5259	6058	6820
62163	Neuroendoscopy, intracranial; with retrieval of foreign body	30.52	1094.10	4432	5244	6043
62164	Neuroendoscopy, intracranial; with excision of brain tumor, including placement of external ventricular catheter for drainage	49.65	1770.19	7100	9721	11322
62165	Neuroendoscopy, intracranial; with excision of pituitary tumor, transnasal or trans-sphenoidal approach	39.06	1392.35	4683	5645	6450

Cerebrospinal Fluid (CSF) Shunt

		Medicare RVU	National Fee	50%	75%	90%
62180	Ventriculocisternostomy (Torkildsen type operation)	39.68	1418.12	4441	5048	5437
62190	Creation of shunt; subarachnoid/subdural-atrial, -jugular, -auricular	22.12	792.44	3623	4109	4504
62192	Creation of shunt; subarachnoid/subdural-peritoneal, -pleural, other terminus	24.11	863.31	3668	3929	4579
62194	Replacement or irrigation, subarachnoid/subdural catheter	9.36	333.12	1288	1618	1933
62200	Ventriculocisternostomy, third ventricle;	34.68	1241.14	4844	5271	5845
62201	Ventriculocisternostomy, third ventricle; stereotactic, neuroendoscopic method	29.31	1050.14	3499	3960	4342
62220	Creation of shunt; ventriculo-atrial, -jugular, -auricular	25.46	911.43	3990	4880	5313
62223	Creation of shunt; ventriculo-peritoneal, -pleural, other terminus	25.60	917.12	4435	5181	5807
62225	Replacement or irrigation, ventricular catheter	11.95	429.76	1617	1986	2411
62230	Replacement or revision of cerebrospinal fluid shunt, obstructed valve, or distal catheter in shunt system	20.76	743.55	2877	3680	4374
62252	Reprogramming of programmable cerebrospinal shunt	2.50	92.09	222	275	315
-26		1.28	45.86	111	138	158
62256	Removal of complete cerebrospinal fluid shunt system; without replacement	14.02	503.66	1882	2178	2595
62258	Removal of complete cerebrospinal fluid shunt system; with replacement by similar or other shunt at same operation	28.16	1008.07	4245	4877	5429

Spine and Spinal Cord

Injection, Drainage, or Aspiration

		Medicare RVU	National Fee	50%	75%	90%
62263	Percutaneous lysis of epidural adhesions using solution injection (eg, hypertonic saline, enzyme) or mechanical means (eg, catheter) including radiologic localization (includes contrast when administered), multiple adhesiolysis sessions; 2 or more days	18.60	680.64	1190	1535	1898

		Medicare RVU	National Fee	PFR Fee Information 50%	75%	90%
62264	Percutaneous lysis of epidural adhesions using solution injection (eg, hypertonic saline, enzyme) or mechanical means (eg, catheter) including radiologic localization (includes contrast when administered), multiple adhesiolysis sessions; 1 day	11.89	433.93	1013	1279	1407
62268	Percutaneous aspiration, spinal cord cyst or syrinx	15.42	566.19	1927	2296	2784
62269	Biopsy of spinal cord, percutaneous needle	18.05	665.10	1224	1693	2270
	(A4550 (Disposable Surgical Tray) can be coded in addition to 62270 in the office setting. Payment is at carrier discretion.)					
62270	Spinal puncture, lumbar, diagnostic	4.27	156.52	238	262	308
62272	Spinal puncture, therapeutic, for drainage of cerebrospinal fluid (by needle or catheter)	5.00	184.18	281	339	402
62273	Injection, epidural, of blood or clot patch	4.73	170.92	395	565	652
62280	Injection/infusion of neurolytic substance (eg, alcohol, phenol, iced saline solutions), with or without other therapeutic substance; subarachnoid	9.18	338.05	445	504	636
62281	Injection/infusion of neurolytic substance (eg, alcohol, phenol, iced saline solutions), with or without other therapeutic substance; epidural, cervical or thoracic	8.01	293.33	506	612	835
62282	Injection/infusion of neurolytic substance (eg, alcohol, phenol, iced saline solutions), with or without other therapeutic substance; epidural, lumbar, sacral (caudal)	9.75	360.78	638	707	931
⊘ **62284**	Injection procedure for myelography and/or computed tomography, spinal (other than C1-C2 and posterior fossa)	6.29	232.69	549	601	680
	(Payment for code 62287 by Medicare is restricted to the presence of the following ICD-9-CM codes: 722.10, 722.11, 722.51 or 722.52.)					
62287	Aspiration or decompression procedure, percutaneous, of nucleus pulposus of intervertebral disc, any method, single or multiple levels, lumbar (eg, manual or automated percutaneous discectomy, percutaneous laser discectomy)	14.64	521.09	3197	3886	4608
62290	Injection procedure for discography, each level; lumbar	9.66	354.72	563	691	839
62291	Injection procedure for discography, each level; cervical or thoracic	8.64	316.44	580	673	778
62292	Injection procedure for chemonucleolysis, including discography, intervertebral disc, single or multiple levels, lumbar	14.11	499.87	2330	2552	2896
62294	Injection procedure, arterial, for occlusion of arteriovenous malformation, spinal	19.59	693.90	1190	1702	1876
62310	Injection, single (not via indwelling catheter), not including neurolytic substances, with or without contrast (for either localization or epidurography), of diagnostic or therapeutic substance(s) (including anesthetic, antispasmodic, opioid, steroid, other solution), epidural or subarachnoid; cervical or thoracic	6.38	234.59	660	850	1062
62311	Injection, single (not via indwelling catheter), not including neurolytic substances, with or without contrast (for either localization or epidurography), of diagnostic or therapeutic substance(s) (including anesthetic, antispasmodic, opioid, steroid, other solution), epidural or subarachnoid; lumbar, sacral (caudal)	5.98	220.94	669	816	1049
62318	Injection, including catheter placement, continuous infusion or intermittent bolus, not including neurolytic substances, with or without contrast (for either localization or epidurography), of diagnostic or therapeutic substance(s) (including anesthetic, antispasmodic, opioid, steroid, other solution), epidural or subarachnoid; cervical or thoracic	7.25	266.80	765	921	1088
62319	Injection, including catheter placement, continuous infusion or intermittent bolus, not including neurolytic substances, with or without contrast (for either localization or epidurography), of diagnostic or therapeutic substance(s) (including anesthetic, antispasmodic, opioid, steroid, other solution), epidural or subarachnoid; lumbar, sacral (caudal)	6.43	236.48	745	897	1058

Catheter Implantation

		Medicare RVU	National Fee	50%	75%	90%
62350	Implantation, revision or repositioning of tunneled intrathecal or epidural catheter, for long-term medication administration via an external pump or implantable reservoir/infusion pump; without laminectomy	13.06	464.24	1460	1672	2502
62351	Implantation, revision or repositioning of tunneled intrathecal or epidural catheter, for long-term medication administration via an external pump or implantable reservoir/infusion pump; with laminectomy	21.08	754.92	2277	2931	3553
62355	Removal of previously implanted intrathecal or epidural catheter	10.58	375.94	1159	1567	1943

Reservoir/pump Implantation

		Medicare RVU	National Fee	50%	75%	90%
62360	Implantation or replacement of device for intrathecal or epidural drug infusion; subcutaneous reservoir	6.89	247.09	598	727	1060
62361	Implantation or replacement of device for intrathecal or epidural drug infusion; non-programmable pump	11.33	404.37	1458	1629	1846
62362	Implantation or replacement of device for intrathecal or epidural drug infusion; programmable pump, including preparation of pump, with or without programming	14.22	506.31	1581	1805	2029

● = New Code ⊗ = Conscious Sedation ✚ = Add-on Code ⊘ = Modifier '51' Exempt ▲ =Revised Code

		Medicare RVU	National Fee	PFR Fee Information 50%	75%	90%
62365	Removal of subcutaneous reservoir or pump, previously implanted for intrathecal or epidural infusion	11.08	394.89	1004	1387	1682
62367	Electronic analysis of programmable, implanted pump for intrathecal or epidural drug infusion (includes evaluation of reservoir status, alarm status, drug prescription status); without reprogramming	1.07	38.66	100	116	162
62368	Electronic analysis of programmable, implanted pump for intrathecal or epidural drug infusion (includes evaluation of reservoir status, alarm status, drug prescription status); with reprogramming	1.48	53.06	152	200	251

Posterior Extradural Laminotomy or Laminectomy For Exploration/decompression of Neural Elements or Excision of Herniated Intervertebral Disks

		Medicare RVU	National Fee	PFR Fee Information 50%	75%	90%
63001	Laminectomy with exploration and/or decompression of spinal cord and/or cauda equina, without facetectomy, foraminotomy or discectomy, (eg, spinal stenosis), one or two vertebral segments; cervical	30.92	1105.09	4850	5855	6660
63003	Laminectomy with exploration and/or decompression of spinal cord and/or cauda equina, without facetectomy, foraminotomy or discectomy, (eg, spinal stenosis), one or two vertebral segments; thoracic	31.24	1116.84	4697	5928	6983
63005	Laminectomy with exploration and/or decompression of spinal cord and/or cauda equina, without facetectomy, foraminotomy or discectomy, (eg, spinal stenosis), one or two vertebral segments; lumbar, except for spondylolisthesis	29.57	1058.48	4412	4977	5553
63011	Laminectomy with exploration and/or decompression of spinal cord and/or cauda equina, without facetectomy, foraminotomy or discectomy, (eg, spinal stenosis), one or two vertebral segments; sacral	27.69	989.12	4250	5114	5977
63012	Laminectomy with removal of abnormal facets and/or pars inter-articularis with decompression of cauda equina and nerve roots for spondylolisthesis, lumbar (Gill type procedure)	30.29	1084.25	4704	5596	6477
63015	Laminectomy with exploration and/or decompression of spinal cord and/or cauda equina, without facetectomy, foraminotomy or discectomy, (eg, spinal stenosis), more than 2 vertebral segments; cervical	37.40	1338.54	5491	6625	7433
63016	Laminectomy with exploration and/or decompression of spinal cord and/or cauda equina, without facetectomy, foraminotomy or discectomy, (eg, spinal stenosis), more than 2 vertebral segments; thoracic	38.35	1369.99	5454	6670	7429
63017	Laminectomy with exploration and/or decompression of spinal cord and/or cauda equina, without facetectomy, foraminotomy or discectomy, (eg, spinal stenosis), more than 2 vertebral segments; lumbar	31.25	1118.73	5170	6015	6495
63020	Laminotomy (hemilaminectomy), with decompression of nerve root(s), including partial facetectomy, foraminotomy and/or excision of herniated intervertebral disc; one interspace, cervical	29.55	1058.86	4672	5691	6529
63030	Laminotomy (hemilaminectomy), with decompression of nerve root(s), including partial facetectomy, foraminotomy and/or excision of herniated intervertebral disc; one interspace, lumbar (including open or endoscopically-assisted approach)	24.54	880.36	4466	5473	6389
✚ 63035	Laminotomy (hemilaminectomy), with decompression of nerve root(s), including partial facetectomy, foraminotomy and/or excision of herniated intervertebral disc; each additional interspace, cervical or lumbar (List separately in addition to code for primary procedure)	5.44	194.04	1327	1747	2242
63040	Laminotomy (hemilaminectomy), with decompression of nerve root(s), including partial facetectomy, foraminotomy and/or excision of herniated intervertebral disc, reexploration, single interspace; cervical	36.29	1298.37	5316	6314	7158
63042	Laminotomy (hemilaminectomy), with decompression of nerve root(s), including partial facetectomy, foraminotomy and/or excision of herniated intervertebral disc, reexploration, single interspace; lumbar	34.07	1220.30	5499	6647	7675
✚ 63043	Laminotomy (hemilaminectomy), with decompression of nerve root(s), including partial facetectomy, foraminotomy and/or excision of herniated intervertebral disc, reexploration, single interspace; each additional cervical interspace (List separately in addition to code for primary procedure)	-	-	1157	1598	2007
✚ 63044	Laminotomy (hemilaminectomy), with decompression of nerve root(s), including partial facetectomy, foraminotomy and/or excision of herniated intervertebral disc, reexploration, single interspace; each additional lumbar interspace (List separately in addition to code for primary procedure)	-	-	1378	1655	2053
63045	Laminectomy, facetectomy and foraminotomy (unilateral or bilateral with decompression of spinal cord, cauda equina and/or nerve root(s), (eg, spinal or lateral recess stenosis)), single vertebral segment; cervical	32.21	1152.84	5736	6605	7172
63046	Laminectomy, facetectomy and foraminotomy (unilateral or bilateral with decompression of spinal cord, cauda equina and/or nerve root(s), (eg, spinal or lateral recess stenosis)), single vertebral segment; thoracic	30.81	1102.44	5493	6382	7220
	(UNBUNDLING ALERT: 63047 cannot be used with 62278, 62279, 63005, or 63012 by the same physician on the same day.)					
63047	Laminectomy, facetectomy and foraminotomy (unilateral or bilateral with decompression of spinal cord, cauda equina and/or nerve root(s), (eg, spinal or lateral recess stenosis)), single vertebral segment; lumbar	28.25	1012.62	5786	6883	7943

● = New Code ⊗ = Conscious Sedation ✚ = Add-on Code ∅ = Modifier '51' Exempt ▲ =Revised Code

		Medicare RVU	National Fee	PFR Fee Information 50%	75%	90%
✛ 63048	Laminectomy, facetectomy and foraminotomy (unilateral or bilateral with decompression of spinal cord, cauda equina and/or nerve root(s), (eg, spinal or lateral recess stenosis)), single vertebral segment; each additional segment, cervical, thoracic, or lumbar (List separately in addition to code for primary procedure)	5.77	205.40	1872	2450	2857
63050	Laminoplasty, cervical, with decompression of the spinal cord, two or more vertebral segments;	37.66	1343.85	6677	7826	8895
63051	Laminoplasty, cervical, with decompression of the spinal cord, two or more vertebral segments; with reconstruction of the posterior bony elements (including the application of bridging bone graft and non-segmental fixation devices (eg, wire, suture, mini-plates), when performed)	43.10	1536.74	7597	8904	10121

Transpedicular or Costovertebral Approach For Posterolateral Extradural Exploration/decompression

		Medicare RVU	National Fee	50%	75%	90%
63055	Transpedicular approach with decompression of spinal cord, equina and/or nerve root(s) (eg, herniated intervertebral disc), single segment; thoracic	41.70	1490.89	6132	7575	8026
63056	Transpedicular approach with decompression of spinal cord, equina and/or nerve root(s) (eg, herniated intervertebral disc), single segment; lumbar (including transfacet, or lateral extraforaminal approach) (eg, far lateral herniated intervertebral disc)	38.80	1387.43	5652	6866	7574
✛ 63057	Transpedicular approach with decompression of spinal cord, equina and/or nerve root(s) (eg, herniated intervertebral disc), single segment; each additional segment, thoracic or lumbar (List separately in addition to code for primary procedure)	8.94	318.72	1635	2033	2406
63064	Costovertebral approach with decompression of spinal cord or nerve root(s), (eg, herniated intervertebral disc), thoracic; single segment	46.01	1644.37	5634	6720	7695
✛ 63066	Costovertebral approach with decompression of spinal cord or nerve root(s), (eg, herniated intervertebral disc), thoracic; each additional segment (List separately in addition to code for primary procedure)	5.51	196.31	1260	1638	2036

Anterior or Anterolateral Approach For Extradural Exploration/decompression

		Medicare RVU	National Fee	50%	75%	90%
63075	Discectomy, anterior, with decompression of spinal cord and/or nerve root(s), including osteophytectomy; cervical, single interspace	35.97	1288.89	4743	5866	6972
✛ 63076	Discectomy, anterior, with decompression of spinal cord and/or nerve root(s), including osteophytectomy; cervical, each additional interspace (List separately in addition to code for primary procedure)	6.93	247.09	1538	1944	2295
63077	Discectomy, anterior, with decompression of spinal cord and/or nerve root(s), including osteophytectomy; thoracic, single interspace	39.15	1396.90	4727	5658	6594
✛ 63078	Discectomy, anterior, with decompression of spinal cord and/or nerve root(s), including osteophytectomy; thoracic, each additional interspace (List separately in addition to code for primary procedure)	5.48	195.17	1381	1592	2038
63081	Vertebral corpectomy (vertebral body resection), partial or complete, anterior approach with decompression of spinal cord and/or nerve root(s); cervical, single segment	45.72	1633.76	6601	7207	8602
✛ 63082	Vertebral corpectomy (vertebral body resection), partial or complete, anterior approach with decompression of spinal cord and/or nerve root(s); cervical, each additional segment (List separately in addition to code for primary procedure)	7.47	266.42	1488	1860	2231
63085	Vertebral corpectomy (vertebral body resection), partial or complete, transthoracic approach with decompression of spinal cord and/or nerve root(s); thoracic, single segment	48.91	1741.77	6494	7600	8915
✛ 63086	Vertebral corpectomy (vertebral body resection), partial or complete, transthoracic approach with decompression of spinal cord and/or nerve root(s); thoracic, each additional segment (List separately in addition to code for primary procedure)	5.27	187.59	1630	2214	2745
63087	Vertebral corpectomy (vertebral body resection), partial or complete, combined thoracolumbar approach with decompression of spinal cord, cauda equina or nerve root(s), lower thoracic or lumbar; single segment	62.44	2223.83	7415	9050	10454
✛ 63088	Vertebral corpectomy (vertebral body resection), partial or complete, combined thoracolumbar approach with decompression of spinal cord, cauda equina or nerve root(s), lower thoracic or lumbar; each additional segment (List separately in addition to code for primary procedure)	7.18	255.81	1721	1921	2206
63090	Vertebral corpectomy (vertebral body resection), partial or complete, transperitoneal or retroperitoneal approach with decompression of spinal cord, cauda equina or nerve root(s), lower thoracic, lumbar, or sacral; single segment	50.58	1799.37	6376	7661	9848
✛ 63091	Vertebral corpectomy (vertebral body resection), partial or complete, transperitoneal or retroperitoneal approach with decompression of spinal cord, cauda equina or nerve root(s), lower thoracic, lumbar, or sacral; each additional segment (List separately in addition to code for primary procedure)	4.89	173.95	1551	1916	2218

Lateral Extracavitary Approach for Extradural Exploration/Decompression

		Medicare RVU	National Fee	50%	75%	90%
63101	Vertebral corpectomy (vertebral body resection), partial or complete, lateral extracavitary approach with decompression of spinal cord and/or nerve root(s) (eg, for tumor or retropulsed bone fragments); thoracic, single segment	58.43	2085.12	7314	9039	11208
63102	Vertebral corpectomy (vertebral body resection), partial or complete, lateral extracavitary approach with decompression of spinal cord and/or nerve root(s) (eg, for tumor or retropulsed bone fragments); lumbar, single segment	58.36	2082.47	7242	8286	10108

● = New Code ⊗ = Conscious Sedation ✛ = Add-on Code ∅ = Modifier '51' Exempt ▲ =Revised Code

		Medicare RVU	National Fee	PFR Fee Information 50%	75%	90%
✚ 63103	Vertebral corpectomy (vertebral body resection), partial or complete, lateral extracavitary approach with decompression of spinal cord and/or nerve root(s) (eg, for tumor or retropulsed bone fragments); thoracic or lumbar, each additional segment (List separately in addition to code for primary procedure)	7.84	278.93	1743	2151	2585

Incision

		Medicare RVU	National Fee	50%	75%	90%
63170	Laminectomy with myelotomy (eg, Bischof or DREZ type), cervical, thoracic, or thoracolumbar	39.05	1395.76	4663	5899	6763
63172	Laminectomy with drainage of intramedullary cyst/syrinx; to subarachnoid space	34.99	1251.00	5078	5839	6775
63173	Laminectomy with drainage of intramedullary cyst/syrinx; to peritoneal or pleural space	42.87	1532.57	5576	6729	7841
63180	Laminectomy and section of dentate ligaments, with or without dural graft, cervical; one or two segments	35.34	1261.61	4543	5621	6379
63182	Laminectomy and section of dentate ligaments, with or without dural graft, cervical; more than two segments	38.02	1354.46	5518	6714	7549
63185	Laminectomy with rhizotomy; one or two segments	27.78	990.26	4781	5686	6533
63190	Laminectomy with rhizotomy; more than two segments	32.17	1147.54	5216	6589	7785
63191	Laminectomy with section of spinal accessory nerve	35.73	1282.45	4166	5190	6015
63194	Laminectomy with cordotomy, with section of one spinothalamic tract, one stage; cervical	36.25	1290.03	3910	4870	5725
63195	Laminectomy with cordotomy, with section of one spinothalamic tract, one stage; thoracic	37.79	1349.91	4299	5180	5919
63196	Laminectomy with cordotomy, with section of both spinothalamic tracts, one stage; cervical	44.48	1589.80	4630	5615	6527
63197	Laminectomy with cordotomy, with section of both spinothalamic tracts, one stage; thoracic	41.88	1495.81	4551	5618	6203
63198	Laminectomy with cordotomy with section of both spinothalamic tracts, two stages within 14 days; cervical	44.76	1582.98	5317	6591	7620
63199	Laminectomy with cordotomy with section of both spinothalamic tracts, two stages within 14 days; thoracic	46.32	1636.04	5370	6574	7745
63200	Laminectomy, with release of tethered spinal cord, lumbar	37.73	1348.77	4745	5885	6772

Excision By Laminectomy of Lesion Other Than Herniated Disk

		Medicare RVU	National Fee	50%	75%	90%
63250	Laminectomy for excision or occlusion of arteriovenous malformation of spinal cord; cervical	73.07	2602.42	7055	8338	9315
63251	Laminectomy for excision or occlusion of arteriovenous malformation of spinal cord; thoracic	77.29	2759.32	7285	8306	9163
63252	Laminectomy for excision or occlusion of arteriovenous malformation of spinal cord; thoracolumbar	77.22	2757.04	7468	8951	9880
63265	Laminectomy for excision or evacuation of intraspinal lesion other than neoplasm, extradural; cervical	42.03	1502.64	5238	6303	7384
63266	Laminectomy for excision or evacuation of intraspinal lesion other than neoplasm, extradural; thoracic	43.35	1549.25	5206	6871	7781
63267	Laminectomy for excision or evacuation of intraspinal lesion other than neoplasm, extradural; lumbar	34.84	1246.83	5060	5824	6688
63268	Laminectomy for excision or evacuation of intraspinal lesion other than neoplasm, extradural; sacral	34.10	1216.51	4741	5632	6016
63270	Laminectomy for excision of intraspinal lesion other than neoplasm, intradural; cervical	52.10	1861.53	5848	6905	8084
63271	Laminectomy for excision of intraspinal lesion other than neoplasm, intradural; thoracic	52.27	1867.21	6053	7583	8714
63272	Laminectomy for excision of intraspinal lesion other than neoplasm, intradural; lumbar	48.21	1722.82	5745	6935	7844
63273	Laminectomy for excision of intraspinal lesion other than neoplasm, intradural; sacral	46.35	1656.12	4899	5878	6949
63275	Laminectomy for biopsy/excision of intraspinal neoplasm; extradural, cervical	45.29	1618.22	5802	7140	8314
63276	Laminectomy for biopsy/excision of intraspinal neoplasm; extradural, thoracic	45.14	1613.30	5737	6893	8116
63277	Laminectomy for biopsy/excision of intraspinal neoplasm; extradural, lumbar	39.75	1421.54	5514	6529	7745
63278	Laminectomy for biopsy/excision of intraspinal neoplasm; extradural, sacral	38.89	1390.08	5247	6311	7241
63280	Laminectomy for biopsy/excision of intraspinal neoplasm; intradural, extramedullary, cervical	53.72	1921.02	6595	8082	9214
63281	Laminectomy for biopsy/excision of intraspinal neoplasm; intradural, extramedullary, thoracic	53.16	1900.94	6868	8311	9715

● = New Code ⊗ = Conscious Sedation ✚ = Add-on Code ∅ = Modifier '51' Exempt ▲ =Revised Code

		Medicare RVU	National Fee	PFR Fee Information 50%	75%	90%
63282	Laminectomy for biopsy/excision of intraspinal neoplasm; intradural, extramedullary, lumbar	50.11	1792.17	6474	7894	8848
63283	Laminectomy for biopsy/excision of intraspinal neoplasm; intradural, sacral	47.47	1697.43	5042	6284	7342
63285	Laminectomy for biopsy/excision of intraspinal neoplasm; intradural, intramedullary, cervical	66.89	2390.57	6886	8158	9769
63286	Laminectomy for biopsy/excision of intraspinal neoplasm; intradural, intramedullary, thoracic	66.40	2373.52	6750	7932	9590
63287	Laminectomy for biopsy/excision of intraspinal neoplasm; intradural, intramedullary, thoracolumbar	69.61	2485.70	7256	8745	10042
63290	Laminectomy for biopsy/excision of intraspinal neoplasm; combined extradural-intradural lesion, any level	70.25	2507.30	7494	9149	10508
✚ 63295	Osteoplastic reconstruction of dorsal spinal elements, following primary intraspinal procedure (List separately in addition to code for primary procedure)	8.22	291.43	1070	1274	1467

Excision, Anterior or Anterolateral Approach, Intraspinal Lesion

63300	Vertebral corpectomy (vertebral body resection), partial or complete, for excision of intraspinal lesion, single segment; extradural, cervical	46.81	1672.42	5465	6583	7229
63301	Vertebral corpectomy (vertebral body resection), partial or complete, for excision of intraspinal lesion, single segment; extradural, thoracic by transthoracic approach	52.29	1861.90	5845	7184	8207
63302	Vertebral corpectomy (vertebral body resection), partial or complete, for excision of intraspinal lesion, single segment; extradural, thoracic by thoracolumbar approach	52.17	1858.87	6120	6688	7304
63303	Vertebral corpectomy (vertebral body resection), partial or complete, for excision of intraspinal lesion, single segment; extradural, lumbar or sacral by transperitoneal or retroperitoneal approach	54.48	1937.32	6310	7015	7270
63304	Vertebral corpectomy (vertebral body resection), partial or complete, for excision of intraspinal lesion, single segment; intradural, cervical	57.40	2046.84	5583	6901	7467
63305	Vertebral corpectomy (vertebral body resection), partial or complete, for excision of intraspinal lesion, single segment; intradural, thoracic by transthoracic approach	59.79	2128.32	6257	7479	8528
63306	Vertebral corpectomy (vertebral body resection), partial or complete, for excision of intraspinal lesion, single segment; intradural, thoracic by thoracolumbar approach	61.05	2178.73	6379	7688	8884
63307	Vertebral corpectomy (vertebral body resection), partial or complete, for excision of intraspinal lesion, single segment; intradural, lumbar or sacral by transperitoneal or retroperitoneal approach	56.36	2003.26	6456	7869	8928
✚ 63308	Vertebral corpectomy (vertebral body resection), partial or complete, for excision of intraspinal lesion, single segment; each additional segment (List separately in addition to codes for single segment)	8.97	319.85	1326	1645	1951

Stereotaxis

63600	Creation of lesion of spinal cord by stereotactic method, percutaneous, any modality (including stimulation and/or recording)	21.72	765.91	2943	3410	3848
	(Medicare fees for the code below are based on Non Facility RVUs. PFR information reflects fee when procedure is performed in a facility.)					
63610	Stereotactic stimulation of spinal cord, percutaneous, separate procedure not followed by other surgery	57.83	2158.26	2273	2805	3359
63615	Stereotactic biopsy, aspiration, or excision of lesion, spinal cord	28.53	1015.65	3605	4477	4908

Neurostimulators (Spinal)

63650	Percutaneous implantation of neurostimulator electrode array, epidural	11.21	396.03	2740	3568	4205
63655	Laminectomy for implantation of neurostimulator electrodes, plate/paddle, epidural	21.02	753.02	4559	5073	5544
63660	Revision or removal of spinal neurostimulator electrode percutaneous array(s) or plate/paddle(s)	11.19	397.92	2140	2687	2955
63685	Insertion or replacement of spinal neurostimulator pulse generator or receiver, direct or inductive coupling	12.95	460.83	1830	2495	2788
63688	Revision or removal of implanted spinal neurostimulator pulse generator or receiver	10.55	376.70	1471	1680	1903

Repair

63700	Repair of meningocele; less than 5 cm diameter	31.05	1110.78	3473	4166	4896
63702	Repair of meningocele; larger than 5 cm diameter	34.42	1230.91	3822	4757	5399
63704	Repair of myelomeningocele; less than 5 cm diameter	39.67	1418.50	4210	4873	5428
63706	Repair of myelomeningocele; larger than 5 cm diameter	45.40	1624.67	4491	5189	5774
63707	Repair of dural/cerebrospinal fluid leak, not requiring laminectomy	22.81	816.69	3825	4926	6044
63709	Repair of dural/cerebrospinal fluid leak or pseudomeningocele, with laminectomy	27.95	1000.12	4751	5777	6621

● = New Code ⊗ = Conscious Sedation ✚ = Add-on Code ∅ = Modifier '51' Exempt ▲ =Revised Code

		Medicare RVU	National Fee	PFR Fee Information 50%	75%	90%
63710	Dural graft, spinal	27.79	994.81	4082	4940	5586

Shunt, Spinal CSF

		Medicare RVU	National Fee	50%	75%	90%
63740	Creation of shunt, lumbar, subarachnoid-peritoneal, -pleural, or other; including laminectomy	23.03	825.03	3711	4338	4661
63741	Creation of shunt, lumbar, subarachnoid-peritoneal, -pleural, or other; percutaneous, not requiring laminectomy	15.46	551.41	2551	2927	3447
63744	Replacement, irrigation or revision of lumbosubarachnoid shunt	16.23	581.35	1942	2374	2734
63746	Removal of entire lumbosubarachnoid shunt system without replacement	12.80	457.42	1439	1678	2210

Extracranial Nerves, Peripheral Nerves, and Autonomic Nervous System

Introduction/injection of Anesthetic Agent (Nerve Block), Diagnostic or Therapeutic

Somatic Nerves

		Medicare RVU	National Fee	50%	75%	90%
64400	Injection, anesthetic agent; trigeminal nerve, any division or branch	2.95	107.63	253	368	428
64402	Injection, anesthetic agent; facial nerve	2.91	105.36	242	296	379
64405	Injection, anesthetic agent; greater occipital nerve	2.79	100.81	239	273	304
64408	Injection, anesthetic agent; vagus nerve	3.06	110.66	265	356	390
64410	Injection, anesthetic agent; phrenic nerve	3.85	140.60	275	297	347
64412	Injection, anesthetic agent; spinal accessory nerve	3.76	137.95	234	271	321
64413	Injection, anesthetic agent; cervical plexus	3.18	115.21	264	341	368
64415	Injection, anesthetic agent; brachial plexus, single	4.04	147.42	291	333	372
64416	Injection, anesthetic agent; brachial plexus, continuous infusion by catheter (including catheter placement) including daily management for anesthetic agent administration	4.90	170.92	334	420	505
64417	Injection, anesthetic agent; axillary nerve	4.20	153.86	258	288	386
64418	Injection, anesthetic agent; suprascapular nerve	3.82	139.84	266	302	375
64420	Injection, anesthetic agent; intercostal nerve, single	4.76	175.84	243	333	390
64421	Injection, anesthetic agent; intercostal nerves, multiple, regional block	7.22	267.18	428	540	691
64425	Injection, anesthetic agent; ilioinguinal, iliohypogastric nerves	3.45	123.92	276	332	422
64430	Injection, anesthetic agent; pudendal nerve	4.04	147.42	269	335	441
64435	Injection, anesthetic agent; paracervical (uterine) nerve	3.99	145.53	213	333	399
64445	Injection, anesthetic agent; sciatic nerve, single	4.00	145.91	270	375	495
64446	Injection, anesthetic agent; sciatic nerve, continuous infusion by catheter, (including catheter placement) including daily management for anesthetic agent administration	4.71	164.85	393	491	594
64447	Injection, anesthetic agent; femoral nerve, single	1.97	68.97	179	225	270
64448	Injection, anesthetic agent; femoral nerve, continuous infusion by catheter (including catheter placement) including daily management for anesthetic agent administration	4.27	148.94	365	456	553
64449	Injection, anesthetic agent; lumbar plexus, posterior approach, continuous infusion by catheter (including catheter placement) including daily management for anesthetic agent administration *(UNBUNDLING ALERT: 64450 cannot be used on the same day by the same physician with 10060, 10061, 11000, 11040-11044, 11700-11732, 20550-20605 and 29580.)*	4.23	147.80	343	435	527
64450	Injection, anesthetic agent; other peripheral nerve or branch	2.65	95.50	210	263	324
64470	Injection, anesthetic agent and/or steroid, paravertebral facet joint or facet joint nerve; cervical or thoracic, single level	8.33	308.49	490	668	829
✚ 64472	Injection, anesthetic agent and/or steroid, paravertebral facet joint or facet joint nerve; cervical or thoracic, each additional level (List separately in addition to code for primary procedure)	3.42	124.68	329	429	564
64475	Injection, anesthetic agent and/or steroid, paravertebral facet joint or facet joint nerve; lumbar or sacral, single level	7.58	281.96	401	495	608

● = New Code ⊗ = Conscious Sedation ✚ = Add-on Code ∅ = Modifier '51' Exempt ▲ =Revised Code

		Medicare RVU	National Fee	PFR Fee Information 50%	75%	90%
✚ 64476	Injection, anesthetic agent and/or steroid, paravertebral facet joint or facet joint nerve; lumbar or sacral, each additional level (List separately in addition to code for primary procedure)	2.91	106.49	301	409	508
64479	Injection, anesthetic agent and/or steroid, transforaminal epidural; cervical or thoracic, single level	8.87	327.81	528	725	856
✚ 64480	Injection, anesthetic agent and/or steroid, transforaminal epidural; cervical or thoracic, each additional level (List separately in addition to code for primary procedure)	4.14	151.21	377	514	625
64483	Injection, anesthetic agent and/or steroid, transforaminal epidural; lumbar or sacral, single level	8.87	328.95	482	665	827
✚ 64484	Injection, anesthetic agent and/or steroid, transforaminal epidural; lumbar or sacral, each additional level (List separately in addition to code for primary procedure)	4.27	156.90	389	531	651

Sympathetic Nerves

64505	Injection, anesthetic agent; sphenopalatine ganglion	2.67	95.88	255	297	342
64508	Injection, anesthetic agent; carotid sinus (separate procedure)	4.15	153.11	254	307	330
64510	Injection, anesthetic agent; stellate ganglion (cervical sympathetic)	4.35	160.31	298	350	447
64517	Injection, anesthetic agent; superior hypogastric plexus	4.76	172.05	429	532	661
64520	Injection, anesthetic agent; lumbar or thoracic (paravertebral sympathetic)	5.93	219.43	392	467	534
64530	Injection, anesthetic agent; celiac plexus, with or without radiologic monitoring	5.66	208.44	438	584	752

Neurostimulators (Peripheral Nerve)

64550	Application of surface (transcutaneous) neurostimulator	0.45	16.30	90	111	150
64553	Percutaneous implantation of neurostimulator electrodes; cranial nerve	5.26	190.62	365	426	499
64555	Percutaneous implantation of neurostimulator electrodes; peripheral nerve (excludes sacral nerve)	5.44	197.45	304	366	457
64560	Percutaneous implantation of neurostimulator electrodes; autonomic nerve	5.19	187.59	393	437	511
64561	Percutaneous implantation of neurostimulator electrodes; sacral nerve (transforaminal placement)	35.09	1302.92	1848	2411	3015
64565	Percutaneous implantation of neurostimulator electrodes; neuromuscular	4.99	182.29	300	324	374
64573	Incision for implantation of neurostimulator electrodes; cranial nerve	15.06	539.66	982	1188	1516
64575	Incision for implantation of neurostimulator electrodes; peripheral nerve (excludes sacral nerve)	7.47	266.42	891	1042	1333
64577	Incision for implantation of neurostimulator electrodes; autonomic nerve	8.85	317.58	762	1035	1193
64580	Incision for implantation of neurostimulator electrodes; neuromuscular	7.84	281.20	735	915	1106
64581	Incision for implantation of neurostimulator electrodes; sacral nerve (transforaminal placement)	20.93	739.38	1809	2163	2656
	(Medicare fees for the code below are based on Non Facility RVUs. PFR information reflects fee when procedure is performed in a facility.)					
64585	Revision or removal of peripheral neurostimulator electrodes	12.18	453.63	482	757	920
▲ 64590	Insertion or replacement of peripheral or gastric neurostimulator pulse generator or receiver, direct or inductive coupling	9.56	353.20	596	821	948
	(Medicare fees for the code below are based on Non Facility RVUs. PFR information reflects fee when procedure is performed in a facility.)					
▲ 64595	Revision or removal of peripheral or gastric neurostimulator pulse generator or receiver	11.35	423.32	475	666	836

Destruction By Neurolytic Agent (eg, Chemical, Thermal, Electrical, Radiofrequency)

Somatic Nerves

64600	Destruction by neurolytic agent, trigeminal nerve; supraorbital, infraorbital, mental, or inferior alveolar branch	12.12	446.05	551	637	683
64605	Destruction by neurolytic agent, trigeminal nerve; second and third division branches at foramen ovale	15.45	563.91	734	804	933
64610	Destruction by neurolytic agent, trigeminal nerve; second and third division branches at foramen ovale under radiologic monitoring	17.75	645.39	1311	1701	2018
64612	Chemodenervation of muscle(s); muscle(s) innervated by facial nerve (eg, for blepharospasm, hemifacial spasm)	4.36	157.65	361	420	531
64613	Chemodenervation of muscle(s); neck muscle(s) (eg, for spasmodic torticollis, spasmodic dysphonia)	4.63	167.89	352	427	481

Code	Description	Medicare RVU	National Fee	PFR Fee Information 50%	75%	90%
64614	Chemodenervation of muscle(s); extremity(s) and/or trunk muscle(s) (eg, for dystonia, cerebral palsy, multiple sclerosis)	5.12	185.70	428	511	629
64620	Destruction by neurolytic agent, intercostal nerve	7.70	280.82	407	515	635
64622	Destruction by neurolytic agent, paravertebral facet joint nerve; lumbar or sacral, single level	10.02	368.36	485	557	751
✚ 64623	Destruction by neurolytic agent, paravertebral facet joint nerve; lumbar or sacral, each additional level (List separately in addition to code for primary procedure)	3.67	135.29	254	310	337
64626	Destruction by neurolytic agent, paravertebral facet joint nerve; cervical or thoracic, single level	11.01	402.85	545	668	808
✚ 64627	Destruction by neurolytic agent, paravertebral facet joint nerve; cervical or thoracic, each additional level (List separately in addition to code for primary procedure)	5.21	192.90	309	378	446
64630	Destruction by neurolytic agent; pudendal nerve	5.98	215.26	384	436	490
64640	Destruction by neurolytic agent; other peripheral nerve or branch	6.82	247.85	412	458	540

Sympathetic Nerves

Code	Description	Medicare RVU	National Fee	PFR Fee Information 50%	75%	90%
64650	Chemodenervation of eccrine glands; both axillae	1.61	58.36	80	132	174
64653	Chemodenervation of eccrine glands; other area(s) (eg, scalp, face, neck), per day	1.86	67.08	92	153	201
64680	Destruction by neurolytic agent, with or without radiologic monitoring; celiac plexus	8.84	324.78	432	711	939
64681	Destruction by neurolytic agent, with or without radiologic monitoring; superior hypogastric plexus	12.23	449.09	593	980	1293

Neuroplasty (exploration, Neurolysis or Nerve Decompression)

Code	Description	Medicare RVU	National Fee	PFR Fee Information 50%	75%	90%
64702	Neuroplasty; digital, one or both, same digit	10.94	391.48	1080	1388	1595
64704	Neuroplasty; nerve of hand or foot	8.51	305.07	1425	1588	1800
64708	Neuroplasty, major peripheral nerve, arm or leg; other than specified	11.91	427.48	1846	2214	2564
64712	Neuroplasty, major peripheral nerve, arm or leg; sciatic nerve	13.79	492.29	2218	2625	3005
64713	Neuroplasty, major peripheral nerve, arm or leg; brachial plexus	19.15	682.53	2349	2893	3286
64714	Neuroplasty, major peripheral nerve, arm or leg; lumbar plexus	16.01	566.95	1832	2521	2922
64716	Neuroplasty and/or transposition; cranial nerve (specify)	13.28	477.13	1941	2463	2876
64718	Neuroplasty and/or transposition; ulnar nerve at elbow	14.17	510.10	2025	2474	2720
64719	Neuroplasty and/or transposition; ulnar nerve at wrist	10.10	364.19	1620	1961	2113
	(UNBUNDLING ALERT: 64721 cannot be used with 29075, or 29125 by the same physician on the same day.)					
64721	Neuroplasty and/or transposition; median nerve at carpal tunnel	10.78	389.97	1691	1956	2229
64722	Decompression; unspecified nerve(s) (specify)	8.21	292.95	1607	1939	2145
64726	Decompression; plantar digital nerve	7.53	269.45	709	781	885
✚ 64727	Internal neurolysis, requiring use of operating microscope (List separately in addition to code for neuroplasty) (Neuroplasty includes external neurolysis)	5.02	178.50	1119	1742	1998

Transection or Avulsion

Code	Description	Medicare RVU	National Fee	PFR Fee Information 50%	75%	90%
64732	Transection or avulsion of; supraorbital nerve	9.50	341.84	1032	1136	1494
64734	Transection or avulsion of; infraorbital nerve	10.55	378.98	1296	1395	1493
64736	Transection or avulsion of; mental nerve	9.64	345.63	1143	1296	1438
64738	Transection or avulsion of; inferior alveolar nerve by osteotomy	11.87	425.97	1297	1509	1735
64740	Transection or avulsion of; lingual nerve	11.76	422.18	1432	1665	1852
64742	Transection or avulsion of; facial nerve, differential or complete	12.11	433.17	1636	1961	2263
64744	Transection or avulsion of; greater occipital nerve	10.78	386.93	1174	1521	1704
64746	Transection or avulsion of; phrenic nerve	11.62	415.74	833	1038	1241
64752	Transection or avulsion of; vagus nerve (vagotomy), transthoracic	12.74	454.01	1997	2375	2690

● = New Code ⊗ = Conscious Sedation ✚ = Add-on Code ∅ = Modifier '51' Exempt ▲ =Revised Code

		Medicare RVU	National Fee	PFR Fee Information 50%	75%	90%
64755	Transection or avulsion of; vagus nerves limited to proximal stomach (selective proximal vagotomy, proximal gastric vagotomy, parietal cell vagotomy, supra- or highly selective vagotomy)	22.48	794.71	3183	3687	4145
64760	Transection or avulsion of; vagus nerve (vagotomy), abdominal	11.85	420.66	1901	2223	2509
64761	Transection or avulsion of; pudendal nerve	11.10	394.13	872	1042	1242
64763	Transection or avulsion of obturator nerve, extrapelvic, with or without adductor tenotomy	13.58	486.22	983	1138	1336
64766	Transection or avulsion of obturator nerve, intrapelvic, with or without adductor tenotomy	15.66	557.85	1481	1730	1981
64771	Transection or avulsion of other cranial nerve, extradural	14.75	528.29	1550	1879	2180
64772	Transection or avulsion of other spinal nerve, extradural	14.17	507.45	1419	1789	2169

Excision

Somatic Nerves

64774	Excision of neuroma; cutaneous nerve, surgically identifiable	10.31	369.12	849	985	1139
64776	Excision of neuroma; digital nerve, one or both, same digit	9.98	356.99	903	1031	1234
+ 64778	Excision of neuroma; digital nerve, each additional digit (List separately in addition to code for primary procedure)	5.00	177.74	447	519	558
64782	Excision of neuroma; hand or foot, except digital nerve	11.48	409.29	1042	1371	1793
+ 64783	Excision of neuroma; hand or foot, each additional nerve, except same digit (List separately in addition to code for primary procedure)	5.95	211.47	611	739	995
64784	Excision of neuroma; major peripheral nerve, except sciatic	18.38	656.38	1782	2029	2282
64786	Excision of neuroma; sciatic nerve	28.38	1014.14	2228	2676	3066
+ 64787	Implantation of nerve end into bone or muscle (List separately in addition to neuroma excision)	6.87	244.06	1122	1428	1840
64788	Excision of neurofibroma or neurolemmoma; cutaneous nerve	9.44	338.05	1044	1334	1545
64790	Excision of neurofibroma or neurolemmoma; major peripheral nerve	21.20	757.95	1953	2286	2725
64792	Excision of neurofibroma or neurolemmoma; extensive (including malignant type)	26.94	961.08	2248	2747	3649
64795	Biopsy of nerve	5.06	180.39	655	836	1254

Sympathetic Nerves

64802	Sympathectomy, cervical	16.44	584.00	2269	2632	3025
64804	Sympathectomy, cervicothoracic	24.80	879.60	3043	3764	3996
64809	Sympathectomy, thoracolumbar	22.09	781.45	2889	3657	4225
64818	Sympathectomy, lumbar	17.60	624.17	2183	2672	3096
64820	Sympathectomy; digital arteries, each digit	19.26	689.36	1634	2093	2720
64821	Sympathectomy; radial artery	17.62	632.89	1823	2167	2501
64822	Sympathectomy; ulnar artery	17.55	630.24	1823	2167	2501
64823	Sympathectomy; superficial palmar arch	20.27	726.87	2042	2428	2801

Neurorrhaphy

64831	Suture of digital nerve, hand or foot; one nerve	18.64	667.37	1407	1838	2060
+ 64832	Suture of digital nerve, hand or foot; each additional digital nerve (List separately in addition to code for primary procedure)	9.30	330.85	817	995	1133
64834	Suture of one nerve, hand or foot; common sensory nerve	19.24	688.22	1756	1893	2113
64835	Suture of one nerve, hand or foot; median motor thenar	20.96	749.99	1762	2175	2610
64836	Suture of one nerve, hand or foot; ulnar motor	20.81	744.31	1958	2297	2889
+ 64837	Suture of each additional nerve, hand or foot (List separately in addition to code for primary procedure)	10.33	367.61	1065	1229	1373
64840	Suture of posterior tibial nerve	22.72	807.97	2343	2866	3138
64856	Suture of major peripheral nerve, arm or leg, except sciatic; including transposition	26.14	933.79	2375	2935	3271

● = New Code ⊗ = Conscious Sedation ✚ = Add-on Code ∅ = Modifier '51' Exempt ▲ =Revised Code

Code	Description	Medicare RVU	National Fee	PFR Fee Information 50%	75%	90%
64857	Suture of major peripheral nerve, arm or leg, except sciatic; without transposition	27.40	978.51	2154	2699	3285
64858	Suture of sciatic nerve	31.71	1134.27	2263	2763	3692
✚ 64859	Suture of each additional major peripheral nerve (List separately in addition to code for primary procedure)	7.05	250.88	1044	1163	1393
64861	Suture of; brachial plexus	36.20	1292.68	2318	2981	3578
64862	Suture of; lumbar plexus	35.90	1280.56	3158	3847	4340
64864	Suture of facial nerve; extracranial	22.94	818.59	2424	2812	3525
64865	Suture of facial nerve; infratemporal, with or without grafting	30.12	1080.46	3019	3591	4055
64866	Anastomosis; facial-spinal accessory	31.73	1138.82	3390	3766	4145
64868	Anastomosis; facial-hypoglossal	27.10	970.55	3514	4069	5306
64870	Anastomosis; facial-phrenic	26.93	955.77	3454	3838	4204
✚ 64872	Suture of nerve; requiring secondary or delayed suture (List separately in addition to code for primary neurorrhaphy)	3.30	117.48	580	687	722
✚ 64874	Suture of nerve; requiring extensive mobilization, or transposition of nerve (List separately in addition to code for nerve suture)	4.86	172.81	760	980	1100
✚ 64876	Suture of nerve; requiring shortening of bone of extremity (List separately in addition to code for nerve suture)	5.34	189.49	510	746	927

Neurorrhaphy With Nerve Graft

Code	Description	Medicare RVU	National Fee	PFR Fee Information 50%	75%	90%
64885	Nerve graft (includes obtaining graft), head or neck; up to 4 cm in length	30.09	1073.64	2960	3719	4162
64886	Nerve graft (includes obtaining graft), head or neck; more than 4 cm length	35.46	1265.02	3199	3824	4328
64890	Nerve graft (includes obtaining graft), single strand, hand or foot; up to 4 cm length	28.21	1007.69	2823	3455	3746
64891	Nerve graft (includes obtaining graft), single strand, hand or foot; more than 4 cm length	27.05	959.56	2622	3259	3815
64892	Nerve graft (includes obtaining graft), single strand, arm or leg; up to 4 cm length	27.01	964.11	2657	3106	3695
64893	Nerve graft (includes obtaining graft), single strand, arm or leg; more than 4 cm length	29.23	1044.08	2916	3356	3737
64895	Nerve graft (includes obtaining graft), multiple strands (cable), hand or foot; up to 4 cm length	32.65	1160.04	3213	3931	4305
64896	Nerve graft (includes obtaining graft), multiple strands (cable), hand or foot; more than 4 cm length	36.23	1290.03	3669	4403	5104
64897	Nerve graft (includes obtaining graft), multiple strands (cable), arm or leg; up to 4 cm length	32.47	1157.01	3310	3978	4550
64898	Nerve graft (includes obtaining graft), multiple strands (cable), arm or leg; more than 4 cm length	35.32	1259.33	3608	4389	4991
✚ 64901	Nerve graft, each additional nerve; single strand (List separately in addition to code for primary procedure)	16.50	586.27	1997	2367	2841
✚ 64902	Nerve graft, each additional nerve; multiple strands (cable) (List separately in addition to code for primary procedure)	18.93	672.30	1855	2722	3125
64905	Nerve pedicle transfer; first stage	25.11	894.38	1869	2374	2648
64907	Nerve pedicle transfer; second stage	34.05	1214.61	2050	2720	3282
● 64910	Nerve repair; with synthetic conduit or vein allograft (eg, nerve tube), each nerve	18.16	645.39	1606	2096	2448
● 64911	Nerve repair; with autogenous vein graft (includes harvest of vein graft), each nerve	22.09	782.96	1953	2550	2977

Other Procedures

Code	Description	Medicare RVU	National Fee	PFR Fee Information 50%	75%	90%
64999	Unlisted procedure, nervous system	-	-	IR	IR	IR

Eye and Ocular Adnexa

Eyeball

Removal of Eye

(For all procedures performed on the eye and related organs (65091 - 68899), indicate the affected eye using the -LT (Left) or -RT (Right) modifier following each code.)

Code	Description	Medicare RVU	National Fee	PFR Fee Information 50%	75%	90%
65091	Evisceration of ocular contents; without implant	15.45	558.23	1437	1700	1916
65093	Evisceration of ocular contents; with implant	15.56	563.16	1635	1828	2045

● = New Code ⊗ = Conscious Sedation ✚ = Add-on Code ∅ = Modifier '51' Exempt ▲ =Revised Code

		Medicare RVU	National Fee	PFR Fee Information 50%	75%	90%
65101	Enucleation of eye; without implant	17.64	637.81	1530	1800	2020
	(To code ocular implants, see HCPCS codes V2624 - V2629.)					
65103	Enucleation of eye; with implant, muscles not attached to implant	18.41	664.72	1660	2176	2510
65105	Enucleation of eye; with implant, muscles attached to implant	20.25	730.28	2035	2636	3104
65110	Exenteration of orbit (does not include skin graft), removal of orbital contents; only	29.41	1055.82	2788	3264	3670
65112	Exenteration of orbit (does not include skin graft), removal of orbital contents; with therapeutic removal of bone	34.88	1252.51	3082	3448	3862
65114	Exenteration of orbit (does not include skin graft), removal of orbital contents; with muscle or myocutaneous flap	36.06	1293.06	3252	3655	4039

Secondary Implant(s) Procedures

		Medicare RVU	National Fee	50%	75%	90%
65125	Modification of ocular implant with placement or replacement of pegs (eg, drilling receptacle for prosthesis appendage) (separate procedure)	11.67	430.14	572	861	974
	(To code ocular implants, see HCPCS codes V2624 - V2629.)					
65130	Insertion of ocular implant secondary; after evisceration, in scleral shell	17.45	629.86	1532	1738	1821
65135	Insertion of ocular implant secondary; after enucleation, muscles not attached to implant	17.75	640.47	1445	1677	2041
65140	Insertion of ocular implant secondary; after enucleation, muscles attached to implant	19.20	692.39	1829	2193	2414
65150	Reinsertion of ocular implant; with or without conjunctival graft	14.24	515.41	1461	1732	2090
65155	Reinsertion of ocular implant; with use of foreign material for reinforcement and/or attachment of muscles to implant	20.46	737.86	1826	2476	3052
65175	Removal of ocular implant	15.72	568.08	1173	1655	2151

Removal of Foreign Body

		Medicare RVU	National Fee	50%	75%	90%
65205	Removal of foreign body, external eye; conjunctival superficial	1.37	49.27	113	149	166
65210	Removal of foreign body, external eye; conjunctival embedded (includes concretions), subconjunctival, or scleral nonperforating	1.67	60.26	128	153	186
65220	Removal of foreign body, external eye; corneal, without slit lamp	1.39	50.02	129	157	201
65222	Removal of foreign body, external eye; corneal, with slit lamp	1.84	66.32	162	177	206
65235	Removal of foreign body, intraocular; from anterior chamber of eye or lens	15.97	571.87	1539	1768	2070
65260	Removal of foreign body, intraocular; from posterior segment, magnetic extraction, anterior or posterior route	22.38	801.15	1927	2164	2445
65265	Removal of foreign body, intraocular; from posterior segment, nonmagnetic extraction	25.15	899.69	2160	2383	2863

Repair of Laceration

		Medicare RVU	National Fee	50%	75%	90%
	(Medicare fees for the code below are based on Non Facility RVUs. PFR information reflects fee when procedure is performed in a facility.)					
65270	Repair of laceration; conjunctiva, with or without nonperforating laceration sclera, direct closure	6.89	253.91	254	297	343
	(Medicare fees for the code below are based on Non Facility RVUs. PFR information reflects fee when procedure is performed in a facility.)					
65272	Repair of laceration; conjunctiva, by mobilization and rearrangement, without hospitalization	12.09	441.13	462	586	730
65273	Repair of laceration; conjunctiva, by mobilization and rearrangement, with hospitalization	8.80	314.17	567	770	1050
65275	Repair of laceration; cornea, nonperforating, with or without removal foreign body	12.75	459.70	666	889	1329
65280	Repair of laceration; cornea and/or sclera, perforating, not involving uveal tissue	15.45	551.79	1683	2273	2644
65285	Repair of laceration; cornea and/or sclera, perforating, with reposition or resection of uveal tissue	24.19	861.79	2298	2703	2863
65286	Repair of laceration; application of tissue glue, wounds of cornea and/or sclera	17.32	631.75	965	1072	1347
65290	Repair of wound, extraocular muscle, tendon and/or Tenon's capsule	11.37	406.64	1148	1337	1682

● = New Code ⊗ = Conscious Sedation ✚ = Add-on Code ∅ = Modifier '51' Exempt ▲ =Revised Code

		Medicare RVU	National Fee	PFR Fee Information 50%	75%	90%

Anterior Segment
Cornea
Excision

(See also HCPCS code S0812 for phototherapeutic keratectomy (PTK).)
(See also HCPCS code S0810 for photorefractive keratectomy (PRK).)

		Medicare RVU	National Fee	50%	75%	90%
65400	Excision of lesion, cornea (keratectomy, lamellar, partial), except pterygium	15.75	569.22	1055	1261	1569
65410	Biopsy of cornea	3.55	128.85	286	400	441
65420	Excision or transposition of pterygium; without graft	12.85	470.69	788	974	1280
65426	Excision or transposition of pterygium; with graft	15.92	580.59	1124	1518	1877

Removal or Destruction

		Medicare RVU	National Fee	50%	75%	90%
65430	Scraping of cornea, diagnostic, for smear and/or culture	2.79	100.05	120	159	185
65435	Removal of corneal epithelium; with or without chemocauterization (abrasion, curettage)	1.93	69.73	153	170	218
65436	Removal of corneal epithelium; with application of chelating agent (eg, EDTA)	8.98	322.51	375	563	816
65450	Destruction of lesion of cornea by cryotherapy, photocoagulation or thermocauterization	7.51	271.73	482	554	697
65600	Multiple punctures of anterior cornea (eg, for corneal erosion, tattoo)	9.15	331.22	667	904	1051

Keratoplasty

		Medicare RVU	National Fee	50%	75%	90%
65710	Keratoplasty (corneal transplant); lamellar	25.75	922.05	2660	3286	3498

(UNBUNDLING ALERT: 65730 cannot be used with 65710, 66030, 67500 or 92504 by the same physician on the same day.)

		Medicare RVU	National Fee	50%	75%	90%
65730	Keratoplasty (corneal transplant); penetrating (except in aphakia)	28.56	1021.34	3227	3872	4652

(UNBUNDLING ALERT: 65750 cannot be used with 65710, 66030, 67500 or 92504 by the same physician on the same day.)

		Medicare RVU	National Fee	50%	75%	90%
65750	Keratoplasty (corneal transplant); penetrating (in aphakia)	29.10	1039.53	3418	3849	4162
65755	Keratoplasty (corneal transplant); penetrating (in pseudophakia)	28.91	1032.71	3415	3848	4040

Other Procedures

(See also HCPCS code S0800 for laser in situ keratomileusis (LASIK).)
(See also HCPCS code S0820 for computerized corneal topography, unilateral.)

		Medicare RVU	National Fee	50%	75%	90%
65760	Keratomileusis	-	-	3056	3674	3937
65765	Keratophakia	-	-	3558	3999	4134
65767	Epikeratoplasty	-	-	2900	3098	3752
65770	Keratoprosthesis	33.24	1185.81	3186	3678	4362
65771	Radial keratotomy	-	-	1528	1750	1896
65772	Corneal relaxing incision for correction of surgically induced astigmatism	10.57	381.63	992	1286	1512
65775	Corneal wedge resection for correction of surgically induced astigmatism	12.85	461.21	1326	1552	1732
65780	Ocular surface reconstruction; amniotic membrane transplantation	20.91	752.64	1960	2288	2711
65781	Ocular surface reconstruction; limbal stem cell allograft (eg, cadaveric or living donor)	31.56	1128.21	2905	3692	4318
65782	Ocular surface reconstruction; limbal conjunctival autograft (includes obtaining graft)	27.26	975.10	2505	3023	3464

Anterior Chamber
Incision

		Medicare RVU	National Fee	50%	75%	90%
65800	Paracentesis of anterior chamber of eye (separate procedure); with diagnostic aspiration of aqueous	3.71	133.40	303	373	412
65805	Paracentesis of anterior chamber of eye (separate procedure); with therapeutic release of aqueous	4.07	147.04	313	376	427
65810	Paracentesis of anterior chamber of eye (separate procedure); with removal of vitreous and/or discission of anterior hyaloid membrane, with or without air injection	10.65	382.01	1045	1235	1475
65815	Paracentesis of anterior chamber of eye (separate procedure); with removal of blood, with or without irrigation and/or air injection	15.64	570.36	1041	1222	1434

● = New Code ⊗ = Conscious Sedation ✚ = Add-on Code ∅ = Modifier '51' Exempt ▲ =Revised Code

		Medicare RVU	National Fee	PFR Fee Information 50%	75%	90%
65820	Goniotomy	17.89	644.64	1533	1959	2522
65850	Trabeculotomy ab externo	20.00	715.13	1667	2263	2545
	(UNBUNDLING ALERT: 65855 cannot be used with 67500 or 92504 by the same physician on the same day.)					
65855	Trabeculoplasty by laser surgery, one or more sessions (defined treatment series)	8.23	297.12	1379	1664	1866
65860	Severing adhesions of anterior segment, laser technique (separate procedure)	7.62	275.14	918	1265	1418

Other Procedures

65865	Severing adhesions of anterior segment of eye, incisional technique (with or without injection of air or liquid) (separate procedure); goniosynechiae	11.38	409.67	1412	1628	1821
65870	Severing adhesions of anterior segment of eye, incisional technique (with or without injection of air or liquid) (separate procedure); anterior synechiae, except goniosynechiae	13.81	495.70	1104	1475	1666
65875	Severing adhesions of anterior segment of eye, incisional technique (with or without injection of air or liquid) (separate procedure); posterior synechiae	14.62	524.88	1154	1563	1849
65880	Severing adhesions of anterior segment of eye, incisional technique (with or without injection of air or liquid) (separate procedure); corneovitreal adhesions	15.44	554.06	1201	1489	1664
65900	Removal of epithelial downgrowth, anterior chamber of eye	22.80	817.45	1470	1805	2357
65920	Removal of implanted material, anterior segment of eye	18.23	653.73	1880	2163	2391
65930	Removal of blood clot, anterior segment of eye	15.24	546.10	1319	1493	1840
66020	Injection, anterior chamber of eye (separate procedure); air or liquid	4.65	170.16	312	365	416
66030	Injection, anterior chamber of eye (separate procedure); medication	4.14	151.97	195	236	384
	(To code medication, see appropriate HCPCS code in the J Section.)					

Anterior Sclera
Excision

66130	Excision of lesion, sclera	17.28	625.31	1135	1430	1685
66150	Fistulization of sclera for glaucoma; trephination with iridectomy	19.97	718.16	1742	2112	2416
66155	Fistulization of sclera for glaucoma; thermocauterization with iridectomy	19.87	714.37	1688	2030	2352
66160	Fistulization of sclera for glaucoma; sclerectomy with punch or scissors, with iridectomy	22.65	812.52	1831	2128	2546
66165	Fistulization of sclera for glaucoma; iridencleisis or iridotasis	19.49	701.10	1601	1974	2278
	(UNBUNDLING ALERT: 66170 cannot be used with 65850, 66030, 66625, 67500 or 92504 by the same physician on the same day.)					
66170	Fistulization of sclera for glaucoma; trabeculectomy ab externo in absence of previous surgery	27.34	980.41	2072	2458	2798
66172	Fistulization of sclera for glaucoma; trabeculectomy ab externo with scarring from previous ocular surgery or trauma (includes injection of antifibrotic agents)	34.21	1226.74	2417	2907	3213

Aqueous Shunt

66180	Aqueous shunt to extraocular reservoir (eg, Molteno, Schocket, Denver-Krupin)	27.35	975.48	2433	2941	3373
66185	Revision of aqueous shunt to extraocular reservoir	17.12	613.18	1528	1921	2177

Repair or Revision

66220	Repair of scleral staphyloma; without graft	16.53	592.34	2110	2765	3276
66225	Repair of scleral staphyloma; with graft	21.61	771.59	2490	3274	3615
66250	Revision or repair of operative wound of anterior segment, any type, early or late, major or minor procedure	18.37	669.65	1417	1633	1881

Iris, Ciliary Body
Incision

66500	Iridotomy by stab incision (separate procedure); except transfixion	8.43	305.07	791	883	963
66505	Iridotomy by stab incision (separate procedure); with transfixion as for iris bombe	9.19	332.36	766	836	883

Excision

66600	Iridectomy, with corneoscleral or corneal section; for removal of lesion	18.64	668.89	1611	1917	2261

● = New Code ⊗ = Conscious Sedation ✚ = Add-on Code ∅ = Modifier '51' Exempt ▲ =Revised Code

		Medicare RVU	National Fee	PFR Fee Information 50%	75%	90%
66605	Iridectomy, with corneoscleral or corneal section; with cyclectomy	24.65	880.74	2269	2705	3229
	(UNBUNDLING ALERT: 66625 cannot be used with 66030, 67500, or 92504 by the same physician on the same day.)					
66625	Iridectomy, with corneoscleral or corneal section; peripheral for glaucoma (separate procedure)	10.09	362.68	1312	1610	1910
66630	Iridectomy, with corneoscleral or corneal section; sector for glaucoma (separate procedure)	13.09	469.17	1270	1496	1815
66635	Iridectomy, with corneoscleral or corneal section; optical (separate procedure)	13.21	473.34	1335	1657	2037

Repair

66680	Repair of iris, ciliary body (as for iridodialysis)	11.78	422.56	1230	1600	1897
66682	Suture of iris, ciliary body (separate procedure) with retrieval of suture through small incision (eg, McCannel suture)	14.16	509.34	1470	1762	2064

Destruction

66700	Ciliary body destruction; diathermy	10.48	377.84	1157	1231	1397
66710	Ciliary body destruction; cyclophotocoagulation, transscleral	10.36	373.29	1295	1366	1486
66711	Ciliary body destruction; cyclophotocoagulation, endoscopic	14.49	519.95	1551	1730	1972
⊗ 66720	Ciliary body destruction; cryotherapy	10.84	392.24	1124	1288	1467
66740	Ciliary body destruction; cyclodialysis	10.28	370.26	1201	1445	1726
	(UNBUNDLING ALERT: 66761 cannot be used with 66762, 67500, or 92504 by the same physician on the same day.)					
66761	Iridotomy/iridectomy by laser surgery (eg, for glaucoma) (one or more sessions)	10.56	381.63	1222	1482	1653
66762	Iridoplasty by photocoagulation (one or more sessions) (eg, for improvement of vision, for widening of anterior chamber angle)	11.04	398.30	1146	1435	1694
66770	Destruction of cyst or lesion iris or ciliary body (nonexcisional procedure)	12.24	441.13	1210	1536	1786

Lens
Incision

66820	Discission of secondary membranous cataract (opacified posterior lens capsule and/or anterior hyaloid); stab incision technique (Ziegler or Wheeler knife)	9.67	351.31	1014	1121	1269
	(UNBUNDLING ALERT: 66821 cannot be used with 67500 by the same physician on the same day.)					
66821	Discission of secondary membranous cataract (opacified posterior lens capsule and/or anterior hyaloid); laser surgery (eg, YAG laser) (one or more stages)	7.48	270.97	1000	1196	1582
	(UNBUNDLING ALERT: 66825 cannot be used with 66030 or 67500 by the same physician on the same day.)					
66825	Repositioning of intraocular lens prosthesis, requiring an incision (separate procedure)	18.03	649.56	1608	1783	1981

Removal Cataract

(UNBUNDLING ALERT: 66830 cannot be used with 66030, 66625, 66820, 66821, 67005, or 67500 by the same physician on the same day.)

66830	Removal of secondary membranous cataract (opacified posterior lens capsule and/or anterior hyaloid) with corneo-scleral section, with or without iridectomy (iridocapsulotomy, iridocapsulectomy)	16.51	590.44	1530	1788	2179
66840	Removal of lens material; aspiration technique, one or more stages	16.16	578.32	2032	2313	2588
66850	Removal of lens material; phacofragmentation technique (mechanical or ultrasonic) (eg, phacoemulsification), with aspiration	18.35	656.01	2454	2673	2992
66852	Removal of lens material; pars plana approach, with or without vitrectomy	19.68	703.38	2335	2813	3266
66920	Removal of lens material; intracapsular	17.58	628.34	2123	2516	2749
66930	Removal of lens material; intracapsular, for dislocated lens	19.93	712.09	2337	2814	3340
66940	Removal of lens material; extracapsular (other than 66840, 66850, 66852)	18.11	647.67	2235	2667	3076

		Medicare RVU	National Fee	PFR Fee Information 50%	75%	90%
66982	Extracapsular cataract removal with insertion of intraocular lens prosthesis (one stage procedure), manual or mechanical technique (eg, irrigation and aspiration or phacoemulsification), complex, requiring devices or techniques not generally used in routine cataract surgery (eg, iris expansion device, suture support for intraocular lens, or primary posterior capsulorrhexis) or performed on patients in the amblyogenic developmental stage *(UNBUNDLING ALERT: 66983 cannot be used with 66030, 66625, 66920, 66985, 67005, or 67500 by the same physician on the same day.)*	25.21	898.93	2807	3276	3626
66983	Intracapsular cataract extraction with insertion of intraocular lens prosthesis (one stage procedure) *(UNBUNDLING ALERT: 66984 cannot be used with 66030, 66625, 66840, 66850, 67005, or 67500 by the same physician on the same day.)*	16.52	587.03	2547	3002	3392
66984	Extracapsular cataract removal with insertion of intraocular lens prosthesis (one stage procedure), manual or mechanical technique (eg, irrigation and aspiration or phacoemulsification) *(UNBUNDLING ALERT: 66985 cannot be used with 66030, 66625, or 67500 by the same physician on the same day.)*	17.99	642.36	2818	3299	3721
66985	Insertion of intraocular lens prosthesis (secondary implant), not associated with concurrent cataract removal	17.53	627.20	2040	2300	2768
66986	Exchange of intraocular lens	21.85	781.45	2373	2890	3175
✚ 66990	Use of ophthalmic endoscope (List separately in addition to code for primary procedure)	2.24	79.21	315	354	397

Other Procedures

66999	Unlisted procedure, anterior segment of eye	-	-	IR	IR	IR

Posterior Segment

Vitreous

		Medicare RVU	National Fee	50%	75%	90%
	(UNBUNDLING ALERT: 67005 cannot be used with 66030 or 67500 by the same physician on the same day.)					
67005	Removal of vitreous, anterior approach (open sky technique or limbal incision); partial removal *(UNBUNDLING ALERT: 67010 cannot be used with 66030, 67005, or 67500 by the same physician on the same day.)*	10.89	390.72	2203	2495	2759
67010	Removal of vitreous, anterior approach (open sky technique or limbal incision); subtotal removal with mechanical vitrectomy	12.64	452.50	2391	3048	3348
67015	Aspiration or release of vitreous, subretinal or choroidal fluid, pars plana approach (posterior sclerotomy)	13.66	491.15	1108	1397	1515
67025	Injection of vitreous substitute, pars plana or limbal approach, (fluid-gas exchange), with or without aspiration (separate procedure)	17.20	621.52	1329	1739	1938
67027	Implantation of intravitreal drug delivery system (eg, ganciclovir implant), includes concomitant removal of vitreous	19.90	710.58	2573	2943	3573
67028	Intravitreal injection of a pharmacologic agent (separate procedure)	5.23	188.73	579	693	735
67030	Discission of vitreous strands (without removal), pars plana approach	11.99	432.03	1423	1618	1814
67031	Severing of vitreous strands, vitreous face adhesions, sheets, membranes or opacities, laser surgery (one or more stages) *(UNBUNDLING ALERT: 67036 cannot be used with 67005, 67010, 67015, 67025, 67028, 67031 or 67500 by the same physician on the same day.)*	9.03	325.54	1362	1692	1868
67036	Vitrectomy, mechanical, pars plana approach; *(UNBUNDLING ALERT: 67038 cannot be used with 67005, 67010, 67015, 67025, 67028, 67031, 67036 or 67500 by the same physician on the same day.)*	22.63	807.60	3578	3893	4450
67038	Vitrectomy, mechanical, pars plana approach; with epiretinal membrane stripping *(UNBUNDLING ALERT: 67039 cannot be used with 67028 by the same physician on the same day.)*	39.50	1408.27	4628	5065	5428
67039	Vitrectomy, mechanical, pars plana approach; with focal endolaser photocoagulation *(UNBUNDLING ALERT: 67040 cannot be used with 67028 by the same physician on the same day.)*	29.04	1038.01	4059	4840	5420
67040	Vitrectomy, mechanical, pars plana approach; with endolaser panretinal photocoagulation	33.49	1196.05	4453	5488	5902

© PFR 2007

● = New Code ⊗ = Conscious Sedation ✚ = Add-on Code ∅ = Modifier '51' Exempt ▲ =Revised Code

		Medicare RVU	National Fee	PFR Fee Information 50%	75%	90%

Retina or Choroid
Repair

		Medicare RVU	National Fee	50%	75%	90%
67101	Repair of retinal detachment, one or more sessions; cryotherapy or diathermy, with or without drainage of subretinal fluid *(UNBUNDLING ALERT: 67105 cannot be used with 67015, 67028, 67101, 67141, 67145, 67208, 67210, 67227, 67228, or 67500 by the same physician on the same day.)*	18.01	649.56	2295	2842	3304
67105	Repair of retinal detachment, one or more sessions; photocoagulation, with or without drainage of subretinal fluid *(UNBUNDLING ALERT: 67107 cannot be used with 67015, 67101, 67105, 67141, 67145, 67208, 67210, or 67500 by the same physician on the same day.)*	16.71	601.43	2294	2781	3215
67107	Repair of retinal detachment; scleral buckling (such as lamellar scleral dissection, imbrication or encircling procedure), with or without implant, with or without cryotherapy, photocoagulation, and drainage of subretinal fluid *(UNBUNDLING ALERT: 67108 cannot be used with 67015, 67025, 67028, 67031, 67036, 67039, 67040, 67101, 67105, 67107, 67141, 67145, 67208, 67210 or 67500 by the same physician on the same day.)*	28.27	1009.21	3488	4397	5118
67108	Repair of retinal detachment; with vitrectomy, any method, with or without air or gas tamponade, focal endolaser photocoagulation, cryotherapy, drainage of subretinal fluid, scleral buckling, and/or removal of lens by same technique	37.73	1344.22	5027	6302	7420
67110	Repair of retinal detachment; by injection of air or other gas (eg, pneumatic retinopexy) *(UNBUNDLING ALERT: 67112 cannot be used with 67028 by the same physician on the same day.)*	20.45	736.73	2637	3257	3723
67112	Repair of retinal detachment; by scleral buckling or vitrectomy, on patient having previous ipsilateral retinal detachment repair(s) using scleral buckling or vitrectomy techniques	30.99	1103.95	3058	3675	4342
67115	Release of encircling material (posterior segment)	11.27	404.37	1014	1257	1344
67120	Removal of implanted material, posterior segment; extraocular	15.55	562.78	1238	1553	1889
67121	Removal of implanted material, posterior segment; intraocular	21.02	750.75	1536	1944	2244

Prophylaxis

		Medicare RVU	National Fee	50%	75%	90%
67141	Prophylaxis of retinal detachment (eg, retinal break, lattice degeneration) without drainage, one or more sessions; cryotherapy, diathermy *(UNBUNDLING ALERT: 67145 cannot be used with 67141 or 67500 by the same physician on the same day.)*	12.06	434.31	1390	1636	1840
67145	Prophylaxis of retinal detachment (eg, retinal break, lattice degeneration) without drainage, one or more sessions; photocoagulation (laser or xenon arc)	12.12	435.82	1446	1738	2032

Destruction

		Medicare RVU	National Fee	50%	75%	90%
67208	Destruction of localized lesion of retina (eg, macular edema, tumors), one or more sessions; cryotherapy, diathermy *(UNBUNDLING ALERT: 67210 cannot be used with 67208 or 67500 by the same physician on the same day.)*	13.89	497.97	1447	1742	1930
67210	Destruction of localized lesion of retina (eg, macular edema, tumors), one or more sessions; photocoagulation	16.27	580.97	1459	1834	2263
67218	Destruction of localized lesion of retina (eg, macular edema, tumors), one or more sessions; radiation by implantation of source (includes removal of source)	33.06	1175.96	2560	3076	3412
67220	Destruction of localized lesion of choroid (eg, choroidal neovascularization); photocoagulation (eg, laser), one or more sessions	25.07	895.90	1570	1905	2240
67221	Destruction of localized lesion of choroid (eg, choroidal neovascularization); photodynamic therapy (includes intravenous infusion)	7.66	277.03	844	1092	1192
✚ 67225	Destruction of localized lesion of choroid (eg, choroidal neovascularization); photodynamic therapy, second eye, at single session (List separately in addition to code for primary eye treatment) *(UNBUNDLING ALERT: 67227 cannot be used with 67141, 67145, 67208, 67210, or 67500 by the same physician on the same day.)*	0.74	26.15	115	145	164
67227	Destruction of extensive or progressive retinopathy (eg, diabetic retinopathy), one or more sessions; cryotherapy, diathermy *(UNBUNDLING ALERT: 67228 cannot be used with 67141, 67145, 67208, 67210, 67227 or 67500 by the same physician on the same day.)*	14.21	510.48	1520	1874	2163
67228	Destruction of extensive or progressive retinopathy (eg, diabetic retinopathy), one or more sessions; photocoagulation (laser or xenon arc)	25.50	914.09	1660	1876	2185

Sclera
Repair

		Medicare RVU	National Fee	50%	75%	90%
67250	Scleral reinforcement (separate procedure); without graft	18.80	676.47	1959	2126	2554

		Medicare RVU	National Fee	PFR Fee Information 50%	75%	90%
67255	Scleral reinforcement (separate procedure); with graft	20.02	720.81	2368	2702	3118

Other Procedures

67299	Unlisted procedure, posterior segment	-	-	IR	IR	IR

Ocular Adnexa
Extraocular Muscles

67311	Strabismus surgery, recession or resection procedure; one horizontal muscle	13.91	498.35	1617	1934	2160
67312	Strabismus surgery, recession or resection procedure; two horizontal muscles	16.60	593.10	2012	2362	2645
67314	Strabismus surgery, recession or resection procedure; one vertical muscle (excluding superior oblique)	15.50	554.82	1677	2006	2312
67316	Strabismus surgery, recession or resection procedure; two or more vertical muscles (excluding superior oblique)	18.66	666.24	2239	2596	2805
67318	Strabismus surgery, any procedure, superior oblique muscle	16.24	581.35	1804	2169	2490
✚ 67320	Transposition procedure (eg, for paretic extraocular muscle), any extraocular muscle (specify) (List separately in addition to code for primary procedure)	7.60	267.56	1765	2153	2588
✚ 67331	Strabismus surgery on patient with previous eye surgery or injury that did not involve the extraocular muscles (List separately in addition to code for primary procedure)	7.20	253.16	995	1225	1505
✚ 67332	Strabismus surgery on patient with scarring of extraocular muscles (eg, prior ocular injury, strabismus or retinal detachment surgery) or restrictive myopathy (eg, dysthyroid ophthalmopathy) (List separately in addition to code for primary procedure)	7.84	275.89	1450	1805	2151
✚ 67334	Strabismus surgery by posterior fixation suture technique, with or without muscle recession (List separately in addition to code for primary procedure)	7.07	248.61	1310	1550	1777
✚ 67335	Placement of adjustable suture(s) during strabismus surgery, including postoperative adjustment(s) of suture(s) (List separately in addition to code for specific strabismus surgery)	3.70	130.75	673	767	922
✚ 67340	Strabismus surgery involving exploration and/or repair of detached extraocular muscle(s) (List separately in addition to code for primary procedure)	8.47	298.25	1556	1803	2256
67343	Release of extensive scar tissue without detaching extraocular muscle (separate procedure)	15.12	541.56	1163	1462	1624
67345	Chemodenervation of extraocular muscle	5.66	203.13	550	713	829
● 67346	Biopsy of extraocular muscle	4.85	172.81	578	704	841

Other Procedures

67399	Unlisted procedure, ocular muscle	-	-	IR	IR	IR

Orbit
Exploration, Excision, Decompression

67400	Orbitotomy without bone flap (frontal or transconjunctival approach); for exploration, with or without biopsy	22.42	807.97	2229	2749	3226
67405	Orbitotomy without bone flap (frontal or transconjunctival approach); with drainage only	18.90	681.78	1949	2406	2863
67412	Orbitotomy without bone flap (frontal or transconjunctival approach); with removal of lesion	21.07	759.84	2346	2722	3050
67413	Orbitotomy without bone flap (frontal or transconjunctival approach); with removal of foreign body	20.92	754.16	2513	2975	3273
67414	Orbitotomy without bone flap (frontal or transconjunctival approach); with removal of bone for decompression	30.49	1087.66	2112	2526	2727
67415	Fine needle aspiration of orbital contents	2.58	90.95	362	452	515
67420	Orbitotomy with bone flap or window, lateral approach (eg, Kroenlein); with removal of lesion	39.50	1414.71	3342	3948	4343
67430	Orbitotomy with bone flap or window, lateral approach (eg, Kroenlein); with removal of foreign body	30.21	1087.66	2744	3175	3504
67440	Orbitotomy with bone flap or window, lateral approach (eg, Kroenlein); with drainage	29.01	1044.08	2988	3425	3895
67445	Orbitotomy with bone flap or window, lateral approach (eg, Kroenlein); with removal of bone for decompression	33.47	1196.05	2877	3444	3732
67450	Orbitotomy with bone flap or window, lateral approach (eg, Kroenlein); for exploration, with or without biopsy	29.99	1078.94	2708	3318	3864

Other Procedures

67500	Retrobulbar injection; medication (separate procedure, does not include supply of medication)	2.15	76.17	172	201	220
67505	Retrobulbar injection; alcohol	1.97	69.73	247	298	343

● = New Code ⊗ = Conscious Sedation ✚ = Add-on Code ∅ = Modifier '51' Exempt ▲ =Revised Code

		Medicare RVU	National Fee	PFR Fee Information 50%	75%	90%
67515	Injection of medication or other substance into Tenon's capsule	2.08	73.52	140	185	216
67550	Orbital implant (implant outside muscle cone); insertion	23.25	837.16	1804	2184	2572
67560	Orbital implant (implant outside muscle cone); removal or revision	23.60	848.90	1691	1857	2104
67570	Optic nerve decompression (eg, incision or fenestration of optic nerve sheath)	27.93	1004.28	2402	2867	3308
67599	Unlisted procedure, orbit	-	-	IR	IR	IR

Eyelids
Incision

(Medicare fees for the code below are based on Non Facility RVUs. PFR information reflects fee when procedure is performed in a facility.)

67700	Blepharotomy, drainage of abscess, eyelid	7.06	262.25	219	254	288
67710	Severing of tarsorrhaphy	6.06	225.87	292	378	477
67715	Canthotomy (separate procedure)	6.30	234.21	290	355	374

Excision

67800	Excision of chalazion; single	3.04	109.90	219	265	366
67801	Excision of chalazion; multiple, same lid	3.89	140.22	294	396	444
67805	Excision of chalazion; multiple, different lids	4.81	173.57	344	416	507
67808	Excision of chalazion; under general anesthesia and/or requiring hospitalization, single or multiple	8.42	302.04	576	673	770
67810	Biopsy of eyelid	5.03	184.94	244	326	454
67820	Correction of trichiasis; epilation, by forceps only	1.32	47.37	100	123	156
67825	Correction of trichiasis; epilation by other than forceps (eg, by electrosurgery, cryotherapy, laser surgery)	3.13	113.31	207	242	279
67830	Correction of trichiasis; incision of lid margin	6.97	257.70	647	782	942
67835	Correction of trichiasis; incision of lid margin, with free mucous membrane graft	10.41	373.29	1614	1771	1950
67840	Excision of lesion of eyelid (except chalazion) without closure or with simple direct closure	7.26	267.18	368	385	430
67850	Destruction of lesion of lid margin (up to 1 cm)	5.14	188.35	334	413	579

Tarsorrhaphy

67875	Temporary closure of eyelids by suture (eg, Frost suture)	4.51	165.61	396	548	747
67880	Construction of intermarginal adhesions, median tarsorrhaphy, or canthorrhaphy;	11.02	400.58	899	1007	1525
67882	Construction of intermarginal adhesions, median tarsorrhaphy, or canthorrhaphy; with transposition of tarsal plate	13.49	488.88	1149	1405	1581

Repair (Brow Ptosis, Blepharoptosis, Lid Retraction, Ectropion, Entropion)

67900	Repair of brow ptosis (supraciliary, mid-forehead or coronal approach)	15.76	571.87	1341	1518	2011
67901	Repair of blepharoptosis; frontalis muscle technique with suture or other material (eg, banked fascia)	14.38	516.54	2030	2370	2645
67902	Repair of blepharoptosis; frontalis muscle technique with autologous fascial sling (includes obtaining fascia)	16.04	571.12	2145	2349	2520
67903	Repair of blepharoptosis; (tarso) levator resection or advancement, internal approach	15.78	573.39	2289	2859	3209

(UNBUNDLING ALERT: 67904 cannot be used with 15822 or 15823 by the same physician on the same day.)

67904	Repair of blepharoptosis; (tarso) levator resection or advancement, external approach	17.58	636.30	2294	2950	3587
67906	Repair of blepharoptosis; superior rectus technique with fascial sling (includes obtaining fascia)	12.25	438.10	2028	2272	2535
67908	Repair of blepharoptosis; conjunctivo-tarso-Muller's muscle-levator resection (eg, Fasanella-Servat type)	11.88	430.52	1826	2233	2473
67909	Reduction of overcorrection of ptosis	13.40	486.98	1618	1944	2137
67911	Correction of lid retraction	12.60	449.46	1983	2222	2452

● = New Code ⊗ = Conscious Sedation ➕ = Add-on Code ∅ = Modifier '51' Exempt ▲ =Revised Code

		Medicare RVU	National Fee	PFR Fee Information 50%	75%	90%
67912	Correction of lagophthalmos, with implantation of upper eyelid lid load (eg, gold weight)	24.00	885.66	3285	3635	4035
67914	Repair of ectropion; suture	9.87	360.03	962	1088	1169
67915	Repair of ectropion; thermocauterization	8.99	328.57	624	798	1023
67916	Repair of ectropion; excision tarsal wedge	13.33	484.71	1339	1495	1800
	(UNBUNDLING ALERT: 67917 cannot be used with 67500, 67914, 67916 or 67950 by the same physician on the same day.)					
67917	Repair of ectropion; extensive (eg, tarsal strip operations)	14.52	527.15	1609	1873	2450
67921	Repair of entropion; suture	9.42	344.11	782	891	1122
	(Medicare fees for the code below are based on Non Facility RVUs. PFR information reflects fee when procedure is performed in a facility.)					
67922	Repair of entropion; thermocauterization	8.79	321.37	554	703	971
67923	Repair of entropion; excision tarsal wedge	14.00	507.83	1498	1622	1741
	(UNBUNDLING ALERT: 67924 cannot be used with 67500, 67921, 67923 or 67950 by the same physician on the same day.)					
67924	Repair of entropion; extensive (eg, tarsal strip or capsulopalpebral fascia repairs operation)	14.62	531.70	1644	2008	2352

Reconstruction

67930	Suture of recent wound, eyelid, involving lid margin, tarsus, and/or palpebral conjunctiva direct closure; partial thickness	9.22	335.77	731	949	1030
67935	Suture of recent wound, eyelid, involving lid margin, tarsus, and/or palpebral conjunctiva direct closure; full thickness	14.80	537.01	1260	1576	1760
	(Medicare fees for the code below are based on Non Facility RVUs. PFR information reflects fee when procedure is performed in a facility.)					
67938	Removal of embedded foreign body, eyelid	6.43	238.38	271	419	635
67950	Canthoplasty (reconstruction of canthus)	14.42	524.12	1576	1896	2548
67961	Excision and repair of eyelid, involving lid margin, tarsus, conjunctiva, canthus, or full thickness, may include preparation for skin graft or pedicle flap with adjacent tissue transfer or rearrangement; up to one-fourth of lid margin	14.35	521.85	1742	2266	2660
67966	Excision and repair of eyelid, involving lid margin, tarsus, conjunctiva, canthus, or full thickness, may include preparation for skin graft or pedicle flap with adjacent tissue transfer or rearrangement; over one-fourth of lid margin	18.14	653.73	2178	2643	3113
67971	Reconstruction of eyelid, full thickness by transfer of tarsoconjunctival flap from opposing eyelid; up to two-thirds of eyelid, one stage or first stage	17.48	624.93	2188	2447	2696
67973	Reconstruction of eyelid, full thickness by transfer of tarsoconjunctival flap from opposing eyelid; total eyelid, lower, one stage or first stage	22.73	812.14	2940	3498	3901
67974	Reconstruction of eyelid, full thickness by transfer of tarsoconjunctival flap from opposing eyelid; total eyelid, upper, one stage or first stage	22.64	808.73	3052	3690	4107
67975	Reconstruction of eyelid, full thickness by transfer of tarsoconjunctival flap from opposing eyelid; second stage	16.49	589.69	1140	1551	1796

Other Procedures

67999	Unlisted procedure, eyelids	-	-	IR	IR	IR

Conjunctiva
Incision and Drainage

68020	Incision of conjunctiva, drainage of cyst	2.83	101.94	159	184	206
68040	Expression of conjunctival follicles (eg, for trachoma)	1.58	56.47	154	186	214

Excision and/or Destruction

68100	Biopsy of conjunctiva	4.46	163.72	251	295	406
68110	Excision of lesion, conjunctiva; up to 1 cm	5.74	210.71	354	474	611
68115	Excision of lesion, conjunctiva; over 1 cm	8.08	297.12	530	585	730
68130	Excision of lesion, conjunctiva; with adjacent sclera	13.48	491.91	909	1020	1170
68135	Destruction of lesion, conjunctiva	3.72	133.78	307	369	488

© PFR 2007

● = New Code ⊗ = Conscious Sedation ✚ = Add-on Code ∅ = Modifier '51' Exempt ▲ =Revised Code

		Medicare RVU	National Fee	PFR Fee Information 50%	75%	90%

Injection

| 68200 | Subconjunctival injection | 1.03 | 37.14 | 168 | 230 | 336 |

Conjunctivoplasty

68320	Conjunctivoplasty; with conjunctival graft or extensive rearrangement	17.53	639.71	1552	1957	2229
68325	Conjunctivoplasty; with buccal mucous membrane graft (includes obtaining graft)	15.33	548.76	2035	2348	2662
68326	Conjunctivoplasty, reconstruction cul-de-sac; with conjunctival graft or extensive rearrangement	14.92	533.98	1988	2620	2885
68328	Conjunctivoplasty, reconstruction cul-de-sac; with buccal mucous membrane graft (includes obtaining graft)	16.94	606.74	2002	2211	2473
68330	Repair of symblepharon; conjunctivoplasty, without graft	14.84	540.80	1103	1318	1543
68335	Repair of symblepharon; with free graft conjunctiva or buccal mucous membrane (includes obtaining graft)	14.96	535.49	1446	1691	1862
68340	Repair of symblepharon; division of symblepharon, with or without insertion of conformer or contact lens	13.47	491.91	1011	1225	1405

Other Procedures

68360	Conjunctival flap; bridge or partial (separate procedure)	12.95	471.44	1015	1153	1349
68362	Conjunctival flap; total (such as Gunderson thin flap or purse string flap)	15.13	541.18	1432	1704	1856
68371	Harvesting conjunctival allograft, living donor	10.02	360.78	920	1071	1207
68399	Unlisted procedure, conjunctiva	-	-	IR	IR	IR

Lacrimal System
Incision

68400	Incision, drainage of lacrimal gland	7.32	270.97	380	494	602
68420	Incision, drainage of lacrimal sac (dacryocystotomy or dacryocystostomy)	8.25	303.94	412	537	634
68440	Snip incision of lacrimal punctum	2.89	105.73	265	354	426

Excision

68500	Excision of lacrimal gland (dacryoadenectomy), except for tumor; total	22.61	809.11	1761	2119	2599
68505	Excision of lacrimal gland (dacryoadenectomy), except for tumor; partial	23.25	833.74	1821	2126	2679
68510	Biopsy of lacrimal gland	11.67	424.83	613	806	1080
68520	Excision of lacrimal sac (dacryocystectomy)	16.20	581.35	1719	1989	2181
68525	Biopsy of lacrimal sac	6.58	232.69	505	603	711
68530	Removal of foreign body or dacryolith, lacrimal passages	11.41	418.39	929	1132	1340
68540	Excision of lacrimal gland tumor; frontal approach	21.70	776.90	2106	2416	2740
68550	Excision of lacrimal gland tumor; involving osteotomy	26.83	960.32	2458	2685	2906

Repair

68700	Plastic repair of canaliculi	13.93	498.73	1508	1844	2221
68705	Correction of everted punctum, cautery	6.09	222.84	334	423	521
68720	Dacryocystorhinostomy (fistulization of lacrimal sac to nasal cavity)	17.91	641.60	2179	2520	2893
68745	Conjunctivorhinostomy (fistulization of conjunctiva to nasal cavity); without tube	18.00	645.02	2073	2365	2502
68750	Conjunctivorhinostomy (fistulization of conjunctiva to nasal cavity); with insertion of tube or stent	18.43	660.93	2331	2444	2681
68760	Closure of the lacrimal punctum; by thermocauterization, ligation, or laser surgery	5.16	188.73	262	381	433
	(Code also HCPCS code A4262 for absorbable lacrimal plug or A4263 for long-term, nonabsorbable plug.)					
68761	Closure of the lacrimal punctum; by plug, each	3.61	131.50	228	288	352
68770	Closure of lacrimal fistula (separate procedure)	12.31	435.82	950	1262	1597

● = New Code ⊗ = Conscious Sedation ✚ = Add-on Code ∅ = Modifier '51' Exempt ▲ =Revised Code

		Medicare RVU	National Fee	PFR Fee Information 50%	75%	90%

Probing and/or Related Procedures

Code	Description	Medicare RVU	National Fee	50%	75%	90%
68801	Dilation of lacrimal punctum, with or without irrigation	2.92	106.87	162	178	206
68810	Probing of nasolacrimal duct, with or without irrigation;	6.35	230.80	236	290	351
68811	Probing of nasolacrimal duct, with or without irrigation; requiring general anesthesia	4.88	175.84	410	508	608
68815	Probing of nasolacrimal duct, with or without irrigation; with insertion of tube or stent	11.23	413.08	624	725	853
68840	Probing of lacrimal canaliculi, with or without irrigation	2.92	105.73	198	238	293
68850	Injection of contrast medium for dacryocystography	1.67	60.26	194	252	298

Other Procedures

Code	Description	Medicare RVU	National Fee	50%	75%	90%
68899	Unlisted procedure, lacrimal system	-	-	IR	IR	IR

Auditory System

External Ear

Incision

Code	Description	Medicare RVU	National Fee	50%	75%	90%
69000	Drainage external ear, abscess or hematoma; simple	4.43	162.20	195	263	355
69005	Drainage external ear, abscess or hematoma; complicated	5.19	188.73	529	618	829
69020	Drainage external auditory canal, abscess	5.58	205.78	250	288	340
69090	Ear piercing	-	-	72	124	158

Excision

Code	Description	Medicare RVU	National Fee	50%	75%	90%
69100	Biopsy external ear	2.59	95.12	159	183	252
69105	Biopsy external auditory canal	3.30	121.65	218	278	376
69110	Excision external ear; partial, simple repair	10.73	393.38	926	1094	1281
69120	Excision external ear; complete amputation	10.37	377.46	1569	2169	2737
69140	Excision exostosis(es), external auditory canal	21.74	793.19	1960	2265	3276
69145	Excision soft tissue lesion, external auditory canal	8.83	324.40	686	833	1025
69150	Radical excision external auditory canal lesion; without neck dissection	27.43	987.99	2566	3009	3498
69155	Radical excision external auditory canal lesion; with neck dissection	43.40	1556.83	3632	4492	4880

Removal of Foreign Body

Code	Description	Medicare RVU	National Fee	50%	75%	90%
69200	Removal foreign body from external auditory canal; without general anesthesia	3.12	115.21	153	194	223
69205	Removal foreign body from external auditory canal; with general anesthesia	2.61	94.36	412	488	632

(UNBUNDLING ALERT: 69210 cannot be used with 92504 by the same physician on the same day.)

(To code 69210 in addition to an E/M code, Medicare requires that the physician perform the actual procedures and the presence of ICD-9-CM codes 380.00 - 389.9. If these conditions are met, use a -25 modifier. Do not use a -50 modifier.)

(See also HCPCS code G0268 for removal of impacted cerumen (one or both ears) by physician on same date of service as audiologic function te)

Code	Description	Medicare RVU	National Fee	50%	75%	90%
69210	Removal impacted cerumen (separate procedure), one or both ears	1.27	45.86	78	94	108
69220	Debridement, mastoidectomy cavity, simple (eg, routine cleaning)	3.27	120.89	128	151	209
69222	Debridement, mastoidectomy cavity, complex (eg, with anesthesia or more than routine cleaning)	5.35	197.45	312	367	490

Repair

(69300 may be reimbursable by Medicare if related to a tumor or interferes with hearing.)

Code	Description	Medicare RVU	National Fee	50%	75%	90%
⊗ 69300	Otoplasty, protruding ear, with or without size reduction	13.02	468.03	1836	2211	2543
69310	Reconstruction of external auditory canal (meatoplasty) (eg, for stenosis due to injury, infection) (separate procedure)	27.49	1000.49	2707	3177	3640
69320	Reconstruction external auditory canal for congenital atresia, single stage	39.36	1426.84	3321	3975	4500

● = New Code ⊗ = Conscious Sedation ✚ = Add-on Code ∅ = Modifier '51' Exempt ▲ =Revised Code

	Medicare RVU	National Fee	PFR Fee Information 50%	75%	90%

Other Procedures

69399 Unlisted procedure, external ear	-	-	IR	IR	IR

Middle Ear
Introduction

69400 Eustachian tube inflation, transnasal; with catheterization	3.17	117.10	145	162	178
69401 Eustachian tube inflation, transnasal; without catheterization	1.98	72.76	103	123	141

(Medicare fees for the code below are based on Non Facility RVUs. PFR information reflects fee when procedure is performed in a facility.)

69405 Eustachian tube catheterization, transtympanic	6.34	230.04	370	465	555

Incision

69420 Myringotomy including aspiration and/or eustachian tube inflation	4.59	168.64	253	311	424
69421 Myringotomy including aspiration and/or eustachian tube inflation requiring general anesthesia	3.95	142.87	372	445	560
69424 Ventilating tube removal requiring general anesthesia	3.10	114.07	226	263	374
69433 Tympanostomy (requiring insertion of ventilating tube), local or topical anesthesia	4.76	174.71	402	494	636
69436 Tympanostomy (requiring insertion of ventilating tube), general anesthesia	4.32	156.14	530	628	783
69440 Middle ear exploration through postauricular or ear canal incision	16.91	611.67	1800	2210	2763
69450 Tympanolysis, transcanal	13.09	474.86	1722	2063	2648

Excision

69501 Transmastoid antrotomy (simple mastoidectomy)	18.58	669.27	1845	2275	2791
69502 Mastoidectomy; complete	24.67	887.56	2579	3099	3730
69505 Mastoidectomy; modified radical	30.73	1114.94	2802	3378	4165
69511 Mastoidectomy; radical	31.53	1142.99	3094	3754	4471
69530 Petrous apicectomy including radical mastoidectomy	42.55	1535.23	3902	4388	4820
69535 Resection temporal bone, external approach	70.30	2522.08	5628	6342	6652
69540 Excision aural polyp	5.03	186.08	311	360	515
69550 Excision aural glomus tumor; transcanal	26.37	957.29	2871	3425	3820
69552 Excision aural glomus tumor; transmastoid	40.97	1477.62	3940	4155	4767
69554 Excision aural glomus tumor; extended (extratemporal)	67.07	2405.73	5200	6075	6619

Repair

69601 Revision mastoidectomy; resulting in complete mastoidectomy	26.63	958.43	2591	3014	3370
69602 Revision mastoidectomy; resulting in modified radical mastoidectomy	27.59	993.67	3337	3635	4459
69603 Revision mastoidectomy; resulting in radical mastoidectomy	32.79	1188.84	3297	3674	4828
69604 Revision mastoidectomy; resulting in tympanoplasty	28.44	1023.99	3477	3801	4873
69605 Revision mastoidectomy; with apicectomy	40.19	1452.23	3688	4357	5136
69610 Tympanic membrane repair, with or without site preparation of perforation for closure, with or without patch	10.09	365.33	411	538	763
69620 Myringoplasty (surgery confined to drumhead and donor area)	17.29	632.51	2060	2462	3001
69631 Tympanoplasty without mastoidectomy (including canalplasty, atticotomy and/or middle ear surgery), initial or revision; without ossicular chain reconstruction	21.78	787.51	3118	3378	3717
69632 Tympanoplasty without mastoidectomy (including canalplasty, atticotomy and/or middle ear surgery), initial or revision; with ossicular chain reconstruction (eg, postfenestration)	27.01	974.72	3574	4282	5001
69633 Tympanoplasty without mastoidectomy (including canalplasty, atticotomy and/or middle ear surgery), initial or revision; with ossicular chain reconstruction and synthetic prosthesis (eg, partial ossicular replacement prosthesis (PORP), total ossicular replacement prosthesis (TORP))	25.95	937.21	3615	4117	5061

© PFR 2007

● = New Code ⊗ = Conscious Sedation ✚ = Add-on Code ∅ = Modifier '51' Exempt ▲ =Revised Code

		Medicare RVU	National Fee	PFR Fee Information 50%	75%	90%
69635	Tympanoplasty with antrotomy or mastoidotomy (including canalplasty, atticotomy, middle ear surgery, and/or tympanic membrane repair); without ossicular chain reconstruction	30.77	1114.94	3554	4278	5282
69636	Tympanoplasty with antrotomy or mastoidotomy (including canalplasty, atticotomy, middle ear surgery, and/or tympanic membrane repair); with ossicular chain reconstruction	35.19	1275.25	4110	5057	5905
69637	Tympanoplasty with antrotomy or mastoidotomy (including canalplasty, atticotomy, middle ear surgery, and/or tympanic membrane repair); with ossicular chain reconstruction and synthetic prosthesis (eg, partial ossicular replacement prosthesis (PORP), total ossicular replacement prosthesis (TORP))	35.00	1268.43	3848	4669	5426
69641	Tympanoplasty with mastoidectomy (including canalplasty, middle ear surgery, tympanic membrane repair); without ossicular chain reconstruction	26.25	946.30	3662	4265	5449
69642	Tympanoplasty with mastoidectomy (including canalplasty, middle ear surgery, tympanic membrane repair); with ossicular chain reconstruction	34.04	1225.61	4162	4901	5713
69643	Tympanoplasty with mastoidectomy (including canalplasty, middle ear surgery, tympanic membrane repair); with intact or reconstructed wall, without ossicular chain reconstruction	31.05	1117.98	4012	4752	6077
69644	Tympanoplasty with mastoidectomy (including canalplasty, middle ear surgery, tympanic membrane repair); with intact or reconstructed canal wall, with ossicular chain reconstruction	38.08	1377.95	4471	5309	6506
69645	Tympanoplasty with mastoidectomy (including canalplasty, middle ear surgery, tympanic membrane repair); radical or complete, without ossicular chain reconstruction	37.21	1346.88	4093	4696	5501
69646	Tympanoplasty with mastoidectomy (including canalplasty, middle ear surgery, tympanic membrane repair); radical or complete, with ossicular chain reconstruction	39.66	1433.66	4626	5502	6406
69650	Stapes mobilization	20.11	724.98	2328	2763	3117
69660	Stapedectomy or stapedotomy with reestablishment of ossicular continuity, with or without use of foreign material;	23.70	852.69	3209	3715	4256
69661	Stapedectomy or stapedotomy with reestablishment of ossicular continuity, with or without use of foreign material; with footplate drill out	31.18	1121.39	3609	4477	5227
69662	Revision of stapedectomy or stapedotomy	29.92	1074.77	3915	4489	5012
69666	Repair oval window fistula	20.32	732.56	2844	3207	4054
69667	Repair round window fistula	20.32	732.56	2740	3221	3777
69670	Mastoid obliteration (separate procedure)	23.90	861.41	3026	3578	4073
69676	Tympanic neurectomy	20.89	755.30	2195	2603	2865

Other Procedures

		Medicare RVU	National Fee	50%	75%	90%
69700	Closure postauricular fistula, mastoid (separate procedure)	17.82	643.88	1276	1724	2042
69710	Implantation or replacement of electromagnetic bone conduction hearing device in temporal bone	-	-	1809	2178	3005
69711	Removal or repair of electromagnetic bone conduction hearing device in temporal bone	21.81	786.37	1630	1917	2315
69714	Implantation, osseointegrated implant, temporal bone, with percutaneous attachment to external speech processor/cochlear stimulator; without mastoidectomy	27.62	992.16	2525	3158	3922
69715	Implantation, osseointegrated implant, temporal bone, with percutaneous attachment to external speech processor/cochlear stimulator; with mastoidectomy	34.59	1239.25	3051	3765	4334
69717	Replacement (including removal of existing device), osseointegrated implant, temporal bone, with percutaneous attachment to external speech processor/cochlear stimulator; without mastoidectomy	29.90	1074.77	2567	3206	3648
69718	Replacement (including removal of existing device), osseointegrated implant, temporal bone, with percutaneous attachment to external speech processor/cochlear stimulator; with mastoidectomy	38.84	1399.18	3249	4086	4649
69720	Decompression facial nerve, intratemporal; lateral to geniculate ganglion	29.85	1075.53	3520	3981	4737
69725	Decompression facial nerve, intratemporal; including medial to geniculate ganglion	49.14	1757.69	5078	5635	6409
69740	Suture facial nerve, intratemporal, with or without graft or decompression; lateral to geniculate ganglion	30.34	1088.04	3990	4406	4884
69745	Suture facial nerve, intratemporal, with or without graft or decompression; including medial to geniculate ganglion	32.29	1159.28	4789	5672	6636
69799	Unlisted procedure, middle ear	-	-	IR	IR	IR

● = New Code ⊗ = Conscious Sedation ✚ = Add-on Code ∅ = Modifier '51' Exempt ▲ =Revised Code

	Medicare RVU	National Fee	PFR Fee Information 50%	75%	90%

Inner Ear
Incision and/or Destruction

Code	Description	RVU	Fee	50%	75%	90%
69801	Labyrinthotomy, with or without cryosurgery including other nonexcisional destructive procedures or perfusion of vestibuloactive drugs (single or multiple perfusions); transcanal	18.61	672.30	2513	3083	3631
69802	Labyrinthotomy, with or without cryosurgery including other nonexcisional destructive procedures or perfusion of vestibuloactive drugs (single or multiple perfusions); with mastoidectomy	26.36	947.82	3295	3568	4244
69805	Endolymphatic sac operation; without shunt	27.07	970.55	3295	3825	4330
69806	Endolymphatic sac operation; with shunt	24.18	868.61	3759	4335	5230
69820	Fenestration semicircular canal	22.19	801.15	2878	3542	4044
69840	Revision fenestration operation	23.92	867.09	2093	2403	2719

Excision

Code	Description	RVU	Fee	50%	75%	90%
69905	Labyrinthectomy; transcanal	23.11	833.37	2962	3414	3772
69910	Labyrinthectomy; with mastoidectomy	26.30	944.03	3580	4094	4782
69915	Vestibular nerve section, translabyrinthine approach	40.09	1432.90	4482	5105	6272

Introduction

Code	Description	RVU	Fee	50%	75%	90%
69930	Cochlear device implantation, with or without mastoidectomy	33.02	1184.30	3995	4905	5822

Other Procedures

Code	Description	RVU	Fee	50%	75%	90%
69949	Unlisted procedure, inner ear	-	-	IR	IR	IR

Temporal Bone, Middle Fossa Approach

Code	Description	RVU	Fee	50%	75%	90%
69950	Vestibular nerve section, transcranial approach	47.79	1706.52	4902	5898	6987
69955	Total facial nerve decompression and/or repair (may include graft)	52.14	1864.56	5215	6284	6846
69960	Decompression internal auditory canal	50.36	1797.10	5038	6092	6940
69970	Removal of tumor, temporal bone	56.60	2022.21	5976	7027	7979

Other Procedures

Code	Description	RVU	Fee	50%	75%	90%
69979	Unlisted procedure, temporal bone, middle fossa approach	-	-	IR	IR	IR

Operating Microscope

Code	Description	RVU	Fee	50%	75%	90%
✚ 69990	Microsurgical techniques, requiring use of operating microscope (List separately in addition to code for primary procedure)	6.02	214.88	693	871	1045

Radiology

Diagnostic Radiology (Diagnostic Imaging)

Head and Neck

(For codes 70010-79999 (Radiology Section), do not use a -50 bilateral modifier. If an x-ray is done bilaterally, use the -LT modifier on the first code and the -RT modifier on the second code. Using a -50 modifier could reduce the reimbursement.)

Code	Description	RVU	Fee	50%	75%	90%
70010	Myelography, posterior fossa, radiological supervision and interpretation	5.66	209.95	387	524	621
-26		1.62	56.85	135	183	217
70015	Cisternography, positive contrast, radiological supervision and interpretation	3.33	121.65	313	382	463
-26		1.65	57.98	125	153	185
70030	Radiologic examination, eye, for detection of foreign body	0.71	26.15	97	109	130
-26		0.24	8.34	39	44	52

		Medicare RVU	National Fee	PFR Fee Information 50%	75%	90%
70100	Radiologic examination, mandible; partial, less than four views	0.80	29.56	85	94	123
-26		0.25	8.72	34	38	49
	(UNBUNDLING ALERT: 70110 cannot be used with 70100 by the same physician on the same day.)					
70110	Radiologic examination, mandible; complete, minimum of four views	1.02	37.52	106	126	162
-26		0.34	11.75	42	50	65
70120	Radiologic examination, mastoids; less than three views per side	0.91	33.73	79	89	112
-26		0.25	8.72	32	36	45
	(UNBUNDLING ALERT: 70130 cannot be used with 70120 by the same physician on the same day.)					
70130	Radiologic examination, mastoids; complete, minimum of three views per side	1.36	50.40	122	132	154
-26		0.47	16.67	49	53	62
70134	Radiologic examination, internal auditory meati, complete	1.26	46.61	134	158	173
-26		0.47	16.67	54	63	69
70140	Radiologic examination, facial bones; less than three views	0.88	32.59	95	111	128
-26		0.26	9.10	38	44	51
	(UNBUNDLING ALERT: 70150 cannot be used with 70140 by the same physician on the same day.)					
70150	Radiologic examination, facial bones; complete, minimum of three views	1.17	43.20	120	135	148
-26		0.35	12.13	48	54	59
70160	Radiologic examination, nasal bones, complete, minimum of three views	0.80	29.56	84	89	103
-26		0.24	8.34	34	36	41
70170	Dacryocystography, nasolacrimal duct, radiological supervision and interpretation	-	-	125	146	183
-26		0.41	14.40	44	51	64
70190	Radiologic examination; optic foramina	0.95	35.24	100	109	118
-26		0.29	10.23	40	44	47
70200	Radiologic examination; orbits, complete, minimum of four views	1.20	44.34	121	139	164
-26		0.38	13.26	48	56	66
70210	Radiologic examination, sinuses, paranasal, less than three views	0.87	32.21	86	94	110
-26		0.24	8.34	34	38	44
70220	Radiologic examination, sinuses, paranasal, complete, minimum of three views	1.13	41.69	118	140	159
-26		0.34	11.75	47	56	64
70240	Radiologic examination, sella turcica	0.73	26.91	77	93	106
-26		0.26	9.10	31	37	42
70250	Radiologic examination, skull; less than four views	0.99	36.76	99	108	141
-26		0.33	11.75	40	43	56
	(UNBUNDLING ALERT: 70260 cannot be used with 70250 by the same physician on the same day.)					
70260	Radiologic examination, skull; complete, minimum of four views	1.38	51.16	135	157	186
-26		0.47	16.67	54	63	74
70300	Radiologic examination, teeth; single view	0.43	15.92	35	45	58
-26		0.16	5.68	14	18	23

© PFR 2007

● = New Code ⊗ = Conscious Sedation ✚ = Add-on Code ∅ = Modifier '51' Exempt ▲ =Revised Code

		Medicare RVU	National Fee	PFR Fee Information 50%	75%	90%
70310	Radiologic examination, teeth; partial examination, less than full mouth	0.77	28.42	61	67	78
-26		0.24	8.34	24	27	31
	(UNBUNDLING ALERT: 70320 cannot be used with 70300 or 70310 by the same physician on the same day.)					
70320	Radiologic examination, teeth; complete, full mouth	1.17	43.58	94	110	136
-26		0.31	10.99	38	44	54
70328	Radiologic examination, temporomandibular joint, open and closed mouth; unilateral	0.77	28.42	99	135	151
-26		0.25	8.72	40	54	60
	(UNBUNDLING ALERT: 70330 cannot be used with 70328 by the same physician on the same day.)					
70330	Radiologic examination, temporomandibular joint, open and closed mouth; bilateral	1.23	45.86	130	161	204
-26		0.33	11.75	52	64	82
70332	Temporomandibular joint arthrography, radiological supervision and interpretation	2.76	102.70	264	331	375
-26		0.75	26.53	92	116	131
70336	Magnetic resonance (eg, proton) imaging, temporomandibular joint(s)	13.81	517.68	1103	1261	1471
-26		2.02	70.87	221	252	294
70350	Cephalogram, orthodontic	0.62	22.74	83	95	115
-26		0.25	8.72	33	38	46
70355	Orthopantogram	0.81	29.94	86	106	131
-26		0.28	9.85	34	42	52
70360	Radiologic examination; neck, soft tissue	0.70	25.77	75	96	126
-26		0.24	8.34	30	38	50
70370	Radiologic examination; pharynx or larynx, including fluoroscopy and/or magnification technique	1.86	69.35	182	217	255
-26		0.43	15.16	64	76	89
70371	Complex dynamic pharyngeal and speech evaluation by cine or video recording	3.14	115.97	325	405	472
-26		1.15	40.55	130	162	189
70373	Laryngography, contrast, radiological supervision and interpretation	2.40	89.44	225	263	301
-26		0.59	20.84	79	92	105
70380	Radiologic examination, salivary gland for calculus	0.97	36.00	101	124	145
-26		0.24	8.34	35	43	51
70390	Sialography, radiological supervision and interpretation	2.49	92.85	211	268	314
-26		0.52	18.19	74	94	110
	(To code contrast material used in all radiological examinations, see HCPCS codes A4644 to A4646.)					
70450	Computed tomography, head or brain; without contrast material	6.05	225.87	648	753	928
-26		1.16	40.55	194	226	278

		Medicare RVU	National Fee	PFR Fee Information 50%	75%	90%
70460	Computed tomography, head or brain; with contrast material(s)	7.54	281.58	785	909	1136
-26		1.54	54.19	235	273	341
	(UNBUNDLING ALERT: 70470 cannot be used with 70450 or 70460 by the same physician on the same day.)					
70470	Computed tomography, head or brain; without contrast material, followed by contrast material(s) and further sections	9.19	343.35	981	1149	1396
-26		1.74	61.01	294	345	419
	(UNBUNDLING ALERT: 70480 cannot be used with 70480 or 70481 by the same physician on the same day.)					
70480	Computed tomography, orbit, sella, or posterior fossa or outer, middle, or inner ear; without contrast material	7.45	277.41	693	828	938
-26		1.75	61.39	208	248	281
70481	Computed tomography, orbit, sella, or posterior fossa or outer, middle, or inner ear; with contrast material(s)	8.69	324.02	864	983	1117
-26		1.88	65.94	259	295	335
70482	Computed tomography, orbit, sella, or posterior fossa or outer, middle, or inner ear; without contrast material, followed by contrast material(s) and further sections	10.24	382.39	1019	1129	1261
-26		1.97	68.97	306	339	378
70486	Computed tomography, maxillofacial area; without contrast material	6.86	255.81	674	822	972
-26		1.55	54.57	202	247	292
70487	Computed tomography, maxillofacial area; with contrast material(s)	8.21	306.21	817	927	1103
-26		1.78	62.53	245	278	331
	(UNBUNDLING ALERT: 70488 cannot be used with 70486 or 70487 by the same physician on the same day.)					
70488	Computed tomography, maxillofacial area; without contrast material, followed by contrast material(s) and further sections	9.96	372.15	965	1144	1265
-26		1.93	67.84	289	343	379
70490	Computed tomography, soft tissue neck; without contrast material	6.98	259.60	753	840	928
-26		1.75	61.39	226	252	278
70491	Computed tomography, soft tissue neck; with contrast material(s)	8.22	306.21	820	928	1038
-26		1.88	65.94	246	278	311
	(UNBUNDLING ALERT: 70492 cannot be used with 70490 or 70491 by the same physician on the same day.)					
70492	Computed tomography, soft tissue neck; without contrast material followed by contrast material(s) and further sections	9.92	370.26	1041	1250	1443
-26		1.97	68.97	312	375	433
70496	Computed tomographic angiography, head, without contrast material(s), followed by contrast material(s) and further sections, including image post-processing	14.84	555.58	974	1178	1285
-26		2.39	83.75	292	353	385
70498	Computed tomographic angiography, neck, without contrast material(s), followed by contrast material(s) and further sections, including image post-processing	14.86	556.34	974	1200	1307
-26		2.39	83.75	292	360	392
▲ 70540	Magnetic resonance (eg, proton) imaging, orbit, face, and/or neck; without contrast material(s)	13.91	521.85	1512	1714	1941
-26		1.84	64.43	302	343	388
70542	Magnetic resonance (eg, proton) imaging, orbit, face, and/or neck; with contrast material(s)	16.25	609.77	1761	2088	2528
-26		2.20	77.31	352	418	506
70543	Magnetic resonance (eg, proton) imaging, orbit, face, and/or neck; without contrast material(s), followed by contrast material(s) and further sequences	26.74	1005.04	2224	2730	3132
-26		2.94	103.08	445	546	626
70544	Magnetic resonance angiography, head; without contrast material(s)	14.30	537.39	1420	1677	1937
-26		1.64	57.60	284	335	387

● = New Code ⊗ = Conscious Sedation ✚ = Add-on Code ∅ = Modifier '51' Exempt ▲ =Revised Code

Code	Description	Medicare RVU	National Fee	PFR Fee Information 50%	75%	90%
70545	Magnetic resonance angiography, head; with contrast material(s)	14.28	536.63	1577	1875	2174
-26		1.63	57.23	315	375	435
70546	Magnetic resonance angiography, head; without contrast material(s), followed by contrast material(s) and further sequences	25.44	957.29	2082	2453	2858
-26		2.45	86.03	416	491	572
70547	Magnetic resonance angiography, neck; without contrast material(s)	14.29	537.01	1434	1731	2042
-26		1.63	57.23	287	346	408
70548	Magnetic resonance angiography, neck; with contrast material(s)	14.49	544.59	1590	1759	1970
-26		1.63	57.23	318	352	394
70549	Magnetic resonance angiography, neck; without contrast material(s), followed by contrast material(s) and further sequences	25.43	956.91	2121	2498	2868
-26		2.45	86.03	424	500	574
70551	Magnetic resonance (eg, proton) imaging, brain (including brain stem); without contrast material	14.34	537.77	1471	1710	1914
-26		2.02	70.87	294	342	383
	(UNBUNDLING ALERT: 70552 cannot be used with 36000 by the same physician on the same day.)					
70552	Magnetic resonance (eg, proton) imaging, brain (including brain stem); with contrast material(s)	16.78	629.10	1781	1933	2274
-26		2.43	85.27	356	387	455
	(UNBUNDLING ALERT: 70553 cannot be used with 70551 or 70552 by the same physician on the same day.)					
70553	Magnetic resonance (eg, proton) imaging, brain (including brain stem); without contrast material, followed by contrast material(s) and further sequences	27.30	1025.51	2202	2516	2927
-26		3.21	112.56	440	503	585
● 70554	Magnetic resonance imaging, brain, functional MRI; including test selection and administration of repetitive body part movement and/or visual stimulation, not requiring physician or psychologist administration	16.52	618.11	1594	1799	2072
-26		2.81	98.53	398	450	518
● 70555	Magnetic resonance imaging, brain, functional MRI; requiring physician or psychologist administration of entire neurofunctional testing	-	-	IR	IR	IR
-26		0.83	31.45	IR	IR	IR
70557	Magnetic resonance (eg, proton) imaging, brain (including brain stem and skull base), during open intracranial procedure (eg, to assess for residual tumor or residual vascular malformation); without contrast material	-	-	IR	IR	IR
-26		4.04	142.12	IR	IR	IR
70558	Magnetic resonance (eg, proton) imaging, brain (including brain stem and skull base), during open intracranial procedure (eg, to assess for residual tumor or residual vascular malformation); with contrast material(s)	-	-	IR	IR	IR
-26		4.49	158.03	IR	IR	IR
70559	Magnetic resonance (eg, proton) imaging, brain (including brain stem and skull base), during open intracranial procedure (eg, to assess for residual tumor or residual vascular malformation); without contrast material(s), followed by contrast material(s) and further sequences	-	-	IR	IR	IR
-26		4.49	158.03	IR	IR	IR

Chest

Code	Description	Medicare RVU	National Fee	PFR Fee Information 50%	75%	90%
71010	Radiologic examination, chest; single view, frontal	0.71	26.15	79	89	101
-26		0.25	8.72	32	36	40
71015	Radiologic examination, chest; stereo, frontal	0.82	30.32	91	106	119
-26		0.29	10.23	36	42	48
71020	Radiologic examination, chest, two views, frontal and lateral;	0.93	34.49	95	107	111
-26		0.30	10.61	38	43	44

CPT® 2006 © American Medical Assoc. All rights reserved.

© PFR 2007

● = New Code ⊗ = Conscious Sedation ✚ = Add-on Code ∅ = Modifier '51' Exempt ▲ =Revised Code

		Medicare RVU	National Fee	PFR Fee Information 50%	75%	90%
71021	Radiologic examination, chest, two views, frontal and lateral; with apical lordotic procedure	1.12	41.31	118	134	165
-26		0.37	12.89	47	54	66
71022	Radiologic examination, chest, two views, frontal and lateral; with oblique projections	1.21	44.72	129	141	157
-26		0.42	14.78	52	56	63
71023	Radiologic examination, chest, two views, frontal and lateral; with fluoroscopy	1.50	55.33	148	164	192
-26		0.52	18.19	59	66	77
71030	Radiologic examination, chest, complete, minimum of four views;	1.25	46.23	137	164	194
-26		0.42	14.78	55	66	78
71034	Radiologic examination, chest, complete, minimum of four views; with fluoroscopy	2.25	83.37	210	242	265
-26		0.64	22.36	84	97	106
71035	Radiologic examination, chest, special views (eg, lateral decubitus, Bucky studies)	0.83	30.70	92	103	120
-26		0.25	8.72	37	41	48
71040	Bronchography, unilateral, radiological supervision and interpretation	2.43	89.82	201	242	296
-26		0.79	27.67	80	97	118
71060	Bronchography, bilateral, radiological supervision and interpretation	3.46	128.47	315	360	432
-26		1.00	35.24	126	144	173
71090	Insertion pacemaker, fluoroscopy and radiography, radiological supervision and interpretation	-	-	255	287	331
-26		0.79	28.04	102	115	132
71100	Radiologic examination, ribs, unilateral; two views	0.90	33.35	104	111	130
-26		0.30	10.61	42	44	52
71101	Radiologic examination, ribs, unilateral; including posteroanterior chest, minimum of three views	1.07	39.41	122	137	158
-26		0.37	12.89	49	55	63
71110	Radiologic examination, ribs, bilateral; three views	1.17	43.20	128	143	168
-26		0.37	12.89	51	57	67
71111	Radiologic examination, ribs, bilateral; including posteroanterior chest, minimum of four views	1.39	51.54	154	170	202
-26		0.43	15.16	62	68	81
71120	Radiologic examination; sternum, minimum of two views	0.94	34.87	100	109	116
-26		0.28	9.85	40	44	46
71130	Radiologic examination; sternoclavicular joint or joints, minimum of three views	1.04	38.66	110	115	129
-26		0.30	10.61	44	46	52
71250	Computed tomography, thorax; without contrast material	7.76	289.54	797	866	1014
-26		1.58	55.33	199	216	254
71260	Computed tomography, thorax; with contrast material(s)	9.16	342.59	943	998	1246
-26		1.69	59.50	189	200	249
	(UNBUNDLING ALERT: 71270 cannot be used with 71250 or 71260 by the same physician on the same day.)					
71270	Computed tomography, thorax; without contrast material, followed by contrast material(s) and further sections	11.26	421.42	1155	1327	1494
-26		1.88	65.94	231	265	299
▲ **71275**	Computed tomographic angiography, chest (noncoronary), without contrast material(s), followed by contrast material(s) and further sections, including image postprocessing	14.93	558.61	1272	1525	1814
-26		2.62	92.09	254	305	363

© PFR 2007

● = New Code ⊗ = Conscious Sedation ✚ = Add-on Code ∅ = Modifier '51' Exempt ▲ =Revised Code

		Medicare RVU	National Fee	PFR Fee Information 50%	75%	90%
71550	Magnetic resonance (eg, proton) imaging, chest (eg, for evaluation of hilar and mediastinal lymphadenopathy); without contrast material(s)	14.62	548.38	1471	1761	1931
-26		1.98	69.35	294	352	386
71551	Magnetic resonance (eg, proton) imaging, chest (eg, for evaluation of hilar and mediastinal lymphadenopathy); with contrast material(s)	17.09	641.23	1758	2219	2570
-26		2.36	83.00	352	444	514
71552	Magnetic resonance (eg, proton) imaging, chest (eg, for evaluation of hilar and mediastinal lymphadenopathy); without contrast material(s), followed by contrast material(s) and further sequences	27.60	1037.25	2293	2654	3142
-26		3.08	108.01	459	531	628
71555	Magnetic resonance angiography, chest (excluding myocardium), with or without contrast material(s)	15.00	561.64	1640	1867	2112
-26		2.48	87.16	328	373	422

Spine and Pelvis

		Medicare RVU	National Fee	PFR Fee Information 50%	75%	90%
72010	Radiologic examination, spine, entire, survey study, anteroposterior and lateral	1.76	64.80	202	236	275
-26		0.61	21.22	81	94	110
72020	Radiologic examination, spine, single view, specify level	0.64	23.50	72	82	99
-26		0.21	7.20	29	33	40
72040	Radiologic examination, spine, cervical; two or three views	0.96	35.62	101	114	129
-26		0.30	10.61	40	46	52
	(UNBUNDLING ALERT: 72050 cannot be used with 72020 or 72040 by the same physician on the same day.)					
72050	Radiologic examination, spine, cervical; minimum of four views	1.38	51.16	144	170	193
-26		0.42	14.78	58	68	77
	(UNBUNDLING ALERT: 72052 cannot be used with 72040 or 72050 by the same physician on the same day.)					
72052	Radiologic examination, spine, cervical; complete, including oblique and flexion and/or extension studies	1.71	63.29	189	207	227
-26		0.50	17.43	76	83	91
72069	Radiologic examination, spine, thoracolumbar, standing (scoliosis)	0.86	31.83	101	127	150
-26		0.31	10.99	40	51	60
72070	Radiologic examination, spine; thoracic, two views	0.96	35.62	103	110	132
-26		0.30	10.61	41	44	53
	(UNBUNDLING ALERT: 72072 cannot be used with 72070 by the same physician on the same day.)					
72072	Radiologic examination, spine; thoracic, three views	1.06	39.41	119	144	165
-26		0.30	10.61	42	50	58
	(UNBUNDLING ALERT: 72074 cannot be used with 72070 or 72072 by the same physician on the same day.)					
72074	Radiologic examination, spine; thoracic, minimum of four views	1.25	46.61	146	180	211
-26		0.30	10.61	51	63	74
72080	Radiologic examination, spine; thoracolumbar, two views	0.99	36.76	110	123	141
-26		0.30	10.61	44	49	56
72090	Radiologic examination, spine; scoliosis study, including supine and erect studies	1.14	42.07	134	153	175
-26		0.38	13.26	54	61	70

		Medicare RVU	National Fee	PFR Fee Information 50%	75%	90%
72100	Radiologic examination, spine, lumbosacral; two or three views	1.02	37.90	108	115	124
-26		0.30	10.61	43	46	50
	(UNBUNDLING ALERT: 72110 cannot be used with 72020 or 72100 by the same physician on the same day.)					
72110	Radiologic examination, spine, lumbosacral; minimum of four views	1.41	52.30	156	172	200
-26		0.42	14.78	62	69	80
72114	Radiologic examination, spine, lumbosacral; complete, including bending views	1.80	66.70	194	233	262
-26		0.50	17.43	78	93	105
72120	Radiologic examination, spine, lumbosacral, bending views only, minimum of four views	1.27	47.37	151	169	189
-26		0.30	10.61	45	51	57
72125	Computed tomography, cervical spine; without contrast material	7.76	289.54	767	855	976
-26		1.58	55.33	192	214	244
72126	Computed tomography, cervical spine; with contrast material	9.13	341.46	937	1054	1313
-26		1.66	58.36	187	211	263
	(UNBUNDLING ALERT: 72127 cannot be used with 72125 or 72126 by the same physician on the same day.)					
72127	Computed tomography, cervical spine; without contrast material, followed by contrast material(s) and further sections	11.09	415.36	1117	1240	1590
-26		1.74	61.01	223	248	318
72128	Computed tomography, thoracic spine; without contrast material	7.76	289.54	781	896	1082
-26		1.58	55.33	195	224	270
72129	Computed tomography, thoracic spine; with contrast material	9.13	341.46	929	1064	1296
-26		1.66	58.36	186	213	259
	(UNBUNDLING ALERT: 72130 cannot be used with 72128 or 72129 by the same physician on the same day.)					
72130	Computed tomography, thoracic spine; without contrast material, followed by contrast material(s) and further sections	11.08	414.98	1106	1349	1575
-26		1.74	61.01	221	270	315
72131	Computed tomography, lumbar spine; without contrast material	7.76	289.54	781	880	1043
-26		1.58	55.33	195	220	261
72132	Computed tomography, lumbar spine; with contrast material	9.13	341.46	921	1034	1231
-26		1.66	58.36	184	207	246
	(UNBUNDLING ALERT: 72133 cannot be used with 72131 or 72132 by the same physician on the same day.)					
72133	Computed tomography, lumbar spine; without contrast material, followed by contrast material(s) and further sections	11.13	416.87	1092	1247	1501
-26		1.74	61.01	218	249	300
72141	Magnetic resonance (eg, proton) imaging, spinal canal and contents, cervical; without contrast material	14.02	525.26	1457	1695	1974
-26		2.18	76.55	291	339	395
72142	Magnetic resonance (eg, proton) imaging, spinal canal and contents, cervical; with contrast material(s)	16.97	635.92	1758	1977	2479
-26		2.63	92.47	352	395	496
72146	Magnetic resonance (eg, proton) imaging, spinal canal and contents, thoracic; without contrast material	15.00	562.40	1556	1777	2139
-26		2.18	76.55	311	355	428
72147	Magnetic resonance (eg, proton) imaging, spinal canal and contents, thoracic; with contrast material(s)	16.47	616.97	1776	2031	2394
-26		2.62	92.09	355	406	479

● = New Code ⊗ = Conscious Sedation ✚ = Add-on Code ∅ = Modifier '51' Exempt ▲ =Revised Code

		Medicare RVU	National Fee	PFR Fee Information 50%	75%	90%
72148	Magnetic resonance (eg, proton) imaging, spinal canal and contents, lumbar; without contrast material	14.85	557.09	1480	1782	2163
-26		2.03	71.25	296	356	433
72149	Magnetic resonance (eg, proton) imaging, spinal canal and contents, lumbar; with contrast material(s)	16.79	629.48	1743	1953	2388
-26		2.44	85.65	349	391	478
72156	Magnetic resonance (eg, proton) imaging, spinal canal and contents, without contrast material, followed by contrast material(s) and further sequences; cervical	27.51	1032.71	2255	2633	2919
-26		3.50	122.79	451	527	584
72157	Magnetic resonance (eg, proton) imaging, spinal canal and contents, without contrast material, followed by contrast material(s) and further sequences; thoracic	27.11	1017.55	2297	2658	3065
-26		3.49	122.41	459	532	613
72158	Magnetic resonance (eg, proton) imaging, spinal canal and contents, without contrast material, followed by contrast material(s) and further sequences; lumbar	27.22	1022.47	2220	2591	2980
-26		3.21	112.56	444	518	596
72159	Magnetic resonance angiography, spinal canal and contents, with or without contrast material(s)	15.85	593.85	1596	1726	2078
-26		2.52	88.68	319	345	416
72170	Radiologic examination, pelvis; one or two views	0.76	28.04	87	95	117
-26		0.24	8.34	35	38	47
72190	Radiologic examination, pelvis; complete, minimum of three views	1.02	37.90	116	144	162
-26		0.29	10.23	46	58	65
72191	Computed tomographic angiography, pelvis, without contrast material(s), followed by contrast material(s) and further sections, including image post-processing	14.43	540.04	1265	1583	1872
-26		2.47	86.79	316	396	468
72192	Computed tomography, pelvis; without contrast material	7.57	282.72	752	849	946
-26		1.49	52.30	188	212	236
72193	Computed tomography, pelvis; with contrast material(s)	8.77	327.81	856	940	1193
-26		1.58	55.33	214	235	298
	(UNBUNDLING ALERT: 72194 cannot be used with 72192 or 72193 by the same physician on the same day.)					
72194	Computed tomography, pelvis; without contrast material, followed by contrast material(s) and further sections	10.76	403.23	1021	1114	1223
-26		1.66	58.36	255	278	306
72195	Magnetic resonance (eg, proton) imaging, pelvis; without contrast material(s)	14.16	530.94	1320	1550	1766
-26		1.99	69.73	264	310	353
72196	Magnetic resonance (eg, proton) imaging, pelvis; with contrast material(s)	16.51	619.25	1592	1849	2102
-26		2.36	83.00	318	370	420
72197	Magnetic resonance (eg, proton) imaging, pelvis; without contrast material(s), followed by contrast material(s) and further sequences	26.99	1014.14	2190	2670	3154
-26		3.08	108.01	438	534	631
72198	Magnetic resonance angiography, pelvis, with or without contrast material(s)	14.88	557.09	1598	1785	2043
-26		2.45	86.03	320	357	409
72200	Radiologic examination, sacroiliac joints; less than three views	0.78	28.80	104	117	124
-26		0.24	8.34	42	47	50
	(UNBUNDLING ALERT: 72202 cannot be used with 72200 by the same physician on the same day.)					
72202	Radiologic examination, sacroiliac joints; three or more views	0.93	34.49	108	120	139
-26		0.26	9.10	42	47	54

● = New Code ⊗ = Conscious Sedation ✚ = Add-on Code ∅ = Modifier '51' Exempt ▲ =Revised Code

		Medicare RVU	National Fee	PFR Fee Information 50%	75%	90%
72220	Radiologic examination, sacrum and coccyx, minimum of two views	0.83	30.70	97	111	117
-26		0.24	8.34	39	44	47
72240	Myelography, cervical, radiological supervision and interpretation	5.57	207.68	464	573	644
-26		1.23	43.20	139	172	193
72255	Myelography, thoracic, radiological supervision and interpretation	5.15	191.76	448	523	572
-26		1.21	42.45	134	157	172
72265	Myelography, lumbosacral, radiological supervision and interpretation	4.92	183.42	456	526	610
-26		1.12	39.41	137	158	183
72270	Myelography, two or more regions (eg, lumbar/thoracic, cervical/thoracic, lumbar/cervical, lumbar/thoracic/cervical), radiological supervision and interpretation	7.53	280.44	625	806	888
-26		1.80	63.29	187	242	266
72275	Epidurography, radiological supervision and interpretation	3.17	117.10	347	451	514
-26		1.00	34.87	104	135	154
72285	Discography, cervical or thoracic, radiological supervision and interpretation	8.56	319.85	845	1011	1102
-26		1.57	54.95	211	253	276
● **72291**	Radiological supervision and interpretation, percutaneous vertebroplasty or vertebral augmentation including cavity creation, per vertebral body; under fluoroscopic guidance	-	-	IR	IR	IR
-26		1.87	65.94	IR	IR	IR
● **72292**	Radiological supervision and interpretation, percutaneous vertebroplasty or vertebral augmentation including cavity creation, per vertebral body; under CT guidance	-	-	IR	IR	IR
-26		1.91	67.08	IR	IR	IR
72295	Discography, lumbar, radiological supervision and interpretation	7.73	289.92	815	924	978
-26		1.15	40.55	204	231	244

Upper Extremities

		Medicare RVU	National Fee	PFR Fee Information 50%	75%	90%
73000	Radiologic examination; clavicle, complete	0.75	27.67	87	94	107
-26		0.22	7.58	30	33	37
73010	Radiologic examination; scapula, complete	0.78	28.80	94	106	120
-26		0.24	8.34	38	42	48
73020	Radiologic examination, shoulder; one view	0.68	25.01	79	85	98
-26		0.21	7.20	32	34	39
	(UNBUNDLING ALERT: 73030 cannot be used with 73020 by the same physician on the same day.)					
73030	Radiologic examination, shoulder; complete, minimum of two views	0.84	31.08	99	112	123
-26		0.25	8.72	40	45	49
73040	Radiologic examination, shoulder, arthrography, radiological supervision and interpretation	2.92	108.77	286	339	387
-26		0.74	26.15	100	119	135
73050	Radiologic examination; acromioclavicular joints, bilateral, with or without weighted distraction	0.98	36.38	100	110	118
-26		0.28	9.85	35	38	41
73060	Radiologic examination; humerus, minimum of two views	0.83	30.70	90	106	112
-26		0.24	8.34	31	37	39
73070	Radiologic examination, elbow; two views	0.74	27.29	80	90	104
-26		0.21	7.20	28	31	36
73080	Radiologic examination, elbow; complete, minimum of three views	0.88	32.59	97	110	123
-26		0.24	8.34	34	38	43

© PFR 2007

● = New Code ⊗ = Conscious Sedation ✚ = Add-on Code ∅ = Modifier '51' Exempt ▲ =Revised Code

		Medicare RVU	National Fee	PFR Fee Information 50%	75%	90%
73085	Radiologic examination, elbow, arthrography, radiological supervision and interpretation	2.83	105.36	272	327	369
-26		0.74	26.15	95	114	129
73090	Radiologic examination; forearm, two views	0.75	27.67	82	95	101
-26		0.22	7.58	33	38	40
73092	Radiologic examination; upper extremity, infant, minimum of two views	0.74	27.29	84	96	105
-26		0.22	7.58	34	38	42
73100	Radiologic examination, wrist; two views	0.74	27.29	82	88	101
-26		0.22	7.58	33	35	40
	(UNBUNDLING ALERT: 73110 cannot be used with 73100 by the same physician on the same day.)					
73110	Radiologic examination, wrist; complete, minimum of three views	0.83	30.70	92	101	117
-26		0.24	8.34	37	40	47
73115	Radiologic examination, wrist, arthrography, radiological supervision and interpretation	2.55	94.74	230	275	326
-26		0.74	26.15	92	110	130
73120	Radiologic examination, hand; two views	0.73	26.91	76	84	96
-26		0.22	7.58	30	34	38
	(UNBUNDLING ALERT: 73130 cannot be used with 73120 by the same physician on the same day.)					
73130	Radiologic examination, hand; minimum of three views	0.80	29.56	87	103	119
-26		0.24	8.34	35	41	48
73140	Radiologic examination, finger(s), minimum of two views	0.67	25.01	70	77	90
-26		0.18	6.44	28	31	36
73200	Computed tomography, upper extremity; without contrast material	6.89	256.95	660	759	887
-26		1.49	52.30	198	228	266
73201	Computed tomography, upper extremity; with contrast material(s)	8.10	302.42	752	832	974
-26		1.58	55.33	226	250	292
	(UNBUNDLING ALERT: 73202 cannot be used with 73000 or 73201 by the same physician on the same day.)					
73202	Computed tomography, upper extremity; without contrast material, followed by contrast material(s) and further sections	10.04	375.94	896	978	1228
-26		1.66	58.36	224	244	307
73206	Computed tomographic angiography, upper extremity, without contrast material(s), followed by contrast material(s) and further sections, including image post-processing	13.50	504.79	1131	1272	1493
-26		2.47	86.79	283	318	373
73218	Magnetic resonance (eg, proton) imaging, upper extremity, other than joint; without contrast material(s)	14.04	526.78	1225	1475	1852
-26		1.84	64.43	245	295	370
73219	Magnetic resonance (eg, proton) imaging, upper extremity, other than joint; with contrast material(s)	16.31	612.04	1452	1738	2023
-26		2.21	77.69	290	348	405
73220	Magnetic resonance (eg, proton) imaging, upper extremity, other than joint; without contrast material(s), followed by contrast material(s) and further sequences	26.81	1007.69	1646	1955	2388
-26		2.94	103.08	329	391	478
73221	Magnetic resonance (eg, proton) imaging, any joint of upper extremity; without contrast material(s)	13.78	516.92	1351	1484	1678
-26		1.84	64.43	270	297	336
73222	Magnetic resonance (eg, proton) imaging, any joint of upper extremity; with contrast material(s)	16.05	602.19	1570	1804	2016
-26		2.21	77.69	314	361	403

● = New Code ⊗ = Conscious Sedation ✚ = Add-on Code ∅ = Modifier '51' Exempt ▲ =Revised Code

		Medicare RVU	National Fee	PFR Fee Information 50%	75%	90%
73223	Magnetic resonance (eg, proton) imaging, any joint of upper extremity; without contrast material(s), followed by contrast material(s) and further sequences	26.47	994.81	1964	2441	3034
-26		2.94	103.08	393	488	607
73225	Magnetic resonance angiography, upper extremity, with or without contrast material(s)	14.80	554.44	1456	1703	1984
-26		2.43	85.65	291	341	397

Lower Extremities

		Medicare RVU	National Fee	PFR Fee Information 50%	75%	90%
73500	Radiologic examination, hip, unilateral; one view	0.72	26.53	80	92	113
-26		0.24	8.34	32	37	45
	(UNBUNDLING ALERT: 73510 cannot be used with 73500 by the same physician on the same day.)					
73510	Radiologic examination, hip, unilateral; complete, minimum of two views	0.93	34.49	98	110	128
-26		0.29	10.23	39	44	51
	(UNBUNDLING ALERT: 73520 cannot be used with 72170, 73500, or 73510 by the same physician on the same day.)					
73520	Radiologic examination, hips, bilateral, minimum of two views of each hip, including anteroposterior view of pelvis	1.07	39.41	120	138	166
-26		0.36	12.51	48	55	66
73525	Radiologic examination, hip, arthrography, radiological supervision and interpretation	2.84	105.73	265	312	378
-26		0.75	26.53	93	109	132
73530	Radiologic examination, hip, during operative procedure	-	-	130	145	167
-26		0.40	14.02	52	58	67
73540	Radiologic examination, pelvis and hips, infant or child, minimum of two views	0.93	34.49	98	110	123
-26		0.28	9.85	39	44	49
73542	Radiological examination, sacroiliac joint arthrography, radiological supervision and interpretation	2.72	100.81	286	328	393
-26		0.78	27.29	100	115	138
73550	Radiologic examination, femur, two views	0.83	30.70	90	106	122
-26		0.24	8.34	36	42	49
73560	Radiologic examination, knee; one or two views	0.78	28.80	84	98	112
-26		0.24	8.34	34	39	45
	(UNBUNDLING ALERT: 73562 cannot be used with 73560 by the same physician on the same day.)					
73562	Radiologic examination, knee; three views	0.88	32.59	97	117	138
-26		0.25	8.72	39	47	55
	(UNBUNDLING ALERT: 73564 cannot be used with 73560 or 73562 by the same physician on the same day.)					
73564	Radiologic examination, knee; complete, four or more views	1.00	37.14	108	132	156
-26		0.30	10.61	43	53	62
73565	Radiologic examination, knee; both knees, standing, anteroposterior	0.77	28.42	103	119	137
-26		0.24	8.34	41	48	55
73580	Radiologic examination, knee, arthrography, radiological supervision and interpretation	3.38	126.20	324	376	443
-26		0.74	26.15	113	132	155
73590	Radiologic examination; tibia and fibula, two views	0.77	28.42	88	103	115
-26		0.24	8.34	35	41	46
73592	Radiologic examination; lower extremity, infant, minimum of two views	0.74	27.29	86	92	115
-26		0.22	7.58	34	37	46

© PFR 2007

● = New Code ⊗ = Conscious Sedation ✚ = Add-on Code ∅ = Modifier '51' Exempt ▲ =Revised Code

		Medicare RVU	National Fee	PFR Fee Information 50%	75%	90%
73600	Radiologic examination, ankle; two views	0.73	26.91	80	90	106
-26		0.22	7.58	32	36	42
	(UNBUNDLING ALERT: 73610 cannot be used with 73600 by the same physician on the same day.)					
73610	Radiologic examination, ankle; complete, minimum of three views	0.81	29.94	93	104	120
-26		0.24	8.34	37	42	48
73615	Radiologic examination, ankle, arthrography, radiological supervision and interpretation	2.86	106.49	261	306	360
-26		0.75	26.53	78	92	108
73620	Radiologic examination, foot; two views	0.73	26.91	78	96	104
-26		0.22	7.58	31	38	42
	(UNBUNDLING ALERT: 73630 cannot be used with 73620 by the same physician on the same day.)					
73630	Radiologic examination, foot; complete, minimum of three views	0.80	29.56	91	101	113
-26		0.24	8.34	36	40	45
73650	Radiologic examination; calcaneus, minimum of two views	0.72	26.53	83	89	100
-26		0.22	7.58	33	36	40
73660	Radiologic examination; toe(s), minimum of two views	0.66	24.63	68	74	94
-26		0.18	6.44	27	29	37
73700	Computed tomography, lower extremity; without contrast material	6.89	256.95	653	845	923
-26		1.49	52.30	196	253	277
73701	Computed tomography, lower extremity; with contrast material(s)	8.12	303.18	747	862	1032
-26		1.58	55.33	224	259	310
	(UNBUNDLING ALERT: 73702 cannot be used with 73700 or 73701 by the same physician on the same day.)					
73702	Computed tomography, lower extremity; without contrast material, followed by contrast material(s) and further sections	10.06	376.70	897	1015	1228
-26		1.66	58.36	179	203	246
73706	Computed tomographic angiography, lower extremity, without contrast material(s), followed by contrast material(s) and further sections, including image post-processing	13.98	522.61	1012	1324	1580
-26		2.60	91.33	202	265	316
73718	Magnetic resonance (eg, proton) imaging, lower extremity other than joint; without contrast material(s)	13.94	522.99	1297	1611	1910
-26		1.84	64.43	259	322	382
73719	Magnetic resonance (eg, proton) imaging, lower extremity other than joint; with contrast material(s)	16.28	610.91	1485	1800	2194
-26		2.20	77.31	297	360	439
73720	Magnetic resonance (eg, proton) imaging, lower extremity other than joint; without contrast material(s), followed by contrast material(s) and further sequences	26.79	1006.94	1777	2132	2514
-26		2.93	102.70	355	426	503
73721	Magnetic resonance (eg, proton) imaging, any joint of lower extremity; without contrast material	13.85	519.57	1300	1590	1786
-26		1.84	64.43	260	318	357
73722	Magnetic resonance (eg, proton) imaging, any joint of lower extremity; with contrast material(s)	16.11	604.47	1523	1753	2279
-26		2.21	77.69	305	351	456
73723	Magnetic resonance (eg, proton) imaging, any joint of lower extremity; without contrast material(s), followed by contrast material(s) and further sequences	26.46	994.43	2197	2549	3024
-26		2.94	103.08	439	510	605
73725	Magnetic resonance angiography, lower extremity, with or without contrast material(s)	14.93	558.99	1416	1597	1801
-26		2.48	87.16	283	319	360

© PFR 2007

● = New Code ⊗ = Conscious Sedation ✚ = Add-on Code ∅ = Modifier '51' Exempt ▲ =Revised Code

		Medicare RVU	National Fee	PFR Fee Information 50%	75%	90%

Abdomen

Code	Description	Medicare RVU	National Fee	50%	75%	90%
74000	Radiologic examination, abdomen; single anteroposterior view	0.76	28.04	85	94	113
-26		0.25	8.72	34	38	45
	(UNBUNDLING ALERT: 74010 cannot be used with 74000 by the same physician on the same day.)					
74010	Radiologic examination, abdomen; anteroposterior and additional oblique and cone views	0.96	35.62	105	125	141
-26		0.32	11.37	42	50	56
	(UNBUNDLING ALERT: 74020 cannot be used with 74000 or 74010 by the same physician on the same day.)					
74020	Radiologic examination, abdomen; complete, including decubitus and/or erect views	1.04	38.28	113	130	152
-26		0.37	12.89	45	52	61
	(UNBUNDLING ALERT: 74022 cannot be used with 71010, 74000, 74010, 74020 by the same physician on the same day.)					
74022	Radiologic examination, abdomen; complete acute abdomen series, including supine, erect, and/or decubitus views, single view chest	1.23	45.48	146	173	201
-26		0.43	15.16	58	69	80
74150	Computed tomography, abdomen; without contrast material	7.51	280.06	736	853	1029
-26		1.62	56.85	184	213	257
74160	Computed tomography, abdomen; with contrast material(s)	9.22	344.49	903	1069	1315
-26		1.74	61.01	226	267	329
	(UNBUNDLING ALERT: 74170 cannot be used with 74150 or 74160 by the same physician on the same day.)					
74170	Computed tomography, abdomen; without contrast material, followed by contrast material(s) and further sections	11.49	430.14	1063	1189	1449
-26		1.91	67.08	266	297	362
74175	Computed tomographic angiography, abdomen, without contrast material(s), followed by contrast material(s) and further sections, including image post-processing	14.76	552.17	1415	1599	1756
-26		2.59	90.95	283	320	351
74181	Magnetic resonance (eg, proton) imaging, abdomen; without contrast material(s)	13.68	512.75	1508	1695	2116
-26		1.98	69.35	302	339	423
74182	Magnetic resonance (eg, proton) imaging, abdomen; with contrast material(s)	16.96	636.30	1743	1944	2475
-26		2.36	83.00	349	389	495
74183	Magnetic resonance (eg, proton) imaging, abdomen; without contrast material(s), followed by with contrast material(s) and further sequences	27.00	1014.52	2418	2661	3009
-26		3.08	108.01	484	532	602
74185	Magnetic resonance angiography, abdomen, with or without contrast material(s)	14.89	557.47	1586	1939	2103
-26		2.45	86.03	317	388	421
74190	Peritoneogram (eg, after injection of air or contrast), radiological supervision and interpretation	-	-	176	194	217
-26		0.66	23.12	70	78	87

Gastrointestinal Tract

Code	Description	Medicare RVU	National Fee	50%	75%	90%
74210	Radiologic examination; pharynx and/or cervical esophagus	1.84	68.22	174	196	239
-26		0.50	17.43	70	78	96
74220	Radiologic examination; esophagus	2.02	74.66	190	228	261
-26		0.63	21.98	76	91	104
	(For non-physician evaluation of dysphagia, see HCPCS code V5364.)					
74230	Swallowing function, with cineradiography/videoradiography	2.19	81.10	216	249	289
-26		0.72	25.39	86	100	116

● = New Code ⊗ = Conscious Sedation ✚ = Add-on Code ∅ = Modifier '51' Exempt ▲ =Revised Code

		Medicare RVU	National Fee	PFR Fee Information 50%	75%	90%
74235	Removal of foreign body(s), esophageal, with use of balloon catheter, radiological supervision and interpretation	-	-	444	514	574
-26		1.63	57.23	178	206	230
74240	Radiologic examination, gastrointestinal tract, upper; with or without delayed films, without KUB	2.60	95.88	234	283	321
-26		0.94	32.97	94	113	128
	(UNBUNDLING ALERT: 74241 cannot be used with 74000, 74010, or 74240 by the same physician on the same day.)					
74241	Radiologic examination, gastrointestinal tract, upper; with or without delayed films, with KUB	2.69	99.29	257	290	347
-26		0.94	32.97	103	116	139
	(UNBUNDLING ALERT: 74245 cannot be used with 74000, 74010, 74240, 74241, or 74250 by the same physician on the same day.)					
74245	Radiologic examination, gastrointestinal tract, upper; with small intestine, includes multiple serial films	4.02	148.94	371	419	511
-26		1.24	43.58	148	168	204
	(UNBUNDLING ALERT: 74246 cannot be used with 74000, 74010, 74240, 74241, or 74245 by the same physician on the same day.)					
74246	Radiological examination, gastrointestinal tract, upper, air contrast, with specific high density barium, effervescent agent, with or without glucagon; with or without delayed films, without KUB	2.88	106.49	258	295	352
-26		0.94	32.97	103	118	141
	(UNBUNDLING ALERT: 74247 cannot be used with 74000, 74010, 74240, 74241, or 74246 by the same physician on the same day.)					
74247	Radiological examination, gastrointestinal tract, upper, air contrast, with specific high density barium, effervescent agent, with or without glucagon; with or without delayed films, with KUB	3.01	111.42	270	314	380
-26		0.94	32.97	108	126	152
74249	Radiological examination, gastrointestinal tract, upper, air contrast, with specific high density barium, effervescent agent, with or without glucagon; with small intestine follow-through	4.26	158.03	375	432	534
-26		1.24	43.58	150	173	214
74250	Radiologic examination, small intestine, includes multiple serial films;	2.24	83.00	184	222	272
-26		0.64	22.36	74	89	109
74251	Radiologic examination, small intestine, includes multiple serial films; via enteroclysis tube	4.31	160.69	237	284	321
-26		0.94	32.97	95	114	128
74260	Duodenography, hypotonic	3.81	142.49	218	265	314
-26		0.68	23.88	87	106	126
	(UNBUNDLING ALERT: 74270 cannot be used with 74000 or 74010 by the same physician on the same day.)					
74270	Radiologic examination, colon; barium enema, with or without KUB	3.12	115.59	275	337	404
-26		0.94	32.97	110	135	162
	(UNBUNDLING ALERT: 74280 cannot be used with 74000, 74010, or 74270 by the same physician on the same day.)					
74280	Radiologic examination, colon; air contrast with specific high density barium, with or without glucagon	4.23	156.52	371	440	496
-26		1.34	46.99	148	176	198
74283	Therapeutic enema, contrast or air, for reduction of intussusception or other intraluminal obstruction (eg, meconium ileus)	5.48	200.10	451	525	616
-26		2.75	96.64	180	210	246
74290	Cholecystography, oral contrast;	1.37	50.78	140	164	185
-26		0.43	15.16	56	66	74
74291	Cholecystography, oral contrast; additional or repeat examination or multiple day examination	0.99	36.76	87	101	114
-26		0.28	9.85	35	40	46

© PFR 2007

● = New Code ⊗ = Conscious Sedation ✚ = Add-on Code ∅ = Modifier '51' Exempt ▲ =Revised Code

		Medicare RVU	National Fee	PFR Fee Information 50%	75%	90%
74300	Cholangiography and/or pancreatography; intraoperative, radiological supervision and interpretation	-	-	205	235	268
-26		0.50	17.43	82	94	107
✚ 74301	Cholangiography and/or pancreatography; additional set intraoperative, radiological supervision and interpretation (List separately in addition to code for primary procedure)	-	-	118	139	148
-26		0.29	10.23	47	56	59
74305	Cholangiography and/or pancreatography; through existing catheter, radiological supervision and interpretation	-	-	172	197	228
-26		0.58	20.46	86	98	114
74320	Cholangiography, percutaneous, transhepatic, radiological supervision and interpretation	3.73	139.46	444	517	652
-26		0.74	26.15	111	129	163
74327	Postoperative biliary duct calculus removal, percutaneous via T-tube tract, basket, or snare (eg, Burhenne technique), radiological supervision and interpretation	3.03	112.18	413	532	598
-26		0.95	33.35	165	213	239
74328	Endoscopic catheterization of the biliary ductal system, radiological supervision and interpretation	-	-	426	475	553
-26		0.96	33.73	128	142	166
74329	Endoscopic catheterization of the pancreatic ductal system, radiological supervision and interpretation	-	-	439	492	569
-26		0.96	33.73	132	148	171
74330	Combined endoscopic catheterization of the biliary and pancreatic ductal systems, radiological supervision and interpretation	-	-	455	513	614
-26		1.23	43.20	136	154	184
74340	Introduction of long gastrointestinal tube (eg, Miller-Abbott), including multiple fluoroscopies and films, radiological supervision and interpretation	-	-	324	372	447
-26		0.74	26.15	97	112	134
74350	Percutaneous placement of gastrostomy tube, radiological supervision and interpretation	4.03	149.70	423	454	492
-26		1.03	36.00	127	136	148
74355	Percutaneous placement of enteroclysis tube, radiological supervision and interpretation	-	-	376	456	531
-26		1.03	36.00	113	137	159
74360	Intraluminal dilation of strictures and/or obstructions (eg, esophagus), radiological supervision and interpretation	-	-	397	513	608
-26		0.76	26.91	159	205	243
74363	Percutaneous transhepatic dilation of biliary duct stricture with or without placement of stent, radiological supervision and interpretation	-	-	558	630	774
-26		1.20	42.07	223	252	310

		Medicare RVU	National Fee	PFR Fee Information 50%	75%	90%

Urinary Tract

(UNBUNDLING ALERT: 74400 cannot be used with 36000, 74000, or 74010 by the same physician on the same day.)

74400	Urography (pyelography), intravenous, with or without KUB, with or without tomography	2.62	97.40	251	305	370
-26		0.67	23.50	100	122	148

(UNBUNDLING ALERT: 74405 cannot be used with 36000, 74010, or 74400 by the same physician on the same day.)

74410	Urography, infusion, drip technique and/or bolus technique;	2.85	106.11	250	292	332
-26		0.67	23.50	87	102	116

(UNBUNDLING ALERT: 74415 cannot be used with 36000, 74000, 74400 or 74410 by the same physician on the same day.)

74415	Urography, infusion, drip technique and/or bolus technique; with nephrotomography	3.12	116.35	295	329	371
-26		0.67	23.50	103	115	130

(UNBUNDLING ALERT: 74420 cannot be used with 53670 by the same physician on the same day.)

74420	Urography, retrograde, with or without KUB	-	-	253	378	462
-26		0.50	17.43	63	94	116
74425	Urography, antegrade, (pyelostogram, nephrostogram, loopogram), radiological supervision and interpretation	-	-	195	253	278
-26		0.50	17.43	68	89	97
74430	Cystography, minimum of three views, radiological supervision and interpretation	1.73	64.43	162	174	201
-26		0.44	15.54	57	61	70
74440	Vasography, vesiculography, or epididymography, radiological supervision and interpretation	1.94	72.01	156	195	224
-26		0.53	18.57	55	68	78
74445	Corpora cavernosography, radiological supervision and interpretation	-	-	244	298	323
-26		1.60	56.47	122	149	162
74450	Urethrocystography, retrograde, radiological supervision and interpretation	-	-	191	236	278
-26		0.46	16.30	67	83	97
74455	Urethrocystography, voiding, radiological supervision and interpretation	2.24	83.75	209	247	278
-26		0.46	16.30	73	86	97
74470	Radiologic examination, renal cyst study, translumbar, contrast visualization, radiological supervision and interpretation	-	-	202	248	282
-26		0.73	25.77	71	87	99
74475	Introduction of intracatheter or catheter into renal pelvis for drainage and/or injection, percutaneous, radiological supervision and interpretation	4.47	167.51	546	618	686
-26		0.74	26.15	191	216	240
74480	Introduction of ureteral catheter or stent into ureter through renal pelvis for drainage and/or injection, percutaneous, radiological supervision and interpretation	4.47	167.51	577	694	840
-26		0.74	26.15	202	243	294
74485	Dilation of nephrostomy, ureters, or urethra, radiological supervision and interpretation	3.77	140.98	368	464	648
-26		0.74	26.15	129	162	227

Gynecological and Obstetrical

74710	Pelvimetry, with or without placental localization	1.45	53.81	149	171	197
-26		0.47	16.67	60	68	79
74740	Hysterosalpingography, radiological supervision and interpretation	1.97	73.14	189	262	287
-26		0.53	18.57	57	79	86

● = New Code ⊗ = Conscious Sedation ✚ = Add-on Code ∅ = Modifier '51' Exempt ▲ =Revised Code

Code	Description	Medicare RVU	National Fee	PFR Fee Information 50%	75%	90%
74742	Transcervical catheterization of fallopian tube, radiological supervision and interpretation	-	-	252	293	338
-26		0.83	29.18	88	103	118
74775	Perineogram (eg, vaginogram, for sex determination or extent of anomalies)	-	-	241	281	341
-26		0.85	29.94	96	112	136

Heart

Code	Description	Medicare RVU	National Fee	PFR Fee Information 50%	75%	90%
75552	Cardiac magnetic resonance imaging for morphology; without contrast material	15.64	586.65	1446	1641	1851
-26		2.20	77.31	289	328	370
75553	Cardiac magnetic resonance imaging for morphology; with contrast material	17.46	654.11	1472	1759	1843
-26		2.79	98.15	294	352	369
75554	Cardiac magnetic resonance imaging for function, with or without morphology; complete study	17.99	674.95	1452	1776	1933
-26		2.58	90.95	290	355	387
75555	Cardiac magnetic resonance imaging for function, with or without morphology; limited study	18.04	676.85	1444	1705	1957
-26		2.50	87.92	289	341	391
75556	Cardiac magnetic resonance imaging for velocity flow mapping	-	-	853	1012	1123

Vascular Procedures

Aorta and Arteries

(See also HCPCS code G0288 for computed tomographic angiography of aorta for surgical planning for vascular surgery.)

Code	Description	Medicare RVU	National Fee	PFR Fee Information 50%	75%	90%
75600	Aortography, thoracic, without serialography, radiological supervision and interpretation	12.36	466.52	724	1057	1281
-26		0.72	25.39	72	106	128
75605	Aortography, thoracic, by serialography, radiological supervision and interpretation	12.47	468.41	1199	1651	2018
-26		1.61	56.85	180	248	303
75625	Aortography, abdominal, by serialography, radiological supervision and interpretation	12.40	465.76	1146	1564	1856
-26		1.59	56.09	172	235	278
75630	Aortography, abdominal plus bilateral iliofemoral lower extremity, catheter, by serialography, radiological supervision and interpretation	13.83	517.30	1395	1859	2192
-26		2.54	89.44	279	372	438
75635	Computed tomographic angiography, abdominal aorta and bilateral iliofemoral lower extremity runoff, radiological supervision and interpretation, without contrast material(s), followed by contrast material(s) and further sections, including image post-processing	18.46	690.49	1439	1941	2307
-26		3.29	115.59	288	388	461

(See also HCPCS code G0278 for angiography of iliac artery performed at the time of cardiac catheterization.)

Code	Description	Medicare RVU	National Fee	PFR Fee Information 50%	75%	90%
75650	Angiography, cervicocerebral, catheter, including vessel origin, radiological supervision and interpretation	12.87	482.06	1458	1864	2200
-26		2.06	72.38	219	280	330
75658	Angiography, brachial, retrograde, radiological supervision and interpretation	12.77	479.02	1349	1927	2340
-26		1.85	65.18	202	289	351
75660	Angiography, external carotid, unilateral, selective, radiological supervision and interpretation	12.75	478.27	1298	1789	2186
-26		1.82	64.05	195	268	328
75662	Angiography, external carotid, bilateral, selective, radiological supervision and interpretation	13.51	505.55	1455	2053	2640
-26		2.34	82.24	218	308	396
75665	Angiography, carotid, cerebral, unilateral, radiological supervision and interpretation	12.81	480.54	1270	1849	2109
-26		1.84	64.80	190	277	316

● = New Code ⊗ = Conscious Sedation ✚ = Add-on Code ∅ = Modifier '51' Exempt ▲ =Revised Code

		Medicare RVU	National Fee	PFR Fee Information 50%	75%	90%
75671	Angiography, carotid, cerebral, bilateral, radiological supervision and interpretation	13.46	503.66	1545	1968	2447
-26		2.29	80.34	232	295	367
75676	Angiography, carotid, cervical, unilateral, radiological supervision and interpretation	12.74	477.89	1322	1684	2028
-26		1.82	64.05	198	253	304
75680	Angiography, carotid, cervical, bilateral, radiological supervision and interpretation	13.34	499.11	1676	2031	2422
-26		2.29	80.34	251	305	363
75685	Angiography, vertebral, cervical, and/or intracranial, radiological supervision and interpretation	12.72	477.13	1266	1658	2100
-26		1.81	63.67	190	249	315
75705	Angiography, spinal, selective, radiological supervision and interpretation	13.91	518.82	1516	1605	1962
-26		3.02	106.11	227	241	294
75710	Angiography, extremity, unilateral, radiological supervision and interpretation	12.58	472.58	1278	1448	1828
-26		1.61	56.85	192	217	274
75716	Angiography, extremity, bilateral, radiological supervision and interpretation	12.99	487.36	1296	1504	1734
-26		1.82	64.05	194	226	260
	(See also HCPCS code G0275 for unilateral or bilateral renal artery angiography at time of cardiac catheterization.)					
75722	Angiography, renal, unilateral, selective (including flush aortogram), radiological supervision and interpretation	12.54	471.07	1267	1436	1688
-26		1.61	56.85	190	215	253
75724	Angiography, renal, bilateral, selective (including flush aortogram), radiological supervision and interpretation	13.34	499.87	1522	1903	2286
-26		2.15	75.80	228	285	343
75726	Angiography, visceral, selective or supraselective, (with or without flush aortogram), radiological supervision and interpretation	12.45	467.66	1311	1475	1801
-26		1.56	54.95	197	221	270
75731	Angiography, adrenal, unilateral, selective, radiological supervision and interpretation	12.51	469.93	1286	1446	1767
-26		1.58	55.71	193	217	265
75733	Angiography, adrenal, bilateral, selective, radiological supervision and interpretation	13.08	490.77	1336	1571	1727
-26		1.85	65.18	200	236	259
75736	Angiography, pelvic, selective or supraselective, radiological supervision and interpretation	12.51	469.93	1273	1432	1750
-26		1.58	55.71	191	215	262
75741	Angiography, pulmonary, unilateral, selective, radiological supervision and interpretation	12.54	470.31	1332	1604	1935
-26		1.80	63.29	200	241	290
75743	Angiography, pulmonary, bilateral, selective, radiological supervision and interpretation	13.06	488.50	1504	1872	2122
-26		2.26	79.21	226	281	318
75746	Angiography, pulmonary, by nonselective catheter or venous injection, radiological supervision and interpretation	12.40	465.76	1262	1419	1734
-26		1.56	54.95	189	213	260
75756	Angiography, internal mammary, radiological supervision and interpretation	12.71	477.51	1267	1425	1742
-26		1.67	59.12	190	214	261
+ 75774	Angiography, selective, each additional vessel studied after basic examination, radiological supervision and interpretation (List separately in addition to code for primary procedure)	11.18	422.18	1097	1316	1609
-26		0.50	17.43	165	197	241

● = New Code ⊗ = Conscious Sedation ✚ = Add-on Code ∅ = Modifier '51' Exempt ▲ =Revised Code

		Medicare RVU	National Fee	PFR Fee Information 50%	75%	90%
75790	Angiography, arteriovenous shunt (eg, dialysis patient), radiological supervision and interpretation	4.21	152.35	430	503	569
-26		2.51	87.92	172	201	228

Veins and Lymphatics

		Medicare RVU	National Fee	50%	75%	90%
75801	Lymphangiography, extremity only, unilateral, radiological supervision and interpretation	-	-	632	743	912
-26		1.15	40.55	126	149	182
75803	Lymphangiography, extremity only, bilateral, radiological supervision and interpretation	-	-	749	863	970
-26		1.58	55.33	187	216	242
75805	Lymphangiography, pelvic/abdominal, unilateral, radiological supervision and interpretation	-	-	796	1032	1147
-26		1.12	39.41	159	206	229
75807	Lymphangiography, pelvic/abdominal, bilateral, radiological supervision and interpretation	-	-	822	998	1234
-26		1.59	55.71	164	200	247
75809	Shuntogram for investigation of previously placed indwelling nonvascular shunt (eg, LeVeen shunt, ventriculoperitoneal shunt, indwelling infusion pump), radiological supervision and interpretation	1.76	64.80	165	226	287
-26		0.64	22.36	82	113	144
75810	Splenoportography, radiological supervision and interpretation	-	-	1275	1593	1744
-26		1.55	54.57	191	239	262
75820	Venography, extremity, unilateral, radiological supervision and interpretation	2.41	88.68	308	362	424
-26		0.97	34.11	123	145	170
75822	Venography, extremity, bilateral, radiological supervision and interpretation	3.31	121.27	448	543	645
-26		1.45	50.78	179	217	258
75825	Venography, caval, inferior, with serialography, radiological supervision and interpretation	12.28	461.21	1286	1467	1726
-26		1.57	55.33	193	220	259
75827	Venography, caval, superior, with serialography, radiological supervision and interpretation	12.27	460.83	1274	1432	1744
-26		1.55	54.57	191	215	262
75831	Venography, renal, unilateral, selective, radiological supervision and interpretation	12.30	461.97	1225	1378	1634
-26		1.56	54.95	184	207	245
75833	Venography, renal, bilateral, selective, radiological supervision and interpretation	12.93	484.33	1479	1825	2170
-26		2.06	72.38	296	365	434
75840	Venography, adrenal, unilateral, selective, radiological supervision and interpretation	12.39	465.38	835	1023	1211
-26		1.60	56.47	167	205	242
75842	Venography, adrenal, bilateral, selective, radiological supervision and interpretation	12.88	482.44	1434	1648	1953
-26		2.03	71.25	287	330	391
75860	Venography, venous sinus (eg, petrosal and inferior sagittal) or jugular, catheter, radiological supervision and interpretation	12.42	466.52	1263	1421	1579
-26		1.60	56.47	126	142	158
75870	Venography, superior sagittal sinus, radiological supervision and interpretation	12.36	464.24	1251	1399	1563
-26		1.58	55.71	125	140	156
75872	Venography, epidural, radiological supervision and interpretation	12.63	474.48	1335	1606	1876
-26		1.67	59.12	134	161	188
75880	Venography, orbital, radiological supervision and interpretation	2.40	88.30	319	387	443
-26		0.96	33.73	96	116	133

		Medicare RVU	National Fee	PFR Fee Information 50%	75%	90%
75885	Percutaneous transhepatic portography with hemodynamic evaluation, radiological supervision and interpretation	12.69	475.61	1385	1662	2030
-26		1.96	68.97	277	332	406
75887	Percutaneous transhepatic portography without hemodynamic evaluation, radiological supervision and interpretation	12.75	477.89	954	1126	1386
-26		1.97	69.35	191	225	277
75889	Hepatic venography, wedged or free, with hemodynamic evaluation, radiological supervision and interpretation	12.28	461.21	1335	1501	1834
-26		1.55	54.57	200	225	275
75891	Hepatic venography, wedged or free, without hemodynamic evaluation, radiological supervision and interpretation	12.28	461.21	1309	1570	1919
-26		1.55	54.57	196	235	288
75893	Venous sampling through catheter, with or without angiography (eg, for parathyroid hormone, renin), radiological supervision and interpretation	11.48	433.17	1177	1324	1619
-26		0.74	26.15	177	199	243

Transcatheter Procedures

		Medicare RVU	National Fee	PFR Fee Information 50%	75%	90%
75894	Transcatheter therapy, embolization, any method, radiological supervision and interpretation	-	-	2556	3008	3834
-26		1.81	63.67	383	451	575
75896	Transcatheter therapy, infusion, any method (eg, thrombolysis other than coronary), radiological supervision and interpretation	-	-	2225	2648	3299
-26		1.82	64.05	334	397	495
75898	Angiography through existing catheter for follow-up study for transcatheter therapy, embolization or infusion	-	-	571	766	960
-26		2.27	79.58	286	383	480
75900	Exchange of a previously placed intravascular catheter during thrombolytic therapy with contrast monitoring, radiological supervision and interpretation	-	-	IR	IR	IR
-26		0.68	23.88	108	121	132
75901	Mechanical removal of pericatheter obstructive material (eg, fibrin sheath) from central venous device via separate venous access, radiologic supervision and interpretation	3.43	128.09	313	401	478
-26		0.67	23.50	63	80	96
75902	Mechanical removal of intraluminal (intracatheter) obstructive material from central venous device through device lumen, radiologic supervision and interpretation	2.71	101.19	329	409	483
-26		0.54	18.95	66	82	97
75940	Percutaneous placement of IVC filter, radiological supervision and interpretation	-	-	1288	1607	2065
-26		0.76	26.91	193	241	310
75945	Intravascular ultrasound (non-coronary vessel), radiological supervision and interpretation; initial vessel	-	-	489	571	697
-26		0.58	20.46	73	86	105
+ 75946	Intravascular ultrasound (non-coronary vessel), radiological supervision and interpretation; each additional non-coronary vessel (List separately in addition to code for primary procedure)	-	-	268	324	423
-26		0.59	20.84	40	49	63
75952	Endovascular repair of infrarenal abdominal aortic aneurysm or dissection, radiological supervision and interpretation	-	-	839	1123	1432
-26		6.36	223.97	629	842	1074
75953	Placement of proximal or distal extension prosthesis for endovascular repair of infrarenal aortic or iliac artery aneurysm, pseudoaneurysm, or dissection, radiological supervision and interpretation	-	-	322	492	594
-26		1.93	67.84	129	197	238
75954	Endovascular repair of iliac artery aneurysm, pseudoaneurysm, arteriovenous malformation, or trauma, radiological supervision and interpretation	-	-	714	987	1307
-26		3.15	110.66	500	691	915

● = New Code ⊗ = Conscious Sedation ✚ = Add-on Code ∅ = Modifier '51' Exempt ▲ =Revised Code

		Medicare RVU	National Fee	PFR Fee Information 50%	75%	90%
75956	Endovascular repair of descending thoracic aorta (eg, aneurysm, pseudoaneurysm, dissection, penetrating ulcer, intramural hematoma, or traumatic disruption); involving coverage of left subclavian artery origin, initial endoprosthesis plus descending thoracic aortic extension(s), if required, to level of celiac artery origin, radiological supervision and interpretation	-	-	IR	IR	IR
-26		10.16	358.51	IR	IR	IR
75957	Endovascular repair of descending thoracic aorta (eg, aneurysm, pseudoaneurysm, dissection, penetrating ulcer, intramural hematoma, or traumatic disruption); not involving coverage of left subclavian artery origin, initial endoprosthesis plus descending thoracic aortic extension(s), if required, to level of celiac artery origin, radiological supervision and interpretation	-	-	IR	IR	IR
-26		8.71	307.35	IR	IR	IR
75958	Placement of proximal extension prosthesis for endovascular repair of descending thoracic aorta (eg, aneurysm, pseudoaneurysm, dissection, penetrating ulcer, intramural hematoma, or traumatic disruption), radiological supervision and interpretation	-	-	IR	IR	IR
-26		5.80	204.65	IR	IR	IR
75959	Placement of distal extension prosthesis(s) (delayed) after endovascular repair of descending thoracic aorta, as needed, to level of celiac origin, radiological supervision and interpretation	-	-	IR	IR	IR
-26		5.08	179.26	IR	IR	IR
75960	Transcatheter introduction of intravascular stent(s), (except coronary, carotid, and vertebral vessel), percutaneous and/or open, radiological supervision and interpretation, each vessel	-	-	1574	2174	2879
-26		1.16	40.93	157	217	288
75961	Transcatheter retrieval, percutaneous, of intravascular foreign body (eg, fractured venous or arterial catheter), radiological supervision and interpretation	14.96	550.65	1388	1587	1786
-26		5.78	202.75	486	555	625
75962	Transluminal balloon angioplasty, peripheral artery, radiological supervision and interpretation	14.20	536.25	1685	2217	2858
-26		0.75	26.53	118	155	200
✚ 75964	Transluminal balloon angioplasty, each additional peripheral artery, radiological supervision and interpretation (List separately in addition to code for primary procedure)	7.78	293.33	1005	1208	1410
-26		0.51	17.81	101	121	141
75966	Transluminal balloon angioplasty, renal or other visceral artery, radiological supervision and interpretation	15.38	577.94	1828	2272	2866
-26		1.86	65.56	183	227	287
✚ 75968	Transluminal balloon angioplasty, each additional visceral artery, radiological supervision and interpretation (List separately in addition to code for primary procedure)	7.80	294.08	958	1204	1451
-26		0.52	18.19	96	120	145
75970	Transcatheter biopsy, radiological supervision and interpretation	-	-	1215	1474	1757
-26		1.15	40.55	122	147	176
75978	Transluminal balloon angioplasty, venous (eg, subclavian stenosis), radiological supervision and interpretation	14.11	532.84	1947	2547	3152
-26		0.74	26.15	136	178	221
75980	Percutaneous transhepatic biliary drainage with contrast monitoring, radiological supervision and interpretation	-	-	742	928	1081
-26		1.96	68.97	223	278	324
75982	Percutaneous placement of drainage catheter for combined internal and external biliary drainage or of a drainage stent for internal biliary drainage in patients with an inoperable mechanical biliary obstruction, radiological supervision and interpretation	-	-	798	915	1110
-26		1.96	68.97	239	274	333
75984	Change of percutaneous tube or drainage catheter with contrast monitoring (eg, gastrointestinal system, genitourinary system, abscess), radiological supervision and interpretation	3.04	112.56	289	336	420
-26		0.98	34.49	101	118	147

© PFR 2007

● = New Code ⊗ = Conscious Sedation ✚ = Add-on Code ∅ = Modifier '51' Exempt ▲ =Revised Code

Code	Description	Medicare RVU	National Fee	PFR Fee Information 50%	75%	90%
75989	Radiological guidance (ie, fluoroscopy, ultrasound, or computed tomography), for percutaneous drainage (eg, abscess, specimen collection), with placement of catheter, radiological supervision and interpretation	4.59	169.40	459	509	616
-26		1.62	56.85	138	153	185

Transluminal Atherectomy

Code	Description	Medicare RVU	National Fee	50%	75%	90%
75992	Transluminal atherectomy, peripheral artery, radiological supervision and interpretation	-	-	2062	2776	3312
-26		0.77	27.29	206	278	331
✚ 75993	Transluminal atherectomy, each additional peripheral artery, radiological supervision and interpretation (List separately in addition to code for primary procedure)	-	-	868	1039	1212
-26		0.52	18.19	87	104	121
75994	Transluminal atherectomy, renal, radiological supervision and interpretation	-	-	1695	1976	2178
-26		1.88	66.32	170	198	218
75995	Transluminal atherectomy, visceral, radiological supervision and interpretation	-	-	2300	2813	3835
-26		1.84	64.80	230	281	384
✚ 75996	Transluminal atherectomy, each additional visceral artery, radiological supervision and interpretation (List separately in addition to code for primary procedure)	-	-	1313	1733	2054
-26		0.51	17.81	131	173	205

Other Procedures

Code	Description	Medicare RVU	National Fee	50%	75%	90%
76000	Fluoroscopy (separate procedure), up to 1 hour physician time, other than 71023 or 71034 (eg, cardiac fluoroscopy)	1.93	72.38	175	210	237
-26		0.23	7.96	61	73	83
76001	Fluoroscopy, physician time more than 1 hour, assisting a nonradiologic physician (eg, nephrostolithotomy, ERCP, bronchoscopy, transbronchial biopsy)	-	-	336	370	404
-26		0.94	32.97	118	129	141
76010	Radiologic examination from nose to rectum for foreign body, single view, child	0.78	28.80	88	116	136
-26		0.25	8.72	35	46	54
76080	Radiologic examination, abscess, fistula or sinus tract study, radiological supervision and interpretation	1.80	66.32	178	202	247
-26		0.74	26.15	71	81	99

(See also HCPCS code G0206 for diagnostic mammography producing direct digital image, unilateral, all views.)

(UNBUNDLING ALERT: 76091 cannot be used with 76090 by the same physician on the same day.)

(See also HCPCS code G0204 for diagnostic mammography producing direct digital image, bilateral, all views.)

(See also HCPCS code G0202 for screening mammography producing direct digital image, bilateral, all views.)

Code	Description	Medicare RVU	National Fee	50%	75%	90%
76098	Radiological examination, surgical specimen	0.62	22.74	79	94	111
-26		0.22	7.58	32	38	44
76100	Radiologic examination, single plane body section (eg, tomography), other than with urography	2.61	96.64	223	289	354
-26		0.80	28.04	100	130	159
76101	Radiologic examination, complex motion (ie, hypercycloidal) body section (eg, mastoid polytomography), other than with urography; unilateral	3.19	118.62	265	303	373
-26		0.80	28.04	106	121	149
76102	Radiologic examination, complex motion (ie, hypercycloidal) body section (eg, mastoid polytomography), other than with urography; bilateral	4.07	151.97	312	354	416
-26		0.80	28.04	125	142	166
76120	Cineradiography/videoradiography, except where specifically included	1.80	66.70	171	208	227
-26		0.53	18.57	68	83	91
✚ 76125	Cineradiography/videoradiography to complement routine examination (List separately in addition to code for primary procedure)	-	-	147	159	188
-26		0.37	12.89	59	64	75

● = New Code ⊗ = Conscious Sedation ✚ = Add-on Code ∅ = Modifier '51' Exempt ▲ =Revised Code

Code	Description	Medicare RVU	National Fee	PFR Fee Information 50%	75%	90%
76140	Consultation on X-ray examination made elsewhere, written report	-	-	79	92	128
76150	Xeroradiography	0.50	18.95	62	72	97
76350	Subtraction in conjunction with contrast studies	-	-	100	111	141
76376	3D rendering with interpretation and reporting of computed tomography, magnetic resonance imaging, ultrasound, or other tomographic modality; not requiring image postprocessing on an independent workstation	3.25	122.41	415	500	613
-26		0.29	10.23	42	50	61
76377	3D rendering with interpretation and reporting of computed tomography, magnetic resonance imaging, ultrasound, or other tomographic modality; requiring image postprocessing on an independent workstation	4.27	158.79	534	642	788
-26		1.13	39.79	134	160	197
76380	Computed tomography, limited or localized follow-up study	5.18	192.52	462	524	705
-26		1.33	46.61	139	157	211
76390	Magnetic resonance spectroscopy	13.00	487.36	1312	1476	1804
-26		1.90	66.70	262	295	361
76496	Unlisted fluoroscopic procedure (eg, diagnostic, interventional)	-	-	IR	IR	IR
-26		-	-	IR	IR	IR
76497	Unlisted computed tomography procedure (eg, diagnostic, interventional)	-	-	IR	IR	IR
-26		-	-	IR	IR	IR
76498	Unlisted magnetic resonance procedure (eg, diagnostic, interventional)	-	-	IR	IR	IR
-26		-	-	IR	IR	IR
76499	Unlisted diagnostic radiographic procedure	-	-	IR	IR	IR
-26		-	-	IR	IR	IR

Diagnostic Ultrasound

Head and Neck

Code	Description	Medicare RVU	National Fee	PFR Fee Information 50%	75%	90%
76506	Echoencephalography, real time with image documentation (gray scale) (for determination of ventricular size, delineation of cerebral contents, and detection of fluid masses or other intracranial abnormalities), including A-mode encephalography as secondary component where indicated	2.69	99.67	275	334	419
-26		0.92	32.59	138	167	210
76510	Ophthalmic ultrasound, diagnostic; B-scan and quantitative A-scan performed during the same patient encounter	4.38	159.93	366	466	547
-26		2.24	78.83	183	233	274
76511	Ophthalmic ultrasound, diagnostic; quantitative A-scan only	3.21	118.24	271	339	404
-26		1.36	48.13	136	170	202
76512	Ophthalmic ultrasound, diagnostic; B-scan (with or without superimposed non-quantitative A-scan)	3.03	111.42	304	361	447
-26		1.36	48.13	137	162	201
76513	Ophthalmic ultrasound, diagnostic; anterior segment ultrasound, immersion (water bath) B-scan or high resolution biomicroscopy	2.53	93.23	310	369	443
-26		0.96	33.73	140	166	199
76514	Ophthalmic ultrasound, diagnostic; corneal pachymetry, unilateral or bilateral (determination of corneal thickness)	0.34	12.13	41	68	84
-26		0.26	9.10	33	55	68

● = New Code ⊗ = Conscious Sedation ✚ = Add-on Code ∅ = Modifier '51' Exempt ▲ =Revised Code

		Medicare RVU	National Fee	PFR Fee Information 50%	75%	90%
76516	Ophthalmic biometry by ultrasound echography, A-scan;	2.01	74.28	259	308	373
-26		0.78	27.67	117	139	168
	(UNBUNDLING ALERT: 76519 cannot be used with 76516 by the same physician on the same day.)					
76519	Ophthalmic biometry by ultrasound echography, A-scan; with intraocular lens power calculation	2.11	78.07	265	305	364
-26		0.78	27.67	119	137	164
76529	Ophthalmic ultrasonic foreign body localization	1.99	73.14	265	300	351
-26		0.82	28.80	119	135	158
	(See also HCPCS code S9024 for paranasal sinus ultrasound.)					
▲ **76536**	Ultrasound, soft tissues of head and neck (eg, thyroid, parathyroid, parotid), real time with image documentation	2.49	92.09	229	278	345
-26		0.75	26.15	103	125	155

Chest

		Medicare RVU	National Fee	50%	75%	90%
▲ **76604**	Ultrasound, chest (includes mediastinum), real time with image documentation	2.18	80.34	238	292	376
-26		0.74	25.77	107	131	169
▲ **76645**	Ultrasound, breast(s) (unilateral or bilateral), real time with image documentation	2.03	75.04	205	244	295
-26		0.73	25.77	92	110	133

Abdomen and Retroperitoneum

(UNBUNDLING ALERT: 76700 cannot be used with 76705 by the same physician on the same day.)

(For measurement of post-voiding residual urine and/or bladder capacity by ultrasound, see code 51798)

(See also HCPCS code G0262 for imaging of the small intestine.)

		Medicare RVU	National Fee	50%	75%	90%
▲ **76700**	Ultrasound, abdominal, real time with image documentation; complete	3.35	123.92	316	375	434
-26		1.11	39.03	142	169	195
76705	Ultrasound, abdominal, real time with image documentation; limited (eg, single organ, quadrant, follow-up)	2.47	91.33	228	277	348
-26		0.81	28.42	103	125	157
	(UNBUNDLING ALERT: 76770 cannot be used with 76775 by the same physician on the same day.)					
▲ **76770**	Ultrasound, retroperitoneal (eg, renal, aorta, nodes), real time with image documentation; complete	3.24	120.14	306	361	446
-26		1.01	35.62	138	162	201
76775	Ultrasound, retroperitoneal (eg, renal, aorta, nodes), real time with image documentation; limited	2.46	90.95	213	261	332
-26		0.80	28.04	96	117	149
● **76776**	Ultrasound, transplanted kidney, real time and duplex Doppler with image documentation	3.35	123.92	308	370	455
-26		1.02	35.62	108	129	159

Spinal Canal

		Medicare RVU	National Fee	50%	75%	90%
76800	Ultrasound, spinal canal and contents	3.15	115.21	311	366	394
-26		1.51	53.06	156	183	197

Pelvis

Obstetrical

		Medicare RVU	National Fee	50%	75%	90%
76801	Ultrasound, pregnant uterus, real time with image documentation, fetal and maternal evaluation, first trimester (14 weeks 0 days), transabdominal approach; single or first gestation	3.58	131.88	277	335	390
-26		1.36	47.75	125	151	176

● = New Code ⊗ = Conscious Sedation ✚ = Add-on Code ∅ = Modifier '51' Exempt ▲ =Revised Code

		Medicare RVU	National Fee	PFR Fee Information 50%	75%	90%
✚ 76802	Ultrasound, pregnant uterus, real time with image documentation, fetal and maternal evaluation, first trimester (14 weeks 0 days), transabdominal approach; each additional gestation (List separately in addition to code for primary procedure)	2.23	81.48	174	201	240
-26		1.15	40.55	78	90	108
	(UNBUNDLING ALERT: 76805 cannot be used with 76816 or 76856 by the same physician on the same day.)					
76805	Ultrasound, pregnant uterus, real time with image documentation, fetal and maternal evaluation, after first trimester (or = 14 weeks 0 days), transabdominal approach; single or first gestation	3.71	136.81	324	358	420
-26		1.36	47.75	146	161	189
✚ 76810	Ultrasound, pregnant uterus, real time with image documentation, fetal and maternal evaluation, after first trimester (or = 14 weeks 0 days), transabdominal approach; each additional gestation (List separately in addition to code for primary procedure)	2.68	97.78	400	512	643
-26		1.34	46.99	180	230	289
76811	Ultrasound, pregnant uterus, real time with image documentation, fetal and maternal evaluation plus detailed fetal anatomic examination, transabdominal approach; single or first gestation	6.35	233.45	547	618	727
-26		2.66	93.61	246	278	327
✚ 76812	Ultrasound, pregnant uterus, real time with image documentation, fetal and maternal evaluation plus detailed fetal anatomic examination, transabdominal approach; each additional gestation (List separately in addition to code for primary procedure)	4.52	164.48	327	371	437
-26		2.48	87.16	147	167	197
● 76813	Ultrasound, pregnant uterus, real time with image documentation, first trimester fetal nuchal translucency measurement, transabdominal or transvaginal approach; single or first gestation	3.43	125.44	281	315	371
-26		1.56	54.57	141	158	185
✚● 76814	Ultrasound, pregnant uterus, real time with image documentation, first trimester fetal nuchal translucency measurement, transabdominal or transvaginal approach; each additional gestation (List separately in addition to code for primary procedure)	2.29	83.00	188	211	248
-26		1.31	45.86	122	137	161
76815	Ultrasound, pregnant uterus, real time with image documentation, limited (eg, fetal heart beat, placental location, fetal position and/or qualitative amniotic fluid volume), one or more fetuses	2.43	89.44	215	231	276
-26		0.90	31.45	86	92	110
76816	Ultrasound, pregnant uterus, real time with image documentation, follow-up (eg, re-evaluation of fetal size by measuring standard growth parameters and amniotic fluid volume, re-evaluation of organ system(s) suspected or confirmed to be abnormal on a previous scan), transabdominal approach, per fetus	2.61	95.50	189	212	251
-26		1.19	41.69	85	95	113
76817	Ultrasound, pregnant uterus, real time with image documentation, transvaginal	2.66	97.78	268	304	358
-26		1.03	36.00	121	137	161
76818	Fetal biophysical profile; with non-stress testing	3.24	118.62	295	323	375
-26		1.47	51.54	133	145	169
76819	Fetal biophysical profile; without non-stress testing	2.71	99.67	279	345	420
-26		1.06	37.14	126	155	189
76820	Doppler velocimetry, fetal; umbilical artery	2.14	79.21	220	250	297
-26		0.71	25.01	99	113	134
76821	Doppler velocimetry, fetal; middle cerebral artery	2.72	100.43	245	280	331
-26		0.98	34.49	110	126	149
76825	Echocardiography, fetal, cardiovascular system, real time with image documentation (2D), with or without M-mode recording;	4.85	177.36	388	441	484
-26		2.31	81.10	194	220	242
76826	Echocardiography, fetal, cardiovascular system, real time with image documentation (2D), with or without M-mode recording; follow-up or repeat study	2.34	85.65	221	272	319
-26		1.14	40.17	110	136	160

● = New Code ⊗ = Conscious Sedation ✚ = Add-on Code ∅ = Modifier '51' Exempt ▲ =Revised Code

		Medicare RVU	National Fee	PFR Fee Information 50%	75%	90%
76827	Doppler echocardiography, fetal, pulsed wave and/or continuous wave with spectral display; complete	2.43	89.82	278	332	390
-26		0.80	28.04	111	133	156
76828	Doppler echocardiography, fetal, pulsed wave and/or continuous wave with spectral display; follow-up or repeat study	1.83	67.08	191	217	262
-26		0.80	28.04	86	98	118

Non-Obstetrical

		Medicare RVU	National Fee	50%	75%	90%
76830	Ultrasound, transvaginal	2.79	103.08	295	372	479
-26		0.94	32.97	133	167	216
76831	Saline infusion sonohysterography (SIS), including color flow Doppler, when performed	2.85	105.36	310	380	472
-26		0.99	34.87	140	171	212
	(UNBUNDLING ALERT: 76856 cannot be used with 76805 or 76857 by the same physician on the same day.)					
▲ 76856	Ultrasound, pelvic (nonobstetric), real time with image documentation; complete	2.81	103.84	277	340	409
-26		0.95	33.35	125	153	184
76857	Ultrasound, pelvic (nonobstetric), real time with image documentation; limited or follow-up (eg, for follicles)	2.45	91.33	195	257	307
-26		0.53	18.57	88	116	138

Genitalia

		Medicare RVU	National Fee	50%	75%	90%
76870	Ultrasound, scrotum and contents	2.74	101.57	268	313	358
-26		0.88	31.08	121	141	161
76872	Ultrasound, transrectal;	3.35	124.30	333	394	437
-26		0.96	33.73	150	177	197
76873	Ultrasound, transrectal; prostate volume study for brachytherapy treatment planning (separate procedure)	4.61	168.64	413	499	564
-26		2.16	75.80	206	250	282

Extremities

		Medicare RVU	National Fee	50%	75%	90%
▲ 76880	Ultrasound, extremity, nonvascular, real time with image documentation	2.67	98.91	252	288	352
-26		0.80	28.04	113	130	158
76885	Ultrasound, infant hips, real time with imaging documentation; dynamic (requiring physician manipulation)	2.95	109.14	285	334	377
-26		1.00	35.24	128	150	170
76886	Ultrasound, infant hips, real time with imaging documentation; limited, static (not requiring physician manipulation)	2.49	92.09	261	296	335
-26		0.84	29.56	117	133	151

Ultrasonic Guidance Procedures

		Medicare RVU	National Fee	50%	75%	90%
76930	Ultrasonic guidance for pericardiocentesis, imaging supervision and interpretation	2.64	97.40	302	349	397
-26		0.96	33.73	121	140	159
76932	Ultrasonic guidance for endomyocardial biopsy, imaging supervision and interpretation	-	-	311	377	404
-26		0.97	34.11	124	151	162
76936	Ultrasound guided compression repair of arterial pseudoaneurysm or arteriovenous fistulae (includes diagnostic ultrasound evaluation, compression of lesion and imaging)	9.13	338.42	904	1017	1278
-26		2.78	97.78	362	407	511
✚ 76937	Ultrasound guidance for vascular access requiring ultrasound evaluation of potential access sites, documentation of selected vessel patency, concurrent realtime ultrasound visualization of vascular needle entry, with permanent recording and reporting (List separately in addition to code for primary procedure)	0.94	34.49	106	125	147
-26		0.43	15.16	53	62	74

● = New Code ⊗ = Conscious Sedation ✚ = Add-on Code ∅ = Modifier '51' Exempt ▲ =Revised Code

		Medicare RVU	National Fee	PFR Fee Information 50%	75%	90%
▲ 76940	Ultrasound guidance for, and monitoring of, parenchymal tissue ablation	-	-	477	562	650
-26		2.94	103.84	262	309	358
76941	Ultrasonic guidance for intrauterine fetal transfusion or cordocentesis, imaging supervision and interpretation	-	-	337	383	420
-26		1.87	65.94	168	192	210
76942	Ultrasonic guidance for needle placement (eg, biopsy, aspiration, injection, localization device), imaging supervision and interpretation	4.23	157.65	327	412	516
-26		0.92	32.21	131	165	206
76945	Ultrasonic guidance for chorionic villus sampling, imaging supervision and interpretation	-	-	332	411	465
-26		0.92	32.21	133	164	186
76946	Ultrasonic guidance for amniocentesis, imaging supervision and interpretation	1.85	68.59	226	272	335
-26		0.53	18.57	68	82	100
76948	Ultrasonic guidance for aspiration of ova, imaging supervision and interpretation	1.84	68.22	301	357	421
-26		0.52	18.19	90	107	126
76950	Ultrasonic guidance for placement of radiation therapy fields	2.11	77.69	271	331	376
-26		0.80	28.04	108	132	150
76965	Ultrasonic guidance for interstitial radioelement application	6.51	241.79	742	917	1279
-26		1.87	65.94	223	275	384

Other Procedures

		Medicare RVU	National Fee	PFR Fee Information 50%	75%	90%
76970	Ultrasound study follow-up (specify)	1.89	70.11	167	198	240
-26		0.55	19.33	67	79	96
76975	Gastrointestinal endoscopic ultrasound, supervision and interpretation	-	-	312	380	414
-26		1.13	39.79	140	171	186
76977	Ultrasound bone density measurement and interpretation, peripheral site(s), any method	0.77	28.80	129	147	167
-26		0.08	2.65	32	37	42
● 76998	Ultrasonic guidance, intraoperative	-	-	IR	IR	IR
-26		0.52	19.71	IR	IR	IR
76999	Unlisted ultrasound procedure (eg, diagnostic, interventional)	-	-	IR	IR	IR
-26		-	-	IR	IR	IR

Radiologic Guidance

Fluoroscopic Guidance

		Medicare RVU	National Fee	PFR Fee Information 50%	75%	90%
✚ ● 77001	Fluoroscopic guidance for central venous access device placement, replacement (catheter only or complete), or removal (includes fluoroscopic guidance for vascular access and catheter manipulation, any necessary contrast injections through access site or catheter with related venography radiologic supervision and interpretation, and radiographic documentation of final catheter position) (List separately in addition to code for primary procedure	2.22	82.62	182	204	240
-26		0.52	18.19	55	61	72
● 77002	Fluoroscopic guidance for needle placement (eg, biopsy, aspiration, injection, localization device)	2.03	75.04	166	187	219
-26		0.72	25.39	67	75	88
● 77003	Fluoroscopic guidance and localization of needle or catheter tip for spine or paraspinous diagnostic or therapeutic injection procedures (epidural, transforaminal epidural, subarachnoid, paravertebral facet joint, paravertebral facet joint nerve, or sacroiliac joint), including neurolytic agent destruction	1.98	72.76	162	182	214
-26		0.78	27.29	73	82	96

© PFR 2007

● = New Code ⊗ = Conscious Sedation ✚ = Add-on Code ∅ = Modifier '51' Exempt ▲ =Revised Code

		Medicare RVU	National Fee	PFR Fee Information 50%	75%	90%
Computed Tomography Guidance						
● 77011	Computed tomography guidance for stereotactic localization	13.06	490.39	1070	1201	1412
-26		1.65	57.98	214	240	282
● 77012	Computed tomography guidance for needle placement (eg, biopsy, aspiration, injection, localization device), radiological supervision and interpretation	8.65	323.27	709	796	935
-26		1.58	55.33	177	199	234
● 77013	Computerized tomography guidance for, and monitoring of, parenchymal tissue ablation	-	-	IR	IR	IR
-26		1.45	54.95	IR	IR	IR
● 77014	Computed tomography guidance for placement of radiation therapy fields	4.58	170.16	375	421	495
-26		1.17	40.93	131	147	173
Magnetic Resonance Guidance						
● 77021	Magnetic resonance guidance for needle placement (eg, for biopsy, needle aspiration, injection, or placement of localization device) radiological supervision and interpretation	13.22	495.32	1083	1216	1429
-26		2.08	73.14	271	304	357
● 77022	Magnetic resonance guidance for, and monitoring of, parenchymal tissue ablation	-	-	IR	IR	IR
-26		1.58	59.88	IR	IR	IR
Other Radiologic Guidance						
● 77031	Stereotactic localization guidance for breast biopsy or needle placement (eg, for wire localization or for injection), each lesion, radiological supervision and interpretation	8.24	306.21	675	758	891
-26		2.18	76.55	236	265	312
● 77032	Mammographic guidance for needle placement, breast (eg, for wire localization or for injection), each lesion, radiological supervision and interpretation	1.91	70.11	157	176	207
-26		0.76	26.53	70	79	93

Breast Mammography

		Medicare RVU	National Fee	PFR Fee Information 50%	75%	90%
✚● 77051	Computer-aided detection (computer algorithm analysis of digital image data for lesion detection) with further physician review for interpretation, with or without digitization of film radiographic images; diagnostic mammography (List separately in addition to code for primary procedure)	0.46	17.05	38	42	50
-26		0.09	3.03	9	11	12
✚● 77052	Computer-aided detection (computer algorithm analysis of digital image data for lesion detection) with further physician review for interpretation, with or without digitization of film radiographic images; screening mammography (List separately in addition to code for primary procedure)	0.46	17.05	38	42	50
-26		0.09	3.03	9	11	12
● 77053	Mammary ductogram or galactogram, single duct, radiological supervision and interpretation	2.73	101.94	224	251	295
-26		0.50	17.43	56	63	74
● 77054	Mammary ductogram or galactogram, multiple ducts, radiological supervision and interpretation	3.91	146.28	320	360	423
-26		0.62	21.60	80	90	106
● 77055	Mammography; unilateral	1.43	54.19	117	132	155
-26		0.25	9.47	29	33	39
● 77056	Mammography; bilateral	2.66	97.40	218	245	288
-26		1.18	41.31	109	122	144
● 77057	Screening mammography, bilateral (2-view film study of each breast)	2.23	81.86	183	205	241
-26		0.95	33.35	91	103	121
● 77058	Magnetic resonance imaging, breast, without and/or with contrast material(s); unilateral	21.38	804.18	1752	1966	2312
-26		2.21	77.69	263	295	347
● 77059	Magnetic resonance imaging, breast, without and/or with contrast material(s); bilateral	26.40	994.43	2163	2428	2855
-26		2.21	77.69	324	364	428

● = New Code ⊗ = Conscious Sedation ✚ = Add-on Code ∅ = Modifier '51' Exempt ▲ =Revised Code

		Medicare RVU	National Fee	PFR Fee Information 50%	75%	90%

Bone/Joint Studies

		Medicare RVU	National Fee	50%	75%	90%
● 77071	Manual application of stress performed by physician for joint radiography, including contralateral joint if indicated	0.80	28.80	66	74	87
● 77072	Bone age studies	0.61	22.36	50	56	66
-26		0.25	8.72	25	28	33
● 77073	Bone length studies (orthoroentgenogram, scanogram)	1.14	42.07	93	105	123
-26		0.37	12.89	37	42	49
● 77074	Radiologic examination, osseous survey; limited (eg, for metastases)	1.73	63.67	142	159	187
-26		0.62	21.60	64	72	84
● 77075	Radiologic examination, osseous survey; complete (axial and appendicular skeleton)	2.40	89.06	197	221	260
-26		0.74	26.15	79	88	104
● 77076	Radiologic examination, osseous survey, infant	1.98	72.38	162	182	214
-26		0.95	33.35	89	100	118
● 77077	Joint survey, single view, 2 or more joints (specify)	1.46	54.19	120	134	158
-26		0.43	15.16	42	47	55
● 77078	Computed tomography, bone mineral density study, 1 or more sites; axial skeleton (eg, hips, pelvis, spine)	3.83	144.01	314	352	414
-26		0.34	11.75	47	53	62
● 77079	Computed tomography, bone mineral density study, 1 or more sites; appendicular skeleton (peripheral) (eg, radius, wrist, heel)	2.73	102.70	224	251	295
-26		0.30	10.61	45	50	59
● 77080	Dual-energy X-ray absorptiometry (DXA), bone density study, 1 or more sites; axial skeleton (eg, hips, pelvis, spine)	2.97	111.80	243	273	321
-26		0.30	10.61	61	68	80
● 77081	Dual-energy X-ray absorptiometry (DXA), bone density study, 1 or more sites; appendicular skeleton (peripheral) (eg, radius, wrist, heel)	1.08	40.17	88	99	117
-26		0.31	10.99	22	25	29
● 77082	Dual-energy X-ray absorptiometry (DXA), bone density study, 1 or more sites; vertebral fracture assessment	0.94	34.87	77	86	102
-26		0.24	8.34	19	22	25
● 77083	Radiographic absorptiometry (eg, photodensitometry, radiogrammetry), 1 or more sites	0.97	36.00	79	89	105
-26		0.28	9.85	20	22	26
● 77084	Magnetic resonance (eg, proton) imaging, bone marrow blood supply	14.50	543.45	1188	1334	1568
-26		2.18	76.55	297	333	392

Radiation Oncology

Consultation: Clinical Management
Clinical Treatment Planning (External and Internal Sources)

		Medicare RVU	National Fee	50%	75%	90%
77261	Therapeutic radiology treatment planning; simple	1.97	69.35	394	472	543
	(UNBUNDLING ALERT: 77262 cannot be used with 77261 by the same physician on the same day.)					
77262	Therapeutic radiology treatment planning; intermediate	2.96	104.22	491	601	694
	(UNBUNDLING ALERT: 77263 cannot be used with 77261 or 77262 by the same physician on the same day.)					
77263	Therapeutic radiology treatment planning; complex	4.40	154.62	681	798	983
77280	Therapeutic radiology simulation-aided field setting; simple	4.81	179.63	491	634	811
-26		0.97	34.11	147	190	243
77285	Therapeutic radiology simulation-aided field setting; intermediate	7.85	293.33	903	1040	1255
-26		1.44	50.40	271	312	376

● = New Code ⊗ = Conscious Sedation ✚ = Add-on Code ∅ = Modifier '51' Exempt ▲ =Revised Code

		Medicare RVU	National Fee	PFR Fee Information 50%	75%	90%
77290	Therapeutic radiology simulation-aided field setting; complex	10.62	396.41	983	1311	1737
-26		2.15	75.42	295	393	521
77295	Therapeutic radiology simulation-aided field setting; 3-dimensional	30.19	1126.69	3155	3670	4486
-26		6.27	220.18	789	918	1122
77299	Unlisted procedure, therapeutic radiology clinical treatment planning	-	-	IR	IR	IR
-26		-	-	IR	IR	IR

Medical Radiation Physics, Dosimetry, Treatment Devices and Special Services

		Medicare RVU	National Fee	PFR Fee Information 50%	75%	90%
77300	Basic radiation dosimetry calculation, central axis depth dose calculation, TDF, NSD, gap calculation, off axis factor, tissue inhomogeneity factors, calculation of non-ionizing radiation surface and depth dose, as required during course of treatment, only when prescribed by the treating physician	2.17	79.96	279	314	368
-26		0.85	29.94	126	141	166
77301	Intensity modulated radiotherapy plan, including dose-volume histograms for target and critical structure partial tolerance specifications	47.12	1755.41	3805	4395	5077
-26		10.98	385.80	1141	1318	1523
77305	Teletherapy, isodose plan (whether hand or computer calculated); simple (one or two parallel opposed unmodified ports directed to a single area of interest)	2.64	97.40	354	401	450
-26		0.97	34.11	124	140	157
77310	Teletherapy, isodose plan (whether hand or computer calculated); intermediate (three or more treatment ports directed to a single area of interest)	3.55	130.37	417	512	595
-26		1.44	50.40	167	205	238
	(UNBUNDLING ALERT: 77315 cannot be used with 76370 by the same physician on the same day.)					
77315	Teletherapy, isodose plan (whether hand or computer calculated); complex (mantle or inverted Y, tangential ports, the use of wedges, compensators, complex blocking, rotational beam, or special beam considerations)	4.68	171.30	523	664	731
-26		2.15	75.42	262	332	366
77321	Special teletherapy port plan, particles, hemibody, total body	4.85	180.01	580	710	802
-26		1.31	45.86	174	213	241
77326	Brachytherapy isodose plan; simple (calculation made from single plane, one to four sources/ribbon application, remote afterloading brachytherapy, 1 to 8 sources)	3.86	142.87	380	425	524
-26		1.29	45.48	152	170	210
77327	Brachytherapy isodose plan; intermediate (multiplane dosage calculations, application involving 5 to 10 sources/ribbons, remote afterloading brachytherapy, 9 to 12 sources)	5.61	207.30	546	639	752
-26		1.91	67.08	218	256	301
77328	Brachytherapy isodose plan; complex (multiplane isodose plan, volume implant calculations, over 10 sources/ribbons used, special spatial reconstruction, remote afterloading brachytherapy, over 12 sources)	7.99	294.84	788	875	1050
-26		2.88	101.19	315	350	420
77331	Special dosimetry (eg, TLD, microdosimetry) (specify), only when prescribed by the treating physician	1.72	61.77	204	256	314
-26		1.19	41.69	153	192	236
77332	Treatment devices, design and construction; simple (simple block, simple bolus)	2.17	80.34	285	324	361
-26		0.75	26.53	114	130	144
77333	Treatment devices, design and construction; intermediate (multiple blocks, stents, bite blocks, special bolus)	2.74	100.81	343	406	454
-26		1.15	40.55	137	162	182
77334	Treatment devices, design and construction; complex (irregular blocks, special shields, compensators, wedges, molds or casts)	4.90	181.15	631	717	884
-26		1.71	60.26	252	287	354
77336	Continuing medical physics consultation, including assessment of treatment parameters, quality assurance of dose delivery, and review of patient treatment documentation in support of the radiation oncologist, reported per week of therapy	2.68	101.57	262	300	350

© PFR 2007

● = New Code ⊗ = Conscious Sedation ✚ = Add-on Code ∅ = Modifier '51' Exempt ▲ =Revised Code

		Medicare RVU	National Fee	PFR Fee Information 50%	75%	90%
77370	Special medical radiation physics consultation	3.56	134.92	332	390	457

Stereotactic Radiation Treatment Delivery

● 77371	Radiation treatment delivery, stereotactic radiosurgery (SRS), complete course of treatment of cerebral lesion(s) consisting of 1 session; multi-source Cobalt 60 based	30.38	1151.33	3519	4122	4830
● 77372	Radiation treatment delivery, stereotactic radiosurgery (SRS), complete course of treatment of cerebral lesion(s) consisting of 1 session; linear accelerator based	23.06	873.92	2671	3129	3666
● 77373	Stereotactic body radiation therapy, treatment delivery, per fraction to 1 or more lesions, including image guidance, entire course not to exceed 5 fractions	43.00	1629.59	4980	5835	6837

Other Procedures

77399	Unlisted procedure, medical radiation physics, dosimetry and treatment devices, and special services	-	-	IR	IR	IR
-26		-	-	IR	IR	IR

Radiation Treatment Delivery

77401	Radiation treatment delivery, superficial and/or ortho voltage	1.56	59.12	164	191	225
77402	Radiation treatment delivery, single treatment area, single port or parallel opposed ports, simple blocks or no blocks; up to 5 MeV	2.48	93.99	185	217	250
77403	Radiation treatment delivery, single treatment area, single port or parallel opposed ports, simple blocks or no blocks; 6-10 MeV	2.38	90.20	186	219	254
77404	Radiation treatment delivery, single treatment area, single port or parallel opposed ports, simple blocks or no blocks; 11-19 MeV	2.49	94.36	186	219	254
77406	Radiation treatment delivery, single treatment area, single port or parallel opposed ports, simple blocks or no blocks; 20 MeV or greater	2.49	94.36	185	217	250
77407	Radiation treatment delivery, two separate treatment areas, three or more ports on a single treatment area, use of multiple blocks; up to 5 MeV	3.05	115.59	215	250	290
77408	Radiation treatment delivery, two separate treatment areas, three or more ports on a single treatment area, use of multiple blocks; 6-10 MeV	2.99	113.31	215	250	290
77409	Radiation treatment delivery, two separate treatment areas, three or more ports on a single treatment area, use of multiple blocks; 11-19 MeV	3.14	119.00	215	250	290
77411	Radiation treatment delivery, two separate treatment areas, three or more ports on a single treatment area, use of multiple blocks; 20 MeV or greater	3.13	118.62	215	250	291
77412	Radiation treatment delivery, three or more separate treatment areas, custom blocking, tangential ports, wedges, rotational beam, compensators, electron beam; up to 5 MeV	3.59	136.05	259	311	359
77413	Radiation treatment delivery, three or more separate treatment areas, custom blocking, tangential ports, wedges, rotational beam, compensators, electron beam; 6-10 MeV	3.59	136.05	259	311	359
77414	Radiation treatment delivery, three or more separate treatment areas, custom blocking, tangential ports, wedges, rotational beam, compensators, electron beam; 11-19 MeV	3.81	144.39	259	311	359
77416	Radiation treatment delivery, three or more separate treatment areas, custom blocking, tangential ports, wedges, rotational beam, compensators, electron beam; 20 MeV or greater	3.81	144.39	259	311	359
77417	Therapeutic radiology port film(s)	0.57	21.60	81	93	113
77418	Intensity modulated treatment delivery, single or multiple fields/arcs, via narrow spatially and temporally modulated beams, binary, dynamic MLC, per treatment session	16.93	641.60	1515	1816	2223
77421	Stereoscopic X-ray guidance for localization of target volume for the delivery of radiation therapy	3.62	135.67	457	544	642
-26		0.54	18.95	114	136	160

Neutron Beam Treatment Delivery

77422	High energy neutron radiation treatment delivery; single treatment area using a single port or parallel-opposed ports with no blocks or simple blocking	4.71	178.50	211	250	295
77423	High energy neutron radiation treatment delivery; 1 or more isocenter(s) with coplanar or non-coplanar geometry with blocking and/or wedge, and/or compensator(s)	3.97	150.45	259	308	363

Radiation Treatment Management

77427	Radiation treatment management, five treatments	5.02	176.22	668	813	958
77431	Radiation therapy management with complete course of therapy consisting of one or two fractions only	2.61	92.09	275	328	368
77432	Stereotactic radiation treatment management of cerebral lesion(s) (complete course of treatment consisting of one session)	11.18	393.38	1780	2070	2707
● 77435	Stereotactic body radiation therapy, treatment management, per treatment course, to one or more lesions, including image guidance, entire course not to exceed 5 fractions	18.30	643.88	2426	2884	3501

● = New Code ⊗ = Conscious Sedation ✚ = Add-on Code ∅ = Modifier '51' Exempt ▲ =Revised Code

		Medicare RVU	National Fee	PFR Fee Information 50%	75%	90%
77470	Special treatment procedure (eg, total body irradiation, hemibody radiation, per oral, endocavitary or intraoperative cone irradiation)	12.14	452.12	1309	1520	1968
-26		2.88	101.19	327	380	492
77499	Unlisted procedure, therapeutic radiology treatment management	-	-	IR	IR	IR
-26		-	-	IR	IR	IR

Proton Beam Treatment Delivery

77520	Proton treatment delivery; simple, without compensation	-	-	IR	IR	IR
77522	Proton treatment delivery; simple, with compensation	-	-	IR	IR	IR
77523	Proton treatment delivery; intermediate	-	-	IR	IR	IR
77525	Proton treatment delivery; complex	-	-	IR	IR	IR

Hyperthermia

⊗ 77600	Hyperthermia, externally generated; superficial (ie, heating to a depth of 4 cm or less)	6.89	255.05	745	878	1138
-26		2.12	74.28	372	439	569
⊗ 77605	Hyperthermia, externally generated; deep (ie, heating to depths greater than 4 cm)	10.34	383.90	888	1149	1324
-26		2.90	101.94	444	574	662
⊗ 77610	Hyperthermia generated by interstitial probe(s); 5 or fewer interstitial applicators	8.73	324.78	579	711	881
-26		2.15	75.42	290	356	440
⊗ 77615	Hyperthermia generated by interstitial probe(s); more than 5 interstitial applicators	12.44	463.49	761	984	1073
-26		2.87	100.81	380	492	536

Clinical Intracavitary Hyperthermia

77620	Hyperthermia generated by intracavitary probe(s)	6.97	258.08	557	671	740
-26		2.25	79.21	278	336	370

Clinical Brachytherapy

77750	Infusion or instillation of radioelement solution (includes 3 months follow-up care)	8.59	306.59	904	1172	1393
-26		6.79	238.38	814	1055	1254
77761	Intracavitary radiation source application; simple	8.42	304.70	809	902	1125
-26		5.14	180.39	607	676	844
77762	Intracavitary radiation source application; intermediate	12.22	441.13	1145	1380	1751
-26		7.88	276.65	859	1035	1313
77763	Intracavitary radiation source application; complex	17.29	622.28	1670	2025	2464
-26		11.81	414.60	1336	1620	1971
77776	Interstitial radiation source application; simple	9.47	341.08	970	1220	1496
-26		6.25	219.05	776	976	1197
77777	Interstitial radiation source application; intermediate	15.02	540.80	1594	1930	2388
-26		10.28	361.16	1196	1448	1791
77778	Interstitial radiation source application; complex	21.45	770.08	2333	2824	3309
-26		15.43	541.93	1866	2259	2647
77781	Remote afterloading high intensity brachytherapy; 1-4 source positions or catheters	19.08	718.54	2024	2404	2910
-26		1.79	63.29	304	361	436
77782	Remote afterloading high intensity brachytherapy; 5-8 source positions or catheters	22.17	832.23	2235	2654	3213
-26		2.94	103.46	447	531	643

● = New Code ⊗ = Conscious Sedation ✚ = Add-on Code ∅ = Modifier '51' Exempt ▲ =Revised Code

		Medicare RVU	National Fee	PFR Fee Information 50%	75%	90%
77783	Remote afterloading high intensity brachytherapy; 9-12 source positions or catheters	26.72	1000.12	2414	2869	3473
-26		4.63	162.96	604	717	868
77784	Remote afterloading high intensity brachytherapy; over 12 source positions or catheters	34.54	1289.27	2771	3292	3984
-26		7.22	253.91	831	988	1195
77789	Surface application of radiation source	2.36	85.27	202	233	273
-26		1.58	55.71	162	186	218
77790	Supervision, handling, loading of radiation source	2.12	76.17	241	285	327
-26		1.44	50.40	193	228	262
77799	Unlisted procedure, clinical brachytherapy	-	-	IR	IR	IR
-26		-	-	IR	IR	IR

Nuclear Medicine

Diagnostic
Endocrine System

		Medicare RVU	National Fee	PFR Fee Information 50%	75%	90%
78000	Thyroid uptake; single determination	1.47	54.95	134	148	169
-26		0.26	9.10	40	44	51
78001	Thyroid uptake; multiple determinations	1.93	72.01	166	191	233
-26		0.36	12.51	50	57	70
78003	Thyroid uptake; stimulation, suppression or discharge (not including initial uptake studies)	1.66	61.77	161	205	252
-26		0.45	15.92	56	72	88
78006	Thyroid imaging, with uptake; single determination	4.02	150.45	319	357	451
-26		0.67	23.50	112	125	158
78007	Thyroid imaging, with uptake; multiple determinations	3.42	127.71	328	428	459
-26		0.68	23.88	98	128	138
78010	Thyroid imaging; only	2.97	111.04	227	261	350
-26		0.54	18.95	68	78	105
78011	Thyroid imaging; with vascular flow	3.59	134.16	315	356	434
-26		0.62	21.60	94	107	130
78015	Thyroid carcinoma metastases imaging; limited area (eg, neck and chest only)	4.22	157.27	422	491	559
-26		0.92	32.21	127	147	168
78016	Thyroid carcinoma metastases imaging; with additional studies (eg, urinary recovery)	5.88	219.81	459	536	615
-26		1.12	39.41	138	161	184
78018	Thyroid carcinoma metastases imaging; whole body	7.35	275.14	691	730	893
-26		1.19	41.69	207	219	268
✚ 78020	Thyroid carcinoma metastases uptake (List separately in addition to code for primary procedure)	2.32	85.65	146	177	200
-26		0.82	28.80	44	53	60
78070	Parathyroid imaging	5.18	193.28	231	296	336
-26		1.13	39.79	92	118	134
78075	Adrenal imaging, cortex and/or medulla	8.08	303.56	456	532	652
-26		1.02	36.00	137	160	196

		Medicare RVU	National Fee	PFR Fee Information 50%	75%	90%
78099	Unlisted endocrine procedure, diagnostic nuclear medicine	-	-	IR	IR	IR
-26		-	-	IR	IR	IR

Hematopoietic, Reticuloendothelial and Lymphatic System

		Medicare RVU	National Fee	50%	75%	90%
78102	Bone marrow imaging; limited area	3.34	124.30	300	370	438
-26		0.75	26.15	105	129	153
78103	Bone marrow imaging; multiple areas	4.80	178.88	444	547	685
-26		1.03	36.00	133	164	205
78104	Bone marrow imaging; whole body	5.80	216.77	589	694	869
-26		1.10	38.66	177	208	261
78110	Plasma volume, radiopharmaceutical volume-dilution technique (separate procedure); single sampling	1.54	57.60	141	182	246
-26		0.27	9.47	42	55	74
78111	Plasma volume, radiopharmaceutical volume-dilution technique (separate procedure); multiple samplings	2.87	108.01	303	356	442
-26		0.31	10.99	76	89	110
78120	Red cell volume determination (separate procedure); single sampling	2.20	82.62	218	258	307
-26		0.32	11.37	54	64	77
78121	Red cell volume determination (separate procedure); multiple samplings	3.26	122.41	359	422	509
-26		0.44	15.54	90	106	127
78122	Whole blood volume determination, including separate measurement of plasma volume and red cell volume (radiopharmaceutical volume-dilution technique)	4.80	180.01	508	597	716
-26		0.62	21.60	127	149	179
78130	Red cell survival study;	3.90	145.53	382	447	555
-26		0.84	29.56	115	134	166
78135	Red cell survival study; differential organ/tissue kinetics, (eg, splenic and/or hepatic sequestration)	6.76	253.91	533	627	753
-26		0.88	31.08	133	157	188
78140	Labeled red cell sequestration, differential organ/tissue, (eg, splenic and/or hepatic)	4.62	172.81	446	525	630
-26		0.83	29.18	112	131	158
78185	Spleen imaging only, with or without vascular flow	3.65	136.81	358	438	477
-26		0.55	19.33	90	110	119
78190	Kinetics, study of platelet survival, with or without differential organ/tissue localization	8.24	308.11	719	803	972
-26		1.55	54.57	180	201	243
78191	Platelet survival study	7.47	280.82	742	829	1003
-26		0.83	29.18	148	166	201
78195	Lymphatics and lymph nodes imaging	6.88	256.19	554	621	750
-26		1.65	57.98	166	186	225
78199	Unlisted hematopoietic, reticuloendothelial and lymphatic procedure, diagnostic nuclear medicine	-	-	IR	IR	IR
-26		-	-	IR	IR	IR

Gastrointestinal System

		Medicare RVU	National Fee	50%	75%	90%
78201	Liver imaging; static only	3.59	134.54	344	414	458
-26		0.60	21.22	103	124	137
78202	Liver imaging; with vascular flow	4.22	158.03	385	500	586
-26		0.69	24.25	115	150	176

● = New Code ⊗ = Conscious Sedation ✚ = Add-on Code ∅ = Modifier '51' Exempt ▲ =Revised Code

		Medicare RVU	National Fee	PFR Fee Information 50%	75%	90%
78205	Liver imaging (SPECT);	6.90	258.84	706	903	1048
-26		0.97	34.11	176	226	262
78206	Liver imaging (SPECT); with vascular flow	9.23	346.00	746	872	1001
-26		1.32	46.23	186	218	250
78215	Liver and spleen imaging; static only	4.11	153.86	449	530	656
-26		0.67	23.50	112	132	164
78216	Liver and spleen imaging; with vascular flow	4.18	156.14	551	607	698
-26		0.77	26.91	138	152	174
78220	Liver function study with hepatobiliary agents, with serial images	4.33	162.20	494	575	669
-26		0.67	23.50	124	144	167
78223	Hepatobiliary ductal system imaging, including gallbladder, with or without pharmacologic intervention, with or without quantitative measurement of gallbladder function	6.02	225.11	519	602	692
-26		1.15	40.55	156	181	208
78230	Salivary gland imaging;	3.32	123.92	310	353	433
-26		0.61	21.22	93	106	130
78231	Salivary gland imaging; with serial images	3.88	145.15	390	445	536
-26		0.71	25.01	98	111	134
78232	Salivary gland function study	4.09	153.11	399	445	540
-26		0.64	22.36	100	111	135
78258	Esophageal motility	4.65	173.57	400	473	573
-26		1.02	36.00	120	142	172
78261	Gastric mucosa imaging	5.62	210.33	511	590	692
-26		0.95	33.35	128	148	173
78262	Gastroesophageal reflux study	5.70	213.36	563	646	762
-26		0.93	32.59	141	162	190
78264	Gastric emptying study	6.01	224.73	520	606	697
-26		1.06	37.14	156	182	209
78267	Urea breath test, C-14 (isotopic); acquisition for analysis	-	-	38	49	62
	(Medicare fees for the code below are based on Non Facility RVUs. PFR information reflects fee when procedure is performed in a facility.)					
78268	Urea breath test, C-14 (isotopic); analysis	-	-	168	208	242
78270	Vitamin B-12 absorption study (eg, Schilling test); without intrinsic factor	1.98	74.28	180	202	244
-26		0.28	9.85	45	50	61
78271	Vitamin B-12 absorption study (eg, Schilling test); with intrinsic factor	2.06	77.31	198	252	284
-26		0.28	9.85	50	63	71
78272	Vitamin B-12 absorption studies combined, with and without intrinsic factor	2.71	101.57	259	309	363
-26		0.37	12.89	65	77	91
78278	Acute gastrointestinal blood loss imaging	7.20	269.07	618	731	836
-26		1.35	47.37	154	183	209
78282	Gastrointestinal protein loss	-	-	408	476	535
-26		0.52	18.19	102	119	134

● = New Code ⊗ = Conscious Sedation ✚ = Add-on Code ∅ = Modifier '51' Exempt ▲ =Revised Code

		Medicare RVU	National Fee	PFR Fee Information 50%	75%	90%
78290	Intestine imaging (eg, ectopic gastric mucosa, Meckel's localization, volvulus)	5.32	198.96	418	505	597
-26		0.93	32.59	104	126	149
78291	Peritoneal-venous shunt patency test (eg, for LeVeen, Denver shunt)	5.06	188.35	425	497	575
-26		1.21	42.45	106	124	144
78299	Unlisted gastrointestinal procedure, diagnostic nuclear medicine	-	-	IR	IR	IR
-26		-	-	IR	IR	IR

Musculoskeletal System

		Medicare RVU	National Fee	50%	75%	90%
78300	Bone and/or joint imaging; limited area	3.79	141.36	358	452	534
-26		0.85	29.94	107	136	160
	(UNBUNDLING ALERT: 78305 cannot be used with 78300 by the same physician on the same day.)					
78305	Bone and/or joint imaging; multiple areas	5.30	197.82	479	580	652
-26		1.14	40.17	144	174	196
	(UNBUNDLING ALERT: 78306 cannot be used with 78300 or 78305 by the same physician on the same day.)					
78306	Bone and/or joint imaging; whole body	5.96	222.46	545	659	734
-26		1.18	41.31	163	198	220
78315	Bone and/or joint imaging; three phase study	7.17	267.94	575	676	811
-26		1.39	48.89	172	203	243
78320	Bone and/or joint imaging; tomographic (SPECT)	7.34	274.38	715	840	1010
-26		1.42	50.02	179	210	252
78350	Bone density (bone mineral content) study, one or more sites; single photon absorptiometry	1.10	40.93	173	226	290
-26		0.30	10.61	52	68	87
78351	Bone density (bone mineral content) study, one or more sites; dual photon absorptiometry, one or more sites	0.42	14.78	255	309	343
78399	Unlisted musculoskeletal procedure, diagnostic nuclear medicine	-	-	IR	IR	IR
-26		-	-	IR	IR	IR

Cardiovascular System

		Medicare RVU	National Fee	50%	75%	90%
78414	Determination of central c-v hemodynamics (non-imaging) (eg, ejection fraction with probe technique) with or without pharmacologic intervention or exercise, single or multiple determinations	-	-	546	676	804
-26		0.63	21.98	218	270	322
78428	Cardiac shunt detection	4.16	154.62	368	434	506
-26		1.12	39.41	147	174	202
78445	Non-cardiac vascular flow imaging (ie, angiography, venography)	3.23	120.51	394	513	653
-26		0.68	23.88	118	154	196
78456	Acute venous thrombosis imaging, peptide	7.04	263.01	452	539	707
-26		1.42	50.02	136	162	212
78457	Venous thrombosis imaging, venogram; unilateral	4.26	158.41	349	411	496
-26		1.05	36.76	105	123	149

		Medicare RVU	National Fee	PFR Fee Information 50%	75%	90%
78458	Venous thrombosis imaging, venogram; bilateral	5.48	204.27	549	634	744
-26		1.24	43.58	165	190	223

(Medicare fees for the code below are based on Non Facility RVUs. PFR information reflects fee when procedure is performed in a facility.)
(For myocardial perfusion imaging studies, see HCPCS codes G0030 - G0047.)

		Medicare RVU	National Fee	PFR Fee Information 50%	75%	90%
78459	Myocardial imaging, positron emission tomography (PET), metabolic evaluation	-	-	2590	2808	3243
-26		2.11	74.28	IR	IR	IR

(UNBUNDLING ALERT: 78460 cannot be used with 36000 by the same physician on the same day.)

		Medicare RVU	National Fee	PFR Fee Information 50%	75%	90%
78460	Myocardial perfusion imaging; (planar) single study, at rest or stress (exercise and/or pharmacologic), with or without quantification	4.13	153.11	515	639	756
-26		1.19	41.69	206	256	302

(UNBUNDLING ALERT: 78461 cannot be used with 78460 by the same physician on the same day.)

		Medicare RVU	National Fee	PFR Fee Information 50%	75%	90%
78461	Myocardial perfusion imaging; multiple studies, (planar) at rest and/or stress (exercise and/or pharmacologic), and redistribution and/or rest injection, with or without quantification	6.34	235.72	755	967	1287
-26		1.70	59.88	226	290	386
78464	Myocardial perfusion imaging; tomographic (SPECT), single study (including attenuation correction when performed), at rest or stress (exercise and/or pharmacologic), with or without quantification	8.53	319.10	882	981	1241
-26		1.54	54.19	176	196	248

(UNBUNDLING ALERT: 78465 cannot be used with 78460, 78461 or 78464 by the same physician on the same day.)

		Medicare RVU	National Fee	PFR Fee Information 50%	75%	90%
78465	Myocardial perfusion imaging; tomographic (SPECT), multiple studies (including attenuation correction when performed), at rest and/or stress (exercise and/or pharmacologic) and redistribution and/or rest injection, with or without quantification	14.21	532.84	1292	1530	1825
-26		2.08	73.14	258	306	365
78466	Myocardial imaging, infarct avid, planar; qualitative or quantitative	4.09	152.35	454	552	667
-26		0.96	33.73	136	166	200
78468	Myocardial imaging, infarct avid, planar; with ejection fraction by first pass technique	5.47	204.27	547	670	770
-26		1.14	40.17	164	201	231
78469	Myocardial imaging, infarct avid, planar; tomographic SPECT with or without quantification	6.93	259.22	639	737	913
-26		1.29	45.48	160	184	228
78472	Cardiac blood pool imaging, gated equilibrium; planar, single study at rest or stress (exercise and/or pharmacologic), wall motion study plus ejection fraction, with or without additional quantitative processing	7.19	268.69	655	763	941
-26		1.37	48.13	196	229	282
78473	Cardiac blood pool imaging, gated equilibrium; multiple studies, wall motion study plus ejection fraction, at rest and stress (exercise and/or pharmacologic), with or without additional quantification	10.41	388.83	1036	1180	1542
-26		2.06	72.38	311	354	463
✚ 78478	Myocardial perfusion study with wall motion, qualitative or quantitative study (List separately in addition to code for primary procedure)	2.16	79.96	225	263	324
-26		0.75	26.53	79	92	113

		Medicare RVU	National Fee	PFR Fee Information 50%	75%	90%
+ 78480	Myocardial perfusion study with ejection fraction (List separately in addition to code for primary procedure)	1.93	72.01	223	263	317
-26		0.52	18.57	89	105	127
	(UNBUNDLING ALERT: 78481 cannot be used with 36000 by the same physician on the same day.)					
78481	Cardiac blood pool imaging, (planar), first pass technique; single study, at rest or with stress (exercise and/or pharmacologic), wall motion study plus ejection fraction, with or without quantification	6.75	252.02	649	764	902
-26		1.41	49.65	195	229	271
	(UNBUNDLING ALERT: 78483 cannot be used with 36000 by the same physician on the same day.)					
78483	Cardiac blood pool imaging, (planar), first pass technique; multiple studies, at rest and with stress (exercise and/ or pharmacologic), wall motion study plus ejection fraction, with or without quantification	9.95	371.40	1158	1293	1634
-26		2.12	74.66	232	259	327
78491	Myocardial imaging, positron emission tomography (PET), perfusion; single study at rest or stress	-	-	IR	IR	IR
-26		2.15	75.80	IR	IR	IR
78492	Myocardial imaging, positron emission tomography (PET), perfusion; multiple studies at rest and/or stress	-	-	IR	IR	IR
-26		2.72	95.88	IR	IR	IR
78494	Cardiac blood pool imaging, gated equilibrium, SPECT, at rest, wall motion study plus ejection fraction, with or without quantitative processing	8.71	325.54	883	1050	1359
-26		1.69	59.50	265	315	408
	(Medicare fees for the code below are based on Non Facility RVUs. PFR information reflects fee when procedure is performed in a facility.)					
+ 78496	Cardiac blood pool imaging, gated equilibrium, single study, at rest, with right ventricular ejection fraction by first pass technique (List separately in addition to code for primary procedure)	6.49	244.06	291	367	440
-26		0.72	25.39	87	110	132
78499	Unlisted cardiovascular procedure, diagnostic nuclear medicine	-	-	IR	IR	IR
-26		-	-	IR	IR	IR

Respiratory System

		Medicare RVU	National Fee	50%	75%	90%
78580	Pulmonary perfusion imaging, particulate	4.92	183.80	464	519	630
-26		1.01	35.62	139	156	189
78584	Pulmonary perfusion imaging, particulate, with ventilation; single breath	4.54	168.26	459	546	624
-26		1.35	47.37	138	164	187
78585	Pulmonary perfusion imaging, particulate, with ventilation; rebreathing and washout, with or without single breath	7.97	297.87	764	836	1002
-26		1.49	52.30	191	209	250
78586	Pulmonary ventilation imaging, aerosol; single projection	3.58	134.16	342	407	468
-26		0.55	19.33	86	102	117
78587	Pulmonary ventilation imaging, aerosol; multiple projections (eg, anterior, posterior, lateral views)	4.16	155.76	391	467	579
-26		0.67	23.50	98	117	145
78588	Pulmonary perfusion imaging, particulate, with ventilation imaging, aerosol, one or multiple projections	6.02	223.97	678	833	1059
-26		1.49	52.30	203	250	318
78591	Pulmonary ventilation imaging, gaseous, single breath, single projection	3.77	141.36	374	421	501
-26		0.55	19.33	94	105	125
78593	Pulmonary ventilation imaging, gaseous, with rebreathing and washout with or without single breath; single projection	4.53	169.78	460	541	634
-26		0.67	23.50	115	135	158

© PFR 2007

● = New Code ⊗ = Conscious Sedation ✚ = Add-on Code ∅ = Modifier '51' Exempt ▲ =Revised Code

		Medicare RVU	National Fee	PFR Fee Information 50%	75%	90%
78594	Pulmonary ventilation imaging, gaseous, with rebreathing and washout with or without single breath; multiple projections (eg, anterior, posterior, lateral views)	5.92	222.46	585	650	781
-26		0.72	25.39	146	162	195
78596	Pulmonary quantitative differential function (ventilation/perfusion) study	9.39	350.93	705	807	856
-26		1.72	60.26	176	202	214
78599	Unlisted respiratory procedure, diagnostic nuclear medicine	-	-	IR	IR	IR
-26		-	-	IR	IR	IR
Nervous System						
78600	Brain imaging, limited procedure; static	4.58	172.05	374	445	528
-26		0.60	21.22	94	111	132
78601	Brain imaging, limited procedure; with vascular flow	4.64	173.95	456	554	630
-26		0.69	24.25	114	138	158
78605	Brain imaging, complete study; static	4.53	169.78	466	603	698
-26		0.72	25.39	116	151	174
78606	Brain imaging, complete study; with vascular flow	5.96	223.60	541	636	796
-26		0.87	30.70	135	159	199
78607	Brain imaging, complete study; tomographic (SPECT)	10.46	391.86	867	975	1190
-26		1.69	59.50	217	244	298
78608	Brain imaging, positron emission tomography (PET); metabolic evaluation	-	-	2332	2399	2622
-26		2.05	72.01	233	240	262
78609	Brain imaging, positron emission tomography (PET); perfusion evaluation	-	-	2506	2841	3342
-26		2.05	72.01	251	284	334
78610	Brain imaging, vascular flow only	2.73	102.32	221	258	290
-26		0.42	14.78	55	64	72
78615	Cerebral vascular flow	4.91	184.56	461	513	614
-26		0.58	20.46	115	128	154
78630	Cerebrospinal fluid flow, imaging (not including introduction of material); cisternography	6.96	261.11	645	744	860
-26		0.93	32.59	161	186	215
78635	Cerebrospinal fluid flow, imaging (not including introduction of material); ventriculography	4.87	182.29	381	456	561
-26		0.85	29.94	114	137	168
78645	Cerebrospinal fluid flow, imaging (not including introduction of material); shunt evaluation	5.48	205.40	472	552	652
-26		0.77	26.91	118	138	163
78647	Cerebrospinal fluid flow, imaging (not including introduction of material); tomographic (SPECT)	9.31	349.41	723	840	999
-26		1.23	43.20	145	168	200
78650	Cerebrospinal fluid leakage detection and localization	6.56	246.33	632	727	794
-26		0.84	29.56	158	182	198
78660	Radiopharmaceutical dacryocystography	3.41	127.34	309	360	423
-26		0.73	25.77	93	108	127
78699	Unlisted nervous system procedure, diagnostic nuclear medicine	-	-	IR	IR	IR
-26		-	-	IR	IR	IR

● = New Code ⊗ = Conscious Sedation ➕ = Add-on Code ∅ = Modifier '51' Exempt ▲ =Revised Code

		Medicare RVU	National Fee	PFR Fee Information 50%	75%	90%

Genitourinary System

		Medicare RVU	National Fee	50%	75%	90%
▲ 78700	Kidney imaging morphology;	4.10	153.48	372	481	546
-26		0.62	21.60	93	120	136
78701	Kidney imaging morphology; with vascular flow	4.75	178.12	426	507	662
-26		0.67	23.50	106	127	166
▲ 78707	Kidney imaging morphology; with vascular flow and function, single study without pharmacological intervention	6.11	227.76	584	682	866
-26		1.31	45.86	175	205	260
▲ 78708	Kidney imaging morphology; with vascular flow and function, single study, with pharmacological intervention (eg, angiotensin converting enzyme inhibitor and/or diuretic)	5.94	220.56	634	755	878
-26		1.65	57.98	190	226	263
▲ 78709	Kidney imaging morphology; with vascular flow and function, multiple studies, with and without pharmacological intervention (eg, angiotensin converting enzyme inhibitor and/or diuretic)	7.49	278.55	669	786	939
-26		1.92	67.46	201	236	282
▲ 78710	Kidney imaging morphology; tomographic (SPECT)	6.85	256.95	709	820	945
-26		0.90	31.45	142	164	189
78725	Kidney function study, non-imaging radioisotopic study	2.51	93.61	336	423	526
-26		0.53	18.57	101	127	158
✚▲ 78730	Urinary bladder residual study (List separately in addition to code for primary procedure)	1.93	72.38	197	218	275
-26		0.28	9.85	59	65	82
78740	Ureteral reflux study (radiopharmaceutical voiding cystogram)	3.74	139.46	321	418	453
-26		0.78	27.29	96	125	136
▲ 78761	Testicular imaging with vascular flow	4.64	173.19	443	530	624
-26		0.97	34.11	133	159	187
78799	Unlisted genitourinary procedure, diagnostic nuclear medicine	-	-	IR	IR	IR
-26		-	-	IR	IR	IR

Other Procedures

		Medicare RVU	National Fee	50%	75%	90%
78800	Radiopharmaceutical localization of tumor or distribution of radiopharmaceutical agent(s); limited area	4.61	172.05	422	501	619
-26		0.91	31.83	106	125	155
78801	Radiopharmaceutical localization of tumor or distribution of radiopharmaceutical agent(s); multiple areas	5.87	219.43	514	612	768
-26		1.10	38.66	128	153	192
78802	Radiopharmaceutical localization of tumor or distribution of radiopharmaceutical agent(s); whole body, single day imaging	7.49	280.44	653	741	972
-26		1.18	41.31	163	185	243
78803	Radiopharmaceutical localization of tumor or distribution of radiopharmaceutical agent(s); tomographic (SPECT)	10.22	383.14	759	858	992
-26		1.50	52.68	190	214	248
78804	Radiopharmaceutical localization of tumor or distribution of radiopharmaceutical agent(s); whole body, requiring two or more days imaging	13.49	507.07	695	811	1003
-26		1.46	51.16	208	243	301
78805	Radiopharmaceutical localization of inflammatory process; limited area	4.67	174.33	431	504	658
-26		1.00	35.24	108	126	164
78806	Radiopharmaceutical localization of inflammatory process; whole body	8.26	309.62	726	817	1042
-26		1.18	41.31	182	204	260

● = New Code ⊗ = Conscious Sedation ✚ = Add-on Code ∅ = Modifier '51' Exempt ▲ =Revised Code

		Medicare RVU	National Fee	PFR Fee Information 50%	75%	90%
78807	Radiopharmaceutical localization of inflammatory process; tomographic (SPECT)	10.04	376.32	770	885	1108
-26		1.50	52.68	192	221	277
78811	Tumor imaging, positron emission tomography (PET); limited area (eg, chest, head/neck)	-	-	IR	IR	IR
-26		2.16	76.17	IR	IR	IR
78812	Tumor imaging, positron emission tomography (PET); skull base to mid-thigh	-	-	IR	IR	IR
-26		2.68	94.36	IR	IR	IR
78813	Tumor imaging, positron emission tomography (PET); whole body	-	-	IR	IR	IR
-26		2.77	97.40	IR	IR	IR
78814	Tumor imaging, positron emission tomography (PET) with concurrently acquired computed tomography (CT) for attenuation correction and anatomical localization; limited area (eg, chest, head/neck)	-	-	IR	IR	IR
-26		3.04	106.87	IR	IR	IR
78815	Tumor imaging, positron emission tomography (PET) with concurrently acquired computed tomography (CT) for attenuation correction and anatomical localization; skull base to mid-thigh	-	-	IR	IR	IR
-26		3.36	117.86	IR	IR	IR
78816	Tumor imaging, positron emission tomography (PET) with concurrently acquired computed tomography (CT) for attenuation correction and anatomical localization; whole body	-	-	IR	IR	IR
-26		3.44	120.89	IR	IR	IR
	(UNBUNDLING ALERT: 78890 cannot be used with 78000 - 78999 by the same physician on the same day.)					
78890	Generation of automated data: interactive process involving nuclear physician and/or allied health professional personnel; simple manipulations and interpretation, not to exceed 30 minutes	1.22	45.86	161	197	235
-26		0.08	2.65	16	20	24
	(UNBUNDLING ALERT: 78891 cannot be used with 78000 - 78999 by the same physician on the same day.)					
78891	Generation of automated data: interactive process involving nuclear physician and/or allied health professional personnel; complex manipulations and interpretation, exceeding 30 minutes	2.46	92.85	252	310	365
-26		0.15	5.31	25	31	37
78999	Unlisted miscellaneous procedure, diagnostic nuclear medicine	-	-	IR	IR	IR
-26		-	-	IR	IR	IR

Therapeutic
(To code the provision of the therapeutic radiopharmaceutical, see code 79900.)

		Medicare RVU	National Fee	50%	75%	90%
79005	Radiopharmaceutical therapy, by oral administration	4.87	177.74	543	668	766
-26		2.46	86.41	326	401	460
79101	Radiopharmaceutical therapy, by intravenous administration	5.16	187.97	561	691	792
-26		2.71	95.12	337	415	475
79200	Radiopharmaceutical therapy, by intracavitary administration	5.23	190.62	557	708	857
-26		2.74	96.26	334	425	514
79300	Radiopharmaceutical therapy, by interstitial radioactive colloid administration	-	-	514	573	642
-26		2.29	80.72	308	344	385
79403	Radiopharmaceutical therapy, radiolabeled monoclonal antibody by intravenous infusion	7.06	258.84	782	945	1098
-26		3.19	112.18	391	472	549
79440	Radiopharmaceutical therapy, by intra-articular administration	5.13	186.83	602	728	785
-26		2.75	96.64	361	437	471

● = New Code ⊗ = Conscious Sedation ✚ = Add-on Code ∅ = Modifier '51' Exempt ▲ =Revised Code

		Medicare RVU	National Fee	PFR Fee Information 50%	75%	90%
79445	Radiopharmaceutical therapy, by intra-arterial particulate administration	-	-	616	756	869
-26		3.31	116.35	370	454	521
79999	Radiopharmaceutical therapy, unlisted procedure			IR	IR	IR
-26		-	-	IR	IR	IR

Pathology and Laboratory

Organ or Disease oriented Panels

80048	Basic metabolic panel This panel must include the following: Calcium (82310) Carbon dioxide (82374) Chloride (82435) Creatinine (82565) Glucose (82947) Potassium (84132) Sodium (84295) Urea nitrogen (BUN) (84520)	-	-	45	50	70
80050	General health panel This panel must include the following: Comprehensive metabolic panel (80053) Blood count, complete (CBC), automated and automated differential WBC count (85025 or 85027 and 85004) OR Blood count, complete (CBC), automated (85027) and appropriate manual differential WBC count (85007 or 85009) Thyroid stimulating hormone (TSH) (84443)	-	-	101	126	135
80051	Electrolyte panel This panel must include the following: Carbon dioxide (82374) Chloride (82435) Potassium (84132) Sodium (84295)	-	-	33	47	69
80053	Comprehensive metabolic panel This panel must include the following: Albumin (82040) Bilirubin, total (82247) Calcium (82310) Carbon dioxide (bicarbonate) (82374) Chloride (82435) Creatinine (82565) Glucose (82947) Phosphatase, alkaline (84075) Potassium (84132) Protein, total (84155) Sodium (84295) Transferase, alanine amino (ALT) (SGPT) (84460) Transferase, aspartate amino (AST) (SGOT) (84450) Urea nitrogen (BUN) (84520)	-	-	56	61	70
80055	Obstetric panel This panel must include the following: Blood count, complete (CBC), automated and automated differential WBC count (85025 or 85027 and 85004) OR Blood count, complete (CBC), automated (85027) and appropriate manual differential WBC count (85007 or 85009) Hepatitis B surface antigen (HBsAg) (87340) Antibody, rubella (86762) Syphilis test, qualitative (eg, VDRL, RPR, ART) (86592) Antibody screen, RBC, each serum technique (86850) Blood typing, ABO (86900) AND Blood typing, Rh (D) (86901)	-	-	103	152	163
80061	Lipid panel This panel must include the following: Cholesterol, serum, total (82465) Lipoprotein, direct measurement, high density cholesterol (HDL cholesterol) (83718) Triglycerides (84478)	-	-	67	82	101
80069	Renal function panel This panel must include the following: Albumin (82040) Calcium (82310) Carbon dioxide (bicarbonate) (82374) Chloride (82435) Creatinine (82565) Glucose (82947) Phosphorus inorganic (phosphate) (84100) Potassium (84132) Sodium (84295) Urea nitrogen (BUN) (84520)	-	-	42	56	77
80074	Acute hepatitis panel This panel must include the following: Hepatitis A antibody (HAAb), IgM antibody (86709) Hepatitis B core antibody (HBcAb), IgM antibody (86705) Hepatitis B surface antigen (HBsAg) (87340) Hepatitis C antibody (86803)	-	-	176	215	248
80076	Hepatic function panel This panel must include the following: Albumin (82040) Bilirubin, total (82247) Bilirubin, direct (82248) Phosphatase, alkaline (84075) Protein, total (84155) Transferase, alanine amino (ALT) (SGPT) (84460) Transferase, aspartate amino (AST) (SGOT) (84450)	-	-	47	63	86

Drug Testing

80100	Drug screen, qualitative; multiple drug classes chromatographic method, each procedure	-	-	78	102	131
80101	Drug screen, qualitative; single drug class method (eg, immunoassay, enzyme assay), each drug class	-	-	71	90	104
80102	Drug confirmation, each procedure	-	-	77	106	122
80103	Tissue preparation for drug analysis	-	-	36	47	59

Therapeutic Drug Assays

80150	Amikacin	-	-	69	80	92
80152	Amitriptyline	-	-	77	97	113
80154	Benzodiazepines	-	-	79	94	106
80156	Carbamazepine; total	-	-	62	77	85
80157	Carbamazepine; free	-	-	62	81	87

© PFR 2007

● = New Code ⊗ = Conscious Sedation ✚ = Add-on Code ∅ = Modifier '51' Exempt ▲ =Revised Code

		Medicare RVU	National Fee	PFR Fee Information 50%	75%	90%
80158	Cyclosporine	-	-	111	134	157
80160	Desipramine	-	-	83	89	100
80162	Digoxin	-	-	61	73	85
80164	Dipropylacetic acid (valproic acid)	-	-	63	73	102
80166	Doxepin	-	-	69	89	104
80168	Ethosuximide	-	-	66	89	102
80170	Gentamicin	-	-	69	82	96
80172	Gold	-	-	64	99	117
80173	Haloperidol	-	-	74	84	108
80174	Imipramine	-	-	90	106	125
80176	Lidocaine	-	-	55	80	97
80178	Lithium	-	-	38	50	62
80182	Nortriptyline	-	-	75	95	119
80184	Phenobarbital	-	-	62	70	83
80185	Phenytoin; total	-	-	63	72	82
80186	Phenytoin; free	-	-	71	86	97
80188	Primidone	-	-	63	76	90
80190	Procainamide;	-	-	63	77	99
80192	Procainamide; with metabolites (eg, n-acetyl procainamide)	-	-	81	94	104
80194	Quinidine	-	-	68	85	100
80195	Sirolimus	-	-	44	62	80
80196	Salicylate	-	-	45	57	76
80197	Tacrolimus	-	-	97	117	128
80198	Theophylline	-	-	60	74	81
80200	Tobramycin	-	-	75	88	105
80201	Topiramate	-	-	67	73	78
80202	Vancomycin	-	-	65	77	89
80299	Quantitation of drug, not elsewhere specified	-	-	46	81	120

Evocative/Suppression Testing

80400	ACTH stimulation panel; for adrenal insufficiency This panel must include the following: Cortisol (82533 x 2)	-	-	131	164	174
80402	ACTH stimulation panel; for 21 hydroxylase deficiency This panel must include the following: Cortisol (82533 x 2) 17 hydroxyprogesterone (83498 x 2)	-	-	254	289	329
80406	ACTH stimulation panel; for 3 beta-hydroxydehydrogenase deficiency This panel must include the following: Cortisol (82533 x 2) 17 hydroxypregnenolone (84143 x 2)	-	-	249	292	323
80408	Aldosterone suppression evaluation panel (eg, saline infusion) This panel must include the following: Aldosterone (82088 x 2) Renin (84244 x 2)	-	-	354	430	529
80410	Calcitonin stimulation panel (eg, calcium, pentagastrin) This panel must include the following: Calcitonin (82308 x 3)	-	-	300	376	444
80412	Corticotropic releasing hormone (CRH) stimulation panel This panel must include the following: Cortisol (82533 x 6) Adrenocorticotropic hormone (ACTH) (82024 x 6)	-	-	852	1105	1473
80414	Chorionic gonadotropin stimulation panel; testosterone response This panel must include the following: Testosterone (84403 x 2 on three pooled blood samples)	-	-	178	204	239
80415	Chorionic gonadotropin stimulation panel; estradiol response This panel must include the following: Estradiol (82670 x 2 on three pooled blood samples)	-	-	189	230	266

● = New Code ⊗ = Conscious Sedation ✚ = Add-on Code ∅ = Modifier '51' Exempt ▲ =Revised Code

		Medicare RVU	National Fee	PFR Fee Information 50%	75%	90%
80416	Renal vein renin stimulation panel (eg, captopril) This panel must include the following: Renin (84244 x 6)	-	-	382	518	572
80417	Peripheral vein renin stimulation panel (eg, captopril) This panel must include the following: Renin (84244 x 2)	-	-	156	190	227
80418	Combined rapid anterior pituitary evaluation panel This panel must include the following: Adrenocorticotropic hormone (ACTH) (82024 x 4) Luteinizing hormone (LH) (83002 x 4) Follicle stimulating hormone (FSH) (83001 x 4) Prolactin (84146 x 4) Human growth hormone (HGH) (83003 x 4) Cortisol (82533 x 4) Thyroid stimulating hormone (TSH) (84443 x 4)	-	-	2069	2267	2642
80420	Dexamethasone suppression panel, 48 hour This panel must include the following: Free cortisol, urine (82530 x 2) Cortisol (82533 x 2) Volume measurement for timed collection (81050 x 2)	-	-	237	293	352
80422	Glucagon tolerance panel; for insulinoma This panel must include the following: Glucose (82947 x 3) Insulin (83525 x 3)	-	-	152	198	238
80424	Glucagon tolerance panel; for pheochromocytoma This panel must include the following: Catecholamines, fractionated (82384 x 2)	-	-	164	213	263
80426	Gonadotropin releasing hormone stimulation panel This panel must include the following: Follicle stimulating hormone (FSH) (83001 x 4) Luteinizing hormone (LH) (83002 x 4)	-	-	399	517	627
80428	Growth hormone stimulation panel (eg, arginine infusion, l-dopa administration) This panel must include the following: Human growth hormone (HGH) (83003 x 4)	-	-	214	286	356
80430	Growth hormone suppression panel (glucose administration) This panel must include the following: Glucose (82947 x 3) Human growth hormone (HGH) (83003 x 4)	-	-	246	307	376
80432	Insulin-induced C-peptide suppression panel This panel must include the following: Insulin (83525) C-peptide (84681 x 5) Glucose (82947 x 5)	-	-	432	494	570
80434	Insulin tolerance panel; for ACTH insufficiency This panel must include the following: Cortisol (82533 x 5) Glucose (82947 x 5)	-	-	279	401	519
80435	Insulin tolerance panel; for growth hormone deficiency This panel must include the following: Glucose (82947 x 5) Human growth hormone (HGH) (83003 x 5)	-	-	324	415	496
80436	Metyrapone panel This panel must include the following: Cortisol (82533 x 2) 11 deoxycortisol (82634 x 2)	-	-	279	378	462
80438	Thyrotropin releasing hormone (TRH) stimulation panel; one hour This panel must include the following: Thyroid stimulating hormone (TSH) (84443 x 3)	-	-	155	185	214
80439	Thyrotropin releasing hormone (TRH) stimulation panel; two hour This panel must include the following: Thyroid stimulating hormone (TSH) (84443 x 4)	-	-	176	223	276
80440	Thyrotropin releasing hormone (TRH) stimulation panel; for hyperprolactinemia This panel must include the following: Prolactin (84146 x 3)	-	-	188	235	282

Consultations (Clinical Pathology)

		Medicare RVU	National Fee	PFR 50%	75%	90%
80500	Clinical pathology consultation; limited, without review of patient's history and medical records	0.59	20.84	58	65	75
80502	Clinical pathology consultation; comprehensive, for a complex diagnostic problem, with review of patient's history and medical records	1.85	65.18	136	155	183

Urinalysis

		Medicare RVU	National Fee	PFR 50%	75%	90%
81000	Urinalysis, by dip stick or tablet reagent for bilirubin, glucose, hemoglobin, ketones, leukocytes, nitrite, pH, protein, specific gravity, urobilinogen, any number of these constituents; non-automated, with microscopy	-	-	20	23	26
81001	Urinalysis, by dip stick or tablet reagent for bilirubin, glucose, hemoglobin, ketones, leukocytes, nitrite, pH, protein, specific gravity, urobilinogen, any number of these constituents; automated, with microscopy	-	-	22	25	30
81002	Urinalysis, by dip stick or tablet reagent for bilirubin, glucose, hemoglobin, ketones, leukocytes, nitrite, pH, protein, specific gravity, urobilinogen, any number of these constituents; non-automated, without microscopy	-	-	16	19	22
81003	Urinalysis, by dip stick or tablet reagent for bilirubin, glucose, hemoglobin, ketones, leukocytes, nitrite, pH, protein, specific gravity, urobilinogen, any number of these constituents; automated, without microscopy	-	-	18	23	29
81005	Urinalysis; qualitative or semiquantitative, except immunoassays	-	-	16	23	26
81007	Urinalysis; bacteriuria screen, except by culture or dipstick	-	-	19	27	31
81015	Urinalysis; microscopic only	-	-	16	18	23
81020	Urinalysis; two or three glass test	-	-	18	21	25
81025	Urine pregnancy test, by visual color comparison methods	-	-	27	30	33
81050	Volume measurement for timed collection, each	-	-	23	28	33

● = New Code ⊗ = Conscious Sedation ✚ = Add-on Code ∅ = Modifier '51' Exempt ▲ =Revised Code

		Medicare RVU	National Fee	PFR Fee Information 50%	75%	90%
81099	Unlisted urinalysis procedure	-	-	IR	IR	IR

Chemistry

82000	Acetaldehyde, blood	-	-	62	72	84
82003	Acetaminophen	-	-	68	89	109
82009	Acetone or other ketone bodies, serum; qualitative	-	-	20	27	32
82010	Acetone or other ketone bodies, serum; quantitative	-	-	36	60	74
82013	Acetylcholinesterase	-	-	56	68	77
82016	Acylcarnitines; qualitative, each specimen	-	-	77	92	103
82017	Acylcarnitines; quantitative, each specimen	-	-	76	88	100
82024	Adrenocorticotropic hormone (ACTH)	-	-	155	178	227
82030	Adenosine, 5-monophosphate, cyclic (cyclic AMP)	-	-	100	124	141
82040	Albumin; serum	-	-	23	31	36
82042	Albumin; urine or other source, quantitative, each specimen	-	-	29	37	45
82043	Albumin; urine, microalbumin, quantitative	-	-	51	61	76
82044	Albumin; urine, microalbumin, semiquantitative (eg, reagent strip assay)	-	-	27	33	35
82045	Albumin; ischemia modified	-	-	IR	IR	IR
82055	Alcohol (ethanol); any specimen except breath	-	-	50	63	87
82075	Alcohol (ethanol); breath	-	-	37	46	51
82085	Aldolase	-	-	46	52	74
82088	Aldosterone	-	-	162	173	188
82101	Alkaloids, urine, quantitative	-	-	93	121	146
	(Payment for code 82103 by Medicare is restricted to the presence of the following ICD-9-CM codes: 277.6 or 492.8.)					
82103	Alpha-1-antitrypsin; total	-	-	63	93	108
	(Payment for code 82104 by Medicare is restricted to the presence of the following ICD-9-CM code: 492.8.)					
82104	Alpha-1-antitrypsin; phenotype	-	-	86	103	114
82105	Alpha-fetoprotein (AFP); serum	-	-	75	83	120
82106	Alpha-fetoprotein (AFP); amniotic fluid	-	-	71	85	96
● 82107	Alpha-fetoprotein (AFP); AFP-L3 fraction isoform and total AFP (including ratio)	-	-	IR	IR	IR
82108	Aluminum	-	-	99	112	122
82120	Amines, vaginal fluid, qualitative	-	-	16	18	22
82127	Amino acids; single, qualitative, each specimen	-	-	54	64	74
82128	Amino acids; multiple, qualitative, each specimen	-	-	44	52	66
82131	Amino acids; single, quantitative, each specimen	-	-	137	176	212
82135	Aminolevulinic acid, delta (ALA)	-	-	67	79	92
82136	Amino acids, 2 to 5 amino acids, quantitative, each specimen	-	-	121	137	151
82139	Amino acids, 6 or more amino acids, quantitative, each specimen	-	-	121	137	158
82140	Ammonia	-	-	67	86	141
82143	Amniotic fluid scan (spectrophotometric)	-	-	56	67	83
82145	Amphetamine or methamphetamine	-	-	72	86	99

© PFR 2007

● = New Code ⊗ = Conscious Sedation ✚ = Add-on Code ∅ = Modifier '51' Exempt ▲ =Revised Code

Code	Description	Medicare RVU	National Fee	PFR Fee Information 50%	75%	90%
82150	Amylase	-	-	30	36	48
82154	Androstanediol glucuronide	-	-	111	123	140
82157	Androstenedione	-	-	128	145	179
82160	Androsterone	-	-	121	140	162
82163	Angiotensin II	-	-	93	109	123
82164	Angiotensin I - converting enzyme (ACE)	-	-	72	87	104
82172	Apolipoprotein, each	-	-	68	80	85
82175	Arsenic	-	-	77	96	117
82180	Ascorbic acid (Vitamin C), blood	-	-	46	56	64
82190	Atomic absorption spectroscopy, each analyte	-	-	74	87	101
82205	Barbiturates, not elsewhere specified	-	-	58	70	85
82232	Beta-2 microglobulin	-	-	81	104	129
82239	Bile acids; total	-	-	66	79	92
82240	Bile acids; cholylglycine	-	-	104	128	148
82247	Bilirubin; total	-	-	22	27	34
82248	Bilirubin; direct	-	-	24	31	38
82252	Bilirubin; feces, qualitative	-	-	14	19	22
82261	Biotinidase, each specimen	-	-	53	75	89
82270	*(See also HCPCS code G0107 for colorectal cancer screening; fecal-occult blood test, 1-3 simultaneous determinations.)* Blood, occult, by peroxidase activity (eg, guaiac), qualitative; feces, consecutive collected specimens with single determination, for colorectal neoplasm screening (ie, patient was provided three cards or single triple card for consecutive collection)	-	-	17	21	25
82271	Blood, occult, by peroxidase activity (eg, guaiac), qualitative; other sources	-	-	15	20	26
82272	Blood, occult, by peroxidase activity (eg, guaiac), qualitative, feces, single specimen (eg, from digital rectal exam)	-	-	15	20	26
82274	Blood, occult, by fecal hemoglobin determination by immunoassay, qualitative, feces, 1-3 simultaneous determinations	-	-	61	75	89
82286	Bradykinin	-	-	100	126	136
82300	Cadmium	-	-	92	111	134
82306	Calcifediol (25-OH Vitamin D-3)	-	-	146	157	204
82307	Calciferol (Vitamin D)	-	-	120	151	171
82308	Calcitonin	-	-	125	157	178
82310	Calcium; total	-	-	24	30	40
82330	Calcium; ionized	-	-	66	76	105
82331	Calcium; after calcium infusion test	-	-	26	40	46
82340	Calcium; urine quantitative, timed specimen	-	-	35	43	47
82355	Calculus; qualitative analysis	-	-	62	71	78
82360	Calculus; quantitative analysis, chemical	-	-	64	77	102
82365	Calculus; infrared spectroscopy	-	-	76	83	93
82370	Calculus; x-ray diffraction	-	-	65	71	77
82373	Carbohydrate deficient transferrin	-	-	46	54	62
82374	Carbon dioxide (bicarbonate)	-	-	23	27	39
82375	Carbon monoxide, (carboxyhemoglobin); quantitative	-	-	58	78	101

		Medicare RVU	National Fee	PFR Fee Information 50%	75%	90%
82376	Carbon monoxide, (carboxyhemoglobin); qualitative	-	-	22	27	33
82378	Carcinoembryonic antigen (CEA)	-	-	88	107	120
82379	Carnitine (total and free), quantitative, each specimen	-	-	87	104	117
82380	Carotene	-	-	52	68	86
82382	Catecholamines; total urine	-	-	91	120	132
82383	Catecholamines; blood	-	-	141	181	215
82384	Catecholamines; fractionated	-	-	150	170	184
82387	Cathepsin-D	-	-	108	124	142
82390	Ceruloplasmin	-	-	57	73	103
82397	Chemiluminescent assay	-	-	65	79	107
82415	Chloramphenicol	-	-	87	100	119
82435	Chloride; blood	-	-	20	24	33
82436	Chloride; urine	-	-	28	31	34
82438	Chloride; other source	-	-	24	30	36
82441	Chlorinated hydrocarbons, screen	-	-	40	51	66
82465	Cholesterol, serum or whole blood, total	-	-	26	31	37
82480	Cholinesterase; serum	-	-	47	55	62
82482	Cholinesterase; RBC	-	-	64	72	90
82485	Chondroitin B sulfate, quantitative	-	-	113	137	154
82486	Chromatography, qualitative; column (eg, gas liquid or HPLC), analyte not elsewhere specified	-	-	98	125	163
82487	Chromatography, qualitative; paper, 1-dimensional, analyte not elsewhere specified	-	-	87	101	116
82488	Chromatography, qualitative; paper, 2-dimensional, analyte not elsewhere specified	-	-	115	134	155
82489	Chromatography, qualitative; thin layer, analyte not elsewhere specified	-	-	82	97	132
82491	Chromatography, quantitative, column (eg, gas liquid or HPLC); single analyte not elsewhere specified, single stationary and mobile phase	-	-	91	111	141
82492	Chromatography, quantitative, column (eg, gas liquid or HPLC); multiple analytes, single stationary and mobile phase	-	-	89	108	125
82495	Chromium	-	-	100	119	134
82507	Citrate	-	-	125	163	200
82520	Cocaine or metabolite	-	-	79	93	103
82523	Collagen cross links, any method	-	-	88	103	118
82525	Copper	-	-	68	82	100
82528	Corticosterone	-	-	109	129	152
82530	Cortisol; free	-	-	98	124	137
82533	Cortisol; total	-	-	84	98	124
82540	Creatine	-	-	29	40	46
82541	Column chromatography/mass spectrometry (eg, GC/MS, or HPLC/MS), analyte not elsewhere specified; qualitative, single stationary and mobile phase	-	-	75	87	103
82542	Column chromatography/mass spectrometry (eg, GC/MS, or HPLC/MS), analyte not elsewhere specified; quantitative, single stationary and mobile phase	-	-	77	90	106
82543	Column chromatography/mass spectrometry (eg, GC/MS, or HPLC/MS), analyte not elsewhere specified; stable isotope dilution, single analyte, quantitative, single stationary and mobile phase	-	-	81	95	112

		Medicare RVU	National Fee	PFR Fee Information 50%	75%	90%
82544	Column chromatography/mass spectrometry (eg, GC/MS, or HPLC/MS), analyte not elsewhere specified; stable isotope dilution, multiple analytes, quantitative, single stationary and mobile phase	-	-	82	97	114
82550	Creatine kinase (CK), (CPK); total	-	-	33	46	53
82552	Creatine kinase (CK), (CPK); isoenzymes	-	-	62	74	89
82553	Creatine kinase (CK), (CPK); MB fraction only	-	-	51	61	64
82554	Creatine kinase (CK), (CPK); isoforms	-	-	53	64	73
82565	Creatinine; blood	-	-	24	30	37
82570	Creatinine; other source	-	-	33	36	49
82575	Creatinine; clearance	-	-	51	64	80
82585	Cryofibrinogen	-	-	36	43	50
82595	Cryoglobulin, qualitative or semi-quantitative (eg, cryocrit)	-	-	33	48	67
82600	Cyanide	-	-	78	93	106
82607	Cyanocobalamin (Vitamin B-12);	-	-	75	97	124
82608	Cyanocobalamin (Vitamin B-12); unsaturated binding capacity	-	-	74	103	117
82615	Cystine and homocystine, urine, qualitative	-	-	45	64	86
82626	Dehydroepiandrosterone (DHEA)	-	-	129	148	214
82627	Dehydroepiandrosterone-sulfate (DHEA-S)	-	-	109	130	139
82633	Desoxycorticosterone, 11-	-	-	149	173	196
82634	Deoxycortisol, 11-	-	-	124	154	211
82638	Dibucaine number	-	-	48	58	72
82646	Dihydrocodeinone	-	-	83	100	116
82649	Dihydromorphinone	-	-	84	107	129
82651	Dihydrotestosterone (DHT)	-	-	106	130	148
82652	Dihydroxyvitamin D, 1,25-	-	-	147	169	213
82654	Dimethadione	-	-	70	98	106
82656	Elastase, pancreatic (EL-1), fecal, qualitative or semi-quantitative	-	-	33	45	57
82657	Enzyme activity in blood cells, cultured cells, or tissue, not elsewhere specified; nonradioactive substrate, each specimen	-	-	75	87	103
82658	Enzyme activity in blood cells, cultured cells, or tissue, not elsewhere specified; radioactive substrate, each specimen	-	-	75	89	105
82664	Electrophoretic technique, not elsewhere specified	-	-	84	114	122
82666	Epiandrosterone	-	-	88	107	123
82668	Erythropoietin	-	-	101	111	116
82670	Estradiol	-	-	98	115	153
82671	Estrogens; fractionated	-	-	126	155	170
82672	Estrogens; total	-	-	107	134	150
82677	Estriol	-	-	92	106	120
82679	Estrone	-	-	112	152	172
82690	Ethchlorvynol	-	-	74	85	98
82693	Ethylene glycol	-	-	72	85	98
82696	Etiocholanolone	-	-	114	136	154
82705	Fat or lipids, feces; qualitative	-	-	30	35	45

© PFR 2007

● = New Code ⊗ = Conscious Sedation   ✚ = Add-on Code   ∅ = Modifier '51' Exempt   ▲ =Revised Code

		Medicare RVU	National Fee	PFR Fee Information 50%	75%	90%
82710	Fat or lipids, feces; quantitative	-	-	85	117	134
82715	Fat differential, feces, quantitative	-	-	51	68	83
82725	Fatty acids, nonesterified	-	-	44	64	70
82726	Very long chain fatty acids	-	-	65	73	86
82728	Ferritin	-	-	63	79	90
82731	Fetal fibronectin, cervicovaginal secretions, semi-quantitative	-	-	IR	IR	IR
82735	Fluoride	-	-	77	92	105
82742	Flurazepam	-	-	84	101	119
82746	Folic acid; serum	-	-	72	86	106
82747	Folic acid; RBC	-	-	87	102	129
82757	Fructose, semen	-	-	44	53	73
82759	Galactokinase, RBC	-	-	57	68	81
82760	Galactose	-	-	49	67	82
82775	Galactose-1-phosphate uridyl transferase; quantitative	-	-	72	81	109
82776	Galactose-1-phosphate uridyl transferase; screen	-	-	27	34	40
82784	Gammaglobulin; IgA, IgD, IgG, IgM, each	-	-	60	67	81
82785	Gammaglobulin; IgE	-	-	74	99	108
82787	Gammaglobulin; immunoglobulin subclasses, (IgG1, 2, 3, or 4), each	-	-	158	221	261
82800	Gases, blood, pH only	-	-	44	53	63
82803	Gases, blood, any combination of pH, pCO2, pO2, CO2, HCO3 (including calculated O2 saturation);	-	-	82	99	133
82805	Gases, blood, any combination of pH, pCO2, pO2, CO2, HCO3 (including calculated O2 saturation); with O2 saturation, by direct measurement, except pulse oximetry	-	-	93	116	135
82810	Gases, blood, O2 saturation only, by direct measurement, except pulse oximetry	-	-	47	56	66
82820	Hemoglobin-oxygen affinity (pO2 for 50% hemoglobin saturation with oxygen)	-	-	59	71	80
82926	Gastric acid, free and total, each specimen	-	-	30	35	39
82928	Gastric acid, free or total, each specimen	-	-	22	29	39
82938	Gastrin after secretin stimulation	-	-	81	99	125
82941	Gastrin	-	-	86	99	122
82943	Glucagon	-	-	92	114	136
82945	Glucose, body fluid, other than blood	-	-	38	41	48
82946	Glucagon tolerance test	-	-	56	69	83
82947	Glucose; quantitative, blood (except reagent strip)	-	-	23	27	32
82948	Glucose; blood, reagent strip	-	-	18	20	25
82950	Glucose; post glucose dose (includes glucose)	-	-	27	37	58
82951	Glucose; tolerance test (GTT), three specimens (includes glucose)	-	-	63	71	79
82952	Glucose; tolerance test, each additional beyond three specimens	-	-	23	38	58
82953	Glucose; tolbutamide tolerance test	-	-	70	88	100
82955	Glucose-6-phosphate dehydrogenase (G6PD); quantitative	-	-	66	72	87
82960	Glucose-6-phosphate dehydrogenase (G6PD); screen	-	-	32	38	47
82962	Glucose, blood by glucose monitoring device(s) cleared by the FDA specifically for home use	-	-	19	23	26

● = New Code ⊗ = Conscious Sedation ✚ = Add-on Code ∅ = Modifier '51' Exempt ▲ =Revised Code

		Medicare RVU	National Fee	PFR Fee Information 50%	75%	90%
82963	Glucosidase, beta	-	-	84	93	110
82965	Glutamate dehydrogenase	-	-	27	34	42
82975	Glutamine (glutamic acid amide)	-	-	52	69	90
82977	Glutamyltransferase, gamma (GGT)	-	-	29	33	41
82978	Glutathione	-	-	58	69	77
82979	Glutathione reductase, RBC	-	-	36	51	62
82980	Glutethimide	-	-	78	94	110
82985	Glycated protein	-	-	52	63	74
83001	Gonadotropin; follicle stimulating hormone (FSH)	-	-	85	102	124
83002	Gonadotropin; luteinizing hormone (LH)	-	-	82	100	113
83003	Growth hormone, human (HGH) (somatotropin)	-	-	82	96	128
83008	Guanosine monophosphate (GMP), cyclic	-	-	94	108	123
83009	Helicobacter pylori, blood test analysis for urease activity, non-radioactive isotope (eg, C-13)	-	-	IR	IR	IR
83010	Haptoglobin; quantitative	-	-	66	80	97
83012	Haptoglobin; phenotypes	-	-	72	103	116
83013	Helicobacter pylori; breath test analysis for urease activity, non-radioactive isotope (eg, C-13)	-	-	202	232	277
83014	Helicobacter pylori; drug administration	-	-	30	36	43
83015	Heavy metal (eg, arsenic, barium, beryllium, bismuth, antimony, mercury); screen	-	-	112	146	165
83018	Heavy metal (eg, arsenic, barium, beryllium, bismuth, antimony, mercury); quantitative, each	-	-	112	131	152
83020	Hemoglobin fractionation and quantitation; electrophoresis (eg, A2, S, C, and/or F)	-	-	65	76	104
-26		0.52	18.19	23	27	36
83021	Hemoglobin fractionation and quantitation; chromatography (eg, A2, S, C, and/or F)	-	-	86	104	123
83026	Hemoglobin; by copper sulfate method, non-automated	-	-	16	18	20
83030	Hemoglobin; F (fetal), chemical	-	-	42	48	57
83033	Hemoglobin; F (fetal), qualitative	-	-	26	30	36
83036	Hemoglobin; glycosylated (A1C)	-	-	51	60	70
83037	Hemoglobin; glycosylated (A1C) by device cleared by FDA for home use	-	-	18	26	33
83045	Hemoglobin; methemoglobin, qualitative	-	-	21	25	29
83050	Hemoglobin; methemoglobin, quantitative	-	-	26	35	47
83051	Hemoglobin; plasma	-	-	30	34	41
83055	Hemoglobin; sulfhemoglobin, qualitative	-	-	26	31	38
83060	Hemoglobin; sulfhemoglobin, quantitative	-	-	40	48	64
83065	Hemoglobin; thermolabile	-	-	29	36	44
83068	Hemoglobin; unstable, screen	-	-	34	42	49
83069	Hemoglobin; urine	-	-	20	23	25
83070	Hemosiderin; qualitative	-	-	24	31	41
83071	Hemosiderin; quantitative	-	-	27	30	35
83080	b-Hexosaminidase, each assay	-	-	58	67	80
83088	Histamine	-	-	137	155	170

© PFR 2007

● = New Code ⊗ = Conscious Sedation ✚ = Add-on Code ∅ = Modifier '51' Exempt ▲ =Revised Code

		Medicare RVU	National Fee	PFR Fee Information 50%	75%	90%
83090	Homocysteine	-	-	66	82	97
83150	Homovanillic acid (HVA)	-	-	83	104	131
83491	Hydroxycorticosteroids, 17- (17-OHCS)	-	-	96	114	137
83497	Hydroxyindolacetic acid, 5-(HIAA)	-	-	82	92	110
83498	Hydroxyprogesterone, 17-d	-	-	127	144	162
83499	Hydroxyprogesterone, 20-	-	-	95	129	147
83500	Hydroxyproline; free	-	-	89	122	147
83505	Hydroxyproline; total	-	-	110	136	161
83516	Immunoassay for analyte other than infectious agent antibody or infectious agent antigen, qualitative or semiquantitative; multiple step method	-	-	68	83	100
83518	Immunoassay for analyte other than infectious agent antibody or infectious agent antigen, qualitative or semiquantitative; single step method (eg, reagent strip)	-	-	39	47	55
83519	Immunoassay, analyte, quantitative; by radiopharmaceutical technique (eg, RIA)	-	-	83	110	146
83520	Immunoassay, analyte, quantitative; not otherwise specified	-	-	73	107	143
83525	Insulin; total	-	-	62	78	132
83527	Insulin; free	-	-	76	91	104
83528	Intrinsic factor	-	-	84	96	110
83540	Iron	-	-	29	34	37
83550	Iron binding capacity	-	-	40	49	57
83570	Isocitric dehydrogenase (IDH)	-	-	43	56	72
83582	Ketogenic steroids, fractionation	-	-	62	86	102
83586	Ketosteroids, 17- (17-KS); total	-	-	71	88	112
83593	Ketosteroids, 17- (17-KS); fractionation	-	-	133	155	191
83605	Lactate (lactic acid)	-	-	51	59	71
83615	Lactate dehydrogenase (LD), (LDH);	-	-	26	29	40
83625	Lactate dehydrogenase (LD), (LDH); isoenzymes, separation and quantitation	-	-	70	77	98
83630	Lactoferrin, fecal; qualitative	-	-	IR	IR	IR
83631	Lactoferrin, fecal; quantitative	-	-	45	64	82
83632	Lactogen, human placental (HPL) human chorionic somatomammotropin	-	-	104	122	136
83633	Lactose, urine; qualitative	-	-	30	34	41
83634	Lactose, urine; quantitative	-	-	43	54	67
83655	Lead	-	-	50	61	79
83661	Fetal lung maturity assessment; lecithin sphingomyelin (L/S) ratio	-	-	123	133	147
83662	Fetal lung maturity assessment; foam stability test	-	-	62	73	88
83663	Fetal lung maturity assessment; fluorescence polarization	-	-	46	57	68
83664	Fetal lung maturity assessment; lamellar body density	-	-	36	39	45
83670	Leucine aminopeptidase (LAP)	-	-	42	49	58
83690	Lipase	-	-	41	50	56
83695	Lipoprotein (a)	-	-	IR	IR	IR
● 83698	Lipoprotein-associated phospholipase A2, (Lp-PLA2)	-	-	IR	IR	IR
83700	Lipoprotein, blood; electrophoretic separation and quantitation	-	-	26	36	48

		Medicare RVU	National Fee	PFR Fee Information 50%	75%	90%
83701	Lipoprotein, blood; high resolution fractionation and quantitation of lipoproteins including lipoprotein subclasses when performed (eg, electrophoresis, ultracentrifugation)	-	-	65	91	117
83704	Lipoprotein, blood; quantitation of lipoprotein particle numbers and lipoprotein particle subclasses (eg, by nuclear magnetic resonance spectroscopy)	-	-	IR	IR	IR
83718	Lipoprotein, direct measurement; high density cholesterol (HDL cholesterol)	-	-	35	43	54
83719	Lipoprotein, direct measurement; VLDL cholesterol	-	-	42	51	63
83721	Lipoprotein, direct measurement; LDL cholesterol	-	-	38	44	52
83727	Luteinizing releasing factor (LRH)	-	-	89	104	130
83735	Magnesium	-	-	29	37	49
83775	Malate dehydrogenase	-	-	35	41	47
83785	Manganese	-	-	95	113	132
83788	Mass spectrometry and tandem mass spectrometry (MS, MS/MS), analyte not elsewhere specified; qualitative, each specimen	-	-	70	84	98
83789	Mass spectrometry and tandem mass spectrometry (MS, MS/MS), analyte not elsewhere specified; quantitative, each specimen	-	-	80	94	109
83805	Meprobamate	-	-	72	90	110
83825	Mercury, quantitative	-	-	85	102	134
83835	Metanephrines	-	-	86	104	140
83840	Methadone	-	-	69	99	111
83857	Methemalbumin	-	-	48	57	65
83858	Methsuximide	-	-	78	92	113
83864	Mucopolysaccharides, acid; quantitative	-	-	51	60	82
83866	Mucopolysaccharides, acid; screen	-	-	35	42	52
83872	Mucin, synovial fluid (Ropes test)	-	-	23	36	48
83873	Myelin basic protein, cerebrospinal fluid	-	-	85	104	133
83874	Myoglobin	-	-	70	86	94
83880	Natriuretic peptide	-	-	99	138	163
83883	Nephelometry, each analyte not elsewhere specified	-	-	58	69	81
83885	Nickel	-	-	85	111	129
83887	Nicotine	-	-	82	102	124
83890	Molecular diagnostics; molecular isolation or extraction	-	-	42	59	80
83891	Molecular diagnostics; isolation or extraction of highly purified nucleic acid	-	-	37	47	53
83892	Molecular diagnostics; enzymatic digestion	-	-	34	41	51
83893	Molecular diagnostics; dot/slot blot production	-	-	38	44	57
83894	Molecular diagnostics; separation by gel electrophoresis (eg, agarose, polyacrylamide)	-	-	46	54	65
83896	Molecular diagnostics; nucleic acid probe, each	-	-	53	63	75
83897	Molecular diagnostics; nucleic acid transfer (eg, Southern, Northern)	-	-	27	35	42
83898	Molecular diagnostics; amplification of patient nucleic acid, each nucleic acid sequence	-	-	126	148	195
83900	Molecular diagnostics; amplification of patient nucleic acid, multiplex, first two nucleic acid sequences	-	-	48	67	87
✚ 83901	Molecular diagnostics; amplification of patient nucleic acid, multiplex, each additional nucleic acid sequence (List separately in addition to code for primary procedure)	-	-	112	125	140
83902	Molecular diagnostics; reverse transcription	-	-	66	93	121

● = New Code ⊗ = Conscious Sedation ✚ = Add-on Code ∅ = Modifier '51' Exempt ▲ =Revised Code

		Medicare RVU	National Fee	PFR Fee Information 50%	75%	90%
83903	Molecular diagnostics; mutation scanning, by physical properties (eg, single strand conformational polymorphisms (SSCP), heteroduplex, denaturing gradient gel electrophoresis (DGGE), RNA'ase A), single segment, each	-	-	67	92	179
83904	Molecular diagnostics; mutation identification by sequencing, single segment, each segment	-	-	70	96	186
83905	Molecular diagnostics; mutation identification by allele specific transcription, single segment, each segment	-	-	71	98	189
83906	Molecular diagnostics; mutation identification by allele specific translation, single segment, each segment	-	-	71	98	189
83907	Molecular diagnostics; lysis of cells prior to nucleic acid extraction (eg, stool specimens, paraffin embedded tissue)	-	-	46	65	84
83908	Molecular diagnostics; signal amplification of patient nucleic acid, each nucleic acid sequence	-	-	46	65	84
83909	Molecular diagnostics; separation and identification by high resolution technique (eg, capillary electrophoresis)	-	-	47	65	85
83912	Molecular diagnostics; interpretation and report	-	-	56	67	88
-26		0.50	17.43	34	40	53
● 83913	Molecular diagnostics; RNA stabilization	-	-	IR	IR	IR
83914	Mutation identification by enzymatic ligation or primer extension, single segment, each segment (eg, oligonucleotide ligation assay (OLA), single base chain extension (SBCE), or allele-specific primer extension (ASPE))	-	-	47	65	85
83915	Nucleotidase 5'-	-	-	45	52	75
83916	Oligoclonal immune (oligoclonal bands)	-	-	87	96	122
83918	Organic acids; total, quantitative, each specimen	-	-	107	127	154
83919	Organic acids; qualitative, each specimen	-	-	87	119	144
83921	Organic acid, single, quantitative	-	-	139	206	268
83925	Opiates, (eg, morphine, meperidine)	-	-	76	87	111
83930	Osmolality; blood	-	-	36	44	52
83935	Osmolality; urine	-	-	49	57	62
83937	Osteocalcin (bone g1a protein)	-	-	107	126	154
83945	Oxalate	-	-	62	73	84
83950	Oncoprotein, HER-2/neu	-	-	193	233	268
83970	Parathormone (parathyroid hormone)	-	-	165	197	236
83986	pH, body fluid, except blood	-	-	21	22	25
83992	Phencyclidine (PCP)	-	-	70	82	94
84022	Phenothiazine	-	-	63	74	101
84030	Phenylalanine (PKU), blood	-	-	25	30	38
84035	Phenylketones, qualitative	-	-	20	23	25
84060	Phosphatase, acid; total	-	-	53	61	71
84061	Phosphatase, acid; forensic examination	-	-	42	48	54
84066	Phosphatase, acid; prostatic	-	-	55	65	72
84075	Phosphatase, alkaline;	-	-	21	32	44
84078	Phosphatase, alkaline; heat stable (total not included)	-	-	36	47	52
84080	Phosphatase, alkaline; isoenzymes	-	-	63	85	102
84081	Phosphatidylglycerol	-	-	87	104	129
84085	Phosphogluconate, 6-, dehydrogenase, RBC	-	-	35	43	56
84087	Phosphohexose isomerase	-	-	43	51	68

● = New Code ⊗ = Conscious Sedation ✚ = Add-on Code ∅ = Modifier '51' Exempt ▲ =Revised Code

		Medicare RVU	National Fee	PFR Fee Information 50%	75%	90%
84100	Phosphorus inorganic (phosphate);	-	-	22	27	35
84105	Phosphorus inorganic (phosphate); urine	-	-	27	34	44
84106	Porphobilinogen, urine; qualitative	-	-	29	36	51
84110	Porphobilinogen, urine; quantitative	-	-	45	55	62
84119	Porphyrins, urine; qualitative	-	-	41	52	64
84120	Porphyrins, urine; quantitation and fractionation	-	-	75	94	114
84126	Porphyrins, feces; quantitative	-	-	76	93	102
84127	Porphyrins, feces; qualitative	-	-	34	47	54
84132	Potassium; serum	-	-	21	26	31
84133	Potassium; urine	-	-	28	35	45
84134	Prealbumin	-	-	49	63	78
84135	Pregnanediol	-	-	80	99	120
84138	Pregnanetriol	-	-	78	92	126
84140	Pregnenolone	-	-	92	114	131
84143	17-hydroxypregnenolone	-	-	98	123	143
84144	Progesterone	-	-	81	96	131
84146	Prolactin	-	-	84	106	131
84150	Prostaglandin, each	-	-	91	121	143
84152	Prostate specific antigen (PSA); complexed (direct measurement)	-	-	75	92	116
	(See also HCPCS code G0103 for prostate cancer screening; prostate specific antigen test (PSA), total.)					
84153	Prostate specific antigen (PSA); total	-	-	80	98	113
84154	Prostate specific antigen (PSA); free	-	-	78	94	119
84155	Protein, total, except by refractometry; serum	-	-	28	36	43
84156	Protein, total, except by refractometry; urine	-	-	20	27	34
84157	Protein, total, except by refractometry; other source (eg, synovial fluid, cerebrospinal fluid)	-	-	20	26	34
84160	Protein, total, by refractometry, any source	-	-	19	22	25
84163	Pregnancy-associated plasma protein-A (PAPP-A)	-	-	IR	IR	IR
84165	Protein; electrophoretic fractionation and quantitation, serum	-	-	59	75	97
-26		0.51	17.81	15	19	24
84166	Protein; electrophoretic fractionation and quantitation, other fluids with concentration (eg, urine, CSF)	-	-	68	85	100
-26		0.51	17.81	17	21	25
84181	Protein; Western Blot, with interpretation and report, blood or other body fluid	-	-	89	110	161
-26		0.52	18.19	31	38	56
84182	Protein; Western Blot, with interpretation and report, blood or other body fluid, immunological probe for band identification, each	-	-	122	162	188
-26		0.54	18.95	43	57	66
84202	Protoporphyrin, RBC; quantitative	-	-	60	76	90
84203	Protoporphyrin, RBC; screen	-	-	26	31	45
84206	Proinsulin	-	-	97	113	127
84207	Pyridoxal phosphate (Vitamin B-6)	-	-	118	141	164

● = New Code ⊗ = Conscious Sedation ✚ = Add-on Code ∅ = Modifier '51' Exempt ▲ =Revised Code

		Medicare RVU	National Fee	PFR Fee Information 50%	75%	90%
84210	Pyruvate	-	-	54	71	79
84220	Pyruvate kinase	-	-	50	59	69
84228	Quinine	-	-	54	69	90
84233	Receptor assay; estrogen	-	-	169	223	287
84234	Receptor assay; progesterone	-	-	172	209	267
84235	Receptor assay; endocrine, other than estrogen or progesterone (specify hormone)	-	-	169	245	286
84238	Receptor assay; non-endocrine (specify receptor)	-	-	162	201	245
84244	Renin	-	-	100	111	139
84252	Riboflavin (Vitamin B-2)	-	-	73	92	107
84255	Selenium	-	-	88	94	121
84260	Serotonin	-	-	148	183	254
84270	Sex hormone binding globulin (SHBG)	-	-	80	119	133
84275	Sialic acid	-	-	70	81	93
84285	Silica	-	-	108	126	148
84295	Sodium; serum	-	-	22	25	33
84300	Sodium; urine	-	-	23	31	47
84302	Sodium; other source	-	-	21	26	31
84305	Somatomedin	-	-	126	150	170
84307	Somatostatin	-	-	88	104	129
84311	Spectrophotometry, analyte not elsewhere specified	-	-	38	43	59
84315	Specific gravity (except urine)	-	-	14	16	17
84375	Sugars, chromatographic, TLC or paper chromatography	-	-	61	70	92
84376	Sugars (mono-, di-, and oligosaccharides); single qualitative, each specimen	-	-	22	26	30
84377	Sugars (mono-, di-, and oligosaccharides); multiple qualitative, each specimen	-	-	22	26	30
84378	Sugars (mono-, di-, and oligosaccharides); single quantitative, each specimen	-	-	46	50	61
84379	Sugars (mono-, di-, and oligosaccharides); multiple quantitative, each specimen	-	-	45	49	59
84392	Sulfate, urine	-	-	18	22	25
84402	Testosterone; free	-	-	128	156	196
84403	Testosterone; total	-	-	112	127	154
84425	Thiamine (Vitamin B-1)	-	-	101	126	147
84430	Thiocyanate	-	-	62	76	101
84432	Thyroglobulin	-	-	82	112	126
84436	Thyroxine; total	-	-	32	39	62
84437	Thyroxine; requiring elution (eg, neonatal)	-	-	36	40	44
84439	Thyroxine; free	-	-	55	82	102
84442	Thyroxine binding globulin (TBG)	-	-	61	82	106
84443	Thyroid stimulating hormone (TSH)	-	-	67	86	102
84445	Thyroid stimulating immune globulins (TSI)	-	-	223	260	290
84446	Tocopherol alpha (Vitamin E)	-	-	65	75	88
84449	Transcortin (cortisol binding globulin)	-	-	78	92	108

● = New Code ⊗ = Conscious Sedation ✚ = Add-on Code ∅ = Modifier '51' Exempt ▲ =Revised Code

		Medicare RVU	National Fee	PFR Fee Information 50%	75%	90%
84450	Transferase; aspartate amino (AST) (SGOT)	-	-	24	32	39
84460	Transferase; alanine amino (ALT) (SGPT)	-	-	24	30	43
84466	Transferrin	-	-	63	66	79
84478	Triglycerides	-	-	26	31	37
84479	Thyroid hormone (T3 or T4) uptake or thyroid hormone binding ratio (THBR)	-	-	30	47	53
84480	Triiodothyronine T3; total (TT-3)	-	-	69	84	103
84481	Triiodothyronine T3; free	-	-	98	115	170
84482	Triiodothyronine T3; reverse	-	-	107	137	178
84484	Troponin, quantitative	-	-	64	76	99
84485	Trypsin; duodenal fluid	-	-	36	42	47
84488	Trypsin; feces, qualitative	-	-	24	30	35
84490	Trypsin; feces, quantitative, 24-hour collection	-	-	23	30	38
84510	Tyrosine	-	-	47	56	66
84512	Troponin, qualitative	-	-	33	44	57
84520	Urea nitrogen; quantitative	-	-	23	27	32
84525	Urea nitrogen; semiquantitative (eg, reagent strip test)	-	-	17	21	26
84540	Urea nitrogen, urine	-	-	30	38	45
84545	Urea nitrogen, clearance	-	-	36	44	58
84550	Uric acid; blood	-	-	24	29	34
84560	Uric acid; other source	-	-	29	40	49
84577	Urobilinogen, feces, quantitative	-	-	50	61	73
84578	Urobilinogen, urine; qualitative	-	-	16	18	21
84580	Urobilinogen, urine; quantitative, timed specimen	-	-	31	40	48
84583	Urobilinogen, urine; semiquantitative	-	-	19	21	23
84585	Vanillylmandelic acid (VMA), urine	-	-	77	86	116
84586	Vasoactive intestinal peptide (VIP)	-	-	158	189	220
84588	Vasopressin (antidiuretic hormone, ADH)	-	-	140	166	190
84590	Vitamin A	-	-	74	93	118
84591	Vitamin, not otherwise specified	-	-	60	68	80
84597	Vitamin K	-	-	72	96	111
84600	Volatiles (eg, acetic anhydride, carbon tetrachloride, dichloroethane, dichloromethane, diethylether, isopropyl alcohol, methanol)	-	-	62	70	94
84620	Xylose absorption test, blood and/or urine	-	-	69	75	80
84630	Zinc	-	-	62	80	111
84681	C-peptide	-	-	98	114	143
84702	Gonadotropin, chorionic (hCG); quantitative	-	-	72	89	101
84703	Gonadotropin, chorionic (hCG); qualitative	-	-	41	53	69
84830	Ovulation tests, by visual color comparison methods for human luteinizing hormone	-	-	47	55	63
84999	Unlisted chemistry procedure	-	-	IR	IR	IR

		Medicare RVU	National Fee	PFR Fee Information 50%	75%	90%

Hematology and Coagulation

Code	Description	Medicare RVU	National Fee	50%	75%	90%
85002	Bleeding time	-	-	33	37	43
85004	Blood count; automated differential WBC count	-	-	26	33	40
85007	Blood count; blood smear, microscopic examination with manual differential WBC count	-	-	21	26	32
85008	Blood count; blood smear, microscopic examination without manual differential WBC count	-	-	13	20	25
85009	Blood count; manual differential WBC count, buffy coat	-	-	20	23	28
85013	Blood count; spun microhematocrit	-	-	16	18	23
85014	Blood count; hematocrit (Hct)	-	-	17	20	25
85018	Blood count; hemoglobin (Hgb)	-	-	17	20	25
85025	Blood count; complete (CBC), automated (Hgb, Hct, RBC, WBC and platelet count) and automated differential WBC count	-	-	33	43	50
85027	Blood count; complete (CBC), automated (Hgb, Hct, RBC, WBC and platelet count)	-	-	31	35	43
85032	Blood count; manual cell count (erythrocyte, leukocyte, or platelet) each	-	-	23	29	36
85041	Blood count; red blood cell (RBC), automated	-	-	16	17	19
85044	Blood count; reticulocyte, manual	-	-	25	29	36
85045	Blood count; reticulocyte, automated	-	-	24	28	36
85046	Blood count; reticulocytes, automated, including one or more cellular parameters (eg, reticulocyte hemoglobin content (CHr), immature reticulocyte fraction (IRF), reticulocyte volume (MRV), RNA content), direct measurement	-	-	22	26	34
85048	Blood count; leukocyte (WBC), automated	-	-	18	21	28
85049	Blood count; platelet, automated	-	-	23	28	33
85055	Reticulated platelet assay	-	-	IR	IR	IR
85060	Blood smear, peripheral, interpretation by physician with written report	0.64	22.36	61	66	73

(A4550 (Disposable Surgical Tray) can be coded in addition to 85095 in the office setting. Payment is at carrier discretion.)

Code	Description	Medicare RVU	National Fee	50%	75%	90%
85097	Bone marrow, smear interpretation	2.74	100.43	163	175	200

(A4550 (Disposable Surgical Tray) can be coded in addition to 85102 in the office setting. Payment is at carrier discretion.)

Code	Description	Medicare RVU	National Fee	50%	75%	90%
85130	Chromogenic substrate assay	-	-	48	59	67
85170	Clot retraction	-	-	19	25	36
85175	Clot lysis time, whole blood dilution	-	-	28	40	48
85210	Clotting; factor II, prothrombin, specific	-	-	55	67	83
85220	Clotting; factor V (AcG or proaccelerin), labile factor	-	-	106	127	145
85230	Clotting; factor VII (proconvertin, stable factor)	-	-	99	127	154
85240	Clotting; factor VIII (AHG), one stage	-	-	108	123	142
85244	Clotting; factor VIII related antigen	-	-	130	136	158
85245	Clotting; factor VIII, VW factor, ristocetin cofactor	-	-	94	114	130
85246	Clotting; factor VIII, VW factor antigen	-	-	107	127	148
85247	Clotting; factor VIII, von Willebrand factor, multimetric analysis	-	-	111	130	153
85250	Clotting; factor IX (PTC or Christmas)	-	-	106	141	163
85260	Clotting; factor X (Stuart-Prower)	-	-	94	109	135
85270	Clotting; factor XI (PTA)	-	-	96	112	139
85280	Clotting; factor XII (Hageman)	-	-	94	120	139

		Medicare RVU	National Fee	PFR Fee Information 50%	75%	90%
85290	Clotting; factor XIII (fibrin stabilizing)	-	-	97	110	124
85291	Clotting; factor XIII (fibrin stabilizing), screen solubility	-	-	49	68	77
85292	Clotting; prekallikrein assay (Fletcher factor assay)	-	-	94	111	131
85293	Clotting; high molecular weight kininogen assay (Fitzgerald factor assay)	-	-	94	111	131
85300	Clotting inhibitors or anticoagulants; antithrombin III, activity	-	-	91	110	143
85301	Clotting inhibitors or anticoagulants; antithrombin III, antigen assay	-	-	90	102	136
85302	Clotting inhibitors or anticoagulants; protein C, antigen	-	-	108	138	171
85303	Clotting inhibitors or anticoagulants; protein C, activity	-	-	104	128	157
85305	Clotting inhibitors or anticoagulants; protein S, total	-	-	118	141	164
85306	Clotting inhibitors or anticoagulants; protein S, free	-	-	113	136	161
85307	Activated Protein C (APC) resistance assay	-	-	100	119	133
85335	Factor inhibitor test	-	-	52	63	74
85337	Thrombomodulin	-	-	54	64	72
85345	Coagulation time; Lee and White	-	-	23	25	29
85347	Coagulation time; activated	-	-	20	24	28
85348	Coagulation time; other methods	-	-	26	32	36
85360	Euglobulin lysis	-	-	46	50	61
85362	Fibrin(ogen) degradation (split) products (FDP)(FSP); agglutination slide, semiquantitative	-	-	37	46	57
85366	Fibrin(ogen) degradation (split) products (FDP)(FSP); paracoagulation	-	-	44	52	60
85370	Fibrin(ogen) degradation (split) products (FDP)(FSP); quantitative	-	-	54	67	75
85378	Fibrin degradation products, D-dimer; qualitative or semiquantitative	-	-	43	50	66
85379	Fibrin degradation products, D-dimer; quantitative	-	-	52	64	78
85380	Fibrin degradation products, D-dimer; ultrasensitive (eg, for evaluation for venous thromboembolism), qualitative or semiquantitative	-	-	42	56	67
85384	Fibrinogen; activity	-	-	38	52	71
85385	Fibrinogen; antigen	-	-	43	49	56
85390	Fibrinolysins or coagulopathy screen, interpretation and report	-	-	40	50	61
-26		0.51	17.81	32	40	49
85396	Coagulation/fibrinolysis assay, whole blood (eg, viscoelastic clot assessment), including use of any pharmacologic additive(s), as indicated, including interpretation and written report, per day	0.54	18.95	60	69	78
85400	Fibrinolytic factors and inhibitors; plasmin	-	-	51	58	70
85410	Fibrinolytic factors and inhibitors; alpha-2 antiplasmin	-	-	51	59	73
85415	Fibrinolytic factors and inhibitors; plasminogen activator	-	-	64	76	91
85420	Fibrinolytic factors and inhibitors; plasminogen, except antigenic assay	-	-	53	66	85
85421	Fibrinolytic factors and inhibitors; plasminogen, antigenic assay	-	-	98	106	123
85441	Heinz bodies; direct	-	-	14	16	19
85445	Heinz bodies; induced, acetyl phenylhydrazine	-	-	27	34	42
85460	Hemoglobin or RBCs, fetal, for fetomaternal hemorrhage; differential lysis (Kleihauer-Betke)	-	-	41	47	56
85461	Hemoglobin or RBCs, fetal, for fetomaternal hemorrhage; rosette	-	-	43	48	56
85475	Hemolysin, acid	-	-	51	60	72
85520	Heparin assay	-	-	67	78	89

● = New Code ⊗ = Conscious Sedation ✚ = Add-on Code ∅ = Modifier '51' Exempt ▲ =Revised Code

		Medicare RVU	National Fee	PFR Fee Information 50%	75%	90%
85525	Heparin neutralization	-	-	61	70	79
85530	Heparin-protamine tolerance test	-	-	69	81	91
85536	Iron stain, peripheral blood	-	-	35	39	45
85540	Leukocyte alkaline phosphatase with count	-	-	45	57	65
85547	Mechanical fragility, RBC	-	-	38	50	60
85549	Muramidase	-	-	78	101	123
85555	Osmotic fragility, RBC; unincubated	-	-	41	49	63
85557	Osmotic fragility, RBC; incubated	-	-	83	90	106
85576	Platelet, aggregation (in vitro), each agent	-	-	78	105	139
-26		0.53	18.57	20	26	35
85597	Platelet neutralization	-	-	66	87	114
85610	Prothrombin time;	-	-	25	29	37
85611	Prothrombin time; substitution, plasma fractions, each	-	-	23	28	33
85612	Russell viper venom time (includes venom); undiluted	-	-	44	57	65
85613	Russell viper venom time (includes venom); diluted	-	-	53	70	83
85635	Reptilase test	-	-	38	48	56
85651	Sedimentation rate, erythrocyte; non-automated	-	-	22	26	28
85652	Sedimentation rate, erythrocyte; automated	-	-	22	27	31
85660	Sickling of RBC, reduction	-	-	27	34	44
85670	Thrombin time; plasma	-	-	33	45	52
85675	Thrombin time; titer	-	-	32	40	53
85705	Thromboplastin inhibition, tissue	-	-	62	73	87
85730	Thromboplastin time, partial (PTT); plasma or whole blood	-	-	31	37	46
85732	Thromboplastin time, partial (PTT); substitution, plasma fractions, each	-	-	35	42	54
85810	Viscosity	-	-	44	57	76
85999	Unlisted hematology and coagulation procedure	-	-	IR	IR	IR

Immunology

		Medicare RVU	National Fee	PFR Fee Information 50%	75%	90%
86000	Agglutinins, febrile (eg, Brucella, Francisella, Murine typhus, Q fever, Rocky Mountain spotted fever, scrub typhus), each antigen	-	-	48	63	76
86001	Allergen specific IgG quantitative or semiquantitative, each allergen	-	-	18	25	32

(Payment for code 86003 by Medicare is restricted to the presence of the following ICD-9-CM codes: 117.3, 691.8, 708.3, 989.5, 995.0, 995.60 - 995.69.)
(Code 86003 should be reimbursed based on the number of allergens per test)

86003	Allergen specific IgE; quantitative or semiquantitative, each allergen	-	-	26	34	46
86005	Allergen specific IgE; qualitative, multiallergen screen (dipstick, paddle or disk)	-	-	51	60	67
86021	Antibody identification; leukocyte antibodies	-	-	115	146	193
86022	Antibody identification; platelet antibodies	-	-	153	194	239
86023	Antibody identification; platelet associated immunoglobulin assay	-	-	92	105	128
86038	Antinuclear antibodies (ANA);	-	-	63	79	103
86039	Antinuclear antibodies (ANA); titer	-	-	61	74	91
86060	Antistreptolysin 0; titer	-	-	39	45	54

● = New Code ⊗ = Conscious Sedation ✚ = Add-on Code ∅ = Modifier '51' Exempt ▲ =Revised Code

		Medicare RVU	National Fee	PFR Fee Information 50%	75%	90%
86063	Antistreptolysin 0; screen	-	-	38	47	58
86077	Blood bank physician services; difficult cross match and/or evaluation of irregular antibody(s), interpretation and written report	1.36	48.13	115	164	214
86078	Blood bank physician services; investigation of transfusion reaction including suspicion of transmissible disease, interpretation and written report	1.41	50.02	128	148	201
86079	Blood bank physician services; authorization for deviation from standard blood banking procedures (eg, use of outdated blood, transfusion of Rh incompatible units), with written report	1.40	49.65	109	134	171
86140	C-reactive protein;	-	-	36	47	64
86141	C-reactive protein; high sensitivity (hsCRP)	-	-	52	62	71
86146	Beta 2 Glycoprotein I antibody, each	-	-	122	144	163
86147	Cardiolipin (phospholipid) antibody, each Ig class	-	-	116	130	150
86148	Anti-phosphatidylserine (phospholipid) antibody	-	-	81	91	103
86155	Chemotaxis assay, specify method	-	-	56	62	79
86156	Cold agglutinin; screen	-	-	35	40	51
86157	Cold agglutinin; titer	-	-	42	49	56
86160	Complement; antigen, each component	-	-	68	98	125
86161	Complement; functional activity, each component	-	-	62	87	107
86162	Complement; total hemolytic (CH50)	-	-	105	135	160
86171	Complement fixation tests, each antigen	-	-	62	83	99
86185	Counterimmunoelectrophoresis, each antigen	-	-	44	54	63
86200	Cyclic citrullinated peptide (CCP), antibody	-	-	43	60	78
86215	Deoxyribonuclease, antibody	-	-	67	81	103
86225	Deoxyribonucleic acid (DNA) antibody; native or double stranded	-	-	78	88	108
86226	Deoxyribonucleic acid (DNA) antibody; single stranded	-	-	74	86	122
86235	Extractable nuclear antigen, antibody to, any method (eg, nRNP, SS-A, SS-B, Sm, RNP, Sc170, J01), each antibody	-	-	83	110	131
86243	Fc receptor	-	-	92	110	129
86255	Fluorescent noninfectious agent antibody; screen, each antibody	-	-	68	85	122
-26		0.52	18.19	41	51	73
86256	Fluorescent noninfectious agent antibody; titer, each antibody	-	-	71	88	118
-26		0.52	18.19	43	53	71
86277	Growth hormone, human (HGH), antibody	-	-	71	86	100
86280	Hemagglutination inhibition test (HAI)	-	-	44	60	78
86294	Immunoassay for tumor antigen, qualitative or semiquantitative (eg, bladder tumor antigen)	-	-	71	81	90
86300	Immunoassay for tumor antigen, quantitative; CA 15-3 (27.29)	-	-	98	117	133
86301	Immunoassay for tumor antigen, quantitative; CA 19-9	-	-	95	113	128
86304	Immunoassay for tumor antigen, quantitative; CA 125	-	-	96	115	137
86308	Heterophile antibodies; screening	-	-	28	36	43
86309	Heterophile antibodies; titer	-	-	37	47	59
86310	Heterophile antibodies; titers after absorption with beef cells and guinea pig kidney	-	-	42	53	67
	(Payment for code 86316 by Medicare is restricted to the presence of the following ICD-9-CM codes: 183.0, 183.8, 184.8, 198.6.)					
86316	Immunoassay for tumor antigen, other antigen, quantitative (eg, CA 50, 72-4, 549), each	-	-	93	107	139

● = New Code ⊗ = Conscious Sedation ✚ = Add-on Code ∅ = Modifier '51' Exempt ▲ =Revised Code

		Medicare RVU	National Fee	PFR Fee Information 50%	75%	90%
86317	Immunoassay for infectious agent antibody, quantitative, not otherwise specified	-	-	55	85	139
86318	Immunoassay for infectious agent antibody, qualitative or semiquantitative, single step method (eg, reagent strip)	-	-	59	85	115
86320	Immunoelectrophoresis; serum	-	-	113	123	132
-26		0.52	18.19	62	68	73
86325	Immunoelectrophoresis; other fluids (eg, urine, cerebrospinal fluid) with concentration	-	-	90	139	158
-26		0.51	17.81	22	35	40
86327	Immunoelectrophoresis; crossed (2-dimensional assay)	-	-	88	102	124
-26		0.61	21.60	62	71	87
86329	Immunodiffusion; not elsewhere specified	-	-	69	80	115
86331	Immunodiffusion; gel diffusion, qualitative (Ouchterlony), each antigen or antibody	-	-	71	83	96
86332	Immune complex assay	-	-	98	137	168
86334	Immunofixation electrophoresis; serum	-	-	97	122	139
-26		0.52	18.19	58	73	83
86335	Immunofixation electrophoresis; other fluids with concentration (eg, urine, CSF)	-	-	101	132	165
-26		0.52	18.19	61	79	99
86336	Inhibin A	-	-	68	85	103
86337	Insulin antibodies	-	-	96	135	167
86340	Intrinsic factor antibodies	-	-	81	95	108
86341	Islet cell antibody	-	-	67	103	131
86343	Leukocyte histamine release test (LHR)	-	-	69	83	92
86344	Leukocyte phagocytosis	-	-	42	49	60
86353	Lymphocyte transformation, mitogen (phytomitogen) or antigen induced blastogenesis	-	-	187	215	254
86355	B cells, total count	-	-	83	116	150
86357	Natural killer (NK) cells, total count	-	-	83	116	150
86359	T cells; total count	-	-	119	159	212
86360	T cells; absolute CD4 and CD8 count, including ratio	-	-	174	204	243
86361	T cells; absolute CD4 count	-	-	120	146	163
86367	Stem cells (ie, CD34), total count	-	-	83	116	150
86376	Microsomal antibodies (eg, thyroid or liver-kidney), each	-	-	71	97	113
86378	Migration inhibitory factor test (MIF)	-	-	81	97	112
86382	Neutralization test, viral	-	-	81	93	108
86384	Nitroblue tetrazolium dye test (NTD)	-	-	58	71	84
86403	Particle agglutination; screen, each antibody	-	-	36	46	57
86406	Particle agglutination; titer, each antibody	-	-	37	46	55
86430	Rheumatoid factor; qualitative	-	-	33	40	50
86431	Rheumatoid factor; quantitative	-	-	40	45	55
86480	Tuberculosis test, cell mediated immunity measurement of gamma interferon antigen response	-	-	IR	IR	IR
86485	Skin test; candida	-	-	28	33	42
86490	Skin test; coccidioidomycosis	0.27	10.23	29	32	37

● = New Code ⊗ = Conscious Sedation ✚ = Add-on Code ∅ = Modifier '51' Exempt ▲ =Revised Code

		Medicare RVU	National Fee	PFR Fee Information 50%	75%	90%
86510	Skin test; histoplasmosis	0.30	11.37	27	30	38
86580	Skin test; tuberculosis, intradermal	0.25	9.47	23	24	29
86586	Unlisted antigen, each	-	-	38	54	71
86590	Streptokinase, antibody	-	-	33	38	48
86592	Syphilis test; qualitative (eg, VDRL, RPR, ART)	-	-	25	31	42
86593	Syphilis test; quantitative	-	-	26	37	43
86602	Antibody; actinomyces	-	-	51	68	76
86603	Antibody; adenovirus	-	-	65	88	103
86606	Antibody; Aspergillus	-	-	78	89	103
86609	Antibody; bacterium, not elsewhere specified	-	-	108	137	172
86611	Antibody; Bartonella	-	-	55	65	73
86612	Antibody; Blastomyces	-	-	67	78	89
86615	Antibody; Bordetella	-	-	76	88	101
86617	Antibody; Borrelia burgdorferi (Lyme disease) confirmatory test (eg, Western Blot or immunoblot)	-	-	99	120	141
86618	Antibody; Borrelia burgdorferi (Lyme disease)	-	-	103	116	136
86619	Antibody; Borrelia (relapsing fever)	-	-	62	81	102
86622	Antibody; Brucella	-	-	42	51	70
86625	Antibody; Campylobacter	-	-	84	101	122
86628	Antibody; Candida	-	-	84	104	122
86631	Antibody; Chlamydia	-	-	64	78	113
86632	Antibody; Chlamydia, IgM	-	-	66	74	90
86635	Antibody; Coccidioides	-	-	82	94	108
86638	Antibody; Coxiella burnetii (Q fever)	-	-	71	80	92
86641	Antibody; Cryptococcus	-	-	54	62	85
86644	Antibody; cytomegalovirus (CMV)	-	-	86	103	119
86645	Antibody; cytomegalovirus (CMV), IgM	-	-	87	101	118
86648	Antibody; Diphtheria	-	-	92	100	108
86651	Antibody; encephalitis, California (La Crosse)	-	-	68	77	89
86652	Antibody; encephalitis, Eastern equine	-	-	66	75	88
86653	Antibody; encephalitis, St. Louis	-	-	66	75	88
86654	Antibody; encephalitis, Western equine	-	-	66	75	88
86658	Antibody; enterovirus (eg, coxsackie, echo, polio)	-	-	81	98	113
86663	Antibody; Epstein-Barr (EB) virus, early antigen (EA)	-	-	82	119	153
86664	Antibody; Epstein-Barr (EB) virus, nuclear antigen (EBNA)	-	-	70	103	125
86665	Antibody; Epstein-Barr (EB) virus, viral capsid (VCA)	-	-	90	109	137
86666	Antibody; Ehrlichia	-	-	58	67	75
86668	Antibody; Francisella tularensis	-	-	51	57	72
86671	Antibody; fungus, not elsewhere specified	-	-	87	109	122
86674	Antibody; Giardia lamblia	-	-	72	83	105
86677	Antibody; Helicobacter pylori	-	-	104	119	132

● = New Code ⊗ = Conscious Sedation ✚ = Add-on Code ∅ = Modifier '51' Exempt ▲ =Revised Code

Code	Description	Medicare RVU	National Fee	PFR Fee Information 50%	75%	90%
86682	Antibody; helminth, not elsewhere specified	-	-	82	103	123
86684	Antibody; Haemophilus influenza	-	-	79	90	107
86687	Antibody; HTLV-I	-	-	72	80	116
86688	Antibody; HTLV-II	-	-	64	75	86
86689	Antibody; HTLV or HIV antibody, confirmatory test (eg, Western Blot)	-	-	110	130	176
86692	Antibody; hepatitis, delta agent	-	-	97	126	145
86694	Antibody; herpes simplex, non-specific type test	-	-	85	101	134
86695	Antibody; herpes simplex, type 1	-	-	73	97	140
86696	Antibody; herpes simplex, type 2	-	-	83	99	126
86698	Antibody; histoplasma	-	-	64	85	98
86701	Antibody; HIV-1	-	-	69	86	112
86702	Antibody; HIV-2	-	-	78	103	140
86703	Antibody; HIV-1 and HIV-2, single assay	-	-	68	81	89
86704	Hepatitis B core antibody (HBcAb); total	-	-	57	75	93
86705	Hepatitis B core antibody (HBcAb); IgM antibody	-	-	74	85	103
86706	Hepatitis B surface antibody (HBsAb)	-	-	58	67	78
86707	Hepatitis Be antibody (HBeAb)	-	-	62	79	90
86708	Hepatitis A antibody (HAAb); total	-	-	61	72	91
86709	Hepatitis A antibody (HAAb); IgM antibody	-	-	61	73	91
86710	Antibody; influenza virus	-	-	61	72	87
86713	Antibody; Legionella	-	-	80	92	107
86717	Antibody; Leishmania	-	-	62	72	85
86720	Antibody; Leptospira	-	-	69	78	89
86723	Antibody; Listeria monocytogenes	-	-	69	78	89
86727	Antibody; lymphocytic choriomeningitis	-	-	67	78	87
86729	Antibody; lymphogranuloma venereum	-	-	64	81	97
86732	Antibody; mucormycosis	-	-	69	78	89
86735	Antibody; mumps	-	-	73	95	130
86738	Antibody; mycoplasma	-	-	73	92	126
86741	Antibody; Neisseria meningitidis	-	-	67	76	90
86744	Antibody; Nocardia	-	-	67	76	90
86747	Antibody; parvovirus	-	-	97	110	118
86750	Antibody; Plasmodium (malaria)	-	-	67	76	88
86753	Antibody; protozoa, not elsewhere specified	-	-	70	83	95
86756	Antibody; respiratory syncytial virus	-	-	65	76	88
86757	Antibody; Rickettsia	-	-	88	105	120
86759	Antibody; rotavirus	-	-	72	84	97
86762	Antibody; rubella	-	-	48	59	72
86765	Antibody; rubeola	-	-	81	99	118
86768	Antibody; Salmonella	-	-	69	81	89

● = New Code ⊗ = Conscious Sedation ✚ = Add-on Code ∅ = Modifier '51' Exempt ▲ =Revised Code

		Medicare RVU	National Fee	PFR Fee Information 50%	75%	90%
86771	Antibody; Shigella	-	-	69	78	89
86774	Antibody; tetanus	-	-	81	103	128
86777	Antibody; Toxoplasma	-	-	69	88	121
86778	Antibody; Toxoplasma, IgM	-	-	88	99	111
86781	Antibody; Treponema pallidum, confirmatory test (eg, FTA-abs)	-	-	56	65	82
86784	Antibody; Trichinella	-	-	64	87	95
86787	Antibody; varicella-zoster	-	-	70	83	114
● 86788	Antibody; West Nile virus, IgM	-	-	IR	IR	IR
● 86789	Antibody; West Nile virus	-	-	IR	IR	IR
86790	Antibody; virus, not elsewhere specified	-	-	105	118	151
86793	Antibody; Yersinia	-	-	65	86	96
86800	Thyroglobulin antibody	-	-	73	95	106
86803	Hepatitis C antibody;	-	-	84	101	114
86804	Hepatitis C antibody; confirmatory test (eg, immunoblot)	-	-	119	134	153

Tissue Typing

86805	Lymphocytotoxicity assay, visual crossmatch; with titration	-	-	235	282	328
86806	Lymphocytotoxicity assay, visual crossmatch; without titration	-	-	172	185	223
86807	Serum screening for cytotoxic percent reactive antibody (PRA); standard method	-	-	126	147	168
86808	Serum screening for cytotoxic percent reactive antibody (PRA); quick method	-	-	111	133	152
86812	HLA typing; A, B, or C (eg, A10, B7, B27), single antigen	-	-	127	160	185
86813	HLA typing; A, B, or C, multiple antigens	-	-	190	220	259
86816	HLA typing; DR/DQ, single antigen	-	-	164	191	219
86817	HLA typing; DR/DQ, multiple antigens	-	-	386	449	534
86821	HLA typing; lymphocyte culture, mixed (MLC)	-	-	372	420	469
86822	HLA typing; lymphocyte culture, primed (PLC)	-	-	146	166	200
86849	Unlisted immunology procedure	-	-	IR	IR	IR

Transfusion Medicine

86850	Antibody screen, RBC, each serum technique	-	-	36	40	43
86860	Antibody elution (RBC), each elution	-	-	51	59	74
86870	Antibody identification, RBC antibodies, each panel for each serum technique	-	-	59	79	114
86880	Antihuman globulin test (Coombs test); direct, each antiserum	-	-	26	34	41
86885	Antihuman globulin test (Coombs test); indirect, qualitative, each antiserum	-	-	26	34	41
86886	Antihuman globulin test (Coombs test); indirect, titer, each antiserum	-	-	32	48	66
86890	Autologous blood or component, collection processing and storage; predeposited	-	-	140	163	187
86891	Autologous blood or component, collection processing and storage; intra- or postoperative salvage	-	-	162	220	287
86900	Blood typing; ABO	-	-	26	29	37
86901	Blood typing; Rh (D)	-	-	26	29	40
86903	Blood typing; antigen screening for compatible blood unit using reagent serum, per unit screened	-	-	31	37	44

● = New Code   ⊗ = Conscious Sedation   ✚ = Add-on Code   ∅ = Modifier '51' Exempt   ▲ = Revised Code

		Medicare RVU	National Fee	PFR Fee Information 50%	75%	90%
86904	Blood typing; antigen screening for compatible unit using patient serum, per unit screened	-	-	33	41	48
86905	Blood typing; RBC antigens, other than ABO or Rh (D), each	-	-	20	23	26
86906	Blood typing; Rh phenotyping, complete	-	-	27	36	48
86910	Blood typing, for paternity testing, per individual; ABO, Rh and MN	-	-	61	73	93
86911	Blood typing, for paternity testing, per individual; each additional antigen system	-	-	30	39	48
86920	Compatibility test each unit; immediate spin technique	-	-	49	62	78
86921	Compatibility test each unit; incubation technique	-	-	54	64	76
86922	Compatibility test each unit; antiglobulin technique	-	-	54	64	75
86923	Compatibility test each unit; electronic	-	-	29	41	52
86927	Fresh frozen plasma, thawing, each unit	-	-	27	33	40
86930	Frozen blood, each unit; freezing (includes preparation)	-	-	162	196	249
86931	Frozen blood, each unit; thawing	-	-	171	208	257
86932	Frozen blood, each unit; freezing (includes preparation) and thawing	-	-	190	230	290
86940	Hemolysins and agglutinins; auto, screen, each	-	-	34	44	50
86941	Hemolysins and agglutinins; incubated	-	-	46	51	59
86945	Irradiation of blood product, each unit	-	-	54	65	84
86950	Leukocyte transfusion	-	-	117	149	185
86960	Volume reduction of blood or blood product (eg, red blood cells or platelets), each unit	-	-	IR	IR	IR
86965	Pooling of platelets or other blood products	-	-	33	46	62
86970	Pretreatment of RBCs for use in RBC antibody detection, identification, and/or compatibility testing; incubation with chemical agents or drugs, each	-	-	45	61	85
86971	Pretreatment of RBCs for use in RBC antibody detection, identification, and/or compatibility testing; incubation with enzymes, each	-	-	29	39	52
86972	Pretreatment of RBCs for use in RBC antibody detection, identification, and/or compatibility testing; by density gradient separation	-	-	34	44	58
86975	Pretreatment of serum for use in RBC antibody identification; incubation with drugs, each	-	-	53	65	82
86976	Pretreatment of serum for use in RBC antibody identification; by dilution	-	-	61	81	96
86977	Pretreatment of serum for use in RBC antibody identification; incubation with inhibitors, each	-	-	56	68	86
86978	Pretreatment of serum for use in RBC antibody identification; by differential red cell absorption using patient RBCs or RBCs of known phenotype, each absorption	-	-	58	85	107
86985	Splitting of blood or blood products, each unit	-	-	40	50	71
86999	Unlisted transfusion medicine procedure	-	-	IR	IR	IR

Microbiology

		Medicare RVU	National Fee	50%	75%	90%
87001	Animal inoculation, small animal; with observation	-	-	51	61	71
87003	Animal inoculation, small animal; with observation and dissection	-	-	63	78	91
87015	Concentration (any type), for infectious agents	-	-	35	42	63
87040	Culture, bacterial; blood, aerobic, with isolation and presumptive identification of isolates (includes anaerobic culture, if appropriate)	-	-	53	62	86
87045	Culture, bacterial; stool, aerobic, with isolation and preliminary examination (eg, KIA, LIA), Salmonella and Shigella species	-	-	47	60	72
87046	Culture, bacterial; stool, aerobic, additional pathogens, isolation and presumptive identification of isolates, each plate	-	-	42	58	70
87070	Culture, bacterial; any other source except urine, blood or stool, aerobic, with isolation and presumptive identification of isolates	-	-	44	52	61

© PFR 2007

● = New Code ⊗ = Conscious Sedation ✚ = Add-on Code ∅ = Modifier '51' Exempt ▲ =Revised Code

		Medicare RVU	National Fee	PFR Fee Information 50%	75%	90%
87071	Culture, bacterial; quantitative, aerobic with isolation and presumptive identification of isolates, any source except urine, blood or stool	-	-	22	30	40
87073	Culture, bacterial; quantitative, anaerobic with isolation and presumptive identification of isolates, any source except urine, blood or stool	-	-	19	26	40
87075	Culture, bacterial; any source, except blood, anaerobic with isolation and presumptive identification of isolates	-	-	49	65	82
87076	Culture, bacterial; anaerobic isolate, additional methods required for definitive identification, each isolate	-	-	53	62	80
87077	Culture, bacterial; aerobic isolate, additional methods required for definitive identification, each isolate	-	-	44	53	60
87081	Culture, presumptive, pathogenic organisms, screening only;	-	-	34	48	56
87084	Culture, presumptive, pathogenic organisms, screening only; with colony estimation from density chart	-	-	31	35	40
	(See also HCPCS code P7001 for culture, bacterial, urine; quantitative, sensitivity study.)					
87086	Culture, bacterial; quantitative colony count, urine	-	-	39	49	56
▲ 87088	Culture, bacterial; with isolation and presumptive identification of each isolate, urine	-	-	37	43	52
87101	Culture, fungi (mold or yeast) isolation, with presumptive identification of isolates; skin, hair, or nail	-	-	37	49	59
87102	Culture, fungi (mold or yeast) isolation, with presumptive identification of isolates; other source (except blood)	-	-	45	54	66
87103	Culture, fungi (mold or yeast) isolation, with presumptive identification of isolates; blood	-	-	46	56	66
87106	Culture, fungi, definitive identification, each organism; yeast	-	-	42	53	85
87107	Culture, fungi, definitive identification, each organism; mold	-	-	43	51	60
87109	Culture, mycoplasma, any source	-	-	83	98	150
87110	Culture, chlamydia, any source	-	-	68	97	116
87116	Culture, tubercle or other acid-fast bacilli (eg, TB, AFB, mycobacteria) any source, with isolation and presumptive identification of isolates	-	-	56	69	85
87118	Culture, mycobacterial, definitive identification, each isolate	-	-	50	57	65
87140	Culture, typing; immunofluorescent method, each antiserum	-	-	28	36	47
87143	Culture, typing; gas liquid chromatography (GLC) or high pressure liquid chromatography (HPLC) method	-	-	59	69	77
87147	Culture, typing; immunologic method, other than immunofluoresence (eg, agglutination grouping), per antiserum	-	-	23	29	38
87149	Culture, typing; identification by nucleic acid probe	-	-	64	80	98
87152	Culture, typing; identification by pulse field gel typing	-	-	21	26	31
87158	Culture, typing; other methods	-	-	21	26	31
87164	Dark field examination, any source (eg, penile, vaginal, oral, skin); includes specimen collection	-	-	49	65	82
-26		0.50	17.43	39	52	66
87166	Dark field examination, any source (eg, penile, vaginal, oral, skin); without collection	-	-	45	53	64
87168	Macroscopic examination; arthropod	-	-	17	21	27
87169	Macroscopic examination; parasite	-	-	13	17	21
	(See also HCPCS code Q0113 for pinworm examination.)					
87172	Pinworm exam (eg, cellophane tape prep)	-	-	21	25	36
87176	Homogenization, tissue, for culture	-	-	30	34	41
87177	Ova and parasites, direct smears, concentration and identification	-	-	44	55	70
87181	Susceptibility studies, antimicrobial agent; agar dilution method, per agent (eg, antibiotic gradient strip)	-	-	25	31	43
87184	Susceptibility studies, antimicrobial agent; disk method, per plate (12 or fewer agents)	-	-	28	40	49
87185	Susceptibility studies, antimicrobial agent; enzyme detection (eg, beta lactamase), per enzyme	-	-	26	39	47

= New Code ⊗ = Conscious Sedation ✚ = Add-on Code ∅ = Modifier '51' Exempt ▲ =Revised Code

Code	Description	Medicare RVU	National Fee	PFR Fee Information 50%	75%	90%
87186	Susceptibility studies, antimicrobial agent; microdilution or agar dilution (minimum inhibitory concentration (MIC) or breakpoint), each multi-antimicrobial, per plate	-	-	35	44	55
✚ 87187	Susceptibility studies, antimicrobial agent; microdilution or agar dilution, minimum lethal concentration (MLC), each plate (List separately in addition to code for primary procedure)	-	-	38	45	55
87188	Susceptibility studies, antimicrobial agent; macrobroth dilution method, each agent	-	-	33	38	46
87190	Susceptibility studies, antimicrobial agent; mycobacteria, proportion method, each agent	-	-	25	32	36
87197	Serum bactericidal titer (Schlicter test)	-	-	54	70	82
87205	Smear, primary source with interpretation; Gram or Giemsa stain for bacteria, fungi, or cell types	-	-	25	28	32
87206	Smear, primary source with interpretation; fluorescent and/or acid fast stain for bacteria, fungi, parasites, viruses or cell types	-	-	37	47	61
87207	Smear, primary source with interpretation; special stain for inclusion bodies or parasites (eg, malaria, coccidia, microsporidia, trypanosomes, herpes viruses)	-	-	40	52	58
-26		0.53	18.57	26	34	38
87209	Smear, primary source with interpretation; complex special stain (eg, trichrome, iron hemotoxylin) for ova and parasites **(See also HCPCS code Q0111 for wet mount.)**	-	-	19	27	35
87210	Smear, primary source with interpretation; wet mount for infectious agents (eg, saline, India ink, KOH preps) **(See also HCPCS code Q0112 for potassium hydroxide (KOH) preparations.)**	-	-	23	27	30
87220	Tissue examination by KOH slide of samples from skin, hair, or nails for fungi or ectoparasite ova or mites (eg, scabies)	-	-	24	29	33
87230	Toxin or antitoxin assay, tissue culture (eg, Clostridium difficile toxin)	-	-	82	103	118
87250	Virus isolation; inoculation of embryonated eggs, or small animal, includes observation and dissection	-	-	85	109	132
87252	Virus isolation; tissue culture inoculation, observation, and presumptive identification by cytopathic effect	-	-	85	109	131
87253	Virus isolation; tissue culture, additional studies or definitive identification (eg, hemabsorption, neutralization, immunofluoresence stain), each isolate	-	-	81	91	101
87254	Virus isolation; centrifuge enhanced (shell vial) technique, includes identification with immunofluorescence stain, each virus	-	-	74	101	127
87255	Virus isolation; including identification by non-immunologic method, other than by cytopathic effect (eg, virus specific enzymatic activity)	-	-	87	111	137
87260	Infectious agent antigen detection by immunofluorescent technique; adenovirus	-	-	50	62	70
87265	Infectious agent antigen detection by immunofluorescent technique; Bordetella pertussis/parapertussis	-	-	50	62	72
87267	Infectious agent antigen detection by immunofluorescent technique; Enterovirus, direct fluorescent antibody (DFA)	-	-	45	61	76
87269	Infectious agent antigen detection by immunofluorescent technique; giardia	-	-	43	54	63
87270	Infectious agent antigen detection by immunofluorescent technique; Chlamydia trachomatis	-	-	54	63	72
87271	Infectious agent antigen detection by immunofluorescent technique; Cytomegalovirus, direct fluorescent antibody (DFA)	-	-	44	57	69
87272	Infectious agent antigen detection by immunofluorescent technique; cryptosporidium	-	-	54	66	75
87273	Infectious agent antigen detection by immunofluorescent technique; Herpes simplex virus type 2	-	-	50	62	70
87274	Infectious agent antigen detection by immunofluorescent technique; Herpes simplex virus type 1	-	-	51	61	72
87275	Infectious agent antigen detection by immunofluorescent technique; influenza B virus	-	-	50	60	70
87276	Infectious agent antigen detection by immunofluorescent technique; influenza A virus	-	-	50	60	70
87277	Infectious agent antigen detection by immunofluorescent technique; Legionella micdadei	-	-	50	60	70
87278	Infectious agent antigen detection by immunofluorescent technique; Legionella pneumophila	-	-	50	60	70
87279	Infectious agent antigen detection by immunofluorescent technique; Parainfluenza virus, each type	-	-	50	60	70
87280	Infectious agent antigen detection by immunofluorescent technique; respiratory syncytial virus	-	-	50	60	70

● = New Code ⊗ = Conscious Sedation ✚ = Add-on Code ∅ = Modifier '51' Exempt ▲ =Revised Code

Code	Description	Medicare RVU	National Fee	PFR Fee Information 50%	75%	90%
87281	Infectious agent antigen detection by immunofluorescent technique; Pneumocystis carinii	-	-	50	60	70
87283	Infectious agent antigen detection by immunofluorescent technique; Rubeola	-	-	50	60	70
87285	Infectious agent antigen detection by immunofluorescent technique; Treponema pallidum	-	-	52	63	74
87290	Infectious agent antigen detection by immunofluorescent technique; Varicella zoster virus	-	-	50	63	73
87299	Infectious agent antigen detection by immunofluorescent technique; not otherwise specified, each organism	-	-	50	62	72
87300	Infectious agent antigen detection by immunofluorescent technique, polyvalent for multiple organisms, each polyvalent antiserum	-	-	24	28	36
87301	Infectious agent antigen detection by enzyme immunoassay technique, qualitative or semiquantitative, multiple-step method; adenovirus enteric types 40/41	-	-	49	59	69
● 87305	Infectious agent antigen detection by enzyme immunoassay technique, qualitative or semiquantitative, multiple-step method; Aspergillus	-	-	IR	IR	IR
87320	Infectious agent antigen detection by enzyme immunoassay technique, qualitative or semiquantitative, multiple-step method; Chlamydia trachomatis	-	-	48	58	68
87324	Infectious agent antigen detection by enzyme immunoassay technique, qualitative or semiquantitative, multiple-step method; Clostridium difficile toxin(s)	-	-	57	72	89
87327	Infectious agent antigen detection by enzyme immunoassay technique, qualitative or semiquantitative, multiple-step method; Cryptococcus neoformans	-	-	49	59	69
87328	Infectious agent antigen detection by enzyme immunoassay technique, qualitative or semiquantitative, multiple-step method; cryptosporidium	-	-	53	63	72
87329	Infectious agent antigen detection by enzyme immunoassay technique, qualitative or semiquantitative, multiple-step method; giardia	-	-	33	43	52
87332	Infectious agent antigen detection by enzyme immunoassay technique, qualitative or semiquantitative, multiple-step method; cytomegalovirus	-	-	51	61	71
87335	Infectious agent antigen detection by enzyme immunoassay technique, qualitative or semiquantitative, multiple-step method; Escherichia coli 0157	-	-	50	60	70
87336	Infectious agent antigen detection by enzyme immunoassay technique, qualitative or semiquantitative, multiple-step method; Entamoeba histolytica dispar group	-	-	50	60	70
87337	Infectious agent antigen detection by enzyme immunoassay technique, qualitative or semiquantitative, multiple-step method; Entamoeba histolytica group	-	-	50	60	70
87338	Infectious agent antigen detection by enzyme immunoassay technique, qualitative or semiquantitative, multiple-step method; Helicobacter pylori, stool	-	-	IR	IR	IR
87339	Infectious agent antigen detection by enzyme immunoassay technique, qualitative or semiquantitative, multiple-step method; Helicobacter pylori	-	-	47	57	66
87340	Infectious agent antigen detection by enzyme immunoassay technique, qualitative or semiquantitative, multiple-step method; hepatitis B surface antigen (HBsAg)	-	-	41	58	67
87341	Infectious agent antigen detection by enzyme immunoassay technique, qualitative or semiquantitative, multiple-step method; hepatitis B surface antigen (HBsAg) neutralization	-	-	39	56	64
87350	Infectious agent antigen detection by enzyme immunoassay technique, qualitative or semiquantitative, multiple-step method; hepatitis Be antigen (HBeAg)	-	-	46	59	81
87380	Infectious agent antigen detection by enzyme immunoassay technique, qualitative or semiquantitative, multiple-step method; hepatitis, delta agent	-	-	59	69	75
87385	Infectious agent antigen detection by enzyme immunoassay technique, qualitative or semiquantitative, multiple-step method; Histoplasma capsulatum	-	-	46	57	65
87390	Infectious agent antigen detection by enzyme immunoassay technique, qualitative or semiquantitative, multiple-step method; HIV-1	-	-	68	83	95
87391	Infectious agent antigen detection by enzyme immunoassay technique, qualitative or semiquantitative, multiple-step method; HIV-2	-	-	67	82	94
87400	Infectious agent antigen detection by enzyme immunoassay technique, qualitative or semiquantitative, multiple-step method; Influenza, A or B, each	-	-	26	36	43
87420	Infectious agent antigen detection by enzyme immunoassay technique, qualitative or semiquantitative, multiple-step method; respiratory syncytial virus	-	-	48	59	70
87425	Infectious agent antigen detection by enzyme immunoassay technique, qualitative or semiquantitative, multiple-step method; rotavirus	-	-	48	59	69
87427	Infectious agent antigen detection by enzyme immunoassay technique, qualitative or semiquantitative, multiple-step method; Shiga-like toxin	-	-	48	58	67
87430	Infectious agent antigen detection by enzyme immunoassay technique, qualitative or semiquantitative, multiple-step method; Streptococcus, group A	-	-	45	55	63
87449	Infectious agent antigen detection by enzyme immunoassay technique qualitative or semiquantitative; multiple step method, not otherwise specified, each organism	-	-	57	69	86
87450	Infectious agent antigen detection by enzyme immunoassay technique qualitative or semiquantitative; single step method, not otherwise specified, each organism	-	-	38	45	56

© PFR 2007

● = New Code ⊗ = Conscious Sedation ✚ = Add-on Code ∅ = Modifier '51' Exempt ▲ =Revised Code

		Medicare RVU	National Fee	PFR Fee Information 50%	75%	90%
87451	Infectious agent antigen detection by enzyme immunoassay technique qualitative or semiquantitative; multiple step method, polyvalent for multiple organisms, each polyvalent antiserum	-	-	37	44	52
87470	Infectious agent detection by nucleic acid (DNA or RNA); Bartonella henselae and Bartonella quintana, direct probe technique	-	-	69	86	105
87471	Infectious agent detection by nucleic acid (DNA or RNA); Bartonella henselae and Bartonella quintana, amplified probe technique	-	-	121	143	166
87472	Infectious agent detection by nucleic acid (DNA or RNA); Bartonella henselae and Bartonella quintana, quantification	-	-	147	161	193
87475	Infectious agent detection by nucleic acid (DNA or RNA); Borrelia burgdorferi, direct probe technique	-	-	69	80	98
87476	Infectious agent detection by nucleic acid (DNA or RNA); Borrelia burgdorferi, amplified probe technique	-	-	106	140	167
87477	Infectious agent detection by nucleic acid (DNA or RNA); Borrelia burgdorferi, quantification	-	-	139	176	206
87480	Infectious agent detection by nucleic acid (DNA or RNA); Candida species, direct probe technique	-	-	68	78	96
87481	Infectious agent detection by nucleic acid (DNA or RNA); Candida species, amplified probe technique	-	-	109	141	170
87482	Infectious agent detection by nucleic acid (DNA or RNA); Candida species, quantification	-	-	155	172	208
87485	Infectious agent detection by nucleic acid (DNA or RNA); Chlamydia pneumoniae, direct probe technique	-	-	71	81	100
87486	Infectious agent detection by nucleic acid (DNA or RNA); Chlamydia pneumoniae, amplified probe technique	-	-	121	133	159
87487	Infectious agent detection by nucleic acid (DNA or RNA); Chlamydia pneumoniae, quantification	-	-	144	165	198
87490	Infectious agent detection by nucleic acid (DNA or RNA); Chlamydia trachomatis, direct probe technique	-	-	67	77	91
87491	Infectious agent detection by nucleic acid (DNA or RNA); Chlamydia trachomatis, amplified probe technique	-	-	110	132	158
87492	Infectious agent detection by nucleic acid (DNA or RNA); Chlamydia trachomatis, quantification	-	-	114	143	170
87495	Infectious agent detection by nucleic acid (DNA or RNA); cytomegalovirus, direct probe technique	-	-	66	87	107
87496	Infectious agent detection by nucleic acid (DNA or RNA); cytomegalovirus, amplified probe technique	-	-	116	128	153
87497	Infectious agent detection by nucleic acid (DNA or RNA); cytomegalovirus, quantification	-	-	148	163	196
● 87498	Infectious agent detection by nucleic acid (DNA or RNA); enterovirus, amplified probe technique	-	-	IR	IR	IR
87510	Infectious agent detection by nucleic acid (DNA or RNA); Gardnerella vaginalis, direct probe technique	-	-	70	87	103
87511	Infectious agent detection by nucleic acid (DNA or RNA); Gardnerella vaginalis, amplified probe technique	-	-	116	125	150
87512	Infectious agent detection by nucleic acid (DNA or RNA); Gardnerella vaginalis, quantification	-	-	139	164	198
87515	Infectious agent detection by nucleic acid (DNA or RNA); hepatitis B virus, direct probe technique	-	-	64	82	101
87516	Infectious agent detection by nucleic acid (DNA or RNA); hepatitis B virus, amplified probe technique	-	-	118	149	178
87517	Infectious agent detection by nucleic acid (DNA or RNA); hepatitis B virus, quantification	-	-	141	187	225
87520	Infectious agent detection by nucleic acid (DNA or RNA); hepatitis C, direct probe technique	-	-	66	85	103
87521	Infectious agent detection by nucleic acid (DNA or RNA); hepatitis C, amplified probe technique	-	-	126	146	176
87522	Infectious agent detection by nucleic acid (DNA or RNA); hepatitis C, quantification	-	-	170	233	278
87525	Infectious agent detection by nucleic acid (DNA or RNA); hepatitis G, direct probe technique	-	-	69	86	105
87526	Infectious agent detection by nucleic acid (DNA or RNA); hepatitis G, amplified probe technique	-	-	108	142	171
87527	Infectious agent detection by nucleic acid (DNA or RNA); hepatitis G, quantification	-	-	140	182	220
87528	Infectious agent detection by nucleic acid (DNA or RNA); Herpes simplex virus, direct probe technique	-	-	64	98	118

● = New Code ⊗ = Conscious Sedation ✚ = Add-on Code ∅ = Modifier '51' Exempt ▲ =Revised Code

		Medicare RVU	National Fee	PFR Fee Information 50%	75%	90%
87529	Infectious agent detection by nucleic acid (DNA or RNA); Herpes simplex virus, amplified probe technique	-	-	113	142	169
87530	Infectious agent detection by nucleic acid (DNA or RNA); Herpes simplex virus, quantification	-	-	152	172	208
87531	Infectious agent detection by nucleic acid (DNA or RNA); Herpes virus-6, direct probe technique	-	-	68	88	106
87532	Infectious agent detection by nucleic acid (DNA or RNA); Herpes virus-6, amplified probe technique	-	-	120	145	172
87533	Infectious agent detection by nucleic acid (DNA or RNA); Herpes virus-6, quantification	-	-	140	179	214
87534	Infectious agent detection by nucleic acid (DNA or RNA); HIV-1, direct probe technique	-	-	63	90	110
87535	Infectious agent detection by nucleic acid (DNA or RNA); HIV-1, amplified probe technique	-	-	109	138	164
87536	Infectious agent detection by nucleic acid (DNA or RNA); HIV-1, quantification	-	-	213	254	323
87537	Infectious agent detection by nucleic acid (DNA or RNA); HIV-2, direct probe technique	-	-	63	94	124
87538	Infectious agent detection by nucleic acid (DNA or RNA); HIV-2, amplified probe technique	-	-	114	148	172
87539	Infectious agent detection by nucleic acid (DNA or RNA); HIV-2, quantification	-	-	158	176	212
87540	Infectious agent detection by nucleic acid (DNA or RNA); Legionella pneumophila, direct probe technique	-	-	67	85	102
87541	Infectious agent detection by nucleic acid (DNA or RNA); Legionella pneumophila, amplified probe technique	-	-	113	136	163
87542	Infectious agent detection by nucleic acid (DNA or RNA); Legionella pneumophila, quantification	-	-	144	174	208
87550	Infectious agent detection by nucleic acid (DNA or RNA); Mycobacteria species, direct probe technique	-	-	69	86	105
87551	Infectious agent detection by nucleic acid (DNA or RNA); Mycobacteria species, amplified probe technique	-	-	114	138	164
87552	Infectious agent detection by nucleic acid (DNA or RNA); Mycobacteria species, quantification	-	-	138	184	220
87555	Infectious agent detection by nucleic acid (DNA or RNA); Mycobacteria tuberculosis, direct probe technique	-	-	66	80	99
87556	Infectious agent detection by nucleic acid (DNA or RNA); Mycobacteria tuberculosis, amplified probe technique	-	-	115	138	166
87557	Infectious agent detection by nucleic acid (DNA or RNA); Mycobacteria tuberculosis, quantification	-	-	155	176	212
87560	Infectious agent detection by nucleic acid (DNA or RNA); Mycobacteria avium-intracellulare, direct probe technique	-	-	65	85	104
87561	Infectious agent detection by nucleic acid (DNA or RNA); Mycobacteria avium-intracellulare, amplified probe technique	-	-	123	136	162
87562	Infectious agent detection by nucleic acid (DNA or RNA); Mycobacteria avium-intracellulare, quantification	-	-	156	180	214
87580	Infectious agent detection by nucleic acid (DNA or RNA); Mycoplasma pneumoniae, direct probe technique	-	-	64	84	98
87581	Infectious agent detection by nucleic acid (DNA or RNA); Mycoplasma pneumoniae, amplified probe technique	-	-	112	139	161
87582	Infectious agent detection by nucleic acid (DNA or RNA); Mycoplasma pneumoniae, quantification	-	-	129	170	204
87590	Infectious agent detection by nucleic acid (DNA or RNA); Neisseria gonorrhoeae, direct probe technique	-	-	68	92	126
87591	Infectious agent detection by nucleic acid (DNA or RNA); Neisseria gonorrhoeae, amplified probe technique	-	-	109	138	164
87592	Infectious agent detection by nucleic acid (DNA or RNA); Neisseria gonorrhoeae, quantification	-	-	148	174	210
87620	Infectious agent detection by nucleic acid (DNA or RNA); papillomavirus, human, direct probe technique	-	-	69	85	103
87621	Infectious agent detection by nucleic acid (DNA or RNA); papillomavirus, human, amplified probe technique	-	-	114	138	164
87622	Infectious agent detection by nucleic acid (DNA or RNA); papillomavirus, human, quantification	-	-	147	170	204
● 87640	Infectious agent detection by nucleic acid (DNA or RNA); Staphylococcus aureus, amplified probe technique	-	-	IR	IR	IR
● 87641	Infectious agent detection by nucleic acid (DNA or RNA); Staphylococcus aureus, methicillin resistant, amplified probe technique	-	-	IR	IR	IR

● = New Code ⊗ = Conscious Sedation ✚ = Add-on Code ∅ = Modifier '51' Exempt ▲ =Revised Code

		Medicare RVU	National Fee	PFR Fee Information 50%	75%	90%
87650	Infectious agent detection by nucleic acid (DNA or RNA); Streptococcus, group A, direct probe technique	-	-	69	84	98
87651	Infectious agent detection by nucleic acid (DNA or RNA); Streptococcus, group A, amplified probe technique	-	-	114	140	164
87652	Infectious agent detection by nucleic acid (DNA or RNA); Streptococcus, group A, quantification	-	-	147	167	198
● 87653	Infectious agent detection by nucleic acid (DNA or RNA); Streptococcus, group B, amplified probe technique	-	-	IR	IR	IR
87660	Infectious agent detection by nucleic acid (DNA or RNA); Trichomonas vaginalis, direct probe technique	-	-	53	67	80
87797	Infectious agent detection by nucleic acid (DNA or RNA), not otherwise specified; direct probe technique, each organism	-	-	66	85	99
87798	Infectious agent detection by nucleic acid (DNA or RNA), not otherwise specified; amplified probe technique, each organism	-	-	114	137	164
87799	Infectious agent detection by nucleic acid (DNA or RNA), not otherwise specified; quantification, each organism	-	-	148	181	218
87800	Infectious agent detection by nucleic acid (DNA or RNA), multiple organisms; direct probe(s) technique	-	-	126	144	178
87801	Infectious agent detection by nucleic acid (DNA or RNA), multiple organisms; amplified probe(s) technique	-	-	128	154	184
87802	Infectious agent antigen detection by immunoassay with direct optical observation; Streptococcus, group B	-	-	41	50	60
87803	Infectious agent antigen detection by immunoassay with direct optical observation; Clostridium difficile toxin A	-	-	41	50	59
87804	Infectious agent antigen detection by immunoassay with direct optical observation; Influenza	-	-	41	50	59
	(Medicare fees for the code below are based on Non Facility RVUs. PFR information reflects fee when procedure is performed in a facility.)					
87807	Infectious agent antigen detection by immunoassay with direct optical observation; respiratory syncytial virus	-	-	40	52	63
● 87808	Infectious agent antigen detection by immunoassay with direct optical observation; Trichomonas vaginalis	-	-	IR	IR	IR
87810	Infectious agent detection by immunoassay with direct optical observation; Chlamydia trachomatis	-	-	46	59	65
87850	Infectious agent detection by immunoassay with direct optical observation; Neisseria gonorrhoeae	-	-	47	57	68
87880	Infectious agent detection by immunoassay with direct optical observation; Streptococcus, group A	-	-	42	51	59
87899	Infectious agent detection by immunoassay with direct optical observation; not otherwise specified	-	-	44	49	57
87900	Infectious agent drug susceptibility phenotype prediction using regularly updated genotypic bioinformatics	-	-	IR	IR	IR
87901	Infectious agent genotype analysis by nucleic acid (DNA or RNA); HIV 1, reverse transcriptase and protease	-	-	557	670	794
87902	Infectious agent genotype analysis by nucleic acid (DNA or RNA); Hepatitis C virus	-	-	533	766	922
87903	Infectious agent phenotype analysis by nucleic acid (DNA or RNA) with drug resistance tissue culture analysis, HIV 1; first through 10 drugs tested	-	-	1024	1195	1365
+ 87904	Infectious agent phenotype analysis by nucleic acid (DNA or RNA) with drug resistance tissue culture analysis, HIV 1; each additional drug tested (List separately in addition to code for primary procedure)	-	-	112	142	173
87999	Unlisted microbiology procedure	-	-	IR	IR	IR

Anatomic Pathology

Postmortem Examination

88000	Necropsy (autopsy), gross examination only; without CNS	-	-	730	973	1125
88005	Necropsy (autopsy), gross examination only; with brain	-	-	895	1170	1242
88007	Necropsy (autopsy), gross examination only; with brain and spinal cord	-	-	1025	1335	1461
88012	Necropsy (autopsy), gross examination only; infant with brain	-	-	844	1080	1159
88014	Necropsy (autopsy), gross examination only; stillborn or newborn with brain	-	-	780	1059	1149
88016	Necropsy (autopsy), gross examination only; macerated stillborn	-	-	730	973	1125
88020	Necropsy (autopsy), gross and microscopic; without CNS	-	-	1022	1323	1450

● = New Code ⊗ = Conscious Sedation ✚ = Add-on Code ∅ = Modifier '51' Exempt ▲ =Revised Code

		Medicare RVU	National Fee	PFR Fee Information 50%	75%	90%
88025	Necropsy (autopsy), gross and microscopic; with brain	-	-	1166	1551	1672
88027	Necropsy (autopsy), gross and microscopic; with brain and spinal cord	-	-	1242	1565	1843
88028	Necropsy (autopsy), gross and microscopic; infant with brain	-	-	1002	1243	1435
88029	Necropsy (autopsy), gross and microscopic; stillborn or newborn with brain	-	-	973	1209	1393
88036	Necropsy (autopsy), limited, gross and/or microscopic; regional	-	-	815	1026	1210
88037	Necropsy (autopsy), limited, gross and/or microscopic; single organ	-	-	612	763	911
88040	Necropsy (autopsy); forensic examination	-	-	2347	3125	3682
88045	Necropsy (autopsy); coroner's call	-	-	132	147	162
88099	Unlisted necropsy (autopsy) procedure	-	-	IR	IR	IR

Cytopathology

		Medicare RVU	National Fee	PFR Fee Information 50%	75%	90%
88104	Cytopathology, fluids, washings or brushings, except cervical or vaginal; smears with interpretation	1.53	55.71	106	127	147
-26		0.80	28.04	64	76	88
▲ 88106	Cytopathology, fluids, washings or brushings, except cervical or vaginal; simple filter method with interpretation	1.99	73.14	87	109	144
-26		0.80	28.04	39	49	65
▲ 88107	Cytopathology, fluids, washings or brushings, except cervical or vaginal; smears and simple filter preparation with interpretation	2.47	90.58	116	145	165
-26		1.10	38.66	64	80	91
88108	Cytopathology, concentration technique, smears and interpretation (eg, Saccomanno technique)	1.87	68.59	116	139	164
-26		0.80	28.04	58	70	82
88112	Cytopathology, selective cellular enhancement technique with interpretation (eg, liquid based slide preparation method), except cervical or vaginal	3.07	111.80	284	368	441
-26		1.66	58.36	156	202	243
88125	Cytopathology, forensic (eg, sperm)	0.55	19.71	89	114	140
-26		0.37	12.89	71	91	112
88130	Sex chromatin identification; Barr bodies	-	-	57	71	86
88140	Sex chromatin identification; peripheral blood smear, polymorphonuclear drumsticks	-	-	43	51	65
88141	Cytopathology, cervical or vaginal (any reporting system), requiring interpretation by physician	0.65	23.12	47	58	68
88142	Cytopathology, cervical or vaginal (any reporting system), collected in preservative fluid, automated thin layer preparation; manual screening under physician supervision	-	-	59	69	93
88143	Cytopathology, cervical or vaginal (any reporting system), collected in preservative fluid, automated thin layer preparation; with manual screening and rescreening under physician supervision	-	-	76	87	98
88147	Cytopathology smears, cervical or vaginal; screening by automated system under physician supervision	-	-	70	84	112
88148	Cytopathology smears, cervical or vaginal; screening by automated system with manual rescreening under physician supervision	-	-	90	116	135

(For 88150-88154, Medicare requires the following ICD-9-CM codes: V01.6, V02.7, V02.8, V10.40-.44, 042, 078.10-.19, 079.4, 099.53, 179-184.9, 218.0-221.9, 233.1-.3, 236.0-.2, 614.0-616.9, 621.4, 622.1-.2, 623.0-.1, 623.5, 626.0-627.1, 795.0.)

		Medicare RVU	National Fee	PFR Fee Information 50%	75%	90%
88150	Cytopathology, slides, cervical or vaginal; manual screening under physician supervision	-	-	35	40	50
88152	Cytopathology, slides, cervical or vaginal; with manual screening and computer-assisted rescreening under physician supervision	-	-	52	63	79
88153	Cytopathology, slides, cervical or vaginal; with manual screening and rescreening under physician supervision	-	-	75	86	112
88154	Cytopathology, slides, cervical or vaginal; with manual screening and computer-assisted rescreening using cell selection and review under physician supervision	-	-	70	109	138
✚ 88155	Cytopathology, slides, cervical or vaginal, definitive hormonal evaluation (eg, maturation index, karyopyknotic index, estrogenic index) (List separately in addition to code(s) for other technical and interpretation services)	-	-	37	45	60

● = New Code ⊗ = Conscious Sedation ✚ = Add-on Code ∅ = Modifier '51' Exempt ▲ =Revised Code

		Medicare RVU	National Fee	PFR Fee Information 50%	75%	90%
88160	Cytopathology, smears, any other source; screening and interpretation	1.39	50.78	75	87	104
-26		0.71	25.01	41	48	57
88161	Cytopathology, smears, any other source; preparation, screening and interpretation	1.53	56.09	90	108	126
-26		0.72	25.39	50	59	69
88162	Cytopathology, smears, any other source; extended study involving over 5 slides and/or multiple stains	1.86	67.46	142	177	198
-26		1.08	37.90	92	115	129
88164	Cytopathology, slides, cervical or vaginal (the Bethesda System); manual screening under physician supervision	-	-	38	49	62
88165	Cytopathology, slides, cervical or vaginal (the Bethesda System); with manual screening and rescreening under physician supervision	-	-	66	76	85
88166	Cytopathology, slides, cervical or vaginal (the Bethesda System); with manual screening and computer-assisted rescreening under physician supervision	-	-	43	50	62
88167	Cytopathology, slides, cervical or vaginal (the Bethesda System); with manual screening and computer-assisted rescreening using cell selection and review under physician supervision	-	-	84	94	106
88172	Cytopathology, evaluation of fine needle aspirate; immediate cytohistologic study to determine adequacy of specimen(s)	1.40	50.78	160	192	240
-26		0.86	30.32	104	125	156
88173	Cytopathology, evaluation of fine needle aspirate; interpretation and report	3.64	132.64	193	226	248
-26		1.98	69.73	116	136	149
88174	Cytopathology, cervical or vaginal (any reporting system), collected in preservative fluid, automated thin layer preparation; screening by automated system, under physician supervision	-	-	71	88	103
88175	Cytopathology, cervical or vaginal (any reporting system), collected in preservative fluid, automated thin layer preparation; with screening by automated system and manual rescreening or review, under physician supervision	-	-	73	99	116
88182	Flow cytometry, cell cycle or DNA analysis	2.81	103.46	250	344	449
-26		1.08	37.90	113	155	202
88184	Flow cytometry, cell surface, cytoplasmic, or nuclear marker, technical component only; first marker	1.62	61.39	120	149	186
+ 88185	Flow cytometry, cell surface, cytoplasmic, or nuclear marker, technical component only; each additional marker (List separately in addition to code for first marker)	0.87	32.97	62	76	96
88187	Flow cytometry, interpretation; 2 to 8 markers	1.81	63.29	162	204	251
88188	Flow cytometry, interpretation; 9 to 15 markers	2.24	78.45	201	251	311
88189	Flow cytometry, interpretation; 16 or more markers	2.92	102.32	264	331	409
88199	Unlisted cytopathology procedure	-	-	IR	IR	IR
-26		-	-	IR	IR	IR

Cytogenetic Studies

88230	Tissue culture for non-neoplastic disorders; lymphocyte	-	-	367	402	515
88233	Tissue culture for non-neoplastic disorders; skin or other solid tissue biopsy	-	-	411	477	548
88235	Tissue culture for non-neoplastic disorders; amniotic fluid or chorionic villus cells	-	-	447	507	627
88237	Tissue culture for neoplastic disorders; bone marrow, blood cells	-	-	379	459	555
88239	Tissue culture for neoplastic disorders; solid tumor	-	-	444	528	618
88240	Cryopreservation, freezing and storage of cells, each cell line	-	-	112	132	145
88241	Thawing and expansion of frozen cells, each aliquot	-	-	122	143	155
88245	Chromosome analysis for breakage syndromes; baseline Sister Chromatid Exchange (SCE), 20-25 cells	-	-	439	500	586
88248	Chromosome analysis for breakage syndromes; baseline breakage, score 50-100 cells, count 20 cells, 2 karyotypes (eg, for ataxia telangiectasia, Fanconi anemia, fragile X)	-	-	426	510	658
88249	Chromosome analysis for breakage syndromes; score 100 cells, clastogen stress (eg, diepoxybutane, mitomycin C, ionizing radiation, UV radiation)	-	-	620	726	824

© PFR 2007

● = New Code ⊗ = Conscious Sedation ✚ = Add-on Code ∅ = Modifier '51' Exempt ▲ =Revised Code

		Medicare RVU	National Fee	PFR Fee Information 50%	75%	90%
88261	Chromosome analysis; count 5 cells, 1 karyotype, with banding	-	-	477	563	662
88262	Chromosome analysis; count 15-20 cells, 2 karyotypes, with banding	-	-	541	628	682
88263	Chromosome analysis; count 45 cells for mosaicism, 2 karyotypes, with banding	-	-	546	620	683
88264	Chromosome analysis; analyze 20-25 cells	-	-	448	531	614
88267	Chromosome analysis, amniotic fluid or chorionic villus, count 15 cells, 1 karyotype, with banding	-	-	631	710	868
88269	Chromosome analysis, in situ for amniotic fluid cells, count cells from 6-12 colonies, 1 karyotype, with banding	-	-	514	638	747
88271	Molecular cytogenetics; DNA probe, each (eg, FISH)	-	-	67	78	91
88272	Molecular cytogenetics; chromosomal in situ hybridization, analyze 3-5 cells (eg, for derivatives and markers)	-	-	111	126	141
88273	Molecular cytogenetics; chromosomal in situ hybridization, analyze 10-30 cells (eg, for microdeletions)	-	-	112	128	143
88274	Molecular cytogenetics; interphase in situ hybridization, analyze 25-99 cells	-	-	116	133	149
88275	Molecular cytogenetics; interphase in situ hybridization, analyze 100-300 cells	-	-	116	133	149
88280	Chromosome analysis; additional karyotypes, each study	-	-	117	139	158
88283	Chromosome analysis; additional specialized banding technique (eg, NOR, C-banding)	-	-	148	206	237
88285	Chromosome analysis; additional cells counted, each study	-	-	65	79	91
88289	Chromosome analysis; additional high resolution study	-	-	116	133	147
88291	Cytogenetics and molecular cytogenetics, interpretation and report	0.74	26.15	56	91	128
88299	Unlisted cytogenetic study	-	-	IR	IR	IR

Surgical Pathology

		Medicare RVU	National Fee	PFR Fee Information 50%	75%	90%
88300	Level I - Surgical pathology, gross examination only	0.59	21.98	57	67	97
-26		0.12	4.17	40	47	68
88302	Level II - Surgical pathology, gross and microscopic examination Appendix, incidental Fallopian tube, sterilization Fingers/toes, amputation, traumatic Foreskin, newborn Hernia sac, any location Hydrocele sac Nerve Skin, plastic repair Sympathetic ganglion Testis, castration Vaginal mucosa, incidental Vas deferens, sterilization	1.26	47.37	98	106	125
-26		0.20	7.20	74	80	94
88304	Level III - Surgical pathology, gross and microscopic examination Abortion, induced Abscess Aneurysm - arterial/ventricular Anus, tag Appendix, other than incidental Artery, atheromatous plaque Bartholin's gland cyst Bone fragment(s), other than pathologic fracture Bursa/synovial cyst Carpal tunnel tissue Cartilage, shavings Cholesteatoma Colon, colostomy stoma Conjunctiva - biopsy/pterygium Cornea Diverticulum - esophagus/small intestine Dupuytren's contracture tissue Femoral head, other than fracture Fissure/fistula Foreskin, other than newborn Gallbladder Ganglion cyst Hematoma Hemorrhoids Hydatid of Morgagni Intervertebral disc Joint, loose body Meniscus Mucocele, salivary Neuroma - Morton's/traumatic Pilonidal cyst/sinus Polyps, inflammatory - nasal/sinusoidal Skin - cyst/tag/debridement Soft tissue, debridement Soft tissue, lipoma Spermatocele Tendon/tendon sheath Testicular appendage Thrombus or embolus Tonsil and/or adenoids Varicocele Vas deferens, other than sterilization Vein, varicosity	1.62	60.64	112	155	195
-26		0.31	10.99	84	116	146

● = New Code ⊗ = Conscious Sedation ✚ = Add-on Code ∅ = Modifier '51' Exempt ▲ =Revised Code

		Medicare RVU	National Fee	PFR Fee Information 50%	75%	90%
88305	Level IV - Surgical pathology, gross and microscopic examination Abortion - spontaneous/missed Artery, biopsy Bone marrow, biopsy Bone exostosis Brain/meninges, other than for tumor resection Breast, biopsy, not requiring microscopic evaluation of surgical margins Breast, reduction mammoplasty Bronchus, biopsy Cell block, any source Cervix, biopsy Colon, biopsy Duodenum, biopsy Endocervix, curettings/biopsy Endometrium, curettings/biopsy Esophagus, biopsy Extremity, amputation, traumatic Fallopian tube, biopsy Fallopian tube, ectopic pregnancy Femoral head, fracture Fingers/toes, amputation, non-traumatic Gingiva/oral mucosa, biopsy Heart valve Joint, resection Kidney, biopsy Larynx, biopsy Leiomyoma(s), uterine myomectomy - without uterus Lip, biopsy/wedge resection Lung, transbronchial biopsy Lymph node, biopsy Muscle, biopsy Nasal mucosa, biopsy Nasopharynx/oropharynx, biopsy Nerve, biopsy Odontogenic/dental cyst Omentum, biopsy Ovary with or without tube, non-neoplastic Ovary, biopsy/wedge resection Parathyroid gland Peritoneum, biopsy Pituitary tumor Placenta, other than third trimester Pleura/pericardium - biopsy/tissue Polyp, cervical/endometrial Polyp, colorectal Polyp, stomach/small intestine Prostate, needle biopsy Prostate, TUR Salivary gland, biopsy Sinus, paranasal biopsy Skin, other than cyst/tag/debridement/plastic repair Small intestine, biopsy Soft tissue, other than tumor/mass/lipoma/debridement Spleen Stomach, biopsy Synovium Testis, other than tumor/biopsy/castration Thyroglossal duct/brachial cleft cyst Tongue, biopsy Tonsil, biopsy Trachea, biopsy Ureter, biopsy Urethra, biopsy Urinary bladder, biopsy Uterus, with or without tubes and ovaries, for prolapse Vagina, biopsy Vulva/labia, biopsy	2.79	102.70	178	215	261
-26		1.08	37.90	125	150	183
88307	Level V - Surgical pathology, gross and microscopic examination Adrenal, resection Bone - biopsy/curettings Bone fragment(s), pathologic fracture Brain, biopsy Brain/meninges, tumor resection Breast, excision of lesion, requiring microscopic evaluation of surgical margins Breast, mastectomy - partial/simple Cervix, conization Colon, segmental resection, other than for tumor Extremity, amputation, non-traumatic Eye, enucleation Kidney, partial/total nephrectomy Larynx, partial/total resection Liver, biopsy - needle/wedge Liver, partial resection Lung, wedge biopsy Lymph nodes, regional resection Mediastinum, mass Myocardium, biopsy Odontogenic tumor Ovary with or without tube, neoplastic Pancreas, biopsy Placenta, third trimester Prostate, except radical resection Salivary gland Sentinel lymph node Small intestine, resection, other than for tumor Soft tissue mass (except lipoma) - biopsy/simple excision Stomach - subtotal/total resection, other than for tumor Testis, biopsy Thymus, tumor Thyroid, total/lobe Ureter, resection Urinary bladder, TUR Uterus, with or without tubes and ovaries, other than neoplastic/prolapse	5.19	190.62	264	327	390
-26		2.28	80.34	198	245	292
88309	Level VI - Surgical pathology, gross and microscopic examination Bone resection Breast, mastectomy - with regional lymph nodes Colon, segmental resection for tumor Colon, total resection Esophagus, partial/total resection Extremity, disarticulation Fetus, with dissection Larynx, partial/total resection - with regional lymph nodes Lung - total/lobe/segment resection Pancreas, total/subtotal resection Prostate, radical resection Small intestine, resection for tumor Soft tissue tumor, extensive resection Stomach - subtotal/total resection for tumor Testis, tumor Tongue/tonsil -resection for tumor Urinary bladder, partial/total resection Uterus, with or without tubes and ovaries, neoplastic Vulva, total/subtotal resection	7.80	284.99	394	471	591
-26		3.82	134.16	296	353	443

© PFR 2007

● = New Code ⊗ = Conscious Sedation ✚ = Add-on Code ∅ = Modifier '51' Exempt ▲ =Revised Code

		Medicare RVU	National Fee	PFR Fee Information 50%	75%	90%
✚ **88311**	Decalcification procedure (List separately in addition to code for surgical pathology examination)	0.49	17.81	46	57	80
-26		0.34	12.13	34	43	60
	(Medicare fees for the code below are based on Non Facility RVUs. PFR information reflects fee when procedure is performed in a facility.)					
✚ **88312**	Special stains (List separately in addition to code for primary service); Group I for microorganisms (eg, Gridley, acid fast, methenamine silver), each	2.33	86.41	93	117	158
-26		0.77	27.29	74	94	126
	(Medicare fees for the code below are based on Non Facility RVUs. PFR information reflects fee when procedure is performed in a facility.)					
✚ **88313**	Special stains (List separately in addition to code for primary service); Group II, all other, (eg, iron, trichrome), except immunocytochemistry and immunoperoxidase stains, each	1.68	62.91	69	90	110
-26		0.34	12.13	52	68	82
	(Medicare fees for the code below are based on Non Facility RVUs. PFR information reflects fee when procedure is performed in a facility.)					
✚ **88314**	Special stains (List separately in addition to code for primary service); histochemical staining with frozen section(s)	2.53	93.99	124	136	171
-26		0.65	22.74	93	102	128
	(Medicare fees for the code below are based on Non Facility RVUs. PFR information reflects fee when procedure is performed in a facility.)					
88318	Determinative histochemistry to identify chemical components (eg, copper, zinc)	2.43	90.58	110	142	160
-26		0.61	21.60	82	106	120
	(Medicare fees for the code below are based on Non Facility RVUs. PFR information reflects fee when procedure is performed in a facility.)					
88319	Determinative histochemistry or cytochemistry to identify enzyme constituents, each	3.93	147.04	166	234	278
-26		0.75	26.53	124	176	208
88321	Consultation and report on referred slides prepared elsewhere	2.46	87.16	159	186	219
88323	Consultation and report on referred material requiring preparation of slides	3.78	136.43	185	206	252
-26		2.42	84.89	139	154	189
88325	Consultation, comprehensive, with review of records and specimens, with report on referred material	5.33	192.52	235	255	292
88329	Pathology consultation during surgery;	1.35	48.51	116	138	167
88331	Pathology consultation during surgery; first tissue block, with frozen section(s), single specimen	2.41	86.79	214	282	341
-26		1.71	60.26	160	212	256
88332	Pathology consultation during surgery; each additional tissue block with frozen section(s)	1.09	39.03	125	139	162
-26		0.84	29.56	94	104	122
88333	Pathology consultation during surgery; cytologic examination (eg, touch prep, squash prep), initial site	2.43	87.54	152	215	278
-26		1.73	61.01	114	161	208
88334	Pathology consultation during surgery; cytologic examination (eg, touch prep, squash prep), each additional site	1.42	51.16	80	112	145
-26		1.00	35.24	60	84	109
88342	Immunohistochemistry (including tissue immunoperoxidase), each antibody	2.50	91.33	168	206	239
-26		1.21	42.45	126	154	179
88346	Immunofluorescent study, each antibody; direct method	2.58	94.36	128	152	183
-26		1.22	42.82	96	114	137
88347	Immunofluorescent study, each antibody; indirect method	2.19	79.58	135	155	184
-26		1.20	42.07	101	116	138
88348	Electron microscopy; diagnostic	13.12	491.53	521	660	755
-26		2.15	75.80	391	495	566

● = New Code ⊗ = Conscious Sedation ✚ = Add-on Code ∅ = Modifier '51' Exempt ▲ =Revised Code

		Medicare RVU	National Fee	PFR Fee Information 50%	75%	90%
88349	Electron microscopy; scanning	5.73	214.12	370	401	451
-26		1.09	38.28	278	301	338
	(Medicare fees for the code below are based on Non Facility RVUs. PFR information reflects fee when procedure is performed in a facility.)					
88355	Morphometric analysis; skeletal muscle	9.39	348.66	386	459	529
-26		2.61	91.71	116	138	159
88356	Morphometric analysis; nerve	8.00	291.81	401	455	538
-26		4.28	150.83	261	296	350
88358	Morphometric analysis; tumor (eg, DNA ploidy)	2.03	73.14	392	415	445
-26		1.39	48.89	294	311	334
88360	Morphometric analysis, tumor immunohistochemistry (eg, Her-2/neu, estrogen receptor/progesterone receptor), quantitative or semiquantitative, each antibody; manual	3.05	111.42	212	263	317
-26		1.58	55.71	148	184	222
88361	Morphometric analysis, tumor immunohistochemistry (eg, Her-2/neu, estrogen receptor/progesterone receptor), quantitative or semiquantitative, each antibody; using computer-assisted technology	4.29	158.03	267	360	448
-26		1.71	60.26	134	180	224
88362	Nerve teasing preparations	7.15	262.63	350	417	503
-26		3.10	109.14	262	313	377
	(For physician interpretation of peripheral blood smear, use 85060)					
88365	In situ hybridization (eg, FISH), each probe	3.57	130.75	213	284	344
-26		1.67	58.74	128	170	206
88367	Morphometric analysis, in situ hybridization, (quantitative or semi-quantitative) each probe; using computer-assisted technology	5.73	212.23	402	500	600
-26		1.82	64.05	161	200	240
88368	Morphometric analysis, in situ hybridization, (quantitative or semi-quantitative) each probe; manual	4.48	164.48	342	423	510
-26		1.96	68.97	205	254	306
88371	Protein analysis of tissue by Western Blot, with interpretation and report;	-	-	71	81	90
-26		0.50	17.43	43	49	54
88372	Protein analysis of tissue by Western Blot, with interpretation and report; immunological probe for band identification, each	-	-	75	90	109
-26		0.53	18.57	19	22	27
88380	Microdissection (eg, mechanical, laser capture)	-	-	IR	IR	IR
-26		-	-	IR	IR	IR
88384	Array-based evaluation of multiple molecular probes; 11 through 50 probes	-	-	170	240	310
-26		-	-	128	180	232
88385	Array-based evaluation of multiple molecular probes; 51 through 250 probes	10.52	393.00	IR	IR	IR
-26		2.10	73.90	IR	IR	IR
88386	Array-based evaluation of multiple molecular probes; 251 through 500 probes	10.88	405.12	IR	IR	IR
-26		2.65	93.23	IR	IR	IR
88399	Unlisted surgical pathology procedure	-	-	IR	IR	IR
-26		-	-	IR	IR	IR

Transcutaneous Procedures

88400	Bilirubin, total, transcutaneous	-	-	15	21	25

● = New Code ⊗ = Conscious Sedation ✚ = Add-on Code ∅ = Modifier '51' Exempt ▲ =Revised Code

		Medicare RVU	National Fee	PFR Fee Information 50%	75%	90%

Other Procedures

89049	Caffeine halothane contracture test (CHCT) for malignant hyperthermia susceptibility, including interpretation and report	5.05	186.08	352	497	642
89050	Cell count, miscellaneous body fluids (eg, cerebrospinal fluid, joint fluid), except blood;	-	-	29	37	51
89051	Cell count, miscellaneous body fluids (eg, cerebrospinal fluid, joint fluid), except blood; with differential count	-	-	33	47	63
89055	Leukocyte assessment, fecal, qualitative or semiquantitative	-	-	30	42	52
▲ 89060	Crystal identification by light microscopy with or without polarizing lens analysis, tissue or any body fluid (except urine)	-	-	36	51	64
-26		0.53	18.57	27	38	48
89100	Duodenal intubation and aspiration; single specimen (eg, simple bile study or afferent loop culture) plus appropriate test procedure	4.21	157.27	136	188	234
89105	Duodenal intubation and aspiration; collection of multiple fractional specimens with pancreatic or gallbladder stimulation, single or double lumen tube	4.08	152.73	164	210	267
89125	Fat stain, feces, urine, or respiratory secretions	-	-	23	30	40
89130	Gastric intubation and aspiration, diagnostic, each specimen, for chemical analyses or cytopathology;	3.49	130.37	113	143	177
89132	Gastric intubation and aspiration, diagnostic, each specimen, for chemical analyses or cytopathology; after stimulation	2.98	112.18	96	130	160
89135	Gastric intubation, aspiration, and fractional collections (eg, gastric secretory study); one hour	4.46	165.99	163	197	235
89136	Gastric intubation, aspiration, and fractional collections (eg, gastric secretory study); two hours	3.27	123.17	123	134	145
89140	Gastric intubation, aspiration, and fractional collections (eg, gastric secretory study); two hours including gastric stimulation (eg, histalog, pentagastrin)	4.23	156.90	196	223	250
89141	Gastric intubation, aspiration, and fractional collections (eg, gastric secretory study); three hours, including gastric stimulation	4.31	159.93	237	258	283
89160	Meat fibers, feces	-	-	18	21	25
89190	Nasal smear for eosinophils	-	-	23	28	35
89220	Sputum, obtaining specimen, aerosol induced technique (separate procedure)	0.43	16.30	39	48	56
89225	Starch granules, feces	-	-	19	29	37
89230	Sweat collection by iontophoresis	0.12	4.55	IR	IR	IR
89235	Water load test	-	-	IR	IR	IR
89240	Unlisted miscellaneous pathology test	-	-	IR	IR	IR

Reproductive Medicine Procedures

89250	Culture of oocyte(s)/embryo(s), less than 4 days;	-	-	1226	1406	1612
89251	Culture of oocyte(s)/embryo(s), less than 4 days; with co-culture of oocyte(s)/embryos	-	-	IR	IR	IR
89253	Assisted embryo hatching, microtechniques (any method)	-	-	IR	IR	IR
89254	Oocyte identification from follicular fluid	-	-	IR	IR	IR
89255	Preparation of embryo for transfer (any method)	-	-	IR	IR	IR
89257	Sperm identification from aspiration (other than seminal fluid)	-	-	IR	IR	IR
89258	Cryopreservation; embryo(s)	-	-	IR	IR	IR
89259	Cryopreservation; sperm	-	-	IR	IR	IR
89260	Sperm isolation; simple prep (eg, sperm wash and swim-up) for insemination or diagnosis with semen analysis	-	-	IR	IR	IR
89261	Sperm isolation; complex prep (eg, Percoll gradient, albumin gradient) for insemination or diagnosis with semen analysis	-	-	IR	IR	IR
89264	Sperm identification from testis tissue, fresh or cryopreserved	-	-	IR	IR	IR
89268	Insemination of oocytes	-	-	IR	IR	IR

● = New Code ⊗ = Conscious Sedation ✚ = Add-on Code ∅ = Modifier '51' Exempt ▲ =Revised Code

		Medicare RVU	National Fee	PFR Fee Information 50%	75%	90%
89272	Extended culture of oocyte(s)/embryo(s), 4-7 days	-	-	IR	IR	IR
89280	Assisted oocyte fertilization, microtechnique; less than or equal to 10 oocytes	-	-	IR	IR	IR
89281	Assisted oocyte fertilization, microtechnique; greater than 10 oocytes	-	-	IR	IR	IR
89290	Biopsy, oocyte polar body or embryo blastomere, microtechnique (for pre-implantation genetic diagnosis); less than or equal to 5 embryos	-	-	IR	IR	IR
89291	Biopsy, oocyte polar body or embryo blastomere, microtechnique (for pre-implantation genetic diagnosis); greater than 5 embryos	-	-	IR	IR	IR
89300	Semen analysis; presence and/or motility of sperm including Huhner test (post coital)	-	-	66	80	127
89310	Semen analysis; motility and count (not including Huhner test)	-	-	57	75	83
89320	Semen analysis; complete (volume, count, motility, and differential)	-	-	86	107	146
89321	Semen analysis, presence and/or motility of sperm	-	-	31	40	50
89325	Sperm antibodies	-	-	133	157	186
89329	Sperm evaluation; hamster penetration test	-	-	332	369	424
89330	Sperm evaluation; cervical mucus penetration test, with or without spinnbarkeit test	-	-	89	96	101
89335	Cryopreservation, reproductive tissue, testicular	-	-	IR	IR	IR
89342	Storage, (per year); embryo(s)	-	-	IR	IR	IR
89343	Storage, (per year); sperm/semen	-	-	IR	IR	IR
89344	Storage, (per year); reproductive tissue, testicular/ovarian	-	-	IR	IR	IR
89346	Storage, (per year); oocyte(s)	-	-	IR	IR	IR
89352	Thawing of cryopreserved; embryo(s)	-	-	IR	IR	IR
89353	Thawing of cryopreserved; sperm/semen, each aliquot	-	-	IR	IR	IR
89354	Thawing of cryopreserved; reproductive tissue, testicular/ovarian	-	-	IR	IR	IR
89356	Thawing of cryopreserved; oocytes, each aliquot	-	-	IR	IR	IR

Medicine

Immune Globulins

		Medicare RVU	National Fee	PFR Fee Information 50%	75%	90%
∅ **90281**	Immune globulin (Ig), human, for intramuscular use	-	∅	39	47	57
∅ **90283**	Immune globulin (IgIV), human, for intravenous use	-	∅	IR	IR	IR
∅ **90287**	Botulinum antitoxin, equine, any route	-	-	IR	IR	IR
∅ **90288**	Botulism immune globulin, human, for intravenous use	-	-	IR	IR	IR
∅ **90291**	Cytomegalovirus immune globulin (CMV-IgIV), human, for intravenous use	-	-	IR	IR	IR
∅ **90296**	Diphtheria antitoxin, equine, any route	-	-	IR	IR	IR
∅ **90371**	Hepatitis B immune globulin (HBIg), human, for intramuscular use	-	-	96	122	150
∅ **90375**	Rabies immune globulin (RIg), human, for intramuscular and/or subcutaneous use	-	-	155	211	242
∅ **90376**	Rabies immune globulin, heat-treated (RIg-HT), human, for intramuscular and/or subcutaneous use	-	-	146	203	256
∅ **90378**	Respiratory syncytial virus immune globulin (RSV-IgIM), for intramuscular use, 50 mg, each	-	-	1339	1554	1900
∅ **90379**	Respiratory syncytial virus immune globulin (RSV-IgIV), human, for intravenous use	-	-	IR	IR	IR
∅ **90384**	Rho(D) immune globulin (RhIg), human, full-dose, for intramuscular use	-	-	137	150	183
∅ **90385**	Rho(D) immune globulin (RhIg), human, mini-dose, for intramuscular use	-	∅	55	66	79
∅ **90386**	Rho(D) immune globulin (RhIgIV), human, for intravenous use	-	-	IR	IR	IR
∅ **90389**	Tetanus immune globulin (TIg), human, for intramuscular use	-	-	127	155	185

		Medicare RVU	National Fee	PFR Fee Information 50%	75%	90%
⊘ **90393**	Vaccinia immune globulin, human, for intramuscular use	-	-	IR	IR	IR
⊘ **90396**	Varicella-zoster immune globulin, human, for intramuscular use	-	-	IR	IR	IR
⊘ **90399**	Unlisted immune globulin	-	-	IR	IR	IR

Immunization Administration for Vaccines/Toxoids

		Medicare RVU	National Fee	50%	75%	90%
90465	Immunization administration younger than 8 years of age (includes percutaneous, intradermal, subcutaneous, or intramuscular injections) when the physician counsels the patient/family; first injection (single or combination vaccine/toxoid), per day	0.53	19.33	27	41	58
✚ **90466**	Immunization administration younger than 8 years of age (includes percutaneous, intradermal, subcutaneous, or intramuscular injections) when the physician counsels the patient/family; each additional injection (single or combination vaccine/toxoid), per day (List separately in addition to code for primary procedure)	0.29	10.23	18	25	37
90467	Immunization administration younger than age 8 years (includes intranasal or oral routes of administration) when the physician counsels the patient/family; first administration (single or combination vaccine/toxoid), per day	0.35	12.51	24	37	48
✚ **90468**	Immunization administration younger than age 8 years (includes intranasal or oral routes of administration) when the physician counsels the patient/family; each additional administration (single or combination vaccine/toxoid), per day (List separately in addition to code for primary procedure)	0.27	9.47	21	28	36
90471	Immunization administration (includes percutaneous, intradermal, subcutaneous, or intramuscular injections); one vaccine (single or combination vaccine/toxoid)	0.53	19.33	20	28	39
✚ **90472**	Immunization administration (includes percutaneous, intradermal, subcutaneous, or intramuscular injections); each additional vaccine (single or combination vaccine/toxoid) (List separately in addition to code for primary procedure)	0.29	10.23	22	34	48
90473	Immunization administration by intranasal or oral route; one vaccine (single or combination vaccine/toxoid)	0.36	12.89	22	29	37
✚ **90474**	Immunization administration by intranasal or oral route; each additional vaccine (single or combination vaccine/toxoid) (List separately in addition to code for primary procedure)	0.25	8.72	18	27	36

Vaccines, Toxoids

		Medicare RVU	National Fee	50%	75%	90%
⊘ **90476**	Adenovirus vaccine, type 4, live, for oral use	-	-	IR	IR	IR
⊘ **90477**	Adenovirus vaccine, type 7, live, for oral use	-	-	IR	IR	IR
⊘ **90581**	Anthrax vaccine, for subcutaneous use	-	-	IR	IR	IR
⊘ **90585**	Bacillus Calmette-Guerin vaccine (BCG) for tuberculosis, live, for percutaneous use	-	-	50	87	137
⊘ **90586**	Bacillus Calmette-Guerin vaccine (BCG) for bladder cancer, live, for intravesical use	-	-	IR	IR	IR
⊘ **90632**	Hepatitis A vaccine, adult dosage, for intramuscular use	-	-	90	104	122
⊘ **90633**	Hepatitis A vaccine, pediatric/adolescent dosage-2 dose schedule, for intramuscular use	-	-	61	82	99
⊘ **90634**	Hepatitis A vaccine, pediatric/adolescent dosage-3 dose schedule, for intramuscular use	-	-	75	88	115
⊘ **90636**	Hepatitis A and hepatitis B vaccine (HepA-HepB), adult dosage, for intramuscular use	-	-	102	123	144
⊘ **90645**	Hemophilus influenza b vaccine (Hib), HbOC conjugate (4 dose schedule), for intramuscular use	-	-	42	52	62
⊘ **90646**	Hemophilus influenza b vaccine (Hib), PRP-D conjugate, for booster use only, intramuscular use	-	-	38	49	66
⊘ **90647**	Hemophilus influenza b vaccine (Hib), PRP-OMP conjugate (3 dose schedule), for intramuscular use	-	-	38	48	56
⊘ **90648**	Hemophilus influenza b vaccine (Hib), PRP-T conjugate (4 dose schedule), for intramuscular use	-	-	40	47	55
⊘ **90649**	Human Papilloma virus (HPV) vaccine, types 6, 11, 16, 18 (quadrivalent), 3 dose schedule, for intramuscular use	-	-	IR	IR	IR
▲ **90655**	Influenza virus vaccine, split virus, preservative free, when administered to children 6-35 months of age, for intramuscular use	-	-	34	44	51
▲ **90656**	Influenza virus vaccine, split virus, preservative free, when administered to 3 years and older, for intramuscular use	-	-	IR	IR	IR

● = New Code ⊗ = Conscious Sedation ✚ = Add-on Code ⊘ = Modifier '51' Exempt ▲ = Revised Code

		Medicare RVU	National Fee	PFR Fee Information 50%	75%	90%
⊘▲ 90657	Influenza virus vaccine, split virus, when administered to children 6-35 months of age, for intramuscular use	-	-	17	21	29
	(See also HCPCS code G0008 for administration of influenza virus vaccine when no physician fee schedule service on the same day.)					
⊘▲ 90658	Influenza virus vaccine, split virus, when administered to 3 years of age and older, for intramuscular use	-	-	16	21	26
⊘ 90660	Influenza virus vaccine, live, for intranasal use	-	-	56	68	76
⊘ 90665	Lyme disease vaccine, adult dosage, for intramuscular use	-	-	80	85	96
	(See also HCPCS code S0195 for pneumococcal conjugate vaccine, polyvalent, intramuscular, for children from 5 years to 9 years of age who ha)					
⊘▲ 90669	Pneumococcal conjugate vaccine, polyvalent, when administered to children younger than 5 years, for intramuscular use	-	-	100	109	131
⊘ 90675	Rabies vaccine, for intramuscular use	-	-	188	223	276
⊘ 90676	Rabies vaccine, for intradermal use	-	-	128	166	197
⊘ 90680	Rotavirus vaccine, pentavalent, 3 dose schedule, live, for oral use	-	-	77	83	90
⊘ 90690	Typhoid vaccine, live, oral	-	-	43	53	64
⊘ 90691	Typhoid vaccine, Vi capsular polysaccharide (ViCPs), for intramuscular use	-	-	52	85	101
⊘ 90692	Typhoid vaccine, heat- and phenol-inactivated (H-P), for subcutaneous or intradermal use	-	-	32	40	44
⊘ 90693	Typhoid vaccine, acetone-killed, dried (AKD), for subcutaneous use (U.S. military)	-	-	IR	IR	IR
⊘ 90698	Diphtheria, tetanus toxoids, acellular pertussis vaccine, haemophilus influenza Type B, and poliovirus vaccine, inactivated (DTaP - Hib - IPV), for intramuscular use	-	-	IR	IR	IR
⊘▲ 90700	Diphtheria, tetanus toxoids, and acellular pertussis vaccine (DTaP), when administered to younger than 7 years, for intramuscular use	-	-	41	52	58
⊘ 90701	Diphtheria, tetanus toxoids, and whole cell pertussis vaccine (DTP), for intramuscular use	-	-	35	45	49
	(Medicare fees for the code below are based on Non Facility RVUs. PFR information reflects fee when procedure is performed in a facility.)					
⊘▲ 90702	Diphtheria and tetanus toxoids (DT) adsorbed when administered to younger than 7 years, for intramuscular use	-	-	22	28	31
⊘ 90703	Tetanus toxoid adsorbed, for intramuscular use	-	-	26	31	43
⊘ 90704	Mumps virus vaccine, live, for subcutaneous use	-	-	36	51	55
⊘ 90705	Measles virus vaccine, live, for subcutaneous use	-	-	36	43	52
⊘ 90706	Rubella virus vaccine, live, for subcutaneous use	-	-	39	49	53
⊘ 90707	Measles, mumps and rubella virus vaccine (MMR), live, for subcutaneous use	-	-	58	70	77
⊘ 90708	Measles and rubella virus vaccine, live, for subcutaneous use	-	-	47	52	60
⊘ 90710	Measles, mumps, rubella, and varicella vaccine (MMRV), live, for subcutaneous use	-	-	60	65	75
⊘ 90712	Poliovirus vaccine, (any type(s)) (OPV), live, for oral use	-	-	35	40	45
⊘ 90713	Poliovirus vaccine, inactivated, (IPV), for subcutaneous or intramuscular use	-	-	45	51	59
⊘▲ 90714	Tetanus and diphtheria toxoids (Td) adsorbed, preservative free, when administered to 7 years or older, for intramuscular use	-	-	26	41	54
⊘▲ 90715	Tetanus, diphtheria toxoids and acellular pertussis vaccine (Tdap), when administered to 7 years or older, for intramuscular use	-	-	53	58	75
⊘ 90716	Varicella virus vaccine, live, for subcutaneous use	-	-	82	92	96
⊘ 90717	Yellow fever vaccine, live, for subcutaneous use	-	-	87	109	127
⊘▲ 90718	Tetanus and diphtheria toxoids (Td) adsorbed when administered to 7 years or older, for intramuscular use	-	-	25	30	35
⊘ 90719	Diphtheria toxoid, for intramuscular use	-	-	23	35	40
⊘ 90720	Diphtheria, tetanus toxoids, and whole cell pertussis vaccine and Hemophilus influenza B vaccine (DTP-Hib), for intramuscular use	-	-	59	65	86
⊘ 90721	Diphtheria, tetanus toxoids, and acellular pertussis vaccine and Hemophilus influenza B vaccine (DtaP-Hib), for intramuscular use	-	-	65	72	88
⊘ 90723	Diphtheria, tetanus toxoids, acellular pertussis vaccine, Hepatitis B, and poliovirus vaccine, inactivated (DtaP-HepB-IPV), for intramuscular use	-	-	90	96	118
⊘ 90725	Cholera vaccine for injectable use	-	-	27	33	36

		Medicare RVU	National Fee	PFR Fee Information 50%	75%	90%
⊘ 90727	Plague vaccine, for intramuscular use	-	-	29	35	40
	(Medicare fees for the code below are based on Non Facility RVUs. PFR information reflects fee when procedure is performed in a facility.) *(See also HCPCS code G0009 for administration of pneumococcal vaccine when no physician fee schedule service on the same day.)*					
▲ 90732	Pneumococcal polysaccharide vaccine, 23-valent, adult or immunosuppressed patient dosage, when administered to 2 years or older, for subcutaneous or intramuscular use	-	-	32	41	49
⊘ 90733	Meningococcal polysaccharide vaccine (any group(s)), for subcutaneous use	-	-	100	114	126
⊘ 90734	Meningococcal conjugate vaccine, serogroups A, C, Y and W-135 (tetravalent), for intramuscular use	-	-	IR	IR	IR
⊘ 90735	Japanese encephalitis virus vaccine, for subcutaneous use	-	-	108	127	163
⊘ 90736	Zoster (shingles) vaccine, live, for subcutaneous injection	-	-	IR	IR	IR
⊘ 90740	Hepatitis B vaccine, dialysis or immunosuppressed patient dosage (3 dose schedule), for intramuscular use	-	-	185	205	221
⊘ 90743	Hepatitis B vaccine, adolescent (2 dose schedule), for intramuscular use	-	-	50	78	90
	(See also HCPCS code G0010 for administration of Hepatitis B vaccine when no physician fee schedule service on the same day.) *(See also HCPCS code Q3021.)*					
⊘ 90744	Hepatitis B vaccine, pediatric/adolescent dosage (3 dose schedule), for intramuscular use	-	-	60	78	97
	(See also HCPCS code Q3022.)					
⊘ 90746	Hepatitis B vaccine, adult dosage, for intramuscular use	-	-	87	101	108
	(See also HCPCS code Q3023.)					
⊘ 90747	Hepatitis B vaccine, dialysis or immunosuppressed patient dosage (4 dose schedule), for intramuscular use	-	-	114	155	193
⊘ 90748	Hepatitis B and Hemophilus influenza b vaccine (HepB-Hib), for intramuscular use	-	-	82	89	99
⊘ 90749	Unlisted vaccine/toxoid	-	-	IR	IR	IR

Hydration, Therapeutic, Prophylactic, and Diagnostic Injections and Infusions
(Excludes Chemotherapy)
Hydration

90760	Intravenous infusion, hydration; initial, up to 1 hour	1.64	61.39	116	155	204
▲ 90761	Intravenous infusion, hydration; each additional hour (List separately in addition to code for primary procedure)	0.51	18.95	38	50	67

Therapeutic, Prophylactic, and Diagnostic Injections and Infusions

90765	Intravenous infusion, for therapy, prophylaxis, or diagnosis (specify substance or drug); initial, up to 1 hour	2.00	75.04	143	190	250
▲ 90766	Intravenous infusion, for therapy, prophylaxis, or diagnosis (specify substance or drug); each additional hour (List separately in addition to code for primary procedure)	0.66	24.25	50	66	88
✚ 90767	Intravenous infusion, for therapy, prophylaxis, or diagnosis (specify substance or drug); additional sequential infusion, up to 1 hour (List separately in addition to code for primary procedure)	1.07	39.79	80	106	139
✚ 90768	Intravenous infusion, for therapy, prophylaxis, or diagnosis (specify substance or drug); concurrent infusion (List separately in addition to code for primary procedure)	0.62	22.74	47	62	82
90772	Therapeutic, prophylactic or diagnostic injection (specify substance or drug); subcutaneous or intramuscular	0.53	19.33	35	47	61
90773	Therapeutic, prophylactic or diagnostic injection (specify substance or drug); intra-arterial	0.50	18.19	37	49	64
90774	Therapeutic, prophylactic or diagnostic injection (specify substance or drug); intravenous push, single or initial substance/drug	1.53	57.23	108	145	189
✚ 90775	Therapeutic, prophylactic or diagnostic injection (specify substance or drug); each additional sequential intravenous push of a new substance/drug (List separately in addition to code for primary procedure)	0.70	26.15	50	66	87

© PFR 2007

● = New Code ⊗ = Conscious Sedation ✚ = Add-on Code ⊘ = Modifier '51' Exempt ▲ =Revised Code

		Medicare RVU	National Fee	PFR Fee Information 50%	75%	90%
90779	Unlisted therapeutic, prophylactic or diagnostic intravenous or intra-arterial injection or infusion	-	-	IR	IR	IR

(For 90780-90799, indicate medication and dosage using the appropriate HCPCS code from the J section.)

(UNBUNDLING ALERT: 90780 cannot be used with 36000 by the same physician on the same day.)

(UNBUNDLING ALERT: 90781 cannot be used with 36000 by the same physician on the same day.)

(UNBUNDLING ALERT: 90784 cannot be used with 36000 by the same physician on the same day.)

Psychiatry

Psychiatric Diagnostic or Evaluative Interview Procedures

90801	Psychiatric diagnostic interview examination	4.11	145.15	193	217	265
90802	Interactive psychiatric diagnostic interview examination using play equipment, physical devices, language interpreter, or other mechanisms of communication	4.36	153.86	194	237	303

Psychiatric Therapeutic Procedures
Office or Other Outpatient Facility
Insight Oriented, Behavior Modifying and/or Supportive Psychotherapy

90804	Individual psychotherapy, insight oriented, behavior modifying and/or supportive, in an office or outpatient facility, approximately 20 to 30 minutes face-to-face with the patient;	1.75	61.77	99	122	160
90805	Individual psychotherapy, insight oriented, behavior modifying and/or supportive, in an office or outpatient facility, approximately 20 to 30 minutes face-to-face with the patient; with medical evaluation and management services	1.93	67.84	120	147	166
90806	Individual psychotherapy, insight oriented, behavior modifying and/or supportive, in an office or outpatient facility, approximately 45 to 50 minutes face-to-face with the patient;	2.56	89.82	143	178	236
90807	Individual psychotherapy, insight oriented, behavior modifying and/or supportive, in an office or outpatient facility, approximately 45 to 50 minutes face-to-face with the patient; with medical evaluation and management services	2.77	97.40	167	213	244
90808	Individual psychotherapy, insight oriented, behavior modifying and/or supportive, in an office or outpatient facility, approximately 75 to 80 minutes face-to-face with the patient;	3.79	133.02	220	282	315
90809	Individual psychotherapy, insight oriented, behavior modifying and/or supportive, in an office or outpatient facility, approximately 75 to 80 minutes face-to-face with the patient; with medical evaluation and management services	3.99	139.84	246	314	359

Interactive Psychotherapy

90810	Individual psychotherapy, interactive, using play equipment, physical devices, language interpreter, or other mechanisms of non-verbal communication, in an office or outpatient facility, approximately 20 to 30 minutes face-to-face with the patient;	1.87	65.94	112	145	181
90811	Individual psychotherapy, interactive, using play equipment, physical devices, language interpreter, or other mechanisms of non-verbal communication, in an office or outpatient facility, approximately 20 to 30 minutes face-to-face with the patient; with medical evaluation and management services	2.13	75.04	134	171	207
90812	Individual psychotherapy, interactive, using play equipment, physical devices, language interpreter, or other mechanisms of non-verbal communication, in an office or outpatient facility, approximately 45 to 50 minutes face-to-face with the patient;	2.76	97.02	157	204	248
90813	Individual psychotherapy, interactive, using play equipment, physical devices, language interpreter, or other mechanisms of non-verbal communication, in an office or outpatient facility, approximately 45 to 50 minutes face-to-face with the patient; with medical evaluation and management services	2.97	104.60	178	221	269
90814	Individual psychotherapy, interactive, using play equipment, physical devices, language interpreter, or other mechanisms of non-verbal communication, in an office or outpatient facility, approximately 75 to 80 minutes face-to-face with the patient;	3.98	139.84	226	290	351
90815	Individual psychotherapy, interactive, using play equipment, physical devices, language interpreter, or other mechanisms of non-verbal communication, in an office or outpatient facility, approximately 75 to 80 minutes face-to-face with the patient; with medical evaluation and management services	4.17	146.28	252	319	357

Inpatient Hospital, Partial Hospital or Residential Care Facility
Insight Oriented, Behavior Modifying Residential Care Facility

90816	Individual psychotherapy, insight oriented, behavior modifying and/or supportive, in an inpatient hospital, partial hospital or residential care setting, approximately 20 to 30 minutes face-to-face with the patient;	1.71	59.88	114	143	163

		Medicare RVU	National Fee	PFR Fee Information 50%	75%	90%
90817	Individual psychotherapy, insight oriented, behavior modifying and/or supportive, in an inpatient hospital, partial hospital or residential care setting, approximately 20 to 30 minutes face-to-face with the patient; with medical evaluation and management services	1.88	65.94	135	168	187
90818	Individual psychotherapy, insight oriented, behavior modifying and/or supportive, in an inpatient hospital, partial hospital or residential care setting, approximately 45 to 50 minutes face-to-face with the patient;	2.56	89.82	160	204	247
90819	Individual psychotherapy, insight oriented, behavior modifying and/or supportive, in an inpatient hospital, partial hospital or residential care setting, approximately 45 to 50 minutes face-to-face with the patient; with medical evaluation and management services	2.71	94.74	176	233	282
90821	Individual psychotherapy, insight oriented, behavior modifying and/or supportive, in an inpatient hospital, partial hospital or residential care setting, approximately 75 to 80 minutes face-to-face with the patient;	3.80	133.40	245	310	344
90822	Individual psychotherapy, insight oriented, behavior modifying and/or supportive, in an inpatient hospital, partial hospital or residential care setting, approximately 75 to 80 minutes face-to-face with the patient; with medical evaluation and management services	3.94	137.95	271	336	383

Interactive Psychotherapy

		Medicare RVU	National Fee	50%	75%	90%
90823	Individual psychotherapy, interactive, using play equipment, physical devices, language interpreter, or other mechanisms of non-verbal communication, in an inpatient hospital, partial hospital or residential care setting, approximately 20 to 30 minutes face-to-face with the patient;	1.84	64.43	115	152	184
90824	Individual psychotherapy, interactive, using play equipment, physical devices, language interpreter, or other mechanisms of non-verbal communication, in an inpatient hospital, partial hospital or residential care setting, approximately 20 to 30 minutes face-to-face with the patient; with medical evaluation and management services	2.02	70.87	145	183	207
90826	Individual psychotherapy, interactive, using play equipment, physical devices, language interpreter, or other mechanisms of non-verbal communication, in an inpatient hospital, partial hospital or residential care setting, approximately 45 to 50 minutes face-to-face with the patient;	2.72	95.50	172	219	265
90827	Individual psychotherapy, interactive, using play equipment, physical devices, language interpreter, or other mechanisms of non-verbal communication, in an inpatient hospital, partial hospital or residential care setting, approximately 45 to 50 minutes face-to-face with the patient; with medical evaluation and management services	2.84	99.29	196	242	276
90828	Individual psychotherapy, interactive, using play equipment, physical devices, language interpreter, or other mechanisms of non-verbal communication, in an inpatient hospital, partial hospital or residential care setting, approximately 75 to 80 minutes face-to-face with the patient;	3.95	138.33	263	323	364
90829	Individual psychotherapy, interactive, using play equipment, physical devices, language interpreter, or other mechanisms of non-verbal communication, in an inpatient hospital, partial hospital or residential care setting, approximately 75 to 80 minutes face-to-face with the patient; with medical evaluation and management services	4.07	142.49	280	342	387

Other Psychotherapy

		Medicare RVU	National Fee	50%	75%	90%
90845	Psychoanalysis	2.36	82.62	143	180	195
90846	Family psychotherapy (without the patient present)	2.49	87.54	150	177	189
90847	Family psychotherapy (conjoint psychotherapy) (with patient present)	3.06	107.63	180	194	214
90849	Multiple-family group psychotherapy	0.89	31.45	103	129	162
90853	Group psychotherapy (other than of a multiple-family group)	0.86	30.32	83	101	105
90857	Interactive group psychotherapy	0.95	33.73	89	112	123

Other Psychiatric Services or Procedures

		Medicare RVU	National Fee	50%	75%	90%
90862	Pharmacologic management, including prescription, use, and review of medication with no more than minimal medical psychotherapy	1.43	50.40	88	106	121
90865	Narcosynthesis for psychiatric diagnostic and therapeutic purposes (eg, sodium amobarbital (Amytal) interview)	4.28	151.21	248	297	342
90870	Electroconvulsive therapy (includes necessary monitoring)	3.85	138.70	231	289	361
90875	Individual psychophysiological therapy incorporating biofeedback training by any modality (face-to-face with the patient), with psychotherapy (eg, insight oriented, behavior modifying or supportive psychotherapy); approximately 20-30 minutes	2.05	73.14	104	133	162
90876	Individual psychophysiological therapy incorporating biofeedback training by any modality (face-to-face with the patient), with psychotherapy (eg, insight oriented, behavior modifying or supportive psychotherapy); approximately 45-50 minutes	2.99	106.11	162	241	286

● = New Code ⊗ = Conscious Sedation ✚ = Add-on Code ∅ = Modifier '51' Exempt ▲ =Revised Code

		Medicare RVU	National Fee	PFR Fee Information 50%	75%	90%
90880	Hypnotherapy	3.16	111.42	175	207	233
90882	Environmental intervention for medical management purposes on a psychiatric patient's behalf with agencies, employers, or institutions	-	-	142	171	199
90885	Psychiatric evaluation of hospital records, other psychiatric reports, psychometric and/or projective tests, and other accumulated data for medical diagnostic purposes	1.32	46.23	171	202	219
90887	Interpretation or explanation of results of psychiatric, other medical examinations and procedures, or other accumulated data to family or other responsible persons, or advising them how to assist patient	2.29	81.10	154	168	188
90889	Preparation of report of patient's psychiatric status, history, treatment, or progress (other than for legal or consultative purposes) for other physicians, agencies, or insurance carriers	-	-	141	184	232
90899	Unlisted psychiatric service or procedure	-	-	IR	IR	IR

Biofeedback

90901	Biofeedback training by any modality	1.04	37.90	115	162	237
90911	Biofeedback training, perineal muscles, anorectal or urethral sphincter, including EMG and/or manometry	2.46	89.82	189	217	251

Dialysis

End Stage Renal Disease Services

90918	End-stage renal disease (ESRD) related services per full month; for patients younger than two years of age to include monitoring for the adequacy of nutrition, assessment of growth and development, and counseling of parents	17.27	612.04	1098	1520	1651
90919	End-stage renal disease (ESRD) related services per full month; for patients between two and eleven years of age to include monitoring for the adequacy of nutrition, assessment of growth and development, and counseling of parents	12.58	444.16	844	1015	1220
90920	End-stage renal disease (ESRD) related services per full month; for patients between twelve and nineteen years of age to include monitoring for the adequacy of nutrition, assessment of growth and development, and counseling of parents	10.99	388.83	752	1045	1313
90921	End-stage renal disease (ESRD) related services per full month; for patients twenty years of age and older	6.86	242.92	523	732	893
90922	End-stage renal disease (ESRD) related services (less than full month), per day; for patients younger than two years of age	0.58	20.46	35	43	49
90923	End-stage renal disease (ESRD) related services (less than full month), per day; for patients between two and eleven years of age	0.41	14.40	32	37	47
90924	End-stage renal disease (ESRD) related services (less than full month), per day; for patients between twelve and nineteen years of age	0.36	12.89	29	38	54
90925	End-stage renal disease (ESRD) related services (less than full month), per day; for patients twenty years of age and older	0.23	7.96	19	26	37

Hemodialysis

90935	Hemodialysis procedure with single physician evaluation	1.90	67.46	266	320	381
90937	Hemodialysis procedure requiring repeated evaluation(s) with or without substantial revision of dialysis prescription	3.11	109.90	482	590	657
90940	Hemodialysis access flow study to determine blood flow in grafts and arteriovenous fistulae by an indicator method	-	-	119	170	211

Miscellaneous Dialysis Procedures

90945	Dialysis procedure other than hemodialysis (eg, peritoneal dialysis, hemofiltration, or other continuous renal replacement therapies), with single physician evaluation	1.98	70.11	277	310	377
90947	Dialysis procedure other than hemodialysis (eg, peritoneal dialysis, hemofiltration, or other continuous renal replacement therapies) requiring repeated physician evaluations, with or without substantial revision of dialysis prescription	3.17	111.80	433	506	595
90989	Dialysis training, patient, including helper where applicable, any mode, completed course	-	-	788	910	1106
90993	Dialysis training, patient, including helper where applicable, any mode, course not completed, per training session	-	-	142	176	206
90997	Hemoperfusion (eg, with activated charcoal or resin)	2.52	88.30	495	592	672
90999	Unlisted dialysis procedure, inpatient or outpatient	-	-	IR	IR	IR

● = New Code ⊗ = Conscious Sedation ✚ = Add-on Code ∅ = Modifier '51' Exempt ▲ =Revised Code

		Medicare RVU	National Fee	PFR Fee Information 50%	75%	90%

Gastroenterology

Code	Description	RVU	Fee	50%	75%	90%
91000	Esophageal intubation and collection of washings for cytology, including preparation of specimens (separate procedure)	1.57	56.85	132	166	185
-26		1.01	35.62	106	133	148
91010	Esophageal motility (manometric study of the esophagus and/or gastroesophageal junction) study;	5.59	206.92	313	354	401
-26		1.78	62.53	110	124	140
91011	Esophageal motility (manometric study of the esophagus and/or gastroesophageal junction) study; with mecholyl or similar stimulant	6.88	255.05	381	470	525
-26		2.15	75.80	133	164	184
91012	Esophageal motility (manometric study of the esophagus and/or gastroesophageal junction) study; with acid perfusion studies	7.28	270.21	384	458	565
-26		2.08	73.14	134	160	198
91020	Gastric motility (manometric) studies	6.15	227.76	273	308	373
-26		2.03	71.63	96	108	131
91022	Duodenal motility (manometric) study	5.65	208.82	365	440	505
-26		2.05	72.38	128	154	177
91030	Esophagus, acid perfusion (Bernstein) test for esophagitis	3.52	129.99	176	211	246
-26		1.30	45.86	62	74	86
91034	Esophagus, gastroesophageal reflux test; with nasal catheter pH electrode(s) placement, recording, analysis and interpretation	6.05	225.49	361	426	498
-26		1.39	48.89	90	106	124
91035	Esophagus, gastroesophageal reflux test; with mucosal attached telemetry pH electrode placement, recording, analysis and interpretation	12.63	472.58	701	827	966
-26		2.25	79.21	175	207	242
91037	Esophageal function test, gastroesophageal reflux test with nasal catheter intraluminal impedance electrode(s) placement, recording, analysis and interpretation;	4.13	152.73	225	266	310
-26		1.39	48.89	90	106	124
91038	Esophageal function test, gastroesophageal reflux test with nasal catheter intraluminal impedance electrode(s) placement, recording, analysis and interpretation; prolonged (greater than 1 hour, up to 24 hours)	3.58	131.50	210	247	288
-26		1.58	55.71	105	124	144
91040	Esophageal balloon distension provocation study	11.76	441.88	743	878	1024
-26		1.38	48.51	149	176	205
91052	Gastric analysis test with injection of stimulant of gastric secretion (eg, histamine, insulin, pentagastrin, calcium and secretin)	3.43	126.96	195	245	307
-26		1.13	39.79	68	86	107
91055	Gastric intubation, washings, and preparing slides for cytology (separate procedure)	3.82	141.36	160	197	271
-26		1.26	44.34	56	69	95
91065	Breath hydrogen test (eg, for detection of lactase deficiency, fructose intolerance, bacterial overgrowth, or oro-cecal gastrointestinal transit)	1.65	61.77	191	219	248
-26		0.28	9.85	48	55	62
	(Medicare fees for the code below are based on Non Facility RVUs. PFR information reflects fee when procedure is performed in a facility.)					
91100	Intestinal bleeding tube, passage, positioning and monitoring	3.78	139.08	139	160	167
91105	Gastric intubation, and aspiration or lavage for treatment (eg, for ingested poisons)	2.41	89.82	110	142	207
91110	Gastrointestinal tract imaging, intraluminal (eg, capsule endoscopy), esophagus through ileum, with physician interpretation and report	25.57	955.02	2034	2364	2668
-26		5.12	180.01	508	591	667

● = New Code ⊗ = Conscious Sedation ✚ = Add-on Code ∅ = Modifier '51' Exempt ▲ =Revised Code

		Medicare RVU	National Fee	PFR Fee Information 50%	75%	90%
● 91111	Gastrointestinal tract imaging, intraluminal (eg, capsule endoscopy), esophagus with physician interpretation and report	19.70	742.79	1064	1272	1539
-26		1.49	52.68	IR	IR	IR
91120	Rectal sensation, tone, and compliance test (ie, response to graded balloon distention)	11.57	434.68	680	814	986
-26		1.37	48.13	170	204	246
91122	Anorectal manometry	6.74	248.61	330	387	447
-26		2.48	87.16	132	155	179
91123	Pulsed irrigation of fecal impaction	-	-	IR	IR	IR

Gastric Physiology

		Medicare RVU	National Fee	50%	75%	90%
91132	Electrogastrography, diagnostic, transcutaneous;	-	-	55	80	97
-26		0.74	26.15	38	56	68
91133	Electrogastrography, diagnostic, transcutaneous; with provocative testing	-	-	IR	IR	IR
-26		0.94	32.97	IR	IR	IR

Other Procedures

		Medicare RVU	National Fee	50%	75%	90%
91299	Unlisted diagnostic gastroenterology procedure	-	-	IR	IR	IR
-26		-	-	IR	IR	IR

Ophthalmology

General Ophthalmological Services

New Patient

(See also HCPCS code G0117 for glaucoma screening for high risk patient furnished by an optometrist or ophthalmologist.)

(See also HCPCS code G0118 for glaucoma screening for high risk patient furnished under the direct supervision of an optometrist or ophthalm)

		Medicare RVU	National Fee	50%	75%	90%
92002	Ophthalmological services: medical examination and evaluation with initiation of diagnostic and treatment program; intermediate, new patient	1.87	67.46	94	108	124
92004	Ophthalmological services: medical examination and evaluation with initiation of diagnostic and treatment program; comprehensive, new patient, one or more visits	3.38	121.65	144	166	199

Established Patient

		Medicare RVU	National Fee	50%	75%	90%
92012	Ophthalmological services: medical examination and evaluation, with initiation or continuation of diagnostic and treatment program; intermediate, established patient	1.70	61.77	84	91	96
92014	Ophthalmological services: medical examination and evaluation, with initiation or continuation of diagnostic and treatment program; comprehensive, established patient, one or more visits	2.52	91.33	105	121	147

Special Ophthalmological Services

(Medicare fees for the code below are based on Non Facility RVUs. PFR information reflects fee when procedure is performed in a facility.)

(See also CPT Category III code 0025T for determination of corneal thickness (e.g., pachymetry) with interpretation and report, bilateral.)

(See also HCPCS code S0830 for ultrasound pachymetry to determine corneal thickness with interpretation and report, unilateral.)

(See also HCPCS code S0820 for computerized corneal topography, unilateral.)

		Medicare RVU	National Fee	50%	75%	90%
92015	Determination of refractive state	1.53	56.47	32	37	46
92018	Ophthalmological examination and evaluation, under general anesthesia, with or without manipulation of globe for passive range of motion or other manipulation to facilitate diagnostic examination; complete	3.61	127.34	284	333	384
92019	Ophthalmological examination and evaluation, under general anesthesia, with or without manipulation of globe for passive range of motion or other manipulation to facilitate diagnostic examination; limited	1.87	65.94	138	176	225
92020	Gonioscopy (separate procedure)	0.70	25.01	52	61	80
● 92025	Computerized corneal topography, unilateral or bilateral, with interpretation and report	0.81	29.18	50	60	75
-26		0.48	16.67	IR	IR	IR

● = New Code ⊗ = Conscious Sedation ✚ = Add-on Code ∅ = Modifier '51' Exempt ▲ =Revised Code

Code	Description	Medicare RVU	National Fee	PFR Fee Information 50%	75%	90%
92060	Sensorimotor examination with multiple measurements of ocular deviation (eg, restrictive or paretic muscle with diplopia) with interpretation and report (separate procedure)	1.47	53.06	76	92	105
-26		0.99	34.87	53	64	73
92065	Orthoptic and/or pleoptic training, with continuing medical direction and evaluation	1.01	36.76	62	75	83
-26		0.52	18.19	37	45	50
92070	Fitting of contact lens for treatment of disease, including supply of lens	1.76	64.05	165	206	242
92081	Visual field examination, unilateral or bilateral, with interpretation and report; limited examination (eg, tangent screen, Autoplot, arc perimeter, or single stimulus level automated test, such as Octopus 3 or 7 equivalent)	1.33	48.89	56	65	90
-26		0.51	17.81	22	26	36
92082	Visual field examination, unilateral or bilateral, with interpretation and report; intermediate examination (eg, at least 2 isopters on Goldmann perimeter, or semiquantitative, automated suprathreshold screening program, Humphrey suprathreshold automatic diagnostic test, Octopus program 33)	1.72	63.67	84	104	132
-26		0.63	22.36	34	42	53
92083	Visual field examination, unilateral or bilateral, with interpretation and report; extended examination (eg, Goldmann visual fields with at least 3 isopters plotted and static determination within the central 30°, or quantitative, automated threshold perimetry, Octopus program G-1, 32 or 42, Humphrey visual field analyzer full threshold programs 30-2, 24-2, or 30/60-2)	1.98	73.14	132	145	161
-26		0.72	25.39	53	58	64

(Medicare fees for the code below are based on Non Facility RVUs. PFR information reflects fee when procedure is performed in a facility.)

(Payment for code 92100 by Medicare is restricted to the presence of the following ICD-9-CM codes: 365.00 to 365.9, 743.20 to 743.22 and 767.8.)

Code	Description	Medicare RVU	National Fee	PFR Fee Information 50%	75%	90%
92100	Serial tonometry (separate procedure) with multiple measurements of intraocular pressure over an extended time period with interpretation and report, same day (eg, diurnal curve or medical treatment of acute elevation of intraocular pressure)	2.27	82.62	75	95	111
92120	Tonography with interpretation and report, recording indentation tonometer method or perilimbal suction method	1.88	68.22	74	90	113
92130	Tonography with water provocation	2.09	76.17	83	104	134
92135	Scanning computerized ophthalmic diagnostic imaging (eg, scanning laser) with interpretation and report, unilateral	1.16	42.45	86	121	162
-26		0.50	17.43	22	30	40
92136	Ophthalmic biometry by partial coherence interferometry with intraocular lens power calculation	2.22	82.24	107	122	138
-26		0.78	27.67	27	30	34
92140	Provocative tests for glaucoma, with interpretation and report, without tonography	1.48	54.19	61	72	79

Ophthalmoscopy

Code	Description	Medicare RVU	National Fee	PFR Fee Information 50%	75%	90%
92225	Ophthalmoscopy, extended, with retinal drawing (eg, for retinal detachment, melanoma), with interpretation and report; initial	0.62	21.98	85	92	114
92226	Ophthalmoscopy, extended, with retinal drawing (eg, for retinal detachment, melanoma), with interpretation and report; subsequent	0.56	20.09	76	84	97
92230	Fluorescein angioscopy with interpretation and report	1.95	71.63	113	151	189

(Payment for code 92235 by Medicare is restricted to the presence of the following ICD-9-CM codes: 362.01, 362.02, 362.12 - 362.16, 362.30 - 362.37, 362.52 - 362.55, 362.81 - 362.84, 363.00 - 363.22.)

Code	Description	Medicare RVU	National Fee	PFR Fee Information 50%	75%	90%
92235	Fluorescein angiography (includes multiframe imaging) with interpretation and report	3.43	126.96	264	325	370
-26		1.19	42.07	79	97	111

(Medicare fees for the code below are based on Non Facility RVUs. PFR information reflects fee when procedure is performed in a facility.)

Code	Description	Medicare RVU	National Fee	PFR Fee Information 50%	75%	90%
92240	Indocyanine-green angiography (includes multiframe imaging) with interpretation and report	6.89	256.95	258	344	392
-26		1.61	56.85	77	103	118
92250	Fundus photography with interpretation and report	1.94	72.01	90	112	134
-26		0.63	22.36	27	34	40
92260	Ophthalmodynamometry	0.46	16.67	77	88	96

© PFR 2007

● = New Code ⊗ = Conscious Sedation ✚ = Add-on Code ∅ = Modifier '51' Exempt ▲ =Revised Code

		Medicare RVU	National Fee	PFR Fee Information 50%	75%	90%

Other Specialized Services

		Medicare RVU	National Fee	50%	75%	90%
92265	Needle oculoelectromyography, one or more extraocular muscles, one or both eyes, with interpretation and report	2.24	81.86	147	166	200
-26		1.12	39.41	59	66	80
92270	Electro-oculography with interpretation and report	2.36	86.41	145	185	221
-26		1.15	40.55	65	83	99
92275	Electroretinography with interpretation and report	3.14	115.21	170	199	257
-26		1.46	51.54	77	90	116
92283	Color vision examination, extended, eg, anomaloscope or equivalent	1.08	40.17	61	67	75
-26		0.25	8.72	46	50	56
92284	Dark adaptation examination with interpretation and report	1.98	74.28	105	144	163
-26		0.33	11.75	26	36	41
92285	External ocular photography with interpretation and report for documentation of medical progress (eg, close-up photography, slit lamp photography, goniophotography, stereo-photography)	1.17	43.58	65	71	89
-26		0.30	10.61	16	18	22
92286	Special anterior segment photography with interpretation and report; with specular endothelial microscopy and cell count	3.53	131.13	215	269	340
-26		0.96	33.73	108	134	170
92287	Special anterior segment photography with interpretation and report; with fluorescein angiography	3.11	114.83	249	302	369

Contact Lens Services

(See HCPCS codes V2020 - V2799 for detailed supply coding for vision services.)

		Medicare RVU	National Fee	50%	75%	90%
92310	Prescription of optical and physical characteristics of and fitting of contact lens, with medical supervision of adaptation; corneal lens, both eyes, except for aphakia	2.31	83.00	169	205	259
92311	Prescription of optical and physical characteristics of and fitting of contact lens, with medical supervision of adaptation; corneal lens for aphakia, one eye	2.25	81.10	159	189	244
92312	Prescription of optical and physical characteristics of and fitting of contact lens, with medical supervision of adaptation; corneal lens for aphakia, both eyes	2.48	89.06	196	241	319
92313	Prescription of optical and physical characteristics of and fitting of contact lens, with medical supervision of adaptation; corneoscleral lens	2.11	76.55	197	241	313
92314	Prescription of optical and physical characteristics of contact lens, with medical supervision of adaptation and direction of fitting by independent technician; corneal lens, both eyes except for aphakia	1.69	61.39	135	173	238
92315	Prescription of optical and physical characteristics of contact lens, with medical supervision of adaptation and direction of fitting by independent technician; corneal lens for aphakia, one eye	1.43	52.30	122	158	199
92316	Prescription of optical and physical characteristics of contact lens, with medical supervision of adaptation and direction of fitting by independent technician; corneal lens for aphakia, both eyes	1.80	65.56	139	178	223
92317	Prescription of optical and physical characteristics of contact lens, with medical supervision of adaptation and direction of fitting by independent technician; corneoscleral lens	1.53	56.09	105	150	212
92325	Modification of contact lens (separate procedure), with medical supervision of adaptation	0.52	19.71	36	46	59
92326	Replacement of contact lens	1.47	55.71	89	123	152

Spectacle Services (Including Prosthesis For Aphakia)

		Medicare RVU	National Fee	50%	75%	90%
92340	Fitting of spectacles, except for aphakia; monofocal	1.02	37.14	55	64	74
92341	Fitting of spectacles, except for aphakia; bifocal	1.15	41.69	65	76	89
92342	Fitting of spectacles, except for aphakia; multifocal, other than bifocal	1.23	44.72	67	81	104
92352	Fitting of spectacle prosthesis for aphakia; monofocal	1.03	37.52	43	55	99
92353	Fitting of spectacle prosthesis for aphakia; multifocal	1.22	44.34	51	64	77
92354	Fitting of spectacle mounted low vision aid; single element system	6.82	258.46	IR	IR	IR
92355	Fitting of spectacle mounted low vision aid; telescopic or other compound lens system	3.37	127.71	IR	IR	IR

● = New Code ⊗ = Conscious Sedation ✚ = Add-on Code ∅ = Modifier '51' Exempt ▲ =Revised Code

		Medicare RVU	National Fee	PFR Fee Information 50%	75%	90%
92358	Prosthesis service for aphakia, temporary (disposable or loan, including materials)	0.84	31.83	73	90	128
92370	Repair and refitting spectacles; except for aphakia	0.85	31.08	46	57	87
92371	Repair and refitting spectacles; spectacle prosthesis for aphakia	0.55	20.84	51	61	71

(For 92392, see HCPCS codes V2600 - V2615 for a more detailed description.)
(For 92395, see HCPCS codes V2100 - V2499 for a more detailed description.)
(For 92396, see HCPCS codes V2500 - V2599 for a more detailed description.)

Other Procedures

		Medicare RVU	National Fee	PFR Fee Information 50%	75%	90%
92499	Unlisted ophthalmological service or procedure	-	-	IR	IR	IR
-26		-	-	IR	IR	IR

Special Otorhinolaryngologic Services

(For non-physician evaluation of dysphagia, see HCPCS code V5364 "Dysphagia Screening". For radiologic evaluation of swallowing function, see CPT code 74230.)

		Medicare RVU	National Fee	PFR Fee Information 50%	75%	90%
92502	Otolaryngologic examination under general anesthesia	2.59	92.47	283	342	404
92504	Binocular microscopy (separate diagnostic procedure)	0.70	25.77	58	89	121

(For non-physician evaluation of language skills, see HCPCS code V5363 "Language Screening".)

		Medicare RVU	National Fee	PFR Fee Information 50%	75%	90%
92506	Evaluation of speech, language, voice, communication, and/or auditory processing	3.65	134.92	140	166	206
92507	Treatment of speech, language, voice, communication, and/or auditory processing disorder; individual	1.67	61.39	79	90	107
92508	Treatment of speech, language, voice, communication, and/or auditory processing disorder; group, 2 or more individuals	0.78	28.42	50	56	64
92511	Nasopharyngoscopy with endoscope (separate procedure)	4.08	151.59	198	234	369
92512	Nasal function studies (eg, rhinomanometry)	1.66	60.64	117	144	201
92516	Facial nerve function studies (eg, electroneuronography)	1.63	60.26	112	150	198
92520	Laryngeal function studies (ie, aerodynamic testing and acoustic testing)	1.38	49.27	219	267	321
92526	Treatment of swallowing dysfunction and/or oral function for feeding	2.22	81.86	113	143	165

Vestibular Function Test, With Observation and Evaluation By Physician, Without Electrical Recording

		Medicare RVU	National Fee	PFR Fee Information 50%	75%	90%
92531	Spontaneous nystagmus, including gaze	-	-	44	56	77
92532	Positional nystagmus test	-	-	47	64	98
92533	Caloric vestibular test, each irrigation (binaural, bithermal stimulation constitutes four tests)	-	-	69	87	129
92534	Optokinetic nystagmus test	-	-	44	54	62

Vestibular Function Tests, With Recording (EG, ENG, PENG), and Medical Diagnostic Evaluation

		Medicare RVU	National Fee	PFR Fee Information 50%	75%	90%
92541	Spontaneous nystagmus test, including gaze and fixation nystagmus, with recording	1.49	54.95	109	134	189
-26		0.59	20.84	82	100	142
92542	Positional nystagmus test, minimum of 4 positions, with recording	1.52	56.47	98	124	185
-26		0.48	17.05	74	93	139
92543	Caloric vestibular test, each irrigation (binaural, bithermal stimulation constitutes four tests), with recording	0.71	26.53	109	140	215
-26		0.16	5.68	76	98	150
92544	Optokinetic nystagmus test, bidirectional, foveal or peripheral stimulation, with recording	1.22	45.10	61	85	120
-26		0.38	13.26	46	64	90
92545	Oscillating tracking test, with recording	1.11	41.31	64	80	106
-26		0.34	12.13	48	60	80

© PFR 2007

● = New Code ⊗ = Conscious Sedation ➕ = Add-on Code ∅ = Modifier '51' Exempt ▲ =Revised Code

		Medicare RVU	National Fee	PFR Fee Information 50%	75%	90%
92546	Sinusoidal vertical axis rotational testing	2.26	84.51	98	146	193
-26		0.42	14.78	74	110	145
✚ 92547	Use of vertical electrodes (List separately in addition to code for primary procedure)	0.15	5.68	58	73	98
92548	Computerized dynamic posturography	2.75	102.32	197	239	273
-26		0.75	26.53	89	108	123

Audiologic Function Tests With Medical Diagnostic Evaluation
(For non-physician hearing services, see HCPCS codes V5008 - V5336.)

		Medicare RVU	National Fee	PFR Fee Information 50%	75%	90%
92551	Screening test, pure tone, air only	0.26	9.85	30	36	49
92552	Pure tone audiometry (threshold); air only	0.51	19.33	39	44	54
92553	Pure tone audiometry (threshold); air and bone	0.73	27.67	55	64	72
92555	Speech audiometry threshold;	0.42	15.92	33	38	44
92556	Speech audiometry threshold; with speech recognition	0.62	23.50	48	58	71
	(UNBUNDLING ALERT: 92557 cannot be used with 69210, 92552, 92553, 92556 by the same physician on the same day.)					
92557	Comprehensive audiometry threshold evaluation and speech recognition (92553 and 92556 combined)	1.33	50.40	93	106	132
92559	Audiometric testing of groups	-	-	50	62	75
92560	Bekesy audiometry; screening	-	-	47	67	75
92561	Bekesy audiometry; diagnostic	0.77	29.18	87	97	135
92562	Loudness balance test, alternate binaural or monaural	0.52	19.71	33	39	58
92563	Tone decay test	0.45	17.05	34	49	66
92564	Short increment sensitivity index (SISI)	0.51	19.33	39	45	62
92565	Stenger test, pure tone	0.40	15.16	40	51	63
92567	Tympanometry (impedance testing)	0.57	21.60	38	48	62
92568	Acoustic reflex testing; threshold	0.36	13.64	34	41	46
92569	Acoustic reflex testing; decay	0.39	14.78	37	49	58
92571	Filtered speech test	0.43	16.30	41	48	64
92572	Staggered spondaic word test	0.23	8.72	37	45	57
92575	Sensorineural acuity level test	0.52	19.71	35	43	64
92576	Synthetic sentence identification test	0.52	19.71	38	48	61
92577	Stenger test, speech	0.67	25.39	42	50	58
92579	Visual reinforcement audiometry (VRA)	0.82	31.08	69	82	102
92582	Conditioning play audiometry	0.88	33.35	69	86	98
92583	Select picture audiometry	0.92	34.87	60	72	82
92584	Electrocochleography	2.35	89.06	247	296	336
92585	Auditory evoked potentials for evoked response audiometry and/or testing of the central nervous system; comprehensive	2.69	100.05	299	368	482
-26		0.72	25.39	150	184	241
92586	Auditory evoked potentials for evoked response audiometry and/or testing of the central nervous system; limited	1.88	71.25	190	222	256
92587	Evoked otoacoustic emissions; limited (single stimulus level, either transient or distortion products)	1.44	54.19	103	120	136
-26		0.20	7.20	31	36	41

● = New Code　⊗ = Conscious Sedation　✚ = Add-on Code　∅ = Modifier '51' Exempt　▲ =Revised Code

		Medicare RVU	National Fee	PFR Fee Information 50%	75%	90%
92588	Evoked otoacoustic emissions; comprehensive or diagnostic evaluation (comparison of transient and/or distortion product otoacoustic emissions at multiple levels and frequencies)	1.98	73.52	148	164	181
-26		0.52	18.19	52	57	63
92590	Hearing aid examination and selection; monaural	-	-	97	132	149
92591	Hearing aid examination and selection; binaural	-	-	145	160	203
92592	Hearing aid check; monaural	-	-	40	47	58
92593	Hearing aid check; binaural	-	-	60	71	82
92594	Electroacoustic evaluation for hearing aid; monaural	-	-	42	48	55
92595	Electroacoustic evaluation for hearing aid; binaural	-	-	58	72	97
92596	Ear protector attenuation measurements	0.74	28.04	49	59	67
92597	Evaluation for use and/or fitting of voice prosthetic device to supplement oral speech	2.58	94.36	196	217	264

Evaluative and Therapeutic Services

		Medicare RVU	National Fee	PFR Fee Information 50%	75%	90%
92601	Diagnostic analysis of cochlear implant, patient younger than 7 years of age; with programming	3.91	148.18	295	353	440
92602	Diagnostic analysis of cochlear implant, patient younger than 7 years of age; subsequent reprogramming	2.69	101.94	208	248	310
92603	Diagnostic analysis of cochlear implant, age 7 years or older; with programming	2.47	93.61	197	235	294
92604	Diagnostic analysis of cochlear implant, age 7 years or older; subsequent reprogramming	1.61	61.01	129	156	193
92605	Evaluation for prescription of non-speech-generating augmentative and alternative communication device	-	-	IR	IR	IR
92606	Therapeutic service(s) for the use of non-speech-generating device, including programming and modification	-	-	IR	IR	IR
92607	Evaluation for prescription for speech-generating augmentative and alternative communication device, face-to-face with the patient; first hour	3.43	129.99	247	294	366
✚ 92608	Evaluation for prescription for speech-generating augmentative and alternative communication device, face-to-face with the patient; each additional 30 minutes (List separately in addition to code for primary procedure)	0.68	25.77	49	59	72
92609	Therapeutic services for the use of speech-generating device, including programming and modification	1.81	68.59	132	160	200
92610	Evaluation of oral and pharyngeal swallowing function	3.06	115.97	212	319	382
92611	Motion fluoroscopic evaluation of swallowing function by cine or video recording	3.12	118.24	212	319	382
92612	Flexible fiberoptic endoscopic evaluation of swallowing by cine or video recording;	4.05	148.56	371	443	553
92613	Flexible fiberoptic endoscopic evaluation of swallowing by cine or video recording; physician interpretation and report only	1.12	39.79	94	111	139
92614	Flexible fiberoptic endoscopic evaluation, laryngeal sensory testing by cine or video recording;	3.75	137.19	304	363	453
92615	Flexible fiberoptic endoscopic evaluation, laryngeal sensory testing by cine or video recording; physician interpretation and report only	0.99	35.24	86	103	128
92616	Flexible fiberoptic endoscopic evaluation of swallowing and laryngeal sensory testing by cine or video recording;	5.21	190.25	413	492	614
92617	Flexible fiberoptic endoscopic evaluation of swallowing and laryngeal sensory testing by cine or video recording; physician interpretation and report only	1.23	43.58	101	120	150
92620	Evaluation of central auditory function, with report; initial 60 minutes	1.38	52.30	96	114	143
92621	Evaluation of central auditory function, with report; each additional 15 minutes	0.35	13.26	27	32	40
92625	Assessment of tinnitus (includes pitch, loudness matching, and masking)	1.36	51.54	96	114	142
92626	Evaluation of auditory rehabilitation status; first hour	2.17	82.24	50	59	74
✚ 92627	Evaluation of auditory rehabilitation status; each additional 15 minutes (List separately in addition to code for primary procedure)	0.54	20.46	48	57	71
92630	Auditory rehabilitation; prelingual hearing loss	-	-	IR	IR	IR
92633	Auditory rehabilitation; postlingual hearing loss	-	-	IR	IR	IR

Special Diagnostic Procedures

		Medicare RVU	National Fee	PFR Fee Information 50%	75%	90%
● 92640	Diagnostic analysis with programming of auditory brainstem implant, per hour	1.41	53.44	79	94	117

● = New Code ⊗ = Conscious Sedation ✚ = Add-on Code ∅ = Modifier '51' Exempt ▲ =Revised Code

		Medicare RVU	National Fee	PFR Fee Information 50%	75%	90%

Other Procedures

92700 Unlisted otorhinolaryngological service or procedure | - | - | IR | IR | IR

Cardiovascular

Therapeutic Services

	Code	Description	RVU	Fee	50%	75%	90%
	92950	Cardiopulmonary resuscitation (eg, in cardiac arrest)	8.03	289.92	483	586	665
⊗	**92953**	Temporary transcutaneous pacing	0.32	11.37	184	204	240
⊗	**92960**	Cardioversion, elective, electrical conversion of arrhythmia; external	8.15	300.15	386	455	520
⊗	**92961**	Cardioversion, elective, electrical conversion of arrhythmia; internal (separate procedure)	7.07	250.50	584	703	807
	92970	Cardioassist-method of circulatory assist; internal	4.87	171.30	495	551	641
	92971	Cardioassist-method of circulatory assist; external	2.74	97.02	224	276	336
⊗ ✚	**92973**	Percutaneous transluminal coronary thrombectomy (List separately in addition to code for primary procedure)	4.93	174.33	478	582	673
⊗ ✚	**92974**	Transcatheter placement of radiation delivery device for subsequent coronary intravascular brachytherapy (List separately in addition to code for primary procedure)	4.52	159.93	510	617	702
⊗	**92975**	Thrombolysis, coronary; by intracoronary infusion, including selective coronary angiography	10.83	382.76	1356	1519	1891
	92977	Thrombolysis, coronary; by intravenous infusion	6.92	262.25	727	839	944
⊗ ✚	**92978**	Intravascular ultrasound (coronary vessel or graft) during diagnostic evaluation and/or therapeutic intervention including imaging supervision, interpretation and report; initial vessel (List separately in addition to code for primary procedure)	-	-	586	739	967
	-26		2.64	93.23	234	296	387
⊗ ✚	**92979**	Intravascular ultrasound (coronary vessel or graft) during diagnostic evaluation and/or therapeutic intervention including imaging supervision, interpretation and report; each additional vessel (List separately in addition to code for primary procedure)	-	-	417	546	665
	-26		2.12	75.04	188	246	299
⊗	**92980**	Transcatheter placement of an intracoronary stent(s), percutaneous, with or without other therapeutic intervention, any method; single vessel	22.50	796.23	3404	3924	4263
⊗ ✚	**92981**	Transcatheter placement of an intracoronary stent(s), percutaneous, with or without other therapeutic intervention, any method; each additional vessel (List separately in addition to code for primary procedure) *(UNBUNDLING ALERT: 92982 cannot be used with 33210 or 36140 by the same physician on the same day.)*	6.25	220.94	1391	1589	1834
⊗	**92982**	Percutaneous transluminal coronary balloon angioplasty; single vessel	16.69	590.82	3067	3624	3877
⊗ ✚	**92984**	Percutaneous transluminal coronary balloon angioplasty; each additional vessel (List separately in addition to code for primary procedure)	4.46	157.65	1214	1474	1608
⊗	**92986**	Percutaneous balloon valvuloplasty; aortic valve	37.05	1317.70	3350	3994	4523
⊗	**92987**	Percutaneous balloon valvuloplasty; mitral valve	38.31	1362.42	3229	3716	4290
	92990	Percutaneous balloon valvuloplasty; pulmonary valve	29.49	1048.62	2589	3000	3443
	92992	Atrial septectomy or septostomy; transvenous method, balloon (eg, Rashkind type) (includes cardiac catheterization)	-	-	4737	5206	5804
	92993	Atrial septectomy or septostomy; blade method (Park septostomy) (includes cardiac catheterization) *(UNBUNDLING ALERT: 92995 cannot be used with 92982 or 92984 by the same physician on the same day.)*	-	-	3668	3992	4373
⊗	**92995**	Percutaneous transluminal coronary atherectomy, by mechanical or other method, with or without balloon angioplasty; single vessel *(UNBUNDLING ALERT: 92996 cannot be used with 92982 or 92984 by the same physician on the same day.)*	18.36	649.94	3246	3775	4057
⊗ ✚	**92996**	Percutaneous transluminal coronary atherectomy, by mechanical or other method, with or without balloon angioplasty; each additional vessel (List separately in addition to code for primary procedure)	4.77	168.26	1282	1447	1681
	92997	Percutaneous transluminal pulmonary artery balloon angioplasty; single vessel	17.31	610.15	2702	3303	3934
✚	**92998**	Percutaneous transluminal pulmonary artery balloon angioplasty; each additional vessel (List separately in addition to code for primary procedure)	8.62	303.94	1346	1644	2019

© PFR 2007

● = New Code ⊗ = Conscious Sedation ✚ = Add-on Code ∅ = Modifier '51' Exempt ▲ =Revised Code

		Medicare RVU	National Fee	PFR Fee Information 50%	75%	90%

Cardiography

		Medicare RVU	National Fee	50%	75%	90%
93000	Electrocardiogram, routine ECG with at least 12 leads; with interpretation and report	0.67	24.63	72	86	95
93005	Electrocardiogram, routine ECG with at least 12 leads; tracing only, without interpretation and report	0.43	16.30	53	68	81
93010	Electrocardiogram, routine ECG with at least 12 leads; interpretation and report only	0.24	8.34	37	46	55
93012	Telephonic transmission of post-symptom electrocardiogram rhythm strip(s), 24-hour attended monitoring, per 30 day period of time; tracing only	5.73	217.15	285	406	549
93014	Telephonic transmission of post-symptom electrocardiogram rhythm strip(s), 24-hour attended monitoring, per 30 day period of time; physician review with interpretation and report only	0.74	26.15	69	114	164
	(UNBUNDLING ALERT: 93015 cannot be used with 93017 or 93018 by the same physician on the same day.)					
93015	Cardiovascular stress test using maximal or submaximal treadmill or bicycle exercise, continuous electrocardiographic monitoring, and/or pharmacological stress; with physician supervision, with interpretation and report	2.84	104.60	360	424	469
93016	Cardiovascular stress test using maximal or submaximal treadmill or bicycle exercise, continuous electrocardiographic monitoring, and/or pharmacological stress; physician supervision only, without interpretation and report	0.66	23.12	109	119	142
93017	Cardiovascular stress test using maximal or submaximal treadmill or bicycle exercise, continuous electrocardiographic monitoring, and/or pharmacological stress; tracing only, without interpretation and report	1.75	66.32	176	206	268
93018	Cardiovascular stress test using maximal or submaximal treadmill or bicycle exercise, continuous electrocardiographic monitoring, and/or pharmacological stress; interpretation and report only	0.43	15.16	132	159	206
93024	Ergonovine provocation test	3.08	112.18	376	429	475
-26		1.70	59.88	226	257	285
93025	Microvolt T-wave alternans for assessment of ventricular arrhythmias	7.56	283.47	726	852	937
-26		1.09	38.28	94	111	122
93040	Rhythm ECG, one to three leads; with interpretation and report	0.38	13.64	44	54	67
93041	Rhythm ECG, one to three leads; tracing only without interpretation and report	0.16	6.06	30	39	44
93042	Rhythm ECG, one to three leads; interpretation and report only	0.22	7.58	30	37	43
	(Payment for 93224 - 93227 by Medicare is restricted to the following ICD-9-CM codes: V67.51, 410.02 - 410.82, 413.0 - 413.9, 427.0 - 427.42, 427.60 - 427.89, 780.2, 780.4, 785.1, 786.50, 786.59.)					
	(Payment for 93224 - 93227 by Medicare is subject to a frequency limitation of one procedure in a 6 month period.)					
93224	Electrocardiographic monitoring for 24 hours by continuous original ECG waveform recording and storage, with visual superimposition scanning; includes recording, scanning analysis with report, physician review and interpretation	4.05	151.59	390	441	522
93225	Electrocardiographic monitoring for 24 hours by continuous original ECG waveform recording and storage, with visual superimposition scanning; recording (includes hook-up, recording, and disconnection)	1.28	48.51	126	154	190
93226	Electrocardiographic monitoring for 24 hours by continuous original ECG waveform recording and storage, with visual superimposition scanning; scanning analysis with report	2.02	76.55	184	215	252
93227	Electrocardiographic monitoring for 24 hours by continuous original ECG waveform recording and storage, with visual superimposition scanning; physician review and interpretation	0.75	26.53	147	173	220
93230	Electrocardiographic monitoring for 24 hours by continuous original ECG waveform recording and storage without superimposition scanning utilizing a device capable of producing a full miniaturized printout; includes recording, microprocessor-based analysis with report, physician review and interpretation	4.27	159.93	385	506	572
93231	Electrocardiographic monitoring for 24 hours by continuous original ECG waveform recording and storage without superimposition scanning utilizing a device capable of producing a full miniaturized printout; recording (includes hook-up, recording, and disconnection)	1.48	56.09	129	155	170
93232	Electrocardiographic monitoring for 24 hours by continuous original ECG waveform recording and storage without superimposition scanning utilizing a device capable of producing a full miniaturized printout; microprocessor-based analysis with report	2.05	77.69	167	203	231
93233	Electrocardiographic monitoring for 24 hours by continuous original ECG waveform recording and storage without superimposition scanning utilizing a device capable of producing a full miniaturized printout; physician review and interpretation	0.74	26.15	143	197	250

● = New Code ⊗ = Conscious Sedation ✚ = Add-on Code ∅ = Modifier '51' Exempt ▲ =Revised Code

		Medicare RVU	National Fee	PFR Fee Information 50%	75%	90%
93235	Electrocardiographic monitoring for 24 hours by continuous computerized monitoring and non-continuous recording, and real-time data analysis utilizing a device capable of producing intermittent full-sized waveform tracings, possibly patient activated; includes monitoring and real-time data analysis with report, physician review and interpretation	-	-	339	396	430
93236	Electrocardiographic monitoring for 24 hours by continuous computerized monitoring and non-continuous recording, and real-time data analysis utilizing a device capable of producing intermittent full-sized waveform tracings, possibly patient activated; monitoring and real-time data analysis with report	-	-	202	239	294
93237	Electrocardiographic monitoring for 24 hours by continuous computerized monitoring and non-continuous recording, and real-time data analysis utilizing a device capable of producing intermittent full-sized waveform tracings, possibly patient activated; physician review and interpretation	0.65	22.74	142	176	233
93268	Patient demand single or multiple event recording with presymptom memory loop, 24-hour attended monitoring, per 30 day period of time; includes transmission, physician review and interpretation	7.82	294.46	418	514	645
93270	Patient demand single or multiple event recording with presymptom memory loop, 24-hour attended monitoring, per 30 day period of time; recording (includes hook-up, recording, and disconnection)	1.08	40.93	131	158	203
93271	Patient demand single or multiple event recording with presymptom memory loop, 24-hour attended monitoring, per 30 day period of time; monitoring, receipt of transmissions, and analysis	6.00	227.38	268	349	444
93272	Patient demand single or multiple event recording with presymptom memory loop, 24-hour attended monitoring, per 30 day period of time; physician review and interpretation only	0.74	26.15	104	129	171
93278	Signal-averaged electrocardiography (SAECG), with or without ECG	1.46	54.19	189	250	334
-26		0.36	12.51	76	100	134

Echocardiography

		Medicare RVU	National Fee	PFR Fee Information 50%	75%	90%
93303	Transthoracic echocardiography for congenital cardiac anomalies; complete	5.98	221.70	514	611	744
-26		1.85	65.18	206	244	298
93304	Transthoracic echocardiography for congenital cardiac anomalies; follow-up or limited study	3.36	124.30	272	339	412
-26		1.06	37.14	109	136	165
	(UNBUNDLING ALERT: 93307 cannot be used with 93308 by the same physician on the same day.)					
93307	Echocardiography, transthoracic, real-time with image documentation (2D) with or without M-mode recording; complete	5.28	196.69	484	557	754
-26		1.33	46.99	194	223	302
93308	Echocardiography, transthoracic, real-time with image documentation (2D) with or without M-mode recording; follow-up or limited study	2.94	109.52	262	302	415
-26		0.77	27.29	105	121	166
	(UNBUNDLING ALERT: 93312 cannot be used with 43200, 43234, 93313, 93314 by the same physician on the same day.)					
⊗ 93312	Echocardiography, transesophageal, real time with image documentation (2D) (with or without M-mode recording); including probe placement, image acquisition, interpretation and report	7.88	290.29	646	734	825
-26		3.13	110.28	258	294	330
	(UNBUNDLING ALERT: 93313 cannot be used with 43200, 43234, or 93314 by the same physician on the same day.)					
⊗ 93313	Echocardiography, transesophageal, real time with image documentation (2D) (with or without M-mode recording); placement of transesophageal probe only	1.20	41.69	210	277	347
⊗ 93314	Echocardiography, transesophageal, real time with image documentation (2D) (with or without M-mode recording); image acquisition, interpretation and report only	6.57	244.06	483	575	667
-26		1.79	62.91	193	230	267
⊗ 93315	Transesophageal echocardiography for congenital cardiac anomalies; including probe placement, image acquisition, interpretation and report	-	-	IR	IR	IR
-26		3.97	139.84	639	735	829
⊗ 93316	Transesophageal echocardiography for congenital cardiac anomalies; placement of transesophageal probe only	1.25	43.58	162	197	237
⊗ 93317	Transesophageal echocardiography for congenital cardiac anomalies; image acquisition, interpretation and report only	-	-	IR	IR	IR
-26		2.60	91.71	491	620	730

● = New Code ⊗ = Conscious Sedation ✚ = Add-on Code ∅ = Modifier '51' Exempt ▲ =Revised Code

		Medicare RVU	National Fee	PFR Fee Information 50%	75%	90%
⊗ **93318**	Echocardiography, transesophageal (TEE) for monitoring purposes, including probe placement, real time 2-dimensional image acquisition and interpretation leading to ongoing (continuous) assessment of (dynamically changing) cardiac pumping function and to therapeutic measures on an immediate time basis	-	-	IR	IR	IR
-26		2.93	102.70	587	740	890
✚ **93320**	Doppler echocardiography, pulsed wave and/or continuous wave with spectral display (List separately in addition to codes for echocardiographic imaging); complete	2.33	86.79	306	372	432
-26		0.55	19.33	122	149	173
✚ **93321**	Doppler echocardiography, pulsed wave and/or continuous wave with spectral display (List separately in addition to codes for echocardiographic imaging); follow-up or limited study (List separately in addition to codes for echocardiographic imaging)	1.28	47.75	168	204	236
-26		0.23	7.96	67	82	94
✚ **93325**	Doppler echocardiography color flow velocity mapping (List separately in addition to codes for echocardiography)	2.65	100.05	244	261	301
-26		0.11	3.79	98	104	120
93350	Echocardiography, transthoracic, real-time with image documentation (2D), with or without M-mode recording, during rest and cardiovascular stress test using treadmill, bicycle exercise and/or pharmacologically induced stress, with interpretation and report	4.69	172.05	687	827	1049
-26		2.16	76.17	275	331	420

Cardiac Catheterization

(UNBUNDLING ALERT: 93501 cannot be used with 33210, 36000, 36010, 36140, 36489, 36491, 76000, 93561, or 93562 by the same physician on the same day.)

		Medicare RVU	National Fee	50%	75%	90%
⊘ **93501**	Right heart catheterization	-	-	2045	2724	3126
-26		4.50	159.17	511	681	782

(UNBUNDLING ALERT: 93503 cannot be used with 36010 by the same physician on the same day.)

⊘ **93503**	Insertion and placement of flow directed catheter (eg, Swan-Ganz) for monitoring purposes	3.74	130.75	624	765	856

(UNBUNDLING ALERT: 93505 cannot be used with 36000, 36010 or 76000 by the same physician on the same day.)

⊘ **93505**	Endomyocardial biopsy	-	-	1037	1468	1727
-26		6.52	230.42	778	1101	1295
⊘ **93508**	Catheter placement in coronary artery(s), arterial coronary conduit(s), and/or venous coronary bypass graft(s) for coronary angiography without concomitant left heart catheterization	-	-	1793	2522	3176
-26		6.50	230.80	628	883	1112

(UNBUNDLING ALERT: 93510 cannot be used with 33210, 36140, 36600, 36620, 36625, 76000, 93561, or 93562 by the same physician on the same day.)

(This code is for a left heart catheterization, but it is rarely used. The code includes introduction, positioning and repositioning of catheter(s). Precise documentation is necessary for this code.)

⊘ **93510**	Left heart catheterization, retrograde, from the brachial artery, axillary artery or femoral artery; percutaneous	-	-	4045	6530	9279
-26		6.84	242.92	809	1306	1856
⊘ **93511**	Left heart catheterization, retrograde, from the brachial artery, axillary artery or femoral artery; by cutdown	-	-	3971	6416	7831
-26		7.87	278.93	794	1283	1566
⊘ **93514**	Left heart catheterization by left ventricular puncture	-	-	3893	5591	7301
-26		10.67	377.46	973	1398	1825

● = New Code ⊗ = Conscious Sedation ✚ = Add-on Code ⊘ = Modifier '51' Exempt ▲ =Revised Code

		Medicare RVU	National Fee	PFR Fee Information 50%	75%	90%
⊗ ∅ **93524**	Combined transseptal and retrograde left heart catheterization	-	-	4247	5309	6370
-26		10.75	380.87	849	1062	1274
	(UNBUNDLING ALERT: 93526 cannot be used with 33210, 36000, 36010, 36013, 36014, 36015, 36489, 36491, 36600, 36620, 36625, 76000, 93501, 93510, 93561 or 93562 by the same physician on the same day.)					
⊗ ∅ **93526**	Combined right heart catheterization and retrograde left heart catheterization	-	-	5341	7717	9260
-26		9.33	330.85	1068	1543	1852
	(UNBUNDLING ALERT: 93527 cannot be used with 36013, 36014 or 36015 by the same physician on the same day.)					
⊗ ∅ **93527**	Combined right heart catheterization and transseptal left heart catheterization through intact septum (with or without retrograde left heart catheterization)	-	-	5361	9000	10510
-26		11.27	399.44	1072	1800	2102
	(UNBUNDLING ALERT: 93528 cannot be used with 36013, 36014 or 36015 by the same physician on the same day.)					
⊗ ∅ **93528**	Combined right heart catheterization with left ventricular puncture (with or without retrograde left heart catheterization)	-	-	4175	5915	7799
-26		13.80	488.88	1044	1479	1950
	(UNBUNDLING ALERT: 93529 cannot be used with 36013, 36014 or 36015 by the same physician on the same day.)					
⊗ ∅ **93529**	Combined right heart catheterization and left heart catheterization through existing septal opening (with or without retrograde left heart catheterization)	-	-	3669	5681	7148
-26		7.48	265.28	550	852	1072
⊗ ∅ **93530**	Right heart catheterization, for congenital cardiac anomalies	-	-	1952	2883	4226
-26		6.43	227.76	586	865	1268
∅ **93531**	Combined right heart catheterization and retrograde left heart catheterization, for congenital cardiac anomalies	-	-	5534	8286	10694
-26		12.55	443.78	1107	1657	2139
∅ **93532**	Combined right heart catheterization and transseptal left heart catheterization through intact septum with or without retrograde left heart catheterization, for congenital cardiac anomalies	-	-	5423	7918	9731
-26		14.89	526.40	1356	1980	2433
∅ **93533**	Combined right heart catheterization and transseptal left heart catheterization through existing septal opening, with or without retrograde left heart catheterization, for congenital cardiac anomalies	-	-	4853	6745	8510
-26		10.03	354.72	971	1349	1702
	(UNBUNDLING ALERT: 93536 cannot be used with 36140, 36489, 36600, or 36620 by the same physician on the same day.)					
⊗ ∅ **93539**	Injection procedure during cardiac catheterization; for selective opacification of arterial conduits (eg, internal mammary), whether native or used for bypass	0.59	20.84	279	315	333
⊗ ∅ **93540**	Injection procedure during cardiac catheterization; for selective opacification of aortocoronary venous bypass grafts, one or more coronary arteries	0.63	22.36	292	321	344
⊗ ∅ **93541**	Injection procedure during cardiac catheterization; for pulmonary angiography	0.42	14.78	288	342	424
⊗ ∅ **93542**	Injection procedure during cardiac catheterization; for selective right ventricular or right atrial angiography	0.42	14.78	247	280	326
⊗ ∅ **93543**	Injection procedure during cardiac catheterization; for selective left ventricular or left atrial angiography	0.42	14.78	272	341	400
⊗ ∅ **93544**	Injection procedure during cardiac catheterization; for aortography	0.37	12.89	262	286	307
⊗ ∅ **93545**	Injection procedure during cardiac catheterization; for selective coronary angiography (injection of radiopaque material may be by hand)	0.59	20.84	396	434	471
⊗ ∅ **93555**	Imaging supervision, interpretation and report for injection procedure(s) during cardiac catheterization; ventricular and/or atrial angiography	-	-	624	722	817
-26		1.19	42.07	94	108	123

© PFR 2007

● = New Code ⊗ = Conscious Sedation ✚ = Add-on Code ∅ = Modifier '51' Exempt ▲ =Revised Code

		Medicare RVU	National Fee	PFR Fee Information 50%	75%	90%
∅ **93556**	Imaging supervision, interpretation and report for injection procedure(s) during cardiac catheterization; pulmonary angiography, aortography, and/or selective coronary angiography including venous bypass grafts and arterial conduits (whether native or used in bypass)	-	-	903	1069	1233
-26		1.22	43.20	135	160	185
	(This code is bundled into 93510 "Left Heart Catheterization." If both codes are submitted, the insurance claim may be denied or delayed.)					
⊗ **93561**	Indicator dilution studies such as dye or thermal dilution, including arterial and/or venous catheterization; with cardiac output measurement (separate procedure)	-	-	222	314	372
-26		0.68	23.88	89	126	149
⊗ **93562**	Indicator dilution studies such as dye or thermal dilution, including arterial and/or venous catheterization; subsequent measurement of cardiac output	-	-	91	128	181
-26		0.22	7.58	36	51	72
✚ **93571**	Intravascular Doppler velocity and/or pressure derived coronary flow reserve measurement (coronary vessel or graft) during coronary angiography including pharmacologically induced stress; initial vessel (List separately in addition to code for primary procedure)	-	-	586	738	964
-26		2.62	92.47	234	295	386
✚ **93572**	Intravascular Doppler velocity and/or pressure derived coronary flow reserve measurement (coronary vessel or graft) during coronary angiography including pharmacologically induced stress; each additional vessel (List separately in addition to code for primary procedure)	-	-	339	582	732
-26		2.04	72.01	136	233	293

Repair of Septal Defect

		Medicare RVU	National Fee	50%	75%	90%
93580	Percutaneous transcatheter closure of congenital interatrial communication (ie, Fontan fenestration, atrial septal defect) with implant	27.19	961.84	9260	11132	12807
93581	Percutaneous transcatheter closure of a congenital ventricular septal defect with implant	36.50	1290.41	9640	11631	14176

Intracardiac Electrophysiological Procedures/Studies

		Medicare RVU	National Fee	50%	75%	90%
∅ **93600**	Bundle of His recording	-	-	692	809	876
-26		3.18	112.56	415	485	526
∅ **93602**	Intra-atrial recording	-	-	468	550	601
-26		3.18	112.56	337	396	433
∅ **93603**	Right ventricular recording	-	-	533	612	669
-26		3.18	112.56	336	386	421
✚ **93609**	Intraventricular and/or intra-atrial mapping of tachycardia site(s) with catheter manipulation to record from multiple sites to identify origin of tachycardia (List separately in addition to code for primary procedure)	-	-	1450	1718	2030
-26		7.49	264.90	1044	1237	1462
∅ **93610**	Intra-atrial pacing	-	-	595	748	844
-26		4.51	159.55	357	449	506
∅ **93612**	Intraventricular pacing	-	-	587	678	830
-26		4.51	159.55	423	488	598
✚ **93613**	Intracardiac electrophysiologic 3-dimensional mapping (List separately in addition to code for primary procedure)	10.51	371.77	1085	1238	1414
∅ **93615**	Esophageal recording of atrial electrogram with or without ventricular electrogram(s);	-	-	141	169	191
-26		1.35	47.37	85	101	115
∅ **93616**	Esophageal recording of atrial electrogram with or without ventricular electrogram(s); with pacing	-	-	275	387	451
-26		2.01	70.49	165	232	271
	(UNBUNDLING ALERT: 93618 cannot be used with 33210, 36140, 36489, 36491, 36600, 36620, 36625, 92950, 92960, 93562, 93603, 93610, or 93612 by the same physician on the same day.)					
∅ **93618**	Induction of arrhythmia by electrical pacing	-	-	1464	1654	2062
-26		6.39	225.87	864	976	1217

		Medicare RVU	National Fee	PFR Fee Information 50%	75%	90%
⊗ ∅ **93619**	Comprehensive electrophysiologic evaluation with right atrial pacing and recording, right ventricular pacing and recording, His bundle recording, including insertion and repositioning of multiple electrode catheters, without induction or attempted induction of arrhythmia	-	-	2455	2784	2994
-26		11.19	396.03	1399	1587	1707
⊗ ∅ **93620**	Comprehensive electrophysiologic evaluation including insertion and repositioning of multiple electrode catheters with induction or attempted induction of arrhythmia; with right atrial pacing and recording, right ventricular pacing and recording, His bundle recording	-	-	IR	IR	IR
-26		17.59	622.66	3445	3615	3927
⊗ ✚ **93621**	Comprehensive electrophysiologic evaluation including insertion and repositioning of multiple electrode catheters with induction or attempted induction of arrhythmia; with left atrial pacing and recording from coronary sinus or left atrium (List separately in addition to code for primary procedure)	-	-	3445	3615	4127
-26		3.15	111.42	2067	2169	2476
⊗ ✚ **93622**	Comprehensive electrophysiologic evaluation including insertion and repositioning of multiple electrode catheters with induction or attempted induction of arrhythmia; with left ventricular pacing and recording (List separately in addition to code for primary procedure)	-	-	IR	IR	IR
-26		4.65	164.48	3295	3626	4000
✚ **93623**	Programmed stimulation and pacing after intravenous drug infusion (List separately in addition to code for primary procedure)	-	-	IR	IR	IR
-26		4.27	150.83	751	1083	1501
⊗ ∅ **93624**	Electrophysiologic follow-up study with pacing and recording to test effectiveness of therapy, including induction or attempted induction of arrhythmia	-	-	1762	1922	2183
-26				1057	1153	1310
∅ **93631**	Intra-operative epicardial and endocardial pacing and mapping to localize the site of tachycardia or zone of slow conduction for surgical correction	-	-	1974	2450	2866
-26		11.33	400.58	1184	1470	1720
⊗ ∅ **93640**	Electrophysiologic evaluation of single or dual chamber pacing cardioverter-defibrillator leads including defibrillation threshold evaluation (induction of arrhythmia, evaluation of sensing and pacing for arrhythmia termination) at time of initial implantation or replacement;	-	-	1580	1894	2311
-26		5.25	185.70	948	1136	1387
⊗ ∅ **93641**	Electrophysiologic evaluation of single or dual chamber pacing cardioverter-defibrillator leads including defibrillation threshold evaluation (induction of arrhythmia, evaluation of sensing and pacing for arrhythmia termination) at time of initial implantation or replacement; with testing of single or dual chamber pacing cardioverter-defibrillator pulse generator	-	-	1946	2163	2442
-26		8.87	313.41	1168	1298	1465
⊗ ∅ **93642**	Electrophysiologic evaluation of single or dual chamber pacing cardioverter-defibrillator (includes defibrillation threshold evaluation, induction of arrhythmia, evaluation of sensing and pacing for arrhythmia termination, and programming or reprogramming of sensing or therapeutic parameters)	14.35	525.26	1831	2077	2474
-26		7.36	260.36	1099	1246	1484
⦿ ∅ **93650**	Intracardiac catheter ablation of atrioventricular node function, atrioventricular conduction for creation of complete heart block, with or without temporary pacemaker placement	16.06	568.46	3191	3556	3899
⊗ ∅ **93651**	Intracardiac catheter ablation of arrhythmogenic focus; for treatment of supraventricular tachycardia by ablation of fast or slow atrioventricular pathways, accessory atrioventricular connections or other atrial foci, singly or in combination	24.32	859.89	3438	3975	4543
⊗ ∅ **93652**	Intracardiac catheter ablation of arrhythmogenic focus; for treatment of ventricular tachycardia	26.46	935.31	3570	4145	4808
∅ **93660**	Evaluation of cardiovascular function with tilt table evaluation, with continuous ECG monitoring and intermittent blood pressure monitoring, with or without pharmacological intervention	4.55	165.23	549	788	1017
-26		2.76	97.40	329	473	610
✚ **93662**	Intracardiac echocardiography during therapeutic/diagnostic intervention, including imaging supervision and interpretation (List separately in addition to code for primary procedure)	-	-	876	1047	1294
-26		4.11	145.15	526	628	776

Peripheral Arterial Disease Rehabilitation

		Medicare RVU	National Fee	50%	75%	90%
93668	Peripheral arterial disease (PAD) rehabilitation, per session	0.41	15.54	158	208	264

⦿ = New Code   ⊗ = Conscious Sedation   ✚ = Add-on Code   ∅ = Modifier '51' Exempt   ▲ =Revised Code

		Medicare RVU	National Fee	PFR Fee Information 50%	75%	90%

Other Vascular Studies

Code	Description	Medicare RVU	National Fee	50%	75%	90%
93701	Bioimpedance, thoracic, electrical	1.10	40.93	146	187	222
-26		0.25	8.72	31	39	47
93720	Plethysmography, total body; with interpretation and report	1.11	41.31	157	201	237
93721	Plethysmography, total body; tracing only, without interpretation and report	0.88	33.35	94	111	146
93722	Plethysmography, total body; interpretation and report only	0.23	7.96	66	80	94
93724	Electronic analysis of antitachycardia pacemaker system (includes electrocardiographic recording, programming of device, induction and termination of tachycardia via implanted pacemaker, and interpretation of recordings)	10.56	381.63	1048	1308	1582
-26		7.12	251.26	681	850	1028
93727	Electronic analysis of implantable loop recorder (ILR) system (includes retrieval of recorded and stored ECG data, physician review and interpretation of retrieved ECG data and reprogramming)	0.85	30.32	73	90	118
93731	Electronic analysis of dual-chamber pacemaker system (includes evaluation of programmable parameters at rest and during activity where applicable, using electrocardiographic recording and interpretation of recordings at rest and during exercise, analysis of event markers and device response); without reprogramming	1.20	43.58	107	152	181
-26		0.65	22.74	64	91	109
	(UNBUNDLING ALERT: 93732 cannot be used with 93731, 93733, 93734, 93735, or 93736 by the same physician on the same day.)					
93732	Electronic analysis of dual-chamber pacemaker system (includes evaluation of programmable parameters at rest and during activity where applicable, using electrocardiographic recording and interpretation of recordings at rest and during exercise, analysis of event markers and device response); with reprogramming	1.93	69.73	144	184	222
-26		1.34	47.37	101	129	155
	(UNBUNDLING ALERT: 93733 cannot be used with 93731, 93734, 93735, or 93736 by the same physician on the same day.)					
93733	Electronic analysis of dual chamber internal pacemaker system (may include rate, pulse amplitude and duration, configuration of wave form, and/or testing of sensory function of pacemaker), telephonic analysis	1.07	39.79	89	112	129
-26		0.25	8.72	31	39	45
93734	Electronic analysis of single chamber pacemaker system (includes evaluation of programmable parameters at rest and during activity where applicable, using electrocardiographic recording and interpretation of recordings at rest and during exercise, analysis of event markers and device response); without reprogramming	0.96	34.87	80	103	113
-26		0.55	19.33	48	62	68
93735	Electronic analysis of single chamber pacemaker system (includes evaluation of programmable parameters at rest and during activity where applicable, using electrocardiographic recording and interpretation of recordings at rest and during exercise, analysis of event markers and device response); with reprogramming	1.58	57.23	116	148	188
-26		1.07	37.90	81	104	132
	(UNBUNDLING ALERT: 93736 cannot be used with 93734 or 93735 by the same physician on the same day.)					
93736	Electronic analysis of single chamber internal pacemaker system (may include rate, pulse amplitude and duration, configuration of wave form, and/or testing of sensory function of pacemaker), telephonic analysis	0.96	35.62	75	89	107
-26		0.22	7.58	38	44	54
93740	Temperature gradient studies	0.33	11.75	108	119	149
-26		0.21	7.20	54	60	74
93741	Electronic analysis of pacing cardioverter-defibrillator (includes interrogation, evaluation of pulse generator status, evaluation of programmable parameters at rest and during activity where applicable, using electrocardiographic recording and interpretation of recordings at rest and during exercise, analysis of event markers and device response); single chamber or wearable cardioverter-defibrillator system, without reprogramming	1.86	67.46	146	165	187
-26		1.17	41.31	73	82	94

		Medicare RVU	National Fee	PFR Fee Information 50%	75%	90%
93742	Electronic analysis of pacing cardioverter-defibrillator (includes interrogation, evaluation of pulse generator status, evaluation of programmable parameters at rest and during activity where applicable, using electrocardiographic recording and interpretation of recordings at rest and during exercise, analysis of event markers and device response); single chamber or wearable cardioverter-defibrillator system, with reprogramming	2.05	74.28	184	206	225
-26		1.34	47.37	92	103	112
93743	Electronic analysis of pacing cardioverter-defibrillator (includes interrogation, evaluation of pulse generator status, evaluation of programmable parameters at rest and during activity where applicable, using electrocardiographic recording and interpretation of recordings at rest and during exercise, analysis of event markers and device response); dual chamber, without reprogramming	2.25	81.48	166	188	213
-26		1.50	53.06	83	94	106
93744	Electronic analysis of pacing cardioverter-defibrillator (includes interrogation, evaluation of pulse generator status, evaluation of programmable parameters at rest and during activity where applicable, using electrocardiographic recording and interpretation of recordings at rest and during exercise, analysis of event markers and device response); dual chamber, with reprogramming	2.45	88.30	207	234	261
-26		1.73	61.01	145	164	183
93745	Initial set-up and programming by a physician of wearable cardioverter-defibrillator includes initial programming of system, establishing baseline electronic ECG, transmission of data to data repository, patient instruction in wearing system and patient reporting of problems or events	-	-	IR	IR	IR
-26		-	-	IR	IR	IR
93760	Thermogram; cephalic	-	-	236	283	340
93762	Thermogram; peripheral	-	-	340	422	530
93770	Determination of venous pressure	0.25	8.72	30	35	41
-26		0.22	7.58	27	32	37
93784	Ambulatory blood pressure monitoring, utilizing a system such as magnetic tape and/or computer disk, for 24 hours or longer; including recording, scanning analysis, interpretation and report	1.95	72.38	364	406	526
93786	Ambulatory blood pressure monitoring, utilizing a system such as magnetic tape and/or computer disk, for 24 hours or longer; recording only	0.91	34.49	68	81	96
93788	Ambulatory blood pressure monitoring, utilizing a system such as magnetic tape and/or computer disk, for 24 hours or longer; scanning analysis with report	0.52	19.71	131	165	195
93790	Ambulatory blood pressure monitoring, utilizing a system such as magnetic tape and/or computer disk, for 24 hours or longer; physician review with interpretation and report	0.52	18.19	146	198	245

Other Procedures

		Medicare RVU	National Fee	50%	75%	90%
93797	Physician services for outpatient cardiac rehabilitation; without continuous ECG monitoring (per session)	0.50	18.19	47	59	68
93798	Physician services for outpatient cardiac rehabilitation; with continuous ECG monitoring (per session)	0.75	27.29	76	108	136
93799	Unlisted cardiovascular service or procedure	-	-	IR	IR	IR
-26		-	-	IR	IR	IR

Non-Invasive Vascular Diagnostic Studies

Cerebrovascular Arterial Studies

(UNBUNDLING ALERT: 93875 cannot be used with 93325 by the same physician on the same day.)

		Medicare RVU	National Fee	50%	75%	90%
93875	Noninvasive physiologic studies of extracranial arteries, complete bilateral study (eg, periorbital flow direction with arterial compression, ocular pneumoplethysmography, Doppler ultrasound spectral analysis)	2.72	102.32	226	285	376
-26		0.31	10.99	90	114	150
93880	Duplex scan of extracranial arteries; complete bilateral study	6.66	250.12	413	495	596
-26		0.84	29.56	165	198	238
93882	Duplex scan of extracranial arteries; unilateral or limited study	4.29	161.06	326	424	482
-26		0.57	20.09	130	170	193

● = New Code ⊗ = Conscious Sedation ✚ = Add-on Code ∅ = Modifier '51' Exempt ▲ =Revised Code

		Medicare RVU	National Fee	PFR Fee Information 50%	75%	90%
93886	Transcranial Doppler study of the intracranial arteries; complete study	8.16	305.83	467	530	654
-26		1.35	47.75	187	212	262
93888	Transcranial Doppler study of the intracranial arteries; limited study	5.30	198.58	309	369	505
-26		0.89	31.45	124	148	202
93890	Transcranial Doppler study of the intracranial arteries; vasoreactivity study	6.65	248.23	482	586	738
-26		1.44	50.78	193	234	295
93892	Transcranial Doppler study of the intracranial arteries; emboli detection without intravenous microbubble injection	7.12	265.28	494	600	756
-26		1.64	57.60	198	240	302
93893	Transcranial Doppler study of the intracranial arteries; emboli detection with intravenous microbubble injection	6.94	258.46	466	567	714
-26		1.64	57.60	186	227	286

Extremity Arterial Studies (Including Digits)

(UNBUNDLING ALERT: 93922 cannot be used with 93325 by the same physician on the same day.)

		Medicare RVU	National Fee	50%	75%	90%
93922	Noninvasive physiologic studies of upper or lower extremity arteries, single level, bilateral (eg, ankle/brachial indices, Doppler waveform analysis, volume plethysmography, transcutaneous oxygen tension measurement)	3.18	119.38	212	301	426
-26		0.35	12.13	85	120	170

(UNBUNDLING ALERT: 93923 cannot be used with 93325 by the same physician on the same day.)

93923	Noninvasive physiologic studies of upper or lower extremity arteries, multiple levels or with provocative functional maneuvers, complete bilateral study (eg, segmental blood pressure measurements, segmental Doppler waveform analysis, segmental volume plethysmography, segmental transcutaneous oxygen tension measurements, measurements with postural provocative tests, measurements with reactive hyperemia)	4.89	183.42	310	384	451
-26		0.64	22.36	124	154	180

(UNBUNDLING ALERT: 93924 cannot be used with 93325 by the same physician on the same day.)

93924	Noninvasive physiologic studies of lower extremity arteries, at rest and following treadmill stress testing, complete bilateral study	5.85	219.81	318	380	422
-26		0.72	25.39	127	152	169
93925	Duplex scan of lower extremity arteries or arterial bypass grafts; complete bilateral study	8.02	301.66	396	483	590
-26		0.82	28.80	158	193	236
93926	Duplex scan of lower extremity arteries or arterial bypass grafts; unilateral or limited study	4.97	186.83	256	297	398
-26		0.56	19.71	102	119	159
93930	Duplex scan of upper extremity arteries or arterial bypass grafts; complete bilateral study	6.41	241.03	400	489	687
-26		0.66	23.12	160	196	275
93931	Duplex scan of upper extremity arteries or arterial bypass grafts; unilateral or limited study	4.22	158.79	255	290	317
-26		0.44	15.54	102	116	127

Extremity Venous Studies (Including Digits)

(UNBUNDLING ALERT: 93965 cannot be used with 93325 by the same physician on the same day.)

93965	Noninvasive physiologic studies of extremity veins, complete bilateral study (eg, Doppler waveform analysis with responses to compression and other maneuvers, phleborheography, impedance plethysmography)	3.32	124.30	233	273	350
-26		0.49	17.05	93	109	140
93970	Duplex scan of extremity veins including responses to compression and other maneuvers; complete bilateral study	6.58	246.71	410	503	602
-26		0.96	33.73	164	201	241

© PFR 2007

● = New Code ⊗ = Conscious Sedation ✚ = Add-on Code ∅ = Modifier '51' Exempt ▲ = Revised Code

		Medicare RVU	National Fee	PFR Fee Information 50%	75%	90%
93971	Duplex scan of extremity veins including responses to compression and other maneuvers; unilateral or limited study	4.42	165.61	275	318	372
-26		0.63	21.98	110	127	149

Visceral and Penile Vascular Studies

93975	Duplex scan of arterial inflow and venous outflow of abdominal, pelvic, scrotal contents and/or retroperitoneal organs; complete study	10.14	377.46	438	548	702
-26		2.53	89.06	175	219	281
93976	Duplex scan of arterial inflow and venous outflow of abdominal, pelvic, scrotal contents and/or retroperitoneal organs; limited study	5.89	218.67	367	465	560
-26		1.65	57.98	147	186	224
93978	Duplex scan of aorta, inferior vena cava, iliac vasculature, or bypass grafts; complete study	5.93	222.08	365	439	530
-26		0.93	32.59	146	176	212
93979	Duplex scan of aorta, inferior vena cava, iliac vasculature, or bypass grafts; unilateral or limited study	4.17	156.52	267	303	379
-26		0.62	21.98	107	121	152

(UNBUNDLING ALERT: 93980 cannot be used with 93325 by the same physician on the same day.)

93980	Duplex scan of arterial inflow and venous outflow of penile vessels; complete study	4.69	172.81	439	544	599
-26		1.76	61.77	176	218	240

(UNBUNDLING ALERT: 93981 cannot be used with 93325 by the same physician on the same day.)

93981	Duplex scan of arterial inflow and venous outflow of penile vessels; follow-up or limited study	3.62	135.67	338	383	418
-26		0.61	21.60	101	115	125

Extremity Arterial - Venous Studies

93990	Duplex scan of hemodialysis access (including arterial inflow, body of access and venous outflow)	4.79	180.39	265	311	324
-26		0.36	12.51	79	93	97

Pulmonary

Ventilator Management

● 94002	Ventilation assist and management, initiation of pressure or volume preset ventilators for assisted or controlled breathing; hospital inpatient/observation, initial day	2.42	84.13	177	210	246
● 94003	Ventilation assist and management, initiation of pressure or volume preset ventilators for assisted or controlled breathing; hospital inpatient/observation, each subsequent day	1.76	61.39	129	153	179
● 94004	Ventilation assist and management, initiation of pressure or volume preset ventilators for assisted or controlled breathing; nursing facility, per day	1.28	44.72	94	111	130
● 94005	Home ventilator management care plan oversight of a patient (patient not present) in home, domiciliary or rest home (eg, assisted living) requiring review of status, review of laboratories and other studies and revision of orders and respiratory care plan (as appropriate), within a calendar month, 30 minutes or more	2.25	79.58	164	196	229

Other Procedures

(UNBUNDLING ALERT: 94010 cannot be used with 94160 or 94200 by the same physician on the same day.)

(See also HCPCS codes A4614, A4627 and S8096 - S8101 for peak flow meter supplies.)

(See also HCPCS code S8110 for peak expiratory flow rate (physician services).)

94010	Spirometry, including graphic record, total and timed vital capacity, expiratory flow rate measurement(s), with or without maximal voluntary ventilation	0.89	32.97	85	97	110
-26		0.23	7.96	34	39	44
94014	Patient-initiated spirometric recording per 30-day period of time; includes reinforced education, transmission of spirometric tracing, data capture, analysis of transmitted data, periodic recalibration and physician review and interpretation	1.32	48.13	82	94	112
94015	Patient-initiated spirometric recording per 30-day period of time; recording (includes hook-up, reinforced education, data transmission, data capture, trend analysis, and periodic recalibration)	0.62	23.50	30	37	45
94016	Patient-initiated spirometric recording per 30-day period of time; physician review and interpretation only	0.70	24.63	54	63	74

● = New Code ⊗ = Conscious Sedation ✚ = Add-on Code ∅ = Modifier '51' Exempt ▲ =Revised Code

		Medicare RVU	National Fee	PFR Fee Information 50%	75%	90%
94060	Bronchodilation responsiveness, spirometry as in 94010, pre- and post-bronchodilator administration	1.51	56.09	124	158	184
-26		0.41	14.40	50	63	74
94070	Bronchospasm provocation evaluation, multiple spirometric determinations as in 94010, with administered agents (eg, antigen(s), cold air, methacholine)	1.59	57.98	220	267	318
-26		0.80	28.04	88	107	127
94150	Vital capacity, total (separate procedure)	0.57	21.22	34	44	50
-26		0.11	3.79	14	18	20
94200	Maximum breathing capacity, maximal voluntary ventilation	0.59	21.98	57	64	81
-26		0.15	5.31	17	19	24
94240	Functional residual capacity or residual volume: helium method, nitrogen open circuit method, or other method	1.02	37.52	90	122	152
-26		0.35	12.13	27	37	46
94250	Expired gas collection, quantitative, single procedure (separate procedure)	0.74	27.67	31	40	51
-26		0.15	5.31	9	12	15
94260	Thoracic gas volume	0.81	30.32	80	105	127
-26		0.18	6.44	24	31	38
94350	Determination of maldistribution of inspired gas: multiple breath nitrogen washout curve including alveolar nitrogen or helium equilibration time	1.04	38.28	89	99	114
-26		0.35	12.13	27	30	34
94360	Determination of resistance to airflow, oscillatory or plethysmographic methods	1.10	40.55	96	118	149
-26		0.35	12.13	29	35	45
94370	Determination of airway closing volume, single breath tests	0.98	36.00	75	100	124
-26		0.35	12.13	22	30	37
94375	Respiratory flow volume loop	0.97	35.62	99	113	124
-26		0.41	14.40	30	34	37
94400	Breathing response to CO2 (CO2 response curve)	1.38	50.78	150	172	232
-26		0.55	19.33	45	52	70
94450	Breathing response to hypoxia (hypoxia response curve)	1.33	48.89	94	131	171
-26		0.53	18.57	28	39	51
94452	High altitude simulation test (HAST), with physician interpretation and report;	1.40	51.92	125	151	196
-26		0.42	14.78	37	45	59
94453	High altitude simulation test (HAST), with physician interpretation and report; with supplemental oxygen titration	1.97	73.14	180	216	280
-26		0.54	18.95	54	65	84
⊘● 94610	Intrapulmonary surfactant administration by a physician through endotracheal tube	1.77	62.53	183	213	266
▲ 94620	Pulmonary stress testing; simple (eg, 6-minute walk test, prolonged exercise test for bronchospasm with pre- and post-spirometry and oximetry)	2.83	104.98	252	302	327
-26		0.86	30.32	76	91	98
94621	Pulmonary stress testing; complex (including measurements of CO2 production, O2 uptake, and electrocardiographic recordings)	4.03	147.42	348	415	466
-26		1.93	67.84	104	124	140
	(94640 is for inhalation treatment (nebulizer). For initial teaching, see 94664.)					
94640	Pressurized or nonpressurized inhalation treatment for acute airway obstruction or for sputum induction for diagnostic purposes (eg, with an aerosol generator, nebulizer, metered dose inhaler or intermittent positive pressure breathing [IPPB] device)	0.34	12.89	41	47	63
94642	Aerosol inhalation of pentamidine for pneumocystis carinii pneumonia treatment or prophylaxis	-	-	145	201	279
● 94644	Continuous inhalation treatment with aerosol medication for acute airway obstruction; first hour	0.94	35.62	97	113	141

		Medicare RVU	National Fee	PFR Fee Information 50%	75%	90%
✚● 94645	Continuous inhalation treatment with aerosol medication for acute airway obstruction; each additional hour (List separately in addition to code for primary procedure)	0.36	13.64	37	43	54
94660	Continuous positive airway pressure ventilation (CPAP), initiation and management	1.49	53.44	181	224	296
94662	Continuous negative pressure ventilation (CNP), initiation and management	1.01	35.24	120	139	161
	(94664 is for initial teaching. For inhalation treatment (nebulizer), see 94640.)					
94664	Demonstration and/or evaluation of patient utilization of an aerosol generator, nebulizer, metered dose inhaler or IPPB device	0.37	14.02	48	60	78
94667	Manipulation chest wall, such as cupping, percussing, and vibration to facilitate lung function; initial demonstration and/or evaluation	0.58	21.98	58	62	71
94668	Manipulation chest wall, such as cupping, percussing, and vibration to facilitate lung function; subsequent	0.48	18.19	43	56	68
94680	Oxygen uptake, expired gas analysis; rest and exercise, direct, simple	2.00	74.66	116	145	172
-26		0.35	12.13	46	58	69
94681	Oxygen uptake, expired gas analysis; including CO2 output, percentage oxygen extracted	2.49	93.61	184	228	289
-26		0.27	9.47	74	91	116
94690	Oxygen uptake, expired gas analysis; rest, indirect (separate procedure)	1.87	70.49	93	120	142
-26		0.10	3.41	19	24	28
94720	Carbon monoxide diffusing capacity (eg, single breath, steady state)	1.37	50.78	108	143	164
-26		0.35	12.13	43	57	66
94725	Membrane diffusion capacity	2.82	105.73	164	194	212
-26		0.35	12.13	66	78	85
94750	Pulmonary compliance study (eg, plethysmography, volume and pressure measurements)	1.71	64.05	105	136	166
-26		0.31	10.99	42	54	66
94760	Noninvasive ear or pulse oximetry for oxygen saturation; single determination	0.07	2.65	38	47	63
94761	Noninvasive ear or pulse oximetry for oxygen saturation; multiple determinations (eg, during exercise)	0.14	5.31	67	76	92
94762	Noninvasive ear or pulse oximetry for oxygen saturation; by continuous overnight monitoring (separate procedure)	0.66	25.01	86	116	151
94770	Carbon dioxide, expired gas determination by infrared analyzer	0.99	36.76	76	90	105
-26		0.20	6.82	30	36	42
94772	Circadian respiratory pattern recording (pediatric pneumogram), 12-24 hour continuous recording, infant	-	-	270	391	477
-26		-	-	108	156	191
● 94774	Pediatric home apnea monitoring event recording including respiratory rate, pattern and heart rate per 30-day period of time; includes monitor attachment, download of data, physician review, interpretation, and preparation of a report	-	-	IR	IR	IR
● 94775	Pediatric home apnea monitoring event recording including respiratory rate, pattern and heart rate per 30-day period of time; monitor attachment only (includes hook-up, initiation of recording and disconnection)	-	-	IR	IR	IR
● 94776	Pediatric home apnea monitoring event recording including respiratory rate, pattern and heart rate per 30-day period of time; monitoring, download of information, receipt of transmission(s) and analyses by computer only	-	-	IR	IR	IR
● 94777	Pediatric home apnea monitoring event recording including respiratory rate, pattern and heart rate per 30-day period of time; physician review, interpretation and preparation of report only	-	-	IR	IR	IR
94799	Unlisted pulmonary service or procedure	-	-	IR	IR	IR
-26		-	-	IR	IR	IR

Allergy and Clinical Immunology

Allergy Testing

95004	Percutaneous tests (scratch, puncture, prick) with allergenic extracts, immediate type reaction, specify number of tests	0.13	4.93	8	10	11
95010	Percutaneous tests (scratch, puncture, prick) sequential and incremental, with drugs, biologicals or venoms, immediate type reaction, specify number of tests	0.47	17.05	23	29	36

		Medicare RVU	National Fee	PFR Fee Information 50%	75%	90%
● **95012**	Nitric oxide expired gas determination	0.49	18.57	34	42	48
95015	Intracutaneous (intradermal) tests, sequential and incremental, with drugs, biologicals, or venoms, immediate type reaction, specify number of tests	0.32	11.37	22	29	34
95024	Intracutaneous (intradermal) tests with allergenic extracts, immediate type reaction, specify number of tests	0.18	6.82	15	17	20
95027	Intracutaneous (intradermal) tests, sequential and incremental, with allergenic extracts for airborne allergens, immediate type reaction, specify number of tests	0.18	6.82	15	18	20
95028	Intracutaneous (intradermal) tests with allergenic extracts, delayed type reaction, including reading, specify number of tests	0.26	9.85	21	23	26
95044	Patch or application test(s) (specify number of tests)	0.20	7.58	17	20	26
95052	Photo patch test(s) (specify number of tests)	0.24	9.10	16	18	20
95056	Photo tests	0.44	16.67	11	13	18
95060	Ophthalmic mucous membrane tests	0.46	17.43	25	29	34
95065	Direct nasal mucous membrane test	0.32	12.13	22	26	29
95070	Inhalation bronchial challenge testing (not including necessary pulmonary function tests); with histamine, methacholine, or similar compounds	1.93	73.14	193	210	230
95071	Inhalation bronchial challenge testing (not including necessary pulmonary function tests); with antigens or gases, specify	2.43	92.09	192	243	317
95075	Ingestion challenge test (sequential and incremental ingestion of test items, eg, food, drug or other substance such as metabisulfite)	1.76	62.91	178	242	275

Allergen Immunotherapy

		Medicare RVU	National Fee	50%	75%	90%
95115	Professional services for allergen immunotherapy not including provision of allergenic extracts; single injection	0.37	14.02	22	23	28
95117	Professional services for allergen immunotherapy not including provision of allergenic extracts; two or more injections	0.46	17.43	26	31	36
	(Medicare fees for the code below are based on Non Facility RVUs. PFR information reflects fee when procedure is performed in a facility.)					
95120	Professional services for allergen immunotherapy in prescribing physicians office or institution, including provision of allergenic extract; single injection	-	-	25	36	40
	(Medicare fees for the code below are based on Non Facility RVUs. PFR information reflects fee when procedure is performed in a facility.)					
95125	Professional services for allergen immunotherapy in prescribing physicians office or institution, including provision of allergenic extract; two or more injections	-	-	35	44	54
95130	Professional services for allergen immunotherapy in prescribing physicians office or institution, including provision of allergenic extract; single stinging insect venom	-	-	42	50	64
95131	Professional services for allergen immunotherapy in prescribing physicians office or institution, including provision of allergenic extract; two stinging insect venoms	-	-	59	76	90
95132	Professional services for allergen immunotherapy in prescribing physicians office or institution, including provision of allergenic extract; three stinging insect venoms	-	-	73	99	121
95133	Professional services for allergen immunotherapy in prescribing physicians office or institution, including provision of allergenic extract; four stinging insect venoms	-	-	86	100	117
95134	Professional services for allergen immunotherapy in prescribing physicians office or institution, including provision of allergenic extract; five stinging insect venoms	-	-	105	127	156
95144	Professional services for the supervision of preparation and provision of antigens for allergen immunotherapy, single dose vial(s) (specify number of vials)	0.28	10.23	15	20	26
95145	Professional services for the supervision of preparation and provision of antigens for allergen immunotherapy (specify number of doses); single stinging insect venom	0.40	14.78	29	41	54
95146	Professional services for the supervision of preparation and provision of antigens for allergen immunotherapy (specify number of doses); two single stinging insect venoms	0.56	20.84	38	48	62
95147	Professional services for the supervision of preparation and provision of antigens for allergen immunotherapy (specify number of doses); three single stinging insect venoms	0.55	20.46	52	72	96
95148	Professional services for the supervision of preparation and provision of antigens for allergen immunotherapy (specify number of doses); four single stinging insect venoms	0.74	27.67	58	80	102
95149	Professional services for the supervision of preparation and provision of antigens for allergen immunotherapy (specify number of doses); five single stinging insect venoms	0.98	36.76	68	96	123
95165	Professional services for the supervision of preparation and provision of antigens for allergen immunotherapy; single or multiple antigens (specify number of doses)	0.28	10.23	16	23	28
95170	Professional services for the supervision of preparation and provision of antigens for allergen immunotherapy; whole body extract of biting insect or other arthropod (specify number of doses)	0.22	7.96	28	37	50
95180	Rapid desensitization procedure, each hour (eg, insulin, penicillin, equine serum)	3.97	142.87	178	250	319

● = New Code ⊗ = Conscious Sedation ✚ = Add-on Code ∅ = Modifier '51' Exempt ▲ =Revised Code

		Medicare RVU	National Fee	PFR Fee Information 50%	75%	90%
95199	Unlisted allergy/clinical immunologic service or procedure	-	-	IR	IR	IR

Endocrinology

95250	Ambulatory continuous glucose monitoring of interstitial tissue fluid via a subcutaneous sensor for up to 72 hours; sensor placement, hook-up, calibration of monitor, patient training, removal of sensor, and printout of recording	3.96	150.07	196	245	294
95251	Ambulatory continuous glucose monitoring of interstitial tissue fluid via a subcutaneous sensor for up to 72 hours; physician interpretation and report	1.08	37.52	68	89	107

Neurology and Neuromuscular Procedures

Sleep Testing

(Medicare fees for the code below are based on Non Facility RVUs. PFR information reflects fee when procedure is performed in a facility.)

95805	Multiple sleep latency or maintenance of wakefulness testing, recording, analysis and interpretation of physiological measurements of sleep during multiple trials to assess sleepiness	17.01	637.44	876	1070	1314
-26		2.59	90.95	350	428	526
95806	Sleep study, simultaneous recording of ventilation, respiratory effort, ECG or heart rate, and oxygen saturation, unattended by a technologist	5.51	202.37	696	933	1170
-26		2.27	79.58	313	420	527
95807	Sleep study, simultaneous recording of ventilation, respiratory effort, ECG or heart rate, and oxygen saturation, attended by a technologist	13.98	523.36	810	1123	1381
-26		2.25	78.83	324	449	552
95808	Polysomnography; sleep staging with 1-3 additional parameters of sleep, attended by a technologist	16.99	633.65	853	1128	1359
-26		3.65	128.09	341	451	544
95810	Polysomnography; sleep staging with 4 or more additional parameters of sleep, attended by a technologist	21.65	807.22	1118	1290	1498
-26		4.81	169.02	447	516	599
95811	Polysomnography; sleep staging with 4 or more additional parameters of sleep, with initiation of continuous positive airway pressure therapy or bilevel ventilation, attended by a technologist	23.72	884.53	1300	1572	1913
-26		5.17	181.53	520	629	765

Routine Electroencephalography (EEG)

95812	Electroencephalogram (EEG) extended monitoring; 41-60 minutes	5.74	213.36	308	358	430
-26		1.56	54.95	123	143	172
95813	Electroencephalogram (EEG) extended monitoring; greater than one hour	7.33	271.35	336	397	479
-26		2.47	87.16	134	159	192
95816	Electroencephalogram (EEG); including recording awake and drowsy	5.34	198.20	333	388	516
-26		1.56	54.95	133	155	206
	(For extended EEG monitoring, see 95812, 95813)					
95819	Electroencephalogram (EEG); including recording awake and asleep	5.00	185.32	274	340	398
-26		1.56	54.95	110	136	159
	(For digital analysis of EEG, see 95957)					
95822	Electroencephalogram (EEG); recording in coma or sleep only	6.09	226.63	279	346	433
-26		1.56	54.95	112	138	173
95824	Electroencephalogram (EEG); cerebral death evaluation only	-	-	487	587	687
-26		1.07	37.90	195	235	275
95827	Electroencephalogram (EEG); all night recording	6.16	229.28	390	494	592
-26		1.51	53.06	156	198	237

© PFR 2007

● = New Code ⊗ = Conscious Sedation ✚ = Add-on Code ∅ = Modifier '51' Exempt ▲ =Revised Code

		Medicare RVU	National Fee	PFR Fee Information 50%	75%	90%
95829	Electrocorticogram at surgery (separate procedure)	36.26	1350.67	1557	2143	2537
-26		8.87	312.65	623	857	1015
95830	Insertion by physician of sphenoidal electrodes for electroencephalographic (EEG) recording	5.02	183.80	246	336	372

Muscle and Range of Motion Testing

95831	Muscle testing, manual (separate procedure) with report; extremity (excluding hand) or trunk	0.73	26.53	54	92	125
95832	Muscle testing, manual (separate procedure) with report; hand, with or without comparison with normal side	0.65	23.50	64	75	90
95833	Muscle testing, manual (separate procedure) with report; total evaluation of body, excluding hands	1.04	37.52	104	124	150
95834	Muscle testing, manual (separate procedure) with report; total evaluation of body, including hands	1.24	44.72	122	137	150
95851	Range of motion measurements and report (separate procedure); each extremity (excluding hand) or each trunk section (spine)	0.51	18.57	61	85	103
95852	Range of motion measurements and report (separate procedure); hand, with or without comparison with normal side	0.37	13.64	50	56	63
95857	Tensilon test for myasthenia gravis	1.15	41.69	114	142	174

Electromyography and Nerve Conduction Tests

95860	Needle electromyography; one extremity with or without related paraspinal areas	2.39	86.79	223	267	352
-26		1.41	49.65	134	160	211
	(UNBUNDLING ALERT: 95861 cannot be used with 95860 by the same physician on the same day.)					
95861	Needle electromyography; two extremities with or without related paraspinal areas	3.15	113.69	322	379	480
-26		2.25	79.58	242	284	360
95863	Needle electromyography; three extremities with or without related paraspinal areas	3.81	137.19	425	512	581
-26		2.71	95.50	319	384	436
95864	Needle electromyography; four extremities with or without related paraspinal areas	4.73	171.68	478	591	713
-26		2.89	101.94	311	384	463
95865	Needle electromyography; larynx	3.11	111.80	318	383	470
-26		2.35	83.00	254	306	376
95866	Needle electromyography; hemidiaphragm	2.25	80.34	215	258	317
-26		1.84	64.80	172	206	254
95867	Needle electromyography; cranial nerve supplied muscle(s), unilateral	1.84	66.70	185	233	262
-26		1.14	40.17	129	163	183
95868	Needle electromyography; cranial nerve supplied muscles, bilateral	2.54	91.71	265	292	385
-26		1.70	59.88	185	204	269
95869	Needle electromyography; thoracic paraspinal muscles (excluding T1 or T12)	0.94	34.11	134	195	233
-26		0.54	18.95	100	146	175
95870	Needle electromyography; limited study of muscles in one extremity or non-limb (axial) muscles (unilateral or bilateral), other than thoracic paraspinal, cranial nerve supplied muscles, or sphincters	0.94	34.11	122	152	208
-26		0.54	18.95	85	106	146
95872	Needle electromyography using single fiber electrode, with quantitative measurement of jitter, blocking and/or fiber density, any/all sites of each muscle studied	4.36	154.24	262	300	345
-26		3.67	128.09	210	240	276
✚ **95873**	Electrical stimulation for guidance in conjunction with chemodenervation (List separately in addition to code for primary procedure)	0.92	33.35	95	121	150
-26		0.54	18.95	71	91	112

		Medicare RVU	National Fee	PFR Fee Information 50%	75%	90%
+ 95874	Needle electromyography for guidance in conjunction with chemodenervation (List separately in addition to code for primary procedure)	0.93	33.73	97	123	152
-26		0.55	19.33	73	92	114
95875	Ischemic limb exercise test with serial specimen(s) acquisition for muscle(s) metabolite(s)	2.62	95.12	157	201	263
-26		1.58	55.71	102	131	171
∅ **95900**	Nerve conduction, amplitude and latency/velocity study, each nerve; motor, without F-wave study	1.64	60.64	116	140	187
-26		0.61	21.60	46	56	75
∅ **95903**	Nerve conduction, amplitude and latency/velocity study, each nerve; motor, with F-wave study	1.80	65.94	171	225	308
-26		0.87	30.70	86	112	154
∅ **95904**	Nerve conduction, amplitude and latency/velocity study, each nerve; sensory	1.41	52.30	132	188	243
-26		0.50	17.81	53	75	97

Intraoperative Neurophysiology

		Medicare RVU	National Fee	50%	75%	90%
+ 95920	Intraoperative neurophysiology testing, per hour (List separately in addition to code for primary procedure)	4.47	161.44	370	446	496
-26		3.14	111.04	296	357	397

Autonomic Function Tests

		Medicare RVU	National Fee	50%	75%	90%
95921	Testing of autonomic nervous system function; cardiovagal innervation (parasympathetic function), including two or more of the following: heart rate response to deep breathing with recorded R-R interval, Valsalva ratio, and 30:15 ratio	1.78	64.05	133	167	187
-26		1.25	43.96	106	134	150
95922	Testing of autonomic nervous system function; vasomotor adrenergic innervation (sympathetic adrenergic function), including beat-to-beat blood pressure and R-R interval changes during Valsalva maneuver and at least five minutes of passive tilt	2.03	73.14	135	171	192
-26		1.38	48.51	108	137	154
95923	Testing of autonomic nervous system function; sudomotor, including one or more of the following: quantitative sudomotor axon reflex test (QSART), silastic sweat imprint, thermoregulatory sweat test, and changes in sympathetic skin potential	2.96	108.77	142	172	197
-26		1.30	45.86	71	86	98

Evoked Potentials and Reflex Tests

		Medicare RVU	National Fee	50%	75%	90%
95925	Short-latency somatosensory evoked potential study, stimulation of any/all peripheral nerves or skin sites, recording from the central nervous system; in upper limbs	2.27	84.13	332	424	495
-26		0.79	28.04	166	212	248
95926	Short-latency somatosensory evoked potential study, stimulation of any/all peripheral nerves or skin sites, recording from the central nervous system; in lower limbs	2.22	82.24	262	363	446
-26		0.78	27.67	131	182	223
95927	Short-latency somatosensory evoked potential study, stimulation of any/all peripheral nerves or skin sites, recording from the central nervous system; in the trunk or head	2.27	84.13	248	336	395
-26		0.81	28.80	124	168	198
95928	Central motor evoked potential study (transcranial motor stimulation); upper limbs	4.84	177.74	440	563	667
-26		2.16	76.17	220	282	334
95929	Central motor evoked potential study (transcranial motor stimulation); lower limbs	5.07	186.46	459	586	694
-26		2.17	76.55	230	293	347
95930	Visual evoked potential (VEP) testing central nervous system, checkerboard or flash	2.72	101.57	178	243	261
-26		0.51	17.81	89	122	130
95933	Orbicularis oculi (blink) reflex, by electrodiagnostic testing	1.73	63.29	146	180	197
-26		0.85	29.94	117	144	158
95934	H-reflex, amplitude and latency study; record gastrocnemius/soleus muscle	1.10	39.79	123	147	193
-26		0.74	26.15	98	118	154

● = New Code ⊗ = Conscious Sedation ✚ = Add-on Code ∅ = Modifier '51' Exempt ▲ =Revised Code

		Medicare RVU	National Fee	50%	75%	90%
95936	H-reflex, amplitude and latency study; record muscle other than gastrocnemius/soleus muscle	1.09	39.03	110	157	194
-26		0.80	28.04	88	126	155
95937	Neuromuscular junction testing (repetitive stimulation, paired stimuli), each nerve, any one method	1.43	51.54	147	179	218
-26		0.98	34.49	118	143	174

Special EEG Tests

		Medicare RVU	National Fee	50%	75%	90%
95950	Monitoring for identification and lateralization of cerebral seizure focus, electroencephalographic (eg, 8 channel EEG) recording and interpretation, each 24 hours	6.20	229.28	659	785	913
-26		2.18	76.93	264	314	365
95951	Monitoring for localization of cerebral seizure focus by cable or radio, 16 or more channel telemetry, combined electroencephalographic (EEG) and video recording and interpretation (eg, for presurgical localization), each 24 hours	-	-	986	1314	1792
-26		8.65	305.07	394	526	717
95953	Monitoring for localization of cerebral seizure focus by computerized portable 16 or more channel EEG, electroencephalographic (EEG) recording and interpretation, each 24 hours	11.42	420.28	772	930	1044
-26		4.68	164.85	309	372	418
95954	Pharmacological or physical activation requiring physician attendance during EEG recording of activation phase (eg, thiopental activation test)	7.02	256.57	370	469	561
-26		3.49	122.79	222	281	337
95955	Electroencephalogram (EEG) during nonintracranial surgery (eg, carotid surgery)	3.66	134.92	306	362	497
-26		1.40	49.27	153	181	248
95956	Monitoring for localization of cerebral seizure focus by cable or radio, 16 or more channel telemetry, electroencephalographic (EEG) recording and interpretation, each 24 hours	19.14	713.61	1105	1337	1743
-26		4.44	156.52	331	401	523
95957	Digital analysis of electroencephalogram (EEG) (eg, for epileptic spike analysis)	5.58	203.89	298	359	456
-26		2.87	101.19	185	223	283
95958	Wada activation test for hemispheric function, including electroencephalographic (EEG) monitoring	8.83	318.34	652	764	1014
-26		6.06	213.36	522	611	811
95961	Functional cortical and subcortical mapping by stimulation and/or recording of electrodes on brain surface, or of depth electrodes, to provoke seizures or identify vital brain structures; initial hour of physician attendance	6.27	226.25	436	536	685
-26		4.67	165.61	349	429	548
✚ 95962	Functional cortical and subcortical mapping by stimulation and/or recording of electrodes on brain surface, or of depth electrodes, to provoke seizures or identify vital brain structures; each additional hour of physician attendance (List separately in addition to code for primary procedure)	6.19	222.46	395	509	593
-26		4.81	170.16	316	407	474
95965	Magnetoencephalography (MEG), recording and analysis; for spontaneous brain magnetic activity (eg, epileptic cerebral cortex localization)	-	-	IR	IR	IR
-26		11.59	408.91	IR	IR	IR
95966	Magnetoencephalography (MEG), recording and analysis; for evoked magnetic fields, single modality (eg, sensory, motor, language, or visual cortex localization)	-	-	IR	IR	IR
-26		5.75	202.75	IR	IR	IR
✚ 95967	Magnetoencephalography (MEG), recording and analysis; for evoked magnetic fields, each additional modality (eg, sensory, motor, language, or visual cortex localization) (List separately in addition to code for primary procedure)	-	-	IR	IR	IR
-26		4.78	167.89	IR	IR	IR

Neurostimulators, Analysis-Programming

		Medicare RVU	National Fee	50%	75%	90%
95970	Electronic analysis of implanted neurostimulator pulse generator system (eg, rate, pulse amplitude and duration, configuration of wave form, battery status, electrode selectability, output modulation, cycling, impedance and patient compliance measurements); simple or complex brain, spinal cord, or peripheral (ie, cranial nerve, peripheral nerve, autonomic nerve, neuromuscular) neurostimulator pulse generator/transmitter, without reprogramming	1.34	48.89	63	81	92

● = New Code ⊗ = Conscious Sedation ✚ = Add-on Code ∅ = Modifier '51' Exempt ▲ =Revised Code

		Medicare RVU	National Fee	PFR Fee Information 50%	75%	90%
95971	Electronic analysis of implanted neurostimulator pulse generator system (eg, rate, pulse amplitude and duration, configuration of wave form, battery status, electrode selectability, output modulation, cycling, impedance and patient compliance measurements); simple spinal cord, or peripheral (ie, peripheral nerve, autonomic nerve, neuromuscular) neurostimulator pulse generator/transmitter, with intraoperative or subsequent programming	1.51	54.19	102	113	126
95972	Electronic analysis of implanted neurostimulator pulse generator system (eg, rate, pulse amplitude and duration, configuration of wave form, battery status, electrode selectability, output modulation, cycling, impedance and patient compliance measurements); complex spinal cord, or peripheral (except cranial nerve) neurostimulator pulse generator/transmitter, with intraoperative or subsequent programming, first hour	2.85	102.32	186	225	278
✚ 95973	Electronic analysis of implanted neurostimulator pulse generator system (eg, rate, pulse amplitude and duration, configuration of wave form, battery status, electrode selectability, output modulation, cycling, impedance and patient compliance measurements); complex spinal cord, or peripheral (except cranial nerve) neurostimulator pulse generator/transmitter, with intraoperative or subsequent programming, each additional 30 minutes after first hour (List separately in addition to code for primary procedure)	1.60	57.23	116	136	170
95974	Electronic analysis of implanted neurostimulator pulse generator system (eg, rate, pulse amplitude and duration, configuration of wave form, battery status, electrode selectability, output modulation, cycling, impedance and patient compliance measurements); complex cranial nerve neurostimulator pulse generator/transmitter, with intraoperative or subsequent programming, with or without nerve interface testing, first hour	4.81	170.92	328	399	465
✚ 95975	Electronic analysis of implanted neurostimulator pulse generator system (eg, rate, pulse amplitude and duration, configuration of wave form, battery status, electrode selectability, output modulation, cycling, impedance and patient compliance measurements); complex cranial nerve neurostimulator pulse generator/transmitter, with intraoperative or subsequent programming, each additional 30 minutes after first hour (List separately in addition to code for primary procedure)	2.68	95.12	214	261	302
95978	Electronic analysis of implanted neurostimulator pulse generator system (eg, rate, pulse amplitude and duration, battery status, electrode selectability and polarity, impedance and patient compliance measurements), complex deep brain neurostimulator pulse generator/transmitter, with initial or subsequent programming; first hour	5.59	198.58	536	684	810
✚ 95979	Electronic analysis of implanted neurostimulator pulse generator system (eg, rate, pulse amplitude and duration, battery status, electrode selectability and polarity, impedance and patient compliance measurements), complex deep brain neurostimulator pulse generator/transmitter, with initial or subsequent programming; each additional 30 minutes after first hour (List separately in addition to code for primary procedure)	2.56	90.95	243	310	367

Other Procedures

95990	Refilling and maintenance of implantable pump or reservoir for drug delivery, spinal (intrathecal, epidural) or brain (intraventricular);	1.59	60.26	111	129	175
95991	Refilling and maintenance of implantable pump or reservoir for drug delivery, spinal (intrathecal, epidural) or brain (intraventricular); administered by physician	2.36	86.41	161	187	254
95999	Unlisted neurological or neuromuscular diagnostic procedure	-	-	IR	IR	IR

Motion Analysis

96000	Comprehensive computer-based motion analysis by video-taping and 3-D kinematics;	2.45	86.03	178	227	289
96001	Comprehensive computer-based motion analysis by video-taping and 3-D kinematics; with dynamic plantar pressure measurements during walking	2.88	100.81	205	252	315
96002	Dynamic surface electromyography, during walking or other functional activities, 1-12 muscles	0.57	20.09	42	52	60
96003	Dynamic fine wire electromyography, during walking or other functional activities, 1 muscle	0.52	18.19	39	46	54
96004	Physician review and interpretation of comprehensive computer-based motion analysis, dynamic plantar pressure measurements, dynamic surface electromyography during walking or other functional activities, and dynamic fine wire electromyography, with written report	3.09	108.77	220	247	272

Functional Brain Mapping

● 96020	Neurofunctional testing selection and administration during noninvasive imaging functional brain mapping, with test administered entirely by a physician or psychologist, with review of test results and report	-	-	IR	IR	IR
-26		1.03	39.03	IR	IR	IR

Medical Genetics and Genetic Counseling Services

● 96040	Medical genetics and genetic counseling services, each 30 minutes face-to-face with patient/family	0.98	37.14	71	86	103

		Medicare RVU	National Fee	PFR Fee Information 50%	75%	90%

Central Nervous System Assessments/tests

(eg, Neuro-Cognitive, Mental Status, Speech Testing)

96101	Psychological testing (includes psychodiagnostic assessment of emotionality, intellectual abilities, personality and psychopathology, eg, MMPI, Rorschach, WAIS), per hour of the psychologist's or physician's time, both face-to-face time with the patient and time interpreting test results and preparing the report	2.49	87.16	450	570	711
96102	Psychological testing (includes psychodiagnostic assessment of emotionality, intellectual abilities, personality and psychopathology, eg, MMPI and WAIS), with qualified health care professional interpretation and report, administered by technician, per hour of technician time, face-to-face	1.31	47.75	206	261	325
96103	Psychological testing (includes psychodiagnostic assessment of emotionality, intellectual abilities, personality and psychopathology, eg, MMPI), administered by a computer, with qualified health care professional interpretation and report	1.02	36.76	130	165	206
96105	Assessment of aphasia (includes assessment of expressive and receptive speech and language function, language comprehension, speech production ability, reading, spelling, writing, eg, by Boston Diagnostic Aphasia Examination) with interpretation and report, per hour	2.01	76.17	182	260	336
96110	Developmental testing; limited (eg, Developmental Screening Test II, Early Language Milestone Screen), with interpretation and report	0.36	13.64	172	214	266
96111	Developmental testing; extended (includes assessment of motor, language, social, adaptive and/or cognitive functioning by standardized developmental instruments) with interpretation and report	3.74	131.88	175	211	252
96116	Neurobehavioral status exam (clinical assessment of thinking, reasoning and judgment, eg, acquired knowledge, attention, language, memory, planning and problem solving, and visual spatial abilities), per hour of the psychologist's or physician's time, both face-to-face time with the patient and time interpreting test results and preparing the report	2.80	98.91	504	639	797
96118	Neuropsychological testing (eg, Halstead-Reitan Neuropsychological Battery, Wechsler Memory Scales and Wisconsin Card Sorting Test), per hour of the psychologist's or physician's time, both face-to-face time with the patient and time interpreting test results and preparing the report	3.29	117.48	602	764	953
96119	Neuropsychological testing (eg, Halstead-Reitan Neuropsychological Battery, Wechsler Memory Scales and Wisconsin Card Sorting Test), with qualified health care professional interpretation and report, administered by technician, per hour of technician time, face-to-face	1.88	68.97	307	390	486
96120	Neuropsychological testing (eg, Wisconsin Card Sorting Test), administered by a computer, with qualified health care professional interpretation and report	1.57	57.60	223	283	353

Health and Behavior Assessment/Intervention

96150	Health and behavior assessment (eg, health-focused clinical interview, behavioral observations, psychophysiological monitoring, health-oriented questionnaires), each 15 minutes face-to-face with the patient; initial assessment	0.67	23.50	67	74	84
96151	Health and behavior assessment (eg, health-focused clinical interview, behavioral observations, psychophysiological monitoring, health-oriented questionnaires), each 15 minutes face-to-face with the patient; re-assessment	0.65	22.74	54	61	67
96152	Health and behavior intervention, each 15 minutes, face-to-face; individual	0.62	21.60	50	62	71
96153	Health and behavior intervention, each 15 minutes, face-to-face; group (2 or more patients)	0.15	5.31	15	21	24
96154	Health and behavior intervention, each 15 minutes, face-to-face; family (with the patient present)	0.61	21.22	44	62	79
96155	Health and behavior intervention, each 15 minutes, face-to-face; family (without the patient present)	0.62	21.98	47	62	73

Chemotherapy Administration

Injection and Intravenous Infusion Chemotherapy

96401	Chemotherapy administration, subcutaneous or intramuscular; non-hormonal anti-neoplastic	1.56	58.36	79	97	115
96402	Chemotherapy administration, subcutaneous or intramuscular; hormonal anti-neoplastic	1.14	42.45	42	52	62
	(Medicare fees for the code below are based on Non Facility RVUs. PFR information reflects fee when procedure is performed in a facility.)					
96405	Chemotherapy administration; intralesional, up to and including 7 lesions	3.26	121.65	119	124	133

= New Code ⊗ = Conscious Sedation ✚ = Add-on Code ∅ = Modifier '51' Exempt ▲ =Revised Code

		Medicare RVU	National Fee	PFR Fee Information 50%	75%	90%
96406	Chemotherapy administration; intralesional, more than 7 lesions	3.91	145.15	164	195	226
	(UNBUNDLING ALERT: 96408 cannot be used with 36000 by the same physician on the same day.)					
96409	Chemotherapy administration; intravenous, push technique, single or initial substance/drug	3.18	119.76	145	179	213
	(UNBUNDLING ALERT: 96410 cannot be used with 36000 by the same physician on the same day.)					
✚ 96411	Chemotherapy administration; intravenous, push technique, each additional substance/drug (List separately in addition to code for primary procedure)	1.84	68.97	84	104	123
	(UNBUNDLING ALERT: 96412 cannot be used with 36000 by the same physician on the same day.)					
96413	Chemotherapy administration, intravenous infusion technique; up to 1 hour, single or initial substance/drug	4.41	165.99	205	253	301
✚▲ 96415	Chemotherapy administration, intravenous infusion technique; each additional hour (List separately in addition to code for primary procedure)	1.00	37.14	47	57	68
96416	Chemotherapy administration, intravenous infusion technique; initiation of prolonged chemotherapy infusion (more than 8 hours), requiring use of a portable or implantable pump	4.76	179.63	220	271	324
✚ 96417	Chemotherapy administration, intravenous infusion technique; each additional sequential infusion (different substance/drug), up to 1 hour (List separately in addition to code for primary procedure)	2.17	81.48	100	123	147

Intra-Arterial Chemotherapy

96420	Chemotherapy administration, intra-arterial; push technique	2.92	109.90	148	171	188
96422	Chemotherapy administration, intra-arterial; infusion technique, up to one hour	4.82	181.91	237	314	391
✚▲ 96423	Chemotherapy administration, intra-arterial; infusion technique, each additional hour (List separately in addition to code for primary procedure)	2.08	78.07	96	118	147
96425	Chemotherapy administration, intra-arterial; infusion technique, initiation of prolonged infusion (more than 8 hours), requiring the use of a portable or implantable pump	4.73	178.50	225	293	360

Other Chemotherapy

(Medicare fees for the code below are based on Non Facility RVUs. PFR information reflects fee when procedure is performed in a facility.)

(UNBUNDLING ALERT: 96440 cannot be used with 32000, 32002, 32005, or 36000 by the same physician on the same day.)

(A4550 (Disposable Surgical Tray) can be coded in addition to 96440 in the office setting. Payment is at carrier discretion.)

96440	Chemotherapy administration into pleural cavity, requiring and including thoracentesis	10.02	370.64	428	581	756
	(UNBUNDLING ALERT: 96445 cannot be used with 36000, 49080 or 49081 by the same physician on the same day.)					
	(A4550 (Disposable Surgical Tray) can be coded in addition to 96445 in the office setting. Payment is at carrier discretion.)					
96445	Chemotherapy administration into peritoneal cavity, requiring and including peritoneocentesis	9.72	360.03	440	567	750
	(UNBUNDLING ALERT: 96450 cannot be used with 36000, 62270 or 62272 by the same physician on the same day.)					
	(A4550 (Disposable Surgical Tray) can be coded in addition to 96450 in the office setting. Payment is at carrier discretion.)					
96450	Chemotherapy administration, into CNS (eg, intrathecal), requiring and including spinal puncture	8.07	300.15	376	491	546
96521	Refilling and maintenance of portable pump	3.87	145.91	181	223	267
96522	Refilling and maintenance of implantable pump or reservoir for drug delivery, systemic (eg, intravenous, intra-arterial)	2.93	110.28	131	162	193
96523	Irrigation of implanted venous access device for drug delivery systems	0.73	27.67	33	41	49
96542	Chemotherapy injection, subarachnoid or intraventricular via subcutaneous reservoir, single or multiple agents	4.89	182.29	258	294	343
96549	Unlisted chemotherapy procedure	-	-	IR	IR	IR

Photodynamic Therapy

96567	Photodynamic therapy by external application of light to destroy premalignant and/or malignant lesions of the skin and adjacent mucosa (eg, lip) by activation of photosensitive drug(s), each phototherapy exposure session	2.44	92.47	IR	IR	IR
✚ 96570	Photodynamic therapy by endoscopic application of light to ablate abnormal tissue via activation of photosensitive drug(s); first 30 minutes (List separately in addition to code for endoscopy for bronchoscopy procedures of lung and esophagus)	1.59	56.09	180	223	257

● = New Code ⊗ = Conscious Sedation ✚ = Add-on Code ∅ = Modifier '51' Exempt ▲ =Revised Code

		Medicare RVU	National Fee	PFR Fee Information 50%	75%	90%
+ 96571	Photodynamic therapy by endoscopic application of light to ablate abnormal tissue via activation of photosensitive drug(s); each additional 15 minutes (List separately in addition to code for endoscopy or bronchoscopy procedures of lung and esophagus)	0.77	26.91	94	110	126

Special Dermatological Procedures

		Medicare RVU	National Fee	50%	75%	90%
96900	Actinotherapy (ultraviolet light)	0.49	18.57	34	44	51
96902	Microscopic examination of hairs plucked or clipped by the examiner (excluding hair collected by the patient) to determine telogen and anagen counts, or structural hair shaft abnormality	0.58	20.46	49	62	73
● 96904	Whole body integumentary photography, for monitoring of high risk patients with dysplastic nevus syndrome or a history of dysplastic nevi, or patients with a personal or familial history of melanoma	1.85	70.11	113	147	176
96910	Photochemotherapy; tar and ultraviolet B (Goeckerman treatment) or petrolatum and ultraviolet B	1.28	48.51	54	63	74
96912	Photochemotherapy; psoralens and ultraviolet A (PUVA)	1.64	62.15	68	87	105
96913	Photochemotherapy (Goeckerman and/or PUVA) for severe photoresponsive dermatoses requiring at least four to eight hours of care under direct supervision of the physician (includes application of medication and dressings)	2.27	86.03	153	222	284
96920	Laser treatment for inflammatory skin disease (psoriasis); total area less than 250 sq cm	3.97	145.91	243	317	380
96921	Laser treatment for inflammatory skin disease (psoriasis); 250 sq cm to 500 sq cm	4.02	147.80	264	344	412
96922	Laser treatment for inflammatory skin disease (psoriasis); over 500 sq cm	5.91	216.02	342	446	537
96999	Unlisted special dermatological service or procedure	-	-	IR	IR	IR

Physical Medicine and Rehabilitation

		Medicare RVU	National Fee	50%	75%	90%
97001	Physical therapy evaluation	1.98	70.49	109	130	150
97002	Physical therapy re-evaluation	1.05	37.52	56	65	74
97003	Occupational therapy evaluation	2.12	75.80	112	122	132
97004	Occupational therapy re-evaluation	1.26	45.48	55	59	71
97005	Athletic training evaluation	-	-	95	133	173
97006	Athletic training re-evaluation	-	-	52	65	81

Modalities
Supervised

		Medicare RVU	National Fee	50%	75%	90%
97010	Application of a modality to one or more areas; hot or cold packs	0.13	4.55	29	38	42
97012	Application of a modality to one or more areas; traction, mechanical	0.39	13.64	40	44	47
97014	Application of a modality to one or more areas; electrical stimulation (unattended)	0.38	13.64	36	42	55
97016	Application of a modality to one or more areas; vasopneumatic devices	0.39	14.02	42	58	63
97018	Application of a modality to one or more areas; paraffin bath	0.19	6.82	37	42	62
97022	Application of a modality to one or more areas; whirlpool	0.42	15.16	37	46	60
97024	Application of a modality to one or more areas; diathermy (eg, microwave)	0.14	4.93	34	39	42
97026	Application of a modality to one or more areas; infrared	0.13	4.55	25	32	43
97028	Application of a modality to one or more areas; ultraviolet	0.16	5.68	28	34	41

Constant Attendance

		Medicare RVU	National Fee	50%	75%	90%
97032	Application of a modality to one or more areas; electrical stimulation (manual), each 15 minutes	0.43	15.16	39	50	56
97033	Application of a modality to one or more areas; iontophoresis, each 15 minutes	0.58	20.84	49	55	67
97034	Application of a modality to one or more areas; contrast baths, each 15 minutes	0.38	13.64	30	38	44
97035	Application of a modality to one or more areas; ultrasound, each 15 minutes	0.32	11.37	41	43	48

		Medicare RVU	National Fee	PFR Fee Information 50%	75%	90%
97036	Application of a modality to one or more areas; Hubbard tank, each 15 minutes	0.64	23.12	47	56	63
97039	Unlisted modality (specify type and time if constant attendance)	-	-	IR	IR	IR

Therapeutic Procedures

		Medicare RVU	National Fee	50%	75%	90%
97110	Therapeutic procedure, one or more areas, each 15 minutes; therapeutic exercises to develop strength and endurance, range of motion and flexibility	0.75	26.53	53	62	73
97112	Therapeutic procedure, one or more areas, each 15 minutes; neuromuscular reeducation of movement, balance, coordination, kinesthetic sense, posture, and/or proprioception for sitting and/or standing activities	0.78	27.67	52	66	82
97113	Therapeutic procedure, one or more areas, each 15 minutes; aquatic therapy with therapeutic exercises	0.88	31.83	51	66	80
97116	Therapeutic procedure, one or more areas, each 15 minutes; gait training (includes stair climbing)	0.66	23.50	48	55	58
97124	Therapeutic procedure, one or more areas, each 15 minutes; massage, including effleurage, petrissage and/or tapotement (stroking, compression, percussion)	0.60	21.22	45	53	65
97139	Unlisted therapeutic procedure (specify)	-	-	IR	IR	IR
97140	Manual therapy techniques (eg, mobilization/ manipulation, manual lymphatic drainage, manual traction), one or more regions, each 15 minutes	0.70	25.01	50	59	66
97150	Therapeutic procedure(s), group (2 or more individuals)	0.47	16.67	36	42	48
97530	Therapeutic activities, direct (one-on-one) patient contact by the provider (use of dynamic activities to improve functional performance), each 15 minutes	0.79	28.42	55	64	75
97532	Development of cognitive skills to improve attention, memory, problem solving, (includes compensatory training), direct (one-on-one) patient contact by the provider, each 15 minutes	0.66	23.50	52	63	71
97533	Sensory integrative techniques to enhance sensory processing and promote adaptive responses to environmental demands, direct (one-on-one) patient contact by the provider, each 15 minutes	0.70	25.01	50	61	71
97535	Self-care/home management training (eg, activities of daily living (ADL) and compensatory training, meal preparation, safety procedures, and instructions in use of assistive technology devices/adaptive equipment) direct one-on-one contact by provider, each 15 minutes	0.80	28.42	49	61	73
97537	Community/work reintegration training (eg, shopping, transportation, money management, avocational activities and/or work environment/modification analysis, work task analysis, use of assistive technology device/adaptive equipment), direct one-on-one contact by provider, each 15 minutes	0.73	25.77	48	53	59
97542	Wheelchair management (eg, assessment, fitting, training), each 15 minutes	0.74	26.15	38	44	50
97545	Work hardening/conditioning; initial 2 hours	-	-	155	197	298
✚ 97546	Work hardening/conditioning; each additional hour (List separately in addition to code for primary procedure)	-	-	72	92	103

Active Wound Care Management

		Medicare RVU	National Fee	50%	75%	90%
97597	Removal of devitalized tissue from wound(s), selective debridement, without anesthesia (eg, high pressure waterjet with/without suction, sharp selective debridement with scissors, scalpel and forceps), with or without topical application(s), wound assessment, and instruction(s) for ongoing care, may include use of a whirlpool, per session; total wound(s) surface area less than or equal to 20 square centimeters	1.40	50.78	72	89	105
97598	Removal of devitalized tissue from wound(s), selective debridement, without anesthesia (eg, high pressure waterjet with/without suction, sharp selective debridement with scissors, scalpel and forceps), with or without topical application(s), wound assessment, and instruction(s) for ongoing care, may include use of a whirlpool, per session; total wound(s) surface area greater than 20 square centimeters	1.76	63.67	95	121	147
97602	Removal of devitalized tissue from wound(s), non-selective debridement, without anesthesia (eg, wet-to-moist dressings, enzymatic, abrasion), including topical application(s), wound assessment, and instruction(s) for ongoing care, per session	-	-	38	46	54
97605	Negative pressure wound therapy (eg, vacuum assisted drainage collection), including topical application(s), wound assessment, and instruction(s) for ongoing care, per session; total wound(s) surface area less than or equal to 50 square centimeters	0.93	32.97	51	68	79
97606	Negative pressure wound therapy (eg, vacuum assisted drainage collection), including topical application(s), wound assessment, and instruction(s) for ongoing care, per session; total wound(s) surface area greater than 50 square centimeters	1.00	35.62	91	119	150

Tests and Measurements

		Medicare RVU	National Fee	50%	75%	90%
97750	Physical performance test or measurement (eg, musculoskeletal, functional capacity), with written report, each 15 minutes	0.79	28.04	63	87	114
97755	Assistive technology assessment (eg, to restore, augment or compensate for existing function, optimize functional tasks and/or maximize environmental accessibility), direct one-on-one contact by provider, with written report, each 15 minutes	0.92	32.59	51	60	69

● = New Code ⊗ = Conscious Sedation ✚ = Add-on Code ∅ = Modifier '51' Exempt ▲ =Revised Code

		Medicare RVU	National Fee	PFR Fee Information 50%	75%	90%

Orthotic Management and Prosthetic Management

Code	Description	RVU	Fee	50%	75%	90%
97760	Orthotic(s) management and training (including assessment and fitting when not otherwise reported), upper extremity(s), lower extremity(s) and/or trunk, each 15 minutes	0.84	29.94	56	72	91
97761	Prosthetic training, upper and/or lower extremity(s), each 15 minutes	0.76	26.91	51	66	83
97762	Checkout for orthotic/prosthetic use, established patient, each 15 minutes	0.77	28.04	46	60	76

Other Procedures

Code	Description	RVU	Fee	50%	75%	90%
97799	Unlisted physical medicine/rehabilitation service or procedure	-	-	IR	IR	IR

Medical Nutrition Therapy

Code	Description	RVU	Fee	50%	75%	90%
97802	Medical nutrition therapy; initial assessment and intervention, individual, face-to-face with the patient, each 15 minutes	0.85	30.32	43	50	62
97803	Medical nutrition therapy; re-assessment and intervention, individual, face-to-face with the patient, each 15 minutes	0.76	27.29	30	38	43
97804	Medical nutrition therapy; group (2 or more individual(s)), each 30 minutes	0.41	14.40	22	26	31

Acupuncture

Code	Description	RVU	Fee	50%	75%	90%
97810	Acupuncture, 1 or more needles; without electrical stimulation, initial 15 minutes of personal one-on-one contact with the patient	0.98	34.87	51	63	81
✚ 97811	Acupuncture, 1 or more needles; without electrical stimulation, each additional 15 minutes of personal one-on-one contact with the patient, with re-insertion of needle(s) (List separately in addition to code for primary procedure)	0.76	26.91	39	48	61
97813	Acupuncture, 1 or more needles; with electrical stimulation, initial 15 minutes of personal one-on-one contact with the patient	1.05	37.14	54	69	79
✚ 97814	Acupuncture, 1 or more needles; with electrical stimulation, each additional 15 minutes of personal one-on-one contact with the patient, with re-insertion of needle(s) (List separately in addition to code for primary procedure)	0.85	29.94	43	55	64

Osteopathic Manipulative Treatment

Code	Description	RVU	Fee	50%	75%	90%
98925	Osteopathic manipulative treatment (OMT); one to two body regions involved	0.78	27.67	53	62	69
98926	Osteopathic manipulative treatment (OMT); three to four body regions involved	1.08	38.28	76	84	91
98927	Osteopathic manipulative treatment (OMT); five to six body regions involved	1.39	49.27	89	111	130
98928	Osteopathic manipulative treatment (OMT); seven to eight body regions involved	1.64	58.36	108	118	138
98929	Osteopathic manipulative treatment (OMT); nine to ten body regions involved	1.89	67.08	126	141	162

Chiropractic Manipulative Treatment

Code	Description	RVU	Fee	50%	75%	90%
98940	Chiropractic manipulative treatment (CMT); spinal, one to two regions	0.69	24.25	48	57	71
98941	Chiropractic manipulative treatment (CMT); spinal, three to four regions	0.95	33.35	58	71	84
98942	Chiropractic manipulative treatment (CMT); spinal, five regions	1.25	43.96	70	93	104
98943	Chiropractic manipulative treatment (CMT); extraspinal, one or more regions	0.63	22.36	43	54	60

Education and Training for Patient Self-Management

Code	Description	RVU	Fee	50%	75%	90%
98960	Education and training for patient self-management by a qualified, nonphysician health care professional using a standardized curriculum, face-to-face with the patient (could include caregiver/family) each 30 minutes; individual patient	0.49	18.57	IR	IR	IR
98961	Education and training for patient self-management by a qualified, nonphysician health care professional using a standardized curriculum, face-to-face with the patient (could include caregiver/family) each 30 minutes; 2-4 patients	0.24	9.10	IR	IR	IR
98962	Education and training for patient self-management by a qualified, nonphysician health care professional using a standardized curriculum, face-to-face with the patient (could include caregiver/family) each 30 minutes; 5-8 patients	0.18	6.82	IR	IR	IR

© PFR 2007

● = New Code ⊗ = Conscious Sedation ✚ = Add-on Code ∅ = Modifier '51' Exempt ▲ =Revised Code

		Medicare RVU	National Fee	PFR Fee Information 50%	75%	90%

Special Services, Procedures, and Reports

Miscellaneous Services

99000	Handling and/or conveyance of specimen for transfer from the physician's office to a laboratory	-	-	20	26	35
99001	Handling and/or conveyance of specimen for transfer from the patient in other than a physician's office to a laboratory (distance may be indicated)	-	-	20	31	44
99002	Handling, conveyance, and/or any other service in connection with the implementation of an order involving devices (eg, designing, fitting, packaging, handling, delivery or mailing) when devices such as orthotics, protectives, prosthetics are fabricated by an outside laboratory or shop but which items have been designed, and are to be fitted and adjusted by the attending physician	-	-	28	38	48
99024	Postoperative follow-up visit, normally included in the surgical package, to indicate that an evaluation and management service was performed during a postoperative period for a reason(s) related to the original procedure	-	-	IR	IR	IR

(Use 99025 in addition to the procedure code when a starred procedure is performed at an initial visit.)

99026	Hospital mandated on call service; in-hospital, each hour	-	-	IR	IR	IR
99027	Hospital mandated on call service; out-of-hospital, each hour	-	-	IR	IR	IR
99050	Services provided in the office at times other than regularly scheduled office hours, or days when the office is normally closed (eg, holidays, Saturday or Sunday), in addition to basic service	-	-	66	92	113
99051	Service(s) provided in the office during regularly scheduled evening, weekend, or holiday office hours, in addition to basic service	-	-	IR	IR	IR
99053	Service(s) provided between 10:00 PM and 8:00 AM at 24-hour facility, in addition to basic service	-	-	IR	IR	IR
99056	Service(s) typically provided in the office, provided out of the office at request of patient, in addition to basic service	-	-	87	113	129
99058	Service(s) provided on an emergency basis in the office, which disrupts other scheduled office services, in addition to basic service	-	-	84	104	127
99060	Service(s) provided on an emergency basis, out of the office, which disrupts other scheduled office services, in addition to basic service	-	-	IR	IR	IR

(Use of this code will result in an inquiry letter from the insurance carrier. Use a more specific code from the HCPCS book to describe the supply or drug.)

99070	Supplies and materials (except spectacles), provided by the physician over and above those usually included with the office visit or other services rendered (list drugs, trays, supplies, or materials provided)	-	-	IR	IR	IR
99071	Educational supplies, such as books, tapes, and pamphlets, provided by the physician for the patient's education at cost to physician	-	-	IR	IR	IR
99075	Medical testimony	-	-	449	665	963
99078	Physician educational services rendered to patients in a group setting (eg, prenatal, obesity, or diabetic instructions)	-	-	52	95	133
99080	Special reports such as insurance forms, more than the information conveyed in the usual medical communications or standard reporting form	-	-	54	108	190
99082	Unusual travel (eg, transportation and escort of patient)	-	-	211	324	404
99090	Analysis of clinical data stored in computers (eg, ECGs, blood pressures, hematologic data)	-	-	139	271	318
99091	Collection and interpretation of physiologic data (eg, ECG, blood pressure, glucose monitoring) digitally stored and/or transmitted by the patient and/or caregiver to the physician or other qualified health care professional, requiring a minimum of 30 minutes of time	1.39	48.51	IR	IR	IR

Qualifying Circumstances For Anesthesia

✚ 99100	Anesthesia for patient of extreme age, younger than 1 year and older than 70 (List separately in addition to code for primary anesthesia procedure)	-	-	IR	IR	IR
✚ 99116	Anesthesia complicated by utilization of total body hypothermia (List separately in addition to code for primary anesthesia procedure)	-	-	IR	IR	IR
✚ 99135	Anesthesia complicated by utilization of controlled hypotension (List separately in addition to code for primary anesthesia procedure)	-	-	112	134	157
✚ 99140	Anesthesia complicated by emergency conditions (specify) (List separately in addition to code for primary anesthesia procedure)	-	-	IR	IR	IR

		Medicare RVU	National Fee	PFR Fee Information 50%	75%	90%

Moderate (Conscious) Sedation

⊘ 99143	Moderate sedation services (other than those services described by codes 00100-01999) provided by the same physician performing the diagnostic or therapeutic service that the sedation supports, requiring the presence of an independent trained observer to assist in the monitoring of the patient's level of consciousness and physiological status; younger than 5 years of age, first 30 minutes intra-service time	-	-	IR	IR	IR
⊘ 99144	Moderate sedation services (other than those services described by codes 00100-01999) provided by the same physician performing the diagnostic or therapeutic service that the sedation supports, requiring the presence of an independent trained observer to assist in the monitoring of the patient's level of consciousness and physiological status; age 5 years or older, first 30 minutes intra-service time	-	-	IR	IR	IR
✚ 99145	Moderate sedation services (other than those services described by codes 00100-01999) provided by the same physician performing the diagnostic or therapeutic service that the sedation supports, requiring the presence of an independent trained observer to assist in the monitoring of the patient's level of consciousness and physiological status; each additional 15 minutes intra-service time (List separately in addition to code for primary service)	-	-	IR	IR	IR
⊘ 99148	Moderate sedation services (other than those services described by codes 00100-01999), provided by a physician other than the health care professional performing the diagnostic or therapeutic service that the sedation supports; younger than 5 years of age, first 30 minutes intra-service time	-	-	IR	IR	IR
⊘ 99149	Moderate sedation services (other than those services described by codes 00100-01999), provided by a physician other than the health care professional performing the diagnostic or therapeutic service that the sedation supports; age 5 years or older, first 30 minutes intra-service time	-	-	IR	IR	IR
✚ 99150	Moderate sedation services (other than those services described by codes 00100-01999), provided by a physician other than the health care professional performing the diagnostic or therapeutic service that the sedation supports; each additional 15 minutes intra-service time (List separately in addition to code for primary service)	-	-	IR	IR	IR

Other Services and Procedures

99170	Anogenital examination with colposcopic magnification in childhood for suspected trauma	3.53	126.96	214	255	297
99172	Visual function screening, automated or semi-automated bilateral quantitative determination of visual acuity, ocular alignment, color vision by pseudoisochromatic plates, and field of vision (may include all or some screening of the determination(s) for contrast sensitivity, vision under glare)	-	-	42	52	72
99173	Screening test of visual acuity, quantitative, bilateral	0.07	2.65	30	46	60
99175	Ipecac or similar administration for individual emesis and continued observation until stomach adequately emptied of poison	1.23	46.61	93	117	148
99183	Physician attendance and supervision of hyperbaric oxygen therapy, per session	5.58	202.37	280	352	421
99185	Hypothermia; regional	0.93	35.24	55	70	100
99186	Hypothermia; total body	2.13	80.72	174	201	208
99190	Assembly and operation of pump with oxygenator or heat exchanger (with or without ECG and/or pressure monitoring); each hour	-	-	795	919	1041
99191	Assembly and operation of pump with oxygenator or heat exchanger (with or without ECG and/or pressure monitoring); 45 minutes	-	-	573	717	849
99192	Assembly and operation of pump with oxygenator or heat exchanger (with or without ECG and/or pressure monitoring); 30 minutes	-	-	384	547	638
99195	Phlebotomy, therapeutic (separate procedure)	1.00	37.90	59	85	99
99199	Unlisted special service, procedure or report	-	-	IR	IR	IR

		Medicare RVU	National Fee	PFR Fee Information		
				50%	75%	90%

Evaluation and Management

Office or Other Outpatient Services

New Patient

(Codes 99201-99285 are documented and assigned based on the Evaluation and Management Documentation Guidelines issued by the Centers for Med)

99201 Office or other outpatient visit for the evaluation and management of a new patient, which requires these three key components: A problem focused history; A problem focused examination; Straightforward medical decision making. Counseling and/or coordination of care with other providers or agencies are provided consistent with the nature of the problem(s) and the patient's and/or family's needs. Usually, the presenting problem(s) are self limited or minor. Physicians typically spend 10 minutes face-to-face with the patient and/or family. — 0.99 | 35.62 | 71 | 85 | 114

99202 Office or other outpatient visit for the evaluation and management of a new patient, which requires these three key components: An expanded problem focused history; An expanded problem focused examination; Straightforward medical decision making. Counseling and/or coordination of care with other providers or agencies are provided consistent with the nature of the problem(s) and the patient's and/or family's needs. Usually, the presenting problem(s) are of low to moderate severity. Physicians typically spend 20 minutes face-to-face with the patient and/or family. — 1.73 | 62.15 | 96 | 111 | 125

99203 Office or other outpatient visit for the evaluation and management of a new patient, which requires these three key components: A detailed history; A detailed examination; Medical decision making of low complexity. Counseling and/or coordination of care with other providers or agencies are provided consistent with the nature of the problem(s) and the patient's and/or family's needs. Usually, the presenting problem(s) are of moderate severity. Physicians typically spend 30 minutes face-to-face with the patient and/or family. — 2.56 | 92.09 | 132 | 149 | 172

99204 Office or other outpatient visit for the evaluation and management of a new patient, which requires these three key components: A comprehensive history; A comprehensive examination; Medical decision making of moderate complexity. Counseling and/or coordination of care with other providers or agencies are provided consistent with the nature of the problem(s) and the patient's and/or family's needs. Usually, the presenting problem(s) are of moderate to high severity. Physicians typically spend 45 minutes face-to-face with the patient and/or family. — 3.92 | 139.84 | 185 | 202 | 225

99205 Office or other outpatient visit for the evaluation and management of a new patient, which requires these three key components: A comprehensive history; A comprehensive examination; Medical decision making of high complexity. Counseling and/or coordination of care with other providers or agencies are provided consistent with the nature of the problem(s) and the patient's and/or family's needs. Usually, the presenting problem(s) are of moderate to high severity. Physicians typically spend 60 minutes face-to-face with the patient and/or family. — 4.93 | 175.47 | 238 | 270 | 312

Established Patient

99211 Office or other outpatient visit for the evaluation and management of an established patient, that may not require the presence of a physician. Usually, the presenting problem(s) are minimal. Typically, 5 minutes are spent performing or supervising these services. — 0.55 | 20.09 | 40 | 45 | 55

99212 Office or other outpatient visit for the evaluation and management of an established patient, which requires at least two of these three key components: A problem focused history; A problem focused examination; Straightforward medical decision making. Counseling and/or coordination of care with other providers or agencies are provided consistent with the nature of the problem(s) and the patient's and/or family's needs. Usually, the presenting problem(s) are self limited or minor. Physicians typically spend 10 minutes face-to-face with the patient and/or family. — 1.02 | 36.76 | 59 | 69 | 77

99213 Office or other outpatient visit for the evaluation and management of an established patient, which requires at least two of these three key components: An expanded problem focused history; An expanded problem focused examination; Medical decision making of low complexity. Counseling and coordination of care with other providers or agencies are provided consistent with the nature of the problem(s) and the patient's and/or family's needs. Usually, the presenting problem(s) are of low to moderate severity. Physicians typically spend 15 minutes face-to-face with the patient and/or family. — 1.66 | 59.50 | 80 | 90 | 103

99214 Office or other outpatient visit for the evaluation and management of an established patient, which requires at least two of these three key components: A detailed history; A detailed examination; Medical decision making of moderate complexity. Counseling and/or coordination of care with other providers or agencies are provided consistent with the nature of the problem(s) and the patient's and/or family's needs. Usually, the presenting problem(s) are of moderate to high severity. Physicians typically spend 25 minutes face-to-face with the patient and/or family. — 2.52 | 90.20 | 119 | 130 | 147

		Medicare RVU	National Fee	PFR Fee Information 50%	75%	90%
99215	Office or other outpatient visit for the evaluation and management of an established patient, which requires at least two of these three key components: A comprehensive history; A comprehensive examination; Medical decision making of high complexity. Counseling and/or coordination of care with other providers or agencies are provided consistent with the nature of the problem(s) and the patient's and/or family's needs. Usually, the presenting problem(s) are of moderate to high severity. Physicians typically spend 40 minutes face-to-face with the patient and/or family.	3.42	122.03	172	193	216

Hospital Observation Services

Observation Care Discharge Services

99217	Observation care discharge day management (This code is to be utilized by the physician to report all services provided to a patient on discharge from "observation status" if the discharge is on other than the initial date of "observation status." To report services to a patient designated as "observation status" or "inpatient status" and discharged on the same date, use the codes for Observation or Inpatient Care Services [including Admission and Discharge Services, 99234-99236 as appropriate.])	1.87	65.94	119	132	158

Initial Observation Care
New or Established Patient

99218	A detailed or comprehensive history; A detailed or comprehensive examination; and Medical decision making that is straightforward or of low complexity. Initial observation care, per day, for the evaluation and management of a patient which requires these three key components: Counseling and/or coordination of care with other providers or agencies are provided consistent with the nature of the problem(s) and the patient's and/or family's needs. Usually, the problem(s) requiring admission to "observation status" are of low severity.	1.77	62.15	138	154	186
99219	Initial observation care, per day, for the evaluation and management of a patient, which requires these three key components: A comprehensive history; A comprehensive examination; and Medical decision making of moderate complexity. Counseling and/or coordination of care with other providers or agencies are provided consistent with the nature of the problem(s) and the patient's and/or family's needs. Usually, the problem(s) requiring admission to "observation status" are of moderate severity.	2.93	102.70	195	216	244
99220	Initial observation care, per day, for the evaluation and management of a patient, which requires these three key components: A comprehensive history; A comprehensive examination; and Medical decision making of high complexity. Counseling and/or coordination of care with other providers or agencies are provided consistent with the nature of the problem(s) and the patient's and/or family's needs. Usually, the problem(s) requiring admission to "observation status" are of high severity.	4.12	144.77	245	281	315

Hospital Inpatient Services

Initial Hospital Care
New or Established Patient

99221	Initial hospital care, per day, for the evaluation and management of a patient, which requires these three key components: A detailed or comprehensive history; A detailed or comprehensive examination; and Medical decision making that is straightforward or of low complexity. Counseling and/or coordination of care with other providers or agencies are provided consistent with the nature of the problem(s) and the patient's and/or family's needs. Usually, the problem(s) requiring admission are of low severity. Physicians typically spend 30 minutes at the bedside and on the patient's hospital floor or unit.	2.43	84.89	152	169	196
99222	Initial hospital care, per day, for the evaluation and management of a patient, which requires these three key components: A comprehensive history; A comprehensive examination; and Medical decision making of moderate complexity. Counseling and/or coordination of care with other providers or agencies are provided consistent with the nature of the problem(s) and the patient's and/or family's needs. Usually, the problem(s) requiring admission are of moderate severity. Physicians typically spend 50 minutes at the bedside and on the patient's hospital floor or unit.	3.40	119.00	205	229	260
99223	Initial hospital care, per day, for the evaluation and management of a patient, which requires these three key components: A comprehensive history; A comprehensive examination; and Medical decision making of high complexity. Counseling and/or coordination of care with other providers or agencies are provided consistent with the nature of the problem(s) and the patient's and/or family's needs. Usually, the problem(s) requiring admission are of high severity. Physicians typically spend 70 minutes at the bedside and on the patient's hospital floor or unit.	4.96	173.57	260	284	299

● = New Code ⊗ = Conscious Sedation ✚ = Add-on Code ∅ = Modifier '51' Exempt ▲ =Revised Code

	Medicare RVU	National Fee	PFR Fee Information 50%	75%	90%

Subsequent Hospital Care

99231 Subsequent hospital care, per day, for the evaluation and management of a patient, which requires at least two of these three key components: A problem focused interval history; A problem focused examination; Medical decision making that is straightforward or of low complexity. Counseling and/or coordination of care with other providers or agencies are provided consistent with the nature of the problem(s) and the patient's and/or family's needs. Usually, the patient is stable, recovering or improving. Physicians typically spend 15 minutes at the bedside and on the patient's hospital floor or unit. — 1.02 | 35.62 | 81 | 94 | 105

99232 Subsequent hospital care, per day, for the evaluation and management of a patient, which requires at least two of these three key components: An expanded problem focused interval history; An expanded problem focused examination; Medical decision making of moderate complexity. Counseling and/or coordination of care with other providers or agencies are provided consistent with the nature of the problem(s) and the patient's and/or family's needs. Usually, the patient is responding inadequately to therapy or has developed a minor complication. Physicians typically spend 25 minutes at the bedside and on the patient's hospital floor or unit. — 1.82 | 63.67 | 109 | 128 | 152

99233 Subsequent hospital care, per day, for the evaluation and management of a patient, which requires at least two of these three key components: A detailed interval history; A detailed examination; Medical decision making of high complexity. Counseling and/or coordination of care with other providers or agencies are provided consistent with the nature of the problem(s) and the patient's and/or family's needs. Usually, the patient is unstable or has developed a significant complication or a significant new problem. Physicians typically spend 35 minutes at the bedside and on the patient's hospital floor or unit. — 2.60 | 90.95 | 160 | 173 | 210

Observation or Inpatient Care Services (Including Admission and Discharge Services)

99234 Observation or inpatient hospital care, for the evaluation and management of a patient including admission and discharge on the same date which requires these three key components: A detailed or comprehensive history; A detailed or comprehensive examination; and Medical decision making that is straightforward or of low complexity. Counseling and/or coordination of care with other providers or agencies are provided consistent with the nature of the problem(s) and the patient's and/or family's needs. Usually the presenting problem(s) requiring admission are of low severity. — 3.56 | 125.06 | 205 | 232 | 269

99235 Observation or inpatient hospital care, for the evaluation and management of a patient including admission and discharge on the same date which requires these three key components: A comprehensive history; A comprehensive examination; and Medical decision making of moderate complexity. Counseling and/or coordination of care with other providers or agencies are provided consistent with the nature of the problem(s) and the patient's and/or family's needs. Usually the presenting problem(s) requiring admission are of moderate severity. — 4.69 | 164.85 | 271 | 303 | 332

99236 Observation or inpatient hospital care, for the evaluation and management of a patient including admission and discharge on the same date which requires these three key components: A comprehensive history; A comprehensive examination; and Medical decision making of high complexity. Counseling and/or coordination of care with other providers or agencies are provided consistent with the nature of the problem(s) and the patient's and/or family's needs. Usually the presenting problem(s) requiring admission are of high severity. — 5.85 | 205.40 | 324 | 360 | 413

Hospital Discharge Services

(99238 - 99239 Hospital Discharge Day Management can be used on a day that is not the actual day of discharge, i.e., preparation for discharge.)

99238 Hospital discharge day management; 30 minutes or less — 1.86 | 65.56 | 133 | 152 | 176

99239 Hospital discharge day management; more than 30 minutes — 2.69 | 94.74 | 202 | 238 | 258

Consultations

Office or Other Outpatient Consultations

New or Established Patient

99241 Office consultation for a new or established patient, which requires these three key components: A problem focused history; A problem focused examination; and Straightforward medical decision making. Counseling and/or coordination of care with other providers or agencies are provided consistent with the nature of the problem(s) and the patient's and/or family's needs. Usually, the presenting problem(s) are self limited or minor. Physicians typically spend 15 minutes face-to-face with the patient and/or family. — 1.34 | 48.51 | 109 | 122 | 134

99242 Office consultation for a new or established patient, which requires these three key components: An expanded problem focused history; An expanded problem focused examination; and Straightforward medical decision making. Counseling and/or coordination of care with other providers or agencies are provided consistent with the nature of the problem(s) and the patient's and/or family's needs. Usually, the presenting problem(s) are of low severity. Physicians typically spend 30 minutes face-to-face with the patient and/or family. — 2.49 | 89.44 | 152 | 163 | 177

		Medicare RVU	National Fee	PFR Fee Information 50%	75%	90%
99243	Office consultation for a new or established patient, which requires these three key components: A detailed history; A detailed examination; and Medical decision making of low complexity. Counseling and/or coordination of care with other providers or agencies are provided consistent with the nature of the problem(s) and the patient's and/or family's needs. Usually, the presenting problem(s) are of moderate severity. Physicians typically spend 40 minutes face-to-face with the patient and/or family.	3.42	122.41	189	210	230
99244	Office consultation for a new or established patient, which requires these three key components: A comprehensive history; A comprehensive examination; and Medical decision making of moderate complexity. Counseling and/or coordination of care with other providers or agencies are provided consistent with the nature of the problem(s) and the patient's and/or family's needs. Usually, the presenting problem(s) are of moderate to high severity. Physicians typically spend 60 minutes face-to-face with the patient and/or family.	5.04	179.63	249	273	298
99245	Office consultation for a new or established patient, which requires these three key components: A comprehensive history; A comprehensive examination; and Medical decision making of high complexity. Counseling and/or coordination of care with other providers or agencies are provided consistent with the nature of the problem(s) and the patient's and/or family's needs. Usually, the presenting problem(s) are of moderate to high severity. Physicians typically spend 80 minutes face-to-face with the patient and/or family.	6.26	222.84	321	353	392

Initial Inpatient Consultations

New or Established Patient

		Medicare RVU	National Fee	PFR Fee Information 50%	75%	90%
▲ 99251	Inpatient consultation for a new or established patient, which requires these three key components: A problem focused history; A problem focused examination; and Straightforward medical decision making. Counseling and/or coordination of care with other providers or agencies are provided consistent with the nature of the problem(s) and the patient's and/or family's needs. Usually, the presenting problem(s) are self limited or minor. Physicians typically spend 20 minutes at the bedside and on the patient's hospital floor or unit.	1.31	45.86	122	136	148
▲ 99252	Inpatient consultation for a new or established patient, which requires these three key components: An expanded problem focused history; An expanded problem focused examination; and Straightforward medical decision making. Counseling and/or coordination of care with other providers or agencies are provided consistent with the nature of the problem(s) and the patient's and/or family's needs. Usually, the presenting problem(s) are of low severity. Physicians typically spend 40 minutes at the bedside and on the patient's hospital floor or unit.	2.09	73.52	168	182	197
▲ 99253	Inpatient consultation for a new or established patient, which requires these three key components: A detailed history; A detailed examination; and Medical decision making of low complexity. Counseling and/or coordination of care with other providers or agencies are provided consistent with the nature of the problem(s) and the patient's and/or family's needs. Usually, the presenting problem(s) are of moderate severity. Physicians typically spend 55 minutes at the bedside and on the patient's hospital floor or unit.	3.10	108.77	207	224	249
▲ 99254	Inpatient consultation for a new or established patient, which requires these three key components: A comprehensive history; A comprehensive examination; and Medical decision making of moderate complexity. Counseling and/or coordination of care with other providers or agencies are provided consistent with the nature of the problem(s) and the patient's and/or family's needs. Usually, the presenting problem(s) are of moderate to high severity. Physicians typically spend 80 minutes at the bedside and on the patient's hospital floor or unit.	4.46	156.52	265	288	309
▲ 99255	Inpatient consultation for a new or established patient, which requires these three key components: A comprehensive history; A comprehensive examination; and Medical decision making of high complexity. Counseling and/or coordination of care with other providers or agencies are provided consistent with the nature of the problem(s) and the patient's and/or family's needs. Usually, the presenting problem(s) are of moderate to high severity. Physicians typically spend 110 minutes at the bedside and on the patient's hospital floor or unit.	5.55	195.17	338	359	379

Emergency Department Services

New or Established Patient

		Medicare RVU	National Fee	PFR Fee Information 50%	75%	90%
99281	Emergency department visit for the evaluation and management of a patient, which requires these three key components: A problem focused history; A problem focused examination; and Straightforward medical decision making. Counseling and/or coordination of care with other providers or agencies are provided consistent with the nature of the problem(s) and the patient's and/or family's needs. Usually, the presenting problem(s) are self limited or minor.	0.56	19.33	82	103	123
99282	Emergency department visit for the evaluation and management of a patient, which requires these three key components: An expanded problem focused history; An expanded problem focused examination; and Medical decision making of low complexity. Counseling and/or coordination of care with other providers or agencies are provided consistent with the nature of the problem(s) and the patient's and/or family's needs. Usually, the presenting problem(s) are of low to moderate severity.	1.07	37.14	118	136	153

● = New Code ⊗ = Conscious Sedation ✚ = Add-on Code ∅ = Modifier '51' Exempt ▲ =Revised Code

		Medicare RVU	National Fee	PFR Fee Information 50%	75%	90%
99283	Emergency department visit for the evaluation and management of a patient, which requires these three key components: An expanded problem focused history; An expanded problem focused examination; and Medical decision making of moderate complexity. Counseling and/or coordination of care with other providers or agencies are provided consistent with the nature of the problem(s) and the patient's and/or family's needs. Usually, the presenting problem(s) are of moderate severity.	1.73	60.64	158	180	204
99284	Emergency department visit for the evaluation and management of a patient, which requires these three key components: A detailed history; A detailed examination; and Medical decision making of moderate complexity. Counseling and/or coordination of care with other providers or agencies are provided consistent with the nature of the problem(s) and the patient's and/or family's needs. Usually, the presenting problem(s) are of high severity, and require urgent evaluation by the physician but do not pose an immediate significant threat to life or physiologic function.	3.17	110.28	224	243	272
99285	Emergency department visit for the evaluation and management of a patient, which requires these three key components within the constraints imposed by the urgency of the patient's clinical condition and/or mental status: A comprehensive history; A comprehensive examination; and Medical decision making of high complexity. Counseling and/or coordination of care with other providers or agencies are provided consistent with the nature of the problem(s) and the patient's and/or family's needs. Usually, the presenting problem(s) are of high severity and pose an immediate significant threat to life or physiologic function.	4.74	165.23	304	341	395

Other Emergency Services

99288	Physician direction of emergency medical systems (EMS) emergency care, advanced life support	-	-	180	216	249

Pediatric Critical Care Patient Transport

99289	Critical care services delivered by a physician, face-to-face, during an interfacility transport of critically ill or critically injured pediatric patient, 24 months of age or less; first 30-74 minutes of hands on care during transport	6.40	224.35	428	558	670
✚ 99290	Critical care services delivered by a physician, face-to-face, during an interfacility transport of critically ill or critically injured pediatric patient, 24 months of age or less; each additional 30 minutes (List separately in addition to code for primary service)	3.28	115.21	212	285	340

Critical Care Services

(UNBUNDLING ALERT: 99291 cannot be used with 36000, 36410, 36415, 36600, 71010, 71020, 91105, 92953, 93561, 93562, 94656, 94657, 94760, 94761, 94762 or HCPCS G0001 by the same physician on the same day.)

99291	Critical care, evaluation and management of the critically ill or critically injured patient; first 30-74 minutes	7.21	256.19	363	414	466

(UNBUNDLING ALERT: 99292 cannot be used with 36000, 36410, 36415, 36600, 71010, 71020, 91105, 92953, 93561, 93562, 94656, 94657, 94760, 94761, 94762 or HCPCS G0001 by the same physician on the same day.)

✚ 99292	Critical care, evaluation and management of the critically ill or critically injured patient; each additional 30 minutes (List separately in addition to code for primary service)	3.25	114.45	182	211	233

Inpatient Neonatal and Pediatric Critical Care Services
Inpatient Pediatric Critical Care

99293	Initial inpatient pediatric critical care, per day, for the evaluation and management of a critically ill infant or young child, 29 days through 24 months of age	21.58	756.81	1350	1551	1802
99294	Subsequent inpatient pediatric critical care, per day, for the evaluation and management of a critically ill infant or young child, 29 days through 24 months of age	10.68	374.43	714	821	951

Inpatient Neonatal Critical Care

99295	Initial inpatient neonatal critical care, per day, for the evaluation and management of a critically ill neonate, 28 days of age or less	24.76	867.85	1550	1879	2077

(PFR research indicates that fees vary considerably in certified High Risk Level III facilities)

99296	Subsequent inpatient neonatal critical care, per day, for the evaluation and management of a critically ill neonate, 28 days of age or less	10.67	374.05	824	915	1065

(PFR research indicates that fees vary considerably in certified High Risk Level III facilities)

Intensive (Non-Critical) Low birth Weight Services

(PFR research indicates that fees vary considerably in certified High Risk Level III facilities)

99298	Subsequent intensive care, per day, for the evaluation and management of the recovering very low birth weight infant (present body weight less than 1500 g)	3.79	133.02	373	438	511
99299	Subsequent intensive care, per day, for the evaluation and management of the recovering low birth weight infant (present body weight of 1500-2500 g)	3.50	123.17	333	402	482

● = New Code ⊗ = Conscious Sedation ✚ = Add-on Code ∅ = Modifier '51' Exempt ▲ =Revised Code

		Medicare RVU	National Fee	PFR Fee Information 50%	75%	90%
99300	Subsequent intensive care, per day, for the evaluation and management of the recovering infant (present body weight of 2501-5000 g)	3.37	118.62	467	557	659
	(Codes 99301-99350 are documented and assigned based on the Evaluation and Management Documentation Guidelines issued by the Centers for Med)					

Nursing Facility Services

Comprehensive Nursing Facility Assessments
New or Established Patient

		Medicare RVU	National Fee	50%	75%	90%
99304	Initial nursing facility care, per day, for the evaluation and management of a patient which requires these three key components: A detailed or comprehensive history; A detailed or comprehensive examination; and Medical decision making that is straightforward or of low complexity. Counseling and/or coordination of care with other providers or agencies are provided consistent with the nature of the problem(s) and the patient's and/or family's needs. Usually, the problem(s) requiring admission are of low severity.	1.73	61.01	101	114	128
99305	Initial nursing facility care, per day, for the evaluation and management of a patient which requires these three key components: A comprehensive history; A comprehensive examination; and Medical decision making of moderate complexity. Counseling and/or coordination of care with other providers or agencies are provided consistent with the nature of the problem(s) and the patient's and/or family's needs. Usually, the problem(s) requiring admission are of moderate severity.	2.30	81.10	134	153	171
99306	Initial nursing facility care, per day, for the evaluation and management of a patient, which requires these three key components: A comprehensive history; A comprehensive examination; and Medical decision making of high complexity. Counseling and/or coordination of care with other providers or agencies are provided consistent with the nature of the problem(s) and the patient's and/or family's needs. Usually, the problem(s) requiring admission are of high severity.	2.83	99.67	166	188	210

Subsequent Nursing Facility Care

		Medicare RVU	National Fee	50%	75%	90%
99307	Subsequent nursing facility care, per day, for the evaluation and management of a patient, which requires at least two of these three key components: A problem focused interval history; A problem focused examination; Straightforward medical decision making. Counseling and/or coordination of care with other providers or agencies are provided consistent with the nature of the problem(s) and the patient's and/or family's needs. Usually, the patient is stable, recovering, or improving.	0.90	31.83	52	59	70
99308	Subsequent nursing facility care, per day, for the evaluation and management of a patient, which requires at least two of these three key components: An expanded problem focused interval history; An expanded problem focused examination; Medical decision making of low complexity. Counseling and/or coordination of care with other providers or agencies are provided consistent with the nature of the problem(s) and the patient's and/or family's needs. Usually, the patient is responding inadequately to therapy or has developed a minor complication.	1.49	52.68	86	97	115
99309	Subsequent nursing facility care, per day, for the evaluation and management of a patient, which requires at least two of these three key components: A detailed interval history; A detailed examination; Medical decision making of moderate complexity. Counseling and/or coordination of care with other providers or agencies are provided consistent with the nature of the problem(s) and the patient's and/or family's needs. Usually, the patient has developed a significant complication or a significant new problem.	2.09	73.90	121	137	163
99310	Subsequent nursing facility care, per day, for the evaluation and management of a patient, which requires at least two of these three key components: A comprehensive interval history; A comprehensive examination; Medical decision making of high complexity. Counseling and/or coordination of care with other providers or agencies are provided consistent with the nature of the problem(s) and the patient's and/or family's needs. The patient may be unstable or may have developed a significant new problem requiring immediate physician attention.	2.62	92.47	152	172	204

Nursing Facility Discharge Services

		Medicare RVU	National Fee	50%	75%	90%
99315	Nursing facility discharge day management; 30 minutes or less	1.62	57.23	111	127	142
99316	Nursing facility discharge day management; more than 30 minutes	2.13	75.04	129	157	184

Other Nursing Facility Services

		Medicare RVU	National Fee	50%	75%	90%
99318	Evaluation and management of a patient involving an annual nursing facility assessment, which requires these three key components: A detailed interval history; A comprehensive examination; and Medical decision making that is of low to moderate complexity. Counseling and/or coordination of care with other providers or agencies are provided consistent with the nature of the problem(s) and the patient's and/or family's needs. Usually, the patient is stable, recovering, or improving.	1.73	61.01	103	118	138

		Medicare RVU	National Fee	PFR Fee Information		
				50%	75%	90%

Domiciliary, Rest Home (eg Boarding Home), or Custodial Care Services

New Patient

99324 Domiciliary or rest home visit for the evaluation and management of a new patient, which requires these three key components: A problem focused history; A problem focused examination; and Straightforward medical decision making. Counseling and/or coordination of care with other providers or agencies are provided consistent with the nature of the problem(s) and the patient's and/or family's needs. Usually, the presenting problem(s) are of low severity. Physicians typically spend 20 minutes with the patient and/or family or caregiver. — 1.54 | 54.57 | 98 | 116 | 138

99325 Domiciliary or rest home visit for the evaluation and management of a new patient, which requires these three key components: An expanded problem focused history; An expanded problem focused examination; and Medical decision making of low complexity. Counseling and/or coordination of care with other providers or agencies are provided consistent with the nature of the problem(s) and the patient's and/or family's needs. Usually, the presenting problem(s) are of moderate severity. Physicians typically spend 30 minutes with the patient and/or family or caregiver. — 2.25 | 79.58 | 144 | 169 | 202

99326 Domiciliary or rest home visit for the evaluation and management of a new patient, which requires these three key components: A detailed history; A detailed examination; and Medical decision making of moderate complexity. Counseling and/or coordination of care with other providers or agencies are provided consistent with the nature of the problem(s) and the patient's and/or family's needs. Usually, the presenting problem(s) are of moderate to high severity. Physicians typically spend 45 minutes with the patient and/or family or caregiver. — 3.25 | 114.45 | 209 | 246 | 293

99327 Domiciliary or rest home visit for the evaluation and management of a new patient, which requires these three key components: A comprehensive history; A comprehensive examination; and Medical decision making of moderate complexity. Counseling and/or coordination of care with other providers or agencies are provided consistent with the nature of the problem(s) and the patient's and/or family's needs. Usually, the presenting problem(s) are of high severity. Physicians typically spend 60 minutes with the patient and/or family or caregiver. — 4.27 | 150.45 | 275 | 323 | 386

99328 Domiciliary or rest home visit for the evaluation and management of a new patient, which requires these three key components: A comprehensive history; A comprehensive examination; and Medical decision making of high complexity. Counseling and/or coordination of care with other providers or agencies are provided consistent with the nature of the problem(s) and the patient's and/or family's needs. Usually, the patient is unstable or has developed a significant new problem requiring immediate physician attention. Physicians typically spend 75 minutes with the patient and/or family or caregiver. — 5.29 | 186.08 | 341 | 400 | 478

Established Patient

99334 Domiciliary or rest home visit for the evaluation and management of an established patient, which requires at least two of these three key components: A problem focused interval history; A problem focused examination; Straightforward medical decision making. Counseling and/or coordination of care with other providers or agencies provided consistent with the nature of the problem(s) and the patient's and/or family's needs. Usually, the presenting problem(s) are self-limited or minor. Physicians typically spend 15 minutes with the patient and/or family or caregiver. — 1.19 | 42.07 | 73 | 82 | 94

99335 Domiciliary or rest home visit for the evaluation and management of an established patient, which requires at least two of these three key components: An expanded problem focused interval history; An expanded problem focused examination; Medical decision making of low complexity. Counseling and/or coordination of care with other providers or agencies are provided consistent with the nature of the problem(s) and the patient's and/or family's needs. Usually, the presenting problem(s) are of low to moderate severity. Physicians typically spend 25 minutes with the patient and/or family or caregiver. — 1.88 | 66.32 | 116 | 129 | 149

99336 Domiciliary or rest home visit for the evaluation and management of an established patient, which requires at least two of these three key components: A detailed interval history; A detailed examination; Medical decision making of moderate complexity. Counseling and/or coordination of care with other providers or agencies are provided consistent with the nature of the problem(s) and the patient's and/or family's needs. Usually, the presenting problem(s) are of moderate to high severity. Physicians typically spend 40 minutes with the patient and/or family or caregiver. — 2.89 | 101.94 | 178 | 200 | 229

99337 Domiciliary or rest home visit for the evaluation and management of an established patient, which requires at least two of these three key components: A comprehensive interval history; A comprehensive examination; Medical decision making of moderate to high complexity. Counseling and/or coordination of care with other providers or agencies are provided consistent with the nature of the problem(s) and the patient's and/or family's needs. Usually, the presenting problem(s) are of moderate to high severity. The patient may be unstable or may have developed a significant new problem requiring immediate physician attention. Physicians typically spend 60 minutes with the patient and/or family or caregiver. — 4.25 | 149.70 | 262 | 294 | 337

● = New Code ⊗ = Conscious Sedation ✚ = Add-on Code ∅ = Modifier '51' Exempt ▲ =Revised Code

| | | Medicare RVU | National Fee | PFR Fee Information |||
				50%	75%	90%

Domiciliary, Rest Home , or Home Care Plan Oversight Services

99339	Individual physician supervision of a patient (patient not present) in home, domiciliary or rest home (eg, assisted living facility) requiring complex and multidisciplinary care modalities involving regular physician development and/or revision of care plans, review of subsequent reports of patient status, review of related laboratory and other studies, communication (including telephone calls) for purposes of assessment or care decisions with health care professional(s), family member(s), surrogate decision maker(s) (eg, legal guardian) and/or key caregiver(s) involved in patient's care, integration of new information into the medical treatment plan and/or adjustment of medical therapy, within a calendar month; 15-29 minutes	1.89	66.70	IR	IR	IR
99340	Individual physician supervision of a patient (patient not present) in home, domiciliary or rest home (eg, assisted living facility) requiring complex and multidisciplinary care modalities involving regular physician development and/or revision of care plans, review of subsequent reports of patient status, review of related laboratory and other studies, communication (including telephone calls) for purposes of assessment or care decisions with health care professional(s), family member(s), surrogate decision maker(s) (eg, legal guardian) and/or key caregiver(s) involved in patient's care, integration of new information into the medical treatment plan and/or adjustment of medical therapy, within a calendar month; 30 minutes or more	2.63	92.85	IR	IR	IR

Home Services

New Patient

99341	Home visit for the evaluation and management of a new patient, which requires these three key components: A problem focused history; A problem focused examination; and Straightforward medical decision making. Counseling and/or coordination of care with other providers or agencies are provided consistent with the nature of the problem(s) and the patient's and/or family's needs. Usually, the presenting problem(s) are of low severity. Physicians typically spend 20 minutes face-to-face with the patient and/or family.	1.53	54.19	103	122	134
99342	Home visit for the evaluation and management of a new patient, which requires these three key components: An expanded problem focused history; An expanded problem focused examination; and Medical decision making of low complexity. Counseling and/or coordination of care with other providers or agencies are provided consistent with the nature of the problem(s) and the patient's and/or family's needs. Usually, the presenting problem(s) are of moderate severity. Physicians typically spend 30 minutes face-to-face with the patient and/or family.	2.25	79.58	115	135	169
99343	Home visit for the evaluation and management of a new patient, which requires these three key components: A detailed history; A detailed examination; and Medical decision making of moderate complexity. Counseling and/or coordination of care with other providers or agencies are provided consistent with the nature of the problem(s) and the patient's and/or family's needs. Usually, the presenting problem(s) are of moderate to high severity. Physicians typically spend 45 minutes face-to-face with the patient and/or family.	3.27	115.21	172	199	232
99344	Home visit for the evaluation and management of a new patient, which requires these three components: A comprehensive history; A comprehensive examination; and Medical decision making of moderate complexity. Counseling and/or coordination of care with other providers or agencies are provided consistent with the nature of the problem(s) and the patient's and/or family's needs. Usually, the presenting problem(s) are of high severity. Physicians typically spend 60 minutes face-to-face with the patient and/or family.	4.28	150.83	209	246	315
99345	Home visit for the evaluation and management of a new patient, which requires these three key components: A comprehensive history; A comprehensive examination; and Medical decision making of high complexity. Counseling and/or coordination of care with other providers or agencies are provided consistent with the nature of the problem(s) and the patient's and/or family's needs. Usually, the patient is unstable or has developed a significant new problem requiring immediate physician attention. Physicians typically spend 75 minutes face-to-face with the patient and/or family.	5.29	186.08	268	300	359

Established Patient

99347	Home visit for the evaluation and management of an established patient, which requires at least two of these three key components: A problem focused interval history; A problem focused examination; Straightforward medical decision making. Counseling and/or coordination of care with other providers or agencies are provided consistent with the nature of the problem(s) and the patient's and/or family's needs. Usually, the presenting problem(s) are self limited or minor. Physicians typically spend 15 minutes face-to-face with the patient and/or family.	1.19	42.07	81	98	107
99348	Home visit for the evaluation and management of an established patient, which requires at least two of these three key components: An expanded problem focused interval history; An expanded problem focused examination; Medical decision making of low complexity. Counseling and/or coordination of care with other providers or agencies are provided consistent with the nature of the problem(s) and the patient's and/or family's needs. Usually, the presenting problem(s) are of low to moderate severity. Physicians typically spend 25 minutes face-to-face with the patient and/or family.	1.88	66.32	111	137	162

= New Code ⊗ = Conscious Sedation ✚ = Add-on Code ∅ = Modifier '51' Exempt ▲ =Revised Code

		Medicare RVU	National Fee	PFR Fee Information 50%	75%	90%

99349 Home visit for the evaluation and management of an established patient, which requires at least two of these three key components: A detailed interval history; A detailed examination; Medical decision making of moderate complexity. Counseling and/or coordination of care with other providers or agencies are provided consistent with the nature of the problem(s) and the patient's and/or family's needs. Usually, the presenting problem(s) are moderate to high severity. Physicians typically spend 40 minutes face-to-face with the patient and/or family. — 2.90 | 102.32 | 159 | 207 | 237

99350 Home visit for the evaluation and management of an established patient, which requires at least two of these three key components: A comprehensive interval history; A comprehensive examination; Medical decision making of moderate to high complexity. Counseling and/or coordination of care with other providers or agencies are provided consistent with the nature of the problem(s) and the patient's and/or family's needs. Usually, the presenting problem(s) are of moderate to high severity. The patient may be unstable or may have developed a significant new problem requiring immediate physician attention. Physicians typically spend 60 minutes face-to-face with the patient and/or family. — 4.28 | 150.83 | 212 | 239 | 318

Prolonged Services

Prolonged Physician Service With Direct (Face - to - Face) Patient Contact

+ 99354 Prolonged physician service in the office or other outpatient setting requiring direct (face-to-face) patient contact beyond the usual service (eg, prolonged care and treatment of an acute asthmatic patient in an outpatient setting); first hour (List separately in addition to code for office or other outpatient Evaluation and Management service) — 2.59 | 91.33 | 177 | 218 | 264

+ 99355 Prolonged physician service in the office or other outpatient setting requiring direct (face-to-face) patient contact beyond the usual service (eg, prolonged care and treatment of an acute asthmatic patient in an outpatient setting); each additional 30 minutes (List separately in addition to code for prolonged physician service) — 2.57 | 90.58 | 147 | 172 | 218

+ 99356 Prolonged physician service in the inpatient setting, requiring direct (face-to-face) patient contact beyond the usual service (eg, maternal fetal monitoring for high risk delivery or other physiological monitoring, prolonged care of an acutely ill inpatient); first hour (List separately in addition to code for inpatient Evaluation and Management service) — 2.38 | 83.75 | 194 | 217 | 267

+ 99357 Prolonged physician service in the inpatient setting, requiring direct (face-to-face) patient contact beyond the usual service (eg, maternal fetal monitoring for high risk delivery or other physiological monitoring, prolonged care of an acutely ill inpatient); each additional 30 minutes (List separately in addition to code for prolonged physician service) — 2.39 | 84.13 | 146 | 169 | 200

Prolonged Physician Service Without Direct (Face - to - Face) Patient Contact

+ 99358 Prolonged evaluation and management service before and/or after direct (face-to-face) patient care (eg, review of extensive records and tests, communication with other professionals and/or the patient/family); first hour (List separately in addition to code(s) for other physician service(s) and/or inpatient or outpatient Evaluation and Management service) — 2.70 | 94.36 | 168 | 233 | 308

+ 99359 Prolonged evaluation and management service before and/or after direct (face-to-face) patient care (eg, review of extensive records and tests, communication with other professionals and/or the patient/family); each additional 30 minutes (List separately in addition to code for prolonged physician service) — 1.30 | 45.48 | 99 | 127 | 171

Physician Standby Services

99360 Physician standby service, requiring prolonged physician attendance, each 30 minutes (eg, operative standby, standby for frozen section, for cesarean/high risk delivery, for monitoring EEG) — 1.25 | 42.82 | 198 | 250 | 294

Case Management Services

Team Conferences

99361 Medical conference by a physician with interdisciplinary team of health professionals or representatives of community agencies to coordinate activities of patient care (patient not present); approximately 30 minutes — - | - | 120 | 156 | 184

99362 Medical conference by a physician with interdisciplinary team of health professionals or representatives of community agencies to coordinate activities of patient care (patient not present); approximately 60 minutes — - | - | 186 | 255 | 282

Anticoagulant Management

● 99363 Anticoagulant management for an outpatient taking warfarin, physician review and interpretation of International Normalized Ratio (INR) testing, patient instructions, dosage adjustment (as needed), and ordering of additional tests; initial 90 days of therapy (must include a minimum of 8 INR measurements) — 3.01 | 107.63 | 174 | 213 | 250

		Medicare RVU	National Fee	PFR Fee Information 50%	75%	90%
● 99364	Anticoagulant management for an outpatient taking warfarin, physician review and interpretation of International Normalized Ratio (INR) testing, patient instructions, dosage adjustment (as needed), and ordering of additional tests; each subsequent 90 days of therapy (must include a minimum of 3 INR measurements)	1.05	37.52	61	74	87

Telephone Calls

99371	Telephone call by a physician to patient or for consultation or medical management or for coordinating medical management with other health care professionals (eg, nurses, therapists, social workers, nutritionists, physicians, pharmacists); simple or brief (eg, to report on tests and/or laboratory results, to clarify or alter previous instructions, to integrate new information from other health professionals into the medical treatment plan, or to adjust therapy)	-	-	38	55	65
99372	Telephone call by a physician to patient or for consultation or medical management or for coordinating medical management with other health care professionals (eg, nurses, therapists, social workers, nutritionists, physicians, pharmacists); intermediate (eg, to provide advice to an established patient on a new problem, to initiate therapy that can be handled by telephone, to discuss test results in detail, to coordinate medical management of a new problem in an established patient, to discuss and evaluate new information and details, or to initiate new plan of care)	-	-	56	79	86
99373	Telephone call by a physician to patient or for consultation or medical management or for coordinating medical management with other health care professionals (eg, nurses, therapists, social workers, nutritionists, physicians, pharmacists); complex or lengthy (eg, lengthy counseling session with anxious or distraught patient, detailed or prolonged discussion with family members regarding seriously ill patient, lengthy communication necessary to coordinate complex services of several different health professionals working on different aspects of the total patient care plan)	-	-	94	132	157

Care Plan Oversight Services

99374	Physician supervision of a patient under care of home health agency (patient not present) in home, domiciliary or equivalent environment (eg, Alzheimer's facility) requiring complex and multidisciplinary care modalities involving regular physician development and/or revision of care plans, review of subsequent reports of patient status, review of related laboratory and other studies, communication (including telephone calls) for purposes of assessment or care decisions with health care professional(s), family member(s), surrogate decision maker(s) (eg, legal guardian) and/or key caregiver(s) involved in patient's care, integration of new information into the medical treatment plan and/or adjustment of medical therapy, within a calendar month; 15-29 minutes	1.81	64.43	91	104	120
99375	Physician supervision of a patient under care of home health agency (patient not present) in home, domiciliary or equivalent environment (eg, Alzheimer's facility) requiring complex and multidisciplinary care modalities involving regular physician development and/or revision of care plans, review of subsequent reports of patient status, review of related laboratory and other studies, communication (including telephone calls) for purposes of assessment or care decisions with health care professional(s), family member(s), surrogate decision maker(s) (eg, legal guardian) and/or key caregiver(s) involved in patient's care, integration of new information into the medical treatment plan and/or adjustment of medical therapy, within a calendar month; 30 minutes or more *(UNBUNDLING ALERT: 99376 cannot be used with 99375 by the same physician on the same day.)*	3.15	112.93	137	158	208
99377	Physician supervision of a hospice patient (patient not present) requiring complex and multidisciplinary care modalities involving regular physician development and/or revision of care plans, review of subsequent reports of patient status, review of related laboratory and other studies, communication (including telephone calls) for purposes of assessment or care decisions with health care professional(s), family member(s), surrogate decision maker(s) (eg, legal guardian) and/or key caregiver(s) involved in patient's care, integration of new information into the medical treatment plan and/or adjustment of medical therapy, within a calendar month; 15-29 minutes	1.81	64.43	97	110	127
99378	Physician supervision of a hospice patient (patient not present) requiring complex and multidisciplinary care modalities involving regular physician development and/or revision of care plans, review of subsequent reports of patient status, review of related laboratory and other studies, communication (including telephone calls) for purposes of assessment or care decisions with health care professional(s), family member(s), surrogate decision maker(s) (eg, legal guardian) and/or key caregiver(s) involved in patient's care, integration of new information into the medical treatment plan and/or adjustment of medical therapy, within a calendar month; 30 minutes or more	3.44	123.92	147	171	205
99379	Physician supervision of a nursing facility patient (patient not present) requiring complex and multidisciplinary care modalities involving regular physician development and/or revision of care plans, review of subsequent reports of patient status, review of related laboratory and other studies, communication (including telephone calls) for purposes of assessment or care decisions with health care professional(s), family member(s), surrogate decision maker(s) (eg, legal guardian) and/or key caregiver(s) involved in patient's care, integration of new information into the medical treatment plan and/or adjustment of medical therapy, within a calendar month; 15-29 minutes	1.80	64.05	86	103	121

		Medicare RVU	National Fee	PFR Fee Information 50%	75%	90%
99380	Physician supervision of a nursing facility patient (patient not present) requiring complex and multidisciplinary care modalities involving regular physician development and/or revision of care plans, review of subsequent reports of patient status, review of related laboratory and other studies, communication (including telephone calls) for purposes of assessment or care decisions with health care professional(s), family member(s), surrogate decision maker(s) (eg, legal guardian) and/or key caregiver(s) involved in patient's care, integration of new information into the medical treatment plan and/or adjustment of medical therapy, within a calendar month; 30 minutes or more	2.72	96.64	142	162	183

Preventive Medicine Services

New Patient

99381	Initial comprehensive preventive medicine evaluation and management of an individual including an age and gender appropriate history, examination, counseling/anticipatory guidance/risk factor reduction interventions, and the ordering of appropriate immunization(s), laboratory/diagnostic procedures, new patient; infant (age younger than 1 year)	2.61	94.36	113	156	180
99382	Initial comprehensive preventive medicine evaluation and management of an individual including an age and gender appropriate history, examination, counseling/anticipatory guidance/risk factor reduction interventions, and the ordering of appropriate immunization(s), laboratory/diagnostic procedures, new patient; early childhood (age 1 through 4 years)	2.82	101.57	122	154	167
99383	Initial comprehensive preventive medicine evaluation and management of an individual including an age and gender appropriate history, examination, counseling/anticipatory guidance/risk factor reduction interventions, and the ordering of appropriate immunization(s), laboratory/diagnostic procedures, new patient; late childhood (age 5 through 11 years)	2.78	100.05	131	174	194

(Use Preventive Medicine (99383-99395) codes for school and sports physicals.)

99384	Initial comprehensive preventive medicine evaluation and management of an individual including an age and gender appropriate history, examination, counseling/anticipatory guidance/risk factor reduction interventions, and the ordering of appropriate immunization(s), laboratory/diagnostic procedures, new patient; adolescent (age 12 through 17 years)	3.02	108.77	146	187	201
99385	Initial comprehensive preventive medicine evaluation and management of an individual including an age and gender appropriate history, examination, counseling/anticipatory guidance/risk factor reduction interventions, and the ordering of appropriate immunization(s), laboratory/diagnostic procedures, new patient; 18-39 years	3.02	108.77	170	199	227
99386	Initial comprehensive preventive medicine evaluation and management of an individual including an age and gender appropriate history, examination, counseling/anticipatory guidance/risk factor reduction interventions, and the ordering of appropriate immunization(s), laboratory/diagnostic procedures, new patient; 40-64 years	3.54	126.96	205	236	267

(See also HCPCS code G0101 for cervical or vaginal cancer screening; pelvic and clinical breast examination.)

(See also HCPCS code G0102 for prostate cancer screening; digital rectal examination.)

(See also HCPCS code Q0091 for screening papanicolaou smear; obtaining, preparing and conveyance of cervical or vaginal smear to laboratory.)

99387	Initial comprehensive preventive medicine evaluation and management of an individual including an age and gender appropriate history, examination, counseling/anticipatory guidance/risk factor reduction interventions, and the ordering of appropriate immunization(s), laboratory/diagnostic procedures, new patient; 65 years and older	3.85	137.95	207	246	296

Established Patient

99391	Periodic comprehensive preventive medicine reevaluation and management of an individual including an age and gender appropriate history, examination, counseling/anticipatory guidance/risk factor reduction interventions, and the ordering of appropriate immunization(s), laboratory/diagnostic procedures, established patient; infant (age younger than 1 year)	2.04	73.52	97	126	151
99392	Periodic comprehensive preventive medicine reevaluation and management of an individual including an age and gender appropriate history, examination, counseling/anticipatory guidance/risk factor reduction interventions, and the ordering of appropriate immunization(s), laboratory/diagnostic procedures, established patient; early childhood (age 1 through 4 years)	2.28	81.86	105	145	171
99393	Periodic comprehensive preventive medicine reevaluation and management of an individual including an age and gender appropriate history, examination, counseling/anticipatory guidance/risk factor reduction interventions, and the ordering of appropriate immunization(s), laboratory/diagnostic procedures, established patient; late childhood (age 5 through 11 years)	2.26	81.10	106	148	176
99394	Periodic comprehensive preventive medicine reevaluation and management of an individual including an age and gender appropriate history, examination, counseling/anticipatory guidance/risk factor reduction interventions, and the ordering of appropriate immunization(s), laboratory/diagnostic procedures, established patient; adolescent (age 12 through 17 years)	2.49	89.06	122	161	185

● = New Code ⊗ = Conscious Sedation ✚ = Add-on Code ∅ = Modifier '51' Exempt ▲ =Revised Code

		Medicare RVU	National Fee	PFR Fee Information 50%	75%	90%
99395	Periodic comprehensive preventive medicine reevaluation and management of an individual including an age and gender appropriate history, examination, counseling/anticipatory guidance/risk factor reduction interventions, and the ordering of appropriate immunization(s), laboratory/diagnostic procedures, established patient; 18-39 years	2.51	89.82	136	151	183
99396	Periodic comprehensive preventive medicine reevaluation and management of an individual including an age and gender appropriate history, examination, counseling/anticipatory guidance/risk factor reduction interventions, and the ordering of appropriate immunization(s), laboratory/diagnostic procedures, established patient; 40-64 years	2.77	99.29	150	178	219
99397	Periodic comprehensive preventive medicine reevaluation and management of an individual including an age and gender appropriate history, examination, counseling/anticipatory guidance/risk factor reduction interventions, and the ordering of appropriate immunization(s), laboratory/diagnostic procedures, established patient; 65 years and older	3.07	109.90	176	206	226

Counseling and/or Risk Factor Reduction Intervention

New or Established Patient

Preventive Medicine, Individual Counseling

		Medicare RVU	National Fee	50%	75%	90%
99401	Preventive medicine counseling and/or risk factor reduction intervention(s) provided to an individual (separate procedure); approximately 15 minutes	1.05	37.90	61	68	83
99402	Preventive medicine counseling and/or risk factor reduction intervention(s) provided to an individual (separate procedure); approximately 30 minutes	1.77	63.29	96	119	143
99403	Preventive medicine counseling and/or risk factor reduction intervention(s) provided to an individual (separate procedure); approximately 45 minutes	2.46	87.54	153	177	190
99404	Preventive medicine counseling and/or risk factor reduction intervention(s) provided to an individual (separate procedure); approximately 60 minutes	3.17	112.56	204	231	259

Preventive Medicine, Group Counseling

		Medicare RVU	National Fee	50%	75%	90%
99411	Preventive medicine counseling and/or risk factor reduction intervention(s) provided to individuals in a group setting (separate procedure); approximately 30 minutes	0.35	12.51	59	70	80
99412	Preventive medicine counseling and/or risk factor reduction intervention(s) provided to individuals in a group setting (separate procedure); approximately 60 minutes	0.51	18.19	94	105	126

Other Preventive Medicine Services

(Medicare fees for the code below are based on Non Facility RVUs. PFR information reflects fee when procedure is performed in a facility.)

		Medicare RVU	National Fee	50%	75%	90%
99420	Administration and interpretation of health risk assessment instrument (eg, health hazard appraisal)	0.23	8.72	123	176	203
99429	Unlisted preventive medicine service	-	-	IR	IR	IR

Newborn Care

		Medicare RVU	National Fee	50%	75%	90%
99431	History and examination of the normal newborn infant, initiation of diagnostic and treatment programs and preparation of hospital records. (This code should also be used for birthing room deliveries.)	1.57	54.95	169	229	265
99432	Normal newborn care in other than hospital or birthing room setting, including physical examination of baby and conference(s) with parent(s)	2.28	81.48	151	186	209
99433	Subsequent hospital care, for the evaluation and management of a normal newborn, per day	0.83	29.18	86	101	125
99435	History and examination of the normal newborn infant, including the preparation of medical records. (This code should only be used for newborns assessed and discharged from the hospital or birthing room on the same date.)	2.12	74.66	252	277	316
99436	Attendance at delivery (when requested by delivering physician) and initial stabilization of newborn	2.00	70.11	253	286	368
99440	Newborn resuscitation: provision of positive pressure ventilation and/or chest compressions in the presence of acute inadequate ventilation and/or cardiac output	3.92	137.57	376	433	503

Special Evaluation and Management Services

Basic Life and/or Disability Evaluation Services

(Medicare fees for the code below are based on Non Facility RVUs. PFR information reflects fee when procedure is performed in a facility.)

		Medicare RVU	National Fee	50%	75%	90%
99450	Basic life and/or disability examination that includes: Measurement of height, weight and blood pressure; Completion of a medical history following a life insurance pro forma; Collection of blood sample and/or urinalysis complying with "chain of custody" protocols; and Completion of necessary documentation/certificates.	-	-	106	140	189

● = New Code ⊗ = Conscious Sedation ✚ = Add-on Code ∅ = Modifier '51' Exempt ▲ =Revised Code

		Medicare RVU	National Fee	PFR Fee Information 50%	75%	90%
Work Related or Medical Disability Evaluation Services						
99455	Work related or medical disability examination by the treating physician that includes: Completion of a medical history commensurate with the patient's condition; Performance of an examination commensurate with the patient's condition; Formulation of a diagnosis, assessment of capabilities and stability, and calculation of impairment; Development of future medical treatment plan; and Completion of necessary documentation/certificates and report.	-	-	275	361	489
99456	Work related or medical disability examination by other than the treating physician that includes: Completion of a medical history commensurate with the patient's condition; Performance of an examination commensurate with the patient's condition; Formulation of a diagnosis, assessment of capabilities and stability, and calculation of impairment; Development of future medical treatment plan; and Completion of necessary documentation/certificates and report.	-	-	430	526	572

Other Evaluation and Management Services

99499	Unlisted evaluation and management service	-	-	IR	IR	IR

Home Health Procedures/Services

99500	Home visit for prenatal monitoring and assessment to include fetal heart rate, non-stress test, uterine monitoring, and gestational diabetes monitoring	-	-	IR	IR	IR
99501	Home visit for postnatal assessment and follow-up care	-	-	IR	IR	IR
99502	Home visit for newborn care and assessment	-	-	IR	IR	IR
99503	Home visit for respiratory therapy care (eg, bronchodilator, oxygen therapy, respiratory assessment, apnea evaluation)	-	-	IR	IR	IR
99504	Home visit for mechanical ventilation care	-	-	IR	IR	IR
99505	Home visit for stoma care and maintenance including colostomy and cystostomy	-	-	IR	IR	IR
99506	Home visit for intramuscular injections	-	-	IR	IR	IR
99507	Home visit for care and maintenance of catheter(s) (eg, urinary, drainage, and enteral)	-	-	IR	IR	IR
99509	Home visit for assistance with activities of daily living and personal care	-	-	IR	IR	IR
99510	Home visit for individual, family, or marriage counseling	-	-	IR	IR	IR
99511	Home visit for fecal impaction management and enema administration	-	-	IR	IR	IR
99512	Home visit for hemodialysis	-	-	IR	IR	IR
99600	Unlisted home visit service or procedure	-	-	IR	IR	IR

Home Infusion Procedures/Services

99601	Home infusion/specialty drug administration, per visit (up to 2 hours);	-	-	IR	IR	IR
✚ 99602	Home infusion/specialty drug administration, per visit (up to 2 hours); each additional hour (List separately in addition to code for primary procedure)	-	-	IR	IR	IR

APPENDIX A GEOGRAPHIC MULTIPLIERS

As stated in the introduction, **PFR** multipliers are national references. To adjust these national references for your area we have provides a list of 3 digit zip code prefix adjustment factors (multipliers). These **PFR** multipliers are based on a modified version of Medicare's RBRVS cost indexes and other government economic data.

The calculation of RBRVS Medicare reimbursement is beyond the scope of this text. DO NOT use these multipliers for Medicare.

PFR multipliers describe overall relative differences of physicians' costs between communities and do not take into consideration economic disparities within large urban areas. This approximation adds a degree of error or uncertainty - perhaps up to +/- 5%. Geographic multipliers have their limitations but are found to be the best available measurement of the relative differences between areas in medical practice costs. Also, multipliers are most accurate at the middle or median (50%) of a distribution.

Zip Prefix	Multiplier	Zip Prefix	Multiplier	Zip Prefix	Multiplier	Zip Prefix	Multiplier
006	0.762	035	0.946	064	1.096	103	1.261
007	0.762	036	0.946	065	1.080	104	1.261
008	0.979	037	0.946	066	1.167	105	1.239
009	0.762	038	0.946	067	1.082	106	1.261
010	1.010	039	0.948	068	1.167	107	1.261
011	1.011	040	0.943	069	1.167	108	1.261
012	1.011	041	0.948	070	1.130	109	1.148
013	0.992	042	0.916	071	1.130	110	1.261
014	1.011	043	0.915	072	1.130	111	1.258
015	1.011	044	0.921	073	1.130	112	1.261
016	1.011	045	0.915	074	1.130	113	1.258
017	1.011	046	0.921	075	1.130	114	1.258
018	1.011	047	0.921	076	1.130	115	1.261
019	1.011	048	0.916	077	1.130	116	1.258
020	1.011	049	0.920	078	1.130	117	1.261
021	1.081	050	0.874	079	1.130	118	1.261
022	1.062	051	0.874	080	0.999	119	1.261
023	1.011	052	0.874	081	0.992	120	0.985
024	1.011	053	0.874	082	0.993	121	0.989
025	0.992	054	0.874	083	0.993	122	0.976
026	0.989	055	1.011	084	0.992	123	0.976
027	1.011	056	0.874	085	1.053	124	1.061
028	1.064	057	0.874	086	1.013	125	1.062
029	1.064	058	0.874	087	1.013	126	1.062
030	0.946	059	0.874	088	1.130	127	1.062
031	0.946	060	1.080	089	1.130	128	0.968
032	0.946	061	1.080	100	1.300	129	0.967
033	0.946	062	1.076	101	1.222	130	0.970
034	0.946	063	1.083	102	1.222	131	0.973

GEOGRAPHIC MULTIPLIERS

Zip Prefix	Multiplier	Zip Prefix	Multiplier	Zip Prefix	Multiplier	Zip Prefix	Multiplier
132	0.976	175	0.923	219	0.989	262	0.899
133	0.971	176	0.923	220	1.062	263	0.900
134	0.971	177	0.972	221	1.047	264	0.900
135	0.976	178	0.925	222	1.077	265	0.910
136	0.971	179	0.931	223	1.075	266	0.898
137	1.003	180	1.026	224	0.868	267	0.899
138	0.991	181	1.032	225	0.868	268	0.899
139	0.976	182	0.931	226	0.875	270	0.872
140	0.977	183	0.935	227	0.882	271	0.886
141	0.977	184	0.951	228	0.871	272	0.872
142	0.978	185	1.032	229	0.875	273	0.869
143	0.978	186	0.931	230	0.870	274	0.886
144	1.004	187	0.931	231	0.875	275	0.895
145	1.004	188	0.923	232	0.882	276	0.895
146	1.010	189	1.032	233	0.874	277	0.895
147	0.972	190	1.035	234	0.901	278	0.866
148	0.972	191	1.087	235	0.943	279	0.866
149	0.966	192	1.089	236	0.943	280	0.867
150	1.023	193	1.032	237	0.943	281	0.868
151	1.056	194	1.032	238	0.869	282	0.886
152	1.056	195	1.028	239	0.867	283	0.866
153	0.928	196	1.032	240	0.870	284	0.866
154	0.934	197	0.992	241	0.869	285	0.866
155	0.929	198	0.992	242	0.868	286	0.866
156	1.021	199	0.992	243	0.867	287	0.869
157	0.926	200	1.104	244	0.870	288	0.886
158	0.923	201	0.962	245	0.871	289	0.866
159	0.932	202	1.104	246	0.867	290	0.858
160	0.930	203	1.104	247	0.897	291	0.858
161	0.940	204	1.104	248	0.897	292	0.858
162	0.923	205	1.104	249	0.897	293	0.858
163	0.929	206	0.996	250	0.913	294	0.858
164	0.989	207	1.073	251	0.914	295	0.858
165	1.032	208	1.109	252	0.908	296	0.858
166	0.924	209	1.108	253	0.939	297	0.858
167	0.923	210	1.046	254	0.899	298	0.858
168	0.927	211	1.046	255	0.935	299	0.858
169	0.923	212	1.046	256	0.898	300	1.005
170	0.927	214	1.046	257	0.939	301	0.968
171	0.931	215	0.991	258	0.897	302	0.980
172	0.928	216	0.989	259	0.897	303	1.007
173	0.931	217	1.001	260	0.912	304	0.936
174	0.931	218	0.989	261	0.901	305	0.939

GEOGRAPHIC MULTIPLIERS

Zip Prefix	Multiplier	Zip Prefix	Multiplier	Zip Prefix	Multiplier	Zip Prefix	Multiplier
306	0.941	354	0.901	397	0.859	444	1.003
307	0.940	355	0.901	398	0.936	445	1.003
308	0.937	356	0.911	400	0.902	446	0.995
309	0.955	357	0.906	401	0.896	447	1.009
310	0.938	358	0.911	402	0.930	448	0.990
311	1.007	359	0.902	403	0.898	449	0.985
312	0.956	360	0.901	404	0.897	450	1.011
313	0.936	361	0.904	405	0.930	451	1.001
314	0.956	362	0.901	406	0.901	452	1.011
315	0.938	363	0.901	407	0.892	453	1.009
316	0.939	364	0.901	408	0.899	454	1.009
317	0.936	365	0.911	409	0.895	455	1.013
318	0.937	366	0.923	410	0.896	456	0.988
319	0.956	367	0.901	411	0.898	457	0.987
320	0.981	368	0.903	412	0.893	458	0.990
321	0.983	369	0.900	413	0.892	459	1.011
322	0.996	370	0.856	414	0.892	460	0.861
323	0.980	371	0.855	415	0.901	461	0.860
324	0.972	372	0.910	416	0.901	462	0.989
325	0.990	373	0.851	417	0.898	463	0.878
326	0.986	374	0.851	418	0.897	464	0.884
327	0.992	375	0.910	420	0.896	465	0.852
328	0.996	376	0.851	421	0.897	466	0.852
329	1.017	377	0.854	422	0.896	467	0.855
330	1.104	378	0.854	423	0.894	468	0.884
331	1.144	379	0.910	424	0.898	469	0.850
332	1.144	380	0.861	425	0.892	470	0.848
333	1.066	381	0.910	426	0.892	471	0.850
334	1.064	382	0.851	427	0.894	472	0.850
335	0.987	383	0.851	430	0.998	473	0.858
336	0.996	384	0.851	431	1.000	474	0.850
337	0.996	385	0.851	432	1.008	475	0.849
338	0.993	386	0.859	433	0.989	476	0.849
339	1.041	387	0.859	434	1.003	477	0.884
341	1.066	388	0.859	435	1.001	478	0.850
342	0.994	389	0.859	436	1.025	479	0.849
344	0.982	390	0.859	437	0.988	480	1.136
346	0.983	391	0.859	438	0.988	481	1.079
347	0.986	392	0.859	439	0.989	482	1.242
349	1.059	393	0.859	440	1.025	483	1.182
350	0.912	394	0.859	441	1.026	484	1.033
351	0.912	395	0.868	442	1.011	485	1.028
352	0.940	396	0.859	443	1.009	486	1.028

GEOGRAPHIC MULTIPLIERS

Zip Prefix	Multiplier	Zip Prefix	Multiplier	Zip Prefix	Multiplier	Zip Prefix	Multiplier
487	1.028	535	0.937	584	0.869	629	0.946
488	1.028	537	0.962	585	0.869	630	0.981
489	1.028	538	0.923	586	0.869	631	1.006
490	1.028	539	0.925	587	0.869	633	0.951
491	1.028	540	0.937	588	0.869	634	0.925
492	1.028	541	0.941	590	0.894	635	0.925
493	1.028	542	0.940	591	0.894	636	0.925
494	1.028	543	0.941	592	0.894	637	0.924
495	1.028	544	0.932	593	0.894	638	0.925
496	1.028	545	0.932	594	0.894	639	0.925
497	1.028	546	0.930	595	0.894	640	0.958
498	1.028	547	0.939	596	0.894	641	0.976
499	1.028	548	0.929	597	0.894	644	0.933
500	0.850	549	0.936	598	0.894	645	0.931
501	0.844	550	0.872	599	0.894	646	0.930
502	0.849	551	0.962	600	1.070	647	0.931
503	0.939	553	0.872	601	1.051	648	0.925
504	0.848	554	0.961	602	1.133	649	0.976
505	0.840	555	0.872	603	1.104	650	0.936
506	0.847	556	0.872	604	1.075	651	1.009
507	0.848	557	0.872	605	1.021	652	0.951
508	0.842	558	0.872	606	1.133	653	0.931
509	0.939	559	0.872	607	1.133	654	0.925
510	0.839	560	0.872	608	1.133	655	0.925
511	0.839	561	0.872	609	0.954	656	0.929
512	0.839	562	0.872	610	0.959	657	0.930
513	0.839	563	0.872	611	1.003	658	1.009
514	0.841	564	0.872	612	0.972	660	0.947
515	0.842	565	0.872	613	0.959	661	0.976
516	0.842	566	0.872	614	0.973	662	0.976
520	0.849	567	0.872	615	0.993	664	0.941
521	0.849	570	0.856	616	1.006	665	0.941
522	0.846	571	0.856	617	0.979	666	0.941
523	0.848	572	0.856	618	0.951	667	0.941
524	0.849	573	0.856	619	0.958	668	0.941
525	0.839	574	0.856	620	1.029	669	0.941
526	0.856	575	0.856	622	1.041	670	0.941
527	0.854	576	0.856	623	0.946	671	0.941
528	0.856	577	0.856	624	0.950	672	0.941
530	0.959	580	0.869	625	0.977	673	0.941
531	0.973	581	0.869	626	0.980	674	0.941
532	0.987	582	0.869	627	0.980	675	0.941
534	0.988	583	0.869	628	0.952	676	0.941

GEOGRAPHIC MULTIPLIERS

Zip Prefix	Multiplier	Zip Prefix	Multiplier	Zip Prefix	Multiplier	Zip Prefix	Multiplier
677	0.941	730	0.857	776	0.944	822	0.896
678	0.941	731	0.857	777	0.976	823	0.896
679	0.941	733	0.936	778	0.913	824	0.896
680	0.839	734	0.857	779	0.921	825	0.896
681	0.839	735	0.857	780	0.913	826	0.896
683	0.839	736	0.857	781	0.915	827	0.896
684	0.839	737	0.857	782	0.925	828	0.896
685	0.839	738	0.857	783	0.916	829	0.896
686	0.839	739	0.857	784	0.932	830	0.896
687	0.839	740	0.857	785	0.905	831	0.896
688	0.839	741	0.857	786	0.916	832	0.873
689	0.839	743	0.857	787	0.935	833	0.873
690	0.839	744	0.857	788	0.897	834	0.873
691	0.839	745	0.857	789	0.914	835	0.873
692	0.839	746	0.857	790	0.894	836	0.873
693	0.839	747	0.857	791	0.913	837	0.873
700	0.963	748	0.857	792	0.894	838	0.873
701	0.998	749	0.857	793	0.894	840	0.892
703	0.892	750	0.985	794	0.898	841	0.904
704	0.889	751	0.949	795	0.896	842	0.890
705	0.896	752	1.041	796	0.911	843	0.890
706	0.893	753	1.041	797	0.923	844	0.890
707	0.894	754	0.907	798	0.902	845	0.890
708	0.923	755	0.904	799	0.925	846	0.890
710	0.899	756	0.911	800	0.931	847	0.890
711	0.922	757	0.919	801	0.931	850	1.018
712	0.889	758	0.907	802	1.028	852	1.008
713	0.891	759	0.914	803	0.931	853	1.001
714	0.890	760	0.923	804	0.931	855	0.976
716	0.842	761	0.942	805	0.931	856	0.980
717	0.842	762	0.926	806	0.931	857	0.990
718	0.842	763	0.903	807	0.931	859	0.975
719	0.842	764	0.901	808	0.931	860	0.968
720	0.842	765	0.909	809	0.931	863	0.963
721	0.842	766	0.908	810	0.931	864	0.976
722	0.842	767	0.910	811	0.931	865	0.976
723	0.842	768	0.895	812	0.931	870	0.918
724	0.842	769	0.901	813	0.931	871	0.918
725	0.842	770	1.083	814	0.931	872	0.918
726	0.842	772	1.083	815	0.931	873	0.918
727	0.842	773	0.961	816	0.931	874	0.918
728	0.842	774	0.946	820	0.896	875	0.918
729	0.842	775	0.983	821	0.896	877	0.918

GEOGRAPHIC MULTIPLIERS

Zip Prefix	Multiplier	Zip Prefix	Multiplier	Zip Prefix	Multiplier
878	0.918	928	1.097	977	0.955
879	0.918	930	1.063	978	0.955
880	0.918	931	1.036	979	0.955
881	0.918	932	1.020	980	1.006
882	0.918	933	1.036	981	1.011
883	0.918	934	1.037	982	0.965
884	0.918	935	1.057	983	0.964
885	0.925	936	1.015	984	0.964
889	1.045	937	1.015	985	0.964
890	1.028	938	1.015	986	0.964
891	1.045	939	1.053	988	0.957
893	0.972	940	1.118	989	0.964
894	1.002	941	1.118	990	0.958
895	1.012	942	1.048	991	0.952
897	0.999	943	1.118	992	0.959
898	0.969	944	1.118	993	0.959
900	1.095	945	1.095	994	0.960
901	1.075	946	1.101	995	1.188
902	1.093	947	1.101	996	1.188
903	1.093	948	1.101	997	1.188
904	1.095	949	1.064	998	1.188
905	1.095	950	1.087	999	1.188
906	1.095	951	1.118		
907	1.095	952	1.026		
908	1.095	953	1.022		
910	1.095	954	1.032		
911	1.093	955	1.030		
912	1.095	956	1.044		
913	1.091	957	1.048		
914	1.094	958	1.048		
915	1.093	959	1.012		
916	1.093	960	1.007		
917	1.077	961	1.024		
918	1.095	967	1.072		
919	1.049	968	1.072		
920	1.049	969	1.072		
921	1.049	970	0.965		
922	1.045	971	0.960		
923	1.044	972	0.973		
924	1.044	973	0.952		
925	1.044	974	0.954		
926	1.097	975	0.950		
927	1.097	976	0.952		

APPENDIX B   GLOBAL FEE PERIODS

In an effort to create national fee guidelines, Medicare's RBRVS fee schedule uses a "global fee period", expressed in days to include certain pre- and post operative care. Unfortunately, there are no universally accepted guidelines among private insurers for global fee periods and for which services are not included in the global fee. For reference we have included Medicare's global fee periods (GFP). Review your private payer's reimbursement guide or physicians' manual for more specific information. **GFP** - **G**lobal **F**ee **P**eriod, 10 & 90 are in days, **YYY** - Individual Consideration to be set by carrier(for example unlisted surgery codes), **ZZZ** - Included in another Service and falls within the global period for the other service, **MMM** - Maternity service furnished in uncomplicated maternity cases including antepartum care, delivery, and postpartum care where the usual global surgical concept does not apply. See the 2007 CPT code book for specific definitions.

Code	GFP	Code	GFP	Code	GFP	Code	GFP	Code	GFP	Code	GFP	Code	GFP	Code	GFP
10040	10	11626	10	12057	10	15221	ZZZ	15789	90	17261	10	19350	90	20912	90
10060	10	11640	10	13100	10	15240	90	15792	90	17262	10	19355	90	20920	90
10061	10	11641	10	13101	10	15241	ZZZ	15793	90	17263	10	19357	90	20922	90
10080	10	11642	10	13102	ZZZ	15260	90	15819	90	17264	10	19361	90	20924	90
10081	10	11643	10	13120	10	15261	ZZZ	15820	90	17266	10	19364	90	20926	90
10120	10	11644	10	13121	10	15300	90	15821	90	17270	10	19366	90	20931	ZZZ
10121	10	11646	10	13122	ZZZ	15301	ZZZ	15822	90	17271	10	19367	90	20937	ZZZ
10140	10	11732	ZZZ	13131	10	15320	90	15823	90	17272	10	19368	90	20938	ZZZ
10160	10	11750	10	13132	10	15321	ZZZ	15830	90	17273	10	19369	90	20955	90
10180	10	11752	10	13133	ZZZ	15330	90	15832	90	17274	10	19370	90	20956	90
11001	ZZZ	11760	10	13150	10	15331	ZZZ	15833	90	17276	10	19371	90	20957	90
11008	ZZZ	11762	10	13151	10	15335	90	15834	90	17280	10	19380	90	20962	90
11010	10	11765	10	13152	10	15336	ZZZ	15835	90	17281	10	19499	YYY	20969	90
11043	10	11770	10	13153	ZZZ	15340	10	15836	90	17282	10	20000	10	20970	90
11044	10	11771	90	13160	90	15341	ZZZ	15837	90	17283	10	20005	10	20972	90
11101	ZZZ	11772	90	14000	90	15360	90	15838	90	17284	10	20100	10	20973	90
11200	10	11922	ZZZ	14001	90	15361	ZZZ	15839	90	17286	10	20101	10	20999	YYY
11201	ZZZ	11960	90	14020	90	15365	90	15840	90	17312	ZZZ	20102	10	21010	90
11400	10	11970	90	14021	90	15366	ZZZ	15841	90	17314	ZZZ	20103	10	21015	90
11401	10	11971	90	14040	90	15400	90	15842	90	17315	ZZZ	20150	90	21025	90
11402	10	12001	10	14041	90	15401	ZZZ	15845	90	17340	10	20240	10	21026	90
11403	10	12002	10	14060	90	15420	90	15847	YYY	17360	10	20245	10	21029	90
11404	10	12004	10	14061	90	15421	ZZZ	15920	90	17999	YYY	20250	10	21030	90
11406	10	12005	10	14300	90	15430	90	15922	90	19001	ZZZ	20251	10	21031	90
11420	10	12006	10	14350	90	15431	ZZZ	15931	90	19020	90	20500	10	21032	90
11421	10	12007	10	15003	ZZZ	15570	90	15933	90	19101	10	20500	10	21034	90
11422	10	12011	10	15005	ZZZ	15572	90	15934	90	19110	90	20520	10	21040	90
11423	10	12013	10	15050	90	15574	90	15935	90	19112	90	20525	10	21044	90
11424	10	12014	10	15100	90	15576	90	15936	90	19120	90	20615	10	21045	90
11426	10	12015	10	15101	ZZZ	15600	90	15937	90	19125	90	20650	10	21046	90
11440	10	12016	10	15110	90	15610	90	15940	90	19126	ZZZ	20661	90	21047	90
11441	10	12017	10	15111	ZZZ	15620	90	15941	90	19260	90	20662	90	21048	90
11442	10	12018	10	15115	90	15630	90	15944	90	19271	90	20663	90	21049	90
11443	10	12020	10	15116	ZZZ	15650	90	15945	90	19272	90	20664	90	21050	90
11444	10	12021	10	15120	90	15731	90	15946	90	19291	ZZZ	20665	10	21060	90
11446	10	12031	10	15121	ZZZ	15732	90	15950	90	19295	ZZZ	20670	10	21070	90
11450	90	12032	10	15130	90	15734	90	15951	90	19297	ZZZ	20670	10	21076	10
11451	90	12034	10	15131	ZZZ	15736	90	15952	90	19300	90	20680	90	21077	90
11462	90	12035	10	15135	90	15738	90	15953	90	19301	90	20690	90	21079	90
11463	90	12036	10	15136	ZZZ	15740	90	15956	90	19302	90	20692	90	21080	90
11470	90	12037	10	15150	90	15750	90	15958	90	19303	90	20693	90	21081	90
11471	90	12041	10	15151	ZZZ	15756	90	15999	YYY	19304	90	20694	90	21082	90
11600	10	12042	10	15152	ZZZ	15757	90	16035	90	19305	90	20802	90	21083	90
11601	10	12044	10	15155	90	15758	90	16036	ZZZ	19306	90	20805	90	21084	90
11602	10	12045	10	15156	ZZZ	15760	90	17000	10	19307	90	20808	90	21085	10
11603	10	12046	10	15157	ZZZ	15770	90	17003	ZZZ	19316	90	20816	90	21086	90
11604	10	12047	10	15170	90	15780	90	17004	10	19318	90	20822	90	21087	90
11606	10	12051	10	15171	ZZZ	15781	90	17106	90	19324	90	20824	90	21088	90
11620	10	12052	10	15175	90	15782	90	17107	90	19325	90	20827	90	21089	90
11621	10	12053	10	15176	ZZZ	15783	90	17108	90	19328	90	20838	90	21100	90
11622	10	12054	10	15200	90	15786	10	17110	10	19330	90	20900	90	21100	90
11623	10	12055	10	15201	ZZZ	15787	ZZZ	17111	10	19340	ZZZ	20902	90	21110	90
11624	10	12056	10	15220	90	15788	90	17260	10	19342	90	20910	90	21120	90

APPENDIX B　　GLOBAL FEE PERIODS

Code	GFP	Code	GFP	Code	GFP	Code	GFP	Code	GFP	Code	GFP	Code	GFP	Code	GFP
21121	90	21299	YYY	21615	90	22534	ZZZ	23150	90	23660	90	24351	90	25025	90
21122	90	21315	10	21616	90	22548	90	23155	90	23665	90	24352	90	25028	90
21123	90	21320	10	21620	90	22554	90	23156	90	23670	90	24354	90	25031	90
21125	90	21325	90	21627	90	22556	90	23170	90	23675	90	24356	90	25035	90
21125	90	21330	90	21630	90	22558	90	23172	90	23680	90	24360	90	25040	90
21127	90	21335	90	21632	90	22585	ZZZ	23174	90	23700	10	24361	90	25065	10
21137	90	21336	90	21685	90	22590	90	23180	90	23800	90	24362	90	25066	90
21138	90	21337	90	21700	90	22595	90	23182	90	23802	90	24363	90	25075	90
21139	90	21338	90	21705	90	22600	90	23184	90	23900	90	24365	90	25076	90
21141	90	21339	90	21720	90	22610	90	23190	90	23920	90	24366	90	25077	90
21142	90	21340	90	21725	90	22612	90	23195	90	23921	90	24400	90	25085	90
21143	90	21343	90	21740	90	22614	ZZZ	23200	90	23929	YYY	24410	90	25100	90
21145	90	21344	90	21742	90	22630	90	23210	90	23930	10	24420	90	25101	90
21146	90	21345	90	21743	90	22632	ZZZ	23220	90	23931	10	24430	90	25105	90
21147	90	21346	90	21750	90	22800	90	23221	90	23935	90	24435	90	25107	90
21150	90	21347	90	21800	90	22802	90	23222	90	24000	90	24470	90	25109	90
21151	90	21348	90	21805	90	22804	90	23330	10	24006	90	24495	90	25110	90
21154	90	21355	10	21810	90	22808	90	23331	90	24065	10	24498	90	25111	90
21155	90	21356	10	21820	90	22810	90	23332	90	24066	90	24500	90	25112	90
21159	90	21360	90	21825	90	22812	90	23395	90	24075	90	24505	90	25115	90
21160	90	21365	90	21899	YYY	22818	90	23397	90	24076	90	24515	90	25116	90
21172	90	21366	90	21920	10	22819	90	23400	90	24077	90	24516	90	25118	90
21175	90	21385	90	21925	90	22830	90	23405	90	24100	90	24530	90	25119	90
21179	90	21386	90	21930	90	22840	ZZZ	23406	90	24101	90	24535	90	25120	90
21180	90	21387	90	21935	90	22842	ZZZ	23410	90	24102	90	24538	90	25125	90
21181	90	21390	90	22010	90	22843	ZZZ	23412	90	24105	90	24545	90	25126	90
21182	90	21395	90	22015	90	22844	ZZZ	23415	90	24110	90	24546	90	25130	90
21183	90	21400	90	22100	90	22845	ZZZ	23420	90	24115	90	24560	90	25135	90
21184	90	21401	90	22101	90	22846	ZZZ	23430	90	24116	90	24565	90	25136	90
21188	90	21406	90	22102	90	22847	ZZZ	23440	90	24120	90	24566	90	25145	90
21193	90	21407	90	22103	ZZZ	22848	ZZZ	23450	90	24125	90	24575	90	25150	90
21194	90	21408	90	22110	90	22849	90	23455	90	24126	90	24576	90	25151	90
21195	90	21421	90	22112	90	22850	90	23460	90	24130	90	24577	90	25170	90
21196	90	21422	90	22114	90	22851	ZZZ	23462	90	24134	90	24579	90	25210	90
21198	90	21423	90	22116	ZZZ	22852	90	23465	90	24136	90	24582	90	25215	90
21199	90	21431	90	22210	90	22855	90	23466	90	24138	90	24586	90	25230	90
21206	90	21432	90	22212	90	22857	90	23470	90	24140	90	24587	90	25240	90
21208	90	21433	90	22214	90	22862	90	23472	90	24145	90	24600	90	25248	90
21209	90	21435	90	22216	ZZZ	22865	90	23480	90	24147	90	24605	90	25250	90
21210	90	21436	90	22220	90	22899	YYY	23485	90	24149	90	24615	90	25251	90
21215	90	21440	90	22222	90	22900	90	23490	90	24150	90	24620	90	25259	90
21230	90	21445	90	22224	90	22999	YYY	23491	90	24151	90	24635	90	25260	90
21235	90	21450	90	22226	ZZZ	23000	90	23500	90	24152	90	24640	10	25263	90
21240	90	21451	90	22305	90	23020	90	23505	90	24153	90	24650	90	25265	90
21242	90	21452	90	22310	90	23030	10	23515	90	24155	90	24655	90	25270	90
21243	90	21453	90	22315	90	23031	10	23520	90	24160	90	24665	90	25272	90
21244	90	21454	90	22318	90	23035	90	23525	90	24164	90	24666	90	25274	90
21245	90	21461	90	22319	90	23040	90	23530	90	24200	10	24670	90	25275	90
21246	90	21462	90	22325	90	23044	90	23532	90	24201	90	24675	90	25280	90
21247	90	21465	90	22326	90	23065	10	23540	90	24300	90	24685	90	25290	90
21248	90	21470	90	22327	90	23066	90	23545	90	24301	90	24800	90	25295	90
21249	90	21485	90	22328	ZZZ	23075	10	23550	90	24305	90	24802	90	25300	90
21255	90	21490	90	22505	10	23076	90	23552	90	24310	90	24900	90	25301	90
21256	90	21495	90	22520	10	23077	90	23570	90	24320	90	24920	90	25310	90
21260	90	21497	90	22520	10	23100	90	23575	90	24330	90	24925	90	25312	90
21261	90	21499	YYY	22521	10	23101	90	23585	90	24331	90	24930	90	25315	90
21263	90	21501	90	22521	10	23105	90	23600	90	24332	90	24931	90	25316	90
21267	90	21502	90	22522	ZZZ	23106	90	23605	90	24340	90	24935	90	25320	90
21268	90	21510	90	22523	10	23107	90	23615	90	24341	90	24940	90	25332	90
21270	90	21550	10	22524	10	23120	90	23616	90	24342	90	24999	YYY	25335	90
21275	90	21555	10	22525	ZZZ	23125	90	23620	90	24343	90	25000	90	25337	90
21280	90	21556	90	22526	10	23130	90	23625	90	24344	90	25001	90	25350	90
21282	90	21557	90	22527	ZZZ	23140	90	23630	90	24345	90	25020	90	25355	90
21295	90	21600	90	22532	90	23145	90	23650	90	24346	90	25023	90	25360	90
21296	90	21610	90	22533	90	23146	90	23655	90	24350	90	25024	90	25365	90

APPENDIX B   GLOBAL FEE PERIODS

Code	GFP	Code	GFP	Code	GFP	Code	GFP	Code	GFP	Code	GFP	Code	GFP	Code	GFP
25370	90	25695	90	26340	90	26548	90	26952	90	27177	90	27335	90	27487	90
25375	90	25800	90	26350	90	26550	90	26989	YYY	27178	90	27340	90	27488	90
25390	90	25805	90	26352	90	26551	90	26990	90	27179	90	27345	90	27495	90
25391	90	25810	90	26356	90	26553	90	26991	90	27181	90	27347	90	27496	90
25392	90	25820	90	26357	90	26554	90	26992	90	27185	90	27350	90	27497	90
25393	90	25825	90	26358	90	26555	90	27000	90	27187	90	27355	90	27498	90
25394	90	25830	90	26370	90	26556	90	27001	90	27193	90	27356	90	27499	90
25400	90	25900	90	26372	90	26560	90	27003	90	27194	90	27357	90	27500	90
25405	90	25905	90	26373	90	26561	90	27005	90	27200	90	27358	ZZZ	27501	90
25415	90	25907	90	26390	90	26562	90	27006	90	27202	90	27360	90	27502	90
25420	90	25909	90	26392	90	26565	90	27025	90	27215	90	27365	90	27503	90
25425	90	25915	90	26410	90	26567	90	27030	90	27216	90	27372	90	27506	90
25426	90	25920	90	26412	90	26568	90	27033	90	27217	90	27380	90	27507	90
25430	90	25922	90	26415	90	26580	90	27035	90	27218	90	27381	90	27508	90
25431	90	25924	90	26416	90	26587	90	27036	90	27220	90	27385	90	27509	90
25440	90	25927	90	26418	90	26590	90	27040	10	27222	90	27386	90	27510	90
25441	90	25929	90	26420	90	26591	90	27041	90	27226	90	27390	90	27511	90
25442	90	25931	90	26426	90	26593	90	27047	90	27227	90	27391	90	27513	90
25443	90	25999	YYY	26428	90	26596	90	27048	90	27228	90	27392	90	27514	90
25444	90	26010	10	26432	90	26600	90	27049	90	27230	90	27393	90	27516	90
25445	90	26010	10	26433	90	26605	90	27050	90	27232	90	27394	90	27517	90
25446	90	26011	10	26434	90	26607	90	27052	90	27235	90	27395	90	27519	90
25447	90	26020	90	26437	90	26608	90	27054	90	27236	90	27396	90	27520	90
25449	90	26025	90	26440	90	26615	90	27060	90	27238	90	27397	90	27524	90
25450	90	26030	90	26442	90	26641	90	27062	90	27240	90	27400	90	27530	90
25455	90	26034	90	26445	90	26645	90	27065	90	27244	90	27403	90	27532	90
25490	90	26035	90	26449	90	26650	90	27066	90	27245	90	27405	90	27535	90
25491	90	26037	90	26450	90	26665	90	27067	90	27246	90	27407	90	27536	90
25492	90	26040	90	26455	90	26670	90	27070	90	27248	90	27409	90	27538	90
25500	90	26045	90	26460	90	26675	90	27071	90	27250	90	27412	90	27540	90
25505	90	26055	90	26471	90	26676	90	27075	90	27252	90	27415	90	27550	90
25515	90	26060	90	26474	90	26685	90	27076	90	27253	90	27418	90	27552	90
25520	90	26070	90	26476	90	26686	90	27077	90	27254	90	27420	90	27556	90
25525	90	26075	90	26477	90	26700	90	27078	90	27256	10	27422	90	27557	90
25526	90	26080	90	26478	90	26705	90	27079	90	27257	10	27424	90	27558	90
25530	90	26100	90	26479	90	26706	90	27080	90	27258	90	27425	90	27560	90
25535	90	26105	90	26480	90	26715	90	27086	10	27259	90	27427	90	27562	90
25545	90	26110	90	26483	90	26720	90	27087	90	27265	90	27428	90	27566	90
25560	90	26115	90	26485	90	26725	90	27090	90	27266	90	27429	90	27570	10
25565	90	26116	90	26489	90	26727	90	27091	90	27275	10	27430	90	27580	90
25574	90	26117	90	26490	90	26735	90	27097	90	27280	90	27435	90	27590	90
25575	90	26121	90	26492	90	26740	90	27098	90	27282	90	27437	90	27591	90
25600	90	26123	90	26494	90	26742	90	27100	90	27284	90	27438	90	27592	90
25605	90	26125	ZZZ	26496	90	26746	90	27105	90	27286	90	27440	90	27594	90
25606	90	26130	90	26497	90	26750	90	27110	90	27290	90	27441	90	27596	90
25607	90	26135	90	26498	90	26755	90	27111	90	27295	90	27442	90	27598	90
25608	90	26140	90	26499	90	26756	90	27120	90	27299	YYY	27443	90	27599	YYY
25609	90	26145	90	26500	90	26765	90	27122	90	27301	90	27445	90	27600	90
25622	90	26160	90	26502	90	26770	90	27125	90	27303	90	27446	90	27601	90
25624	90	26170	90	26508	90	26775	90	27130	90	27305	90	27447	90	27602	90
25628	90	26180	90	26510	90	26776	90	27132	90	27306	90	27448	90	27603	90
25630	90	26185	90	26516	90	26785	90	27134	90	27307	90	27450	90	27604	90
25635	90	26200	90	26517	90	26820	90	27137	90	27310	90	27454	90	27605	10
25645	90	26205	90	26518	90	26841	90	27138	90	27323	10	27455	90	27606	10
25650	90	26210	90	26520	90	26842	90	27140	90	27324	90	27457	90	27607	90
25651	90	26215	90	26525	90	26843	90	27146	90	27325	90	27465	90	27610	90
25652	90	26230	90	26530	90	26844	90	27147	90	27326	90	27466	90	27612	90
25660	90	26235	90	26531	90	26850	90	27151	90	27327	90	27468	90	27613	10
25670	90	26236	90	26535	90	26852	90	27156	90	27328	90	27470	90	27614	90
25671	90	26250	90	26536	90	26860	90	27158	90	27329	90	27472	90	27615	90
25675	90	26255	90	26540	90	26861	ZZZ	27161	90	27330	90	27475	90	27618	90
25676	90	26260	90	26541	90	26862	90	27165	90	27331	90	27477	90	27619	90
25680	90	26261	90	26542	90	26863	ZZZ	27170	90	27332	90	27479	90	27620	90
25685	90	26262	90	26545	90	26910	90	27175	90	27333	90	27485	90	27625	90
25690	90	26320	90	26546	90	26951	90	27176	90	27334	90	27486	90	27626	90

APPENDIX B   GLOBAL FEE PERIODS

Code	GFP	Code	GFP	Code	GFP	Code	GFP	Code	GFP	Code	GFP	Code	GFP	Code	GFP
27630	90	27810	90	28107	90	28309	90	28750	90	29888	90	31070	90	31830	90
27635	90	27814	90	28108	90	28310	90	28755	90	29889	90	31075	90	31899	YYY
27637	90	27816	90	28110	90	28312	90	28760	90	29891	90	31080	90	32035	90
27638	90	27818	90	28111	90	28313	90	28800	90	29892	90	31081	90	32036	90
27640	90	27822	90	28112	90	28315	90	28805	90	29893	90	31084	90	32095	90
27641	90	27823	90	28113	90	28320	90	28810	90	29894	90	31085	90	32100	90
27645	90	27824	90	28114	90	28322	90	28820	90	29895	90	31086	90	32110	90
27646	90	27825	90	28116	90	28340	90	28825	90	29897	90	31087	90	32120	90
27647	90	27826	90	28118	90	28341	90	28890	90	29898	90	31090	90	32124	90
27650	90	27827	90	28119	90	28344	90	28899	YYY	29899	90	31200	90	32140	90
27652	90	27828	90	28120	90	28345	90	29799	YYY	29900	90	31201	90	32141	90
27654	90	27829	90	28122	90	28360	90	29800	90	29901	90	31205	90	32150	90
27656	90	27830	90	28124	90	28400	90	29804	90	29902	90	31225	90	32151	90
27658	90	27831	90	28126	90	28405	90	29805	90	29999	YYY	31230	90	32160	90
27659	90	27832	90	28130	90	28406	90	29806	90	30000	10	31239	10	32200	90
27664	90	27840	90	28140	90	28415	90	29807	90	30020	10	31290	10	32215	90
27665	90	27842	90	28150	90	28420	90	29819	90	30110	10	31291	10	32220	90
27675	90	27846	90	28153	90	28430	90	29820	90	30115	90	31292	10	32225	90
27676	90	27848	90	28160	90	28435	90	29821	90	30117	90	31293	10	32310	90
27680	90	27860	10	28171	90	28436	90	29822	90	30118	90	31294	10	32320	90
27681	90	27870	90	28173	90	28445	90	29823	90	30120	90	31299	YYY	32402	90
27685	90	27871	90	28175	90	28450	90	29824	90	30124	90	31300	90	32440	90
27686	90	27880	90	28190	10	28455	90	29825	90	30125	90	31320	90	32442	90
27687	90	27881	90	28192	90	28456	90	29826	90	30130	90	31360	90	32445	90
27690	90	27882	90	28193	90	28465	90	29827	90	30140	90	31365	90	32480	90
27691	90	27884	90	28200	90	28470	90	29830	90	30150	90	31367	90	32482	90
27692	ZZZ	27886	90	28202	90	28475	90	29834	90	30160	90	31368	90	32484	90
27695	90	27888	90	28208	90	28476	90	29835	90	30210	10	31370	90	32486	90
27696	90	27889	90	28210	90	28485	90	29836	90	30220	10	31375	90	32488	90
27698	90	27892	90	28220	90	28490	90	29837	90	30300	10	31380	90	32491	90
27700	90	27893	90	28222	90	28495	90	29838	90	30300	10	31382	90	32500	90
27702	90	27894	90	28225	90	28496	90	29840	90	30310	10	31390	90	32501	ZZZ
27703	90	27899	YYY	28226	90	28505	90	29843	90	30320	90	31395	90	32503	90
27704	90	28001	10	28230	90	28510	90	29844	90	30400	90	31400	90	32504	90
27705	90	28002	10	28232	90	28515	90	29845	90	30410	90	31420	90	32540	90
27707	90	28003	90	28234	90	28525	90	29846	90	30420	90	31580	90	32650	90
27709	90	28005	90	28238	90	28530	90	29847	90	30430	90	31582	90	32651	90
27712	90	28008	90	28240	90	28531	90	29848	90	30435	90	31584	90	32652	90
27715	90	28010	90	28250	90	28540	90	29850	90	30450	90	31587	90	32653	90
27720	90	28011	90	28260	90	28545	90	29851	90	30460	90	31588	90	32654	90
27722	90	28020	90	28261	90	28546	90	29855	90	30462	90	31590	90	32655	90
27724	90	28022	90	28262	90	28555	90	29856	90	30465	90	31595	90	32656	90
27725	90	28024	90	28264	90	28570	90	29860	90	30520	90	31599	YYY	32657	90
27727	90	28035	90	28270	90	28575	90	29861	90	30540	90	31610	90	32658	90
27730	90	28043	90	28272	90	28576	90	29862	90	30545	90	31611	90	32659	90
27732	90	28045	90	28280	90	28585	90	29863	90	30560	10	31613	90	32660	90
27734	90	28046	90	28285	90	28600	90	29866	90	30560	10	31614	90	32661	90
27740	90	28050	90	28286	90	28605	90	29867	90	30580	90	31620	ZZZ	32662	90
27742	90	28052	90	28288	90	28606	90	29868	90	30600	90	31632	ZZZ	32663	90
27745	90	28054	90	28289	90	28615	90	29870	90	30620	90	31633	ZZZ	32664	90
27750	90	28055	90	28290	90	28630	10	29871	90	30630	90	31637	ZZZ	32665	90
27752	90	28060	90	28292	90	28635	10	29873	90	30801	10	31750	90	32800	90
27756	90	28062	90	28293	90	28636	10	29874	90	30802	10	31755	90	32810	90
27758	90	28070	90	28294	90	28645	90	29875	90	30915	90	31760	90	32815	90
27759	90	28072	90	28296	90	28660	10	29876	90	30920	90	31766	90	32820	90
27760	90	28080	90	28297	90	28665	10	29877	90	30930	10	31770	90	32851	90
27762	90	28086	90	28298	90	28666	10	29879	90	30999	YYY	31775	90	32852	90
27766	90	28088	90	28299	90	28675	90	29880	90	31000	10	31780	90	32853	90
27780	90	28090	90	28300	90	28705	90	29881	90	31002	10	31781	90	32854	90
27781	90	28092	90	28302	90	28715	90	29882	90	31020	90	31785	90	32900	90
27784	90	28100	90	28304	90	28725	90	29883	90	31030	90	31786	90	32905	90
27786	90	28102	90	28305	90	28730	90	29884	90	31032	90	31800	90	32906	90
27788	90	28103	90	28306	90	28735	90	29885	90	31040	90	31805	90	32940	90
27792	90	28104	90	28307	90	28737	90	29886	90	31050	90	31820	90	32999	YYY
27808	90	28106	90	28308	90	28740	90	29887	90	31051	90	31825	90	33015	90

APPENDIX B   GLOBAL FEE PERIODS

Code	GFP	Code	GFP	Code	GFP	Code	GFP	Code	GFP	Code	GFP	Code	GFP	Code	GFP
33020	90	33413	90	33645	90	33881	90	35103	90	35521	90	35800	90	37186	ZZZ
33025	90	33414	90	33647	90	33883	90	35111	90	35522	90	35820	90	37206	ZZZ
33030	90	33415	90	33660	90	33884	ZZZ	35112	90	35525	90	35840	90	37208	ZZZ
33031	90	33416	90	33665	90	33886	90	35121	90	35526	90	35860	90	37215	90
33050	90	33417	90	33670	90	33910	90	35122	90	35531	90	35870	90	37216	90
33120	90	33420	90	33675	90	33915	90	35131	90	35533	90	35875	90	37250	ZZZ
33130	90	33422	90	33676	90	33916	90	35132	90	35536	90	35876	90	37251	ZZZ
33140	90	33425	90	33677	90	33917	90	35141	90	35537	90	35879	90	37500	90
33141	ZZZ	33426	90	33681	90	33920	90	35142	90	35538	90	35881	90	37501	YYY
33202	90	33427	90	33684	90	33922	90	35151	90	35539	90	35883	90	37565	90
33203	90	33430	90	33688	90	33924	ZZZ	35152	90	35540	90	35884	90	37600	90
33206	90	33460	90	33690	90	33925	90	35180	90	35548	90	35901	90	37605	90
33207	90	33463	90	33692	90	33926	90	35182	90	35549	90	35903	90	37606	90
33208	90	33464	90	33694	90	33935	90	35184	90	35551	90	35905	90	37607	90
33212	90	33465	90	33697	90	33945	90	35188	90	35556	90	35907	90	37609	10
33213	90	33468	90	33702	90	33961	ZZZ	35189	90	35558	90	36218	ZZZ	37615	90
33214	90	33470	90	33710	90	33971	90	35190	90	35560	90	36248	ZZZ	37616	90
33215	90	33471	90	33720	90	33974	90	35201	90	35563		36260	90	37617	90
33216	90	33472	90	33722	90	33977	90	35206	90	35565	90	36261	90	37618	90
33217	90	33474	90	33724	90	33978	90	35207	90	35566	90	36262	90	37620	90
33218	90	33475	90	33726	90	33980	90	35211	90	35571		36299	YYY	37650	90
33220	90	33476	90	33730	90	33999	YYY	35216	90	35572	ZZZ	36470	10	37660	90
33222	90	33478	90	33732	90	34001	90	35221	90	35583	90	36471	10	37700	90
33223	90	33496	90	33735	90	34051	90	35226	90	35585	90	36476	ZZZ	37718	90
33225	ZZZ	33500	90	33736	90	34101	90	35231	90	35587	90	36479	ZZZ	37722	90
33233	90	33501	90	33737	90	34111	90	35236	90	35600	ZZZ	36557	10	37735	90
33234	90	33502	90	33750	90	34151	90	35241	90	35601	90	36557	10	37760	90
33235	90	33503	90	33755	90	34201	90	35246	90	35606	90	36558	10	37765	90
33236	90	33504	90	33762	90	34203	90	35251	90	35612	90	36558	10	37766	90
33237	90	33505	90	33764	90	34401	90	35256	90	35616	90	36560	10	37780	90
33238	90	33506	90	33766	90	34421	90	35261	90	35621	90	36561	10	37785	90
33240	90	33507	90	33767	90	34451	90	35266	90	35623	90	36563	10	37788	90
33241	90	33508	ZZZ	33768	ZZZ	34471	90	35271	90	35626	90	36565	10	37790	90
33243	90	33510	90	33770	90	34490	90	35276	90	35631	90	36566	10	37799	YYY
33244	90	33511	90	33771	90	34501	90	35281	90	35636	90	36570	10	38100	90
33249	90	33512	90	33774	90	34502	90	35286	90	35637	90	36571	10	38101	90
33250	90	33513	90	33775	90	34510	90	35301	90	35638	90	36576	10	38102	ZZZ
33251	90	33514	90	33776	90	34520	90	35302	90	35642	90	36578	10	38115	90
33254	90	33516	90	33777	90	34530	90	35303	90	35645	90	36581	10	38120	90
33255	90	33517	ZZZ	33778	90	34800	90	35304	90	35646	90	36582	10	38129	YYY
33256	90	33518	ZZZ	33779	90	34802	90	35305	90	35647	90	36583	10	38230	10
33261	90	33519	ZZZ	33780	90	34803	90	35306	ZZZ	35650	90	36585	10	38300	10
33265	90	33521	ZZZ	33781	90	34804	90	35311	90	35651	90	36589	10	38305	90
33266	90	33522	ZZZ	33786	90	34805	90	35321	90	35654	90	36590	10	38308	90
33282	90	33523	ZZZ	33788	90	34808	ZZZ	35331	90	35656	90	36818	90	38380	90
33284	90	33530	ZZZ	33800	90	34813	ZZZ	35341	90	35661	90	36819	90	38381	90
33300	90	33533	90	33802	90	34825	90	35351	90	35663	90	36820	90	38382	90
33305	90	33534	90	33803	90	34826	ZZZ	35355	90	35665	90	36821	90	38500	10
33310	90	33535	90	33813	90	34830	90	35361	90	35666	90	36822	90	38510	10
33315	90	33536	90	33814	90	34831	90	35363	90	35671	90	36823	90	38520	90
33320	90	33542	90	33820	90	34832	90	35371	90	35681	ZZZ	36825	ZZZ	38525	90
33321	90	33545	90	33822	90	34900	90	35372	90	35682	ZZZ	36830	ZZZ	38530	90
33322	90	33548	90	33824	90	35001	90	35390	ZZZ	35683	ZZZ	36831	90	38542	90
33330	90	33572	ZZZ	33840	90	35002	90	35400	ZZZ	35685	ZZZ	36832	90	38550	90
33332	90	33600	90	33845	90	35005	90	35500	ZZZ	35686	ZZZ	36833	90	38555	90
33335	90	33602	90	33851	90	35011	90	35501	90	35691	90	36834	90	38562	90
33400	90	33606	90	33852	90	35013	90	35506	90	35693	90	36835	90	38564	90
33401	90	33608	90	33853	90	35021	90	35508	90	35694	90	36838	90	38570	10
33403	90	33610	90	33860	90	35022	90	35509	90	35695	90	36870	90	38571	10
33404	90	33611	90	33861	90	35045	90	35510	90	35697	ZZZ	37140	90	38572	10
33405	90	33612	90	33863	90	35081	90	35511	90	35700	ZZZ	37145	90	38589	YYY
33406	90	33615	90	33870	90	35082	90	35512	90	35701	90	37160	90	38700	90
33410	90	33617	90	33875	90	35091	90	35515	90	35721	90	37180	90	38720	90
33411	90	33619	90	33877	90	35092	90	35516	90	35741	90	37181	90	38724	90
33412	90	33641	90	33880	90	35102	90	35518	90	35761	90	37185	ZZZ	38740	90

APPENDIX B   GLOBAL FEE PERIODS

Code	GFP	Code	GFP	Code	GFP	Code	GFP	Code	GFP	Code	GFP	Code	GFP	Code	GFP
38745	90	41006	90	42235	90	42970	90	43633	90	44143	90	45000	90	46261	90
38746	ZZZ	41007	90	42260	90	42971	90	43634	90	44144	90	45005	10	46262	90
38747	ZZZ	41008	90	42280	10	42972	90	43635	ZZZ	44145	90	45020	90	46270	90
38760	90	41009	90	42281	10	42999	YYY	43640	90	44146	90	45100	90	46275	90
38765	90	41010	10	42299	YYY	43020	90	43641	90	44147	90	45108	90	46280	90
38770	90	41015	90	42300	10	43030	90	43644	90	44150	90	45110	90	46285	90
38780	90	41016	90	42305	90	43045	90	43645	90	44151	90	45111	90	46288	90
38794	90	41017	90	42310	10	43100	90	43647	YYY	44155	90	45112	90	46320	10
38999	YYY	41018	90	42320	10	43101	90	43648	YYY	44156	90	45113	90	46500	10
39000	90	41100	10	42330	10	43107	90	43651	90	44157	90	45114	90	46505	10
39010	90	41105	10	42335	90	43108	90	43652	90	44158	90	45116	90	46700	90
39200	90	41108	10	42340	90	43112	90	43653	90	44160	90	45119	90	46705	90
39220	90	41110	10	42405	10	43113	90	43659	YYY	44180	90	45120	90	46706	10
39400	10	41112	90	42408	90	43116	90	43750	10	44186	90	45121	90	46710	90
39499	YYY	41113	90	42409	90	43117	90	43770	90	44187	90	45123	90	46712	90
39501	90	41114	90	42410	90	43118	90	43771	90	44188	90	45126	90	46715	90
39502	90	41115	10	42415	90	43121	90	43772	90	44202	90	45130	90	46716	90
39503	90	41116	90	42420	90	43122	90	43773	90	44203	ZZZ	45135	90	46730	90
39503	90	41120	90	42425	90	43123	90	43774	90	44204	90	45136	90	46735	90
39520	90	41130	90	42426	90	43124	90	43800	90	44205	90	45150	90	46740	90
39530	90	41135	90	42440	90	43130	90	43810	90	44206	90	45160	90	46742	90
39531	90	41140	90	42450	90	43135	90	43820	90	44207	90	45170	90	46744	90
39540	90	41145	90	42500	90	43280	90	43825	90	44208	90	45190	90	46746	90
39541	90	41150	90	42505	90	43289	YYY	43830	90	44210	90	45395	90	46748	90
39545	90	41153	90	42507	90	43300	90	43831	90	44211	90	45397	90	46750	90
39560	90	41155	90	42508	90	43305	90	43832	90	44212	90	45400	90	46751	90
39561	90	41250	10	42509	90	43310	90	43840	90	44213	ZZZ	45402	90	46753	90
39599	YYY	41251	10	42510	90	43312	90	43842	90	44227	90	45499	YYY	46754	10
40500	90	41252	10	42600	90	43313	90	43843	90	44238	YYY	45500	90	46760	90
40510	90	41500	90	42665	90	43314	90	43845	90	44300	90	45505	90	46761	90
40520	90	41510	90	42699	YYY	43320	90	43846	90	44310	90	45540	90	46762	90
40525	90	41520	90	42700	10	43324	90	43847	90	44312	90	45541	90	46900	10
40527	90	41599	YYY	42720	10	43325	90	43848	90	44314	90	45550	90	46910	10
40530	90	41800	10	42725	90	43326	90	43850	90	44316	90	45560	90	46916	10
40650	90	41805	10	42800	10	43330	90	43855	90	44320	90	45562	90	46917	10
40652	90	41806	10	42802	10	43331	90	43860	90	44322	90	45563	90	46922	10
40654	90	41822	10	42804	10	43340	90	43865	90	44340	90	45800	90	46924	10
40700	90	41823	90	42806	10	43341	90	43870	90	44345	90	45805	90	46934	90
40701	90	41825	10	42808	10	43350	90	43880	90	44346	90	45820	90	46935	10
40702	90	41826	10	42809	10	43351	90	43881	YYY	44602	90	45825	90	46936	90
40720	90	41827	90	42810	90	43352	90	43882	YYY	44603	90	45900	10	46937	10
40761	90	41828	10	42815	90	43360	90	43886	90	44604	90	45905	10	46938	90
40799	YYY	41830	10	42820	90	43361	90	43887	90	44605	90	45910	10	46940	10
40800	10	41872	90	42821	90	43400	90	43888	90	44615	90	45915	10	46942	10
40801	10	41874	90	42825	90	43401	90	43999	YYY	44620	90	45999	YYY	46945	10
40804	10	41899	YYY	42826	90	43405	90	44005	90	44625	90	46020	10	46946	90
40805	10	42000	10	42830	90	43410	90	44010	90	44626	90	46030	10	46947	90
40808	10	42100	10	42831	90	43415	90	44015	ZZZ	44640	90	46040	90	46999	YYY
40810	10	42104	10	42835	90	43420	90	44020	90	44650	90	46045	90	47001	ZZZ
40812	10	42106	10	42836	90	43425	90	44021	90	44660	90	46050	10	47010	90
40814	90	42107	90	42842	90	43496	90	44025	90	44661	90	46060	90	47015	90
40816	90	42120	90	42844	90	43499	YYY	44050	90	44680	90	46070	90	47100	90
40818	90	42140	90	42845	90	43500	90	44055	90	44700	90	46080	10	47120	90
40819	90	42145	90	42860	90	43501	90	44110	90	44701	ZZZ	46083	10	47122	90
40820	10	42160	10	42870	90	43502	90	44111	90	44799	YYY	46200	90	47125	90
40830	10	42180	10	42890	90	43510	90	44120	90	44800	90	46210	90	47130	90
40831	10	42182	10	42892	90	43520	90	44121	ZZZ	44820	90	46211	90	47135	90
40840	90	42200	90	42894	90	43605	90	44125	90	44850	90	46220	10	47136	90
40842	90	42205	90	42900	10	43610	90	44126	90	44899	YYY	46221	10	47140	90
40843	90	42210	90	42950	90	43611	90	44127	90	44900	90	46230	10	47141	90
40844	90	42215	90	42953	90	43620	90	44128	ZZZ	44950	90	46250	90	47142	90
40845	90	42220	90	42955	90	43621	90	44130	90	44955	ZZZ	46255	90	47144	90
40899	YYY	42225	90	42960	10	43622	90	44139	ZZZ	44960	90	46257	90	47300	90
41000	10	42226	90	42961	90	43631	90	44140	90	44970	90	46258	90	47350	90
41005	10	42227	90	42962	90	43632	90	44141	90	44979	YYY	46260	90	47360	90

APPENDIX B   GLOBAL FEE PERIODS

Code	GFP	Code	GFP	Code	GFP	Code	GFP	Code	GFP	Code	GFP	Code	GFP	Code	GFP
47361	90	48153	90	49568	ZZZ	50547	90	51585	90	53442	90	54390	90	55680	90
47362	90	48154	90	49570	90	50548	90	51590	90	53444	90	54400	90	55705	10
47370	90	48155	90	49572	90	50549	YYY	51595	90	53445	90	54401	90	55720	90
47371	90	48400	ZZZ	49580	90	50562	90	51596	90	53446	90	54405	90	55725	90
47379	YYY	48500	90	49582	90	50590	90	51597	90	53447	90	54406	90	55801	90
47380	90	48510	90	49585	90	50592	10	51705	10	53448	90	54408	90	55810	90
47381	90	48520	90	49587	90	50600	90	51710	10	53449	90	54410	90	55812	90
47382	10	48540	90	49590	90	50605	90	51800	90	53450	90	54411	90	55815	90
47399	YYY	48545	90	49600	90	50610	90	51820	90	53460	90	54415	90	55821	90
47400	90	48547	90	49605	90	50620	90	51840	90	53500	90	54416	90	55831	90
47420	90	48548	90	49606	90	50630	90	51841	90	53502	90	54417	90	55840	90
47425	90	48554	90	49610	90	50650	90	51845	90	53505	90	54420	90	55842	90
47460	90	48556	90	49611	90	50660	90	51860	90	53510	90	54430	90	55845	90
47480	90	48999	YYY	49650	90	50688	10	51865	90	53515	90	54435	90	55860	90
47490	90	49000	90	49651	90	50700	90	51880	90	53520	90	54440	90	55862	90
47510	90	49002	90	49659	YYY	50715	90	51900	90	53850	90	54505	10	55865	90
47511	90	49010	90	49900	90	50722	90	51920	90	53850	90	54512	90	55866	90
47525	10	49020	90	49904	90	50725	90	51925	90	53852	90	54520	90	55873	90
47525	10	49040	90	49905	ZZZ	50727	90	51940	90	53852	90	54522	90	55875	90
47530	90	49060	90	49906	90	50728	90	51960	90	53853	90	54530	90	55899	YYY
47530	90	49062	90	49999	YYY	50740	90	51980	90	53899	YYY	54535	90	56405	10
47550	ZZZ	49200	90	50010	90	50750	90	51990	90	54000	10	54550	90	56420	10
47562	90	49201	90	50020	90	50760	90	51992	90	54001	10	54560	90	56440	10
47563	90	49215	90	50040	90	50770	90	51999	YYY	54015	10	54600	90	56441	10
47564	90	49220	90	50045	90	50780	90	52400	90	54050	10	54620	10	56501	10
47570	90	49250	90	50060	90	50782	90	52450	90	54055	10	54640	90	56515	10
47579	YYY	49255	90	50065	90	50783	90	52500	90	54056	10	54650	90	56606	ZZZ
47600	90	49320	10	50070	90	50785	90	52510	90	54057	10	54660	90	56620	90
47605	90	49321	10	50075	90	50800	90	52601	90	54060	10	54670	90	56625	90
47610	90	49322	10	50080	90	50810	90	52606	90	54065	10	54680	90	56630	90
47612	90	49323	90	50081	90	50815	90	52612	90	54105	10	54690	90	56631	90
47620	90	49324	10	50100	90	50820	90	52614	90	54110	90	54692	90	56632	90
47630	90	49325	10	50120	90	50825	90	52620	90	54111	90	54699	YYY	56633	90
47700	90	49326	ZZZ	50125	90	50830	90	52630	90	54112	90	54700	10	56634	90
47701	90	49329	YYY	50130	90	50840	90	52640	90	54115	90	54830	90	56637	90
47711	90	49402	90	50135	90	50845	90	52647	90	54120	90	54840	90	56640	90
47712	90	49419	90	50205	90	50860	90	52647	90	54125	90	54860	90	56700	10
47715	90	49421	90	50220	90	50900	90	52648	90	54130	90	54861	90	56740	10
47719	90	49422	10	50225	90	50920	90	52700	90	54135	90	54865	90	56800	10
47720	90	49425	90	50230	90	50930	90	53000	10	54160	10	54900	90	56805	90
47721	90	49426	90	50234	90	50940	90	53010	90	54161	10	54901	90	56810	10
47740	90	49428	10	50236	90	50945	90	53040	90	54162	10	55040	90	57000	10
47741	90	49429	10	50240	90	50947	90	53060	10	54163	10	55041	90	57010	90
47760	90	49435	ZZZ	50250	90	50948	90	53080	90	54164	10	55060	90	57022	10
47765	90	49436	10	50280	90	50949	YYY	53085	90	54200	10	55100	10	57023	10
47780	90	49491	90	50290	90	51010	10	53210	90	54205	90	55110	90	57061	10
47785	90	49492	90	50320	90	51020	90	53215	90	54300	90	55120	90	57065	10
47800	90	49495	90	50340	90	51030	90	53220	90	54304	90	55150	90	57105	10
47801	90	49496	90	50360	90	51040	90	53230	90	54308	90	55175	90	57106	90
47802	90	49500	90	50365	90	51045	90	53235	90	54312	90	55180	90	57107	90
47900	90	49501	90	50370	90	51050	90	53240	90	54316	90	55200	90	57109	90
47999	YYY	49505	90	50380	90	51060	90	53250	90	54318	90	55200	90	57110	90
48000	90	49507	90	50400	90	51065	90	53260	10	54322	90	55250	90	57111	90
48001	90	49520	90	50405	90	51080	90	53265	10	54324	90	55400	90	57112	90
48020	90	49521	90	50500	90	51500	90	53270	10	54326	90	55450	10	57120	90
48100	90	49525	90	50520	90	51520	90	53275	10	54328	90	55500	90	57130	10
48102	10	49540	90	50525	90	51525	90	53400	90	54332	90	55520	90	57135	10
48105	90	49550	90	50526	90	51530	90	53405	90	54336	90	55530	90	57155	90
48120	90	49553	90	50540	90	51535	90	53410	90	54340	90	55535	90	57180	10
48140	90	49555	90	50541	90	51550	90	53415	90	54344	90	55540	90	57200	90
48145	90	49557	90	50542	90	51555	90	53420	90	54348	90	55550	90	57210	90
48146	90	49560	90	50543	90	51565	90	53425	90	54352	90	55559	YYY	57220	90
48148	90	49561	90	50544	90	51570	90	53430	90	54360	90	55600	90	57230	90
48150	90	49565	90	50545	90	51575	90	53431	90	54380	90	55605	90	57240	90
48152	90	49566	90	50546	90	51580	90	53440	90	54385	90	55650	90	57250	90

APPENDIX B   GLOBAL FEE PERIODS

Code	GFP	Code	GFP	Code	GFP	Code	GFP	Code	GFP	Code	GFP	Code	GFP	Code	GFP
57260	90	58293	90	58999	YYY	60522	90	61538	90	61700	90	62264	10	63196	90
57265	90	58294	90	59100	90	60540	90	61539	90	61702	90	62280	10	63197	90
57267	ZZZ	58345	10	59120	90	60545	90	61540	90	61703	90	62281	10	63198	90
57268	90	58346	90	59121	90	60600	90	61541	90	61705	90	62282	10	63199	90
57270	90	58350	10	59130	90	60605	90	61542	90	61708	90	62287	90	63200	90
57280	90	58353	10	59135	90	60650	90	61543	90	61710	90	62292	90	63250	90
57282	90	58353	10	59136	90	60659	YYY	61544	90	61711	90	62294	90	63251	90
57283	90	58356	10	59140	90	60699	YYY	61545	90	61720	90	62350	90	63252	90
57284	90	58356	10	59150	90	61105	90	61546	90	61735	90	62351	90	63265	90
57287	90	58400	90	59151	90	61108	90	61548	90	61750	90	62355	90	63266	90
57288	90	58410	90	59160	10	61120	90	61550	90	61751	90	62360	90	63267	90
57289	90	58520	90	59400	MMM	61140	90	61552	90	61760	90	62361	90	63268	90
57291	90	58540	90	59409	MMM	61150	90	61556	90	61770	90	62362	90	63270	90
57292	90	58541	90	59410	MMM	61151	90	61557	90	61790	90	62365	90	63271	90
57295	90	58542	90	59412	MMM	61154	90	61558	90	61791	90	63001	90	63272	90
57296	90	58543	90	59414	MMM	61156	90	61559	90	61793	90	63003	90	63273	90
57300	90	58544	90	59425	MMM	61215	90	61563	90	61795	ZZZ	63005	90	63275	90
57305	90	58545	90	59426	MMM	61250	90	61564	90	61850	90	63011	90	63276	90
57307	90	58546	90	59430	MMM	61253	90	61566	90	61860	90	63012	90	63277	90
57308	90	58548	90	59510	MMM	61304	90	61567	90	61863	90	63015	90	63278	90
57310	90	58550	90	59514	MMM	61305	90	61570	90	61864	ZZZ	63016	90	63280	90
57311	90	58552	90	59515	MMM	61312	90	61571	90	61867	90	63017	90	63281	90
57320	90	58553	90	59525	ZZZ	61313	90	61575	90	61868	ZZZ	63020	90	63282	90
57330	90	58554	90	59610	MMM	61314	90	61576	90	61870	90	63030	90	63283	90
57335	90	58565	90	59612	MMM	61315	90	61580	90	61875	90	63035	ZZZ	63285	90
57415	10	58578	YYY	59614	MMM	61316	ZZZ	61581	90	61880	90	63040	90	63286	90
57425	90	58579	YYY	59618	MMM	61320	90	61582	90	61885	90	63042	90	63287	90
57505	10	58600	90	59620	MMM	61321	90	61583	90	61886	90	63043	ZZZ	63290	90
57510	10	58605	90	59622	MMM	61322	90	61584	90	61888	10	63044	ZZZ	63295	ZZZ
57511	10	58611	ZZZ	59812	90	61323	90	61585	90	62000	90	63045	90	63300	90
57513	10	58615	10	59820	90	61330	90	61586	90	62005	90	63046	90	63301	90
57520	90	58660	90	59821	90	61332	90	61590	90	62010	90	63047	90	63302	90
57522	90	58661	10	59830	90	61333	90	61591	90	62100	90	63048	ZZZ	63303	90
57530	90	58662	90	59840	10	61334	90	61592	90	62115	90	63050	90	63304	90
57531	90	58670	90	59841	10	61340	90	61595	90	62116	90	63051	90	63305	90
57540	90	58671	90	59850	90	61343	90	61596	90	62117	90	63055	90	63306	90
57545	90	58672	90	59851	90	61345	90	61597	90	62120	90	63056	90	63307	90
57550	90	58673	90	59852	90	61440	90	61598	90	62121	90	63057	ZZZ	63308	ZZZ
57555	90	58679	YYY	59855	90	61450	90	61600	90	62140	90	63064	90	63600	90
57556	90	58700	90	59856	90	61458	90	61601	90	62141	90	63066	ZZZ	63615	90
57558	10	58720	90	59857	90	61460	90	61605	90	62142	90	63075	90	63650	90
57700	90	58740	90	59870	90	61470	90	61606	90	62143	90	63076	ZZZ	63655	90
57720	90	58750	90	59897	YYY	61480	90	61607	90	62145	90	63077	90	63660	90
58110	ZZZ	58752	90	59898	YYY	61490	90	61608	90	62146	90	63078	ZZZ	63685	90
58120	10	58760	90	59899	YYY	61500	90	61609	ZZZ	62147	90	63081	90	63688	90
58140	90	58770	90	60000	10	61501	90	61610	ZZZ	62148	ZZZ	63082	ZZZ	63700	90
58145	90	58800	90	60200	90	61510	90	61611	ZZZ	62160	ZZZ	63085	90	63702	90
58146	90	58805	90	60210	90	61512	90	61612	ZZZ	62161	90	63086	ZZZ	63704	90
58150	90	58820	90	60212	90	61514	90	61613	90	62162	90	63087	90	63706	90
58152	90	58822	90	60220	90	61516	90	61615	90	62163	90	63088	ZZZ	63707	90
58180	90	58825	90	60225	90	61517	ZZZ	61616	90	62164	90	63090	90	63709	90
58200	90	58900	90	60240	90	61518	90	61618	90	62165	90	63091	ZZZ	63710	90
58210	90	58920	90	60252	90	61519	90	61619	90	62180	90	63101	90	63740	90
58240	90	58925	90	60254	90	61520	90	61630	90	62190	90	63102	90	63741	90
58260	90	58940	90	60260	90	61521	90	61635	90	62192	90	63103	ZZZ	63744	90
58262	90	58943	90	60270	90	61522	90	61641	ZZZ	62194	10	63170	90	63746	90
58263	90	58950	90	60271	90	61524	90	61642	ZZZ	62200	90	63172	90	64416	10
58267	90	58951	90	60280	90	61526	90	61680	90	62201	90	63173	90	64446	10
58270	90	58952	90	60281	90	61530	90	61682	90	62220	90	63180	90	64448	10
58275	90	58953	90	60500	90	61531	90	61684	90	62223	90	63182	90	64449	10
58280	90	58954	90	60502	90	61533	90	61686	90	62225	90	63185	90	64472	ZZZ
58285	90	58956	90	60505	90	61534	90	61690	90	62230	90	63190	90	64476	ZZZ
58290	90	58957	90	60512	ZZZ	61535	90	61692	90	62256	90	63191	90	64480	ZZZ
58291	90	58958	90	60520	90	61536	90	61697	90	62258	90	63194	90	64484	ZZZ
58292	90	58960	90	60521	90	61537	90	61698	90	62263	10	63195	90	64553	10

APPENDIX B   GLOBAL FEE PERIODS

Code	GFP	Code	GFP	Code	GFP	Code	GFP	Code	GFP	Code	GFP	Code	GFP	Code	GFP
64555	10	64787	ZZZ	65235	90	66700	90	67334	ZZZ	67999	YYY	69505	90	75774	ZZZ
64560	10	64788	90	65260	90	66710	90	67335	ZZZ	68020	10	69511	90	75774	ZZZ
64561	10	64790	90	65265	90	66711	90	67340	ZZZ	68110	10	69530	90	75946	ZZZ
64565	10	64792	90	65270	10	66720	90	67343	90	68115	10	69535	90	75946	ZZZ
64573	90	64802	90	65270	10	66740	90	67345	10	68130	90	69540	10	75964	ZZZ
64575	90	64804	90	65272	90	66761	90	67399	YYY	68135	10	69550	90	75964	ZZZ
64577	90	64809	90	65272	90	66762	90	67400	90	68320	90	69552	90	75968	ZZZ
64580	90	64818	90	65273	90	66770	90	67405	90	68325	90	69554	90	75968	ZZZ
64581	90	64820	90	65275	90	66820	90	67412	90	68326	90	69601	90	75993	ZZZ
64585	10	64821	90	65280	90	66821	90	67413	90	68328	90	69602	90	75993	ZZZ
64585	10	64822	90	65285	90	66825	90	67414	90	68330	90	69603	90	75996	ZZZ
64590	10	64823	90	65286	90	66830	90	67420	90	68335	90	69604	90	75996	ZZZ
64595	10	64831	90	65290	90	66840	90	67430	90	68340	90	69605	90	76125	ZZZ
64595	10	64832	ZZZ	65400	90	66850	90	67440	90	68360	90	69610	10	76125	ZZZ
64600	10	64834	90	65420	90	66852	90	67445	90	68362	90	69620	90	76802	ZZZ
64605	10	64835	90	65426	90	66920	90	67450	90	68371	10	69631	90	76802	ZZZ
64610	10	64836	90	65436	90	66930	90	67550	90	68399	YYY	69632	90	76810	ZZZ
64612	10	64837	ZZZ	65450	90	66940	90	67560	90	68400	10	69633	90	76810	ZZZ
64613	10	64840	90	65600	90	66982	90	67570	90	68420	10	69635	90	76812	ZZZ
64614	10	64856	90	65710	90	66983	90	67599	YYY	68440	10	69636	90	76812	ZZZ
64620	10	64857	90	65730	90	66984	90	67700	10	68500	90	69637	90	76937	ZZZ
64622	10	64858	90	65750	90	66985	90	67700	10	68505	90	69641	90	76937	ZZZ
64623	ZZZ	64859	ZZZ	65755	90	66986	90	67710	10	68520	90	69642	90	77001	ZZZ
64626	10	64861	90	65770	90	66990	ZZZ	67715	10	68530	10	69643	90	77001	ZZZ
64627	ZZZ	64862	90	65772	90	66999	YYY	67800	10	68540	90	69644	90	77051	ZZZ
64630	10	64864	90	65775	90	67005	90	67801	10	68550	90	69645	90	77051	ZZZ
64640	10	64865	90	65780	90	67010	90	67805	10	68700	90	69646	90	77052	ZZZ
64680	10	64866	90	65781	90	67015	90	67808	90	68705	10	69650	90	77052	ZZZ
64681	10	64868	90	65782	90	67025	90	67825	10	68720	90	69660	90	77750	90
64702	90	64870	90	65810	90	67027	90	67830	10	68745	90	69661	90	77750	90
64704	90	64872	ZZZ	65815	90	67030	90	67835	90	68750	90	69662	90	77761	90
64708	90	64874	ZZZ	65820	90	67031	90	67840	10	68760	10	69666	90	77761	90
64712	90	64876	ZZZ	65850	90	67036	90	67850	10	68761	10	69667	90	77762	90
64713	90	64885	90	65855	10	67038	90	67880	90	68770	90	69670	90	77762	90
64714	90	64886	90	65860	90	67039	90	67882	90	68801	10	69676	90	77763	90
64716	90	64890	90	65865	90	67040	90	67900	90	68810	10	69700	90	77763	90
64718	90	64891	90	65870	90	67101	90	67901	90	68811	10	69711	90	77776	90
64719	90	64892	90	65875	90	67105	90	67902	90	68815	10	69714	90	77776	90
64721	90	64893	90	65880	90	67107	90	67903	90	68840	10	69715	90	77777	90
64722	90	64895	90	65900	90	67108	90	67904	90	68899	YYY	69717	90	77777	90
64726	90	64896	90	65920	90	67110	90	67906	90	69000	10	69718	90	77778	90
64727	ZZZ	64897	90	65930	90	67112	90	67908	90	69005	10	69720	90	77778	90
64732	90	64898	90	66020	10	67115	90	67909	90	69020	10	69725	90	78020	ZZZ
64734	90	64901	ZZZ	66030	10	67120	90	67911	90	69110	90	69740	90	78020	ZZZ
64736	90	64902	ZZZ	66130	90	67121	90	67912	90	69120	90	69745	90	78496	ZZZ
64738	90	64905	90	66150	90	67141	90	67914	90	69140	90	69799	YYY	78496	ZZZ
64740	90	64907	90	66155	90	67145	90	67915	90	69145	90	69801	90	78496	ZZZ
64742	90	64910	90	66160	90	67208	90	67916	90	69150	90	69802	90	78730	ZZZ
64744	90	64911	90	66165	90	67210	90	67917	90	69155	90	69805	90	78730	ZZZ
64746	90	64999	YYY	66170	90	67218	90	67921	90	69205	10	69806	90	88185	ZZZ
64752	90	65091	90	66172	90	67220	90	67922	90	69222	10	69820	90	90466	ZZZ
64755	90	65093	90	66180	90	67225	ZZZ	67922	90	69300	YYY	69840	90	90468	ZZZ
64760	90	65101	90	66185	90	67227	90	67923	90	69310	90	69905	90	90472	ZZZ
64761	90	65103	90	66220	90	67228	90	67924	90	69320	90	69910	90	90474	ZZZ
64763	90	65105	90	66225	90	67250	90	67930	10	69399	YYY	69915	90	90761	ZZZ
64766	90	65110	90	66250	90	67255	90	67935	90	69405	10	69930	90	90766	ZZZ
64771	90	65112	90	66500	90	67299	YYY	67938	10	69405	10	69949	YYY	90767	ZZZ
64772	90	65114	90	66505	90	67311	90	67938	10	69420	10	69950	90	90768	ZZZ
64774	90	65125	90	66600	90	67312	90	67950	90	69421	10	69955	90	90775	ZZZ
64776	90	65130	90	66605	90	67314	90	67961	90	69433	10	69960	90	92547	ZZZ
64778	ZZZ	65135	90	66625	90	67316	90	67966	90	69436	10	69970	90	92621	ZZZ
64782	90	65140	90	66630	90	67318	90	67971	90	69440	90	69979	YYY	92627	ZZZ
64783	ZZZ	65150	90	66635	90	67320	ZZZ	67973	90	69450	90	69990	ZZZ	92973	ZZZ
64784	90	65155	90	66680	90	67331	ZZZ	67974	90	69501	90	74301	ZZZ	92974	ZZZ
64786	90	65175	90	66682	90	67332	ZZZ	67975	90	69502	90	74301	ZZZ	92978	ZZZ

APPENDIX B   GLOBAL FEE PERIODS

Code	GFP	Code	GFP	Code	GFP	Code	GFP	Code	GFP	Code	GFP	Code	GFP	Code	GFP
92978	ZZZ	99290	ZZZ												
92979	ZZZ	99292	ZZZ												
92979	ZZZ	99354	ZZZ												
92981	ZZZ	99355	ZZZ												
92984	ZZZ	99356	ZZZ												
92986	90	99357	ZZZ												
92987	90	99358	ZZZ												
92990	90	99359	ZZZ												
92992	90														
92993	90														
92996	ZZZ														
92998	ZZZ														
93320	ZZZ														
93320	ZZZ														
93321	ZZZ														
93321	ZZZ														
93325	ZZZ														
93325	ZZZ														
93571	ZZZ														
93571	ZZZ														
93572	ZZZ														
93572	ZZZ														
93609	ZZZ														
93609	ZZZ														
93613	ZZZ														
93621	ZZZ														
93621	ZZZ														
93622	ZZZ														
93622	ZZZ														
93623	ZZZ														
93623	ZZZ														
93662	ZZZ														
93662	ZZZ														
94774	YYY														
94775	YYY														
94776	YYY														
94777	YYY														
95873	ZZZ														
95873	ZZZ														
95874	ZZZ														
95874	ZZZ														
95920	ZZZ														
95920	ZZZ														
95962	ZZZ														
95962	ZZZ														
95967	ZZZ														
95967	ZZZ														
95973	ZZZ														
95975	ZZZ														
95979	ZZZ														
96411	ZZZ														
96415	ZZZ														
96417	ZZZ														
96423	ZZZ														
96570	ZZZ														
96571	ZZZ														
97546	ZZZ														
97811	ZZZ														
97814	ZZZ														
99100	ZZZ														
99116	ZZZ														
99135	ZZZ														
99140	ZZZ														
99145	ZZZ														
99150	ZZZ														

Comprehensive Coding Resources

From the publishers of the Official CPT®

CPT® 2007 Standard Edition
Softbound, 8½ x 11", 560 pages
ISBN#: 1-57947-790-9
Authors: American Medical Association
List Price: $69.95 SALE PRICE: $57.95
This softbound edition of CPT contains all the revised 2007 codes, modifiers, and guidelines in an efficient two-column format. An extensive index helps you locate codes by procedure, service, eponym, synonym, and abbreviation.

CPT® 2007 Professional Edition
Spiral bound, 8½ x 11", 700 pages
ISBN#: 1-57947-791-7
Authors: American Medical Association
List Price: $98.95
SALE PRICE: $82.95

CPT® 2007 Electronic Professional Edition
CD ROM   This is the single user license version
ISBN#: 1-57947-792-5
Authors: American Medical Association
List Price: $179.95
SALE PRICE: $145.95

Stay in compliance with the hundreds of code changes each year with the AMA's official coding resource for procedural codes, rules, and guidelines. Exclusive features include color-coded symbols and highlights, procedural and anatomical illustrations, many new for 2007, and CPT® Assistant newsletter and CPT® Changes book citations, directing you to in-depth information you need to code accurately.

AMA Physician ICD-9-CM 2007 Volumes 1 & 2
8½ x 11", 810 pages
Authors: American Medical Association
Spiralbound   ISBN 1-57947-824-7
Softbound   ISBN 1-57947-823-9
List Price $92.95 SALE PRICE: $78.95

Compact Edition
Softbound, 6 x 9", 1,520 pages
ISBN#: 1-57947-827-1
List Price: $74.95
SALE PRICE: $57.95

Significant changes made yearly, you'll want to reserve your 2007 copy now! Don't miss out on this best selling codebook, contains a complete and comprehensive approach to medical diagnosis coding. HIPAA regulations require the use of the current standard code set, use of the official coding guidelines, and adherence to official coding advice.

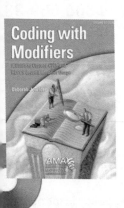

NEW!! Coding With Modifiers 2nd Edition: A Guide to Correct CPT® and HCPCS Modifier Usage
Spiral bound, 8-1/2 x 11", 350 pages with CD ROM
ISBN#: 1-57947-771-2
Authors: Deborah J Grider
List Price: $89.95 SALE PRICE: $75.95

- 45 New Clinical Examples - Guide readers in determining the correct modifier to use
- New CD-ROM - PowerPoint Presentations for each chapter, including the Test-Your-Knowledge quizzes, are provided as an aid to instructors.
- 30 additional Test-Your-Knowledge questions - Test your comprehension of the material through more than 190 questions
- Additional Chapter and appendix on Genetic Testing Modifiers and Category II modifiers - Provides explanation on these areas
- Modifiers Approved for Hospitals and ASCs - Complete information at your fingertips for both professional service and hospital reporting requirements

Comprehensive Coding Resources

From the publishers of the Official CPT®

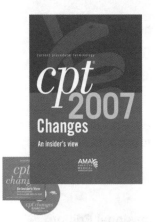

CPT® Changes 2007: An Insider's View
Softbound, 7 x 10", 300 pages
ISBN#: 1-57947-799-2
Authors: American Medical Association
List Price: $64.95
SALE PRICE: $54.95

CPT® Changes Archives: An Insider's View 2000
CD ROM, This is the single user license version
ISBN#: 1-57947-800-X
Authors: American Medical Association
List Price: $184.95
SALE PRICE: $139.95

Written by the CPT coding staff, this book provides the official AMA interpretations and explanations for each CPT code and guideline change in CPT® 2007.
• Detailed rationales provide an explanation behind every code addition, revision, and deletion
• Understand the guideline changes
• Real-life clinical examples and procedural descriptions plus illustrations help you understand the practical situations for which the codes would be appropriately reported

Principles of CPT® Coding Fourth Edition
Spiral bound, 8-1/2 x 11", 580 pages
Authors: American Medical Association
ISBN 1-57947-679-1
List Price: $64.95 SALE PRICE: $59.95

This new edition is a comprehensive training and educational textbook that provides in-depth review of the entire CPT codebook. Principles explains the use of the codes and t application of the guidelines in an easy-to-read-style, making it broad enough to educate t beginning coder, while still serving as a useful tool for those with more experience.

AMA Hospital ICD-9-CM 2007, Volumes 1, 2 & 3
Full-Size Edition
Spiral bound, 8 ½ x 11", 1,040 pages
ISBN#: 1-57947-825-5
Authors: American Medical Association
List Price: $102.95 SALE PRICE: $87.95

Compact Edition
Softbound, 6 x 9", 1,837 pages
ISBN#: 1-57947-826-3
Authors: American Medical Association
List Price: $79.95
SALE PRICE: $62.95

This spiral full-size edition provides critical coding citations, payment system edit details, an manifestation, complex diagnosis, and major complication code alerts on the same page as the code themselves.
  • DRG Indicators - Special symbol alerts coders to whether or not they need special documentation to justify DRG assignment
  • Valid Three-digit Code Table
  • Color Fourth-and Fifth-Digit - Requirement Symbols

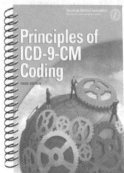

Principles of ICD-9-CM Coding, Third Edition
Spiralbound, 8-1/2 x 11", 400 pages
ISBN#: 1-57947-658-9
Authors: Deborah J Grider
List Price: $69.95 SALE PRICE: $64.95

Phone orders 800 669-33
FAX 414 272-6666
www.medfees.com

  • A CD-ROM to facilitate the learning process - This CD-ROM contains additional questions and answers, answer keys for checkpoint exercises and test your knowledge quizzes, mid-term and final exams with answer keys and Power Point presentations taken from each section of the book
  • Expert analysis - Written by an expert in coding training and instruction, Principles teaches ICD-9-CM coding in a clear, concise way
  • New and updated content - New, deleted and revised ICD-9-CM coding policy is introduced and explained

Medical Coding Software Solutions

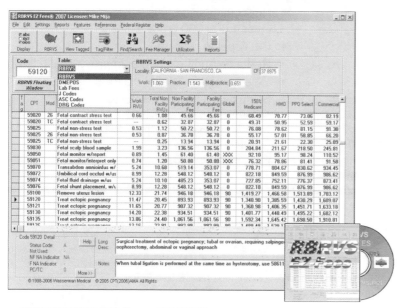

2007 RBRVS EZ-Fees CD ROM
ISBN#: 1-59891-009-4
Authors: Wasserman Medical Publishers
List Price: Standard $199
      Pro Version $399
      Pro Plus Version $499

- Easy-to-use Windows solution for creating and managing Medicare and other RBRVS based fee schedules
- ALL U.S. Localities (including National Values), set your own conversion factors
- HPSA bonus indicator by zipcode
- Fees for facility, non facility, participating, non participating, and limiting charge
- Excellent for Medicare, Managed Care (HMOs & PPOs), and some Workers' Comp
- Over 10,000 CPT® Codes including HCPCS Level II Codes
- Injections - J Codes, DMEPOS, & Lab Fees (Professional Version Only)
- ASC & DRG (Professional Plus Version Only)
- Full and Short CPT Descriptions - Locate any Code in Seconds
- Export codes, unit values & fees to ASCII, dBASE, Excel, Access
- Windows® 95/98/NT/2000/ME/XP Version - CD ROM
- User Friendly - FREE Tech Support

Now have all the features of the PFR book at your fingers. The Physicians' Fee Reference Pricing Program is customized for your five digit zipcode. This low cost software product combines all the information in the PFR book with dozens of features available only in a software product. Create customized fee schedules for your area with the click of a button!

- Preset for your zip code area
- Excellent for "What If?" Calculations
- Full Custom Report Generator
- Frequency analysis feature
- Search for and tag procedures based on CPT keywords
- Import/Export to ASCII, Access, Excel, or dBase
- 50th, 75th, 90th % Fees in **U.S. $$$**
- User friendly - **FREE** Tech Support

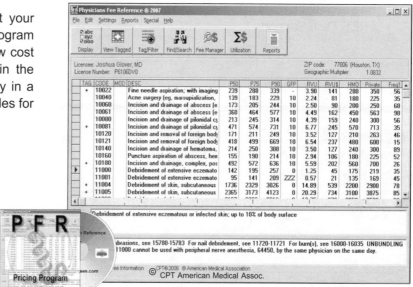

2007 Physicians Fee Reference® Pricing Program
ISBN#: 1-59891-017-5
Authors: Wasserman Medical Publishers
List Price: $199-$799

Professional Versions

- Each Additional 3 digit zip prefix **$50**
- All U.S. Zips **$499**
- Developers (includes full export privileges) **$799**

CPT® is a registered trademark of the American Medical Assoc.

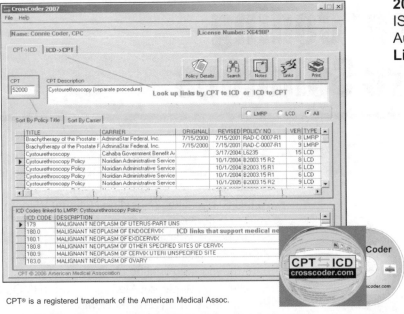

CPT® is a registered trademark of the American Medical Assoc.

2007 CrossCoder CD ROM
ISBN#: 1-59891-022-1
Authors: Wasserman Medical Publishers
List Price: $199.00

- Low cost solution for medical (CPT®) cross coding and diagnosis (ICD) coding
- Look up any CPT® or HCPCS code and instantly find a supporting ICD code
- Helps establish Medical Necessity
- Over 1,000,000 cross walks
- Cut & paste reports
- Reduces audit exposure, improves cash flow
- Helps create a "clean" claim
- Exclusive Software Features
  * Search for key words
  * Reverse look-up ICD → CPT
  * LMRP Look-up
- Free Tech Support

2007 Physicians' Insurance Reference® Contact Manager
ISBN#: 1-59891-020-5
Authors: Wasserman Medical Publishers
List Price: $99.00

- A low cost solution for managing communications with private insurance companies, government agencies, HMOs, & PPOs
- Log all phone calls with automatic date and time stamps
- Over 10,000 listings confirmed for 2007
- Thousands of FAX, 800 Numbers, & Internet Web Sites & e-mails
- Search for companies/contacts based on a key word, state, zipcode, etc.
- **New!** Patient ID field
- **FREE** Tech Support

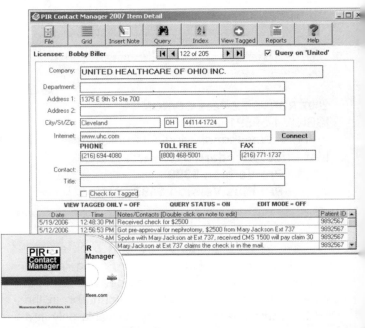

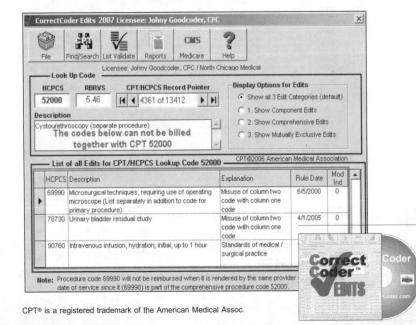

CPT® is a registered trademark of the American Medical Assoc.

2007 Correct Coder CD ROM
ISBN#: 1-59891-019-1
Authors: Wasserman Medical Publishers
List Price: $159

- Medicare National Correct Coding Initiative (C
- Comprehensive, Component & Mutually Exclusive Edits Display options
- Over 280,000 Edit Pairs
- Create & Save Your Own Validation Lists
- Eliminate Unbundling & Reduce Audit Exposu
- Cut & Paste into other Applications
- Search for Keyword using full CPT/HCPCS description
- One Main Screen, No Complicated Manual
- FREE Tech Support
- CD-ROM for Win95/98/NT/2000/ME/XP
- **30-Day Money Back Guarantee**

2007 Physicians Fee Reference®
Softbound, 8½ x 11", 380 pages
ISBN#: 1-59891-012-4
Authors: Wasserman Medical Publishers
List Price: $139

- Provides Updated 50th (median), 75th, & 90th Percentiles in U.S. Dollars - the only fee reference on the Market with this information
- Medicare RBRVS & Global Fee Periods
- Thousands of CPT® Coding & Billing Tips, Hints, Alerts, Warnings, and Traps
- Fees for All U.S. Zipcode Prefixes
- Official 2007 CPT Full Descriptions with Starred Procedures
- Excellent for Negotiating Managed Care Contracts
- Helps Review, Fine-Tune, or Design a Fee Schedule
- An Essential Tool for Practice Management

2007 HCPCS Level II Book
ISBN#: 1-59891-016-7
Authors: Wasserman Medical Publishers
List Price: $59.00

- Codes & Fees for durable medical equipment, prosthetics, orthotics, and supplies (DMEPOS)
- Fees for new, used, and monthly rental for supplies and equipment
- Coding tips and government regulations
- Required for Medicare/Medicaid and many private insurance carriers
- Comprehensive table of drugs available with generic cross reference
- Index of codes, cross coding to CPT®

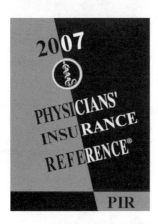

2007 Physicians Insurance Reference®
ISBN#: 1-59891-015-9
Authors: Wasserman Medical Publishers
List Price: $69.00

- Over 10,000 confirmed listings for 2007 (more than any other directory)
- Private Insurance, BC/BS, CMS, HMO's, PPO's, & Claims Offices
- All Health Related U.S. State & Federal Agencies
- Thousands of FAX, 800 Numbers, & Internet sites
- CMS 1500 tips and traps

Phone orders 800 669-3337
FAX 414 272-6666
www.medfees.com

2007 CorrectCoder for Edits Book
ISBN#: 1-59891-014-0
Authors: Wasserman Medical Publishers
List Price: $129

- CMS's **National Correct Coding Initiative (CCI)**
- Eliminate Coding/Unbundling Errors & Reduce Audit Exposure
- Lists all Comprehensive, Component & Mutually Exclusive codes
- Over 280,000 Surgical, Radiology, Laboratory, & E&M Unbundling Alerts
- Used by Medicare and Commercial Insurance
- Includes CPT Procedure Descriptions *exclusive feature!*
- Includes Modifier Indicators (e.g. -59 for same day service)
- Comply with all the latest CMS regulations
- Easy to use - Spiral Bound

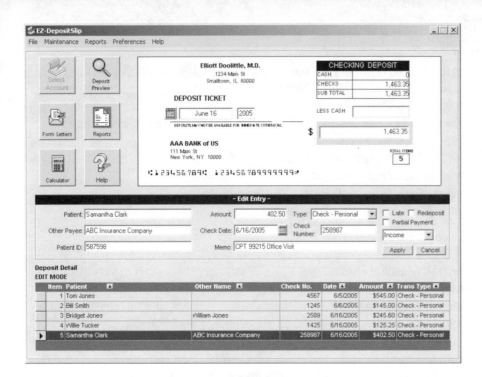

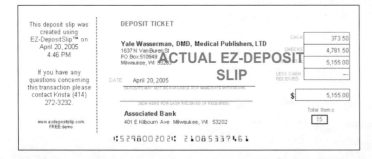

2007 Dental Coding & Reimbursement Products

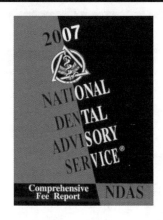

2007 National Dental Advisory Service
ISBN#: 1-59891-013-2
Authors: Wasserman Medical Publishers
Price: $89

- 2007 Fees Based on **NEW!! CDT-2007/2008 Codes and Nomenclature**
- Compare Your Fees with NDAS 40th, 50th, 60th, 70th, 80th, 90th, & 95th Percentile Fees in U.S. Dollars
- Medical (CPT) & Dental (CDT) Cross Reference Codes for Medical Insurance Billing
- Frequently Asked Questions (FAQs) and Answers on CDT-2007/2008 Coding
- National Directories of State Licensing, Insurance Commissioners, and Dental Societies
- ADA Claim Form instructions
- Internet Resource Guide for Dentists
- Glossary of Dental Benefit Terminology
- Get Paid For Your Work: A Third Party Guide to Collections
- Glossary of Medical Terminology for TMJ and Oral Surgery
- Helps Maximize Reimbursement
- Excellent for "what if" calculations

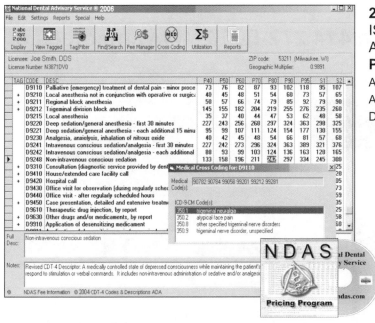

2007 National Dental Advisory Service CD Rom
ISBN#: 1-59891-018-3
Authors: Wasserman Medical Publishers
Price: $129 Standard (includes one zip code prefix)
Additional zip prefix **$20**
All US Zip Codes **$299**
Developers Version **$499** (includes All Zips & Full Export Privileges)

Special Software Features

- Create user defined fee schedules
- Apply global increases/decreases
- Procedure utilization/frequency analysis
- Enter your zip code, compare your fees to the NDAS
- Import and Export to Excel, dBASE, ACCESS, ASCII
- Locate, search, and filter codes based on ADA descriptions, key words or codes
- Windows 95/98/NT/2000/ME/XP, CD ROM
- Easy to Use!! **FREE tech support**

CDT-2007/2008 Current Dental Terminology Book
Authors: American Dental Association
Price: $52.45
- NEW! CDT-2007/2008
- Official Code on Dental Procedures and Nomenclature, published by the ADA
- Effective for services provided on or after January 1, 2007.
- Completely revised and updated
- New procedure codes, revisions, and deleted procedure codes.
- NEW! Highly detailed reference sections including changes to the coding system and completing the ADA dental claim form.
- Be prepared for 2007 coding changes!
- Required for HIPAA Compliance
- Spiral Bound Book

PACKAGE DEALS

FREE HCPCS

THREE BOOK SPECIAL

Includes: Physicians' Fee Reference, Physicians' Insurance Reference, and FREE HCPCS Level II Codebook
Special#: 1011
Package Price: $208 *(SAVE $59)*

FREE CCI

BILLER'S SPECIAL

Includes: 2007 CPT, 2007 ICD-9, 2007 PFR, and FREE CorrectCoder Book.
Special#: 1033
Package Price: $298 *(SAVE $129)*

Phone orders 800 669-3337   FAX 414 272-6666   www.medfees.cor

SAVE 25%

COMPLETE CODERS SPECIAL

Includes: Physicians' Fee Reference, Physicians' Insurance Reference2007, CorrectCoder 2007, CPT® 2007, ICD-9-CM 2007, and 2007 HCPCS Level II Codebook
Special#: 1022
Package Price: $417 *(SAVE $147)*

SAVE 25%

COMPLETE CD SPECIAL

Includes: PFR CD, PIR Contact Manager, CorrectCoder CD, CrossCoder CD, and RBRVS EZ-Fees
Special#: 1044
Package Price: $641 *(SAVE $214)*

Publication	Price	Qty	Total Price
Physicians' Fee Reference® 2007 Book	$139		
Physicians' Fee Reference® 2007 on CD 1st 3 digit prefix n/c ___ ___ ___	$199		
2nd extra 3 digit zip prefix ___ ___ ___	$50		
3rd extra 3 digit zip prefix ___ ___ ___	$50		
Physicians' Fee Reference® 2007 on CD (All U.S. Zip Codes)	$499		
Physicians' Fee Reference® 2007 on CD (Developers Version*)	$799		
AMA CPT® 2007 Standard Version	$57.95		
AMA CPT® 2007 Professional Version	$82.95		
CPT® 2007 Electronic Professional Edition CD ROM	$145.95		
AMA Physician ICD-9-CM 2007 Volumes 1 & 2 ☐ Spiral ☐ Softbound	$78.95		
AMA Physician ICD-9-CM 2007 Volumes 1 & 2 COMPACT EDITION	$57.95		
AMA Hospital ICD-9-CM 2007 Volumes 1, 2 & 3	$87.95		
AMA Hospital ICD-9-CM 2007 Volumes 1, 2 & 3 COMPACT EDITION	$62.95		
AMA CPT® Changes 2007: An Insider's View	$54.95		
CPT® Changes Archives: An Insider's View 2000-2007 CD ROM	$139.95		
Principles of CPT® Coding, 4th Edition	$59.95		
Physicians' Insurance Reference 2007 Book	$69		
Physicians' Insurance Reference 2007 Contact Manager on CD	$99		
HCPCS Level II Codes Book 2007	$59		
CrossCoder on CD 2007	$199		
CorrectCoder For Edits 2007 Book ☐ Quarter ☐ Annual	$129/$299		
CorrectCoder For Edits 2007 on CD Rom ☐ Quarter ☐ Annual	$159/$499		
Coding with Modifiers	$75.95		
RBRVS EZ-Fees 2007 Standard Version	$199		
RBRVS EZ-Fees 2007 Pro Version	$399		
RBRVS EZ-Fees 2007 Pro Plus Version	$499		
National Dental Advisory Service® 2007 on CD 1st 3 digit prefix n/c ___ ___ ___	$129		
2nd extra 3 digit zip prefix ___ ___ ___	$20		
3rd extra 3 digit zip prefix ___ ___ ___	$20		
ADA CDT-2007/2008 Coding Book	$52.45		
National Dental Advisory Service® 2007 on CD (All U.S. Zip Codes)	$299		
National Dental Advisory Service® 2007 on CD (Developers Version*)	$499		
National Dental Advisory Service® Book	$89		
EZ-DepositSlip	$99		
PACKAGE DEAL SPECIAL # _____	$ _____		
	Shipping & Handling		$11.95
	TOTAL		

100% 30-Day Money Back Guarantee

Orders are shipped via UPS for lower 48 states and USPS for PO Boxes, PR, GU, AK, HI, & VI.

one Orders: (800) 669-3337

x Orders: (414) 272-6666

cure Online Orders: www.medfees.com

Method of Payment:

☐ Check   ☐

___e   Title/Degree

___ress

___   State   Zip

___it Card Account #   Exp. Date

___e   Fax   e-mail (for UPS tracking notification)

___ature (for credit card orders)

Prepayment Required.
**Mail orders remit payment
with order form to:**
Wasserman Medical
Publishers
P.O. Box 510949
Milwaukee, WI 53203